CAREER OPPORTUNITIES IN THE INTERNET, VIDEO GAMES, AND MULTIMEDIA

CAREER OPPORTUNITIES IN THE INTERNET, VIDEO GAMES, AND MULTIMEDIA

ALLAN TAYLOR

JAMES ROBERT PARISH

Foreword by
DAN FIDEN

✓Checkmark Books
An imprint of Infobase Publishing

Career Opportunities in the Internet, Video Games, and Multimedia

Copyright © 2007 by Allan Taylor and James Robert Parish

Checkmark Books
An imprint of Infobase Publishing
132 West 31st Street
New York NY 10001

ISBN-10: 0-8160-6315-X
ISBN-13: 978-0-8160-6315-4

Library of Congress Cataloging-in-Publication Data
Taylor, T. Allan.
   Career opportunities in the Internet, video games, and multimedia / Allan Taylor and James Robert Parish.
      p. cm.
   Includes bibliographical references and index.
   ISBN 0-8160-6314-1 (hc)   ISBN 0-8160-6315-X (pb : alk.paper)
   1. Internet—Vocational guidance. 2. Video games—Vocational guidance. 3. Multimedia communications—Vocational guidance. 4. Digital video—Vocational guidance. 5. Web site development—Vocational guidance. I. Parish, James Robert. II. Title.

   TK5105.875.I57T376 2007
   006.7′023—dc22   2006031860

To Chris, Jeff, and Dan Barnes
It Is Their Generation to Whom This Book Truly Speaks

CONTENTS

FOREWORD

Like the industry in which I work, I'm not a kid anymore. Flecks of gray have begun to appear on my temples, probably courtesy of the "crunch times"—seven-day weeks of twelve-hour days—for which my industry is infamous. However, on my best days, you could say that I've matured. And you could say the same thing about the video game, Internet, and multimedia businesses.

In the mid-1990s, when I got an internship doing everything from fixing computers to writing in-game dialogue for a small Chicago game developer, the video game and various Internet industries were being referred to collectively as the "New Media" by an old media that seemed equal parts befuddled and dismissive of the potential of businesses run by a bunch of geeky kids in slippers. And while video games, web development, e-commerce, or any of the myriad tangential businesses with names prefixed by *e* or *i* or suffixed by *.com* often have little to do with one another, explaining the difference to people outside of New Media was like explaining the difference between Quake and Excel to my mom.

It's only been a decade, but it's amazing how things have changed. New Media is old hat. E-mail is now the dominant form of communication for everyone from preschoolers to grandmothers. And the New Media companies are starting to act a lot like old media, with corporate consolidation, sophisticated strategic planning, and huge marketing investments. But not everything's changed. I'm happy to say that I'm still wearing slippers.

Though the video game industry has been around since the 1960s, in those days it was largely the domain of relatively few entrepreneurial technologists. Even by the time the Atari 2600 game console captured the imagination of American consumers in 1979, there were still few people who aspired to undertake the arcane craft of those geeky computer programmers cloistered in Northern California's Silicon Valley. Children of the 1950s and '60s hadn't grown up with the technology. In those days, computers were either room-sized data processors solely the domain of NASA engineers or gimmicky toys like the hula hoop. Few households had them, and few kids had the opportunity to tinker with them. But the 1980s dawned, and with them came Atari and Apple. So when Generation X began looking for jobs in the 1990s, things were much different.

For the first time a large number of people who had grown up with personal computers and video games were entering the workforce. For them, Nintendo wasn't like the hula-hoop or a lava lamp. Video games were as important a part of their free time as television, movies, and music had been in prior decades. This generation didn't see computers the same way their parents did—as mysterious boxes of questionable practical value taking up desk space at the office or home. To Generation X, a desk was taking up space *unless* it had a computer on it.

It was in this environment that I entered the workforce—the typical Gen X "slacker," armed with my degree in English and Cinema from Denison University, a Pavement T-shirt, and an unwillingness to cut my hair, I quickly determined that I was unlikely to unseat the thoroughly entrenched baby-boomer bank president, especially if I continued to prefer slippers to wing tips. In fact, virtually all forms of traditional employment seemed unlikely. I had to do what I now recognize everyone entering the workplace has to do—assess my competitive advantages.

So, while I realized that my preference in footwear might preclude me from much of a future in, say, the international finance field, I understood computers. I hadn't been formally trained in computers, but like many of my friends, I was a tinkerer. I taught myself things like HTML and the basics of networking as my personal curiosity dictated. I also could write pretty well, had years of experience playing Super Mario Brothers, and devotedly watched television. Granted, this isn't the kind of stuff traditionally highlighted on a résumé, to be sure, but it and a pop-culture magazine I edited in college were enough to land me that internship at Chicago game developer Jellyvision. The internship became a job as a writer for the successful You Don't Know Jack series. It was my first job, and, looking back, I was lucky. When I started, the company had only 20 or so employees and was less than two years old. But riding the success of the You Don't Know Jack franchise, the company grew quickly. With that growth came opportunity. By the time I left Chicago for Los Angeles, I'd been a writer, editor, sound designer, and creative director.

While in Los Angeles, I was asked to speak to a small game design class at University of Southern California (USC). I'll admit that the notion of a game design class was bizarre to me, but it was further proof of how quickly the business was maturing. Familiar with my work at Jellyvision, the instructors of the class offered me a job as creative director at their startup interactive television company. Since then, I moved back to Chicago, where I worked on children's electronic learning toys at a large Hong Kong–based company called VTech and later designed slot machines for WMS Gaming—a company formerly called Williams and known for pinball machines. And now I'm living in the epicenter of the video game business, the San Francisco Bay area, producing games for Electronic Arts, the biggest video game company in the world.

When I started in the business a decade ago, I wasn't a programmer or an animator. I didn't have specialized training and I didn't know someone like me could make a living in the field. I was just a guy eager to earn a very modest paycheck and gain any useful experience I could. As it turned out, I was lucky enough to get into an emerging industry on the ground floor.

But that was in the 1990s—the days when anyone with a laptop, a URL, and a halfway compelling presentation on buying tires over the Web could walk out of a venture capitalist's office with a $20 million check and a profile in *Wired* magazine. The good news is that things are much harder now.

That might not seem like good news for people hoping to break into the business, but it's important to remember that in the 1990s both the video game and Internet industries were very unstable. Ambitious game developers without any business experience were taking on tremendous venture capital and using it to pursue ideas that were at best highly speculative. Sometimes they worked, like in the cases of Amazon.com and eBay. Other times, they didn't. And when they failed, they often failed spectacularly. Does anyone remember DEN?

There's no one reason why these companies failed. Sometimes it was poor management, sometimes it was an idea before its time, and sometimes it was just a bad idea. Regardless of why these companies failed, many employees who had opted for modest salaries in favor of large stock option grants, and who had worked 100-hour weeks or more to make those grants valuable, were left with little more than promotional baseball hats and mugs. The New Media companies of those days were gilded sweatshops where people put their personal lives on hold for a payoff that very often never came.

Fortunately for the industry, both employers and employees learned the lessons of the dot-com bust. As a result, these businesses are now better run. Venture capitalists are much less hesitant to fund a completely half-baked idea and corporate management is more risk averse. So while that means employees are somewhat less free to spend large sums in pursuit of the slightest whim, it also means that they're less likely to be unemployed when that whim proves commercially implausible. Today's workforce is less eager to accept stock instead of hard money, so salary and benefits packages are more balanced. In addition, employers recognize the value of retaining talent and experience, so the industry is working hard to move away from the long hours that for so long have defined it. In short, while landing that

first job might be tougher than it used to be, that job is more worthwhile getting.

While the video game and Internet industries today retain many of the trappings associated with the nascent Atari days and the heady dot-com heyday of the late 1990s—things like offices with video arcades, firehouse poles, and machines stocked with free soda—don't expect to find many nerds with taped glasses and pocket protectors. In actuality, the workforce of today's New Media companies looks much more like that of a movie studio, and with good reason. As the large entertainment conglomerates see New Media less like a profitable fad and more like the burgeoning behemoth it is, there is increased cross-pollination of workforces. For example, as more video games are made based on movies and TV licenses, and as more movies are made based on video game licenses, the more it makes sense for individuals exposed to that process to switch from one industry to the other. That is to say, these days you're as likely to see a coworker in a power suit as you are one in slippers.

Also gone are the days when the programmer reigned supreme. It used to be that a game's lead programmer would also serve as the project's producer, the human resources department, and the company's CEO. But as projects, teams, companies, and budgets have become significantly larger, roles have developed that require skill sets other than writing great computer code. That means the need for managers, and lots of them, but not just paper-pushers. The video game business in particular is struggling to find creative project leaders. We haven't yet seen the Martin Scorsese of video games, but the industry sure is looking for such a visionary creative force.

Meanwhile, in the new millennium, programmers in the United States face strong competition from much cheaper teams in places like India and China. The same goes for graphic artists and animators. But those countries are also places with massive tech-savvy populations and economies that will soon afford those populations the disposable income to spend on games. As the new media industry globalizes, some of the most successful artists and programmers are the ones who have made an effort to gain experience in managing global production processes. Competition from abroad is increasing, and the days of measuring success by domestic or English-speaking markets are gone. A game is a hit when it's a hit in the United States, European Union, Japan, South Korea, and China.

Certainly this is an industry that's changing quickly—perhaps more quickly than any other. Ten years ago most of today's new media industry veterans were cutting class to play Madden on PlayStation, technologies on which we base our work today had yet to be developed, and virtually no one had considered consumer markets like China that today represent the industry's most explosive growth potential. It's important that those who want to break into the business stay on top of trends that move at a remarkable pace. We're moving from hard goods to online content delivery, from PC and game consoles to portable devices and cell phones, and from subscription services to microtransactions and virtual currencies. But what's next?

On the other hand, some things don't change. Those who hope to begin a career in video games and/or the Internet would still be well served to do what I did when I first beat the street with my slippered feet: Identify what your competitive advantages are and then capitalize on them. Regardless of whether you're a programmer, an artist, a Web developer, or a writer, focus on what sets you apart from the rest of the applicants for any single job. It might be your foreign language skills or the magazine you edited in college. You never know what will resonate with a potential employer, but you can count on the fact that the same old résumé won't. The new media business was built by visionaries, geeks, and oddballs. The good news is that there's still plenty of room for them.

—Dan Fiden, Half Moon Bay, 2005

Dan Fiden holds a B.A. in English and Cinema from Denison University in Granville, Ohio, and has worked as a producer, game designer, creative director, writer, and sound designer in the interactive TV, gambling, toy, and video game industries. He currently lives in Half Moon Bay, California, with his wife Priscilla and dog Gary.

INDUSTRY OUTLOOK

The more than 80 jobs described in *Career Opportunities in the Internet, Video Games, and Multimedia* are all concerned with job positions in the fastest growing industry sectors in the United States, that of multimedia, the Internet, and electronic games. Nielsen/NetRatings, a research/ratings firm, stated that Web purchases (including spending on online auction sites like eBay) totaled $30.1 billion for just the months of November and December 2005 alone (the highest spending months due to the seasonal holidays). This represented an increase of 30 percent over the same time period of the previous year. Nielsen noted that Yahoo!'s online service in November 2005 continued its domination on the Internet with 104 million unique users, topping MSN (91 million), Google (85 million), and America Online (AOL) (74 million). While e-commerce today still represents less than 6 percent of all retail sales in the United States, these statistics indicate that online commerce has become an important part of mainstream American shopping—and is still on the rise.

JMP Securities, a Wall Street firm, expected that the online ad market would grow to $26.4 billion worldwide in 2006 and $33.2 billion in 2007. Furthermore, JMP expects online advertising spending will soar to $35 billion by 2010, when the Internet will command 11.1 percent of all advertising dollars spent (as opposed to 4.7 percent during 2005).

As for the computer and video (electronic) game industry, a survey conducted by the Entertainment Software Association in 2006 found that 69 percent of American heads of household play computer or video games, and that the average age of a player is 33. Thirty-five percent of American parents responded that they play computer and video games, and 47 percent of those gamer parents are women. The typical gamer parent is 37 years old, and has been playing games for an average of 13 years (with one-third of them having played for 20 years or more). Among gamer parents, 80 percent report that they play video games with their children, and 66 percent feel that such activity has brought their families closer together. It was also found that the amount of time gamers spend playing games each week is triple that which they devote in total to exercising, playing sports, volunteering in the community, religious activities, creative endeavors, cultural activities, or reading. Clearly, electronic game playing has become a major form of entertainment for a wide number of Americans.

Multimedia, as the name implies, is the seamless integration of multiple forms of media (e.g., text, audio, graphics, animation, video, and interactivity) to convey information and/or entertainment. It is important to realize that humans retain 20 percent of what they see, 30 percent of what they hear, 50 percent of what they both see and hear, and 80 percent of what they see, hear, and do—thus, multimedia is an extremely effective way of communicating data. Multimedia also refers to the use of computer technology to create, store, and experience multimedia content. As the information is presented in various formats, multimedia expands on the user experience and makes it easier and faster to grasp information. Although presenting information (or entertainment) in assorted formats is nothing new, multimedia generally implies presenting information in various digital formats.

Multimedia finds its application in many areas, including art, education, entertainment, engineering, medicine, mathematics, business, and scientific research and training. For example, in education, multimedia is used to produce computer-based training courses (popularly called CBTs) and the creation of online reference books like encyclopedias and almanacs. A CBT lets the user proceed through a series of presentations: text about a particular topic and associated illustrations in various information formats. The Multimedia Messaging System (or MMS) is a multimedia application that allows a user to send and receive messages containing multimedia-related content, and is a common feature of most cell phones. An electronic multimedia encyclopedia can present information differently (and, some say, better) than a traditional encyclopedia by presenting hyperlinks to related articles on the subject being researched, and presenting illustrations, maps, and video or aural presentations on the subject in an order chosen by the user. Hyperlinks let a user access information in a nonlinear fashion (skipping through various aspects of the subject being investigated or between it and other related subjects) as opposed to print materials, which are essentially linear (in which such skipping must be done with the aid of an index or, if necessary, consultation with other sources of information). Multimedia is also heavily used in the entertainment industry, especially to develop special effects in movies and animation, as well as electronic (video) games. Finally, interactive multimedia applications allow users to participate actively instead of just sitting by as passive recipients of information.

The Internet is a vast cooperative enterprise, unique in the history of business and human communication as being an organic thing controlled by no single person, company, or entity. The Internet is an interconnected set of computers and computer networks, linked to each other by copper wires, fiber-optic cables, microwave links, and so forth. It was originally developed by the U.S. Department of Defense in 1969 as a way for U.S. research scientists to experiment with methods for computers to communicate with each other. Their creation, the Advanced Research Projects Agency Network (ARPANET), originally linked only four separate computer sites at U.S. universities and research institutes, where primarily scientists used it. In the early 1970s, other countries began to join ARPANET, and within a decade, it was widely accessible to researchers, administrators, and students throughout the world.

This Internet (or Net) grew at a fast pace in the 1990s as the general population discovered the power of the new medium (thanks to the expanded availability of relatively low-price computer hardware for the consumer marketplace). A significant portion of the Net's content is written text, in the form of both electronic mail (e-mail) and articles posed in an electronic discussion forum known as the Usenet news groups. Until this great surge in the growth of the Internet, the major online services (AOL, CompuServe, and so forth) provided e-mail, but only to customers of the same service. When these services began to connect to the Internet for e-mail exchange, the Internet took on the role of a global switching center, and, effectively, glued the world together for electronic mail.

In the mid-1990s, the appearance of the World Wide Web (WWW) made the Internet even more popular. The World Wide Web is an interconnected set of documents and files linked together by hyperlinks. Specifically, the Web is a multimedia interface and hypertext system that allows for the transmission of text, pictures, audio, and video together, known as Web pages, which commonly resemble pages in a magazine. With the advent of graphics-based Web browsers, such as Mosaic, Netscape Navigator, and, soon after, Microsoft's Internet Explorer, the use of the World Wide Web took off. Now the Web was easily accessible for all users of computers (both Macintosh, or Macs, and Personal Computers, or PCs) rather than just largely scientists and researchers. At the same time, new Internet service providers (ISPs) started to offer access to individuals and companies. An Internet service provider is any organization through which Internet access can be arranged. Most ISPs are typically commercial or community organizations offering dial-up access (or fast-speed access through Digital Subscriber Line [DSL] access), usually along with other services such as Web hosting (the creation and management of personalized Web pages) and e-mail. Together these various elements have made the Internet a multimedia medium for communication and for the retrieval of information on virtually any topic.

Besides the complex physical connections that make up its infrastructure, the Internet is held together by bilateral or multilateral commercial contracts and by technical specifications, or protocols, that describe how to exchange data over the network. Each computer that is directly connected to the Internet is uniquely identified by a 32-bit binary number, called its IP. (The IP protocol defines the packets that carry blocks of data from one node to another.) As this address is usually seen as a four-part decimal number, it was found to be difficult to remember. Thus, a system of Internet addresses, or domain names, was developed in the 1980s. Reading from left to right, the parts of a domain name go from specific to general. For example, www.irs.ustreas.gov is a World Wide Web site at the U.S. Internal Revenue Service, which is part of the U.S. Treasury Department, which is a government agency. The rightmost part of the domain name designates either a country (*ca* for Canada, or *uk* for United Kingdom) or a specialized abbreviation, such as *edu* (educational institution), *gov* (government), *com* (commercial), *int* (international), *net* (network), or *org* (organization). The 32-bit binary number (IP) is translated into a specific IP address by a domain-name server, a computer program running on an Internet-connected computer. Since 1998, the Internet Corporation for Assigned Names and Numbers (ICANN), a nonprofit U.S. corporation, has been responsible for overseeing the domain name system.

Other protocols for the Internet include Transmission Control Protocol (TCP) and User Datagram Protocol (UDP), related to the sending of data from one host to another. The former makes a virtual "connection," which gives some level of guarantee of reliability. The latter is a best-effort, connection-less transport, in which data packets that are lost in transit will not be re-sent. On top of these comes the application protocol, which defines the specific messages and data formats sent and understood by the computer application programs running at each end of the communication. This Internet group of protocols was designed to be independent of the underlying physical medium being used to send the data. Any communications network, wired or wireless, that can carry two-way digital data can carry Internet traffic. All these networks, whether wired (by copper wire, coaxial cable, or fiber optic) or wireless (as through such wireless networks as Wi-Fi or cell-phones), share the same protocols and, hence, ARE the Internet.

It is estimated that as of January 2006, over 1 billion people were using the Internet. The public information stored in the multitude of computer networks throughout the world connected to the Internet forms a huge electronic library, but the enormous quantity of data and number of linked computer networks also make it difficult to find where the desired information resides and then to retrieve it. A number of progressively easier-to-use interfaces and tools have been developed to facilitate online searching. Among these Internet search engine utilities are Archie, Gopher, and WAIS (Wide Area Information Server). Additionally, there are also a number of commercial search engine indexes, such as Google or Yahoo!, which are a collection of complex computer programs that use a proprietary algorithm or other means to search a large collection of keywords and quickly return to the searcher a list of documents or Web sites containing one or more of the keywords. In addition, Telnet is a computer program that allows users of one computer to connect with another, distant computer in a different network, and the File Transfer Protocol (FTP) is used to transfer such information between computers in different networks. Thus, through keyword-driven search methods, millions of people worldwide now have easy, instant access to a vast and diverse amount of online information. The World Wide Web has enabled a sudden and extreme decentralization of information and data.

In turn, the Internet has drastically altered the way society conducts its personal and business life. With its high-speed connections, Internet has significantly altered the way many people work. Contrary to the traditional nine-to-five workday where employees commute to and from work, the Internet has allowed greater flexibility in terms of both working hours and work location. Today, many employees work from home, on either a part-time or a full-time basis, by telecommuting their work to their company. Additionally, many individuals (and some companies and groups) have adopted the use of "weblogs" or blogs, which are largely used as easily updatable online diaries. They give employees a forum from which to voice their opinions about their jobs, employers, and coworkers (as well as opinions about almost anything else on their mind). Some commercial companies encourage their staff to fill them with advice on their areas of specialization in the hope that online visitors to these blogs will be impressed by the expert knowledge, advice, and information and, thus, be attracted to the firm (and its services and/or products) as well. Technorati, a search engine that tracks the "blogosphere," estimates that the number of blogs on the Web amount to 28.7 million, though that number may soon be peaking, as growth in the numbers has lessened in the last year or so.

The Internet has also become a larger market for companies, which have taken advantage of the efficient nature of low-cost advertising and commerce through the Internet, now known commonly as e-commerce (electronic-based commerce). Such a use of the Internet has proved to be the fastest way to spread information about services and products to a vast number of people simultaneously. The Internet has subsequently revolutionized the process of shopping. For example, an individual can order anything online (at any hour of the day or night, including weekends) and usually receive it in the mail within a few days, or, in the case of software, articles, or research, even download it directly to their computer. The Internet has also greatly facilitated personalized marketing, which allows a company to market a product to a targeted person or group of people more efficiently than any other advertising medium allows. Examples of personalized marketing include online communities (such as MySpace, Friendster, and others), which thousands of Internet users join to advertise themselves and make friends online. Many of these users are young teens and young adults ranging from 13 to 25 years old. In turn, when they advertise themselves they indicate their interests and hobbies, which online marketing companies can then use as information as to what those users will purchase online, and thus advertise their own products to these potential buyers.

In matters of remote access, the Internet allows computer users to connect to other computers and information stores easily, wherever they may be in the world. They may do this with or without the use of security, or authentication and encryption technologies, depending upon their requirements. Thus, an accountant sitting at home can audit the books of a company based in another country, on an Internet access provider (server) based in a third country that is remotely maintained by information technology (IT) specialists in a fourth country. While some of these situations were possible *before* the Internet, they would have been so costly as to be infeasible in practice. Now, individuals away from their desks, or perhaps on the other side of the world on a business trip or a holiday, can open remote desktop sessions into their normal office or home personal computers, using a secure Virtual Private Network (VPN) connection (via the Internet), and have access to their own files and data, including e-mail.

In addition, the Internet offers the possibility for individuals to undertake and gain online educational degrees from accredited colleges. (This was greatly amplified in March 2006 when the U.S. Congress dropped the requirement that colleges offer at least half their courses face-to-face to receive federal student aid.) Furthermore, the Internet is providing job seekers some exciting new alternatives to explore. Job Web sites have proliferated, many of them capitalizing on search engine technology to provide job offerings of all kinds and from areas throughout the United States and other countries to those individuals looking for positions, or to change jobs. Studies indicate that an increasing number of people are being hired through Web postings and employee referrals, rather than through traditional methods like printed want ads.

Another advantage of the Internet is that it allows computer files to be e-mailed to customers, colleagues, or friends as an attachment, which can be uploaded to a Web site or an FTP server for easy downloading by others. The attachment can be put into a "shared location" or onto a file server for instant use by colleagues. In addition, access to the file can be controlled by user authentication, or the transit of the file over the Internet can be obscured by encryption until money can be exchanged for access to the file. These simple features of the Internet are changing the very nature of the production, sales, and distribution of many types of products and services, wherever they can be reduced to a computer file for transmission. This includes all manner of office documents, publications, software products, music, photography, video, animations, graphics, and most of the other arts.

In terms of leisure, many individuals use the Internet to access and download music, movies, and other works—such as e-books (electronic books)—for their enjoyment and relaxation. There are paid and unpaid sources for all of these, using centralized servers and distributed, peer-to-peer technologies. The World Wide Web is also used to access news, weather, stock, and sports reports, to plan and book holidays, and to explore ideas and casual interests. One other main area of leisure on the Internet is multiplayer gaming. This form of leisure activity creates communities, bring people of all ages and origins together online to enjoy the fast-paced world of multiplayer games, ranging from role-playing games to online gambling. This has revolutionized the way many people interact and spend their free time on the Internet.

Videotape is a means of recording pictures from television or film and their accompanying sound onto magnetic tape as opposed to movie film. Videotape is used in both videotape recorders (VTRs or, more common, video cassette recorders [VCRs]) and video cameras. Tape is a linear method of storing information. While videotape machines go back to 1956, Sony introduced in 1969 the first widespread video cassette (prior formats had used open reels). The first domestic videocassette recorders were introduced in the early 1970s, but it was not until the Japanese systems, Sony's Beta and JVC's VHS, were launched, that videotape moved into the mass market, resulting in what came to be known as the "videotape format war," which VHS finally won. It is still the leading consumer VCR format. However, it has lost the battle against the nonlinear and disc-based DVD, and is fairly rapidly slipping into obsolescence.

DVD is an acronym for *digital video disc.* The first DVD players and discs were made available in November 1996 in Japan, in March 1997 in the United States, and in 1998 in Europe. By the spring of 1999 the price of a DVD player had dropped below $300. At that point, large retailers, such as Wal-Mart, began to offer DVD players for sale, but DVDs still represented only a small part of their video inventory, with VHS tapes of films making up the remainder. With their increased availability, DVDs began to increase in popularity with American consumers.

DVD player sales exceeded VCR sales in the United States in 2001, and DVD rentals topped those of VHS in 2003. In 2005, Wal-Mart and several other large retailers announced plans to phase out the VHS format entirely, in favor of the more popular DVD format. The primary advantages of DVD over VHS are video quality, surround sound, extra features beyond the film or show, and the assertion that, unlike videotape, DVDs will not degrade with age or after many playings. In addition, there is no need to rewind, they provide a quick access to any part of the recording, and they boast of fundamentally lower technology costs for both hardware and disc production. As of 2006, many retailers, such as Circuit City and Target, no longer offer titles on the VHS medium, instead concentrating solely on DVDs. The price of DVD players has dropped to below the level of a typical VCR player, although DVD recorders are still usually more expensive than VCR recorders. In addition, most game play stations, from Microsoft's X-Box series to Sony's PlayStation series, are equipped to handle DVD formats, thus ending VHS's reign, probably forever.

Moreover, there are promising and exciting new trends in the DVD marketplace. For one, there is a new breed of DVD players and discs geared to high definition quality. For another, there is the availability on many DVD recorders to store programming on a hard drive (and the storage capability of such drives is constantly increasing). Meanwhile, DVD stores and Internet outlets which sell DVDs are coping with the latest marketing competitions: DVD rentals by mail (such as from Netflix and Blockbuster) and the availability of Web sites that allow users, for a fee, to legitimately download films, TV shows, and so forth, to burn onto blank DVDs.

Gaming is arguably one of the most interactive and progressive electronic entertainment mediums in existence today. It certainly is a widely recognized part of our cultural landscape. (It should be noted that the popular term, video game, could just as well be designated electronic game, particularly as most games today can be played on many different types of electronic devices. These two terms mean the same thing and are used interchangeably throughout this book.)

Gaming itself goes back thousands of years. Artifacts from ancient Sumeria and Egypt have shown that our ancestors enjoyed playing board games. Electronic (or video) games, however, required the invention of the computer. The earliest computers were slow, failure-prone monsters that took over entire rooms and had less power than a modern pocket calculator. Nonetheless, early programmers on those machines felt compelled to use their free time by making these computers do things like playing tic-tac-toe. When computers moved out of the realm of cutting-edge laboratories after World War II and into universities and large corporations, many university students became the first game programmers, transforming their ideas into digital adventures.

In 1971, Intel invented the microprocessor, which changed the nature of computing and, indeed, society, forever. Because microprocessors were relatively cheap and increasingly efficient and compact, and could be manufactured in large quantities, they made it possible to use the power of the computer in all kinds of new ways. Two of the earliest computer games were a coin-operated video game named *Pong* and a home console version of essentially the same game, the Magnavox Odyssey. The latter had the additional facility of being able to be hooked up to a television set. It was primitive and only displayed spots of light on the

TV screen, requiring translucent plastic overlays to simulate the appearance of a game. Nonetheless, video gaming proved to be a huge success, and a new form of mass-market entertainment was born.

The earliest consoles could play only one or two games that were hardwired into them, but, in 1976, Fairchild Camera and Instrument introduced a machine that accepted ROM (read-only memory) cartridges. This important advantage allowed game players to buy new games without having to buy a whole new console machine on which to play them. By the 1980s, the market for new games was growing at a tremendous rate, and there were several different home console machines available. The two most popular were Atari's 2600 and Mattel's Intellivision. Since anyone could make ROM cartridges for these machines, new game publishers sprang up overnight. Since the games had to fit within only 4K of memory, it was possible for one person to write an entire game in just a few months! As more and more games were introduced to meet the demand, quality began to be sacrificed. They became replete with errors (bugs) and began to look too much like one another. In 1983, the public became bored and the industry nearly crashed. For most of 1984 and 1985, the home video game industry was nearly dead, although arcade machines continued to be successful, but at a slower pace.

In 1986, a Japanese company, little-known in America, brought out a new home console, the Nintendo Entertainment System. Almost single-handedly, Nintendo rebuilt the home console industry and made their name synonymous with video games. Nintendo made three important changes to the way that the games were produced and sold. First, they strictly controlled who could and could not make games for their machine. Second, they instituted quality standards by rigorous testing methods. Third, they instituted content standards, as they considered themselves producers of entertainment for children. As a by-product of these rules, Nintendo tends to restrict the total number of games for the Nintendo console that are available on the market at any given time to avoid any glut and major price slashing.

At the same time, the personal computer side of the game industry continued to grow slowly in the late 1970s. IBM finally introduced its microcomputer in 1982, first primarily as a machine for small businesses, but at last, the general public began to take personal computing seriously. With the introduction of better color graphics cards for the PC and a new digital sound card, personal computer game development continued to expand, even if nowhere near as profitable as console games. Home consoles were still definitely considered toys, and the games for them were correspondingly simpler and more focused on action than strategy. In the early 1990s, however, a great change swept through the personal computer industry with the introduction of the compact disc as a data storage medium. CD-ROM (CD read-only memory) discs changed the PC game landscape

enormously and, a little later, the console game landscape as well. It was now possible to create really large games with photorealistic graphics and high-quality sound.

In the mid-1990s, Hollywood studios entered the game business. They already owned a lot of audiovisual content from their libraries of movies and television shows, and they thought that computer games would be a good, easy place for them to make more money out of the material. A new game concept was born, the so-called interactive movie. By the use of the CD-ROM, they presented pictures and sound that were better than anything else before. However, the CD-ROM, large as it is, still doesn't have enough room for the video that a truly branching story line requires. As a result the story lines remained relatively simplistic, and the interactivity was minimal. Today, such video is used mostly for the opening and closing sequences in a game, or as transitions between levels.

The introduction of 3-D graphics hardware in the 1990s again changed the game industry. In a 3-D accelerator, a special-purpose processor takes over the work of computing and displaying the game environment. This frees up the CPU to do other things, so games can become richer and deeper in look, sound, and content. This technology makes games today more immersive: it gives game players the sense of being *in* the world rather than just looking at it. In the mid-1980s a few PC games began to allow networked play. Most supported only two players, and required them to phone each other directly via modem. The Internet changed all that. The Internet was not designed for gaming, so it has some technical disadvantages over proprietary game networks, but these are more than made up for by its wide diversity. The Internet gave game developers a common worldwide standard for data communications, and relieved game publishers of the burden of designing and maintaining their own networks. Shortly thereafter came the next step forward: the creation of the massively multiplayer online role-playing game (MMORPG), sometimes called a *persistent world* because it continues to exist even when one player logs off.

Most of the changes in the worlds of multimedia, Internet, and the electronic games industry have been brought about by new hardware of one kind or another. There are two reasons why hardware makes such an impact. First, the computer is still such a relatively new entertainment medium that any change to it has a big effect on the kinds of things users can do. Secondly, games are primarily about interactivity, and computing hardware is what makes interactivity possible.

So where is this constant of dynamic change leading the multimedia, Internet, and game development industries? And how does that affect employment and careers in these industries? Many leaders in these arenas believe that in the near future, the principle of convergence is going to come into play in these fields, as well as most other media industries. A present example of convergence is the electronic games industry itself. There are few industries that bring together as many wildly divergent disciplines. In order to make a successful computer game, it is necessary to combine the logical, systematic disciplines of computer programming and project management with the creative disciplines of art, music composition, and writing, along with the commercial factors of sales and marketing. Another part of this convergence is the benefits that electronic games can provide—in training, education, and productivity—through technology transfers to other industries, such as advertising, hospitality, medicine, nursing, real estate, and the military. Other signs of convergence can be seen in the present-day tentative moves toward bringing the television industry and the computer industry together for the general benefit of their respective customers, as well as the introduction of Integrated Services Digital Network (ISDN) with its digital phone system, voice/video conferencing/mail capabilities, and shared technology affecting e-mail, faxing, and printing. Then, there is the potential convergence of the Web with the cell phone industry whereby future cell phone users may be able to take a snapshot of a barcode of a product which will lead to information about the product, what other similar products might interest the user, potential deals, or what companies are involved in making the product. This information can be made to flow both ways, and it would be significant for Internet advertising. The impact of all these changes on the jobs detailed in this volume will be tremendous, but also it will open even more job opportunities for those with the necessary education, background, and training to take advantage of these golden opportunities.

During his speech at the International Consumer Electronics Show in Las Vegas in 2006, Bill Gates (Microsoft Corporation's Chairman) outlined a digital world in which many devices, including cell phones, computers, and televisions, seamlessly complement each other. As he said, "Technology has revolutionized how we listen to music, watch TV, play games, communicate and manage and share personal information." He predicted a very bright future for a "digital lifestyle."

HOW TO USE THIS BOOK

Purpose

The 82 careers described in *Career Opportunities in the Internet, Video Games, and Multimedia* make it one of the most inclusive directories of multimedia, Internet, and video game jobs available in a single volume. These careers are involved in some of the most exciting technological developments in today's high-tech world. Whether our current environment is labeled the "information age" or the "electronic era," there is no doubt that the multimedia, Internet, and video game industries are major components in our ever-expanding digital economy.

The tremendous number of electronic devices that affect, influence, and, to some degree, define our lives represents a new entertainment and information society that is vital and dynamic. Within the multimedia, Internet, and video game industries the underlying critical factor behind the technical equipment, programming, and technological processes is people. The continual technical and communicative expansion of these industries relies on trained technicians; talented programming, production, and marketing/promotional professionals; skilled craftspeople; persevering clerical staffs; and aggressive managers.

The purpose of *Career Opportunities in the Internet, Video Games, and Multimedia* is to serve as a guide to the most common occupations within these industries. By consulting this volume, high school and college students interested in a career in multimedia, in Internet and Web development, or in the continuously growing electronic game business can learn who does what within the complex superstructures of these industries. Those who are currently employed in a professional capacity in multimedia development, Internet and Web design, or in some part of the electronic game business will also find the information contained in this book helpful as they expand and/or redefine their career paths.

In *Career Opportunities in the Internet, Video Games, and Multimedia,* jobs are explained in detail, including duties, alternate titles, salary ranges, employment and advancement prospects (with a Career Ladder detailing typical routes to and from the position), prerequisites (including education and training, experience, and skills requirements), organizations to join, and helpful tips for entering the job arena under discussion. Thus, this volume is geared to assist both those seeking to start a career in any of these industries and to those experienced members already working within one or more of them who are looking to make career shifts or changes within their profession.

Many of the jobs detailed in this book are available to individuals with appropriate education credentials (typically at least a high school diploma and often a bachelor's degree, or, for the more technical jobs, a more advanced degree) and from one to five or more years of experience. Job positions discussed in this volume cover entry- and mid-level posts and those that require more training and/or education, as well as more years of experience within their field, both mid-level and high-end posts.

Sources of Information

Research for this book includes the authors' own experiences, interviews with professionals within the multimedia, Internet, and games industries, and facts, reports, surveys, and other data obtained from job data banks, professional guilds and associations, the federal government, and educational institutions.

The job descriptions provided are based on representative samples of actual job posts, employment documents, research studies, salary surveys, and tables of organization from many sources in the appropriate industries. Thus, the career descriptions detailed are not theoretical, but represent current practice and reflect the actual structure of jobs in all three of these industries.

How the Book Is Organized

The job profiles in *Career Opportunities in the Internet, Video Games, and Multimedia* are organized into four main sections: Internet and the Web; Video Games; Multimedia and Consumer Electronics: Video and DVD; and Multimedia and Education. The Internet and the Web section has seven subsections: Audio, Design, Editorial, Management, Marketing and Sales, Production, and Technical (which includes programming). The Video Games section has eight subsections: Artwork, Audio, Design, Management, Production, Programming, Quality Assurance and Testing, and Sales and Distribution. The Multimedia and Consumer Electronics section has two subsections: Distribution and Sales, and Production. The Multimedia and Education section is complete unto itself. This organization is designed to reflect the different aspects of each of these industries. An Industry Outlook provides an overview of these related, but different, industries, and the career opportunities available in each of them.

While the careers discussed in this book are the most frequent positions found within all these industries, job titles are not universally consistent and their definitions will vary and often overlap from setting to setting. While most of the positions are unique, some may exist in two or more industries and are presented separately by industry. For example, a graphics designer may work for an electronics game developer or publisher but may also work in designing Web sites for individuals or companies. Each job description notes when there are opportunities for a position in other related areas.

The Job Profile

Each job profile starts with a Career Profile, a brief description of the position's major duties, any alternate job titles for the position, salary ranges, employment prospects, opportunities for promotion, and the job prerequisites, such as education and training, job experience, special skills, and personality traits. A Career Ladder graphically illustrates a typical career path to and from the position described, including the positions below and above each job. The rest of the profile is in an extended narrative format with more detailed information on the job that contains the following:

- Position description, including typical major duties and responsibilities, and any optional duties that may or may not be part of the given job
- Salary ranges from entry-level to top earnings, including the factors (such as individual skills or geographic location) that often affect how much a particular position may pay, and indicating any minimum wage levels set by union/guild regulations
- Employment expectations or job forecast, indicating how difficult the post may be to obtain
- Possibilities and suggestions for advancement, and whether such work progression is unusually difficult
- Education required and any special training necessary for the particular job
- Whether any licensing or certification training may be required
- Necessary and/or useful experience, skills, and personal attributes that enhance the potential for success in the job
- Whether there are any union or guild requirements for holding the particular job and/or suggested professional associations related to the job that may be useful
- Tips and practical suggestions for obtaining that initial job in this job category

The Appendixes

Four appendixes offer further resources for individuals seeking any of the job positions described in *Career Opportunities in the Internet, Video Games, and Multimedia.* Appendix I, "Educational Institutions," lists colleges, universities, and educational institutions, in every state and the District of Columbia, which offer undergraduate degrees (four-year programs) in computer programming, electrical and communications engineering, graphic design, and web/multimedia management, as well as other specialties, such as animation, applied mathematics, cinematography and film/video production, cognitive science, communication technology, computer engineering, computer graphics, data processing technology, design/visual communications, digital media, drafting and design technology, information technology, LAN/WAN management, mathematics/computer science, playwriting/screenwriting, sales/distribution, software engineering, technical and business writing, and webpage/multimedia design. The listing does not include *every* four-year institution that offers courses or undergraduate degrees in various areas of the multimedia, Internet, and video games industry. (In addition, not included are such overlapping general majors as computer science or marketing, which most colleges/universities offer, or such tangential specialties as creative writing, fine/studio arts, physics, or speech.) The listings provide each institution's address, telephone number, fax number, e-mail address, and Web site, as well as the major programs relevant to the multimedia, Internet, and electronic game industries.

Appendix II, "Periodicals, Newsletters, and Directories," offers a useful resource list of magazines, newsletters, and directories concerned with multimedia and Internet interests and issues and technologies related to electronic games and their industry in general. (Note that books are not included in this Appendix, but are part of the Bibliography.)

Appendix III, "Professional, Industry, and Trade Associations," lists professional and trade associations related to the multimedia, Internet/World Wide Web, and electronic game industries. For each entry, the address, telephone number, fax number, e-mail, and Web site are provided. Appendix IV, "Useful Web Sites," offers a wide range of Internet resources in many categories that are useful for job searching, trade news and information, and networking, as well as a list of general search engines that will help in researching these industries.

A Glossary of terms relevant to all three industries includes technical terminology, buzzwords, and names used frequently in the industry. The Glossary is followed by a Bibliography, which includes sources utilized in researching this book. In those instances where online sources are cited, it may be necessary to check the particular Web site to determine whether new updates on the topic are now available. Also included with these sources is an expansive list of current useful books on careers in multimedia, the Internet and World Wide Web, and electronic games, as well as on the expanding technological innovations now pervasive throughout these industries.

The Index provides a quick source for locating particular job titles (including cross-references to alternate job names), organizations cited in the text (but not in the Appendixes), and other relevant information appearing in the chapters of this volume.

Lastly, please keep in mind that the Internet is in a constant state of flux, and Web sites sometimes change their Web addresses or, on occasion, cease to exist. If a URL stated in this book—each of which was verified as this volume was written—does not produce the desired Web site, it may be necessary to do a search engine query using the name of the Web site to locate its new home.

ACKNOWLEDGMENTS

First and foremost, we want to acknowledge James Chambers and Sarah Fogarty at Facts On File for their enthusiastic guidance on this project. We also want to thank our literary agent, Stuart Bernstein, for his help, encouragement, and suggestions on this project. In addition, we, of course, want to express thanks to Dan Fiden for the informative and delightful Foreword to this book and for his general feedback on questions about our topic.

Furthermore, we would like to thank the following individuals for their assistance with this project: Mark Allen, Brad Schreiber, Nat Segaloff, Stephen M. Silverman, James Tobey, Michael Tunison, Steven Whitney, and Don Wigal. We also are grateful to the reference librarians at the Beverly Hills Public Library for aiding our research for this book.

INTERNET AND THE WEB

AUDIO

COMPOSER

CAREER PROFILE

Duties: Composes music to be used as background for a Web site or individual webpage

Alternate Title(s): Musician

Salary Range: $10,000 to $60,000 or more

Employment Prospects: Poor to Fair

Advancement Prospects: Fair

Prerequisites:

Education or Training—College degree in music recommended, but not required

Experience—Work as a Composer and/or a songwriter for film, music videos, or theater

Special Skills and Personality Traits—Able to express emotions in musical terms; background in classical music training

CAREER LADDER

```
┌─────────────────────────────────────┐
│   Music Director or Supervisor       │
└─────────────────────────────────────┘

┌─────────────────────────────────────┐
│            Composer                  │
└─────────────────────────────────────┘

┌─────────────────────────────────────┐
│   Musician; Orchestra Conductor      │
│   or Arranger; Songwriter            │
└─────────────────────────────────────┘
```

Position Description

Composers create a music score, songs, or thematic melodies that underscore the action of what is appearing on the webpage or the entire Web site. The music or song is intended to heighten the visuals and/or the words that are used to convey the message(s) of the Web site, or are used to establish an atmosphere or mood in which the visuals take place. Music rhythm can intensify the action of the visual and help to both create and dissipate tension for emphasis. In other instances, music may be used strictly to add further entertainment value to the webpage or Web site, or to create viewer interest during the slower-paced visuals. Not all Web sites utilize the additional feature of musical sounds, but many of the commercial Web sites do.

In planning Web sites that utilize music, visual images can be selected and ordered into a pattern that is prescribed by the prerecorded music by the Composer. Fast-paced music might accompany brisk cutting of visual images and rapid action on the webpage, and slow-paced music might coincide with slower movements. The timing of the visuals can be made to coincide with the timing of the music so that both begin and end at the same points and achieve a parallel structure throughout the webpage or Web site. On the other hand, original music can be composed to accompany specific visuals already planned for a webpage or a Web site.

To compose a musical score for a Web site (as for a television production or film), Composers first have to gain a creative perspective of what variety of musical themes will be needed by studying a rough cut of the webpages. They work with the webpage designers to determine on which webpage the music should emerge and when it should fade out. With all these decisions made, the Composer can begin creating the music that has been decided will accompany the visuals and where this will occur on the Web site.

Today, many musical scores are created first on a computer using a computer language known as the Musical Instrument Digital Interface (MIDI), which allows a computer to control all kinds of musical electronics, including keyboards, synthesizers, and drum machines. These computer music programs and synthesizers can make it easier to have original music composed, played, and recorded by one person, usually the Composer. Having this type of computerized orchestra, so to speak, allows the Composer and the webpage designers to make changes at will, quickly and easily cutting and pasting and shifting music around until it fits the planned concept of the Web site and its various webpages. In other instances, live musicians may be called upon to perform the music created for the Web site.

Most Composers who create music for Web sites also create musical scores for television and, at times, film productions. In those instances, the musical score is more extensive and the entire production process of wedding the score to the visual action is lengthier.

Salaries

Salaries vary widely and depend greatly upon the requirements of the individual Web site and the concepts of the development team. Generally, Composers are not covered by the American Federation of Musicians (AFM) and are customarily paid a flat fee for their composition for the product. If they are a part of the performance group producing the music, they may be compensated through a package deal that may include the union scale due for any union-covered services they perform beyond the composing. Composers may also write for television, music videos, and for computer games and may have annual earnings that range from $10,000 to $60,000 or more. In some cases, beginning Composers may receive a deferred salary and use the opportunity to showcase their talents in order to obtain work on other projects.

Employment Prospects

The competition for music scoring of Internet Web sites is strong and there are not that many Web sites that use original music scores. Nonetheless, opportunities do exist for newcomers in the field. Most Composers work in many arenas, from music videos to television, from electronic games to films.

Advancement Prospects

There are very few advancement prospects for a Composer, as it is a top position for most such individuals. In some cases, they may move on to become a music director (or a music supervisor) for a television station, or a production company that produces music videos. Once they work for a music production firm, there may be openings in the higher management of the organization.

Education and Training

It would be helpful to have music training in the classics. Taking courses in composing for other media, such as films

and television, and in the art of orchestrating also would be useful. Most Composers are adept at playing piano, as well as other instruments. In addition, they may be accomplished with a sequencer or a synthesizer and have the technique of producing the music they write.

Experience, Skills, and Personality Traits

Successful Composers need to be able to create memorable melodies (and often lyrics, as many Composers are also songwriters). They must be musically oriented and be able to create music that will form an emotional undertone to the images utilized on the Web site. Composing, itself, is a very solitary type of art, and Composers usually work alone and within their own time frames. However, in working with webmasters and webpage designers, they must be patient in the process of editing and be able to produce results under tight deadline schedules. Good computer skills are another asset.

Unions and Associations

Composers are not represented by the main music union, the American Federation of Musicians (AFM). Many Composers are members of such performing rights organizations as the American Society of Composers, Authors and Publishers (ASCAP), Broadcast Music, Inc. (BMI), or SESAC, Inc., which greatly aid their guarantees of fair earnings on their compositions.

Tips for Entry

1. Work as a musician in a television studio orchestra or a band to gain practical experience in working with and hearing musical textures.
2. Contact film schools and volunteer to write music for student or low-budget films or public access cable shows to gain practical experience in writing music to fit visual scenes and images.
3. Prepare a sample CD recording, audiotape, or digital file of your work to help you to create interest in your composing at production companies that specialize in Web design.

SOUND DESIGNER

CAREER PROFILE

Duties: Create voice and sound effects, and integrate the music, for Web sites

Alternate Title(s): Sound Coordinator; Sound Producer

Salary Range: $35,000 to $70,000 or more

Employment Prospects: Limited

Advancement Prospects: Fair

Prerequisites:

Education or Training—High school diploma usually required, as well as courses in music or sound production; additional training in computer programming, graphics, and multimedia helpful

Experience—Some sound studio participation or sound production in film, video, or television

Special Skills and Personality Traits—Ability to integrate sound with visual images in Web site production; capacity to work under deadline pressure; knowledge of sound production techniques

CAREER LADDER

Sound Producer; Supervisory Sound Editor

Sound Designer

Sound Technician; Trainee, Sound Production

Position Description

Sound Designers have the task of creating/manipulating the necessary nonmusical sound elements utilized to underline the visual elements presented on a Web site. They design the nonmusical special sound effects, integrate the musical elements, and work with the Web designer and producer to create the overall design and shape of the sound track to complement the theme and tone of the Web site and its webpages.

The work of Sound Designers begins in the beginning stages of the Web design process with a critical appraisal of the producer's script or program for the Web site to determine how sound is, or can be, involved in the creation of the webpages. This script will have specific references to sounds, either directly or indirectly, such as implied sounds of running water, the rustling of leaves, sounds of birds, or even background recorded human speech. All of these sounds are utilized to emphasize the visuals on the webpages. Sound Designers must have a good grasp of what the Web site's message or theme is (and their target audience) and how the Web designer has set out to accomplish these goals.

Sound Designers must work with sounds from a variety of sources: recorded archives of human speech, live recordings of talent hired for the project, digitized sounds and effects, synthesized music, and so forth. Another concern is that the finished Web site will have sound that will play well on the kinds of hardware that likely customers will have and use in accessing the Web site. In addition, they must be familiar with the tools used for digitally recording, mixing, and modifying sound. That is why most Sound Designers are also sound editors.

In creating sound effects, Sound Designers working on a Web site are similar to those individuals working on sound in television, film, or electronic games, in that they utilize computer programs to manipulate sound effects. The current industry standard is a software program called "Pro Tools," made by Digidesign. Pro Tools allows a Sound Designer to capture sound digitally and then move the elements around as easily as a writer uses a word processor. Sound Designers need to know how to synchronize the sound and edit the sound cues onto the scene, in the case of a Web site, as visualized on the webpage.

Most professional Sound Designers work on various types of jobs, from multimedia projects and Web sites to television, video, electronic game, and film productions.

Salaries

Earnings may vary somewhat from project to project depending upon the complexity of sounds needed or the size of the Web site. Experienced and well-known Sound Designers may earn up to six figures a year. The average weekly salary ranges from $700 to $1,400.

Employment Prospects

As most Web sites still do not utilize extensive sound effects, the available jobs for Sound Designers are somewhat limited, mostly to the larger commercial Web sites or other high profile, more elaborate Web productions. Few Sound Designers work exclusively on Web site production, but supplement their other design activities in the video, television, or film industries by working with individual Web site designers or Web site design production companies on a project-by-project basis.

Advancement Prospects

Advancing from Sound Designer to more advanced sound positions in media production or in postproduction companies is possible, but usually requires some management experience, as most higher positions, to a degree, are supervisory, and these positions become vacant relatively seldom. Thus, competition is stiff.

Education and Training

While a thorough understanding of the physics and production of sound is essential, a diverse liberal arts background is recommended as well. Such a background will enable Sound Designers to deal well with the various subjects and needs of Web site designs created for diverse clients and their audiences. Training in music, sound, film, and any other subjects in which audio ideas are expressed is equally important. Training in the use of microphones, as well as recording and sound mixing equipment, is essential.

Experience, Skills, and Personality Traits

Working as a sound technician for a radio or a television station is good background experience for a Sound Designer, as is working as part of the sound crew for a theatrical play or a low-budget film. A thorough knowledge of computers, audio mixing consoles, digital audio workstations, audio recording techniques, theory of sound, and concepts of audio technology are important skills.

Sound Designers have to be good listeners, well organized, creative, but also able to work closely with Web site designers and producers on what they want for the Web site. Sound Designers have to be able to think of sound as an art form explaining and underlining the written ideas expressed and the visuals displayed on the Web site.

Unions and Associations

There is no union for Sound Designers. However, some Sound Designers may belong to either the Sound Technicians Local, Local 700, of the International Alliance of Theatrical Stage Employees (IATSE) or the Sound Editors Union. Other industry associations, such as the International Association of Audio/Video Communicators, may be beneficial for networking purposes.

Tips for Entry

1. Look for courses in acoustics (physics of sound) and electronic sound production. A music school or a college music department may be your best bet.
2. While in school, work in a music or sound studio to acquire experience in the latest techniques of sound recording.
3. Work on your computer skills, as they will be necessary for your position as Sound Designer.
4. Be willing to accept a low-paid beginning post at a sound effects company, or on a postproduction crew, to gain needed experience, knowledge, and contacts.

DESIGN

FLASH DESIGNER

CAREER PROFILE

Duties: Animate images, shapes, texts, and SWF (shockwave flash) clips for Web sites

Alternate Title(s): Flash Developer

Salary Range: $40,000 to $80,000 or more

Employment Prospects: Fair

Advancement Prospects: Fair to Good

Prerequisites:

Education or Training—Minimum of two-year college degree with computer and art-related courses; recommended four-year college degree in graphic design or fine arts with training in industry-standard flash and graphic design programming applications and applicable programming languages

Experience—One to two years' experience in traditional graphic design and one or more years' work in multimedia design; general familiarity with computer programs and interface design

Special Skills and Personality Traits—Ability to take direction from Web designer, art director, or producer to develop flash design elements for multimedia Web sites that meet the needs of the client; capacity to think in a nonlinear way that anticipates and then facilitates the end user's experience on the Web site; creativity within the framework of detailed specifications; familiarity with various genres or styles of flash art; good communication and customer service skills; sense of artistic style and composition

Special Requirements—Certification as a Macromedia Flash MX 2004 Designer may be recommended

CAREER LADDER

```
┌─────────────────────────────────┐
│   Art Director (multimedia);     │
│     Producer (multimedia)        │
└─────────────────────────────────┘

┌─────────────────────────────────┐
│         Flash Designer           │
└─────────────────────────────────┘

┌─────────────────────────────────┐
│    Graphics Art Technician;      │
│    Commercial Graphics Artist    │
└─────────────────────────────────┘
```

Position Description

A Flash Designer is an animation designer (or programmer) who specializes in flash animation. Flash is a Web-oriented vector animation tool and an authoring, or computer-based training, program that was created by Macromedia. Like the Macromedia Director's software program, itself long a staple interactive multimedia tool for CD-ROM applications and other computer content, Flash provides exciting animation content, animated menus, banners, and the like. It can also be utilized for Web menus (the lists that become animated by clicking on given buttons on the screen) and other types of interactive content online.

Flash files are usually coupled with powerful scripting language (known as ActionScripting), and compressed vector output, which enables Flash Designers to create fast-loading, streaming content for the Web, as well as other screen-based media. The media that Flash creates can be embedded in Web sites, played back from CD-ROM discs, or even exported into video productions. In addition, development is continuing to be done on making Flash's content available on small screens like Palm Pilots and cell phones.

Flash files are stored on Web servers as .swf files. When a visitor goes to a Web site that has been designed with Flash animation, the user's browser program will open the webpage containing a Flash animation. It will load a Flash player (if already installed on the user's computer), and the Flash animation will play automatically. One of the problems that Web designers face is that of compatibility. With the many different Internet browsers on the market, Web designers have the job of making their Web sites compatible on all platforms to account for the differences. Flash files do not have this problem as they use plug-ins to ensure that Web sites created with Flash are identical no matter the platform being used.

Flash Designers employ a variety of tools to design their flash animation, from the oval, rectangle, and polystar tools (which draw circles and ovals, rectangles and squares, polygons and stars—allowing for the creation of complex vector shapes) to the pen tool (which creates lines and shapes by creating one point of the line or shape at a time), the line tool (which allows the Flash Designer to alter shapes by using lines to bisect and distort the shapes), the basic selection tool (to choose the objects or portions of the objects for further editing), and the eraser tool (to be able to get rid of any shape in the editing process or to get rid of whatever has been drawn in order to start over).

Most Flash Designers start designing within a wide range of media, even including some print design. Many become involved in a mixture of TV/film production and marketing and then jump into multimedia. Most Flash Designers learn and use the Macromedia Director program, which was the pre-Web, preeminent multimedia application. After working with Hypertext Markup Language (HTML), the scripting language used to create documents on the Web, they utilize the Macromedia Flash programs in conjunction with other popular design and development tools such as Photoshop, After Effects, Dreamweaver, 3D Studio Max, HTML, and JavaScript to help create their final output. However, the core designing experience when working with Flash is its authoring environment and the utilization of Action Scripting, its programming language. One of the great new features in ActionScripting is an ability to make it easier for Flash to communicate with other multimedia applications such as Macromedia Director, or with back-end Web-based databases.

Flash Designers may work as independent freelancers, but most Flash page designers work for Flash site design firms which build professional custom (or template) Web sites, or Web portal applications for clients, and offer free initial consultations, Web site hosting, and Web site templates.

Salaries

While graphic designers generally earn between $30,000 and $65,000 annually, Flash Designers, due to the more specific and detailed training needed, tend to have a higher range of earnings possibilities, from a yearly $40,000 to $80,000 or higher, with an average annual salary being $62,000.

Employment Prospects

As the demand for more sophisticated graphics and art for Web sites and other multimedia outlets grows, there is a corresponding increased demand for designers who can effectively utilize the latest techniques, particularly in flash animation, in order to create interesting and enticing Web designs. According to the U.S. Department of Labor, employment of graphic designers is expected to grow about as fast as the average for all occupations through the year 2014, but the demand for more specific Flash Designers in the rapidly expanding market for Web-based information is as great or greater and will increase prospects for employment for those who have the necessary skills. Flash Designers with the requisite experience will be able to work on design projects not just for the interactive media of Web sites, but also for video games, personal digital assistants (PDAs), and other interactive technology as it develops.

Advancement Prospects

Seasoned and successful Flash Designers can look for advancement to positions of art directors (or their equivalent) in Flash design firms, in game production companies, or other multimedia operations. Where advanced techniques of Flash design are needed, so will be needed those experienced individuals to supervise them: art directors, creative directors, and producers.

Education and Training

A minimum of a two-year college degree in communications with computer and art-related courses may suffice for an entry-level position, but it is recommended that applicants have a four-year college degree in graphic design or fine arts with training in industry-standard Flash and graphic design programming applications (such as Adobe Photoshop, Adobe Illustrator, After Effects, Dreamweaver, and Macromedia Flash with ActionScript) and applicable programming languages (such as HTML, JavaScript, PHP, and CGI).

Special Requirements

While Flash Designers may not be required to be certified in their techniques in order to find employment, such certification as a Macromedia Flash MX 2004 designer may be desirable, as the examination for such represents a professional level of expertise for a designer. Macromedia, in conjunction with Virtual University Enterprise (VUE), offers the Certified Macromedia Flash MX 2004 Designer Exam worldwide at any one of the more than 2,500 worldwide testing facilities. To find the nearest facility, visit their Web site at http://www.vue.com/macromedia.

Experience, Skills, and Personality Traits

Flash Designers should have one to two years of conventional design work and/or at least one year of experience in multimedia design. Flash Designers who look to work in multimedia and Flash design applications (either as a freelancer or an employee of a Flash design firm) need to have hands-on experience with major software packages such as PhotoShop, Quark, PageMaker, Adobe Illustrator, and other similar software, as well as such programming languages as HTML, DHTML, JavaScript, PHP, and CGI, as well as specific training in the use of Macromedia Flash MX 2004.

Flash Designers need to be creative, but also be able to follow the detailed specifications and needs of each Web site they help to design. Flash Designers have to be able to communicate their ideas in writing, visually, and verbally. They must have problem-solving skills, be highly self-disciplined and very detail-oriented, and be able to work rapidly and meet deadlines.

Unions and Associations

While there are no unions that represent Flash Designers specifically, there are designer professional associations that may be of interest, such as the American Institute of Graphic Arts (AIGA), the special interest group on graphic arts of the Association for Computing Machinery (ACM), and the Associated Web Artists Guild (AWAG).

Tips for Entry

1. Take courses in computer graphics, if available at your school, or a course in general graphics art and any vocational-type courses you can find in some of the basic graphics software packages.
2. Peruse a variety of business, educational, and entertainment software and study how animated images are used both to communicate with the user and to provide particular information. Browse various Web sites to determine how well they do these jobs.
3. Volunteer to create art and design for local organizations that are working on Web sites, electronic kiosks, or other multimedia projects.
4. Look into available Flash and ActionScript tutorials that are available on the Internet for both basic, intermediate, and advanced coursework in Flash applications in Web site design.

GRAPHIC DESIGNER

CAREER PROFILE

Duties: Design images for use in Web sites, ensuring that their aesthetic appeal and functionality meet the objectives set by the producer, Web designer, art director, and/or client

Alternate Title(s): Computer Graphic Designer; Graphic Artist; Interactive Designer

Salary Range: $25,000 to $65,000 or more

Employment Prospects: Good to Excellent

Advancement Prospects: Fair to Good

Prerequisites:

Education or Training—Minimum of two-year college degree with computer and art-related courses; recommended four-year college degree in graphic design or fine arts with training in industry-standard design programming applications (such as Adobe Photoshop or Adobe Illustrator) and applicable programming languages (such as HTML, Java, and CGI)

Experience—One to two years' experience in traditional graphic design and one or more years' work in multimedia design; general familiarity with program and interface design

Special Skills and Personality Traits—Ability to take direction from the Web designer, art director, or producer to develop design elements that will meet the Web site needs of the client; capacity to think in a nonlinear way that anticipates and then facilitates the experience of the Web site's end user; creativity within the framework of detailed specifications; familiarity with various genres or styles of art; good communication skills; sense of artistic style and composition

CAREER LADDER

```
┌─────────────────────────────────┐
│   Art Director (multimedia);     │
│   Producer (multimedia)          │
└─────────────────────────────────┘

┌─────────────────────────────────┐
│      Graphic Designer            │
└─────────────────────────────────┘

┌─────────────────────────────────┐
│   Graphic Art Technician;        │
│   Commercial Graphic Artist      │
└─────────────────────────────────┘
```

Position Description

Graphic Designers and graphic artists are principally illustrators of concepts and ideas. In the early years of the computer world, there were very few software programs that used graphics as part of the user information or to illustrate the textual information they presented to the user. With the advent of the Macintosh and Windows operating systems, graphical user interface was introduced and both systems supported graphic icons and other images. With the introduction of the Compact Disc (CD), CD-ROMs, and multimedia software, extensive computer graphics are available to Graphic Designers. Their job is to translate the thoughts and perceptions of a Web designer, an art director, the software engineer, or the producer into finished art and designs that enhance the visual image of a program or a webpage and thereby communicate these ideas directly to the end user.

Web Graphic Designers determine the aesthetic appeal of a Web site, as well as ensuring its user-friendliness. They establish how the computer interface should be constructed to simplify navigation within the Web site and linking to other Web sites. Graphic Designers are involved in the planning discussions and must absorb the key design objectives of the projected Web site. They then combine such traditional design knowledge as color theory and layout with programming and computer design tools that convert the ideas into a functional product.

In addition, they have to consider the multitude of paths that an end user might follow in exploring a Web site, and take into account issues of data compression and the functionality of a variety of computer systems and applications. They create the images used for program buttons and icons, help files, splash screens (that depict two-dimensional images of customer products), box sets (that set those product images into a three-dimensional figure), and other illustrative art that appears on the webpages. Designers choose images that are both attractive and intuitive for the end user and are appropriate for the Web site in question.

While Graphic Designers can call upon many libraries of clip art or scanned photos for much of their basic computer graphics needs, some clients who want their Web sites to be unique may contract for original art. Such unique visuals are now used extensively in advertising that is found on the Internet. While there are some freelance designers, the majority of Graphic Designers work for companies that specialize in graphics production.

Salaries

The American Institute of Graphic Arts (AIGA) reported 2005 median annual total cash compensation for Graphic Designers according to levels of responsibility. Entry-level designers earned a median annual salary of $32,000 in 2005, while staff-level Graphic Designers earned $42,500 per year. Senior designers, who may supervise junior staff or have some decision-making authority that reflects their knowledge of graphic design, earned $56,000 a year. Solo designers, who freelanced or worked under contract to another company, reported median annual earnings of $60,000. Design directors, the creative heads of design companies or in-house corporate design departments, earned $90,000 annually. The U.S. Bureau of Labor Statistics reported income in May 2004 for Graphic Designers that ranged from a yearly low of $23,220 to a high of $65,940.

Employment Prospects

As there is a growing need for art for Web sites and other multimedia outlets, there is a strong demand for Graphic Designers who can demonstrate their skill and already know the software tools utilized in producing interesting Web designs. According to the U.S. Department of Labor, employment of Graphic Designers is expected to grow about as fast as average for all occupations through the year 2014, but the demand

for Graphic Designers in the rapidly expanding market for Web-based information will increase prospects for employment for those who have the necessary skills. Graphic Designers with Web site design and animation experience especially will be needed as demand for design projects increases for the interactive media of Web sites, video games, personal digital assistants (PDAs), and other technology.

Advancement Prospects

Experienced and successful Graphic Designers can expect to advance to positions of art directors (or their equivalent) in game production or other multimedia companies. Where Graphic Designers are needed, so are needed experienced individuals to supervise them: art directors, creative directors, and producers.

Education and Training

A bachelor's degree is usually required for most entry-level and advanced graphic design positions. However, a two-year degree in a computer-related field with courses in the graphic arts may be a good entry-level qualification. Art major students wishing to find employment as Graphic Designers for Web sites should have courses in computer graphics techniques and related software. Advanced work in user interface or educational program design may require a four-year degree with background in computer science as well as communications and graphic design. A solid liberal arts education, including courses in art history, writing, psychology, sociology and cultural studies, marketing, and business, should prove useful for Graphic Designers who have to communicate effectively a wide variety of subjects to just as wide an audience.

Experience, Skills, and Personality Traits

Graphic Designers should have one to two years of conventional design work and/or at least one year of experience in multimedia design. Graphic Designers who look to work in multimedia and Web site design need to have hands-on experience with major software packages such as PhotoShop, Quark, PageMaker, Adobe Illustrator, and other similar software, as well as such programming languages as HTML, DHTML, Java, and CGI.

Graphic Designers must be creative, but also be able to work as part of a design team to detailed specifications. Designers have to be able to communicate their ideas in writing, visually and verbally. They must have problem-solving skills, be self-disciplined and very detail-oriented, and be able to work rapidly and meet deadlines.

Unions and Associations

While there are no unions that represent Graphic Designers, there are associations that support their professional development, such as the American Institute of Graphic Arts, the special interest group on graphic arts of the Association for Computing Machinery (ACM), the Associated Web Artists Guild (AWAG), and the Society for Technical Communications (STC) for those Graphics Designers who deal with user documentation.

Tips for Entry

1. Broaden your educational background by taking liberal arts courses in history, the social sciences, business, and writing to provide you with a background to handle design and artistic challenges presented by potential Web content for which you will need to design images.

2. Take courses in computer graphics, if available at your school, or a course in general graphics art and any vocational-type courses you can find in some of the basic graphics software packages. If you are interested in a particular kind of design software, contact the company and find out if it has a special "student" or "learning" version (usually cheaper than the full commercial version).

3. Peruse a variety of business, educational, and entertainment software and study how images are used both to communicate with the user and to provide information. Look at Web sites and see how well they do these jobs.

4. Volunteer to create art and design for local organizations that are working on Web sites, electronic kiosks, or other multimedia projects.

INTERFACE DESIGNER

CAREER PROFILE

Duties: Design the icons, menus, and other design interactive features for a Web site, ensuring good customer interface with the site

Alternate Title(s): Human Factors Specialist; Information Architect; Interactive Media Production Designer; Usability Engineer; User Interface Designer; User Interface Visual Designer

Salary Range: $35,000 to $75,000 or more

Employment Prospects: Fair to Good

Advancement Prospects: Fair to Good

Prerequisites:

Education or Training—Four-year college degree in design, graphic design, industrial design, human-computer interaction (HCI), cognitive science, or computer science, with courses in psychology, graphical arts, semiotics (signs and symbols), and business operations useful; master's degree may be required in some cases

Experience—Three to five years design experience, preferably in graphic or industrial design, and some experience with Web development and Web product design

Special Skills and Personality Traits—Ability to collaborate actively with others in a cross-functional team; excellent interpersonal and leadership skills; highly organized and capacity to act independently; solid computer talents; strong analytical and oral communication skills; thorough understanding of graphic design and Web design principles, color theory, composition, iconography, and typography; understanding of and empathy with computer users

CAREER LADDER

```
┌─────────────────────────────────┐
│   Product Development Director;  │
│      Web Product Manager;        │
│      Web Systems Director        │
└─────────────────────────────────┘

┌─────────────────────────────────┐
│        Interface Designer        │
└─────────────────────────────────┘

┌─────────────────────────────────┐
│ Graphic Designer; Webpage Designer │
└─────────────────────────────────┘
```

Position Description

Human-computer interaction (or HCI) is a relatively new field of research within computer science and Web site design, as it addresses both ergonomic and interaction issues between users and computers in computer design. Interface Designers utilize human factors, engineering, graphic design theory, and other methodologies to design the user interface of a computer system or a Web site. This user interface is the communication structure between the user and the computer, and consists of several components: what you see on the computer screen when you use a program or visit a Web site, and a set of decisions the Interface Designer makes about that interaction. The interface determines how a user is led through a software program or Web site, setting up a likely path or paths for the user to navigate. It also provides a conceptual structure for organizing large amounts of information. Furthermore, interfaces offer tools for filtering information and then retrieving it at a later point, according to criteria that the user will access.

The key job function of an Interface Designer is to provide ways to manipulate data and visual images on Web sites that more nearly mirror the things people do with real-world objects. Interfaces are delicate balancing acts between graphic, information, and interaction solutions to any design problem. To get that proper balance, the Interface Designer must understand all of the issues that need to be resolved within these three interrelated specialized areas. From this perspective, Interface Designers design and build webpages and Web links using an assortment of graphics software applications, techniques, and tools. They develop and implement the "look and feel" of user interfaces on the Web site.

Consistency, feedback, the ability to recover from errors, and user control are just a few of the principles of good user-interface design. While graphic design focuses on the aesthetics of the interface and the webpage as a whole, interface design is concerned with how effectively users can complete the tasks of obtaining desired information and viewing wanted visuals and how effective their interaction with the computer (and the Web site) proves to be. Visitors to a Web site should be able to figure it out with little explanation or training, and user navigation within the Web site should be as efficient as possible. Another example of good interface design is the creation of icons (to be used on a Web site), where an Interface Designer should always ensure that the icon is simple and appropriate to the action to be taken on the Web site and its meaning clear to users. In addition, the webpage should be of a reasonable byte size for the average user to download, and the graphics large enough to distinguish them on the user's monitor.

Most modern operating systems, such as MS Windows, provide many built-in features that regular programmers and designers utilize to provide Web site basic menus, dialogue boxes, and other parts of their program's interface. While simple Web sites that require little interaction with users or are designed to be utilized by only a few people often do not use an Interface Designer, most major commercial Web sites include a user interface specialist as a part of the design team. As a part of this group, the Interface Designer works closely with the program designers, the graphic designers, and the actual programmers.

Interface Designers should be able to draw icons/symbols, lay out complex information, determine pleasing color systems, create the visual language that flows through the product, optimize a workflow, create simple ways for users to rebound from their own errors in using the site, and organize the site's content so that it can be utilized effectively by the user. In addition, they need to gain experience in color, typography, logo design, data visualization, workflow patterns, hierarchies, database architecture, and industrial design. Thus, to be successful, Interface Designers must, even if not programmers themselves, be familiar with the technical requirements of Web site design and the computer software needed for the project.

Salaries

Salaries vary substantially, depending upon the project's requirements. Large commercial Web sites demand a great deal of attention, and Interface Designers can command relatively hefty salaries, ranging from $60,000 to $85,000 or more a year. Designers working on Web sites with fewer interface design requirements may have lower salaries, from $35,000 to $60,000 yearly. Freelance Interface Designers working as consultants can make an hourly rate of $50 to $125, depending upon their expertise and the size of the project.

Employment Prospects

Computer programmers and developers frequently emphasize how important a good user interface is in guaranteeing good communication between the user and the computer. The application of user interface design in the development and design of Web sites is still in a nascent stage. Nonetheless, there is already a demand for Interface Designers for most commercial Web sites, and the need of interface design to ensure that the Web site is user-friendly is present even in personal Web sites of moderate size and complexity. An Interface Designer who has strong general programming and graphic design skills will readily find employment. As veteran Interface Designer Andrei Herasimchuk has pointed out, work on high technology products (that require front-end computer work) makes it evident that graphic design issues meld into information design issues, which, in turn, turn into interaction issues and point right back to graphic design issues. Because of this interrelationship between the visual, the information, and the interaction in the development of high technology products (such as Web site design), Herasimchuk believes that these projects need Interface Designers, either as managers of the design teams or the driving vision in the overall design.

For these reasons, demand for Interface Designers will only increase.

Advancement Prospects

Basically, there are two possible paths of advancement for Interface Designers. If they work within a corporate structure, Interface Designers can become either lead designers or corporate managers, such as product development managers, or Web systems directors. The alternative path is to become a consultant and compile a growing reputation and record of accomplishment that can command larger and better-paid jobs that, in turn, may lead to higher management responsibilities in a corporate environment.

Education and Training

A liberal arts background is useful for an Interface Designer, as interface design requires an understanding of many seemingly unrelated fields, such as business operation, graphic design, learning theory, and psychology. However, a bachelor's degree in graphic design or computer science with post-graduate course work (or a master's degree) in interactive design or cognitive science and human-computer interaction (HCI) would be an ideal educational background.

Experience, Skills, and Personality Traits

Interface design is both an art and a science, in that Interface Designers need strong visual and graphic design abilities as well as solid software development skills. They must work collaboratively with other designers, programmers, and team design members and be receptive to feedback and direction from others. Conversely, if they are the team leaders, they must have excellent interpersonal and leadership talents. They should have experience in Web application production and the use of such operating computer system software as Photoshop, Illustrator, JavaScript, QuarkXPress, PowerPoint, Dreamweaver, PageMaker, Flash design, and other such design techniques, as well as a basic working knowledge of Hypertext Markup Language (HTML) and Cascading Style Sheets (CSS).

They must be creative problem-solvers and effective communicators (both verbal and written), presenters, and negotiators. They must be extremely detail-oriented and have an obsession for accuracy and consistency. Their analytical skills should include both task analysis and use case creation. (Use case may be defined as a progressive, articulated description of possible sequences or interactions, or requirements, between the system or computer software and its external users, whether a person or another computer.) Their well-rounded understanding of the three major Web design considerations—interaction, organization, and presentation—is key to their success, as visual communication in Web interface design is really about making use of graphic information to "talk" to an audience, offering them information or services that the Web site can provide and how they can make use of them.

Unions and Associations

An Interface Designer may belong to a variety of organizations reflecting different aspects of the design process, in particular the Associated Web Artists Guild (AWAG), the special interest group on graphic arts and design (SIGGRAPH) of the Association for Computing Machinery (ACM), or the Society for Technical Communications (STC) for concerns involving user communications and documentation.

Tips for Entry

1. In your undergraduate education, take a broad variety of courses, including ones in business and customer service, graphic design, computer science, psychology, and writing (composition techniques).
2. Be prepared to go beyond your bachelor's degree for course work (and, potentially, a master's degree) in computer science, human-computer interaction, or a related field.
3. Since the best preparation for becoming a designer of any kind is to design, consider developing a personal Web site, such as a blog (which is a frequent, chronological Web publication of personal thoughts and Web links). It is the easiest way to learn about Web design for the simple reason that you will be constantly tweaking and fiddling with it and thinking of ways to improve its user-friendliness.
4. Investigate various Web sites, both personal and commercial, to note their strong and weak points in communicating their products, services, or ideas, and how, from the perspective of a user, you would modify them.

INTERNET ADVERTISING DESIGNER

CAREER PROFILE

Duties: Create effective advertising features for Web sites, including animation, sound, and text

Alternate Title(s): Interactive Advertising Designer; Internet Graphics Specialist

Salary Range: $30,000 to $65,000 or more

Employment Prospects: Fair

Advancement Prospects: Fair

Prerequisites:

Education or Training—Bachelor's degree useful, with liberal arts background and some programming, writing, and graphic design course work

Experience—One to two years' experience with web-page design, working with graphics and animation; programming skills in Java helpful

Special Skills and Personality Traits—Creative in design and graphics; good programming abilities and writing skills; imaginative; knowledgeable in marketing and social psychology; self-starter

CAREER LADDER

```
┌─────────────────────────────────┐
│  Director, Internet Advertising  │
└─────────────────────────────────┘

┌─────────────────────────────────┐
│  Internet Advertising Designer   │
└─────────────────────────────────┘

┌─────────────────────────────────┐
│  Graphic Artist; Graphic Designer │
└─────────────────────────────────┘
```

Position Description

Advertising on the Internet and the World Wide Web has become one of the most widespread means for businesses to publicize their products and/or services. As the Web has such a profusion of Web sites, companies need to do all they can to attract the attention of casual browsers (known as "Web surfers") and motivate them to read and assimilate the detailed text of their site. While some businesses may use their webmaster to design a logo and animation to enliven their Web site, those companies that advertise extensively on the Internet often consider using a specialist designer to create their needed interactive advertising. Similarly, advertising agencies have learned the efficacy of hiring such specialists to work with their clients.

The Internet Advertising Designer has to combine traditional advertising techniques (such as determining potential target audiences and polling them to find out what types of presentations appeal to them) with the requirements of the new interactive medium of the Internet. Features of this medium that have proved to increase the power and the effect of online advertising include the use of striking graphic symbols or logos, dazzling animation, and catchy audio bytes. Using promotions (such as a contest where viewers fill out a survey on the screen to get a prize), free services (such as Internet search facilities and interactive Web guides for users to access information available on other Web sites), customized information, and lists of recommendations (such as books for further reading) can also impact the effectiveness of online advertising. Despite all these enticements, users of the Internet are notoriously quick to move on to another Web site as soon as their attention wavers. While techniques utilized in print media and on television may be useful for Internet advertising, the Internet Advertising Designer has to be extremely creative and not just rely on known methods and rules.

Another important part of the Internet Advertising Designer's work is to test constantly the effectiveness of the advertising beyond just looking at how many "hits" the webpage in question has from viewers. Such statistics make no distinction between those viewers who have returned continuously to the webpage and those who have visited once only. Thus, the Advertising Designer, along with the webmaster, must find ways to get viewers to respond to surveys about what they liked about the webpage, what they did not like, or what on the webpage they wanted to know more about. Reliable information culled from these responses can be used to modify Web sites and their webpages, as well as provide the business a chance to discover ways to establish a relationship with its Internet audience that can ensure repeat business.

More sophisticated design software can demonstrate what parts of a Web site customers frequent, as well as what types of products the customers may more likely buy. However, some consumers are concerned with the potential invasion of privacy in these methods, and some viewers just plainly object to such things as pop-up ads, banner ads, and other garish animation techniques to grab their attention. Software to suppress these techniques has become very popular. Thus, the Internet Advertising Designer has to be extraordinarily creative to find subtler techniques to measure audience approval (or disapproval) and to devise new means of conveying the Web site's message, possibly by combining advertising more naturally within the main text of the site.

Some Internet Advertising Designers have all the necessary programming skills to formulate the required advertising for the Web site, while others may outline the process and establish the criteria for Internet applications programmers to follow. Many advertising agencies now have Internet Advertising Designers on their staff. In addition, Internet-based businesses (such as Amazon.com) have designers on their in-house advertising staff.

Salaries

Earnings for Internet Advertising Designers at advertising agencies generally depend mainly on the size of the agency and the amount of its commitment to advertising on such interactive media as the Internet. At the same time, there are not that many Internet-based businessesthat are large enough and successful enough to have a full-time Internet Advertising Designer on staff.

Nonetheless, according to the U.S. Department of Labor's Bureau of Labor Statistics, median annual earnings in May 2004 of graphic designers (which an Internet Advertising Designer is) were $40,010, and the salaries ranged from a yearly low of $24,000 to a high of $66,000.

Employment Prospects

While the failures of many electronic commerce ("e-commerce") businesses and the resultant economic downturn in the early 2000s have discouraged investment in such companies devoted exclusively to sales on the Internet, the World Wide Web is increasing in importance in the business community and is still *the* place to advertise. Nonetheless, most Internet Advertising Designers will most likely find employment working for advertising agencies or for busi-

nesses who have a presence on the Internet but do not sell their products or services exclusively on the Web (with a few exceptions, such as Amazon.com or priceline.com).

Skills gained in creating online advertising can be applied to other sectors of the economy, such as the educational, government, or nonprofit businesses. The basic demand for advertising professionals who have Internet skills remains strong, and it is up to individual designers to sell themselves and their skills to prospective employers who may not yet be convinced that online advertising works or do not yet know what they may want their company to do on the Internet.

Advancement Prospects

Unfortunately, the spectacular growth of Internet-based businesses has been accompanied by many failures. Internet Advertising Designers employed to work in-house for such businesses may find that they are working for a series of start-up (dot-com) businesses, within which they need patiently to build up their skills and experience. An attractive alternative for these individuals may be to become a consultant. Those designers who work for advertising agencies may have more job stability and a more defined career path to higher positions of authority within the agency. The competition, however, is stiff in both cases.

Education and Training

A liberal arts education, or even a graphic arts degree, with some basic computer and Internet course work, may be a better bet than a computer science degree. Writing and graphic design courses are necessary. In addition, training is always gained on the job working with actual Web sites and their design needs.

Experience, Skills, and Personality Traits

Some years of Web design work, or experience as a webmaster, might prove to be useful. Some Internet advertising design positions (particularly with smaller firms) may combine both design and programming as a job requirement. However, most large firms separate these two functions into different jobs.

Necessary skills for Internet Advertising Designers include animation techniques, graphic arts, layout, marketing, psychology, and writing, as well as a comfortable familiarity with the general capabilities of Web servers, Internet browsers, and plug-in controls. In addition, Internet Advertising Designers need to be creative and imaginative (sometimes in the extreme), but also disciplined and highly self-motivated to grab opportunities as they present themselves.

Unions and Associations

While there are no unions that represent Internet Advertising Designers, there are designer professional associations that may be of interest, such as the American Institute of Graphic Arts (AIGA), the special interest group on graphic arts of the Association for Computing Machinery (ACM), and the Associated Web Artists Guild. In addition, advertising professional organizations should be contacted to find out whether they have any members who are already working on the Internet. Organizations for Internet graphic artists, webpage designers, and webmasters may also be of interest.

Tips for Entry

1. Take courses in advertising and study the industry, exploring the traditional advertising techniques used. Ask yourself how they could be applied to the interactive world of Web advertising.
2. Browse the Web and note what catches your attention and why. What on a Web site makes you want to explore that site more fully, and what annoys or distracts you? Look for techniques used to get feedback from you and what special effects are used to maintain your interest and prod you into participation.
3. Be willing to take beginner design positions working on webpages or as a webmaster for a small Web site, in order to gain the skills and experience necessary to get a position as an Internet Advertising Designer.

SITE FLOW ARCHITECT

CAREER PROFILE

Duties: Responsible for the aesthetic and functional design of an Internet Web site that will enable the end user to navigate it in a multitude of ways with ease and effectiveness

Alternate Title(s): Information Architect; Information Designer; Web Navigation Expert

Salary Range: $45,000 to $95,000 or more

Employment Prospects: Good

Advancement Prospects: Fair to Good

Prerequisites:

Education or Training—Undergraduate degree in computer engineering, graphic design, industrial design, or a related area

Experience—Two to five years in computer software development, preferably in the areas of functional design

Special Skills and Personality Traits—Ability to work as a team member; excellent organizational skills; process orientation

CAREER LADDER

```
┌─────────────────────────────────┐
│        Web Producer;            │
│  Product Development Manager     │
└─────────────────────────────────┘

┌─────────────────────────────────┐
│       Site Flow Architect        │
└─────────────────────────────────┘

┌─────────────────────────────────┐
│ Graphic Designer; Interface Designer │
└─────────────────────────────────┘
```

Position Description

Site Flow Architects are responsible for organizing a multimedia product and/or Web sites so that users can travel from one screen to another in a medium that is nonlinear and has extensive storage capacity. Unlike designing the layout of a book, which a reader knows will follow a logical, ordered path from start to finish through a limited number of pages, the Site Flow Architect has to plan for numerous options for exploration in both a linear and nonlinear manner that will be made available to the user of the Web site. In addition, the information in this exploration has to connect in a seamless and sensible way. This is known as setting up a navigation scheme for the Web site.

During the beginning years of multimedia development, it seemed enough simply to transfer printed information to a digital platform through basic computer design and coding. However, now multimedia and Web site developers have to make their products as easy to use and consumer-friendly as possible. Today, throughout the planning and analysis phase of the product development, the Site Flow Architect must determine whom the end-users will be and what they will be

trying to attain through their use of the product. Architects work with the producer, software engineers, programmers, and content developers to identify the pieces of information to be disseminated, the many ways these pieces of information relate to one another, and how to enable the end-user to access them via the graphical user interface (GUI) programs to be utilized in the product.

From the beginning analysis stage through the final testing phases of the product, the Site Flow Architect must have a keen sense of organization that will refine the various paths in which the information may flow and will anticipate the seemingly unpredictable progression of a consumer through the product. Hardly a two-dimensional matrix containing solutions or "destinations," the possible courses to chart in a multimedia product are vast and challenging, with as many tangents or paths as a creative mind can envision. The Site Flow Architect must be equipped to devise systems to structure these potential routes, allowing the end user to walk each path (figuratively speaking), while always able to return to the starting point or move back and forth to other relevant screens with ease. The aim is always to strike a balance between technical capabilities, aesthetic considerations, and the accessibility of content.

In this process, the Site Flow Architect's primary concern is that the user does not get lost or confused by the extensive possibilities of multimedia products and of Web sites. In addition, architects need to know what types of navigation schemes visitors to the site prefer—text-based or graphics-based navigation, or a mixture of both. Some users might also prefer multimedia effects and pull-down menus, while others may find that confusing. The client for which the Web site is being designed needs to determine the nature of the typical site user's preferences, so that the Site Flow Architect (and the Web site designers) can determine the nature of each page of the site and the navigational techniques that will be used in the site's overall design. In order for a Web site to be successful, it needs to satisfy its target audience, and the navigation architecture utilized for that site is crucial in that satisfaction.

Salaries

According to the U.S. Department of Labor's Bureau of Labor Statistics, median annual earnings of applications software engineers (which Site Flow Architects are) who worked full time in May 2004 were about $74,980. The middle 50 percent earned between $59,130 and $92,130 per year. The lowest 10 percent earned less than $46,520 yearly, and the highest 10 percent earned more than $113,830. Site Flow Architects working in the larger metropolitan areas, such as the San Francisco Bay area, New York City, Los Angeles, and the greater Boston area, typically earn at the high end of the scale.

Employment Prospects

Job possibilities for Site Flow Architects are good. Both the multimedia industry and the Internet have grown faster that anyone projected. The multiple uses of Web sites to advertise businesses and for personal use are continuing to expand exponentially. Each Web site, whether of a personal or a business nature, needs a navigation expert, along with programming engineers and design specialists, to create the pages, balance the Web site architecture, and optimize the navigational experience for the end user.

Advancement Prospects

Prospects for advancement for Site Flow Architects are fair to good. Most architects bring other design or programming skills to bear on their multimedia or Web site task, and can move forward to a management position of Web producer or product development manager within a multimedia company.

Education and Training

A minimum of a bachelor's degree, usually with a major in a process-oriented field such as engineering, graphic design, or industrial design, is the usual requirement for employment as a Site Flow Architect. For some employers, a fine arts or liberal arts undergraduate degree with further courses in graphic design or computer engineering is advantageous, as it provides a platform for cultivating cognitive abilities as well as a foundation in the inborn interrelatedness of form and function.

Experience, Skills, and Personality Traits

While the discipline of site flow architecture is still relatively new, individuals who are able to structure a Web or multimedia project for clear navigation and communication also have to have experience in graphic design, user interface design, and process engineering. They need to be able to organize enormous amounts of information into manageable, accessible, and logical segments, with clear connections between all the elements. In addition, systems administration and database management are necessary adjunct skills for this position.

Personal skills include creativity, imagination, incredible attention to detail, flexibility, and the understanding of the needs of both the individuals presenting the information and the needs and habits of the end users of the information.

Unions and Associations

There are no unions that represent Site Flow Architects. However, many join such professional associations as the Interactive Multimedia Association (IMA) or the Association Web Artists Guild (AWAG).

Tips for Entry

1. During your educational years, take courses in graphic arts, logic, psychology, programming (such as basic HTML, and then various scripting programming languages), and basic business principles, all of which are necessary components of your career as a Web site architect.
2. Volunteer to help create pages for your school's Web site. In addition, look for local nonprofit groups or businesses that are willing to let you try out your budding Web skills.
3. Spend some time on the Internet, studying various Web sites and noting how they display text, links to other pages of information, and links to other data areas. Check out whether the given Web site is appropriately laid out for its stated purpose and the ease of its linkage to its various components, and think how you might design it differently.

WEBPAGE DESIGNER

CAREER PROFILE

Duties: Create pages of animation, graphics, and text linked together for display on the World Wide Web

Alternate Title(s): Web Author; Web Designer; Web Developer

Salary Range: $36,000 to $70,000 or more

Employment Prospects: Fair

Advancement Prospects: Good

Prerequisites:

    Education or Training—No formal requirements, but courses in composition, graphic arts and multimedia, programming, and typography recommended

    Experience—Some preparation of documents via desktop publishing and use of graphics programs helpful

    Special Skills and Personality Traits—Artistic capabilities, but with discipline and great attention to detail; ability to work with a range of artistic tools and resources to create a unified whole product; excellent composition skills; patience and persistence

CAREER LADDER

```
┌─────────────────────────────────┐
│ Webmaster; Internet Consultant/  │
│     Applications Programmer      │
└─────────────────────────────────┘

┌─────────────────────────────────┐
│        Webpage Designer          │
└─────────────────────────────────┘

┌─────────────────────────────────┐
│     Graphic Artist (Internet)    │
└─────────────────────────────────┘
```

Position Description

The World Wide Web, the graphical portion of the Internet, originally started out as a system with only text and no graphics. It has evolved, as the technology has become available, into a true multimedia experience that can include animation, interactive design, sound, and video.

Webpage Designers (or Web Developers) are responsible for the day-to-day Web site creation and design. They create attractive pages to be displayed on their clients' Web sites. Simple webpages may consist of text, graphics, and links so that readers can click on an object and move on to other pages of the Web site (or even other URLs). More advanced webpages may have animated graphics, created sounds, sections of the page (called frames) that can be scrolled separately, or even separate programs (called applets) that can be downloaded to the user's computer to be run in that user's browser. These applets or an earlier similar technology (called CGI scripts) can make webpages more interactive by requesting data from the user or creating customized information displays for the user to view.

Designers have first to consider what information is to be presented on the page or pages of the Web site, what the intended audience for this information is, and how readers of each page typically will interact with it. For example, a simple webpage that just lists names and phone numbers will be quite different from a page that displays examples of a graphic arts studio's creations.

Previously, Webpage Designers had to encode webpages manually using Hypertext Markup Language (HTML). Today, however, matters are much more sophisticated, with word processing programs available to Webpage Designers to accomplish many of these tasks. These programs include a variety of pre-designed page layouts, called templates. The layouts provide the means to insert or arrange both text and graphics, and even to add interactive features such as forms and tables. Often, designers can adapt one of these standard page layouts to the specific needs of a particular client.

Experienced and advanced Webpage Designers may have the option of writing scripts or programs that can be attached to the page (or pages) of the Web site. These scripts or programs can provide such services as database searches, requesting and receiving feedback from the user of the Web site, placing orders for products and verifying credit card purchases, or playing any one of a variety of electronic games. Webpage Designers who have advanced in their craft to this point are verging on becoming applications programmers.

Salaries

Simple webpage composition or maintenance (or revision) of existing pages usually commands only an entry-level salary. Higher salaries result from the designer's ability to write original text and work with complex layouts (with or without scripting or programming).

According to the U.S. Bureau of Labor Statistics' *Occupational Outlook Handbook,* median annual earnings in May 2004 for network systems and data communication analysts (which include Webpage Designers and developers) were $60,600, with the lowest (and entry-level) 10 percent of these positions earning less than $36,260 yearly, and the highest 10 percent earning more than $95,040 per year. According to Robert Half International, a firm providing specialized staffing services, salaries in 2005 for Web developers ranged from $51,750 to $74,520 annually.

Webpage Designers can work full time in-house at companies, but many are freelance consultants or work for an Internet-based "design house." Small organizations may hire a single person who does Webpage design but also may be asked to act as Webmaster and oversee the whole Web site.

Employment Prospects

The incredible growth in the use of the World Wide Web during the 1990s for commerce, education, and entertainment created a strong demand for people who could create original webpage material, adapt existing material, or set up Web-based links to existing databases. Today, however, the availability of various software packages that can put many kinds of information, all custom designed for the client, on the Web automatically has reduced the demand for routine webpage design. Furthermore, the economic shakeout in the e-commerce industry during the first two years of the new millennium greatly reduced the number of start-up Web-based businesses. Individuals looking for positions as webpage designers should widen their search beyond commerce, education, and entertainment, to government, health care, science, and other sectors of the economy.

Advancement Prospects

Advancement usually comes with the mastery of more complex skills of drafting, composition, or programming.

Webpage Designers who learn the technical details of maintaining a Web site may become webmasters. Alternatively, a Webpage Designer who wants to specialize in types of programming (such as in Java, or a scripting language) may, with training, become an Internet applications programmer. Either of these two career moves likely will mean a substantial increase in salary, or in consulting fees.

Education and Training

As with most jobs related to the Internet, employers are more interested in what applicants can show about what they can do than in what type of degree they hold. A liberal arts college degree, however, is a good start for individuals who wish to become Webpage Designers, along with an interest in writing or graphics, and, of course, a solid basic knowledge of computerized design techniques. High school graduates can certainly pick up these skills, at either a community college or an art academy.

Experience, Skills, and Personality Traits

The best way to begin to get experience is to start designing webpages on your own, beginning with simple headings and text and then, gradually, becoming proficient in graphics, link organization, and interactive features. In order to accomplish this, Webpage Designers need to be able to write text for the pages, edit existing text for Web site display (such as breaking it down into logical sections to be displayed on the monitor screen), manipulate graphics (by sizing and placing the graphics on the page), create linking (the logical links that allow the user of the page to explore and find related information on topics of related interest), and design interfaces (the visual methods displayed to facilitate the user's navigation through the linked pages of the Web site). In addition, Webpage Designers need to be well skilled in composition, so that the different elements of the webpage (text, graphics, headings, and frames) fit well together on the page and are easy for the user to work with and to read.

Webpage Designers should be highly creative and imaginative, but also attentive to detail. They need to be flexible and understand the needs of their clients who want to present information to user and also the needs of the end users in their search of the material presented to them on the webpage(s).

Unions and Associations

There are no unions that represent or bargain for Webpage Designers. Many of them join consultant groups or various other groups that are beginning to emerge for Internet content creators. Webpage Designers with a strong artistic bent may find it useful to check out the Associated Web Artists Guild (AWAG).

Tips for Entry

1. Look at a variety of webpages belonging to different types of organizations or individuals for their design, appropriateness (for their content, presentation, and usefulness), and how you might improve them.

2. While in school or college, volunteer to help create pages for the Web site of your school (or college) or a local charity. In addition, look for local nonprofit groups or businesses that are willing to let you try out your webpage skills (but start with simple projects that don't require programming or other advanced skills).

3. Obtain one of the word-processor-type webpage creation programs (such as Microsoft's FrontPage) and work with it to explore assorted page design ideas.

EDITORIAL

MANAGING EDITOR (ONLINE PUBLICATION)

CAREER PROFILE

Duties: Manage day-to-day content, development, and production of Web sites

Alternate Title(s): Editor-in-Chief (online publication); Executive Editor (online publication)

Salary Range: $40,000 to $75,000 or more

Employment Prospects: Fair

Advancement Prospects: Fair

Prerequisites:

Education or Training—Bachelor's degree in communications, English, journalism, or online publishing with marketing-related coursework; technical knowledge of Hypertext Markup Language (HTML) and word processing and graphics production software

Experience—Five to 10 years editorial experience with magazines or newspapers, with some of those years in a managerial position

Special Skills and Personality Traits—Able to prioritize and work independently; cogent writing abilities; detail-oriented; excellent management and leadership skills; highly motivated and able to meet deadlines; strong analytical and problem-solving skills

CAREER LADDER

```
┌─────────────────────────────────────┐
│      Director of Publications;       │
│  Executive Editor (print publication);│
│       Editor (print publication)     │
└─────────────────────────────────────┘

┌─────────────────────────────────────┐
│  Managing Editor (online publication)│
└─────────────────────────────────────┘

┌─────────────────────────────────────┐
│       Online Editor; Associate       │
│   or Senior Editor (print publication)│
└─────────────────────────────────────┘
```

Position Description

A Managing Editor is a person who supervises all editorial operations and the production of printed products and/or online publications. An online publication may be an electronic version of a printed publication, either a newspaper or a magazine, or it may be an electronic version of material broadcast over radio or television, or an original publication designed to appeal to certain target audiences (such as businesspeople, entertainment audiences, or the scientific community).

In the multimedia world of Web site publication, Managing Editors supervise the overall information architecture of a Web site and online publication endeavors, oversee the writing and editing of material, and may themselves participate in the writing and editing of content for the target audience of the publication. The creative text needs to be integrated with still images, audio and video components, interactive elements (including Flash animation), and links to relevant Internet resources. Managing Editors develop story and visual ideas that are interactive, oversee the online marketing of the publication, and frequently manage the budget while developing the skills of the writers for the publication. They establish and implement the editorial procedures needed to ensure that the content of the online publication or publications is completed in a timely and accurate manner. In addition, Managing Editors oversee the updating of the Web site throughout the day (if it is a news-oriented publication), or on a periodic basis as set by the publication's management.

In some cases, online Managing Editors may evaluate what material is be featured online and from what source, as well as how promotion elements should be produced (video, text, forum, surveys, sidebars, and so forth). Managing Editors work with graphics personnel in their supervision of the production of the online publication, as well as assist marketing personnel on the development of metrics and measurements of the success and the perception of the online publication by its readers. They usually attend promotions meetings with top management, help to innovate and implement new technologies and tools in the development of the Web site, and contribute ideas for cross-promotional projects from the Web site to the printed publication (or the television broadcast, or other printed material) and back again (such as contests, creation of online tie-ins, co-sponsorship opportunities, topical promotions, and the like). In addition, Managing Editors perform routine maintenance tasks for the Web site and/or the online publications, such as moderating discussion forums on the site, answering viewer e-mail, and generally keeping the site fresh in content and image.

Salaries

According to the U.S. Bureau of Labor Statistics' *Occupational Outlook Handbook,* median annual earnings for salaried editors (in general) were $43,890 in May 2004. The middle 50 percent earned between $33,130 and $58,850 per year. The lowest 10 percent earned less than $25,780 yearly and the highest 10 percent earned more than $80,020. In addition, the median annual earnings of those editors working for newspaper, periodical, book, and directory publishers were $43,620. Wage earnings for Managing Editors, due to their supervisory tasks and technical skills, are at the high end of these ranges.

Employment Prospects

While every online publication and Web site needs an editorial oversight, only the larger companies can afford to have both a Managing Editor and an editor for the publication. In cases where the online publication is allied with print publications (or broadcasts, if the Web site derives from TV or radio), the Managing Editor may oversee both print and online content. As the growth of Web sites on the Internet has increased so exponentially in the last several years, there should be many opportunities for Managing Editors who have the requisite skills and experience. However, the competition for this coveted and powerful position is tough, and prospects for employment are only fair.

Advancement Prospects

Prospects for advancement to higher management levels in the publication arms of companies who have online publications on their Web sites are only fair, and are greatly dependent upon vacancies becoming available. A Managing Editor may have to switch to another company in order to move up into higher editorial or management posts.

Education and Training

A bachelor's degree, preferably with a major or concentration in communications or journalism, is required. In some instances, a master's degree may be required, usually in communications, journalism, or writing. Training in a media organization, with some years in a management role, is usually necessary. Some hands-on familiarity with major project management, content review, and desktop publishing software packages is a plus.

Experience, Skills, and Personality Traits

Most companies require a Managing Editor to have had at least five to eight years of editorial or marketing communications experience in a media organization, with at least two to three years of staff managerial responsibility.

Online Managing Editors need to have a practical understanding of how content integrates with visual design and have the ability to provide design direction to creators and designers of that content. They need to possess excellent organizational, time-management, project and process management, and editing/proofreading skills, as well as the ability to manage multiple projects and deadlines. They need to be able to effectively prioritize work and be able to communicate clearly and diplomatically both verbally and in writing. While programming and Hypertext Markup Language (HTML) knowledge is not usually required, a strong familiarity with the use of online social media tools (such as blogging platforms and tagging) is frequently important.

Unions and Associations

A Managing Editor is usually a member of the management team of a publication, either print or online, and does not have a union to represent or bargain for him/her. Associations that might be useful for Managing Editors include the American Society of Journalists and Authors (ASJA); the American Society of Magazine Editors (ASME); the American Society of Newspaper Editors (ASNE); the Association for Women in Communications (AWC); and the Society of Professional Journalists (SPJ).

Tips for Entry

1. Read a variety of Web sites for newspapers and magazines, as well other online sites, and note the kinds of material found on them. Look at how the content is arranged and presented, and how you might better that layout.
2. While in college, look for internships at newspapers or magazines, particularly those with online departments. Contacts at these organizations may be available through your journalism classes.
3. When working for a newspaper or a magazine, get assigned as an assistant Managing Editor, or look for a Managing Editor position for a smaller paper or magazine owned by a newspaper or publishing chain, and work your way up to larger papers in the chain, particularly those with online divisions.

ONLINE EDITOR

CAREER PROFILE

Duties: Edit online publications (or online version of print publications)

Alternate Title(s): Associate Editor; Content Editor; Interactive Editor; Web Editor; Web site News Editor

Salary Range: $28,000 to $60,000 or more

Employment Prospects: Fair to Good

Advancement Prospects: Fair

Prerequisites:

Education or Training—College degree in journalism or liberal arts; master's degree in journalism may be required; technical training in Internet technology and Web design helpful

Experience—Work on a newspaper, a magazine, or in broadcasting and/or have some experience in creating Web material

Special Skills and Personality Traits—Communication skills; creativity and good writing abilities; interpersonal skills; research and analytical talents; video/audio editing abilities

CAREER LADDER

```
┌─────────────────────────────────────┐
│  Managing Editor (online publications);│
│  Executive Editor or Editor-in-Chief  │
│       (online publications)           │
└─────────────────────────────────────┘

┌─────────────────────────────────────┐
│            Online Editor              │
└─────────────────────────────────────┘

┌─────────────────────────────────────┐
│     Online Assistant Editor;          │
│  Online Writer; Editorial Assistant   │
│        (print publications)           │
└─────────────────────────────────────┘
```

Position Description

At the present time nearly every news print publication, from national dailies like the *New York Times* to local shopping newspapers, has its own Web site (and often adjunct blog sites). Typically, these online sites include selected articles from the current print version of the publication, breaking news, and special features that may be available online only. In addition, there are magazine-styled publications that appear only in an online format.

Online publications require editors who can adapt existing material for online presentation, as well as edit material written specifically to appear on the Internet. Readers of online material have different expectations and needs from readers of traditional printed material. For example, the typical computer monitor screen cannot currently hold as much text as a newspaper page (or even some magazine pages), so material that is to be presented on the webpage must be arranged so it can be presented one screen at a time, or scrolled from screen to screen in a Web browser window. On the other hand, the online format is not restricted by the limited space available to most material in a printed publication. Another advantage with an online publication is that there is no longer a need to jump from the first page to some inner page to continue the article or material. Additionally, related material in a story can be highlighted for the reader and linked to other stories or to other relevant Web sites for the reader to pursue the same or related subjects and materials. Thus, a reader of a report on a music group's concert can follow a link to a related story giving biographical details, or to another Web site detailing further concerts by the group. Online, there is also the opportunity to blend multimedia (sound, animation, and so forth) within links in the text.

The responsibilities of editors include examining proposals for articles, interviews, and other materials of interest to the readers of a magazine or a newspaper (either print or electronic) and selecting the pieces for publication. They review, revise, and rewrite a writer's work, and, at times, prepare articles or news items themselves for publication. They nurture and maintain various sources for information to be able to use these personal contacts to check the information provided by the online writers in their columns and to gain a reputation for their site (and themselves) for accuracy, efficiency, and currency.

Online Editors do all these tasks as well as adapt the written material (which may have appeared already in print, or may be original to the online publication) to the format considerations of an online publication. In addition, they develop story ideas for the Web site.

Online Editors work on both magazine and newspaper Web sites, as well as newsletters and other online sites of technology-based content (including blogs). They create and organize new content and make appropriate updates to existing content displayed on the Web site. On media Web sites that publish news items and news articles, Online Editors manage the development, editing, and production of online news content, including, but not limited to, newscasts, feature stories from broadcasts, daily newsletters, news reports, articles, interviews, and other media material that they edit and adapt for online presentation. They may write display copy (headlines, subheads, product reviews, and so forth) that will be seen on the webpages, as well as generate potential story ideas or develop them in partnership with newsroom staff. In this process they must be able to assess whether an idea is story-worthy and cost-justified based on the anticipated online audience and the editorial strategy of the online publication. They utilize all the elements available in an online environment to advance the story or thrust of the Web site's content by incorporating still images, audio- and video-file components, and links to relevant Internet resources into an appealing and thoughtful online package.

In some instances, Online Editors may be asked to assist Web designers or Web producers in the development of the Web site, in its maintenance and its updating procedures, using standard Web production tools, including Hypertext Markup Language (HTML) and image editing software such as HomeSite, Imageready, and Photoshop.

Most Online Editors report directly to the managing editor of the online site or publication, or the executive editor in charge of the publication.

Salaries

According to the U.S. Bureau of Labor Statistics' *Occupational Outlook Handbook,* median annual earnings for salaried editors (in general) were $43,890 in May 2004. The middle 50 percent earned between $33,130 and $58,850 a year. The lowest 10 percent earned less than $25,780 yearly and the highest 10 percent earned more than $80,020. In addition, the median annual earnings of those editors working for newspaper, periodical, book, and directory publishers were $43,620. The wages of salaried Online Editors generally reflect the same range as those of their print publication colleagues.

Employment Prospects

According to the *Occupational Outlook Handbook, 2006-07 Edition,* writers and editors held about 320,000 jobs in 2004. About one-half of the salaried posts for writers and editors were in the information sector of the economy, which includes newspaper, periodical, book, and directory publishers; radio and television broadcasting; software publishers; motion picture and sound-recording industries; Internet service providers, Web search portals, and data-processing services; and Internet publishing. According to the *Handbook,* employment of salaried writers and editors for newspapers, periodicals, and book publishers is expected to increase and exceed the average for all occupations through the year 2014. Businesses and other organizations are continuously developing their Web sites and their electronic newsletters, and online publications and services are growing rapidly both in number and sophistication, spurring the demand for writers and, above all, editors who have hands-on experience in online editing and Web development.

Advancement Prospects

Advancing from an Online Editor to becoming a Managing Editor or an Executive Editor of an online Web site or publication is possible, but the competition for the higher-paying job with the additional overall responsibilities is stiff. Nonetheless, it is the logical next step for Online Editors who have gained experience. Moving from one organization with its Web site or online publication to another may make such a transition easier, once a reputation as an expert Online Editor is gained.

Education and Training

An undergraduate degree in communications, liberal arts, or journalism is an absolute requirement, and a master's degree in journalism is usually preferred. Some technical training in Web technology and the tools used in Web site production is recommended.

Experience, Skills, and Personality Traits

Online Editors are usually required to have three to five or more years' experience in either broadcast or print journalism. A writing background is a plus, and editing experience with print or online publications is highly recommended. Fluency with standard Web production tools and a demonstrable visual and aural awareness of the ever-expanding potentials of the Internet are necessary. Online Editors working within the news medium should be able to work well and productively in an environment where news is constantly changing and being updated at a fast clip, and where the pressure to maintain the currency of information on Web sites is paramount.

Online Editors must be able to develop, structure, and maintain content for their information-rich Web site(s).

They also need to have the flair and imagination to construct original multimedia material to build and maintain multimedia Web sites. They have to be able to prioritize work and make resource decisions in a fast-paced environment. They need to be heavily detail-oriented and have the capacity to meet deadlines effectively and multitask efficiently. They must be hardworking, focused, reliable, and have strong research, organizational, writing, and communication abilities. Above all, they need to exhibit excellent interpersonal and time management skills.

Unions and Associations

There are no unions that represent or bargain for Online Editors. Associations that might be useful for Online Editors include the American Society of Journalists and Authors (ASJA); the American Society of Magazine Editors (ASME); the American Society of Newspaper Editors (ASNE); the Association for Women in Communications (AWC); and the Society of Professional Journalists (SPJ).

Tips for Entry

1. All the journalistic experience you can acquire during college will help you in gaining a beginning position with a print or online publication. Writing and editing experience on campus print and online publications is preferable.

2. Become proficient on the Internet and examine various Web sites to obtain a sense of how they are organized and of the styles of writing on the sites.

3. Consider volunteering to create or to edit news or features for Web sites for community organizations, for your school newspaper, or for nonprofit groups. You can utilize this opportunity to master webpage creation software and to understand the fast-changing technology.

ONLINE WRITER

CAREER PROFILE

Duties: Writes for online publications (or online versions of printed publications) or creates other written material for Web sites

Alternate Title(s): Online Content Provider; Online Feature Writer; Online Journalist; Online Reporter

Salary Range: $20,000 to $65,000 or more

Employment Prospects: Fair

Advancement Prospects: Fair

Prerequisites:

Education or Training—College degree in journalism or liberal arts, some technical training in Internet technology helpful

Experience—Work on a newspaper or magazine and/or creating Web material is recommended, and a portfolio of writing is useful

Special Skills and Personality Traits—Communication skills; flexibility; motivation and perseverance; research and analytic skills; writing skills

CAREER LADDER

```
┌─────────────────────────────────┐
│  Assistant Editor; Managing Editor │
│       (online publication)       │
└─────────────────────────────────┘

┌─────────────────────────────────┐
│          Online Writer           │
└─────────────────────────────────┘

┌─────────────────────────────────┐
│        Journalist; Writer         │
└─────────────────────────────────┘
```

Position Description

With the exciting opportunities and challenges that the Internet increasingly presents, most newspapers, as well as most trade and specialty magazines, now have their own dedicated Web sites (including blogs). Typically, these online offerings include breaking news items, commentary, selected articles and interviews from the print publication, and other features that may be available only online, such as downloadable multimedia materials that may contain both video and audio clips. Industry, trade, business, and health journals similarly have found that many of their readers want a daily dose of news from their particular industry, rather than waiting for a printed version to become available. In addition, there are now magazine-like publications that appear only in an online form. Much of this data is offered without charge, or at only moderate cost, to Internet users. This dramatic change in the way information and analysis is distributed to the public has, in turn, opened up many new opportunities for journalists, writers, and freelancers.

Online publications need writers who can provide original reports or feature articles or interviews that can delve into the stories behind the news and can cover their subjects in much greater depth than most daily or weekly reporting and include more sources and background research. Readers of online material generally have different expectations and needs from readers of traditional printed material.

On the one hand, the typical computer monitor screen currently cannot hold as much text as in a printed newspaper or journal. For this reason, the material must be arranged so that it can be presented succinctly on one screen at a time or easily scrolled in a Web browser window from page to page. The emphasis in this type of journalistic writing is brevity. On the other hand, the online format is not confined by the limited space that most newspapers or magazines have to present their reports or articles. An additional feature is that the reader does not have to jump to other pages later in the publication to find the continuation of the article being read, but can scroll through the article directly or do a search/find for particular buzz words/topics in the piece.

Another great feature of this type of online presentation is that related material in a story can be highlighted and linked to other stories or relevant Web sites. Thus, a reader of a report on a new museum exhibition can follow a link to other similar exhibitions or click on another link for descriptions of the artist's work and life and still be able to go back to the original article quickly. Thus, this type of online material introduces an interactive element for the benefit of the reader.

Online news publications can combine a newspaper's breadth of coverage with the immediacy of a television broadcast. However, this means that Online Writers (or reporters) for such news sites, unlike their brethren in a newspaper's newsroom who have daily or weekly deadlines on their work, may have to gather material and write a story within an hour or two of a major news event (although some online publications use, instead, copy from the news services which they sometimes supplement with follow-up pieces). After completing their work, online reporters move on to their next assignment, which may be on a completely different subject from the one just finished. Online reporters may work directly for a specific Web site, or their reporting may be made available on the Web site, even though it had been assembled for another journalistic medium.

Writers who have special expertise or reputation can become either online feature writers or online columnists. Both these types of writers submit regular essays on controversial political or social issues, scientific developments, reviews of the latest books and movies, or other matters of interest to the readership of the Web and/or blog site. Some online publications, such as Salon (at http://www.salon.com) or Truthout (at http://www.truthout.org), emphasize original content (in the case of Salon) and diversity of opinion (at both Web sites).

Online Writers do not need to be experts in computer technology, but they need to be fully capable in several relevant technologies. Besides their regular use of word processing and e-mail programs, Online Writers need to be able to seek out information on the Web quickly and efficiently (and verify the data they are utilizing). They must be familiar with the major Web search engines and their Web portals, such as Yahoo!, Google, or MSN that organize information into a hierarchy of categories for ease of use, and know their way around specialized Web sites in areas such as economics, military affairs, or science and technology.

While a detailed understanding of Hypertext Markup Language (HTML), the language used for formatting webpages, is not essential, Online Writers should be familiar with the basic elements of webpage design. The capacity of using page design software (such as Dreamweaver or Microsoft FrontPage) can be helpful, particularly if the writer is performing a number of tasks for a small Web site.

Salaries

Individuals who write small items for news Web sites usually receive modest salaries in the $18,000 to $20,000 annual range, similar to beginning reporters at traditional print publications. Experienced writers who create feature-length material for a Web site will earn more yearly, anywhere from $25,000 to $50,000 or more. Those who have special expertise in particular subject areas (such as business, politics, or science and technology) can earn even more, from $30,000 to $65,000 or more. Some Online Writers work freelance, which allows them to combine their online work with other forms of employment.

Employment Prospects

The employment of reporters generally is expected to grow more slowly than average for all occupations through the year 2014, according to the U.S. Bureau of Labor Statistics' *Occupational Outlook Handbook, 2006-07 Edition.* Nevertheless, the expanding growth of the Internet and abundance of Web sites providing news information as well as other material does open some job opportunities for those seeking to establish careers as Online Writers. The steadiest work is with an online operation for a successful (and prestigious) print publication, but competition for these posts will stay very competitive.

The problem is further exacerbated by the inability of many online publications to find a reliable source of revenue, particularly after the dot-com downturn of 2002 and 2003. Some online publications have resorted to asking readers for a monthly subscription fee (or sometimes a per-article charge) to access full versions of their quality online writing, but this has been only moderately successful to date. Nonetheless, the online world will continue to expand, and talented and motivated writers will be able to find opportunities.

Advancement Prospects

Advancing to a more responsible position as an assistant editor or a managing editor of the online publication comes infrequently. To receive a higher salary (or higher fees as a freelancer) and gain a seniority status as a writer with the online publication, writers have to develop one or more areas of expertise and a positive reputation with online readers. Writers need to be extremely adept at accessing relevant research sources, and cultivate personal contacts to add to their expertise and relevancy as online feature writers and columnists.

Education and Training

Most publications (either online or print) require from any reporter or writer an undergraduate degree in communications, English, or liberal arts. This education should be supplemented by courses in computer technology and journalism. A journalism degree is helpful for individuals who want to work with online sites for newspapers. For online industry trade publications, feature writers will likely need to have further education (and possibly a degree) in the particular subject area(s) of the publication, such as a master's degree in business administration for a publication concerned with financial and business matters. However, online publications (like print publications) look for solid writing skills and consider them as important as educational credentials.

Experience, Skills, and Personality Traits

Constructive writing experience on a school paper, or as a writing intern with a newspaper or magazine, is of significant help in obtaining employment as a writer for online publications. In addition, some experience with designing or providing content for Web sites is valuable background for both writers and editors of online publications. Online reporters need to be proficient on the Internet, be extremely knowledgeable about information available on the Internet and how to locate it, and display initiative by networking through e-mail, chat groups, and news/user groups.

It is essential for online writers (and, especially, those employed as reporters) to be detail-oriented, good listeners, exhibit a healthy curiosity, and have acute observational skills. Their writing, researching, and communications skills need to be exemplary. They need self-discipline and self-motivation, as employment frequently remains uncertain and, when found, can be both hectic and stressful. They must also be well-organized to meet deadlines and to be able to stay ahead of potential competing pieces on the same topic.

Unions and Associations

Online Writers working with print publications as well may belong to the newspaper workers' union, The Newspaper Guild-Communications Workers of America (CWA). Most online writers, however, are not members of any guild. Possible associations of interest include such journalistic organizations as the American Society of Journalists and Authors (ASJA), Investigative Reporters and Editors (IRE), the Online News Association (ONA), and the Society of Professional Journalists (SPJ).

Tips for Entry

1. During college, consider volunteering to create news or features for Web sites for local community organizations or nonprofit businesses or for your college newspaper. This is a good opportunity to become proficient in webpage creation software.
2. Read assorted Internet newspapers, magazines, and blogs, as well as other online sites, to note the kind of materials found and how the stories are arranged and presented, and consider how you might do it differently.
3. Look for internships at print newspapers or magazines, particularly those who now have online departments. You may find these contacts through your journalism classes.
4. Consider creating your own Web-based blogs. Besides helping you practice your online writing, you can link with, and comment on, other blogs which can be both a professional and enjoyable social experience.

MANAGEMENT

BUSINESS DEVELOPMENT DIRECTOR

CAREER PROFILE

Duties: Identify, negotiate, and control strategic business relationships with content and technological partners; manage the marketing, sales, and product development teams to implement business development initiatives

Alternate Title(s): Business Development Manager

Salary Range: $65,000 to $120,000 or more

Employment Prospects: Fair

Advancement Prospects: Fair to Good

Prerequisites:

Education or Training—A B.A. or B.S. degree in business, finance, or marketing; M.B.A. degree usually preferred and often required

Experience—Minimum of two to five years' business experience in business development, e-commerce, marketing, sales, and/or strategic planning

Special Skills and Personality Traits—Ability to develop and execute strategic business development plans; excellent written/oral communication talents and interpersonal abilities; highly motivated and innovative problem solver; strong strategic thinking and negotiation skills

CAREER LADDER

```
┌─────────────────────────────────────────┐
│          E-commerce Manager;             │
│  Vice President, Business Development;    │
│     Vice President, Marketing/Sales       │
└─────────────────────────────────────────┘

┌─────────────────────────────────────────┐
│      Business Development Director       │
└─────────────────────────────────────────┘

┌─────────────────────────────────────────┐
│       Sales or Marketing Associate       │
└─────────────────────────────────────────┘
```

Position Description

The primary responsibility for Business Development Directors is to identify potential business partners and negotiate agreements. For their firm and its Web sales, they assess, evaluate, establish, and develop business opportunities with companies, dealing with either content or technology. They are responsible for reviewing and analyzing all information about these companies and developing the new initiatives and partnerships. They handle the complex negotiations relating to revenue sharing with these new potential partners and also oversee the marketing programs behind the introduction of new products and/or services. In so doing, they work closely with the company's legal staff in the negotiations leading to the execution of contracts. Besides their authority over generating new business, they may also have management duties over existing agreements. In addition, they work with marketing, sales, and product development teams and their managers to implement business development initiatives.

Business Development Directors establish, maintain, and plan the overall policies and goals for a business development department, which may consist of several associates or other business professionals, and establish and maintain the relevant business development budget.

In the developing of new products or services, Business Development Directors manage their introduction to the Internet sales team and work with the marketing professionals to develop the sales materials and product promotional materials to guarantee usage by visitors to the company's Web site(s). During this process, they review all the new business objects on an ongoing basis to ensure these product developments remain in line with the firm's business strategy. They may also be required to direct cross-functional development teams, or individual team members, to achieve scheduled delivery dates and successful performance. Thus, they help to control new products and business developments by using product management methodology from initial concept to post delivery review.

Business Development Directors need to conduct research and marketplace intelligence to be on top of trends and issues within both the industry in which their company is a part and the technological environment of new media. In addition, they are always on the lookout for potential market opportunities. Directors usually provide financial analyses to be included with sales reports to top management. They also write memos and presentations for the new product/service launches. In their review of these new products and services, Business Development Directors provide valuable feedback to product teams to aid in the process of defining content attributes, positioning, selection, and pricing. In their ongoing analysis of available products and services, they also identify and recommend opportunities for improvement in terms of productivity and sales performance. Thus, they are mainly responsible for the operational viability of these products and services.

Salaries

For their responsible position and important duties, Business Development Directors are compensated well. According to Salary Wizard's salary.com Web site, annual earnings as of March 2006 for Business Development Directors ranged from a low of $67,000 to a high of $123,000. The national median average salary was $105,000 per year. These salaries are very dependent upon both geographic location and the scope of the responsibilities of the job.

Employment Prospects

As companies expand the sales of their products and/or the availability of their services into the Internet marketplace, it becomes increasingly apparent that they need Business Development Directors to aid them in contracting with other businesses for content or technology to use in the electronic display of their products/services. Job opportunities for individuals with solid backgrounds in marketing and product development and proficiency in Internet technologies are fair to good.

Advancement Prospects

Business Development Managers usually find advancement by moving to senior business, financial, or marketing positions within their company. As an alternative, they may decide to work for a firm that offers business development

consulting work under contract with organizations, or they may even become independent consultants. Advancement can also occur from obtaining a similar position with a larger company.

Education and Training

The minimum educational requirement for a Business Development Director is a bachelor's degree in business, finance, or marketing. Most companies hiring individuals for this post will also require a master's degree in business administration. As Business Development Directors also have to be technically savvy and proficient with Internet technologies, some courses in Web site design and Internet technology and solid computer skills are additional requirements. Proficiency in Microsoft Excel and PowerPoint is often a requisite.

Experience, Skills, and Personality Traits

Most Business Development Directors have to have at least three to five years' experience in marketing and product development. Prior background in Internet business development or large account sales experience is often preferred by companies looking at individuals for this position. Sales experience with online e-commerce services, in either the public or private sector, is a plus.

Business Development Directors must be strategic thinkers and inveterate problem solvers. They need to have a comprehensive understanding of business operations and of corporate marketing and advertising. Strong oral and written communication and presentation skills as well as organization and attention to detail are essential. They need strong analytical skills, as they will develop and execute strategic business development plans. In addition, directors should be able to develop and maintain excellent relationships with senior executives of potential business partners. Finally, they must be able to work well in a fast-paced, high-energy, demanding environment.

Unions and Associations

There are no unions or associations that directly represent Business Development Directors. However, many may belong to such umbrella industry associations as the American Marketing Association (AMA), the International Association of Business Communicators (IABC), or the Software and Information Industry Association (SIIA).

Tips for Entry

1. While in college earning your business degree, take courses in computer design and new media technology to become familiar with both software and design technologies.

2. Take any sales or marketing position you can find with a company, preferably with one that does online selling, to familiarize yourself with marketing tools and techniques, and to begin building your background in marketing.

3. Volunteer your services in researching the marketplace for the marketing or sales department of the company for which you are working to become familiar with research and analysis techniques.

4. Attend local business conferences or meetings to establish contact with business associates from other companies that may become useful to you as you move into a business development position at your firm.

E-COMMERCE EXECUTIVE MANAGER

CAREER PROFILE

Duties: Manage the development, release, and maintenance of Web systems and services that support an organization's online business and mail order sales (e-commerce) and business strategy, providing customer service and maximizing revenue

Alternate Title(s): Internet Store Manager; Manager of Information Systems; Program Manager—E-commerce

Salary Range: $90,000 to $130,000 or more

Employment Prospects: Fair to Good

Advancement Prospects: Fair

Prerequisites:

Education or Training—Bachelor's degree in business or marketing required; advanced degree in business administration or computer science recommended

Experience—Management experience in customer service, call center, or catalog environment; supervisory experience with retail or mail order company, preferably in a Web-related environment

Special Skills and Personality Traits—Basic Internet proficiency; computer programming experience; excellent communication skills; good business judgment; highly energetic and organized; strong leadership and management skills; thorough understanding of retailing practices as applied to online products/services and sales

CAREER LADDER

```
┌─────────────────────────────────────┐
│   Director of Business Development;  │
│      Vice President, Marketing;      │
│   Other Online Executive Positions   │
└─────────────────────────────────────┘

┌─────────────────────────────────────┐
│     E-commerce Executive Manager     │
└─────────────────────────────────────┘

┌─────────────────────────────────────┐
│      Sales or Marketing Assistant    │
└─────────────────────────────────────┘
```

Position Description

E-commerce (i.e., commerce that is transacted electronically) is used today especially for retail selling via the Internet, with advertisements on Web sites and/or e-mail ads that sell products and services. There are two kinds of e-commerce. One is business-to-customer, such as Amazon. com or Ebay.com. The other is business-to-business and is the more significant one today in terms of volume and monetary value, with millions of transactions occurring behind the scenes every day.

Internet business, just like the rest of the business world, is highly competitive. For every successful e-commerce business, there are dozens that fail, usually the product of bad planning. A successful e-commerce business needs to establish its identity clearly by its name (otherwise known as its domain name), or URL, to distinguish it from competitors or other Internet businesses. Such operations need to find the right kind of Web server and build an attractive Web site that is easy to access and fun to roam through (or "navigate"). E-businesses need to establish a trust with potential customers, who will be communicating private information, such as mailing and e-mail addresses, credit card numbers, or phone numbers, in order to buy products and/or services offered on the Web site. Thus, the site has to be secure, and the customers have to know that. Customers also must find it easy to pay for the products or services on the Web site, and, above all, they need to know about the existence of the e-commerce site via its successful promotion of its products and services.

This is where the position of E-commerce Executive Manager comes in. E-commerce Executive Managers head the development and execution of all online business initiatives, usually through a Web site store, and control all warehousing and merchandising operations related to that store. As such, they are responsible for both the day-to-day operation of the online boutique and mail order operation and manage the catalog of products and/or services by adding and removing products or services as necessary, maintaining accurate release dates and prices. They work closely with vendors that supply the store, and they develop and execute marketing and promotional activities, such as pay-per-click advertising, e-mail campaigns, link and banner exchanges, and comparison sites to increase sales at the store Web site. As Web site administrators, they manage the merchant credit card process, any charge backs, inventory updates, and new merchandising placement on the Web site. They usually are also responsible for determining the security methods, such as digital signatures or encryption, firewalls, or virtual private networks, which might be utilized to protect business-to-business or business-to-customer interactions.

They act as the liaison between the company and the marketing, merchandising, accounting, and warehousing departments involved in the online merchandising activities. They recruit, hire, and train additional staff as needed and prepare Web site statistics reports, inventory status reports, analyses, and evaluations as needed. Their regular reports to the firm's top management will include profit and loss (P&L) statements as well as sales forecasts for newly released material applicable to the products or services already available at the company's Web store. In addition, they review and approve all invoices from e-commerce vendors providing shipping, handling, customer service, Web development, and site hosting. They work with the hosts of the Web site to resolve any site technical problems and direct the development and growth of the company site. In addition, they usually formulate and develop the operations manual to be used for the online mail order business of the Web store.

E-commerce Executive Managers identify and develop the processes for pursuing new customers through marketing tools and Web site development. Finally, they must keep abreast of market trends, consumer trends, competition for their products and/or services, customer service issues, as well as e-commerce technology, techniques, and dynamics.

E-commerce Executive Managers who work for large firms may be in charge of a sizeable information technology department and typically interact with higher-level executives. Managers who work for smaller firms typically have responsibility for another company department, such as network management. They even may be responsible for all the computer activities of a smaller corporation.

Salaries

The relatively high salaries of E-commerce Executive Managers reflect the varied and heavy responsibilities of their job. According to salary studies made by Salary.com, the median annual earnings of E-commerce Executive Managers in the United States during March 2006 were $116,984, with the median salaries ranging from a low of $99,157 to a high of $119,306. In the larger urban areas, such as Los Angeles and New York City, the median annual salaries were $133,000 or higher, and the earnings ranged from a low of $112,769 to a high of $142,058.

Some managers may receive a commission or a combination of salary and commission. Under a commission system, managers receive a percentage of store sales. Thus, their earnings depend upon the ability to sell the online products and/or services as well as the condition of the economy in general.

Employment Prospects

As online businesses have flourished on the World Wide Web, employment prospects for those individuals qualified to manage such online sales operations have increased greatly. However, it is a volatile market, with downsizing of operations for purposes of economy or because of mergers. Thus, there are limits on the possibilities for employment as E-commerce Executive Managers, and experience and knowledge will be deciding factors in most such job opportunities.

Advancement Prospects

Successful E-commerce Executive Managers may find opportunities for advancement into the top executive hierarchy (most often the marketing or sales departments) of the company for which they work, or they may enter the management ranks of an Internet service provider, online information service, or other large Internet-based businesses. However, competition for higher management positions is always stiff.

Education and Training

While there may be no specific educational requirements for running an online business, it is highly recommended to have at least a bachelor's degree in business administration or marketing, as well as extensive courses, if not a degree, in computer science. The federal Small Business Administration (http://www.sba.gov) is a good source for information on small business management techniques and processes.

Experience, Skills, and Personality Traits

Companies needing an executive manager of e-commerce operations are seeking individuals who have had marketing (and management, if possible) experience in a customer-oriented environment and some background and awareness of the particular nature and the challenging dynamics of marketing products and services electronically. They also need to have a thorough understanding of how consumer Internet Web sites work and how users surf them and search engine Web sites.

E-commerce Executive Managers should have experience with programs such as Microsoft Office, Adobe Photoshop, Front Page, SQL, Access, Excel, or equivalent software, as well as be proficient in HTML. They need a strong understanding of online marketing, affiliate marketing, paid search and organic search techniques, and marketing analysis procedures. They should possess strong analytical abilities coupled with problem solving skills. They need to have excellent verbal and written communication skills and leadership abilities and be well organized, with a flexible approach in order to manage a team as well as being confident in their decision-making. Finally, they must be equipped to work under intense deadlines and in a fast-paced work environment.

Unions and Associations

There are no unions or associations that directly represent E-commerce Executive Managers. However, many may belong to such umbrella industry associations as the Software and Information Industry Association (SIIA) or the Software Publishers Association (SPA). Specific business information pertaining to online e-commerce may be obtained from such organizations as CommerceNet, Data Interchange Standards Association (DISA), or the Electronic Funds Transfer Association (EFTA).

Tips for Entry

1. Become very familiar with the Internet. Look for different kinds of products or services on the Web. Note how easy or hard it is to find each kind of product, and what techniques the online sites employ to attract visitors to the site. Note how products/services are listed or displayed and how the order and shipping procedures are explained. Are they clear enough, and, if not, how would you do them differently?

2. Work within a retail environment that is heavily customer-oriented to absorb the details of running a retail business, including dealing with taxes, regulations, and employment.

3. Consider subscribing to such Web e-mail newsletters as *Web Marketing Today* (http://www.wilsonweb.com/wmt) and examine the many books available about online retail sales and e-commerce to gain an understanding of the business and what experience you will need to gain a management position.

HUMAN RESOURCES DIRECTOR

CAREER PROFILE

Duties: Plans, directs, and implements policies relating to all phases of personnel activity

Alternate Title(s): Director of Human Resources

Salary Range: $45,000 to $130,000 or more

Employment Prospects: Fair to Good

Advancement Prospects: Poor

Prerequisites:

Education or Training—Bachelor's degree in human resources or industrial and labor relations, with an emphasis on social psychology and business

Experience—Minimum of five years' human resources management experience in technology environment

Special Skills and Personality Traits—Excellent verbal and written communication capabilities; good business and professional judgment; high level of computer and problem solving skills; initiative and adaptability; self-motivated; aptitude to work in a team and multi-task environment; strong attention to detail; excellent conflict-resolution talents

Special Requirements—Professional in Human Resources (PHR) or Senior Professional in Human Resources (SPHR) certification usually required

CAREER LADDER

```
┌─────────────────────────────────────┐
│  Vice President, Human Resources     │
└─────────────────────────────────────┘

┌─────────────────────────────────────┐
│  Human Resources Director            │
└─────────────────────────────────────┘

┌─────────────────────────────────────┐
│  Human Resources                     │
│  Departmental Manager                │
└─────────────────────────────────────┘
```

Position Description

In the past, Human Resources Directors have been associated with performing the employee administrative functions of an organization, such as handling the staff's questions about benefits, as well as recruiting, interviewing, and hiring new team members in accordance with policies and requirements that have been established by top management. While Human Resources Directors still manage these tasks, today they increasingly consult with top executives regarding strategic planning for the organization as well. In order to enhance morale and productivity, limit job turnover, and help organizations increase performance and improve business results, they also help their firms effectively utilize employee skills, provide training and opportunities to improve those abilities, and increase employees' satisfaction with their jobs and working environment.

In a small organization, a single Human Resources Director may handle all aspects of human resources work. In larger organizations, the Human Resources Director may supervise several departments (such as those dealing specifically with compensation and benefits, employee assistance plans, training and development projects, affirmative action coordination, and recruitment and placement of new employees), each headed by an experienced manager.

Other responsibilities of Human Resources Directors include extracting and compiling a variety of personnel data for consolidation into management reports, working with supervisors and managers to ensure accuracy in the completed data dealing with personnel, overseeing verifications of employment and government reporting, answering routine human resources and benefits questions, overseeing employee training regimens, managing the process of compiling annual performance statistics for the use of managers, facilitating exit interviews, and directing policies and objectives relative to benefit programs. In addition, they may prepare and distribute standard management reports on personnel matters, take an active role in exploring business issues and develop and recommend approaches and solutions to upper management, oversee the production of employee newsletters and other communications, and develop and recommend personnel plan changes and enhancements. They keep records of insurance coverage, pension plan and personnel transactions, and investigate any accidents and prepare reports for insurance carriers. They conduct wage surveys of labor markets to determine wage rates for positions that are competitive with the marketplace and prepare the budget for personnel operations. Basically, they provide customer service to all employees and managers of the organization.

Salaries

Annual salary rates for Human Resources Directors vary somewhat according to the scope of their duties and the size of the firm for which they work. According to the U.S. Department of Labor's Bureau of Labor Statistics, median yearly earnings of human resources managers in May 2004 were $92,590. Their study showed that the middle 50 percent earned between $62,080 and $106,440 per year. The lowest 10 percent earned annually less than $48,060, and the highest 10 percent earned more than $136,000. In companies with extensive multimedia operations, the scope of the duties of a Human Resources Director usually is reflected in compensation figures that will be at the high end of these salary ranges.

Employment Prospects

Demand for human resources, training, and labor relations managers and specialists is governed by the staffing needs of the organization for which they work. Most Human Resources Directors began as a specialist in one branch of human resources or another. Individuals with specific human resources specialties should look for posts with larger organizations that have a full-fledged human resources department or division and then work their way up to becoming head of the section as Director.

Demand may be particularly strong for certain specialists, such as job-specific training programs in response to the increasing complexity of many positions, the aging of the workforce, and technological advances that can leave employees with obsolete skills. A rapidly expanding business is likely to hire additional human resources workers, while a firm that has experienced a merger or a reduction in its workforce will require fewer human resources staff members. However, there are also operations involved in management, consulting, and employment service that are hired by businesses that contract out human resources functions, such as training and development programs and the administering of complex employee benefits and compensation packages.

Advancement Prospects

The position of Human Resources Director is a high-level executive position and is usually the culmination of a career in human resources management. For some directors at larger organizations, a move to higher management levels within the organization may be possible, based on their successful career as administrators. For those directors working for smaller firms, advancement can occur by transferring to a larger organization with resultant higher responsibilities and compensation.

Education and Training

The minimum educational requirement for Human Resources Directors is usually a Bachelor of Science (B.S.) or Bachelor of Arts (B.A.) degree in human resources, psychology, business administration, or industrial and labor relations. Many colleges and universities have programs leading to a degree in personnel, human resources, or labor relations. Some offer programs in human resources administration or human resources management of training and development or of compensation and benefits. Because an interdisciplinary background is appropriate in this field, a combination of courses in the behavioral sciences, business, and technical sciences is useful.

Some organizations also prefer a candidate to have a master's degree in a similar field. Human Resource Directors who deal with personnel involved with computer operations should have some technical background as well.

Special Requirements

Most organizations require a candidate for Human Resources Director to have a certification in human resource management. The two most common certifications are Professional in Human Resources (PHR) and Senior Professional in Human Resources (SPHR). With the finishing of course work and the successful completion of a PHR examination, the certification is awarded by the Human Resources Certification Institute of the Society for Human Resource Management (SHRM). Another organization that offers certification is the American Society for Training & Development Certification Institute (ASTD) (http://www.astd.org). In addition, the International Foundation of Employee Benefit Plans (IFEBP) (http://www.ifebp.org) confers a designation to individuals who complete a series of college-level courses and pass exams covering employee benefit plans.

Experience, Skills, and Personality Traits

Organizations seeking a Human Resources Director usually demand four to seven years of progressive human resources experience, and prefer some previous management experience as well. The candidate's background should include compensation, benefits, employee relations, recruitment, organizational development and training, and experience with labor relations and union negotiations. Directors should also be conversant with pertinent federal and state employment laws.

Human Resources Directors must have strong communication skills, both verbal and written, and be able to handle simultaneously a multitude of tasks and projects. They need to be highly organized and detail-oriented, self-motivated, and exhibit excellent prioritization and interpersonal skills. They need to be problem solvers and possess strong conflict-resolution abilities. Their technical skills should include fluency in PC, word-processing, database, and spreadsheet systems, as well as office computer applications such as Microsoft Word, Excel, PowerPoint, and Outlook software programs.

Unions and Associations

While there are no specific unions or associations that represent Human Resources Directors (particularly as they are usually considered management), membership in such industry associations as the Society for Human Resource Management (SHRM) may be useful for networking purposes.

Tips for Entry

1. During your college course work leading to your B.A. or B.S. degree in human resources management, decide on a specialty in the field (such as benefits analysis or labor relations) to use as a means to your first job in a human resources department of a firm.
2. Do not neglect your familiarity with computer programs and Internet technology, as this knowledge will be useful to you when you work at firms that have an expanding multimedia department.
3. Getting a PHR certification will expand your job possibilities and enhance your reputation as a human resources professional.

IT (INFORMATION TECHNOLOGY) SYSTEMS DIRECTOR

CAREER PROFILE

Duties: Responsible for the administration, management, trouble-shooting, and operation of an organization's technology system, data center, Web applications, and network infrastructure

Alternate Title(s): Director, Information Systems; IT Director; IT Manager

Salary Range: $70,000 to $130,000 or more

Employment Prospects: Fair to Good

Advancement Prospects: Poor to Fair

Prerequisites:

Education or Training—B.A. degree in business administration with emphasis on information science, or a B.S. degree (in computer science) and an information science graduate degree or an M.B.A. with technology as a core component is either recommended or required

Experience—Extensive experience managing information systems departments; background in enterprise networking, computer operating systems and applications; familiarity with budgeting, planning, and policy making at a corporate level

Special Skills and Personality Traits—Ability to think strategically, plan, and delegate authority; aptitude at coordinating with professionals and managers and working well in a team environment; energetic, self-motivated, and a capacity for resolute focus and multi-tasking; strong interpersonal, communication, and leadership talents

Special Requirements—Industry certifications are usually necessary

CAREER LADDER

```
┌─────────────────────────────────┐
│  Chief Information Officer (large │
│  corporation); senior management  │
│  positions (small corporations)   │
└─────────────────────────────────┘

┌─────────────────────────────────┐
│   IT (Information Technology)     │
│        Systems Director           │
└─────────────────────────────────┘

┌─────────────────────────────────┐
│   Manager (of a data processing   │
│  or computer design department)   │
└─────────────────────────────────┘
```

Position Description

Information systems managers play a vital role in the technological direction of their organizations. They manage all information technology (IT) functions, from constructing the business plan and strategic planning of IT solutions and services to overseeing network security to directing Internet operations. They are executive managers who are concerned mainly with the "larger picture" of corporate development rather than the day-to-day computer and Internet operations that are handled by various departments or operations center managers. They work with top management to budget for all information technology needs of the company, and they set organization-wide standards for equipment used, software purchased, staff training, auditing of processes, and other computer-related concerns of the business.

They may direct the work of systems analysts, computer programmers, support specialists, and other computer-related workers. Besides managing the planning activities related to computer hardware and software, they coordinate the work actions of the programming and systems design staffs and the development and implementation of the organization's computer networks and Internet and intranet (in-house) sites. They analyze the computer and information needs of their organizations from an operational and strategic perspective and determine immediate and long-range personnel and equipment requirements. In coordination with the heads of appropriate departments, they establish security and disaster recovery procedures and proper staff and training development programs.

They may also be required to coordinate and oversee all contracted IT vendors and developers under contract with the organization. They frequently oversee and administer WAN (wide area network) and LAN (local area network) networks, client computers, backup systems, and any shared applications throughout the organization's main office and any satellite offices nationwide or international. They may be tasked with documenting and updating company IT information schematics, information processing (IP), addressing methodologies, and documenting all IT systems and procedures. They may be required to perform security and performance audits of the organization's networks and Internet systems, analyzing them for trends and any anomalies.

The IT Systems Director is frequently at the top of the ladder in information systems management for most small- or medium-sized corporations and organizations. Some larger businesses may have a chief information officer, or CIO, as their top-level executive to whom the IT Systems Director reports. Otherwise, IT Systems Directors usually report directly to the general manager of the corporation. They may be required to travel with other team members charged with installing and maintaining local networks for clients or to represent the organization with professional groups or contractors and equipment/materials suppliers.

Salaries
Earnings for IT Systems Directors vary by specialty and level of responsibility. According to the U.S. Department of Labor's Bureau of Labor Statistics, the median annual earnings of these managers in May 2004 were $92,570. The middle 50 percent earned between $71,650 and $118,330 yearly. In a study by Robert Half International, a professional staffing and consulting services firm, average starting salaries in 2005 for high-level information technology managers ranged from $80,250 to $112,250 per year. Finally, according to salary studies by Netscape, as of April 2006, the national median annual salary for this position was $100,539, and earnings ranged from a low of $79,530 to a high of $139,652.

Employment Prospects
While there is a strong demand for IT Systems Directors, it is not easy to find a candidate who has the right mix of technical and managerial skills. Many excellent computer programmers and technicians do not possess the requisite management abilities, and managers who do not sufficiently understand technical requirements of computer, network, and Internet systems could bring these operations to a halt. Individuals who have already gained a reputation as good system administrators in an information department or assistant information system managers may be able to work their way into this post. The technical and managerial requirements are stiff, which is where patience and good contacts may be helpful for someone looking to move into this responsible position. Nonetheless, it is estimated by the U.S. Department of Labor that employment of information systems managers is expected to grow faster than the average for all occupations through the year 2014.

Advancement Prospects
In many large corporations, IT Systems Directors who have demonstrated outstanding abilities are well positioned to move on to becoming directors of information services for the organization, supervising all the information systems throughout the organization. However, such openings do not occur very often. For IT managers in smaller organizations, advancement may come by moving on to larger corporations in similar positions.

Education and Training
A four-year degree program that emphasizes information processing and business administration rather than computer science theory may prove more useful for individuals looking to move into the field of information technology. While an IT Systems Director must be familiar with computer programming, networking procedures, security techniques, and system analysis, as well as accounting and auditing techniques, the emphasis in the position is on management skills. Nonetheless, in some cases, a master's degree in computer science or electrical engineering may provide additional necessary educational background.

Special Requirements
Required training for this position may also include industry certification for the major networks and operating systems. Many certification programs are available from Learning Tree International (http://www.learning-tree.com), including Certified Local Area Network Professional, Certified Wide Area Network Professional, and Certified Internet-working Professional. Other certification programs include those from Novell (Certified Novell Engineer, or CNE, and Master Certified Novell Engineer,

or MCNE) (http://www.novell.com/training), from Microsoft (Microsoft Certified Systems Engineer) (http://www.microsoft.com/learning/mcp/mcse), and various Cisco network certifications (http://www.cisco.com/Web/learning/le3/learning_career_certifications_and_learning_paths_home.html).

Experience, Skills, and Personality Traits

Active and personal experience with computer operations and information technology procedures is essential. Most companies require at least five years' experience, usually working with specific systems (such as Microsoft and Unix), networking administration, and Web design and management. However, all this technical background has to be supplemented with experience helping to supervise operators or other personnel, as well as aiding the planning of budgets and the preparation of analysis reports.

IT Systems Directors need to have a hands-on approach to strategic planning and problem solving. They must have a mastery of a variety of technical issues and applications. Their communication and leadership skills must be exemplary, as they will need to supervise subordinates and to interface with other managers. Thus, while they must be self-motivated, they also need to work well in a team environment, have the ability to multitask, be energetic, and be capable of taking responsibility.

Unions and Associations

At this level of management, individuals are more likely to belong to management and executive organizations as well as technical groups concerned with their specialties. Membership in such general industry associations as the American Management Association (AMA) may be useful, but belonging to such information systems management organizations as the American Society for Information Science (ASIS) may be even more helpful for networking purposes.

Tips for Entry

1. In order to apply for this type of executive position, you need to have extensive IT and management experience. As you plan your career moves, be sure that you take positions that have significant management responsibilities, while keeping up-to-date with technical issues.

2. When applying for a position as IT Systems Director, thoroughly research your prospective employer to be sure that your skills and areas of experience closely match the employer's special priorities.

3. Be willing to put in five or more years in IT positions to gain necessary knowledge (of applications, network, and telecommunication systems) and expertise (in such areas as maintaining systems and resolving problems related to both local area network [LAN] and wide area network [WAN] systems).

NETWORK SYSTEMS ADMINISTRATOR

<table>
<tr><td>CAREER PROFILE</td><td>CAREER LADDER</td></tr>
</table>

Duties: Manage the operation and planning for a computer system's local (LAN) or wide area network (WAN); deal with connection between local network and the Internet; establish procedures for support staff and users; organize technical support and training for network features (such as data backup and security protections, performance monitoring, and modem connections); supervise technicians and programmers

Alternate Title(s): Network Manager

Salary Range: $40,000 to $55,000 for small local area networks; $60,000 to $80,000 or more for large or wide area networks

Employment Prospects: Fair to Good

Advancement Prospects: Fair

Prerequisites:

Education or Training—Bachelor's degree in computer science or information systems required; business and communications courses recommended

Experience—Three to five years' experience aiding the running of computer networks, with evidence of increasing responsibilities

Special Skills and Personality Traits—Good management and communications talents; programming and systems analysis skills; problem-solving and troubleshooting aptitude; self-starter; ability to assume accountability

Special Requirements—Industry certifications are necessary

```
         Manager, Information Systems

        Network Systems Administrator

      Network Analyst; Network Control
      Operator; Applications Programmer
```

Position Description

Network Systems Administrators are both company managers and systems administrators, as well as technical problem solvers. While their basic tasks are mostly concerned with the maintenance, management, operation, and growth of either local or wide area networks, they are also concerned with their network's connection to the Internet. This connection usually is accomplished through one of several available "firewall" security systems that prevent direct (and, most likely, unauthorized) access to a computer network and that monitor transfers of information to and from the network. In this task, they often work in tandem with a Webmaster.

Besides their concerns with the computer network's Internet connection, Network Systems Administrators' duties extend to both the administration of the network system and to the technical support of that system. To that extent, they need to ensure that all routine tasks, such as data backup, antivirus and other security protections, and performance of the system are monitored regularly and function properly. Typically, they select the major application software packages to be run on the network. They work with their company's department managers to meet their needs with additional capacity on the system (such as additional workstations, file servers, or modem connections for telecommunication needs) and help in the preparation of budget requests and reports directed to upper management. They investigate any non-routine problems with the network (with the help of network analysts), install new versions of network software, and prepare training materials for network users.

They are continuously solving problems under pressure from both the users and their managers. In addition, they help upper management to fit the network and its connections with the Internet into the organization's overall business strategy, as well as convince top management to maintain (and expand, if possible) adequate funding and support for the network organization.

They must be fully aware of the ever-changing specifications for computer hardware and for the rapid changes in both networking and Internet technology. Web application servers, database platforms, and programming languages (such as the scripting software languages PHP, Perl, CGI, and their like) are constantly modified, updated, and changed, and Network Systems Administrators must keep abreast of these technological modifications and recommend the necessary alterations to their network procedures.

Salaries
Network Systems Administrators of small local area networks such as those serving a single company office or work group usually receive the lowest annual salaries, ranging from $35,000 to around $50,000. Administrators of large LANs usually get intermediate salaries from $50,000 to $60,000 per year, and the highest yearly salaries ($60,000 to $80,000 or more) go to administrators of wide area networks (such as those run by corporations with nationwide and/or international branches).

Employment Prospects
Most desktop computers utilized in business (even small businesses) are part of a local area network, or internal computer network system, known as an intranet. With the extensive use of the ever-expanding Internet, electronic mail as an instant communicator, and networked databases for ease of information search, the need and demand for experienced Network Systems Administrators has increased greatly, especially for those capable of managing the larger or more complex networks.

Advancement Prospects
Career advancements open to Network Systems Administrators are usually into higher management levels or to management of larger or more complex networks. In either case,

the competition for such positions increases with each step of advancement.

Education and Training
While some computer programmers may find themselves elevated to Network Systems Administrators on the strength of their computer skills alone, most corporations and business organizations are looking for candidates who have a solid technical education (four-year and, most likely, graduate degrees in computer science or information systems, with courses in network design and engineering). In addition, candidates need to have the requisite technical skills and knowledge about servers, software, databases, operating systems, and hardware. Some management and business administration courses would also be helpful as background for this administrative position.

Special Requirements
Many certification programs are available from Learning Tree International (http://www.learningtree.com), including Certified Local Area Network Professional, Certified Wide Area Network Professional, and Certified Internet-working Professional. Other certification programs include those from Novell (Certified Novell Engineer, or CNE, and Master Certified Novell Engineer, or MCNE) (http://www.novell.com/training), from Microsoft (Microsoft Certified Systems Engineer) (http://www.microsoft.com/learning/mcp/mcse), and various Cisco network certifications (http://www.cisco.com/web/learning/le3/le2/le0/le9/learning_certification_type_home.html).

Experience, Skills, and Personality Traits
Most Network Systems Administrators have several years of experience as information technology (IT) professionals, usually working as network technicians or assistants. Basic requirements for this position include basic programming (or script writing) skills, familiarity with network utilities and configuration menus, good analytical skills, initiative, and innovative (but cost effective) approaches to problem solving. In addition, Network Systems Administrators need to have excellent written and verbal communication abilities, good customer service talents, and the facility to adapt to a rapidly changing technical and business environment.

Unions and Associations
Many professional Network Systems Administrators belong to the Association for Computing Machinery (ACM) and/or the Institute of Electrical and Electronics Engineers (IEEE) as a matter of course and join special interest groups devoted to networking issues important to them, such as security, user training, and Internet/Network interface. Membership

in information systems management organizations may also be helpful for networking purposes.

Tips for Entry

1. During the course of your education, be sure to take courses in all of the following areas: computer science and computer operations (including network architecture, programming, and systems analysis), management (including both budgeting and business administration), and communications (including both employee relations and technical writing). You may even find that you can concentrate on networking and Internet development in your computer course structure.

2. Look for internships where you can work on the network of your school or of a business.

3. It is critical that you get the most appropriate certification for the network systems work that you are looking for. Check with the Association for Computing Machinery (ACM) for guidance on possible certification programs that are available in your area and that meet your career goals.

PRODUCT DEVELOPMENT DIRECTOR

CAREER PROFILE

Duties: Manage the development and planning (life cycle) of an online product line or service, including strategy formulation, product configuration, procurement, competitive analysis, and market planning

Alternate Title(s): Content Producer; Electronic Product Development Director; Product Management Director

Salary Range: $85,000 to $155,000 or more

Employment Prospects: Good

Advancement Prospects: Fair

Prerequisites:

Education or Training—Bachelor's degree with emphasis on business, marketing, and media development; advanced business degree a plus

Experience—Minimum of three to five years in product development environment, preferably with Internet product development; background in managing multiple complex projects; experience as a market assistant preparing materials; some Internet sales background a plus

Special Skills and Personality Traits—Ability to translate high-level product ideas into detailed business requirements; conscientious and adaptable; effective communicator with good presentation skills; excellent problem-solving and leadership skills; goal-oriented self-starter with outstanding time management and organizational talents; strong written and oral communication skills

CAREER LADDER

```
┌─────────────────────────────────────┐
│      Director (or Vice President)    │
│  of Marketing; E-commerce Manager;   │
│     Online Marketing Consultant      │
└─────────────────────────────────────┘

┌─────────────────────────────────────┐
│    Product Development Director      │
└─────────────────────────────────────┘

┌─────────────────────────────────────┐
│        Marketing Assistant           │
└─────────────────────────────────────┘
```

Position Description

Product Development Directors are responsible for the full development or life-cycle management of an online product line or services, usually reporting to top management. They participate in overall product strategy with the company's decision makers, exploring research and development requirements for new and emerging products, and analyzing product ideas in terms of whether they fit into the operation's basic business strategy, capabilities, and resources. They gather the approved product's technical requirements and prepare the requirements documents used by production. Thereafter, they coordinate product development, establishing estimates of potential profits and release dates for production.

They coordinate marketing analyses to develop product definitions and collaborate with a wide variety of functional areas such as sales, technology, marketing, customer service, and operations. In addition, they provide documentation expertise and training for these other departments in support of the product development. They generate and maintain the initial prioritized list of customer and market requirements for the product or service, providing financial and market justification for product selection and definition that is responsive to customer needs and market opportunities. They then manage the day-to-day progress of the product or service's development. In this process, Product Development Directors essentially define the marketing requirements for the company Web site and manage the course of product development by translating user testing and customer support feedback into feature and function requirements for the Web site.

Product Development Directors prepare objectives and schedules for all phases of product development and introduction onto the company's e-commerce Web site(s). They coordinate with marketing and research to identify and track market trends within their firm's industry as related specifically to the company's products and/or services. They also identify partnering opportunities for complementary third-party products to broaden their company's online product line. In addition, they establish dealer networks, as well as create and manage alliances with partners and affiliates, all for the purposes of maintaining communications with contacts and collecting and analyzing technical, financial, scheduling, and sales information for each product and/or service.

Salaries

For their highly responsible position and its varied duties, Product Development Managers are well compensated. According to Salary Wizard's Salary.com Web site, annual earnings for Product Development (or Management) Directors in March 2006 ranged from a low of about $90,000 to a high of $178,254, with a general median yearly salary ranging from $124,000 to $155,000, greatly dependent upon geographic location.

Employment Prospects

With the continued growth and expansion of online Web sites offering sales of products and services, the need for Product Development Directors for companies extending their sales efforts in the technology of new media via the Internet is on the increase. Companies seek Product Development Directors who have backgrounds both in business and marketing and in online product development to aid their e-commerce business. Employment prospects for qualified individuals, then, are good.

Advancement Prospects

Product Development Managers may advance to more senior marketing or production posts within their company, may decide to work for a firm that offers market consulting and development work, or may even become independent consultants. Advancement can also come from gaining a similar position with a larger company.

Education and Training

Most Product Development Managers have, as a basic minimum, a four-year college degree in business with an emphasis on marketing and media development. Courses in economics, mathematics (for market analysis), communica-

tions, and media production and design are helpful. In addition, course work in computer information systems, or even computer engineering, is recommended. An M.B.A. degree is a strong plus in a candidate for this position.

Experience, Skills, and Personality Traits

Product Development Managers must have knowledge of and/or experience with Internet product development including a demonstrated skill in writing product specifications, as they will need to translate product ideas into detailed business and design requirements. They should have prior experience in developing Web services with engineering, visual design, and other cross-functional production teams, as well as work experience in online shopping or advertising environments. Managers must be able to quantitatively and qualitatively analyze product concepts, strategic opportunities, competitive threats, and finances, as well as supervise several complex projects at the same time. They should have a working knowledge and mastery of MS Office (Excel, Word, and PowerPoint) programs, as well as HTML and other database management software. In addition, they should have strong written and verbal communication abilities and excellent problem-solving talents. They need a high level of initiative and self-motivation and should be able to collaborate easily with varied marketing, production, and technical personnel.

Unions and Associations

There are no unions or associations that directly represent Product Development Directors. However, many may belong to such umbrella industry associations as the American Electronics Association (AEA), the Computer and Electronics Marketing Association (CEMA), and the Software and Information Industry Association (SIIA).

Tips for Entry

1. In college, gain a broad business background but focus especially on marketing, communications, and online media development. Look at case studies or simulations that can aid you in feeling how marketing works.
2. Study publications dealing with the computer, the Internet, and new media and examine company Web sites that are promoting and selling exciting new products and services. Study how they have designed their promotion, how customer-friendly their Web site is, and how you might develop their product promotion differently.
3. Be willing to take lower-paying marketing or sales positions with companies that are actively selling online to gain experience in online promotion.

WEB SECURITY MANAGER

CAREER PROFILE	CAREER LADDER

Duties: Responsible for designing, implementing, and maintaining security measures for an organization's Web site

Alternate Title(s): Web Security Administrator

Salary Range: $60,000 to $150,000 or more

Employment Prospects: Poor to Fair

Advancement Prospects: Poor

Prerequisites:

Education or Training—Bachelor's degree in communications, computer science, or Internet technology

Experience—Three to seven years in Web development and Internet technology

Special Skills and Personality Traits—Close attention to detail; effective communication skills (both verbal and written); excellent organization and problem solving abilities; thorough familiarity with Internet technology, programming, and Web site design techniques

---

> **Web Systems Director**

> **Web Security Manager**

> **Internet Applications Programmer; Webpage Designer**

Position Description

As more and more organizations and institutions are determining that the Internet is a viable venture for them, security of their Web site(s), programs, and data files has become a hot-button issue. Problems still plague Web sites today in the form of CGI (Common Gateway Interface) vulnerabilities, mobile content vulnerabilities in Web browsers, buffer-overflow conditions on many Web servers, and Web sites not running current server patches (programs that facilitate Internet connections) or up-to-date software. A Web Security Manager's duties are to identify the problems, answer the questions, and provide the needed Web security for the organization or institution.

Web Security Managers develop, enable, and maintain firewall technology (which prevents direct, and possibly unauthorized, access to a computer in use) that secures their organization's Web site. They define network security issues and formulate security procedures to prevent, detect, and respond to both internal and external security threats to an organization's data files, access points, network procedures, and software programs. Evaluating

potential problems of security attacks, they develop plans and procedures to ensure the safety and privacy of the organization's Internet and intranet sites and local area computer network (LAN).

Web Security Managers perform periodic security audits of an organization's files, Web site(s), programs, and hardware to ensure security has not been breached or compromised. In this process, they create, modify, and delete user profiles and other access controls, as well as review security logs and violation reports on a daily basis. If e-commerce sales are a part of the Web activity of the organization, Web Security Managers set up the procedures of securing credit card transactions with such techniques as the SET (Secure Electronic Transaction) protocol and document encryption with the SSL (Secure Sockets Layer) protocol. They guard all end users (within or without the company) against the dangers of active content and cookies. (A cookie is a small file stored on an individual computer—often without the user's knowledge—allowing a site to tag any browsing done on that computer with a unique identification. When an individual visits a Web site, the site's server requests a unique ID from that individual's browser program. If this browser does not have an ID the server delivers one, which is called "passing the cookie." In this way, cookies are similar to the Caller ID feature on phone systems. Just as someone can track the origin of a phone call, companies can use cookies to track information about user behavior. Many individuals and organizations feel this is an invasion of their privacy and seek methods to secure against this cookie procedure.)

Besides their ongoing performance of protecting the organization's Web-based technology, Web Security Managers research and evaluate new or improved security measures that can be implemented for Web systems' security. They frequently are called upon to draw up disaster recovery plans for the use of the organization's Web production team. After discussing these plans with top management and gaining their approval, the Web Security Manager briefs the Internet and Web production personnel.

In some organizations, the Web security work is done by the network systems administrator or the Web systems director as a part of their regular duties. In other companies, particularly large organizations with complex Internet and intranet needs, these security duties are held exclusively by the security manager (or administrator). Web Security Managers may also be required to maintain security protocols on the organization's computer systems as well as its Web and Internet systems.

Salaries

The annual compensation of Web Security Managers reflects the importance of their responsibilities for the well-being of an organization's computer and Internet systems. According to the salary Web site of HotJobs.com, the median national annual salary in 2006 for Web Security Managers was $114,847. Depending upon geographic location and depth of responsibilities, yearly incomes range from a low of about $60,000 to a high of $154,000. This remuneration is affected also by the size of the organization and the type of industry involved, as well as the employee's credentials and years of experience.

Employment Prospects

Most small to medium organizations entrust their security protocols to their network systems administrators or Web systems directors. Larger firms and government organizations may prefer to have a single individual responsible for the security of their Internet, intranet, Web, and network systems. Thus, while openings for this position are somewhat limited, there is a guaranteed need (and growing one due to the continual incursions of computer viruses over

the last several years) for expert security for businesses and government institutions.

Advancement Prospects

A Web Security Manager desiring to advance further in the Internet management of an organization will look to becoming the Web systems director, the network systems administrator, or the IT (information technology) systems director, as all three posts share an overall systems control function, similar in nature, if not duties, to that of the Web Security Manager.

Education and Training

At a minimum, an undergraduate degree is necessary, in communications, computer science, or information science. Training in computer networking, hardware installation and maintenance, and Internet technology and techniques are all necessary background.

Experience, Skills, and Personality Traits

The job of Web Security Manager requires anywhere from three to seven years experience in Web and Internet development, network administration, hardware and software installation and maintenance, and e-mail and open source mail systems (such as qmail and sendmail) that are used by many larger organizations for internal communications.

They need to be familiar with Internet load balancing devices and protocols and have a thorough understanding of Internet server architectures and hardware. In addition, they should have a working knowledge of computer management tools (such as SnapMirror, SnapVault, and Cluster Failover) that provide high availability of data but also protection for that data.

Web Security Managers should have strong analytical and creative problem solving skills. They need to be highly aggressive in meeting their security commitments, and be able to work both independently and as part of an overall team. Self-motivated, energetic, and tenacious, they must have strong communication skills (both verbal and written). They must be very flexible and responsive to changing circumstances, but handle potential pressure-filled situations always in a professional manner.

Unions and Associations

There are no specific unions or associations that represent Web Security Managers. However, some of them may belong to such umbrella industry associations as the Software and Information Industry Association (SIIA) or the Software Publishers Association (SPA). In addition, the Internet Society (ISOC) is one of the oldest and most prestigious groups for professionals involved in the Internet and Web matters.

Tips for Entry

1. During your technical education, search for courses in all types of Web programming languages, as well as introductory courses in Internet writing, layout, and graphic arts.

2. Look for opportunities to help with the expansion or maintenance of a Web site at your college or university or at a local nonprofit organization to gain immediate practical experience in dealing with Internet and Web development problems, including security protocols.

3. Consider taking jobs as a Webpage designer or an Internet applications programmer to obtain necessary hands-on experience that also involves data security issues.

WEB SYSTEMS DIRECTOR

CAREER PROFILE

Duties: Directs and oversees all aspects of an organization's Web systems (Internet and intranet), including design, release, and maintenance

Alternate Title(s): Technology Director; Web Director; Web Group Director; Web Systems Manager; Web Site Administrator

Salary Range: $130,000 to $185,000 or more

Employment Prospects: Fair

Advancement Prospects: Poor

Prerequisites:

Education or Training—Bachelor's degree in computer science, communications, or Web/Internet development required; master's degree preferred

Experience—Ten to 14 years of Web development and/or marketing experience that is primarily Internet-oriented

Special Skills and Personality Traits—Ability to work independently and handle multiple tasks; close attention to detail; effective communication abilities (both verbal and written); excellent problem solving and project management skills; familiarity with Internet technology and Web site design; highly organized; knowledge and understanding of database theory and application and system process flows

CAREER LADDER

```
┌─────────────────────────────────┐
│      Director of Technology;     │
│   Vice President of Technology;  │
│    Vice President, Development    │
└─────────────────────────────────┘

┌─────────────────────────────────┐
│       Web Systems Director       │
└─────────────────────────────────┘

┌─────────────────────────────────┐
│   Webmaster; Webpage Designer;   │
│     Web Software Developer       │
└─────────────────────────────────┘
```

Position Description

Web Systems Directors are top-level administrators who manage Web sites and their design, implementation, and maintenance. Many of them have been webpage designers or Web site programmers who have accelerated into the management post of director. As directors, they are primarily responsible for the success of an organization's public Web sites, Internet accesses, and the intranet sites utilized internally by the organization, its various offices, and designated personnel.

Web Systems Directors manage Web site content and coordinate all Web marketing initiatives. They work with the Information Technology (IT) systems director to coordinate all information technology initiatives. They provide leadership for Web site development activities and are tasked with the day-to-day management of the organization's Web sites, including the supervision of personnel who manage these Web sites. In addition, they are usually responsible for Web site delivery, ensuring that there are no delays by the Internet service provider in hosting the Web site to the public, and they are involved in any necessary problem resolution. They may manage overall IT hardware and software systems, including routine network administraion, and identify any need for IT improvement, making recommendations to top management. In addition, they analyze all organizational initiatives that may affect the strategic direction(s) that the organization's Web site(s) might take and make recommendations for modifications for potential renovation and future development.

They work directly with Web project managers on overall project proposals, estimates, and budgets, gathering accurate and complete project requirements to be able to provide well-researched hardware, software, and programming language recommendations to top management. In that process they will write, or oversee the writing of, comprehensive technical specifications and functional descriptions, including logic streams, flow charts, site architecture maps, and interface wireframes. During the implementation process they will locate and manage appropriate resources for the developing projects, overseeing the design and programming of the Web-based applications, and facilitate, design, and organize user-testing scenarios for those applications.

Web Systems Directors must constantly review current Web site trends, any changes in industry standards, and new techniques in design and functionality in order to maintain a competitive edge for the organization. They provide top management with progress reports on both current operations and potential future developments. They may also be involved in the evaluation of current Web sites and their financial return. Organizations demand that their Web sites provide a return on the investment in developing them. Sites must perform a commercial as well as a branding and marketing function to justify continued investment. If a financial benefit can be established, it is much easier to receive continued funding for existing Web projects or to undertake new ones. The Web Systems Director is in a unique position of managing and funneling reports and evaluations to top management.

Salaries

Web Systems Directors are usually well remunerated for their high-level responsibilities within the organization. According to Salary.com's job salary studies, as of March 2006, the median expected salary of a typical Web Systems Director in the United States is $145,291 annually, with the range of yearly income starting with a low of about $121,000 to a high of $215,000. As with many Web-based jobs, these salaries vary according to geographic location as well as size of the organization.

Employment Prospects

Most medium- to large-sized organizations that have well-defined Web-based programs understand the necessity to have a Web Systems Director to administer such programs. Smaller companies, however, frequently assign all their Web site needs (design, implementation, maintenance, and management) to one or more people, usually called Webmasters, who will report to a top executive, usually a programs or product development director. Thus, job opportunities for even highly qualified Web Systems Directors are somewhat limited.

Advancement Prospects

The position of Web Systems Director is typically the highest technical executive post within the corporate structure. Directors may decide to advance into higher management positions in business development or administration in their organization. In addition, they may be able to advance by looking for positions in larger organizations or in companies that do all or most of their business online.

Education and Training

The minimum educational requirement for this position is a bachelor's degree, preferably a B.S. degree in computer science, communications, or Web/Internet technology and development. Most organizations will insist upon a master's degree as well, possibly in business administration. The important point is that this job requires a thorough knowledge of, and experience with, Web development processes and procedures including hardware and software programming tools.

Experience, Skills, and Personality Traits

Most organizations require their Web Systems Director to have from 10 to 14 years of Web development and/or marketing experience that is primarily Internet-oriented. This experience should include several years of project management of Web technology initiatives. Web Systems Directors need to be familiar with content management systems and with search engine optimization techniques, as well as Web measurement tools. Their technical background should include the implementation of Web architectures, some experience with and current knowledge of server-side technologies (such as J2EE, ASP.NET, Cold Fusion, RDBMS, and so forth), browser/platform limitations (to be found in such systems as Mac, PC, Unix and Linux), content and asset management systems, and data-access languages, such as HTML, Perl (for UNIX systems), ActiveX controls (for Windows-based systems), JavaScript, and XML. In addition, they should be familiar with streaming video protocols, compression types, delivery mechanisms, design applications (such as MS Word, Dreamweaver, and Adobe Photoshop), available hosting services, and Internet technology in general. This technical knowledge will let them better supervise the organization's Web personnel and process of development.

Web Systems Directors need to have good spelling, grammar, and writing skills, as well as excellent verbal abilities to communicate effectively with all levels of an organization. They must have excellent problem solving and project management skills. They need to be able to independently research solutions for IT-related problems and make solid and cost-effective recommendations to top management. They should be highly organized, be able to handle multiple tasks simultaneously, be very detail-oriented, and be able to prioritize varied tasks and projects.

Unions and Associations

Web Systems Directors must keep in touch with many aspects of the continuously evolving Web and Internet industry. The Internet Society (ISOC) is one of the oldest and most prestigious groups for professionals involved in the Internet and Web matters. There are other trade groups for Web Systems Directors, such as the Internet Developer Group in California, the U.S. Internet Industry Association (USIIA), or Wise-Women, an association and resource for female (and male) Web designers, developers, and programmers.

Tips for Entry

1. During your technical education, look for courses in all types of Web programming languages, as well as introductory classes in writing, layout, and graphic arts.

2. Search out opportunities to help with the expansion or maintenance of a Web site at your college or university or at a local nonprofit organization to gain immediate practical experience while completing your coursework.

3. Be prepared to work as a Web developer or designer at a small business or other organization that is looking for part-time technical support for their own technical staff. This may be your start of the hands-on practical experience you will need for your advancement, eventually, to the administrative position of Web Systems Director.

MARKETING AND SALES

E-COMMERCE STRATEGY MANAGER

CAREER PROFILE

Duties: Identify and design an organization's strategic and long-range e-commerce goals

Alternate Title(s): E-commerce Web Content Manager; Marketplace Strategy Manager; Online Strategy Manager

Salary Range: $92,000 to $145,000 or more

Employment Prospects: Poor to Fair

Advancement Prospects: Fair

Prerequisites:

Education or Training—B.A. degree in business, communications, or marketing required; M.B.A. or other graduate degree in a field related to competitive analysis and product strategy preferred

Experience—Minimum three to five years of working knowledge of strategic and competitive analysis, preferably in an online or interactive Web marketing environment

Special Skills and Personality Traits—Excellent verbal and written communication skills; keen analytical abilities; proficiency in Web development languages, Web editor programs, and browsers; solid statistical knowledge and business intuition; strong interpersonal, management, and organizational talents; substantial computer aptitude; very customer-oriented

CAREER LADDER

```
┌─────────────────────────────────┐
│   Online Marketing Manager;     │
│  E-commerce Executive Manager    │
└─────────────────────────────────┘

┌─────────────────────────────────┐
│   E-commerce Strategy Manager    │
└─────────────────────────────────┘

┌─────────────────────────────────┐
│  Marketing Associate; Marketing  │
│    Specialist or Researcher      │
└─────────────────────────────────┘
```

Position Description

E-commerce Strategy Managers play a key role in providing top management with insights into the market dynamics of the online retail business. They work with various teams of cross-functional department managers, external sources, and other internal sources to identify key data points and trends that will affect the organization's online competitive positioning and competitive sales strategy. In this process, they help to create and publish periodical competitive update reports that are reviewed by senior management to set (or revise) policies and procedures.

Thus, E-commerce Strategy Managers aid in the development of an Internet strategy and help coordinate efforts across all information technology (IT) functions to support

the organization's comprehensive long-range (and short-range) business strategy. They develop annual and/or semi-annual plans for refreshing and updating the operation's online content. In this process, they coordinate with product marketing, tactical marketing, sales, and applications personnel to drive and develop the overall structure, navigation, and content of the organization's Web site(s). They may be asked to implement content updates and promotion of all newsworthy items as well as maintain targeted URLs, coordinating development as appropriate with individual corporate group Web sites.

They may work with internal groups such as product marketing and sales teams, as well as interactive marketing agencies, to determine the featured online products, offers, positioning, and creative messaging that meet the organization's program objectives, and are consistent with product brand positioning and/or vertical markets. Thus, they help ensure that technical and product Web content for assigned product lines is written clearly and concisely and is updated on a regular basis. They may also develop and manage relationships with interactive marketing agencies and third-party Web site partners to ensure maximization of those resources to the benefit of the organization.

They support various finance and product operations teams in market modeling, competitive product evaluations and benchmarking, data collection, analysis, reporting, and the providing of operational recommendations to top management. They assist in the completion of monthly/quarterly competitive metrics reports, and assist in the preparation of presentation material to divisional and corporate executive management.

Salaries

Commensurate with their value in the planning and strategy process for an organization, E-commerce Strategy Managers are paid relatively well. According to salary analyses made by HotJobs.com, annual national median salaries in 2006 for this position were $111,692, with the earnings ranging from a low of about $92,000 to a high of about $151,500 per year. As is usual, earnings can be dramatically affected by geography (as well as employer size and employee years of experience). For example, according to this salary analysis, earnings for this position in Killeen, Texas, ranged from $92,303 to a high of $115,594 yearly, with a median annual salary of $101,640. In contrast, earnings in New York City for this position ranged from a yearly low of $121,044 to a high of $151,587.

Employment Prospects

Possibilities of openings for the position of E-commerce Strategy Manager are poor to fair. Only larger organizations with well-defined e-commerce operations can afford to fund a separate position on their management team for a marketing and sales strategy executive. In smaller companies, this function of planning/strategy is held usually by either the online marketing manager and his/her staff or by an executive group under the direct supervision of top management.

Advancement Prospects

The most obvious path of advancement for an E-commerce Strategy Manager within an organization is elevation to the level of either online marketing manager or e-commerce executive manager. Advancement (and the resultant higher remuneration and expansion of responsibilities) can also be reached by taking a similar post with a larger firm. Another possibility is to become a recognized consultant to companies in need of statistical analysis on a regular basis.

Education and Training

The educational basic requirement for this job is a B.A. or B.S. degree in business, communications, or marketing. Some organizations may require a master's in business administration or a graduate degree in a field related to competitive analysis and product strategy. E-commerce Strategy Managers also need to have training (and become proficient) in Web development languages (such as HTML, JavaScript, and Perl), Web editor programs (such as Dreamweaver), and Web browsers.

Experience, Skills, and Personality Traits

Most organizations hiring an E-commerce Strategy Manager will require a minimum of three to five years of working knowledge of strategic and competitive analysis with a proven record of accomplishment using trend analysis scenarios in the decision-making process. A basic understanding of Internet technologies is a plus, as is a working knowledge of marketing services and planning as well as product development and management processes. Managers must have solid statistical knowledge and intuition.

Their strong analytical skills must provide them with the ability to analyze raw data while keeping in mind the larger corporate picture, draw conclusions from their analysis, and develop viable recommendations. They have to be able to translate (or formulate) business challenges/goals into analytical terms, and to spot incorrect solutions that look reasonable but are erroneous. Their market research background should include expertise in competitive analysis, product concept validation, and prototype testing procedures.

They need excellent verbal and written communication skills, as well as strong organizational and management talents with the ability to handle multiple projects simultaneously in a high-speed business environment. Their strong interpersonal skills should include the ability to build consensus of opinions, particularly in their cross-functional team capacity. Their solid computer knowledge should include familiarity with Excel and PowerPoint, as well as MS Access. Above all, they must be customer focused and creative.

Unions and Associations

E-commerce Strategy Managers may find it useful to belong to such umbrella associations as the American Marketing Association (AMA), the Computer and Electronics Marketing Association (CEMA), and the Software and Information Industry Association (SIIA) or the more specific American Statistical Association (ASA) and the Statistics Division of the American Society for Quality (ASQ) for the purposes of networking, keeping up to date on the latest technology, and addressing common concerns.

Tips for Entry

1. While in college, compiling results of experiments in a science lab or entering mathematically oriented projects in a science fair are good ways to gain experience using statistical analysis methodologies.

2. During your studies, search for marketing research companies that may need part-time help conducting surveys in your geographic area. Another possibility is to work part time for the U.S. Census Department to gain practical experience in the gathering (and analysis) of statistics.

3. Membership in such specific associations as the American Statistical Association or the American Society for Quality can yield valuable contacts or job leads as well as keep you current with the latest software products and statistical analysis procedures.

ONLINE CUSTOMER SERVICE MANAGER

CAREER PROFILE

Duties: Supervise responses to customer inquiries regarding orders, billing inquiries, and technical problems, ensuring that customers are retained and satisfied and that their needs are satisfactorily fulfilled

Alternate Title(s): Client Support Manager; E-commerce Customer Support Manager

Salary Range: $50,000 to $105,000 or more

Employment Prospects: Fair

Advancement Prospects: Fair to Good

Prerequisites:

Education or Training—Four-year college degree usually required, with emphasis on business and retail marketing, supplemented with computer courses

Experience—Two to five years customer service background, preferably in an e-commerce environment or with a catalog company; experience with technical support and knowledge of client server platforms support and various systems applications; familiarity with customer call center and telephone systems

Special Skills and Personality Traits—Ability to work at a high level in a fast-paced and intense environment; excellent oral communication and problem-solving skills; exceptional client service aptitude and demonstrable team player abilities; extremely well organized, diligent, detail-oriented, and self-motivated, with ability to manage effectively multiple projects or activities; solid grammar, spelling, and writing skills

CAREER LADDER

```
┌─────────────────────────────┐
│  Online Marketing Manager;  │
│  Online Product Manager;    │
│  Online Sales Manager       │
└─────────────────────────────┘

┌─────────────────────────────┐
│ Online Customer Service Manager │
└─────────────────────────────┘

┌─────────────────────────────┐
│  Online Marketing Assistant; │
│  Online Marketing Specialist │
└─────────────────────────────┘
```

Position Description

Online Customer Service Managers manage a staff of customer service representatives, often referred to as the client support team, whose main goal is to guarantee that customers are retained, that they remain satisfied, and that their needs are suitably met. Under the manager's guidance, these representatives respond to customer inquiries about orders, billing problems, and any technical problems that have occurred. They document customer trouble in reports according to established standard operating procedures as set by the Online Customer Service Manager.

It is the manager's task to see to it that customer inquiries are handled effectively and expeditiously, and all product information requests are fulfilled as quickly as possible. Additionally, the Online Customer Service Manager is ultimately responsible for all customer communication, including order confirmation, shipping, and tracking information, and supervises all customer satisfaction tracking, returns, replacement requests, refunds, credits, and any necessary voiding of charges. The managers supervise all e-mailing of customers and responses to e-mails from customers and vendors, as well as preside over the staff handling telephone calls to and from customers and vendors.

In some cases, Online Customer Service Managers have the duty to provide leadership for not only all aspects of retail e-commerce, but also all Web customer service programs. The latter may involve technical aspects, such as creating and updating Web site content on a daily basis across platforms (either PC or Mac). They may generate custom graphics, using such software programs as Dreamweaver to create pages, import text, and fix products. They may also design, create, test, and send out weekly HTML and plain text e-mail newsletters to a subscription list of customers and/or vendors. In all these matters, they may have the help of a technical support representative as a member of the client support team. This individual will have expertise in e-commerce software, search engine optimization, and graphical design services.

Finally, Online Customer Service Managers compile daily sales metrics, usually in the form of an Excel spreadsheet, for marketing and sales managers and participate in the design and improvement of customer service database tools. They are responsible for designing and implementing any improved processes or operational policies, and they recommend to upper management any necessary changes to the organization's Web site, products, or services that would help to fulfill customer needs in a better manner.

Salaries
The annual earnings of Online Customer Service Managers typically are more modest than those of sales and marketing managers. According to HotJobs.com, as of January 2006, median annual salaries of Online Customer Service Managers nationally were $76,556, with a range from a low of $66,726 to a high of $92,391 per year. As geography has an important part to play in earnings, HotJobs.com found that the range extends in some parts of the country from an income low of approximately $50,000 to a high of $110,000 or more.

Employment Prospects
Most organizations, small or large, are acutely aware of the need for good customer relations and the helpful and timely response to customer (and vendor) complaints and requests. As such, the demand for individuals who can handle customer relations well is strong. However, this responsibility often is made a part of other managers' duties (such as those in sales or marketing), especially in smaller organizations. For larger companies and institutions, it frequently is easier and more effective to have these duties (and the managing of a separate client support team of representatives) centered in one individual. Understandably, competition for this position is often stiff.

Advancement Prospects
Online Customer Service Managers may find the easiest path of advancement is to the post of online sales manager, online marketing manager, or product manager, as their skills are directly related to any of these jobs.

Education and Training
A bachelor of arts degree from a four-year college or university is the usual educational requirement for an Online Customer Service Manager. If involved with the more technical aspects of Web site management, this individual may need a bachelor of science degree in computer technology, with additional coursework in business and marketing.

Experience, Skills, and Personality Traits
Experience dealing with the public within a retail environment, or even working as an assistant in a media organization, is helpful background for online customer relations, and experience in an e-commerce environment is a strong plus. Customer service representatives need to be able to troubleshoot customer problems right at the point of contact with the customer and to obtain a detailed level of information from them to be able to resolve the problems or to recognize that the problem necessitates a higher level of authority to be resolved successfully.

Online Customer Service Managers usually are required to have two to five years of prior customer service experience, preferably in an e-commerce, an e-retail, or catalog company (where items are sold out of a printed or an online catalog). They need to be extremely knowledgeable about e-commerce techniques and technology, such as domain registry issues, forum management functions, Search Engine Operations (SEO) processes, and SSL certificates. (An SSL certificate is a digital certificate that authenticates the identity of a Web site to Web browser users and enables encrypted communications using a Secure Sockets Layer process.) In addition, they should have some familiarity with Adobe Photoshop and other image-editing software programs. As they are likely to be responsible for both customer service and for Web-related design functions, they should have two to five years experience in writing and editing HTML (Dreamweaver or any other applicable program) and Javascript and have worked with .ASP pages.

Online Customer Service Managers need to have excellent people skills, have limitless patience, and be able to maintain both a calm demeanor and a high performance level in a fast-paced and intense business environment. They need to have outstanding verbal and written communication skills in order to communicate with customers and vendors effectively over the phone and via e-mail. They must be able to develop strong professional relationships and to influence their peers, managers, and other team members. While being able to work independently, they also should have a team orientation, with a focus on training and coaching as part of their management skills. They need to be highly organized and display excellent decision-making, problem solving, and conflict resolution talents. They must be highly self-motivated, diligently detail-oriented, and able to manage effectively multiple projects or activities simultaneously.

Unions and Associations

Online Customer Service Managers may find it useful to belong to such associations as the American Marketing Association (AMA), or, if involved in the technical aspects of customer relations, the Computer and Electronics Marketing Association (CEMA) and the Software and Information Industry Association (SIIA) for the purposes of networking, keeping up to date on the latest technology, and addressing common concerns.

Tips for Entry

1. While earning your college degree in marketing or business administration, take computer courses to become familiar with programs utilized in the e-retail business for which you are studying.

2. Take a course or two in psychology or sociology to learn how to deal with human variables in a retail environment.

3. Explore Internet Web sites that sell products or services to examine the marketing techniques used to capture online users and the techniques utilized in satisfying customer complaints or problems, and consider how you would react to them as a customer and how effective they are.

ONLINE MARKETING MANAGER

CAREER PROFILE

Duties: Direct and oversee the implementation of an organization's online marketing policies, objectives, and initiatives

Alternate Title(s): Director of Internet Marketing and E-Retailing; E-commerce Marketing Director; E-commerce Marketing Manager; Online Marketing Director

Salary Range: $65,000 to $180,000 or more

Employment Prospects: Fair to Good

Advancement Prospects: Fair

Prerequisites:

Education or Training—B.A. or B.S. in computer science, marketing, or network technology required; M.B.A. recommended

Experience—Four to eight years of experience in online marketing, direct marketing channels, or e-commerce usually required; experience in interactive marketing/advertising and some experience in search engine marketing, online media buying, and Internet advertising metrics recommended

Special Skills and Personality Traits—Ability to organize and prioritize while juggling multiple projects simultaneously, and to work in a fast-paced environment; capacity of being a creative, conceptual, problem-solving, and strategic thinker; computer proficiency; excellent oral/written communication and presentation skills; exceptional quantitative/analytical skills and attention to detail; strong aptitude for negotiation, business development sense, and project management skills

CAREER LADDER

```
┌─────────────────────────────────┐
│   Vice President, Marketing     │
└─────────────────────────────────┘

┌─────────────────────────────────┐
│   Online Marketing Manager      │
└─────────────────────────────────┘

┌─────────────────────────────────┐
│  Marketing Assistant; Marketing │
│   Specialist or Researcher;     │
│       Product Manager           │
└─────────────────────────────────┘
```

Position Description

Online Marketing Managers administer all aspects of an organization's online marketing, including its Web site (and its online store if any), and keyword (words included in a product Webpage that are designed to match words commonly utilized by customers) marketing programs, online advertising, partnerships, affiliate marketing programs, any international marketing promotions, e-mail campaigns, online programs for e-business and internal customers, and demand generation programs. These managers are the drive behind the creation and implementation of the organization's online marketing plan, and they review and recommend online strategies, including e-mail, media placement, and search engine marketing, to support the organization's programming, Web site, and advertising objectives. They usually contribute to and oversee the creative process for all online marketing campaigns, including artwork, written copy, and implementation strategy.

Online Marketing Managers manage the customer survey process and provide recommendations and action plans to upper management. They manage vendor relationships to ensure timely and accurate creation of online components within the pre-determined budget limits. They measure all online campaigns and e-marketing programs against monthly revenue targets, conducting ongoing return on investment (ROI) analysis of these programs and instituting any needed improvements to achieve revenue goals.

Other marketing programs in which the Online Marketing Manager may be involved are:

- PPC, or Pay Per Click, where advertisers are charged for the number of clicks or hits received on their ads
- CPC, or Cost Per Click, which is the cost of one click, or hit, on a listing, keyword, banner (the most visible of all Web advertisements in the style of a long skinny ad running along the top of a Web site's page), or advertisement for which the advertiser would pay each time the online user selects it on the hyperlink
- SEO, or Search Engine Optimization, the process of improving Web site pages so that they rank higher in search engine protocols for targeting keywords with the ultimate goal of generating more revenue from the Web site
- SEM, or Search Engine Marketing, the process of researching, submitting, and positioning a Web site within search engines to achieve maximum exposure of that Web site

Managers assess online user behavior by implementing tracking systems to identify Web site visitation and transaction patterns, as well as success with keyword marketing on the site, working closely with the Web site management team. They liaise with the product development team to ensure smooth online introduction of new products they work with the Web site development and design teams to maintain the clarity of the organization's message or navigational links on the Web site and to make certain that the organization's values are reflected on the Web site. In addition, they work with customer service teams or contracted fulfillment agencies to be sure that the fulfillment of customer orders is accurate and timely.

Finally, they are responsible for ongoing competitive analysis on the organization's services and products offered on its Web site(s), including price studies, SWOT analyses (studies that look at the Strengths and Weaknesses of the organization, as well as Opportunities and Threats that are external to the organization that are either helpful or harmful to the organization's achievement of its objectives), costing analyses, and market trend studies. In this process, they determine new paid channels of opportunity, provide recommendations, and launch test programs of products and services. They provide strategic analysis, information, and recommendations to upper marketing and sales management so that the organization's decisions can be optimized.

In most cases, Online Marketing Managers report directly to a senior marketing manager, usually a vice president of marketing.

Salaries

Commensurate with the measure of their duties and responsibilities, Online Marketing Managers are paid quite well. According to studies made by salary.hotjobs.com, expected annual salaries nationwide for Online (or, as they say, e-commerce) Marketing Managers and directors, as of 2006, range from a low of $72,415 to a high of $163,694. Earnings are greatly affected by geography, size of company, employee's years of experience, and the scope of their duties. In the larger urban cities, the annual salary range moves upward to a low of $82,536 and a high of $195,344.

Employment Prospects

The highly competitive nature of online marketing and sales creates an extremely urgent demand for adept marketing specialists, researchers, and managers. Some companies offer internships or training programs for new graduates starting as researchers for their online marketing team. To reach the responsible position of Online Marketing Manager, however, takes years of marketing and direct hands-on experience with a wide variety of programs, techniques, and procedures. Nonetheless, the strong need for accomplished and successful marketing professionals as Online Marketing Managers provides opportunities for knowledgeable and skilled marketing persons to advance into this responsible and highly satisfying management position.

Advancement Prospects

Online Marketing Managers most frequently advance either by moving to larger companies where they take on a more expanded line of responsibilities (at higher salaries) or by moving into a higher management level of marketing within their organization, such as vice president of marketing for the overall organization.

Education and Training

Nearly every person entering the field of online marketing has a four-year degree in business with emphasis on marketing, either a B.A. or a B.S. degree. Many organizations prefer (or require) an M.B.A. as well. In addition, knowledge of common Web languages and programs (Excel, HTML, Word, PowerPoint, Dreamweaver, and Adobe Photoshop) and techniques, as well as a strong familiarity with the Internet, are important skills.

Experience, Skills, and Personality Traits

Organizations hiring Online Marketing Managers look for individuals with five to as much as 10 years experience in online marketing. They need to have one or two years of experience with search engine marketing and mobile marketing, as well as knowledge of and experience with the common ad servers, ad networks, and online service providers.

Some additional background in direct marketing channels, such as direct mail, Web media, direct response TV, affiliate programs, and e-mail marketing, is a plus.

Online Marketing Managers need to have experience with Web analytics software (such as Hitwise and Websidestory), be familiar with quantitative analysis skills, and have an understanding of trending and forecasting. Their experience should include taking new concepts to market with a strong understanding of customer segmentation and online market dynamics. They need to be conversant with prevailing Internet and Web technologies and trends including streaming media, ad tagging, Flash, and podcasting/blogging, just to name a few.

Online Marketing Managers must enjoy and be skilled at analysis, data manipulation, and data presentation. They have to be highly detail-oriented, with excellent analytical and problem solving skills, and highly organized and efficient in their time management proficiency. They need strong business development and project management talents, with excellent oral/written communication, presentation, and interpersonal abilities as well. They need strong negotiating skills, working directly with salespeople and clients to ensure ad campaign successes. They will be working in a fast-paced and deadline-oriented environment, and they must be able to address successfully all management issues as related to online marketing.

Unions and Associations

As Online Marketing Managers are a part of management, there are no unions that represent them. However, such associations as the American Marketing Association (AMA), the Computer and Electronics Marketing Association (CEMA), and the Software and Information Industry Association (SIIA) are valuable to their marketing members for the purposes of networking and addressing common concerns.

Tips for Entry

1. After receiving your four-year college degree, consider earning an M.B.A. degree with a marketing emphasis to give you an extra advantage in job seeking for online marketing positions.

2. Explore the marketing industry press and, above all, Web sites to locate organizations involved in exciting new online products that are seeking marketing assistants.

3. Look at Internet Web sites that sell products or services to examine the marketing techniques employed to capture online users, and then learn through your training as a marketing assistant how these techniques are put into place and which ones succeed and which ones do not for which user market.

ONLINE SALES MANAGER

CAREER PROFILE

Duties: Manage and direct an online (e-commerce) sales force to achieve an organization's online sales and profit goals

Alternate Title(s): E-commerce Sales Manager; Online Ad Sales Manager; Web Sales Manager

Salary Range: $50,000 to $110,000 or more

Employment Prospects: Fair to Good

Advancement Prospects: Fair

Prerequisites:

Education or Training—B.A. or B.S. degree usually required, or, in some cases, equivalent training and experience

Experience—Two to five years (or more) online ad sales experience and/or traditional marketing and sales experience preferred

Special Skills and Personality Traits—Ability to articulate the differential advantages of online advertising; capable of working in a fast-paced environment and handling multiple projects simultaneously; excellent negotiation, analytical, and organizational skills with diligent attention to detail; exceptional oral and written communication proficiency; flexible and entrepreneurial, but also a team member; good computer skills; strong analytical and problem-solving talents; vigorous and creative problem-solving aptitude

CAREER LADDER

```
┌─────────────────────────────┐
│   Online Sales Director;     │
│   Vice President of Sales    │
└─────────────────────────────┘

┌─────────────────────────────┐
│    Online Sales Manager      │
└─────────────────────────────┘

┌─────────────────────────────┐
│ Sales Assistant; Sales Representative │
└─────────────────────────────┘
```

Position Description

Internet advertising has become one of the most powerful ways to reach audiences, and organizations of all sizes and sorts are bombarding such online portals as AOL, MSN, and Yahoo! with bookings for banners, buttons, and pop-ups to advertise their services and products, as well as developing such on their own Web sites. It is the production, scheduling, and continuous re-evaluation and revision of these online advertising strategies that becomes the major responsibility of the Online Sales Manager.

Online Sales Managers develop, implement, and control these advertising strategies on a daily basis by utilizing the organization's Web site and those other online portals with which the organization has a contract for such advertising, all to generate revenue. Usually under the guidance of the online sales director or the vice president of sales, Online Sales Managers plan the budget and make projections on revenue return by determining pricing and promotion of online advertising opportunities. To do this, they must be knowledgeable of such online media pricing models as:

- CPM, which stands for "Cost Per 1,000 Impressions," which defines the average amount of revenue a Web site receives for every 1,000 impressions on it
- CPC, which stands for "Cost Per Click," which defines how much revenue is generated each time a user clicks an advertisement link on the Web site

- CPL, which stands for "Cost Per Lead," which defines how much revenue is generated when an organization's Web site creates a lead for an advertiser when a user clicks on the advertisement link
- CPA, which stands for "Cost Per Action," which defines how much revenue is generated when a user clicks on an advertisement on the Web site and then completes a certain action, such as filling out a form or taking a survey

In addition, managers are tasked with establishing strategic partners as well as identifying key market targets that will ultimately drive fresh revenue and play an integral part in the ongoing success of the organization's online properties.

Online Sales Managers serve as the primary point of contact within the organization for advertising inquiries, advertising campaign planning, and any requests pertaining to new and existing advertiser campaigns. They prospect new advertisers and advertising outlets, developing/maintaining their own account bases, generating new leads, and following up with prospective advertisers to finalize deals. In the process, they develop and maintain business and social relationships with current and potential clients. Much of their generated sales come through these personal networks, in addition to their "cold calling" (uninvited sales calls) of potential clients.

In most cases, Online Sales Managers lead the sales efforts for all Web sponsorship and advertising sales. In some cases, they lead the strategic and tactical sales initiatives by managing the Web site, including planning, design, development, e-commerce functionality, metrics, and measurement. In addition, they execute strategic and tactical Internet marketing efforts to include e-mail campaigns, search engine marketing programs, and online ads. They prepare strategies for up-selling (suggesting alternative higher-value products to those already selected by the customer) and cross-selling (suggesting new products to current customers based on their past purchases) to existing clients.

Online Sales Managers maintain records and prepare reports for upper management on advertising campaign results and Web metrics. They may be tasked with the negotiation of contracts and the monitoring of commissions on ad transactions. They coordinate and track ad placements to ensure client satisfaction. In addition, they may prepare ad performance and ad campaign reports for clients, maintaining good customer relations before, during, and after the particular sale. They prepare timely intelligence for top management on competitive challenges, sales obstacles and objects, and detail any customer requests for new (or different) online advertising products. They are frequently called upon to travel to participate in client functions, industry events, and meetings of professional associations.

Salaries
Earnings for Online Sales Managers are usually in the middle range of online management salaries. According to studies made by HotJobs.com (sponsored by Yahoo!), annual median salaries at the beginning of 2006 throughout the United States for Online (e-commerce) Sales Managers were $75,643. Yearly salaries ranged from a low of about $50,000 to a high of over $110,000, dependent greatly upon geography, size of the organization, and scope of responsibilities.

Employment Prospects
With the explosion of Internet activity in recent years, the Internet has become one of the most potent areas for advertising and sales of products and services, vying with the print media for revenue-making possibilities. Therefore, there is a growing demand for qualified online sales personnel, individuals with a thorough knowledge of online advertising and the direct marketing industry. Employment opportunities are good for online sales personnel who have gained the necessary experience.

Advancement Prospects
As with most sales personnel, the "bottom line" (total sales) is the most important factor in an Online Sales Manager's career. Success with one ad campaign can lead to an expansion of duties. Further triumphs can lead to a national sales management position, such as director of sales, within an organization or a career jump to a larger organization with an expanded potential of advancement into the upper reaches of sales management.

Education and Training
Online Sales Managers generally need a bachelor's degree in business or in a computer-related field with strong preparation through business-related courses. For the upper range of sales management posts, employers often prefer individuals who have both a technical degree and an M.B.A. Beginning sales personnel often continue their education at night or online to gain the necessary qualifications for higher positions in the sales management team.

Experience, Skills, and Personality Traits
Due to the demanding and competitive nature of retail sales and the relentless pace of the Internet, Online Sales Managers must have a thorough knowledge of the online advertising and direct marketing industries. They must also have an in-depth understanding of the Web sales process for business development, managing of sales results in customer acquisition and retention, content development and management, user-interface, and site usability. They need to know about targeting techniques, response rates, banner advertising, e-commerce advertising campaign metrics, spreadsheet manipulation, basic statistical analysis

and have a thorough familiarity with Web architecture. Often, they will be required to sell a broad portfolio of media and services, as well as identify new opportunities. In this process, they will need to develop and execute their job duties based on a deep understanding of clients' businesses, needs, success metrics, budgets, and timelines. In addition, they should have a strong comprehension of all online media pricing models and be able to explain them to clients.

Online Sales Managers must have good computer skills (knowledgeable, at least, in Microsoft Windows, Word, Excel, PowerPoint, and Access); excellent negotiation, analytical, and organizational abilities; heavy detail orientation; solid written/verbal communication capabilities; resourceful problem-solving abilities; and strong customer service talents. They must be able to work quickly and accurately on multiple tasks in a fast-paced environment and present complicated ideas effectively. They need to be flexible and entrepreneurial, but also be team players, able to merge their efforts and skills with those of other aggressive and highly skilled sales personnel.

Unions and Associations

Online Sales Managers may find it useful to belong to sales (such as the Direct Marketing Association [DMA]), marketing (such as the American Marketing Association [AMA]), or general management organizations or associations for networking, professional opportunities, and skills development.

Tips for Entry

1. In college, consider working toward a technical degree (computer science or network technology), but also include basic courses in marketing, retail sales, and business management.

2. Once you obtain an entry-level job in online advertising, strive to find time to work toward earning an M.B.A. degree, as your successful sales track record plus that degree can greatly aid your advancement to higher sales management positions.

3. In your technical education, become knowledgeable in Microsoft Office, Work, PowerPoint, and Excel software, and acquire some experience in such research tools as Media Metrix and Nielsen NetRatings.

PRODUCTION

EXECUTIVE PRODUCER

CAREER PROFILE

Duties: Manage the overall production process of the creation of multimedia and Internet products and services, from preparing budgets and schedules to hiring and supervision of the project execution by the creative and production teams

Alternate Title(s): Multimedia Developer; Internet Producer

Salary Range: $55,000 to $100,000 or more

Employment Prospects: Good to Excellent

Advancement Prospects: Fair

Prerequisites:

Education or Training—Bachelor's degree in business, design, media arts, mass communications, or computer science required; master's degree in new media and/or Internet production preferred as well

Experience—Five to 10 years experience in media production, either television or multimedia

Special Skills and Personality Traits—Ability to manage all facets of production process; heavy detail orientation; extremely strong organizational skills

CAREER LADDER

```
┌─────────────────────────────────┐
│   Vice President, Production;    │
│  other Senior Executive Positions│
└─────────────────────────────────┘

┌─────────────────────────────────┐
│       Executive Producer         │
└─────────────────────────────────┘

┌─────────────────────────────────┐
│     Producer; Project Manager    │
└─────────────────────────────────┘
```

Position Description

An Executive Producer for both Internet and multimedia projects is the top decision maker in the process of creating the product, whether it is a Web site, an interactive electronic game, or a CD-ROM for use with either Windows software or on a Macintosh. Typically, a company hires an Executive Producer to be the chief planner for one or more Web sites and a line of Internet products. In that capacity, Executive Producers prepare short- and long-range plans to build the line of products, or the creation of interlinked Web sites, by identifying the appropriate products for the company to make available online. They hire production and creative teams that are best suited to design and produce this particular sequence of products, and set time lines and budgets for the completion of the various steps in the process.

In smaller companies and nonprofit organizations, Executive Producers may take on direct operational responsibilities besides their managerial tasks. These responsibilities may include researching funding institutions or options and writing proposals to secure adequate financing, negotiating rights and contracts with authors and vendors who provide content (which, in turn, may include audio bytes, stock photographs, text, video footage, and other materials), and cultivating relationships with other entities, such as distributors and cross-marketing partners.

Executive Producers are responsible on a day-to-day basis for ensuring that the final product (Web site and Internet advertising of Web products and services) is of the best quality possible and has been produced/created as efficiently and cost-effectively as possible. Basically, that means that Executive Producers ensure that the assignment is done right, is finished on schedule, and remains within budget guidelines. To accomplish this, they must maintain a close watch on all details of a project while also keeping in mind, and keeping the execution of the product in line with, the broader goals of the line development as set down by the company for which they work. By working closely with the producer, Executive Producers keep apprised of the work flow of animators, computer programmers, graphic designers, sound designers, and writers so that they can apply pressure where needed in any part of this process to guarantee a seamless and successful conclusion.

Executive Producers are also the key coordinators of communication, as well as project information and product implementation, between the production and creative teams and senior management. They usually are designated as the chief spokespersons for the Web site(s) or Internet products when media inquiries are received by the company. During this production progression, they will constantly assess how all aspects are proceeding and explore how to maximize the use of all available resources.

Salaries

Top executives are among the highest paid workers in the U.S. economy. Salary levels, however, depend greatly upon the extent of managerial responsibility, length of service in the particular industry, and the type, size, and location of the company. According to the U.S. Department of Labor's *Occupational Outlook Handbook,* median annual earnings of general and operations managers (of which an Executive Producer of Web sites and Internet products is a member) in May 2004 were $77,420. The middle 50 percent earned between $52,420 and $118,310. The study notes that the median annual earnings in the computer systems design and related services for general and operations managers were $117,730 yearly. Well-qualified and successful Executive Producers should be able to earn incomes within this middle 50 percent grouping.

Employment Prospects

Beyond the obvious spheres of electronic games and entertainment, the evolution of the Internet and the World Wide Web—much like the development of the telephone and the video before them—has affected nearly every industry. Thus, the possibilities for Executive Producers to oversee the creation of imaginative Web sites and manage the development of advertising and product availability on the Internet for organizations as diverse as the federal government (in any one of its numerous agencies or departments), product manufacturers of all types, or creative organizations (such as art museums, rock band groups, or ballet companies) become nearly endless. The exponential growth of the Internet as both a communication medium and a purveyor of diverse products for a highly varied customer base will help to guarantee production positions for years to come.

Once experience is gained in the production and creation of Web sites and Internet product bases, producers can look forward to gaining the higher position (with its concomitant higher prestige and salary) of Executive Producer.

Advancement Prospects

For most Executive Producers their position is near or at the top of the organizational structure in which they have moved upward professionally. Once this level has been achieved, there are few positions higher that can be attained. Nonetheless, movement to larger companies or to a top executive post at a smaller organization remains a possibility.

Education and Training

Executive Producers may come from a wide range of educational backgrounds, but all will have bachelor's degrees in either humanities, business, or mass communications. Many may also have backgrounds in computer programming and have worked in computer graphic design or programming at one time or another in their careers. Many Executive Producers of Internet and Web-based products have worked for years within the television industry and decided to make the transition to the new media technologies of the Web. A solid background (undergraduate degree and, in many cases, a graduate degree as well) in media arts or the humanities coupled with experience as a project manager will give an advantage to any producer to move upward to the position of Executive Producer.

Experience, Skills, and Personality Traits

Any Executive Producer should have worked as a producer, project manager, or production manager of Internet services and products and learned, as a result, the detailed type of planning that is involved in getting a project completed. Executive Producers must have the ability to anticipate and overcome typical disruptions to the workflow in addition to a command of project management methods, including reasonable budgeting and realistic scheduling of the components and the people involved with them. Other skills include comprehension of how the project is going to take shape long before the production process has begun and the knack for managing various types of contributors to the project, from illustrators and animators to Web navigation experts and computer programmers. In addition, Executive Producers of Web-based projects need to be able to work under extreme pressure, as deadlines are nearly always extremely demanding. Patience, persistence, and extreme attention to detail are all vital elements of the post.

Unions and Associations

There are no unions or associations that represent Executive Producers specifically, though many of them are members of the Software Publishers Association (SPA) and/or the Software & Industry Information Association (SIIA), as well as a wide variety of regional industry councils or groups.

Tips for Entry

1. A broad-based liberal arts education is useful, but be sure to include business and computer programming courses as well.

2. Gain as much Internet project development experience as you can, including computer graphic design and participation in techniques used to advertise and promote products and services on the Internet.

3. As producer, study the business management techniques used by the Executive Producer to whom you report to learn and explore how you would manage the project yourself.

PRODUCTION ASSISTANT

CAREER PROFILE

Duties: Under supervision of the producer, monitors and maintains the daily production of a Web site

Alternate Title(s): Web Production Assistant; Web Production Coordinator

Salary Range: $30,000 to $58,000 or more

Employment Prospects: Good

Advancement Prospects: Good

Prerequisites:

Education or Training—B.A. college degree usual requirement; in some cases B.S. degree recommended

Experience—One to two years' Web production experience recommended; some computer skills and knowledge of both hardware and software; some working knowledge of Web graphics creation programs and HTML editing programs, as well as working knowledge of Web-specific coding

Special Skills and Personality Traits—A self-starter with attention to detail and well organized; able to take direction and multi-task; excellent communication (verbal and written) and interpersonal talents; good time management abilities and capable of meeting deadlines

CAREER LADDER

```
+------------------------------------+
|  Producer; Project Manager;        |
|  Web Producer                      |
+------------------------------------+

+------------------------------------+
|  Production Assistant               |
+------------------------------------+

+------------------------------------+
|  College Intern                     |
+------------------------------------+
```

Position Description

A Production Assistant's main duty is to monitor and maintain the correct daily production of an organization's Web site. Assistants work with the Web developer or Web producer to ensure that the site is operating appropriately and that all front-end programming interfaces correctly with existing site functionality. Their job responsibilities include implementing HTML modifications and corrections to current pages, editing any Active Server Pages (ASP) modifying JavaScript as directed, performing quality assurance checks, and updating relevant databases. The checks usually include cross-browser and cross-platform testing of the Web site. Production Assistants troubleshoot any problems with the Web site, access, or downtime, communicating these difficulties to the correct personnel in the information technology (IT) department, and assist with implementing network and Web site upgrades, including backend integration and redesigns.

In addition, Production Assistants assist with the flow of information for the Web site production group and help with the development and maintenance of intranet (the network within the organization) pages for various departments and/or branch offices. They frequently are part of the team overseeing production/distribution of digital audio and video products for use on the organization's Web site and any partner sites. They may be required to code and send monthly or bimonthly e-mail newsletters and assist Web producers (or content managers) with Webcast production for small to mid-sized company events, as well as staff Web services desks onsite at conferences. The latter may include demonstrating online capabilities to clients, associates, and the general public.

Production Assistants may aid with researching, securing approval for, and purchasing necessary software and hardware. They may be required to assist the IT project manager in project coordination, the scheduling of meetings, and the planning for further project development and Web production. Additionally, they may be tasked with attending ongoing training sessions (either within the organization or at a designated learning center) designed to enhance their knowledge of Web-related issues, software, and new technology.

Salaries

As this post is frequently an entry-level position, or one with minimal experience requirements (one to two years of Web production involvement), salaries for Production Assistants are relatively low in comparison to those for experienced Web technicians. According to Salary.com's Hotjobs Web site, annual earnings of Production Assistants as of January 2006 ranged from a low of $34,000 to a high of $58,600. The national median yearly salary was $50,305.

Employment Prospects

IT departments of any size organization need Production Assistants to support their technical personnel. Some such openings may require little background, with employers preferring to take qualified college graduates (with the necessary knowledge of applicable software and hardware) and train them within the organization. Other employers may require a year or two of Web production experience. In either case, the prospects for jobs are good for qualified individuals.

Advancement Prospects

With the necessary training and experience, Production Assistants can expect confidently to move upward into more responsible levels within the Web production team. They may find that some specialization aids career advancement, such as becoming expert in user interface, graphic design, or e-mail, direct mail, and online marketing technologies.

Education and Training

Nearly all organizations hiring Web Production Assistants expect candidates to have a bachelor's degree, and some may expect a bachelor of science degree. Production Assistants are expected to have exemplary computer skills and be at least somewhat knowledgeable about Macintosh and/or IBM-compatible computers, scanners, word processing programs, image editing, creation and manipulation programs, desktop publishing programs, and Web design programs.

Experience, Skills, and Personality Traits

Production Assistants have to be conversant with HTML, as well as have practical knowledge of the Internet. They should be familiar with Web graphics creation programs (such as Adobe Photoshop, Adobe Illustrator, Quark XPress, Macromedia Fireworks, and MS Paint), and an understanding of HTML editing programs (such as Macromedia Dreamweaver and BB Edit) is a bonus. A working knowledge of Web-specific coding (HTML, DHTML, and JavaScript) and a familiarity with Web hosting procedures are additional pluses.

Production Assistants need to be highly organized, pay close attention to detail, be self-starters, and be equipped to handle multiple projects while adhering to all established schedules. In addition, they must have excellent reading, verbal, and writing skills.

Unions and Associations

While there are no unions or associations that represent Production Assistants, many of them may find it useful to belong to such organizations as the Software Publishers Association (SPA), the Internet Developer Group in California, the U.S. Internet Industry Association (USIIA), or Wise-Women, an association and resource for female (and male) Web designers, developers, and programmers, for networking and possible additional training.

Tips for Entry

1. During college look for courses in the various Web programming languages listed above, but also take introductory class work in writing, layout, and graphic design, as these will be directly applicable to your future work with Web sites.
2. Search out opportunities to gain practical experience in helping with the expansion or maintenance of a Web site at your school or at a local nonprofit group.
3. Document all your achievements in Web production and design to build a résumé to aid you in your applications to organizations needing Production Assistants.

PRODUCER

Duties: Manage the day-to-day production process of material to be made available on the Internet and on one or more Web sites, which involves coordination with engineers, computer programmers, and the Web site creative team as well as the physical implementation and packaging of the product

Alternate Title(s): Production Manager

Salary Range: $45,000 to $90,000 or more

Employment Prospects: Good to Excellent

Advancement Prospects: Good

Prerequisites:

Education or Training—Bachelor's degree in media arts, mass communications, or computer science required; master's degree in new media and/or Web site production highly desirable

Experience—Two to five years' experience in the production of multimedia and Internet products

Special Skills and Personality Traits—Capacity to manage the production cycle and to oversee quality assurance of Internet products; experience with authoring multimedia and Internet software; strong electronic design skills with industry-standard tools

```
┌─────────────────────────────────────┐
│ Executive Producer; Project Manager  │
└─────────────────────────────────────┘

┌─────────────────────────────────────┐
│              Producer                │
└─────────────────────────────────────┘

┌─────────────────────────────────────┐
│   Internet Production Coordinator    │
└─────────────────────────────────────┘
```

Position Description

The Producer of Internet products is the hands-on manager of the production process from inception to completion. Producers need to be well versed in multimedia and Web site development, which encompasses programming, Internet navigation techniques, Web design and content, and quality management. In addition, Producers must be good managers of a diverse staff and be able to work with diverse professionals. The position holds direct responsibility for production scheduling and staffing and, for smaller organizations, usually is accountable for project budgets and overall scheduling. It is also common for Producers to shape the creative direction of a Web product, much as a director does on a film or television production. Above all, the Producer has to understand the specifics of the Web product and its intended market, must be able to coordinate logistics with grace and understanding, and must manage people effectively. Producers usually report to an executive producer who, for smaller productions, may be a vice president of the company whose Web site is being developed.

Excellent communication skills are essential for Producers, who have to maintain production schedules and ensure that the various contributors to the product are accomplishing their assigned tasks on time, within specs boundaries and budgets, and up to the standard set for the project. Among such participants to the production process that the Producer oversees are production coordinators (who, in larger organizations, often are assigned specific supervision of particular production groups), animators and graphic designers, sound designers, Web content writers and technicians, software engineers, net navigation experts, and computer programmers. Most of the production steps happen simultaneously, while others have to occur in a sequential mode, as they are directly dependent upon each other. It is the Producer who sees that the entire process moves along at the designated pace.

Producers have to have a working knowledge of industry-standard computer and design tools, including such programs as Macromedia Director, Visual Basic, Adobe Photoshop and Illustrator, Quark, and PageMaker, as well as applicable programming languages, such as HTML, Java, and CGI. However, with the constant introduction of new programming and design tools, as well as the refining of given ones, Producers have to stay on top of all these emerging technologies and industry directions. Their regular searching is greatly aided by visiting such information-rich Web sites as http://www.zdenet.com and http://www.outlook.com.

Salaries

According to the U.S. Department of Labor, Bureau of Labor Statistics and their *Occupational Outlook Handbook,* in May 2004, the median annual earnings of database administrators (which would include Internet Producers) employed in computer systems design and related services were $70,530, with the yearly salaries ranging from $44,490 to $81,140. According to a study by Robert Half International, a firm that provides specialized staffing services, starting salaries in 2005 for database administrators ranged per year from $67,750 to $95,500.

Employment Prospects

Employment possibilities for qualified Producers are good to excellent, as Web-based products and services have expanded exponentially over the last several years. Both large and small companies continue to make their presence known on the Internet with their products and services. On March 13, 2006, Microsoft Corporation, the world's largest computer software maker, announced a new emphasis on Web-based services that, they project, will provide steadier and faster-growing income streams for the company than the usual prepackaged software sales have done.

Thus, this still burgeoning and expanding field that is influencing virtually every area of work and play in modern society translates into an abundance of job opportunities for those individuals who are willing to gain the needed expertise and make the effort to keep up with the technological changes. According to the U.S. Bureau of Labor Statistics, computer-related occupations (including computer scientists and database administrators) are expected to be among the fastest growing occupations through 2014, and expected to grow much quicker than the average for all occupations.

Advancement Prospects

Possibilities for advancement are good. As more and more large, medium, and small companies begin producing their own Web sites and make their services and products available via those sites, the need for Producers and higher management production positions increases. As the World Wide Web and Internet services continue to expand, Producers who want to move into project management or into a post as executive producer will be able to find work, often at first as independent contractors but also on a permanent basis with companies that are developing their Internet exposure.

Education and Training

Some Producers may emerge from the ranks of television or film production. Increasingly, however, many have earned their bachelor's or master's degrees in multimedia/new media programs that, as a discipline, bring together the creation and production of animation, audio, photography, text, and video by way of the computer interface. In addition, Producers with degrees (or at least large course exposure) in business will find this background beneficial in their jobs. Some computer training is also useful, and background with computer design techniques is an additional benefit. Experience in media production may be more important to some employers than an advanced degree.

Experience, Skills, and Personality Traits

An Internet or multimedia Producer is expected to have two to five years' experience in the production of multimedia products and Internet applications, usually as a project director, a production coordinator, computer programmer, or a computer graphics designer. Producers need a broad range of skills, including the ability to communicate effectively, the aptitude to manage demanding and multifaceted projects, a leadership quality that allows them to lead a team of varied collaborators, and the savvy to work well in a fast-paced and deadline-driven environment. While Producers have to be versatile, they must also have (or gain) a knowledge of the particular industry for which they are developing Internet and Web site products/services. Another useful skill is the ability to speak more than one language, as so much business in the present world is being conducted on an international basis.

Unions and Associations

There are no unions that represent either multimedia or Internet Producers for bargaining purposes. Many Producers belong to the Software Publishers Association (SPA) as well as appropriate state and regional multimedia and Internet organizations for networking, additional training, and just to be visible participants in the industry.

Tips for Entry

1. While completing your bachelor's and/or master's degree in media arts, mass communications, or computer science, add some business courses to your schedule, as a working knowledge of business management techniques will be invaluable to you as a Producer.
2. Volunteer to work on the development or enhancement of your school's Web site, or look for computer internships with local businesses that have Web sites, to gain experience in the techniques used to advertise and promote products and services on the Internet.
3. Join local or regional multimedia and computer design organizations to keep abreast of technical developments and to network with professionals dealing with Web site and Internet concerns.

TECHNICAL
(INCLUDES PROGRAMMING)

ANIMATOR

CAREER PROFILE

Duties: Create moving sequences of computer images that portray lifelike scenes for Web sites and other multimedia products

Alternate Title(s): Animation Designer; Flash Animator; Special Effects Programmer; Web Animator

Salary Range: $35,000 to $86,000 or more

Employment Prospects: Fair to Good

Advancement Prospects: Fair

Prerequisites:

Education or Training—Bachelor of Fine Arts degree with emphasis on graphic arts and illustration; coursework in computer design software (e.g., Adobe PhotoShop and Adobe Illustrator) and techniques recommended; some small business management classes helpful

Experience—One- or two-year internship in an art studio recommended; illustration background helpful

Special Skills and Personality Traits—Ability to visualize flow of a scene and its precise details; capacity to work under deadline pressure; creativity, concentration, and dedication; excellent communication skills; good eye for form, composition, and perspective; solid figure drawing abilities; strong illustration and drafting talents

CAREER LADDER

```
┌─────────────────────────────┐
│  Animation Director; Director,│
│    Multimedia Production;     │
│       Lead Animator           │
└─────────────────────────────┘

┌─────────────────────────────┐
│         Animator              │
└─────────────────────────────┘

┌─────────────────────────────┐
│   Animation Assistant;        │
│    Production Designer        │
└─────────────────────────────┘
```

Position Description

Animators create the motion of characters or moving images (the dimension of movement) by programming or generating computer graphic images. The most obvious use of spectacular computer graphics is found in computer games, but animation and related special effects are found in all types of multimedia products (dealing with such areas as business, education, and science).

Traditional animation (as in movie cartoons) was created by the drawing of thousands of pictures (known as *cels*) that depicted the change of poses and positions that shifted slightly from frame to frame of the film. In this process, each image or frame is hand-drawn. Projecting the frames in rapid succession created the semblance of movement. Another type of classical animation—which is still occasionally used—is stop-motion animation (sometimes known as Claymation), where Animators build models or puppets and move them slightly for each frame, which is photographed or digitized. These frames are assembled to create the illusion of movement. However, traditional animation is being replaced quite rapidly by computer-generated imagery (CGI). The advantages of computer animation, such as speed, larger volume of images available to be developed simultaneously, and easier revisions, have largely supplanted traditional cel animation and stop motion animation.

Some computer-based animation still uses drawings, but they are made a part of the automated process by being scanned into the computer, then adding colors, shadings, and textures to the initial drawings. For much of today's animation, and particularly that animation used extensively in Web programming, the images are created entirely in the computer. The Animator interactively instructs the computer about the image, what movements it must make, and how characteristics of the image, such as shading and coloring, should shift as the image progresses through the playing out of the scene. Sophisticated computer software (such as Adobe Photoshop, Adobe Illustrator) can automatically modify the initial image to create the set of images that will be cycled through to produce the animated motion desired.

Other than the traditional stop-motion animation or cel animation, most Animators specialize in one of several areas. The most common type, 2-D animation, creates moving pictures using computerized animation software to create a sequence of consecutive images or frames to create the cartoon to be utilized on a Web site (or in a film or on television). In 3-D animation, the animator designs images and uses a computer to build models and to give them texture, coloration, animation, and multi-level dimension. Motion graphics Animators prepare graphics for film or television (and some of the more sophisticated Web sites) by scanning images and working with color, visual effects, graphics, and topography on a computer.

Web animation requires more skills than just being able to work with a computer program. The Animator must first create a storyboard, which is a series of sketches showing the progression of the action in a Web site scene, in an electronic game, or other program. This storyboard becomes the plan of action for the animation project. They may work with creative directors, art directors, or other Animators in this creative process. As Chris Wing, an Animator at a graphic design firm, states, "Animators like those at Disney don't come up with the ideas—storyboard artists do that. It's usually the animator's job to take that two-dimensional image and bring it into three dimensions. What we do in Web [animation] is very similar. I get a layout from an artist and we talk about how it should be animated: what should work, what buttons should trigger what effects, etc. It's then my job to make that two-dimensional presentation into a moving representation."

In addition to the actual animation itself, the Animator must create lights, shading, and color changes to enhance the effect of the story and the animation. Other special effects may also be added, such as wipes, dissolves, or "morphings," which is a technique whereby an image may be changed into something completely different (such as a butterfly into a fairy princess).

Animators may work independently as contractors of their work, or they may be part of a graphics design company supplying Web designs for clients. At all times, their labor is heavily detailed and intense in nature, and they most often are working under strict deadline pressure.

Salaries

Animators familiar with 3-D animation and the software used at the more advanced computer workstations will receive the higher salaries. Salaries are often dependent upon the number of years of experience the individual Animator may have. For Animators with one to three years' background, salaries can range from a yearly low of $35,000 to a high of $57,000 or more. For those Animators who have five or more years of experience, annual salaries can range from a low of $52,000 to a high of $86,000 or more. Entry-level income for Animators who work initially on simpler animation jobs (such as those for educational institutions) may range per year from $25,000 to $30,000.

Employment Prospects

Employment demand for skilled Animators is high. However, while employment of artists overall is expected to grow by about 10 to 20 percent through 2012, according to the U.S. Department of Labor's *Occupational Outlook Handbook,* competition for Animator positions (whether in film, television, or on the Web) is expected to remain fierce. While the post (with its distinctive skills) is highly specialized, there is a continuously growing demand for accomplished Animators as the Web and the electronic games industry both grow. Many Animators in the marketplace are flexible, working in both film/television and Web animation. It is also not uncommon for Animators to be hired as independent contractors.

Nevertheless, some Animators in the industry feel there is a tremendous future for animation on the Web. One of these is John Nack, who discusses the crossover of innovation and inspiration that the Web provides. He feels that "we're moving toward a future where different media types—animation, video, and sound—can be integrated seamlessly. Designers will be able to pick the best medium to express their ideas. If text is the best way to express some information and animation is good for the rest, then designers will be able to integrate the two inside of a Webpage. … Animation … will enable businesses to present information in a nonstatic, animated format (which is more interesting for customers to view) while continuously populating that format with updated information from a central server." Not too far in the future, "Animation will be taken for granted just like graphics or HTML text is now."

Advancement Prospects

Skilled and hardworking Animators with several years of experience may find they can progress to positions as animation directors of their design firms or supervisors of other Animators. Advancement can also come either through upgrading skills or through moving into a wider industry management position (such as becoming a multimedia producer).

Education and Training

The basic educational requirement for an Animator is an undergraduate degree in graphic arts or a bachelor of fine arts in animation or illustration. This education should also include courses in computer technology and software, with an emphasis on animation, graphics, and illustration. Talent is especially important in Animation, as the field is so highly competitive. Natural ability is an absolute requirement. Animators should keep their basic skills fresh as well by drawing and painting whenever possible. Ongoing art classes, as well as model-drawing, figure-drawing, painting, and other animation-related courses are recommended. In addition, Animators need to keep up to date with new techniques and computer software in their specialty area.

Experience, Skills, and Personality Traits

For Animators, a portfolio of illustration and graphic designs (as well as a CD with sample graphics and animation sequences) is a necessity, as most employers depend heavily on what they can see about a candidate's work. The actual creating of art and animation, such as for class projects, can be the best way to get started in developing a portfolio. Some employers will give art tests and even train promising entry-level applicants.

Animators need to have drawing, painting, and design skills, as well as knowledge of drawing and animation techniques. They need to be familiar with the different styles of animation, a knowledge of the history of art and design, and a thorough understanding of design and layout. They should appreciate how people and animals move and express their emotions (and, thus, be able to create different moods and feelings in the characters involved in their animation) and how inanimate and animate objects are perceived by people (so as to better create viable animation of such objects). A basic understanding of Web design is highly desirable.

Animators need to be creative and innovative, but also focused, disciplined, and highly motivated. They should be versatile and adaptable, able to accept criticism, and capable of working within a team environment. They should be observant, with an eye for detail, and a sense of humor will not be out of place. They should have good hand-eye coordination and be skilled in using computers.

Unions and Associations

Animators can join such umbrella industry associations as the American Institute of Graphic Arts (AIGA) and the Society of Illustrators (SI) for educational resources, conferences, access to animation festivals, and general professional support. In addition, Animators may find it advantageous to become members of general programmers' organizations, such as the Association for Computer Machinery (ACM) and its SIGGRAPH graphics special interest group, as well as other groups devoted to multimedia and game development.

Tips for Entry

1. Make sure you have become skilled in basic drawing and composition, as well as gaining technical expertise in computer graphics.
2. As you create still art or animation for class projects, set aside the best examples for inclusion in your future portfolio. Think about creating a CD of your animation projects that gain attention and approval within the classroom environment. Above all, keep your portfolio updated with your strongest work, even when you are fully employed. Many animators keep up to 20 pieces in their active portfolios.
3. When you are exploring Web sites, or playing computer games, take note of how animation and other special effects are used and how effective they are. Read computer and gaming magazines for further examples of creative uses of animation and for reviews of animation.

CONTENT SPECIALIST

CAREER PROFILE

Duties: Develop, design, and manage the interface, the pages (including the design of their content), and the tools to navigate a Web site.

Alternate Title(s): Web Content Specialist

Salary Range: $36,800 to $145,000 or more

Employment Prospects: Fair to Good

Advancement Prospects: Fair

Prerequisites:

Education or Training—Bachelor's degree required; in some cases a master's degree in business administration preferred as well

Experience—Three to five or more years of communications experience including experience with Web development technologies and e-mail and e-commerce marketing strategies; knowledge of Web content development processes; thorough understanding of standard Internet protocols; good grasp of marketing practices and how to create persuasive marketing messages as applied to Web content

Special Skills and Personality Traits—Able to work in a highly unstructured and rapidly changing environment; capable of managing numerous projects simultaneously; extremely detail-oriented; good communication skills; strong computer aptitude

CAREER LADDER

```
┌─────────────────────────────┐
│   Web Project Manager;       │
│   Web Systems Director       │
└─────────────────────────────┘

┌─────────────────────────────┐
│     Content Specialist       │
└─────────────────────────────┘

┌─────────────────────────────┐
│  Applications Programmer;    │
│  Assistant Manager           │
└─────────────────────────────┘
```

Position Description

With over 70 million Americans surfing the World Wide Web daily and a search engine such as Google processing some 3,000 searches per second, the need for businesses and other organizations to have a professional and informative Web site is absolutely essential. This necessity is underlined by the realization that one out of every two Internet users relies on search engines as a primary source of locating data on products and services. Businesses want to win customers and prospects over from the first moment of their visit to their Web site and to keep them there for as long as possible. This growing reliance on the Internet has also triggered an explosion of Internet advertising. (In mid-2005, the *San Francisco Chronicle* reported that spending on Internet advertising had increased to $12.3 billion annually.)

For a while, Web site content relied on the premise of keywords. Companies were crowding keywords into the content and code of their Web sites in the hope that search engines would assign a high rate of relevance to their Web content and, in turn, lead Internet users to their home pages. As search engines grew increasingly sophisticated, it became apparent that they were being geared to evaluate a Web site's usefulness based on the volume and relevancy of its supplied data, not the amount of keywords it contained or how colorful the site was. Likewise, the industry strategy of pay-per-click (where each Web vistor/user who clicks, or "hits," on an item, product, or service displayed on the Web site pays some fee) methodology did deliver results, but they proved to be excessively costly to set up and maintain. In short, it became clear that business Web sites, in particular, need to be relevant and provide a flow of fresh content.

More and more search engine marketing experts advocate content-based ranking strategies for business Web sites looking to optimize their content for Google, MSN, Yahoo!, and the myriad of other search engines. Unfortunately, building content that effectively targets and positions the company's products or services for the major search engines is a highly complex task, as the search engines are constantly updating and reworking their own systems and algorithms. To create a successful search engine optimization (SEO) plan requires the use of Content Specialists: content engineers and content managers.

Content engineers develop and design the interface, the front pages, and the tools to navigate the Web site. They identify application platform (e.g., infrastructure) needs of the Web site project and assess the ability of existing Internet infrastructure to support the company's application needs. They engineer the cross platform (between the consumer e-commerce and internal electronic communication needs of the company) interaction of applications and the Web infrastructure. They ensure that Webpages on the site are functional across different browser types and initiate improvements in processes and workflow by incorporating feedback into the overall Web site design. They perform unit testing at the page level, set code standards for the programs utilized, and review those codes continuously. They assess all specifications and provide time estimates on the development of specific Web features and the completion of designated Web projects. Finally, they document the Web project architecture and research emerging Web technologies with a strong focus on practical use, including lab evaluation.

Content managers assist in the management of current and projected Web site content, ensuring accuracy, appropriateness, and timeliness of the data provided, and work with content engineers in dealing with technical challenges in displaying and updating the content. They work with graphic designers to define, develop, and guarantee that the Web site adheres to its style guide and content rules that provide a consistent voice, tone, and style to the online content. They interact with marketing managers to understand the company's objectives and the development of appropriate Web solutions to meet those objectives. They may be responsible for the development and creation of appropriate new content and aid in the analysis of, and recommendations for, improvement of the overall effectiveness of the site's design and usability. In addition, they may be tasked with the development of e-mail marketing strategies to increase advertiser retention and may manage the deployment of e-mail communications and the evaluation of outbound e-mail campaigns that interface with e-mail-monitoring tools.

Junior Content Specialists assist in the development and implementation of content on the Web site(s). They may be involved in the integration of the work of writers and designers to produce a final layout for the Web site that is compatible with corporate standards. Therefore, they need to have knowledge of HTML, DHTML, and, possibly, the JavaScript programming language.

Content engineers and other content personnel may work as a part of a team for an organization or may work for a consulting firm that specializes in the creation of Web content and the design of Web sites. These companies supply a Web content management system that may go beyond just the design of the Web site to aid clients in managing and maintaining their Web sites and their e-commerce business.

Salaries

Due to their special skills and computer expertise, salaries for content engineers tend to be higher than those of other Web content personnel. According to Salary.com's salary surveys, as of April 2006, annual salaries for content engineers started from a low of $60,400 for junior personnel to a high starting income for more experienced content engineers of $95,600. The total range of salaries for content engineers ranged from the low of $60,400 to a high of $150,000.

Reflective of their lesser technical job requirements, yearly salaries for Web content managers ranged from a low of $55,000 to a high of $108,000, and those of junior Content Specialists were lower still, from a low of $36,800 to a high of $67,800.

Employment Prospects

With the explosion of advertising on the Internet, the demand for professional Web site designers, managers, programmers, and specialists is very strong. Engineers (programmers) who specialize in content management are in particular demand as the sophistication of Web technology and search engine capabilities continue to grow. At the same time, as with most business enterprises, the competition for these technical positions is fierce.

Advancement Prospects

Experienced content specialists may find advancement, accompanied by more responsibility and higher salary, by migrating to larger organizations that have more varied Web site needs. Instead, they may find joining a consulting firm specializing in Web management an even better advancement move. As their technical expertise increases, they may look to moving on to higher management positions such as Web project manager or Web systems director, with overall control of the direction and design of a company's total e-commerce ventures.

Education and Training

A bachelor's degree in computer science and/or business administration is a basic requirement. In addition, Web content engineering and management positions require a minimum of three to seven years of communication experience, including familiarity with Web site and e-mail marketing strategies, Web content development processes, and Web technologies, along with a solid understanding of user experience practices.

Experience, Skills, and Personality Traits

Content Specialists need experience with Web development technology architectures, such as NSASPI, ISAPI, Apache Mod, CGI, Servlet Engines and J2EE application servers. They must have background in deploying and debugging Web infrastructure technologies, including load balancers, firewalls, HTTP proxy/caching servers, Web browsers (such as Netscape and Internet Explorer), and disaster recovery procedures. They must understand standard Internet protocols, Web security principles (such as Internet DMZs), and Web authentication and authorization systems. They should be able to design and/or develop Web applications that require mapping user profiles, user sessions, and access to database and/or legacy systems. Obviously, they must have strong computer skills and a thorough understanding of HTML procedures.

Content engineers must be able to work in a rapidly changing environment that requires constant monitoring. They must be capable of managing numerous projects at the same time. They are extremely detail-oriented individuals, with good communication skills and excellent self-discipline. They must have exceptionally strong computer talents and be highly self-motivated. Content managers need strong computer proficiency (usually including experience with Excel, Word, Access, and PowerPoint) and a thorough understanding of the Web content development process, Web technologies, and Web user experience practices. They also must be extremely detail-oriented and understand how to leverage qualitative and quantitative information to drive marketing strategy and create persuasive marketing messages within the information displayed on Web sites.

Unions and Associations

Content engineers may find it advantageous to belong to umbrella computer science or Web development-related professional organizations such as the Association for Computing Machinery (ACM) and the Institute for Electronic and Electrical Engineers (IEEE) and their affiliated special interest groups. Content managers may also belong to a general umbrella association such as the American Marketing Association (AMA) or one of its affiliated special interest groups involved with e-commerce concerns.

Tips for Entry

1. In your college experience, be sure to include computer courses (if you are aiming at a business administration degree) or business management classes (if you are a computer science major), as both knowledge platforms will be essential in your Web site content development work.
2. Examine Web sites to analyze how they are set up to attract and hold the attention of customers and how their products and/or services are displayed. Check the relevancy of the information given on the Web site and its appropriateness to the stated purposes of the site, and decide how you might do it differently.
3. As you master your specific programming tools to be used in your content engineering work, look for acquaintances, local businesses, or nonprofit organizations that need help in developing or improving their Web sites to gain initial experience in dealing with Web site technology.

INTERNET APPLICATIONS PROGRAMMER

CAREER PROFILE

Duties: Develop computer programs that create dynamic features such as animation and forms for Web sites or that provide tools to help users optimize their Internet experience

Alternate Title(s): Internet Software Developer; Software Engineer (Internet); Web Application Programmer; Web Software Developer

Salary Range: $45,000 to $90,000 or more

Employment Prospects: Good

Advancement Prospects: Fair to Good

Prerequisites:

Education or Training—Four-year degree in computer science usually required; courses in computer network systems, computer architecture and multimedia applications; knowledge of HTML, XML, CGI, Virtual Basic, and other scripting languages and Java programming language

Experience—Two to five years' experience implementing network software or webpage support

Special Skills and Personality Traits—Capacity to handle multiple tasks simultaneously and deal with a rapidly changing technology and industry; detail-oriented; good time management and communication skills; strong programming and problem-solving abilities; thorough knowledge of Internet business, educational, and entertainment applications

CAREER LADDER

```
┌─────────────────────────────────┐
│  Director of Computer Engineering; │
│  Senior Program Analyst, Internet  │
│           Applications             │
└─────────────────────────────────┘

┌─────────────────────────────────┐
│  Internet Applications Programmer  │
└─────────────────────────────────┘

┌─────────────────────────────────┐
│        Software Engineer           │
└─────────────────────────────────┘
```

Position Description

Today, the Internet is a pervasive force in the business world as well as in the private lives of most individuals. The business sector uses the Internet (its tools and its public face, the World Wide Web) as its own internal network (known as "intranet") and its outreach arm to the public. Home PC users are relying on the Internet—among other uses—as a reference source, as a source for entertainment (rivaling television), and for shopping. The vast and ever-increasing expansion of the Internet (and development of Web sites) is guaranteeing a demand for sophisticated computer programming to support all its features.

Internet and Web Applications Programmers write the computer programs used for such Internet applications as browsing or surfing (through Web browsers), finding information on the net (through search engines), and saving the contents of a particular Internet site to the computer hard drive or to a backup source. Other generalized tasks include providing regular updates of information to users (known as "subscription" or "push" technology), letting shoppers find and safely pay for products or services online (e-commerce), and adding features to e-mail such as the ability to include video and audio clips and other presentational material. Internet application programs are also used to connect users to multiplayer (electronic) games, to provide live chat or conferencing on the net (which may also include videoconferencing employed frequently by businesses to interconnect its various offices via its intranet), and to create interactive forms and further customize Internet sites for users' special needs. With all these capacities, Internet-based businesses are constantly providing new features for users in order to compete for their attention and to persuade them to "hit" (click) on their sites.

Internet Applications Programmers are responsible for writing clean, readable, well-documented, modular, and reusable programming code for Web site features as well as the tools to support those features. They analyze software requirements to determine feasibility of design within given time and cost constraints. They sustain the current Web site functionality by modifying, enhancing, and improving existing software code and develop software system testing procedures, programming, and documentation.

Many Internet Applications Programmers work for large Web-based companies such as Microsoft and Netscape, which have created strong and effective browser packages that combine Web browsing and searching capabilities with news, e-mail, and interactive features, such as chat rooms. Other programmers work for smaller companies that create the tools that supplement browser features. However, most Internet Applications Programmers work with webmasters and webpage developers to develop the programs (or scripts) that allow individual Web sites to interact with their users. (A good example is an Internet bookstore Web site that offers books, recordings, and related material to be purchased by users. Such a site utilizes powerful search engines that can locate books and recording materials from millions of possible titles and then provides the online shopper a "shopping cart" that accumulates the user's purchases along with the ability to change or modify the purchases anytime during the shopping process. In addition, these sites provide a secure credit card form for completing orders, keep track of information such as addresses and various user preferences so that the user can return to the site without having to reenter the data, and have the means of tracking purchases and creating customer profiles.)

While some Internet Applications Programmers still use such traditional programming languages as C or C++ to provide these features, most now use scripting languages such as ASP.net, JavaScript, JSP, Perl (mod_perl), PHP, SQL, VBScript, or the older CGI scripts, as well as special plug-in Windows controls called ActiveX. They need to be able to write Structured Query Language (SQL) statements— SQL works with relational databases, which store data in tables—and be able to write Action Scripting for Flash applications to be employed on Web sites. Thus, programmers need to have experience with and deep knowledge of database design. In addition, the Applications Programmer must be fluent in Hypertext Markup Language (HTML),

the set of codes that tells Web browsers how to display text and images on the screen, and Extensible Markup Language (XML), which allows information on a webpage to be structured in such a way that it can be searched and analyzed in the same manner as a database.

In building and developing the database-oriented Web applications, Internet Applications Programmers need to comprehend how much data must be moved between Web site and user to make any given Web feature function properly. The more data that must be transferred, the slower the site will be in responding to the user's requests. The programmer must make decisions on what is acceptable for the end user in this impact on speed of access. Despite how effective the graphics, sound, and interactive dialogues may be for a Web site, if the speed of access is severely compromised, that Web site may not attract many "hits" from potential users.

The growing variety of computer programs and tools and the ever-changing needs of Web site developers will continue to provide new challenges to Internet Applications Programmers.

Salaries

In general, an Internet Applications Programmer is likely to be paid a salary similar to that of a traditional computer applications software engineer. According to the U.S. Department of Labor's Bureau of Labor Statistics, median annual earnings of full-time computer applications software engineers in May 2004 were about $74,980. The middle 50 percent earned between $59,130 and $92,130. The lowest 10 percent earned less than $46,520, and the highest 10 percent earned more than $113,830. According to Robert Half International, a firm providing specialized staffing services, starting salaries in 2005 for Web developers (including applications programmers) ranged from $51,750 to $74,520.

Employment Prospects

Despite the economic downturn and the failure of many dot-com businesses (including those involved in Internet development) that began in 2000, the continued tremendous expansion in the growth of Internet and Web-based applications is playing a major role in many businesses and organizations throughout the world. There is a steady demand for qualified Internet Applications Programmers in businesses seeking to expand and upgrade their Web-based sales and with other more traditional organizations that realize their need to establish their own Internet presence. The electronic games industry is another Internet-based business requiring qualified Web-based computer professionals. Outside the world of e-commerce, the biotech, government, health-care, and security sectors of the economy also have particularly strong needs for Internet professionals.

Advancement Prospects

Presently, there is not a clear career ladder progression for this position, other than moving on into more senior programming or computer engineering positions within a firm. Another common path is to build a career as a computer programming consultant, gradually mastering the various tools and programming languages in order to take on increasingly more ambitious contracts leading to higher salary earnings and, even, possible full-time employment with a Web-based Internet development company.

Education and Training

Many employers are more interested in what a candidate for this post can do (what computer program languages he/she knows and what experience in applications work is a part of the background of the candidate) than in what type of college work has been accomplished. However, a four-year degree in computer science, information technology, or computer engineering is a definite plus, if not a requirement. Sometimes equivalent computer experience can be a substitute for a full four-year computer science degree.

Experience, Skills, and Personality Traits

Besides a general programming experience, an Internet Applications Programmer must have specific programming language experience, particularly with such applications as hand-coded HTML and XML, SQL database applications, and background in developing consumer-facing Web applications for e-commerce and data-driven Web sites. Skill in such programming languages as ASP.net, JavaScript, JSP, Perl, PHP, Source Safe, Vignette, Visual Basic, and Websphere may be an additional requirement. Familiarity with user interface design and development and experience with cross-browser compatibility is another useful skill, as well as practical experience interfacing front-end webpages to databases and developing Web-based applications.

Besides having programming and problem-solving skills, Internet Applications Programmers need to be able to work independently and proactively but also to interface well with business development, engineering, and creative personnel in a team-oriented environment. They should be able to multi-task effectively and meet all internal deadlines. They must be able to communicate effectively both in verbal and written formats and be able to evaluate various software options and present the best solution to solve the company's business needs. Their familiarity with software design methodologies will be constantly challenged with new techniques that must be analyzed for effectiveness and potential application in their work.

Unions and Associations

Internet and Web developers may find it advantageous to belong to computer science or networking-related professional organizations such as the Association for Computing Machinery (ACM) and the Institute for Electronic and Electrical Engineers (IEEE) and their affiliated special interest groups. In addition, there is the Internet Society (ISOC), one of the oldest and most prestigious groups for individuals concerned about the future of the Net.

Tips for Entry

1. Besides looking for courses specifically geared to Internet applications programming, take classes in such specific programming languages as HTML, XML, Java, Virtual Basic, and such scripting languages as CGI, CSS, JavaScript, Perl, and SQL where available (either at your college or at an industry-based educational institution).
2. Use school projects and internship, work-study, or volunteer opportunities to gain actual programming experience.
3. As you master your specific programming tools, look for acquaintances, local businesses, or nonprofit organizations that need help in developing or improving their Web sites. For smaller Web sites, you may be able to create a job as a combined webmaster and computer applications developer.

INTERNET SERVICE PROVIDER OWNER/OPERATOR

CAREER PROFILE

Duties: Own or operate an Internet service provider business (ISP) that supplies access to the Internet and provides hosting for Web sites, Internet e-commerce, and related services

Alternate Title(s): Internet Access Provider; Network Service Provider; Online Service Provider

Salary Range: $0 to $150,000 or more

Employment Prospects: Poor

Advancement Prospects: Poor to Fair

Prerequisites:

Education or Training—College background in business management, computer science, and marketing extremely helpful; basic requirement for owners is financial, with start-up costs estimated from $30,000 to $120,000 or more

Experience—Practical experience running a small business and familiarity with Internet services and features

Special Skills and Personality Traits—Must be a disciplined self-starter and a quick learner willing to work an excessive number of hours; need to have imagination and persistence to market services against the competition

CAREER LADDER

```
┌─────────────────────────────────────┐
│  Manager (at a large ISP); Director of│
│  Online Services (at a corporation    │
│  or nonprofit agency)                 │
└─────────────────────────────────────┘

┌─────────────────────────────────────┐
│  Internet Service Provider Owner      │
│  or Operator (of small to medium ISP) │
└─────────────────────────────────────┘

┌─────────────────────────────────────┐
│  Support Staff (at an ISP);           │
│  Computer Programmer                  │
└─────────────────────────────────────┘
```

Position Description

An Internet Service Provider (ISP) is a business or organization that offers home and/or business customers an account through which they can both gain access to the Internet and receive other related services. This access usually includes space for the user's Web site. Generally, an ISP charges a monthly access fee to the consumer, though some of the large commercial services, like America Online, may charge by the hour. For this fee, the ISP provides its customers with a software package to access the Internet, validates the customer's username and password, and supplies an access phone number by which customers can log on to the Internet and browse the World Wide Web, as well as send and receive e-mail. For business customers, most ISPs provide a direct connection from the company's networks (or intranets) to the Internet. The speed at which the data from and to the Internet is transferred varies widely and is dependent upon the type of Internet connection used.

Internet connection speed is generally divided into two types: dial-up and broadband. Dial-up connections require the use of a phone line and usually have connections of 56 kilobits per second or less. Broadband connections can be either Integrated Services Digital Network (ISDN), which is a circuit switching technology, Broadband wireless access, cable modem, Digital Subscriber Line (DSL), Fiber Optics, Satellite, or Ethernet. Broadband is continuously open, unlike Dialup, and, except ISDN, varies in speed between 64 kb per second and 20 Mb per second or more. With the increasing demand among Internet users for extensive file sharing, downloading of music, and a general demand for faster page loads, higher (and faster) bandwidth connections are becoming more popular and less costly.

Internet Service Providers buy access to the Internet from an "upstream provider" (a larger ISP). Eventually, the signal is passed to one or more "backbone providers" (organizations that supply ISPs with access to the high-speed transmission lines that connect users to the Internet), which have the capability of sending signals across the country or around the world. Wholesale ISP companies, such as Net Access, buy connectivity from one or more backbone providers and resell it to their customers. They are normally much cheaper than going directly through backbone providers (which give more direct access and, therefore, slightly faster connections), and they can have more redundant connectivity as well. Most of them are "multi-homed"—that is, they rely on more than one backbone for connectivity, so they can switch from one to another when one of them goes down, ending the connection. The Internet was designed in such a way as to make these kinds of connections smooth and seamless by routing connections around damage.

The most basic challenge facing an ISP operator is, first, to attract enough paying customers, and second, to make sure service (and customer support) is reliable enough so customers will stay. Typically, service must be provided 24 hours a day, seven days a week. ISP operators need to judge what is the right amount of phone line capacity (if dial-up where the connection to the Internet is through special, expensive, high-capacity phone lines) or the amount of broadband connection (and what type) needed for their business. Buying too much capacity can tie up needed cash, but not having enough capacity can cause frustration to customers and potential loss of accounts. Then, business arrangements need to be made with one or more Internet backbone providers to pass their customer's traffic through to the net. ISP operators must set up and configure the Internet server machine and the modems that pick up customers' calls, and constantly monitor all the local connections in order to create alternate routes to the Internet if there are blockages. Finally, ISP operators set up accounts for their customers, providing them with instruction and technical support when needed, and create "added value" features for them (such as e-mail service, support for customers' webpages as a Web and domain name server, consulting, Internet e-commerce services, providing a news service—most effectively done by using a commercial news service like Avi Freedman's Newsread column found at http://avi.freedman.net—and other related resources).

As for owners of ISPs, as their business grows, they will find it best to hire technical support staff or consultants, marketing/advertising personnel, and, perhaps, a systems administrator. Thus, the owner becomes more of a manager, but always a "hands-on" type.

Salaries

As a business owner, the ISP operator's "salary" is the profits left over after all expenses of running the operation are paid and funds are set aside for emergencies and future expansion. With no guarantee for success, the economic welfare of the operation is entirely in his/her hands. If successful, owner/operators may earn up to $100,000 annually.

According to the U.S. Bureau of Labor Statistics' *Occupational Outlook Handbook,* as of May 2004, median hourly earnings of computer systems administrators (which would include ISP managers, as opposed to owners) were $28.57, which translates into weekly earnings of $1,142.80 or an annual salary of about $59,425. Successful managers may have annual salaries ranging from $70,000 to $87,000 or more.

Employment Prospects

Anyone with sufficient money can start up a business, but the prospects of success for small ISPs are definitely problematic. In the early days (say before 1996 or so) as the Internet really got started, there were endless opportunities for clever people with money and computer backgrounds to set up their own ISP businesses. With some effort, they could establish ISPs, provide reasonably reliable service, and secure sufficient profits from them. However, today, the large telephone companies, the massive cable companies, large information service providers (such as America Online), and even Microsoft represent intense competition, as they offer unlimited Internet access at reasonable rates, as well as low fees for hosting customers' webpages and providing continuous customer support.

In order to compete with these big players, small, local ISPs have to offer such "added value" services as quality technical support, help in setting up and designing Web sites, securing e-commerce facilities, providing exclusive content, and offering conferencing systems for customers, as well as other customized services oriented toward the local community.

Advancement Prospects

An ISP owner who has built a successful business can add service capacity to that business and hire a larger staff, both technical and support, all hopefully leading to larger profits. Other individuals, either owners or operators, might decide to use their gained expertise to apply for a job as a director for a larger ISP, or move on to a position as a director of online services for a corporation or a nonprofit agency.

Education and Training

While there is no specific college degree requirement for individuals seeking to set up their own ISP businesses, a good preparation for this field should include basic courses in information processing, Internet technology, and telecommunications. In addition, courses in business administration, management, marketing, and advertising are highly advisable. The federal Small Business Administration (SBA) provides information and helps with a variety of small business needs and can greatly aid in the procedures of setting up such an enterprise. In addition, a basic love of tinkering with computers is a necessary component of setting up an ISP business.

Experience, Skills, and Personality Traits

Familiarity with running a small business is directly transferable to the job of operating an ISP. Also helpful would be a job in customer support or marketing for an established Internet business. Computer expertise is an additional necessary skill.

As with most business entrepreneurs, potential ISP business owners (and operators) must be highly self-motivated, be willing to work hard, be able to learn many different skills, and have excellent communication abilities. In addition, they should be accomplished in judging people and in supervising employees and in staying abreast of changing trends in the marketplace.

Unions and Associations

Owners of small ISPs may belong to small business organizations, such as the American Small Business Association (ASBA) or the National Business Association (NBA).

Operators or managers working in either small or large ISPs might join umbrella professional organizations such as the Association for Computing Machinery (ACM), management organizations such as the American Management Association (AMA), or other emerging ISP trade organizations.

Tips for Entry

1. While in school or college, make sure your course work includes both introductory technical classes in Internet/Web technology and computer science, as well as general business courses.
2. Before embarking on your enterprise as an ISP owner, be sure you have adequate savings or alternate income to live on while the business becomes established and begins to turn a profit.
3. Before making final decisions on starting an ISP, do research on potential demand within your community and whether you will be able to compete with the multiservices of the large, nationwide online service providers.
4. In establishing your ISP business, look to find an area not already well served by existing ISP services, such as disabled or elderly people, or specific ethnic or business groups.

NETWORK CONTROL OPERATOR

CAREER PROFILE

Duties: Perform regular monitoring and maintenance for a computer network (local or wide area); install and configure new network connections; maintain logs and produce reports

Alternate Title(s): Network Support Specialist; Network Technician

Salary Range: $40,000 to $80,000 or more

Employment Prospects: Good

Advancement Prospects: Good

Prerequisites:

Education or Training—Minimum two-year college degree; four-year college degree and/or vocational certificate in communications technology, computer science, or information processing usually preferred; detailed knowledge of network physical components, services, and operating procedures

Experience—Active experience with networking systems, utilities, and related software

Special Skills and Personality Traits—Ability to work alone and under stress; advanced computer knowledge; attention to detail; excellent communication abilities, including report-writing skills; self-motivated with excellent trouble-shooting capabilities

Special Requirements—Industry certification usually required

CAREER LADDER

```
┌─────────────────────────────────────┐
│   Data Communications Manager;       │
│   Network Administrator;             │
│   Network Engineer                   │
└─────────────────────────────────────┘

┌─────────────────────────────────────┐
│   Network Control Operator           │
└─────────────────────────────────────┘

┌─────────────────────────────────────┐
│   Telecommunications Technician;     │
│   Technical Assistant                │
└─────────────────────────────────────┘
```

Position Description

Networks are an integral part of the computer infrastructure in today's world. Most business, educational, government, and health organizations maintain one or more networks that connect their computer equipment (PCs and/or workstations) used by individual personnel to the organization's information resources (databases, document archives, software, e-mail, and so forth). These computer networks can exist in a single office or department (where they are known as local area networks, or LANs, usually with connections that are wired directly), or computer terminals in many different offices in one area or throughout the country (which are linked using telephone lines over a wide area network, or WAN).

Each network has its own control programs, operating system software, and utilities. Most businesses use one of three common network operating systems: Microsoft Windows XP, Linux, or Novell Netware. Many academic and scientific institutions have networks based on some version of the UNIX operating system. The Transmission Control Protocol/Internet Protocol (TCP/IP) is a protocol (a set of rules governing the format of messages that are exchanged between computers) used on the Internet and is often employed as the basis for local organizational networks (LANs), creating an intranet.

The Network Control Operator is responsible for handling the tasks needed to ensure the daily operation of the network. They include monitoring the performance of the network (how fast data is traveling throughout the network and how long it takes programs to load at individual PCs or workstations), checking the connections between the LAN and the Internet, and running regular backups of each file or database server (the larger computer that supplies data to the PCs or workstations). In addition, they watch for unauthorized network access or other security problems, as well as inspect all communications wires and cables for any (potential) problems. Network Control Operators confer with data processing and project managers to obtain information on capabilities and limitations of the existing system, on the capacities required for projected data processing projects and workload, on the number of departments serviced by the network, on the reporting formats that are required, and on the volume of transactions within the given time requirements and cost constraints. They analyze the information to determine, recommend, and plan layout for the necessary computers and peripheral equipment, or the needed modifications to existing equipment, which will provide the capability for the proposed project and its estimated workload.

In addition, Network Control Operators make sure there is enough storage space on file and on the database servers for the projected workload and configure peripheral devices to be used in the system (such as printers to be shared by network users). They wire new PCs or workstations into the network, set up accounts for new users and ensure the correct network environment is present for each user by creating appropriate login scripts, perform system upgrades, and manage the network file system by salvaging and purging files, setting up volume and directory space limitations, tracking volume space usage, and moving directory structures. They are responsible for entering data into a computer terminal to store, retrieve, and manipulate the data for analysis of the system's capabilities and requirements. They prepare reports logging errors and other problems and update documentation of new equipment installed, of new sites, and any changes to computer configurations. They inform maintenance personnel about any equipment malfunctions.

Most Network Control Operators work in a business information processing department or in academic or government computer centers. Some, however, are hired as technical consultants and representatives for vendors who provide the network hardware, software, and support systems. In this capacity, they aid new customers in setting up their networks and make service calls in response to indications of problems.

Salaries

Beginning salaries for this position are usually in the range of $40,000 to $45,000 per year. Salaries usually increase with the size of the organization, the size and complexity of the network, and the individual operator's experience and skills. For experienced Network Control Operators, earnings can move quickly into higher five-figure salaries within a few years.

Employment Prospects

As networking is now a major component of most medium to large businesses, as well as educational, governmental, and health organizations, the demand for network support services is very strong and growing. Employment for Network Control Operators is most plentiful in large cities that have universities and major corporate headquarters but also is available everywhere there is a corporate or educational need for a network.

Advancement Prospects

Network Control Operators who have gained two to five years' experience and have a four-year college degree and an industry certification are in a good position to advance to a position of network engineer, network administrator, or a higher position in network management, with a concomitant increase in salary. Above all, Network Control Operators must keep their skills and certifications up to date, as new versions of network operating systems are constantly entering the market.

Most local networks today are set up as intranets (using the same TCP/IP protocol found on the public Internet). The use of broadband (cable or DSL) and wireless networks has become very common, and operators will often find themselves dealing with several different interconnected networks. Besides keeping up with this constantly changing technical infrastructure, it is also important to keep abreast of proper security procedures, all of which can aid in potential advancement.

Education and Training

Either a two- or four-year undergraduate degree in a computer-related major is the usual requirement set by employers as necessary to indicate good background preparation for this position. Nonetheless, the focus will be primarily on experience and demonstrated technical competence in individual networking systems, such as those from Microsoft, Novell, and/or the UNIX/Linux systems, as well as advanced computer capabilities.

Special Requirements

Many organizations may insist that applicants for the position of Network Control Operator have received an industry certification such as the Microsoft Certified Systems Engineer (MCSE), or their Microsoft Certified Professional (MCP) certification. Other certification programs include the Certified Novell Administrator (CNA), the Cisco Certified Networking Associate (CCNA), and the CompTia Network+ certification.

Experience, Skills, and Personality Traits

Network Control Operators must have a working knowledge of Local Area Networks (LANs) and their application within Wide Area Networks (WANs), as well as WANs and their interconnectivity to nodes, servers, and other end-user devices. They must be totally familiar with the Internet, the technology of its connectivity to LANs and WANs, and Web server management. Their technical knowledge and experience needs to encompass managing systems and client software, webpage integration and creation, network security measures, user accounting, and monitoring of network events and their problem resolution.

Operators must be willing to work at all hours when problems occur. They must be able to work systematically, focusing on details, but also able to recognize anything that looks out of play or wrong. They must be highly self-motivated and able to perform their duties well alone and under considerable stress. They must demonstrate their ability to read and interpret troubleshooting guides, service manuals, and other technical reference handbooks. They should have some mechanical aptitude (for opening computers, installing circuit cards, and running cable wires), problem-solving skills, clear writing abilities (for logs and reports), and excellent verbal communication talents (for answering user questions and keeping managers well informed). Their people skills need to be exemplary. As their job is crucial in keeping the network running (and thus, the operation of the organization moving smoothly), the Network Control Operator needs to be consistent, reliable, and very self-disciplined.

Unions and Associations

In a few organizations, Network Control Operators may be classified as clerical or paraprofessional employees and, as such, be members of labor unions, but it is rare. Most Network Control Operators are in the process of working their way toward network administration positions and may find it useful to join a computer umbrella organization, like the Association for Computing Machinery (ACM) and Usenix: The Advanced Computing Systems Association, or other associations specifically for network engineers and consultants.

Tips for Entry

1. During your college education, make sure you take courses that focus on the most prevalent network systems, but also become familiar with other major systems to increase your chances to be hired for a job.

2. Seek out nonprofit organizations or schools that would likely welcome volunteers to help run their networks to gain practical experience in this field. In searching for job posts, look for ones that offer you a variety of learning experiences and challenges.

3. Seriously consider taking certification courses in Microsoft, Cisco, Linux, and other network systems. Employers usually view such certifications as a guarantee of your basic competence and a measure of your self-discipline, initiative, and hard work.

PROJECT MANAGER

CAREER PROFILE

Duties: Oversee the logistics of the Web project and interface with all team members to ensure work is accomplished in a timely, appropriate manner; act as liaison between client and team staff and determine all project schedules and budgets

Alternate Title(s): Lead Programmer; Web Project Manager

Salary Range: $65,000 to $105,000 or more

Employment Prospects: Poor to Fair

Advancement Prospects: Fair

Prerequisites:

Education or Training—Bachelor's degree in computer science, electrical engineering, or marketing

Experience—Minimum of two to four years of project management experience in Web- or software-related field and application development-related experience; working knowledge of Web-based Internet technology; some experience in financial services or e-commerce desirable

Special Skills and Personality Traits—Ability to compose budgets and schedules; capable of working with multiple projects under tight deadlines; customer-service oriented; excellent verbal presentation and writing skills; organized, detail-oriented, and self-disciplined; strong administrative and management abilities

CAREER LADDER

```
┌─────────────────────────────┐
│   IT Systems Director;       │
│   Web Systems Director       │
└─────────────────────────────┘

┌─────────────────────────────┐
│      Project Manager         │
└─────────────────────────────┘

┌─────────────────────────────┐
│ Applications Programmer; Webmaster │
└─────────────────────────────┘
```

Position Description

Web site development in today's demanding Internet environment frequently does not follow any clearly defined methods or standards of practice. As a result, most Web developers or design shops draw from their own experiences in the field to create effective methods of development as applied to particular clients. As valid as these means might be for one organization, they may not translate well to the next. One suggested solution is to use media production techniques that are employed for film, TV programs, and advertising package branding: that is, dividing the work among teams involved in preproduction (in which the approach, content, site map, interface, and technological needs are determined), production (in which content is refined, graphics production started, HTML and scripts produced, and server administration and hosting is organized), publication (in which cross-platform and cross-browser compatibility is tested, review codes and links are checked, a spelling and grammar review site is set up, and the Web site is uploaded to a live server where it will reside), and, finally, post-publication (in which routine maintenance is done, upgrades are added, and the promotion of the site is undertaken with either the public or within the organization if the site is on an intranet instead of an Internet).

The Project Manager for the Web site is at the center of this operation, responsible for the project from start to finish (and often beyond). Project Managers oversee the project through all its phases, assigning tasks, running meetings, and setting the tone/course of the project. They coordinate internal and external programming, design, and any other needed resources. They act as liaisons among all the diverse specialists on the teams. Therefore, they must be well-versed in a variety of fields, as they will be interfacing with Web graphic designers and content developers, programmers, service and system administrators, and marketing professionals. In addition, the Project Manager is frequently the contact person with the client, working to gather, formulate, and communicate the system requirements for the Web site based on the client's business needs.

In their management of this intricate process, Project Managers set up timelines, schedules, and budgets for each step, as well as identify the process milestones, what the deliverables will be at each step, and the deadlines for final delivery of the Web site project. Project Managers ensure that the right resources are allocated to each step of the task and create the appropriate quality assurance plans. They are responsible for the project documentation (site diagrams, statement of work, and so forth) and provide status reports to upper management and clients. Their basic understanding of business management and the technology and design of Web site development, along with their ability to see both logistical details and long-term results, allows them to make appropriate decisions regarding a given project, build a consensus among diverse and dissenting viewpoints, and convey a professional calm and expertise to all members of the project teams.

Salaries

Project Managers for Web site development are key people in this type of enterprise. Thus, they command an annual salary ranging from about $65,000 to $100,000 or more according to industry sources. As with many information technology positions, the larger urban areas usually have the higher salaries.

Employment Prospects

Since the position of Project Manager is a prestigious one, the competition among applications programmers for the position is stiff. Programmers (and webmasters) need to accrue years of experience and be methodical about gaining their necessary qualifications.

Advancement Prospects

One type of advancement for Project Managers is to transition from the Web development team to an organization's upper levels of management. The successful Project Manager can move into becoming the overall manager in charge of Web systems development or, eventually, the organization's chief information technology manager.

Education and Training

A four-year college degree in computer science or electrical engineering with some business management courses is the usual minimum requirement. In some cases, a four-year degree in marketing with extensive computer expertise is an acceptable substitute. In other instances, a graduate degree is preferred for a job of this level of responsibility and proficiency. The educational background in computer science should emphasize methodology and computer systems management.

Experience, Skills, and Personality Traits

Individuals seeking a Project Manager post need to have two or more years of project management experience in the Web or a software-related field, and four or more years of Web or application development-related experience. They must have a strong understanding of Web-based terminology, technologies (such as HTML, ASP.NET, SQL, C#, and IIS), and script languages (such as VB Script and JavaScript). They should have a practical knowledge of Web site hosting procedures, e-mail technology, and server/networking execution. A familiarity with various graphics and printing specs, such as Adobe Illustrator, PDF, Adobe Photoshop, and Quark would be helpful. Furthermore, a working experience with full Web development and search engine optimization (SEO)/online marketing procedures constitute an additional bonus.

Project Managers must be heavily detail-oriented with excellent written and verbal communication skills. They need to be able to manage and juggle multiple projects in a fast-paced and challenging environment. They must be highly organized to handle multiple details and be able to work with and supervise a diverse set of creative individuals. Additionally, they need to be customer-oriented to deal effectively with clients. They should have experience in quality assurance (QA) procedures and in managing and allocating resources effectively. While they need to possess an understanding of the business environment and decision-making processes, they also need to be flexible and open to feedback with excellent follow-through skills.

Unions and Associations

Due to their multiple task environments, Project Managers tend to be interested both in technical organizations, such as the Association for Computing Machinery (ACM), and organizations focused on business needs and management, such as American Business Association (ABA) or the Management Information Systems (MIS).

Tips for Entry

1. While in college, take business management courses in addition to your solid computer science program. If

you are majoring in business administration, enhance your computer skills with extensive computer science course work.

2. After obtaining an entry-level job as a programmer (or programmer/analyst), work toward acquiring software engineering skills in Web and Internet system development that go well beyond low-level programming tasks.

3. Look for opportunities to assist a Project Manager in coordinating or managing Web development processes. In addition, spend time in the marketing department to gain a feel for their work priorities.

SOFTWARE TEST ENGINEER

CAREER PROFILE	CAREER LADDER

Duties: Design and write complex computer programs to test Internet and Web site development software

Alternate Title(s): Quality Assurance Engineer; Software Quality Assurance Engineer

Salary Range: $55,000 to $110,000 or more

Employment Prospects: Good

Advancement Prospects: Good

Prerequisites:

Education or Training—Bachelor of science degree in computer science, computer engineering, or electrical engineering; in some cases, a master's degree in computer science or electrical engineering may be required

Experience—Minimum of two to four years' working experience in quality assurance and testing; background as a software developer recommended; preferred testing experience should be with Web-based applications

Special Skills and Personality Traits—Exemplary organizational and analytical abilities; firm attention to detail and ability to master new concepts quickly; good interpersonal, verbal, and written communication skills; highly motivated and strong self starter; steadfast problem-solving talents and good understanding of the quality assurance process

Special Requirements—Industry certification usually required

CAREER LADDER

```
┌─────────────────────────────┐
│      Project Manager;        │
│    Web Systems Director      │
└─────────────────────────────┘

┌─────────────────────────────┐
│    Software Test Engineer    │
└─────────────────────────────┘

┌─────────────────────────────┐
│  Applications Programmer;    │
│     Software Engineer        │
└─────────────────────────────┘
```

Position Description

The term "software engineer" is commonly used for an individual who plays a major role in designing software instead of the more customary job title of programmer/analyst. This change reflects a shift in computer science toward viewing software development as an exacting discipline—similar to traditional engineering. The increasing cost and complexity of software development is leading software organizations within the industry to seek new or improved ways for enhancing the quality of the software they develop/deliver, and the testing process is the key instrument in this search.

Traditionally, software testing has been viewed by many in the software industry as unpleasant but unavoidable, a task dreaded by both software developers and management. In addition, testing has not generally been seen as a critical component of the software process. For many, software testers are software developers who could not make it as programmers. However, becoming a good Software Test Engineer requires a skill as equally complex as that of a first-rate software developer.

Software quality engineering has two basic related components: quality assurance (otherwise known as *process level quality*) and testing (otherwise known as *product-oriented quality*). As software systems quality specialist Thomas Drake has pointed out, "Process level quality establishes the techniques, procedures, and tools that help promote, encourage, facilitate, and create a software development environment in which efficient, optimized, acceptable, and as fault-free as possible software code is produced. Product level quality focuses on ensuring that the software delivered is as error-free as possible, functionally sound, and meets or exceeds the real user's needs." Thus, testing becomes the process of executing a software program or system under controlled conditions—including both normal and abnormal situations—to uncover any possible errors. Testing should intentionally attempt to make things go wrong to determine any glitches in the product.

Web sites are essentially client/server applications, with Web servers and "browser" clients. Client/server application software can be quite complex due to the diverse dependencies among clients (users of the Web site), data communications, hardware, and servers. For these reasons, testing requirements can be both extensive and lengthy. Both load/stress/performance testing (to determine client/server application limitations and capabilities) and integration and system testing are of primary importance even when time is limited for the testing process. There are many commercial tools (for automated testing) to assist with the process. Some of these are described at the Software QA and Testing Resource Center at http://www.softwareqatest.com.

Software Test Engineers work closely with software design engineers and program managers to understand Web site requirements and functionality. They establish software test requirements and performance goals, and create and implement test plans and test cases. A test plan is a document that describes the approach, focus, objectives, and scope of a software testing effort. The process of preparing a test plan helps the engineer to objectify the efforts needed to validate the acceptability of a software product. A test case is a document that describes an input, action, or event presented by the software and an expected response from its user, to establish whether a particular feature of a software application is working correctly. The process of developing test cases can help locate problems in the requirements or design of an application, since it necessitates a complete analysis of the operation of the software application.

Software Test Engineers develop quality assurance standards and define and track quality assurance metrics, such as defect densities and open defect counts. Specifically for Web site testing, engineers consider the interactions between HTML pages, TCP/IP communicants, Internet connections, firewalls (hardware and software security devices), software applications that operate in webpages (such as applets, which are software components that run in the context of another program, Javascript, and plug-in applications), and applications that run on the server side (such as CGI scripts, database interfaces, and logging applications). In addition, Software Test Engineers need to understand the expected loads on the server (e.g., number of user hits per unit time),

what kind of performance is required under such loads (such as Web server response time), who the target audience is and what kind of browsers they will be using, what level of performance is expected on the client side (e.g., how fast should webpages and their features appear), what kinds of security will be demanded, and how reliable the Web site's Internet connections must be. The end result of these and other such considerations is that the testing of Web sites can become major ongoing efforts.

During this testing process, Software Test Engineers develop the tools necessary to assist in the software development and testing and assist product development personnel with validation procedures. Their duties may also include assisting Web personnel in troubleshooting software problems that have occurred in already active Web sites. Throughout this process, Software Test Engineers generate and maintain software test reports and regularly communicate their results to the Web developers and managers through ongoing verbal exchanges, demonstrations, and formal written reports. In the course of their work, software testing professionals may also identify key business improvement opportunities and potential future projects.

Salaries

Annual salaries for intermediate-level quality assurance programmers and Software Test Engineers start at around $55,000 and may range as high as $85,000. Experienced engineers and programmers can expect to have incomes ranging from a low of $73,000 to $110,000 or more, depending upon their skills and their geographic locations (with the larger urban areas offering higher salaries). Commercial software development companies tend to pay better salaries than those organizations developing and testing in-house software for their own purposes.

Employment Prospects

According to the U.S. Department of Labor's Bureau of Labor Statistics, computer software engineers are projected to be one of the fastest-growing occupations from the present to 2014. The Bureau states that demand for computer software engineers will increase as computer networking accelerates. This, along with the expanding integration of Internet technologies (with its proliferation of Web sites) and the escalation of e-commerce businesses will result in an increasing demand for computer software engineers to develop, test, and maintain relevant applications. In addition, as expanding electronic data-processing systems in business, telecommunications, government, and other settings continue to become more sophisticated, growing numbers of systems software engineers (which include Software Test Engineers) will be required to develop, implement, protect, and update systems and resolve problems on a continuing basis.

As with other information technology jobs, employment growth for software engineers may be tempered a bit as more software development and testing is contracted out abroad.

Advancement Prospects

Software Test Engineers may look to advance to working full time as Software Engineers on the development of Web-based software applications, from the "nuts and bolts" aspect of testing to the more theoretical plane of computer software design. Some experienced Software Test Engineers with proven skills may prefer to work as independent contractors. Within a corporate environment, a typical advancement track for software engineers moves through positions as senior programmer, then lead programmer on specific projects, to becoming a project manager or a director of Web systems for the organization.

Education and Training

The basic educational requirement for Software Test Engineers is a bachelor's degree in computer science, computer engineering, or electrical engineering. Courses in mathematics and business operations are also recommended. For senior posts, it is recommended that an individual earn a master's degree in computer science, computer engineering, or electrical engineering, as many companies may require such a degree. Specialized training in specific operating systems (such as Novell, Windows XP, and Unix) may be required by employers, depending on the platform (type of computer) for which they are developing Web software.

Special Requirements

The American Society for Quality (ASQ) offers training for the main industry certification, that of Certified Software Quality Engineer (CSQE). In addition, this association, as well as the Quality Assurance Institute (QAI), has programs for other industry certifications, such as Certified Software Test Engineer (CSTE) and Certified Software Project Manager (CSPM). Technical programs are also offered by the Software Engineering Institute (SEI). Many companies now require a certification of their Software Test Engineers.

Experience, Skills, and Personality Traits

Even for intermediate-level Software Test Engineers, most companies expect one to three years' background in software testing, with a preference for test experience with Web-based software applications, Web content testing, and e-commerce applications or client/server applications. Software Test Engineers need a strong knowledge and understanding of network management environment and processing systems, online translation processing, and real-time update procedures to plan their testing. They need experience with software automated testing tools and test automation procedures, including design, development, and execution of test and verification systems. They should have experience with Web browsers and be conversant in HTML, XML, and computer programming languages such as DOS, Visual Basic (VB), and C and its derivatives (C++ and C#). Some familiarity with Linux server environments may also be useful. Above all, they must understand the entire software development process and how it can fit into the business approach and goals of the organization for which they work.

Software Test Engineers must have strong problem-solving and design skills, as well as excellent verbal and written communication capabilities. They should exhibit good time management and analytical abilities and be willing to work in an open, collaborative team environment. They must be methodical, highly motivated, and very detail-oriented. They need to meet deadlines and, learning quickly, adjust to changing priorities in a fast-paced environment.

Unions and Associations

Software Test Engineers may belong to several professional organizations, such as the American Society for Quality (ASQ), the Association for Computing Machinery (ACM), the Institute of Electrical and Electronics Engineers (IEEE), and the Society for Software Quality (SSQ).

Tips for Entry

1. As you work toward your bachelor's degree in computer science or electrical engineering, take courses in business as well to prepare you for a necessary understanding of business companies and their organizational structures.

2. If you do not have much programming experience, seek an entry-level programming job or a possible internship to build up your knowledge and your résumé.

3. Accept a position as a software developer, as previous software development experience can be helpful by providing a deeper understanding/appreciation of the software development process, and may help reduce the learning curve in automated test tool programming.

WEBMASTER

CAREER PROFILE

Duties: Create or maintain the control of all technical aspects of a Web site; provide content and programming, or supervise writers and programmers, for the site; monitor the performance and usage of the site; provide secure forms and transactions for Internet-based business on the site

Alternate Title(s): Web Site Administrator; Web System Administrator

Salary Range: $45,000 to $95,000 or more

Employment Prospects: Fair to Good

Advancement Prospects: Fair

Prerequisites:

Education or Training—Undergraduate degree with computer-related major usually required, but, in some cases, experience in Web design can be substituted for education; master's degree in business or a related field sometimes preferred

Experience—Two to five years' experience designing Webpages, developing and maintaining Web Sites; experience related to Webserver administration, multiple operating systems, relational databases, and application development considered a bonus

Special Skills and Personality Traits—Ability to work well in a team environment; excellent verbal and written communication skills; good online writing abilities; familiarity with computer graphic arts design techniques; flexible problem solver; must be self-motivated and a quick learner

Special Requirements—Relevant technical certification may be required

CAREER LADDER

```
┌─────────────────────────────┐
│   IT Systems Director;       │
│   Web Systems Director       │
└─────────────────────────────┘

┌─────────────────────────────┐
│        Webmaster            │
└─────────────────────────────┘

┌─────────────────────────────┐
│   Webpage Designer;          │
│   Applications Programmer    │
└─────────────────────────────┘
```

Position Description

First started as a network linking university researchers and government laboratories, the Internet is now a major means by which individuals and organizations around the world advertise their diverse presence, offer their services or products, and provide useful information. The World Wide Web is the center of the Internet, as it links documents (which include text, pictures, sound, and videos) together so that individuals can browse through them using easily obtainable software.

A Web site consists of a "home page," which serves as an introduction or a table of contents and index to what follows, which in turn is linked to one or more pages of text and graphics. The contents of these pages will vary greatly, depending on the site and its purpose.

Creating and maintaining a Web site is the primary task of a Webmaster. Webmasters are practitioners of Web communication. They are responsible for all aspects of an organization's (or individual's) Web presence, including Web content development, technical operation (which encompasses performance issues, such as speed of access), and business management (which may include advertising, marketing, and order fulfillment). A Webmaster is system administrator, application programmer, technical communicator, and graphic and media design specialist all rolled into one person. On smaller Web sites, the Webmaster may be the sole owner, designer, developer, programmer, and writer, performing all these functions. On larger sites, the Webmaster usually acts as a coordinator and overseer of the activities of other people working on the site, and is usually an employee of the owner of the Web site.

At the start, Webmasters analyze and develop specifications of the project, determine feasibility, cost, and time required, as well as computer capabilities and compatibility with the current system (if a revision of an already created Web site). They prepare flowcharts and diagrams to illustrate the sequence of steps the programming for the Web site must follow, and describe the logical operations involved. They provide specifications, using flowcharts and diagrams in creating a sequence of detailed instructions and logical steps for coding the specifications into language that can be processed by a computer.

The creation and maintenance of a Web site involves designing the overall structure of the site, which includes the content of the site—the topics to be covered, the kinds of information, and other features to be provided. (Content placement on the site is part of every Webmaster's responsibilities, while content creation, typically, may or may not be a part of what a Webmaster does.) Webmasters create the documents (the webpages) that contain the text, its graphics, and other features, and create the links that take readers from one page to another. These links may be highlighted text or "buttons" of graphic images, and they can go to other pages on the same Web site, or they can refer to other Web sites, similar or otherwise, that might interest readers. In addition, Webmasters write the programs ("scripts") that provide the additional features in the Web site, such as forms that readers can fill out to request more information, apply for membership, or use to order goods. Some of these features are of a generic nature and available as standard software (which can be "plugged in" to the Web site), while others require custom programming.

Webmasters then enter all their commands into the computer to run and test the programs for the site to ensure that all instructions and links are working properly. (The testing of links is a task that has to be done periodically, as outside Web sites linked to the Web site's webpage may change or even disappear.) In this process, Webmasters examine the webpages to detect any syntax or logic errors during the program testing or use diagnostic software to detect potential errors and replace, delete, or modify program codes to correct errors. They write the documentation to describe the program development, logic, coding, and correction methodologies. They write a manual describing the installation and operating procedures of the Web site, detailing how they deal with such technical issues as network congestion and security problems.

They monitor the number of individuals who visit (or "hit") the Web site, which is important for evaluating the effectiveness of the presentation and of the advertising that may appear on the site. At the same time, they respond to feedback from readers (there is usually a webpage for readers to describe their reactions or problems in an e-mail to the Webmaster or Web site administrator) by adding or revising material as appropriate.

Salaries

In some of the smaller organizations, a systems administrator or a public relations specialist may fulfill the duties of a Webmaster as a sideline to his or her other duties. However, larger organizations are more complex (as are their Web sites) and need to have a Webmaster (and, possibly, backup personnel as well). Companies that use the Web as an essential part of their business strategy (such as online e-commerce stores) require the most experienced, reliable Webmasters to satisfy their more sophisticated site needs and are more likely to pay the highest salaries. Computer software companies that use the Web to publicize their products and to provide technical support frequently hire Webmasters to manage their Web sites.

According to the *Wall Street Journal*'s Cobrand Reports, found on their Web site at http://www.careerjournal.com, the national average of annual salaries for Webmasters in May 2006 ranged from a low of $47,747 to a high of $89,353. For states with the larger urban areas, such as California and New York, the range was from a low of $52,434 to a high of $98,639.

Employment Prospects

With the rapid growth of the Internet and the development of highly varied, sophisticated Web sites (for both business and pleasure), demand remains high for technical individuals who have the variety of skills to create and manage a large Web site. While the ability to generate simple Web sites using across-the-board word-processor-like software has made it simpler for people with limited skills to create their own Web sites, there is still a demand for professional Webmasters to enhance and expand smaller Web sites to attract customers and display more effectively their information and images.

Advancement Prospects

With the enhanced status accorded them in many organizations, Webmasters may find that this increased status brings higher pay and more responsibilities, thus allowing them to "advance" without really changing jobs. Others may look for positions in larger organizations as their technical skills grow or work for companies who do most or all of their business online. Finally, some Webmasters may have the opportunity of accelerating to higher management positions in larger companies that have extended information technology requirements.

Education and Training

Smaller organizations are often less demanding of a formal education and are willing to hire as Webmasters individuals who have the requisite hands-on experience. Larger organizations, or ones requiring sophisticated and advanced design and programming skills, may require a four-year college degree with a major in computer science or information processing.

In addition to a college degree, many companies expect the applicant to have a minimum of two to three years' experience related to Web application development and Web-server administration, as well as an industry certification.

Special Requirements

Many organizations now require their Webmasters to have studied and received one of the Certified Web Professional (CWP) certificates, indicating they have attained a professional status within their field based on examination, professionalism, and experience. Programs of study for these certificates are given by various organizations, such as the International Webmasters Association (IWA).

Experience, Skills, and Personality Traits

Webmasters generally are required to have from two to five years' (or more) experience in Web site design concepts, practices, and procedures, as well as familiarity with Web servers and higher-level Web technologies. This background should include a working knowledge of Web development (including such programs as ASP, .NET or PHP), Web application servers (including IIS, Apache, iPlanet, or Tomcat), multiple operating systems (including Windows Server, and Linux), Web site network infrastructure (including firewalls, load balancing, and log analysis tools), and relational databases (such as SQL Server, Oracle, or MySQL).

Webmasters' necessary skills should include writing, basic layout, and graphics manipulation, familiarity with HTML and XML, knowledge of such languages as JavaScript, CGI,

or Visual Basic, and mastery of the various utilities employed to maintain webpages. More advanced skills might include data access languages, such as Perl (for UNIX systems), ActiveX controls (for Windows-based systems), XML, and Web authoring tools/software, such as Macromedia, Dream-Weaver/MS FrontPage, Adobe Photoshop, and Corel Photopaint (or its equivalent). In addition, they should have an understanding of Web encryption technologies, such as SSL Certificates and https. They may be required to have had at least a year of experience working in a client-server environment using such industry standard network protocols as TCP/IP or NOVELL Netware.

Webmasters need to exhibit good verbal and written communication skills, and be able to work well in a team environment. They must be highly self-disciplined, quite self-motivated, and exemplary problem-solvers, with superior attention to detail.

Unions and Associations

Webmasters must stay abreast of the many aspects of the Internet and Web design and technology through such organizations as the International Webmasters Associations (IWA) or The Internet Society (ISOC), the latter one of the oldest and most prestigious groups catering to people concerned about the future of the Net.

Tips for Entry

1. In your college studies preparing you for a career in Web technology, start with introductory courses in writing, layout, and graphic arts before turning to studying any of the Web programming languages mentioned above.
2. Look for opportunities to aid in the expansion or maintenance of a Web site on campus, or at a local nonprofit organization.
3. Search out Web sites devoted to aiding Webmasters, such as WebReference.com, a Web information site (at http://www.webreference.com); NetMechanic, a Webmaster Tips Newsletter (at http://www.netmechanic.com); or Webmaster Toolkit (at http://www.webmaster-toolkit.com) and Webmaster Tools Central.com at two different sites (http://www.creativearena.com/websitedesign/node/3 and http://www.bigwebmaster.com/193.html), both of which feature free and for-fee Webmaster tools and resources.

VIDEO GAMES

ARTWORK

ANIMATOR

CAREER PROFILE

Duties: Design and create moving sequences of computer images that portray characters, backgrounds, and props for electronic games and other multimedia projects

Alternate Title(s): Animation Designer; Computer Games Animator; Special Effects Game Programmer

Salary Range: $35,000 to $90,000 or more

Employment Prospects: Good

Advancement Prospects: Fair

Prerequisites:

Education or Training—Bachelor of fine arts (B.F.A.) degree, with emphasis on graphic arts and illustration; courses in computer design software (e.g., Adobe PhotoShop and Adobe Illustrator) and techniques required; classwork in small business management recommended

Experience—One- or two-year internship in art studio recommended; illustration background helpful; portfolio of art or animation projects, such as work done in school, usually required

Special Skills and Personality Traits—Ability to visualize flow of a scene and its precise details; capable of working under deadline pressure with concentration and dedication; creativity; first-rate communication skills; good eye for form, composition, and perspective; solid illustration and drafting talents; strong figure drawing abilities; background Animators should understand perspective; character Animators should know how to draw figures in all types of action

CAREER LADDER

```
┌─────────────────────────────────────┐
│   Animation Director; Director,       │
│   Multimedia Production;              │
│   Lead Animator                       │
└─────────────────────────────────────┘

┌─────────────────────────────────────┐
│   Animator                            │
└─────────────────────────────────────┘

┌─────────────────────────────────────┐
│   Animation Assistant;                │
│   Production Designer                 │
└─────────────────────────────────────┘
```

Position Description

Art and animation work is the most significant part of electronic game development, whether measured by the number of people the project employs, the megabytes of content produced for the game, or the size of the project's budget. It is the part of the project that brings the game to the player and makes an abstract design idea concrete and visible. Animators create the motion of life in characters or creatures in the game and give motion to images (the dimension of movement) by generating computer graphic images. The most spectacular use of computer graphics is in electronic games, but animation is to be found in all types of multimedia products on the Internet.

Some computer-based animation still uses drawings, but they are now scanned into the computer, where colors, shadings, and textures are added to the drawings. For most of the animation employed in electronic games, the images are created entirely on the computer. The animator interactively instructs the computer about the image, what movements it must make, and how such characteristics as shading and color should shift as the image progresses through the playing out of the scene. Animators receive a list of all the activities the creature or character will perform within the game, and they create a series of appropriate movements for them. Before creating any of the action of a game, Animators devise a storyboard, which is a series of detailed sketches displaying the progression of the action. The storyboard lays out the user interfaces, maps the branching flow of the action of the game, and even may specify the behavior of any of the game's computer-controlled characters or creatures. Thus, the storyboard becomes the plan of action for the animation work, much as a programmer's flowchart maps the program that he or she is writing.

Animators require a good knowledge of anatomy, especially knowing how muscles and bones interact. Skeletal animation software now allows characters to move more realistically than ever before. In addition to natural movement, a lot of character development can take place in animation. How a character (or creature) moves from one side of the scene to the other (i.e., strutting, strolling, darting, swaggering, or staggering) reveals character and reaction to the current "situation" in the game. One way to achieve very believable movement is through motion capture, instead of trying to duplicate movements, sometimes extremely complex, by the Animator's hand drawing. In a motion capture studio, sensors are placed on key spots of an actor's body. The actor performs the desired movement, and his skeletal information is captured, imported into a graphics package, and then later manipulated by the Animator. This process is expensive, but it results in the most accurate depiction of the human body in motion and is now widely used for sports games, as well as fighting and action games.

There are two basic types of animation: 3-D animation and 2-D animation. The 3-D Animator creates online what is called an *armature,* which is, in effect, the skeleton of the creature or character. The armature includes data that defines at what angles each joint may move and for what distance. The Animator then creates a 3-D model of the character's surface and attaches it to the armature, showing how all the parts move in relation to each other. Defining these details and creating and testing animation cycles for walking, running, climbing, and all the other actions that the character can take is the job of the 3-D Animator. The four leading 3-D animation tools used by the game industry are *3-Ds max* (from Discreet), *Maya* (from Alias Wavefront), *Light Wave 3-D* (from NewTek), and *Softimage 3-D* (from Softimage), with the first two being the most popular.

Two-dimensional animation is simpler in that the images created online are used for creating textures and user interface elements, such as menus, buttons, icons, and other items that appear in the game but do not require a 3-D model. They are also used as backgrounds in static screens such as mission briefings and recaps within the story line of the action game, transitions between gameplay modes, maps, inventories, and dashboard instruments. Tools used by 2-D

Animators include Adobe PhotoShop, Adobe Illustrator, and Corel's Graphics Suite, though there are also many free 2-D painting and design tools available on the Internet.

Video game art is subject to numerous technical limitations based on the graphics processing power and the memory that is available to the hardware on which the game will be played. Animators work closely with programmers to ensure that the animation they create will actually work in the game no matter what choices the user makes in playing the game. Some Animators work independently as contractors of their work, but most are employed as part of a game developer group. Game developer groups may exist as companies separate from the publishers of the game, or as wholly or partially owned subsidiaries of the publishers.

Salaries

Animators knowledgeable of 3-D animation and the software used for the more advanced computer playstations will receive the higher salaries. Income is often dependent upon the number of years of experience that the individual Animator may have. Entry-level annual salaries for Animators who work on 2-D or other simpler animation jobs may range from $25,000 to $30,000. For Animators with one to three years' background, salaries can start from a low of $35,000 to a high of about $60,000, according to industry sources. For those Animators who have five or more years of experience, salaries can range from a low of $55,000 to a high of $90,000 or more.

Employment Prospects

While this position (with its distinctive skills) is highly specialized, there is a continuously growing demand for accomplished Animators within the game industry. However, while employment of artists overall is expected to grow by about 10 to 20 percent through 2012, according to the U.S. Bureau of Labor Statistics (in its *Occupational Outlook Handbook),* competition for Animator positions in the electronic games industry is expected to remain strong. Some Animators choose to be flexible by working in film/television or Web site development, as well as electronic game work. However, animation work is both demanding and time-consuming, leading many Animators to concentrate their career efforts on just one of the fields.

Advancement Prospects

Entry-level Animators and those with one to three years' background may find they can advance to a lead Animator position either within their game development group or by moving to another company. Other skilled Animators with five or more years of experience may look for opportunities to become animation directors of their game development group or supervisors of other Animators in a design firm.

Career improvement can also occur through moving into a wider industry management position (such as multimedia producer).

Education and Training

The basic educational requirement for an Animator is an undergraduate degree in graphics arts or a Bachelor of Fine Arts in animation or illustration. Students looking to become Animators should also include courses in computer technology, as well as animation and graphics software. Talent is of paramount importance in animation, as the field is so highly competitive. Natural ability is an absolute requirement. Animators need to keep their skills fresh by drawing and painting whenever possible. Ongoing art classes, as well as model-drawing, figure-drawing, painting, and other animation-related courses are recommended. In addition, Animators need to keep up to date with changes made in their animation-based computer tools and new techniques that may be applicable to their area of specialty.

Experience, Skills, and Personality Traits

Building a portfolio of illustration and graphic designs (as well as a CD with sample graphics and animation sequences) is important, as most employers depend heavily on what they can see about a candidate's work. The actual creation of art and animation, such as for class projects, is a good way to start such a portfolio.

Animators need the basic art skills of drawing, painting, sculpting, and design, as well as expertise in animation. They have to be familiar with both kinds of animation (3-D and 2-D), have a familiarity with the history of art and design, and possess a thorough understanding of design and layout. They must comprehend how people and animals move and express their feelings (thus, allowing them to create different moods and feelings in the characters or creatures involved in their animation) and how inanimate and animate objects are perceived by individuals (so as to better create viable animation of such objects during the course of the game story). Their understanding of human and animal anatomy is an important component of their success as Animators.

Animators need to be creative and innovative, but also focused, disciplined, and highly motivated. They should be versatile but also adaptable in accepting criticism and comfortable working in a team environment. They need to be observant, with a fine eye for detail, and must have good hand-eye coordination. Their computer skills must be exemplary, along with a comprehensive understanding of the latest design and animation software.

Unions and Associations

Animators will find it beneficial to join such umbrella industry associations as the American Institute of Graphic Arts (AIGA) and the Society of Illustrators (SI) for educational resources, conferences, access to animation festivals, and general professional support. In addition, Animators should consider joining a general software/computer organization, such as the Association for Computer Machinery (ACM) and its SIGGRAPH graphics special interest group, as well as other associations devoted to multimedia and game development, such as the International Game Developers Association (IGDA).

Tips for Entry

1. Before you gain your technical expertise in computer graphics, make sure you have become skilled in the basic skills of drawing, painting, sculpting, illustration, and composition, so that you can convert an imaginary, or even real, object into an appropriate image.

2. As you create your still art or animation for classroom projects, set aside the best and most successful examples for inclusion in your future portfolio. Consider creating a CD of your animation projects that gain attention and admiration within your classroom. Most importantly, keep your portfolio updated with your strongest work, even when you are fully employed. Many Animators retain up to 20 pieces in their active portfolios.

3. When you are playing computer and electronic games, take note how the animation and other special effects are used and how effective they are. Think about how you would improve the animation of these games. Read computer and gaming magazines for further examples of creative uses of animation and for reviews of animation.

ARTIST POSITIONS

Duties: Character Artist: create various characters and creatures for electronic games; Concept Artist: devise characters and environment for electronic games by the use of storyboards; Environment Artist: create background environments of scale and proportion for electronic games, ranging from architectural elements to props and vegetation; Lighting Artist: create lighting effects for the scenes of electronic games; Special Effects Artist: devise a variety of special effects and effects sequences for electronic games; Technical Artist: provide a communications bridge between the art and technology teams in electronic game development projects and solve technology issues related to art production; Texture Artist: create and apply textures to characters and objects in electronic games; User Interface Artist: design and execute a user interface strategy that supports electronic game design goals

Alternate Title(s): Character Setup Artist; Character Texture Artist; Conceptual Artist; Level Artist; Object Artist, 3-D Environmental Artist; FX Artist; Art Technician

Salary Range: $40,000 to $75,000 or higher

Employment Prospects: Fair to Good

Advancement Prospects: Fair

Prerequisites:

Education or Training—Bachelor of Fine Arts or Graphic Arts degree with technical emphasis preferred, or bachelor's degree in computer science with art background

Experience—Broad knowledge of computing technology; familiarity with 2-D and 3-D applications and software in game development; minimum of one to three years in electronic game development; PC or console game experience helpful; portfolio of work is crucial

Special Skills and Personality Traits—Ability to work as part of a team; creative problem-solving abilities; deep passion for games as a craft; effective oral and written communication skills; excellent knowledge of human anatomy; meticulous and highly organized; responsive to schedules and deadlines and able to work under pressure; self-driven with positive attitude and outlook; strong interpersonal talents

Art Director; Lead Artist; Producer

Artist Positions (various)

Art Student; Beginning Graphic Artist

Position Description

Artists affect every aspect of game design, from the user interface to the visual presentation of the gameworld on the screen to the special effects. Creating that art has become increasingly complex as game development has evolved and expanded, as have the tools used to generate the creation of game content. Game artists need high-end computers and sophisticated software to create their images, as well as a working understanding of the limitations of the target hardware platform so that they can tailor their work to its strengths and avoid its weaknesses.

Game artists are primarily responsible for creating art assets (computer data files). Games require the creation of many types of art assets, such as character models and textures, environmental modeling and textures, prop models and textures, character and prop animation, and special effects, as well as interface and power-up details. Art production creates thousands of these files of all different kinds: still images, 3-D models, and both 2-D and 3-D animations. Entire software packages are written to manage the workflow of all these assets. These assets regularly must be modified, redone, or deleted altogether. An art team is usually tasked with creating hundreds or thousands of art assets, covering each little icon, cursor or screen element and every single power-up, projectile type, and special effect throughout the game. Furthermore, video game art is always affected by technical limitations based on the graphics processing power and memory available in the target machine on which the game will be played. Thus, the artists must work closely with game programmers to ensure the artwork (assets) they create will actually work in the game.

Art creation necessitates many steps to bring a game to life from the beginning concept to 3-D modeling, motion-capture, animation, texturing, and generating the final files (assets) that the program will actually employ in creating the game. Because no two games are quite the same, this process, known as the production pipeline, is not identical on any two projects. Both art creation and animation work obviously requires a strong visual sense and an understanding of design color and movement, as well as the imagination and skill to turn ideas and their descriptions into actual drawings and models. Therefore, game artists must first be able to draw, before learning how to use the art software tools that make their work that much easier. As Michelle Sullivan, production artist at Turbine Entertainment, has pointed out, "A key thing to know about this job is … it is important to be an artist who just happens to be using the medium of computers."

As with computer programming, there are numerous types of artwork jobs that require their own skills. Most artwork in game development today is more complex than when the industry, in its infancy, had just one or two artists creating all the necessary assets. There are many separate functions within an art team, and most artists specialize in one field or another but, out of necessity, usually are versatile enough to handle more than one function within the team. As established by the lead artist (or art director), each artist is given the chance to contribute to the vision that becomes the final game.

Character Artists build and texture a wide range of creatures and characters. They develop a general character framework, which will include workflow definitions and user interface suggestions for programmers. They develop skeletal, facial, and musculature systems and are responsible for motion and deformation (the alteration of shape) systems for the designed creatures and characters. They usually participate in preproduction planning to determine and address technical design requirements and issues. Obviously, they must have an excellent working knowledge of human and animal anatomy.

Concept Artists do the initial sketching and visualizations of the characters, creatures, and world of the planned game. They create these characters and environments first on paper (or on a computer file) as rough concepts, and then by the use of storyboards. Similar to the picture panels in a comic strip, storyboards are a series of drawings used to plan the progression of action or events in the story line of the game, and to depict the characters and creatures within their environment. These storyboards are used to lay out user interfaces, map the branching flow of a game, and even specify the behavior of a computer-controlled character. They are usually computer-generated, using a design programming application such as Adobe Photoshop. Color is introduced so that the Texture Artist can create the correct textures for the game's "world" and its characters/creatures. Thus, the Concept Artist is responsible for the game's basic "look." Once the concept artwork is completed, it is passed on to the 3-D model builder (or to an animator, if the character/creature is to be animated).

In some cases, concept artwork will be taken a further step beyond a storyboard and will be generated into a high quality cinematic movie sequence. Cutscene artists are responsible for this process, either through prerendered full-screen animation (frequently outsourced to an animation company), or with in-game scripted scenes prepared by using the game's engine processes. Linear cutscenes (non-interactive exposition in the game) require virtual camera movement, lighting, character and object animation, special effects, backgrounds, and props. In turn, these cutscenes may be produced by the art game team during the cycle as a part of the overall development of the game rather than by a specific cutscene artist.

Environment Artists are skilled in level construction and building of realistic models of architecture, terrain, vegetation, and props, accurate in scale and proportions, for high quality "real world" content (background) of the action within the game. They model, texture, and light these 3-D environments and manage the technical aspects of these environments, including high-resolution source geometry, shade creation, damage states, and collision. They must understand the elements of real-world ecosystems and natural phenomena enough to translate them with fidelity into an original in-game world. Their understanding of color theory will allow them to create balanced and appealing color palettes. Along with their comprehension of the aesthetics of environment and of function versus form relationships, they need to appreciate what makes a game level fun and intriguing to its players. A solid grasp of illustration, modeling, texturing, animation, and concept drawing must be joined with a working knowledge of related software tools, such as Maya and Adobe Photoshop.

Lighting Artists add the final touch to the designed environments of a game by using vertex coloring to light up the environment, making it vibrant and effervescent. They lay out lights and various lighting effects throughout the game to enhance the overall atmosphere of the locations and provide different lighting "layers" which will then be applied in the game for special effects.

Special Effects Artists (commonly known as FX Artists) work with the art and design teams to create special effects that are harmonious with the art direction, game design, and the story line of the game. They create, texture, animate, and polish a wide variety of in-game special effects and effects sequences, ranging from environment and character to weapon and combat effects. Special Effects Artists create these special effects using a combination of off-the-shelf products and proprietary tools.

Technical Artists (otherwise known as art technicians) provide a communications bridge between the art and technology teams. They aid in the interface between the artists, the programmers, and management when it comes to software and hardware issues. They usually have the skills to generate tools and workflow enhancements that would otherwise require the aid of a full programmer. They are problem solvers, helping art teams overcome technological obstacles and software quirks. They use scripting languages to create productivity and error reduction tools and provide character tools and animation controls. They educate and train art staff in tools and processes, and they check assets for technical integrity before they are integrated into the game. Often, they are the art team's software and hardware buyer, serving as liaisons with graphics software companies to help corporate management decide which software packages to buy for their game. For all these duties, they need a broad knowledge of computing technology and console hardware, as well as extensive knowledge about the art packages used by the game developer and any content tools or plug-ins employed by the game engine.

Texture Artists design the visible surfaces that cover the architecture, environments, creatures, and objects in a 3-D electronic game. From the marble wall to the faces of characters, from the reptilian skin of a creature to the poisonous leafy fronds of local fauna, the believability of the electronic game is largely in their hands. In this digital painting, their primary tools are Adobe Photoshop and one or more 3-D programs, and they work closely with Environment Artists. There are several techniques that can be used to create textures, and, while they need to know all of them, Texture Artists must choose the one that is most appropriate for the game project at hand. Some of the more common methods are photo manipulation, hand-painting, flattening detailed models, algorithmic textures, and bump mapping. The latter is a technique for making the surface of an object appear bumpy rather than smooth by adding additional polygons to the object. A polygon is a region in 3-D space described by three or four points called vertices. The points make up a triangle or quadrilateral. Three-dimensional game models are built up out of hundreds or thousands of polygons to create the surface seen on the screen. The reduction of necessary polygons is an ongoing concern for all artists and designers in order to keep within the parameters and memory limitations of electronic games. Texture Artists always have to find innovative ways to stretch limited texture memory, while not neglecting to fill in details that may be missing in the original concept art.

User Interface Artists work closely with the game designer and the lead artist (or art director) to design and execute a user interface vision/strategy that supports the game design goals as well as enhancing the player immersion experience. They work within the established technical specifications and process to analyze and design the layout and architecture of the interface to guarantee an intuitive and user-friendly experience. They design and implement such user interface components as front-end menus and screens, the in-game heads up display (HUD) elements, and any mini-games that may occur. Their primary duty is to ensure consistency with overall art style while still achieving the most efficient and user-friendly user interface for the game.

Salaries

In a 2004 survey of salaries in the video game industry done by DeVry University, it was found that video game artists with three years' or less experience made an average of $42,512 a year. Video game artists with three to six years of experience averaged $55,594, and a video game artist with six or more years of experience had an average annual income of $64,870. Salaries for beginning artists may be as low as $30,000, but salaries for experienced game artists may reach $80,000 or more a year, according to industry sources.

Employment Prospects

While game developers always need good artists, there are frequently more people interested in, and ready for, art positions than there are positions available. It is a very competitive field. Game developers are not looking for just artists; they are looking for individuals with art skills that they can utilize to create game assets that help to sell games. The most essential requirement for winning a job in the games business is an incredible portfolio. Vision and raw talent count for a lot, even if the game developer must shoulder the burden of training artists in particular software packages. However, even with a great portfolio and experience with 2-D and 3-D software, an artist usually is hired as an art technician or a low-level artist in order to learn the basics and how to navigate the commercial world of the game industry, as opposed to the world of their own art.

Advancement Prospects

Given the constant need for talented, well-rounded, and fast-working artists, newly hired artists can expect to move up from the more static tasks to a position as a specialized artist, animator, or modeler. Eventually, they may get the opportunity of climbing further up the management ladder to the higher posts of more authority and responsibility, such as lead artists or art director, or even further to becoming a producer.

Education and Training

Most Artist Positions require a minimum of a bachelor of fine arts (B.F.A.) degree, or one of graphic arts (B.G.A.). An alternative is a Bachelor of Computer Science degree with an emphasis on the graphic or illustrative arts. In some cases, an associate degree in fine arts, or several years' equivalent industry experience, along with an extensive portfolio of work, can be a substitute for a bachelor's degree.

Game artists should be reasonably comfortable with mathematical concepts. Although the nature of their work is primarily creative and aesthetic, they often have to adjust their creations to account for the technical limitations imposed by the hardware. When they are advised by programmers that they have only so many polygons or so much memory available for their creations, it will be up to them to decide how to allocate them to different parts of the artwork most effectively.

Experience, Skills, and Personality Traits

Most artist positions other than that of Technical Artist (the lowest member of the artistic totem pole in game design) require three to five years' professional experience in game development. This background must include a thorough understanding of 3-D graphics and 3-D programs, such as Maya or Studio Max, as well as the more common 2-D software. They must have a superior eye for light, shade, color, and detail in creating their textures. In addition, they need an exceptional understanding of anatomy, form, shape, structure, and silhouette in creating their characters/creatures and backgrounds. Knowledge of animation principles and kinematics would be helpful. They should have good traditional art skills and a basic familiarity with design elements, drawing, and painting.

Besides utilizing 3-D tools (such as Maya, Studio Max, LightWave 3-D, and Softimage3-D) and 2-D tools (such as Adobe Photoshop, Adobe Illustrator, and Corel Graphics Suite), artists use other hardware in their day-to-day jobs. Such equipment includes scanners (letting artists digitize graphic scrap from printed sources and scan pencil/marker drawings from computerized reproductions), drawing tablets (which allow artists to draw with a pressure-sensitive pen instead of a mouse, allowing them to really "paint" their objects), and digital cameras (both still and video), which provide artists with the means of storing images they may use, or even creating photo-realistic textures for their 3-D objects.

Game artists need to be creative self-starters and heavily detail-oriented. They must be meticulous and organized in their approach to their tasks, files, and storage of their material. They should have excellent communication skills, both verbal and written, and good interpersonal abilities as they have to work as part of a team. They should be objective in the critiquing of their work and the work of other members of the team and be willing to observe, absorb, and modify their own work based on many avenues of feedback. They must have excellent problem-solving skills and, above all, a genuine enthusiasm for and interest in video games.

Unions and Associations

Most game artists may find it beneficial to belong to the major association for game developers, the International Game Developers Association (IGDA), as well as SIGGRAPH, which is the graphics Special Interest Group of the Association for Computing Machinery (ACM). They may also belong to other industry groups that cater to their own specialties.

Tips for Entry

1. Start with a solid foundation of a bachelor of arts (B.A.) or bachelor of fine arts (B.F.A.) degree in art and design. Draw plenty of humans, vehicles, and animals to establish your traditional art skills.

2. Examine your favorite electronic games to see what kind of art requirements those products demand, as you will be asked, when hired as a game artist, to provide many kinds of in-game art assets, and you need to be versatile.

3. After you establish your traditional skills of drawing, painting, sculpting, and animation, then move on to the technical tools used by game artists. Many of them offer online instruction or free tutorial versions that will let you become familiar with their features and user interface.

LEAD ARTIST

CAREER PROFILE

Duties: Devise an electronic game's visual style and direct the artist team in the production of all visual material throughout the game's development

Alternate Title(s): Art Director; Creative Manager

Salary Range: $50,000 to $80,000 or more

Employment Prospects: Fair to Good

Advancement Prospects: Fair

Prerequisites:

Education or Training—Bachelor's degree in fine arts, graphic arts, or a related field generally preferred; an associate degree may be acceptable; in some cases, an art certificate from an art institute may be sufficient in lieu of an associate's or bachelor's degree

Experience—Minimum of four to seven years' electronic games experience; extensive experience with mainstream 2-D texture maps and 3-D models and environments and their industry art software packages (Adobe PhotoShop, Adobe Illustrator, 3-D Studio Max, and Maya); some project management background

Special Skills and Personality Traits—Ability to work within a team environment; effective project management capabilities, including ability to create and maintain schedules and manage the art team to deliver on those schedules; excellent technical skills; in-depth understanding of color theory, lighting, and composition; strong communication, interpersonal, and organizational abilities; superior art design and illustration skills

CAREER LADDER

```
┌─────────────────────────────────────┐
│         Producer; Product            │
│     Development Director             │
└─────────────────────────────────────┘

┌─────────────────────────────────────┐
│           Lead Artist                │
└─────────────────────────────────────┘

┌─────────────────────────────────────┐
│        Animator; Artist;             │
│   Computer Graphics Designer         │
└─────────────────────────────────────┘
```

Position Description

The Lead Artist is responsible for the overall visual look of an electronic game project and is sometimes known as the art director. At a larger company producing different products, the duties of Lead Artists are frequently shared with art directors, with the latter concentrating upon the management aspects of the product line.

Lead Artists coordinate and supervise the efforts of a variety of artists to achieve the "look" of the project. The types of personnel they supervise include concept artists, character artists, environment artists, animators, cinematic artists, FX artists, and designers, and they ensure their efforts all fit cohesively into a visually compelling electronic game. In some cases, they may be delegated to hire the talent needed for the project. They oversee the work of the art team on a daily basis, communicating the art direction for the project and delivering constructive feedback to the group's progress. They supervise regular team meetings and art reviews, resolving any timeline and artistic discrepancies.

Lead Artists work with the project producer to make certain that the artistic goals for the project are manageable within the overall project budget and schedule. They collaborate with the designer and programmers, analyzing the design needs and establishing the production path, then determining the scope of the art tasks, how many people will be needed, and what kind of artists are required. Then Lead Artists assemble the art and animation team, help to define and specify which pieces of art and animation need to be produced by whom and when, and make decisions on how to guarantee that all tasks meet the established timelines. Additionally, Lead Artists set and maintain the project's art quality and standards, help in determining the best tools and techniques to deploy, and are usually tasked with overseeing any art production that is sourced to an outside art and design vendor.

When interfacing with the designer, one of the goals of the Lead Artist is to develop a consistent style that extends throughout all elements of the game, from the initial splash screen to the characters and environments, and even to the menu interfaces with the eventual players of the game. The look of the game is then codified in a style guide (usually called *the bible*), which is the visual resource to which all artists will refer. This guide will cover the project's overall art style, present both inspirational and technical conceptual art, and will discuss issues of color usage, camera use, lighting, the look of the user interface, and a projected asset list covering the major environments, characters, objects, opponents, and so forth, based on the macro design document for the project. An ongoing task during production is updating and maintaining this list. Most big projects have a dozen or more people working on thousands of assets, so management and revision control is necessary. Keeping this list up to date and the art assets integrated with the programming code all along the way helps to avoid all types of production problems.

The styling for each project is often communicated through concept art, and Lead Artists supervise, if not actually undertake themselves, the production of illustrative material that indicates the visual atmosphere and graphical design for the game. In addition, during the preproduction phase of the project, Lead Artists research and test out different modeling, texturing, animation, rendering, and lighting techniques and tools appropriate to the game technology, with input from the lead programmer. During the production process, Lead Artists work closely with the programming team to make sure that all art and animation assets produced by the art team can be easily imported into the programmers' game engine.

It is this combination of research, design, creative development, and management that makes the position of Lead Artist so unique in game development.

Salaries

The position of Lead Artist is usually the highest-paid position in the art department, reflecting the skills and experience required. In a 2004 salary survey of the video game industry done by DeVry University, researchers found that Lead Artists with three years' or less experience make an average annual income of $62,411. Those with three to six years of experience average $64,036 annually, and Lead Artists with six or more years of experience average $78,700, with a highest salary reported in the study of $220,000 per year.

Employment Prospects

As the position of Lead Artist is not an entry-level one, competition for this sought-after job is strong. Candidates need to have the requisite years of experience as artists or animators and be able to display project management skills to be considered for promotion to this post. Lead Artists must have the ability to create and texture high quality 2-D and 3-D models and be able to document production processes in order to manage the overall design and production of the artistic side of game development.

Advancement Prospects

Since Lead Artists are high on the career ladder of the game development team, advancement prospects are limited. They may be able to elevate further into management as producers or product development managers within their companies or move on to larger game development organizations that provide more responsibilities and higher salaries.

Education and Training

A bachelor's degree in fine arts or graphic arts is a frequent requirement for most artist positions in the games industry. However, for smaller companies, an associate degree in art, or even an art certification, may be all that is required. To reach the position of Lead Artist, hands-on experience is vastly more important than an academic degree of whatever nature.

Experience, Skills, and Personality Traits

Lead Artists are required to have at least three, and usually between five and 10, years of game development industry experience, either as artists or animators. They need to demonstrate strong traditional art design and illustration skills coupled with a strong command of the use of lighting, color, perspective, scale, and composition. In addition, they need to demonstrate a strong technical aptitude related to 2-D hand-rendered textures and art, as well as 3-D modeling tools (such as Studio Max or Maya) and game engine technologies.

Lead Artists must have leadership and management capabilities and be equipped to create a stimulating team environment that encourages the ideas of all artists on the project. They need to communicate their concepts clearly and effectively both orally and in writing. They must be skilled decision makers and problem solvers, with excellent organizational and conflict resolution abilities. They need both tact and diplomacy and must be able to share their techniques while mentoring the team's less-experienced artists. They must have a solid understanding of game creation limitations and dependencies and be able to judge when it is necessary to sacrifice quality or quantity to adhere to budgets, schedules, and milestone delivery dates. Above all, their passion for games must be paramount, and they should have a solid understanding of what ingredients make a game visually appealing and fun to play.

Unions and Associations

Lead Artists may find it beneficial to belong to the major association for game developers, the International Game Developers Association (IGDA), as well as SIGGRAPH, which is the graphics Special Interest Group of the Association for Computing Machinery (ACM).

Tips for Entry

1. While completing your art education, take at least one course in business management, as you will need a knowledge of management techniques in supervising your art team when you become a Lead Artist.

2. Before you acquire your technical expertise in 2-D and 3-D modeling and animation, which you will need to obtain artist positions in the game development industry, make sure you have become skilled in the traditional abilities of drawing, painting, sculpting, illustration, and composition.

3. As you will need considerable games industry experience as a Lead Artist, be willing to develop your own distinctive and original style in a variety of artist jobs in game development before progressing into this team leadership senior role.

MODELER POSITIONS

CAREER PROFILE

Duties: Background Modeler: Build the worlds of an electronic game through which a game player moves; Character Modeler: Design and create characters, creatures, and objects of an electronic game using 3-D imaging software packages; Level Modeler: Lay out the levels of the game that have been designed by the designers

Alternate Title(s): Environmental Artist; Environmental Modeler; Object Artist; 3-D Model Builder; Character Artist; Level Builder

Salary Range: $40,000 to $70,000 or more

Employment Prospects: Fair to Good

Advancement Prospects: Fair

Prerequisites:

Education or Training—Bachelor of fine arts (B.F.A.) or graphic arts degree with technical emphasis recommended, or bachelor of computer science degree with extensive art background; some training in industrial or mechanical design, as well as architecture, may be helpful

Experience—Broad knowledge of computing technology; experience with creating 3-D models and familiarity with 2-D texture maps from 2-D concept art; minimum of one to three years in electronic game development; PC or console game experience helpful; portfolio of work is crucial

Special Skills and Personality Traits—Ability to work as part of a team; creative problem-solving abilities; deep passion for games as a craft; excellent oral and written communication skills; meticulous and highly organized; responsive to schedules and deadlines while working under pressure; self-driven with positive attitude and outlook; strong interpersonal capabilities; thorough knowledge of human and animal anatomy

CAREER LADDER

Art Director; Lead Artist; Producer

Modeler Positions

Intern Artist; Art Student

Position Description

No area of game development is evolving more rapidly than artwork. Artists must constantly keep up with their craft and be ready to adapt or be left behind. Not only do they need high-end computers and sophisticated software to create their images, but also they must have a working understanding of the limitations of the target hardware platform of the end user-player so they can adjust their work accordingly. Their contribution to game design is there on the screen for all to see. Ninety percent of the feedback in a game is visual, and if something proves impossible to draw, then it will be dropped from the scenario of the game. Most artists have a specialty, and, in some cases, two. One of the important specialties among artists is that of modeling.

Modelers sculpt the objects, characters, buildings, and everything else that will appear in the 3-D electronic game. These modeler assets comprise just about everything the player will see in the game, apart from such user interface elements as menus.

Character Modelers are frequently both artists and modelers. They design and create people, creatures, and objects, using sophisticated 3-D software imaging packages, such as 3-D Studio Max and Maya. (Many Character Modelers confine themselves to drawing characters and creatures only, leaving the objects to be done by Background Modelers.) These creatures, characters, and objects can be either low- or high-resolution models, depending upon the platform and the design of the game.

Working from the concept art as established by concept artists and programmers (and approved by the game developer), Character Modelers make a digital 3-D wire mesh design of the character, creature, or object. They then usually apply textures to that mesh (though sometimes this "skinning" is a separate subspecialty handled by another artist). Animation may be added at this point or not, but Character Modelers still need to be familiar with the entire animation process in order to generate a character that will move naturally after the skeletal bones are added. They must have a thorough understanding of animal and human anatomy (as well as the appropriate shape of objects) in order to make fantastic characters/creatures/objects believable. In this process, Character Modelers start entirely from scratch in developing their models. Another method they may use is the 3-D scanner. In this process they create a real-world 3-D model in clay (an actual physical model sculpted by the Modeler), and then scan it into the computer. At this point the character/creature/object can be "cleaned up" by computer programming and then textured, either by the Modeler or by a texture artist.

Background Modelers build the worlds the player of the game moves through. They usually start with basic geometric shapes (called "primitives"), and then combine and deform them to create the rooms and objects that make up the game's environment. They create real life urban situations and natural outdoor environments to scale, often from photographic reference material. This photographic material can be found on Web sites or such printed materials as magazines like *National Geographic* or architectural books. Another source that Background Modelers rely on is the digital camera. As Andrew Holdun, an experienced artist/modeler for game developers, notes, "You never know when you'll see a grain silo or a rust-covered industrial tank that will just excite your imagination. One should also always have a sketch book and pen handy … so you can draw what you see and play with variations on a theme." After the mesh of the environment is completed, Background Modelers add flat shading, then textures, and finally lights so that this newly created world comes alive.

Background Modelers may also create physical objects, such as vehicles, furniture, and weapons. Their task of building models should become quicker over time as they generate a solid library of basic pieces that can be used on different projects. They also need to know when to end their work on the models, as the amount of detail appropriate for a game and visible in the software may have a particular threshold. They need to develop a sense of what is possible and stop themselves before wasting time on unnoticeable details. Many Background Modelers have an architecture background. In addition, many of the best object Modelers have some training in industrial or mechanical design, and therefore understand machinery, balance, gearing, materials science, and other elements of physical engineering. In some cases, both Background Modelers and Character Modelers may be animators as well.

The last category of Modelers is the Level Modeler. Depending on the type of software packages used to create the game, there may be a need for an artist skilled in one of the common 3-D packages, such as 3-DSMax, to lay out the levels of the game that have been structured by the designers. This position usually has less responsibility than either the 3-D modeler or the game designer, but combines aspects of both jobs. On large art teams, Level Modelers work closely with the level designer to place structures, objects, and characters/creatures into the actual game levels. They handle such technical details as fixing seams if things do not join up properly, set triggers for doors and characters, and test to ensure the level performs the way it is intended to do. They need strong technical knowledge and command of 3-D modeling and texturing tools as well as current game engine technologies. The job is a great introduction to (and a way to become part of) the design or art teams. However, many companies use proprietary world-building tools rather than high-end 3-D packages to create the game's basic architecture and levels, so this post is not as widespread as most other art and modeling roles.

Salaries

A 2004 survey of salaries within the video game industry done by DeVry University noted that video game artists and modelers with three years' or less experience made an average of $42,512 a year. Artists with three to six years of experience averaged incomes of $55,594, while an artist with six or more years of experience had average earnings of $64,870. Salaries for beginning artists may be as low as $30,000, but income for experienced game artists and modelers may reach $80,000 or more a year, according to industry sources.

Employment Prospects

While game developers always need good artists and modelers, there are frequently more people interested in, and ready for, such jobs in the game industry than there are positions available. It is a very competitive field. Game developers are not searching for just artists; they are looking for artistically talented individuals upon whom they can rely to create game assets that help sell games. The most essential requirement for getting a job in the electronic games business is an incredible portfolio. Vision and raw talent count for a lot, even if the game developer must shoulder the burden of training artists in particular software packages. In the case of Modelers, however, a strong technical background in 3-D modeling and texturing is also important.

Advancement Prospects

Modelers may take on more responsibilities as animators or texture artists in addition to modeling activities. Eventually, they may find the opportunity of climbing further up the management ladder to higher positions of more authority and responsibility, such as that of lead artist or art director, or even further, to that of a producer.

Education and Training

A Modeler Position usually requires a minimum of a Bachelor of Fine Arts degree, or one of graphic arts. An alternative is a Bachelor of Computer Science degree with an emphasis on the graphic or illustrative arts. In some cases, an associate degree in fine arts or several years' equivalent industry experience, along with an extensive portfolio of work, can be a substitute for a bachelor's degree. For Background Modelers, some professional exposure in architecture, even to the extent of a bachelor of art (B.A.) degree, would be extremely helpful. In addition, some training in industrial or mechanical design is recommended, in order to understand machinery, balance, gearing, and other elements of physical engineering.

Experience, Skills, and Personality Traits

Candidates for Modeler Positions should have two to four years' professional experience in game development, preferably in 3-D modeling. This background must include a thorough understanding of 3-D graphics and 3-D programs, such as Maya or Studio Max, as well as the more common 2-D programs, such as Adobe Photoshop. They should be highly skilled in the traditional art forms: fine arts, drawing and painting, lighting, and color. They must have a superior eye for light, shade, color, and detail in their creations as well as in their texturing activities. In addition, they should exhibit an exceptional understanding of anatomy, form, shape, structure, and silhouette in creating their characters/creatures/objects and backgrounds. Knowledge of animation principles and kinematics would be helpful. They should have good traditional art skills and a basic familiarity with design elements, drawing, and painting.

Game Modelers need to be creative self-starters and heavily detail-oriented. They must be meticulous and organized in their approach to their tasks, files, and storage of their material. They should have excellent communication skills, both verbal and written, and good interpersonal abilities. They should be receptive to art direction and to performing easily within a team setting. They should be willing to observe, absorb, and modify their own work based on many avenues of feedback. They must have excellent problem-solving capacities, and, above all, a genuine excitement for gaming.

Unions and Associations

Most Modelers may find it beneficial to belong to the major association for game developers, the International Game Developers Association (IGDA), as well as SIGGRAPH, which is the graphics Special Interest Group of the Association for Computing Machinery (ACM). They may also belong to other industry groups that cater to their own specialty.

Tips for Entry

1. Develop a strong portfolio of your work, showing only the absolute best and keeping the presentation simple and to the point.
2. Draw all the time. In addition, continually research art, architecture, and sculpture. Keep a folio of your photographs of the outside world and objects for future use in projects.
3. From time to time, step away from the computer and experience the world, so that what you do in 3-D is expressive of real environments rather than rehashing a computer game's look.

AUDIO

COMPOSER

CAREER PROFILE

Duties: Create the music to accompany an electronic game

Alternate Title(s): None

Salary Range: $15,000 to $75,000 or more

Employment Prospects: Fair

Advancement Prospects: Poor

Prerequisites:

Education or Training—Bachelor's degree in music recommended, but not required; some courses in business administration may be helpful

Experience—Work as a Composer for film or television, creating music that reflects a wide range of emotions

Special Skills and Personality Traits—Able to express emotions musically; background in classical music training; some business experience helpful

CAREER LADDER

```
┌─────────────────────────────────────┐
│   Audio Engineer; Sound Producer     │
└─────────────────────────────────────┘

┌─────────────────────────────────────┐
│              Composer                │
└─────────────────────────────────────┘

┌─────────────────────────────────────┐
│    Music Arranger; Musician          │
└─────────────────────────────────────┘
```

Position Description

For the game player, music is a critical part of carrying emotion throughout the gaming experience. Without music, even action scenes can seem flat and disjointed. Music is a way of telling the game player how he or she should be reacting to the visual images of the game. Music can heighten the thrill of action, highlight for the player when danger is lurking around a corner, or set a lighter tone for more comic moments.

Composing for electronic games is different from composing for film or television. Unlike those media, Composers of music for games cannot be entirely sure what is precisely happening on the screen at any given moment, unless they are composing for a cut-scene to be inserted or other non-interactive sequence. That means the music must be sufficiently general to work with whatever is happening. Unlike classical composing, however, the music cannot be entirely abstract, as it must support the game experience at all times.

Generally, game Composers' work is accomplished at a keyboard (sometimes attached to a computer to annotate and save what they play), utilizing special synthesizers that put an entire orchestra at their fingertips. They can compose a hi-tech soundtrack for a science fiction game or a more naturalistic score for a fantasy. Just like in movie or television scoring, they can compose individual themes for different characters, or, by creating aural cues, highlight action scenes and create tense music at moments of suspense, or romantic music during love scenes.

Music appears in games in two forms: as compressed wave data files (MP3s) and as MIDI files. Music is integrated into games in one of two methods, either from ("live") recordings of actual musicians, or from a synthesized music made with a MIDI sequencer. A MIDI sequencer is a piece of software that takes information about the notes to be played and the instruments on which they are to be played and combines these two strands of information to drive a synthesizer to produce music. This synthesizer can do all kinds of other things as well, such as changing the dynamics and the quality of the artificial "room" in which the music is originating (simulating everything from a bathroom to a concert hall).

Before starting to compose a score for a game, a Composer needs to know all the game's potential target hardware platforms and what kind of music they support. PC computers and all next-generation consoles allow the use of regular CD audio files, but handhelds and Internet-delivered games most likely still will require MIDI music, which may be inferior in quality but uses much smaller data files to run. Composers also need to know as much as possible about the game materials. If they are composing for a specific scene to be cut in, they need to see the animation so they can score it like a movie, with the rise and fall of the music paralleling the action at hand. For general game music, Composers need to sense the shifting moods of the game so that they can interpret them for the player.

Some games use looping music to provide a continuous soundtrack. Composers try to make the individual loops sufficiently long so the player does not notice that the music is repeating. Another method is to create different themes with identical starts and finishes, putting them together to provide variety. A more difficult technical and creative musical task is to write adaptive music, which changes its feel to match the game character's actions. This requires writing music in quite small segments and embedding flags into the code to signal the rapidly changing mood states of the game. For example, when the game player is approaching a hidden monster, the music expresses a rising tension, and when the player sees and attacks the monster, the music shifts into an action mode. When the player defeats the monster, the music heard is a victory theme. Creating this kind of music requires close coordination between the game designer, programmer, and the Composer.

One other aspect of composing music for video games is payment schedules and rights. These items can be tricky to negotiate. In television and films there are established norms whereby Composers are generally paid by the song (or score), and they retain several royalty rights that provide an income stream from their music for years to come. However, in the electronic games industry, game developers want to acquire all the rights and avoid any kind of royalty accounting/continuous payment scheduling. They aim to manage the game through its normal life cycle to be able to repackage it in the future without any restrictions. The usual compromise agreed upon by the game developer and the Composer is that the Composer receives a one-time payment for the acquisition of all rights for the life of the game, while the Composer or musicians involved retain the right to use the music in arenas outside the game industry.

Obviously, Composers must understand music in all its aspects: how it creates rhythm and pace and sets an emotional tone for the listener, and how it relates to what is seen on the screen during the playing of the game. They must be able to play an instrument, preferably the piano, since synthesizers are all keyboard-based. In composing for electronic games, Composers must keep in mind that they are often assembling many versions of each sound that is requested for audition by the game developer. They are composing different versions of a music theme or movement for this tryout, and, hopefully, for assembly into the game.

Salaries

Salaries may vary greatly from Composer to Composer, and usually depend greatly upon the game's budget. According to the U.S. Department of Labor's *Occupational Outlook Handbook,* in May 2004 median annual earnings of composers were $34,570. The middle 50 percent earned between $24,040 and $51,770. The lowest 10 percent received less than $15,960, and the highest 10 percent earned more than $75,380. Of course, these are generalized salary statistics for the entire entertainment industry, and they apply to salaried, not freelance, Composers. Nonetheless, they do give an indication of what to expect on a yearly basis. Composers working as independent contractors taking on work for games and other venues concurrently may be able to earn more.

Employment Prospects

With the ongoing expansion of the electronic games industry (and most games need music to accompany their story lines), there is plenty of work for Composers. Still, it remains a highly competitive field. One way to discover who is hiring is to check game companies' Web sites for employment announcements and to look at sites that cover the industry, as many of them carry employment ads as well.

Advancement Prospects

There are almost no musical advancement prospects for a Composer supplying music to the electronics game industry. Most Composers create music for a wide variety of venues other than games. Some Composers may want to become more involved in the technical aspects of sound production for games. With the technical background gained from their synthesizer activities, it may be a natural progression to become an audio engineer and then look to advance to the managerial level of a sound producer.

Education and Training

It would be helpful to have training in classical music, even opera. Taking courses in composing for films and in the art of orchestrating also would be useful. Composers should be adept at several musical instruments, especially the piano, as synthesizers that they most likely will use in their musical creations for games are keyboard-based. Knowledge of how instruments sound and blend is critical in creating their sounds on synthesizers.

Experience, Skills, and Personality Traits

Any job as a Composer on a student (or a low-budget) film or television production will provide good experience in composing for an electronic medium. In addition, such work will aid a Composer to provide a sample CD or audiotape to use in auditioning for work in the game industry. The sample should demonstrate the Composer's capacity to create themes and musical sketches that reflect a wide range of distinctive emotions.

Composing and editing music is a distinct specialty. While it traditionally is thought of as a purely artistic talent, modern synthesized music (most commonly used in the game industry) involves considerable technical ability as well. Nonetheless, Composers working on electronic games must understand music in all its aspects (its rhythms, pace, and emotional tone) and how the music can be meshed with what is seen on the screen.

Unions and Associations

Composers are not represented by the main music union, the American Federation of Musicians (AFM), but orchestrators and arrangers are. Many Composers are members of the American Society of Composers, Authors and Publishers (ASCAP), Broadcast Music, Inc. (BMI), or SESAC, Inc., which can greatly aid them in their negotiations over payments and royalty rights on their compositions used in the game industry. Other associations, such as the National Academy of Recording Arts and Sciences (NARAS), or Screen Composers of America, may be helpful for networking purposes. In addition, membership in the International Game Developers Association (IGDA) may provide job information and contacts.

Tips for Entry

1. Contact film schools and volunteer to write music for a student or low-budget film to gain actual experience in writing music to fit visual scenes.
2. In your employment search, beyond checking the Web sites of individual electronic game publishers, browse sites of development companies or even the sites dedicated to individual game projects for clues as to employment opportunities.
3. Look for internship programs that some music publishers may offer. Once you are on the inside, make personal contacts in any way you can, as the electronic game business, like any other, is all personal.

SOUND PRODUCER

CAREER PROFILE

Duties: Create the voice and sound effects, blending them with music, for electronic games; integrate sound into the overall design of the game

Alternate Title(s): Audio Lead; Electronic Sound Producer; Sound Designer; Sound Director

Salary Range: $40,000 to $90,000 or more

Employment Prospects: Fair to Good

Advancement Prospects: Poor to Fair

Prerequisites:

    Education or Training—High school degree required; college (or technical school) courses in sound production, computer programming, graphics, and multimedia techniques extremely useful; usually a college degree is not required

    Experience—Minimum of one to two years' experience at a sound studio and familiarity with game development techniques and procedures

    Special Skills and Personality Traits—Ability to integrate sound (voice, music, and sound special effects) into electronic games; comfortable working under deadline pressures; strong auditory, creative, and communication skills; thorough understanding of sound production techniques and procedures

CAREER LADDER

```
┌─────────────────────────────────────┐
│   Art Director; Technical Producer   │
└─────────────────────────────────────┘

┌─────────────────────────────────────┐
│            Sound Producer            │
└─────────────────────────────────────┘

┌─────────────────────────────────────┐
│   Apprentice Sound Technician;       │
│   Production Assistant               │
└─────────────────────────────────────┘
```

Position Description

Sound design has a central role in overall electronic game design. Sounds can be used to help immerse game players in the game world, provide feedback for their actions, and give clues that help them along the way. The pictures of the game tell players what is happening, but the sound tells them how the events feel and even what they mean.

Today, games can have hundreds of different sound effects and ambient noises, as well as the voices of the characters within the game and a full musical score. The musical background will change to reflect the mood or level of tension in the game scenes, and the game characters will "speak" with realistic voices (usually recorded from performances by actors). In the real world, background noises are everywhere. No matter where we go, there is a constant hum of background clatter. In games, background sound effects

establish the ambiance and atmosphere of the game. They become part of the stream of concrete details that combine to help make the fictional world of the game seem far more real. Some games, of course, won't have such ambient sounds—board games, card games, and trivia games seldom have an audio background, although they may have event-based sound effects and some background music.

Unlike background sounds, event-based sounds serve as feedback to the actions that the player takes while playing the game. These can be realistic sounds, such as a golf club swishing through the air and hitting a golf ball, or artificial sounds, such as the *ka-ching* of an arcade-style game that lets players know when they rack up points. Sounds can also provide gameplay hints. If a game user comes to a door and hears a monster roaring behind it, there is a certainty of danger when the player opens the door.

Contrary to movies and television, where the production of sound effects is divided between the sound special effects (FX) editor and the foley artist (who creates the small noises), both big and small sound effects in games are selected or created by the Sound Producer (sometimes known as the sound designer). Sound Producers work with sounds from a variety of sources: archives of recorded sounds, live recordings of actors voicing the game's scripted dialogue, digitized sounds and effects, synthesized or prerecorded music, and even natural sounds captured by the producer by going out into the world armed with a microphone and a digital recorder. While there may be recording engineers who do the actual sound processing, the Sound Producer is responsible for the final sound and its integration into the game. This assimilation includes ensuring that the finished product will reproduce well on the kind of hardware (sound cards and speakers) likely to be used by the game player. The problem with projecting high-quality sound is that it requires very large data files. In order to conserve space and enable the necessary fast streaming that a game requires, the sounds are generally sampled at a lower rate and compressed, which reduces the overall quality. Sound Producers and audio programmers have to collaborate on reaching the compromise that best suits the majority of the sounds in the game.

In addition, with all these layers of game sounds available—including voice and music—the Sound Producer needs to be careful to focus the player's attention on the proper sound at the right time. Background noises should not drown out dialogue, nor should the musical score cover over vital sound clues. Thus, Sound Producers should have a good overall grasp of the structure and objectives of the game in order to select the most appropriate type and quality of sound to be used. They must be very familiar with the tools employed for digitally recording, mixing, and modifying sound. Above all, there has to be a close coordination with the designers, artists, and animators who are creating the game's on-screen action.

Sound Producers frequently also have some management responsibilities, as they supervise (and sometimes hire) recording engineers and/or technicians. Most importantly, Sound Producers need to make sure the sound part of the game project keeps up with the overall schedule. On many larger projects, the Sound Producer works in tandem with the lead artist (or art director) who has the comprehensive responsibility for the artistic side of the game development.

Salaries

Full-time Sound Producers in game development have annual incomes ranging from a low of about $40,000 to a high of $90,000 or more. Many of them can earn more as independent contractors, taking on work for games and other venues concurrently. If the Sound Producer is a union

member of the International Alliance of Theatrical Stage Employees (IATSE), minimum salary rates are set by a contract negotiated by that union, and average about $53.66 per hour (or $482.04 for an eight-hour day). Sound Producers working under contract for game developers on specific game products are often paid based on the number (and type) of sounds that they are asked to provide.

In a 2006 survey of the electronic games industry, the magazine *Game Developer* found that Sound Producers' salary averages ranged from $60,000 (for those with three to six years of experience working within the industry) to $90,000 or more yearly (for those with more than six years experience).

Employment Prospects

The audio department at most game-developing companies is quite compact. Some developers choose to contract out their audio requirements to professionals who specialize in preparing sound for various game platforms. If the audio specialist works as a Sound Producer in-house with a developer, the audio department is typically very small. This means that only a few individuals per company are employed full-time creating audio sounds for game development. It also means that competition for these positions is very heavy. Nonetheless, with the incredible expansion of the game development industry, the need for experienced Sound Producers is acute.

Advancement Prospects

A Sound Producer with excellent skills and a time-tested record of accomplishments can become a well-paid consultant. Other Sound Producers that have some familiarity with graphic arts and animation may search out higher positions on the art team of game development, such as that of art director, or even aspire to a more senior management position as technical producer.

Education and Training

Formal education is of minimal importance for this kind of job. However, course work (and, possibly, a degree) in sound production, computer programming, and graphics should prove extremely useful. Most game developers are looking for demonstrated sound skills, so a portfolio of selections of sounds on a CD can be helpful in seeking employment. Training in a sound studio is an excellent background for a Sound Producer in the game industry, although an impressive portfolio of sounds might make up for limited experience.

Experience, Skills, and Personality Traits

Audio work requires good ears. This is not just the ability to hear quiet or distant sounds, but also the ability to mix sounds together and make them sound right. A large part of audio engineering on the part of Sound Producers consists of matching different sounds to achieve a desired overall experience. Needed skills include recording, mixing, and editing. Recording ambient sounds in an open area requires different gear and different settings on that gear from recording, say, an actor in a sound booth or a band in a studio. Combining (mixing) sounds to create an integrated audio experience, applying digital effects (such as echoes) to change the way the results are interpreted by the human ear, is another key skill. In addition, Sound Producers need to be able to cut and paste sound effects, music, and dialogue. Editing dialogue out of individual words or phrases so that it seems natural is a difficult job. It requires a close working relationship between the writer (or designer), who creates the script to be recorded, and the Sound Producer who edits the sounds.

Other skills needed include a sense of dramatic structure and an allied ability to integrate the sound with the visual part of that dramatic structure. Sound Producers must be extremely familiar with the latest sound-related hardware and software tools. They should also be equipped to supervise, manage, and communicate well with other management personnel within the game development process.

Unions and Associations

Some Sound Producers may find it advantageous to be members of the Production Sound Technicians, Local 695, of the International Alliance of Theatrical Stage Employees (IATSE) for the guarantee of wage scales and benefits, as well as other job support. Other industry associations, such as the International Association of Audio/Video Communicators, may be beneficial for networking purposes.

Tips for Entry

1. While in school or college, consider working part time in a music or sound studio to acquire experience in the technique and technology of sound recording.
2. Alternatively, when looking for employment as a sound technician, be willing to accept any low-paid position at a sound effects company to gain seasoning, knowledge, and contacts (who may prove to be critical in your search for employment with game developers).
3. Analyze the sounds you encounter when playing electronic games. In particular, note how the sounds enhance the game experience and help to involve you in the action. Consider what sounds you, as a Sound Producer, would add to enhance the game experience.

DESIGN

GAME DESIGNER

CAREER PROFILE

Duties: Responsible for the overall vision, design, and mechanics of an electronic game

Alternate Title(s): None

Salary Range: $35,000 to $75,000 or more

Employment Prospects: Fair

Advancement Prospects: Fair to Good

Prerequisites:

Education or Training—Four-year college degree in graphic arts or technical design, with computer courses (in some cases, two-year degree with computer and art-related courses and design work experience may be acceptable); portfolio of game development work and one to three years' previous experience in game development critical

Experience—Hands-on familiarity with existing game engines and concepts/terminology for computer graphics; knowledge of programming scripting languages; wide-ranging background designing and using tools for game development

Special Skills and Personality Traits—Ability to maintain project-related documents using commercial software; capacity of working within tech environment; creativity, innovative thinking, and problem solving capabilities; extremely strong organizational, interpersonal, and communication skills (both verbal and writing); high enthusiasm for games and an understanding of what makes them work

CAREER LADDER

```
┌─────────────────────────────────────┐
│   Lead Designer; Creative Director   │
└─────────────────────────────────────┘

┌─────────────────────────────────────┐
│           Game Designer              │
└─────────────────────────────────────┘

┌─────────────────────────────────────┐
│    Level Designer; Junior Artist     │
└─────────────────────────────────────┘
```

Position Description

Game Designers are involved in game development from the first concept to the release of the game product. The Game Designer is usually the "vision" person who, throughout the maze of game development, comprehends how all the pieces will eventually come together, and how the game player (customer) will experience using the product. Game Designers, generally, are not programmers or artists, but they must have a working understanding of all disciplines involved in game development.

Game design is one of the most highly sought-after roles in the game industry. Game Designers may spend some part of their day thinking up fresh and fun ideas for games. However, their primary duty is defining the way a specific game in development works and setting up the rules that will govern the game. They devise the core mechanics of the game and create the world in which the game occurs. They describe the key characters (and/or creatures) and spell out how these characters (and/or creatures) will behave and, generally, how they will look. Game Designers define the rules that game players will use and all the sights/sounds that the player will experience and convey that information to the development team. (The actual task of creating those sights and sounds is up to the artists and audio designers on the development team.)

Game design is a highly collaborative process, even more so than any other part of the development route. Every designer on the project wants to make a creative contribution, and ideas and suggestions are presented continuously. Part of the Game Designer's job is take this material, decide which of it is genuinely useful and which will not work, and then integrate the best into the game design. This process demands compromise, which means that Game Designers need good people skills and leadership ability in addition to their other design and technical qualities. However, Game Designers must remain flexible. Each hardware platform (on which the game will run) has limitations, no budget is bottomless, and no schedule is limitless. Game Designers have to be practical and ready to adapt their vision to what can be implemented by the rest of the development team. If changes are requested, Game Designers must stop and think through why that feature was put into the game plan in the first place. Game Designers have to be careful that their approval of such a request does not create a portion of the game that no longer makes sense because the one element was altered. At the same time, if a team argues passionately to eliminate or change a feature that doesn't affect the core of the game, Game Designers should entertain the possibility that the game may be better off by following the suggestion.

Game Designers need to have experience in designing and using design tools, level geometry (to understand the creation of each self-contained mission or scenario within a game, which is known as a level and has its own starting conditions and victory conditions), and scripting systems and languages (which enable non-programming designers to input their ideas directly into the game and see how they work out). Game Designers are responsible for scheduling and prioritizing gameplay tasks among the team, as well as managing their creative input. In addition, they have to be able to document game design using word processing programs and art software packages. They are responsible for the creation and updating of the game's concept proposal, the design document, and all functional specifications provided to the artists and programmers to create the actual game.

Game Designers also do competitive analyses of similar games in the marketplace. They collaborate with the public relations department of the game company (or publisher) on appropriate product data to be added to the company's Web site, the marketing department as it creates advertisements and the box in which the game will be sold, and the sales group as it generates its promotional materials. Game Designers frequently design demos for all these groups to use, and make themselves available for media interviews when required.

Salaries

The salary range for Game Designers, like many other game development positions, varies greatly. Entry-level designers, who usually start out at a lower position, such as level designer, might make $25,000 to $30,000 yearly, while more experienced designers may have salaries that range from $35,000 to $75,000 or more, depending upon their skills and responsibilities. Successful Game Designers typically earn far more than their range would suggest, but very few game developers fall into this classification.

Employment Prospects

Securing a game design job of any kind is never easy, as the competition is always fierce. On any given development team, there may be as many as 25 developers. However, most of these posts are those of programmers and artists. This means that game productions have relatively few designers. In addition, the position of Game Designer is seldom an entry-level position, not only because it is such a highly sought-after post, but also because of the game development and managerial experience that is required to handle the assignment. Earning a job as a Game Designer involves demonstrating previous design experience. This can take the form of completed games, design documents, and design materials, all of which require solid seasoning in actual game development.

Advancement Prospects

Experienced Game Designers may look to advance to positions as lead designers (if involved with large projects that require such a position to manage the entire development process). Alternatively, they may want to move into the upper levels of company management as a creative director and, eventually, the chief creative officer of the company or publisher. Game Designers with great designing skills would need to persuade company management that they have both excellent management skills and financial savvy.

Education and Training

A four-year college degree in graphics or technical design, with computer and art-related courses, is the basic educational requirement for the position of Game Designer. Relatively few educational programs teach game design principles; however, both trade schools and some postgraduate programs can be found that are dedicated specifically to the game and new media industries.

More importantly, actual experience in game development is a necessity. Most Game Designers come from other areas of game development and most likely will have to demonstrate their design abilities before they can achieve this position.

Experience, Skills, and Personality Traits

Game Designers should have three or more years' experience in gameplay development, particularly design experience in collaborating on premises, scripts, and character descriptions. They need to know existing game engines and have an understanding of concepts and terminology for computer graphics, as well as programming/scripting languages (such as Perl or C++). They should be able to use 3-D software and be able to maintain all project-related documents, using commercial software such as Microsoft Office and FileMaker Pro. Their technical awareness of computer programming does not have to be exhaustive, but it helps greatly to have done some programming, even if only in a scripting language.

Game Designers should be comfortable with basic mathematics and need to display an analytical competence. A game is a system, a set of rules governing the relations between elements. In order to devise, fine-tune, and balance such systems, Game Designers must be able to think logically about cause and effect. They should be both creative and imaginative. They need visual and auditory imagination to invent new objects and imagine how they will look and sound. They need a creative mindset to devise characters, plots, scenes, and relationships. Conceptual imagination enables them to visualize ideas and their interrelationships, while lateral thinking enables them to produce unexpected twists on familiar formulas and material.

Game Designers must have excellent writing skills, as they are responsible for most game development documentation. In addition, they need to have good verbal communication abilities and be able to both work with designers, programmers, and artists and have interpersonal interaction with varied audiences. Game Designers must be problem solvers and be highly organized. Above all, they must have a terrific excitement for games and an understanding of how they work.

Unions and Associations

While there are no unions that represent Game Designers, there are several associations that support their professional development, including The American Institute of Graphic Arts (AIGA), the Association for Computer Machinery's (ACM) special interest group on computer graphics, and, above all, the International Game Developers Association (IGDA).

Tips for Entry

1. Along with your graphics and other art-related courses, take computer programming, English composition, and basic mathematics classes, as you will need these skills in game design.

2. When job searching, check game companies' Web sites for employment announcements. In addition, as many game development companies who do contract work for larger game publishers do not advertise, go to their Web sites, or even to sites dedicated to specific game projects, to search for potential job openings. Also, attend industry trade shows that may be in your region.

3. Be willing to accept any game development position (entry-level), both to gain experience and to begin developing your portfolio of finished game development and design work. Such a portfolio of your best work is critical in your advancement within the game design team.

GAME WRITER

Duties: Write character dialogue, sports commentary, cutscene narratives, journals, or any other portion of an electronic game where words are needed; write technical manuals, design documents, or similar material

Alternate Title(s): Scripter; Scriptwriter; Technical Writer

Salary Range: $30,000 to $60,000 or more

Employment Prospects: Fair

Advancement Prospects: Poor

Prerequisites:

    Education or Training—Undergraduate degree in communications, creative writing, English, fine arts, or liberal arts

    Experience—Any media writing, such as writing for film or television, is helpful; some technical background in computer programming or game design useful for preparing manuals and documents

    Special Skills and Personality Traits—Creative writing skills with aptitude for writing dialogue to fit specific styles and preset formats; excellent grammar and spelling; imagination; technical writing talents, including clarity, conciseness, and thoroughness

```
┌─────────────────────────────────┐
│     Full-time Writer (for Game   │
│       Development Company)       │
└─────────────────────────────────┘

┌─────────────────────────────────┐
│          Game Writer             │
└─────────────────────────────────┘

┌─────────────────────────────────┐
│  Freelance Writer; Technical Writer │
└─────────────────────────────────┘
```

Position Description

Writing is an important aspect of game design. Games are fiction and require a writer's creative skills. This means the ability to create plots, characters, scenes, and dialogue; to build dramatic tension, evoke emotion, and set pace of action through words; and to narrate events.

While some designers prefer to write the game content themselves, more often freelance writers are brought in to assist in framing the game's story. Writers must consult with the lead designer and the director—as well as members of the design team—to gain a comprehensive overview of the project. Freelance Game Writers are seldom with the team full time. They are usually contracted in at specific times to work on various stages of the game. Each time they return to the job, they must confer with the designers to learn if new changes require modifications to the narration and/or dialogue being written for the game.

Game writers are concerned with such elements as story structure, setting, dialogue, character development, setups and payoffs, plot twists, and pacing. They understand the use of the traditional dramatic story arc: call to action, conflict, and resolution. As veteran interactive scriptwriter Susan O'Connor states, "I used to think that scriptwriting would be the core function of my job; more often, it's just icing on the cake. Story design and story structure—that's where the real work lies." The telling of the story and the backstory in games is supposed to support and extend the game-playing experience, not imitate the story-telling qualities of film or television. Developing rich story lines, accessible story logic, and complex characters is not an easy task for screenwriters. Likewise, developing innovative, replayable, highly addictive, and lasting play mechanics in a story line is not easy for Game Writers.

Game Writers face the additional challenge of incorporating direct audience participation into the game experience. In this respect, writing for games is unlike writing for any other medium. In games, players can go through the same section of a game multiple times, which means they can encounter the same words many times. Thus, Game Writers need to write with repetition in mind and work with programmers to introduce variations. Then, different game players may take different paths through the game, so not everyone will encounter information in the same order. This means Game Writers need to write modular segments that make sense in whichever order they are read. As game players want to be *doing* something as they play, dialogue and exposition should be kept short, preferably distributing the background information across an environment. Game Writers must always keep in mind that every line of dialogue has a dual purpose: establish character and provide information. In addition, characters may provide voiceover narration to accompany introductions, segues from scene to scene, mission endings, level endings, and game endings and will sometimes make directional or guidance commentary, even teaching the player how to use the game.

Text in games may be found in mission or level briefings, journals, background information, or introductory narrative, all the responsibilities of a Game Writer. If there is speech involved in the game, then every word that is spoken must be recorded in a sound studio, which means the necessity for a script. The Game Writer has to be skillful in handling these demands.

In addition to story structure and dialogue, Game Writers may be asked to provide other kinds of writing for a project. While designers themselves usually document the game design, they sometimes hire Game Writers to do it for them. In this case, Game Writers must attend design meetings, take copious notes, ask questions, and then organize all this information into a document. This becomes the source that everyone involved in the development process will use to understand the game's details. This design document must be the most current representation of everything known about what a player will experience in the game. It frequently is kept as a set of computer webpages for ease of update and access. Besides the design document, Game Writers may also be hired to write manuals, especially for highly technical games like flight simulators. Finally, marketing departments need writers to create ad copy, box copy, and other promotional material to help sell the product and frequently turn to freelance Game Writers to do these tasks.

Salaries

According to the U.S. Department of Labor's Bureau of Labor Statistics, median annual earnings for salaried writers were $44,350 in May 2004. Salaries ranged from a low of $23,330 to over $90,000. However, Game Writers, generally, are freelance writers hired for specific game projects.

Freelance writers, in turn, usually work on a variety of projects, writing for games and other media. Versatile freelance writers can earn anywhere from $35,000 to $70,000, or considerably more, depending upon their workload of projects.

Employment Prospects

Employment opportunities for freelance writers as Game Writers are only fair. On most small projects, it is the game designer who undertakes most of the writing, both dialogue and documentation, as well as the story structure, elements, and mechanics. On larger projects, or where licensed titles are involved (e.g., *Star Wars*), a freelance writing specialist is frequently brought in as the Game Writer. This employment may extend for a period of time (like six months to a year) or may be only from time to time to work on various stages of the game. It is rare for a writer to have a full-time job with a game publisher or game developer doing nothing but writing on the game. Game Writers tend to be freelance or be occupied in other tasks in the process (technical writing, or marketing) in which their writing skills are useful.

Advancement Prospects

Since most Game Writers are freelance and not full-time salaried workers, the only real advancement open to them is a full-time position as a writer at a game development company or publisher that has been extremely successful with its product line and needs a full-time staff writer to handle the expanded workload. This is not a common situation, and most Game Writers continue to be freelancers.

Education and Training

Most freelance Game Writers have an undergraduate degree in communications, creative writing, English, or liberal arts. Game Writers who are also technical writers need to have training and background in computer technology and be comfortable with standard office software. In addition, Game Writers need to be game players to know what the current hot products are. This requires both fairly up-to-date computer equipment (no more than three or four years old) and practice playing games. Besides the technical tools, Game Writers must have a library (dictionary, thesaurus, style manual, and books on storytelling) to support their work needs.

Experience, Skills, and Personality Traits

Game Writers need to demonstrate a first-rate grasp of English, specifically an excellent command of grammar, punctuation, and spelling. Experience as a writer of fiction is helpful, as they need to create plots, characters, scenes, and dialogue, build dramatic tension, and evoke emotion with their words. In their documentation of the game story and design, they have to be able to create structured, intelligently organized documents that explain, flow naturally from topic to topic, and make sense.

Ideally, Game Writers should have some experience writing within the game industry. However, when starting out as a freelance writer for a game developer or publisher, a familiarity with games by playing them, along with a basic understanding of what makes games function and the role of dialogue in the process, may be sufficient substitutes for actual game writing. Besides their writing skills, Game Writers should have strong interpersonal, communication, and problem solving abilities and a keen attention to detail. They need to have a solid understanding of dramatic structure and a demonstrable ability to write dialogue. In addition, they should be proficient in basic writing software programs, such as MS Office Suite. They should appreciate the basic collaborative nature of game design and work well with designers and programmers. If they also write for the marketing department of a game development company, they should have some experience in writing ad and promotional copy.

Unions and Associations

Major national associations applicable for freelance writers include the American Society of Journalists and Authors (ASJA), the Authors Guild (AG), and the National Writers Association (NWA). Game Writers who also work within the film, radio, or television industries may belong to the Writers Guild of America (WGA), a union that represents primarily scriptwriters. Game Writers may also find it worthwhile belonging to the umbrella association for the game industry, the International Game Developers Association (IGDA).

Tips for Entry

1. Take as many writing courses as possible throughout your academic career, and gain firsthand experience in writing for high school and college publications.
2. In addition, take English literature courses, as they provide a foundation in storytelling, and history courses, as many games are set in historical periods and you need to know what it was like to live during a given historical period.
3. Obviously, familiarity with computers is vital, and you should become well acquainted with a wide variety of games, their stories, strategies, and design, as this working knowledge will be crucial in your future work as a Game Writer.

LEAD DESIGNER

CAREER PROFILE

Duties: Manage the entire design process and guarantee that creative integrity is maintained on large game development projects

Alternate Title(s): Creative Game Director; Lead Game Designer; Senior Designer

Salary Range: $40,000 to $90,000 or more

Employment Prospects: Fair to Good

Advancement Prospects: Poor to Fair

Prerequisites:

Education or Training—Bachelor's degree in graphic arts or technical design, with courses in computer programming required; portfolio of game development work critical for initial employment; three to five years' experience in game design usually required

Experience—Familiarity with existing game engines and concepts/terminology for computer graphics; knowledge of programming scripting languages and ability to use 3-D software; experience with designing and employing tools for game development

Special Skills and Personality Traits—Ability to function within a collaborative technical design environment and to work closely with programming and artist personnel; capable of maintaining project-related documentation, schedules, lists, and so forth, using commercial software; creativity and innovative thinking; excellent interpersonal and communication skills (both verbal and writing); excitement about games and an understanding of what makes them effective; strong organizational, administrative, and problem solving talents

CAREER LADDER

```
┌─────────────────────────────────┐
│      Chief Creative Officer      │
└─────────────────────────────────┘

┌─────────────────────────────────┐
│          Lead Designer           │
└─────────────────────────────────┘

┌─────────────────────────────────┐
│  Assistant Designer; Associate   │
│      Producer; Programmer;       │
│     Quality Assurance Tester     │
└─────────────────────────────────┘
```

Position Description

Lead Designers usually are contracted only for large projects, where they manage the overall design process (the game designer's job on smaller projects). In such instances, the Lead Designer's role is to determine the large-scale vision of the game and to establish the elements that would attract a player to trying the game in the first place. Lead Designers plot out the major areas that need work in the game development and then assign these tasks to designers for refinement. Thus, for major projects, Lead Designers become the individuals tasked with establishing and maintaining the overall creative vision of the project. (Game designers typically accomplish these functions for smaller projects.) The Lead Designer ensures that a creative consistency exists in the execution of the project, from the all-embracing game structure down to the smallest detail.

As the title of the position suggests, part of the Lead Designer's duties are managerial. Lead Designers are responsible for making certain that everyone on the design team—including themselves—fulfills their tasks on time. They assist upper management in the recruiting of core design team members, and ensure that all designers understand the overall architecture and vision of the game. Aspiring Lead Designers need to have several years of seasoning in game design before they can advance to this higher post.

In addition, as supervisors of all design aspects of the game, Lead Designers are tasked with the creation and implementation of the detailed game design document (which will include a technical design portion that will become a task document for the programming team). Game design documentation (and its modifications and add-ons) is geared to be a guide for the design team during the various stages of the game development. Lead Designers are responsible for all revisions, documenting all changes so that there is an accurate, up-to-date record of how each game feature works and/or why a unit or character behaves in a particular fashion. They ensure that the designers have the proper amount of reference material (from movies, books, and other games) and that other development teams (artists, programmers) have the same reference material, thus maintaining a consistent voice and style in the game's overall design and its documentation.

Lead Designers may also be in charge of an ongoing creative design review, which should include a "use case scenario" that illustrates, step by step, just how the gameplayer is intended to use a system in the playing process. This use case scenario will help define the interactions between players and the game system and will help guarantee the inclusion of all functional requirements in a game's design. In addition, Lead Designers frequently supervise all debugging processes and handle any needed post-release technical support.

Salaries

According to a 2005 survey of salaries of video game makers done by DeVry University, Lead Designers with three years' or less experience make an average of $43,778 per year. Those with three to six years of experience averaged $51,777 and those with six or more years of experience averaged $78,913. Another study indicated that Lead Designers, due to their supervisory responsibilities and overall management of the design process, might earn from $65,000 to $95,000 or more, based on their experience and skills. The DeVry survey also found that the highest reported annual salary of a Lead Designer was $190,000.

Employment Prospects

Lead Designer is seldom an entry-level position, not only because it is such a highly sought-after assignment, but also because of the extensive game development experience required. In addition, Lead Designers must have sufficient background to be able to manage the entire design process and its personnel. Most Lead Designers come up through the ranks of the development or production teams. Often Lead Designers have been artists or programmers, which allows them to understand all of the technical and aesthetic tradeoffs as they put the design together.

Advancement Prospects

Some Lead Designers may decide to advance into the higher management echelons, seeking to become the chief creative officer of the development company or publisher. Depending upon their game development background, they may opt instead for advancement into another area of game development, such as production (as an executive producer) or programming (as a director of technology).

Education and Training

The basic educational requirement of most game design positions is a four-year college degree in graphics or technical design, with computer and art-related courses. Designers also need to be well acquainted with mathematics. While there are relatively few educational programs that teach game design principles, trade schools and some postgraduate programs exist that are dedicated specifically to the game and new media industries.

More importantly, actual experience in game development is a necessity. Most applicants for design positions, and especially Lead Designers, come from other areas of game development and most likely will have to demonstrate their design abilities to obtain their position as Lead Designer.

Experience, Skills, and Personality Traits

Lead Designers should have three to five years' background in gameplay development, particularly in helping to create scenarios, scripts, and character descriptions for games. They need to know existing game engines and understand concepts and terminology for computer graphics, as well as programming/scripting languages (such as Perl or C++). In addition, they should be able to use 3-D software. Their technical awareness of computer programming need not be exhaustive, but it helps greatly to have done some programming, even if only in a scripting language.

In addition, Lead Designers should have strong people management and project management talents. Their communication skills must be excellent to aid in their supervising the creation of the detailed game design document, as well as their maintaining of project-related documents, ongoing schedules, and risk assessment studies. They need to be avid game players themselves, as they will be expected to analyze and understand competitive game products. Their management duties also require them to be good problem solvers and to be highly organized (to ensure the design process stays on time and that all aspects of the project are properly integrated).

Unions and Associations

Lead Designers should find such associations as The American Institute of Graphic Arts (AIGA), the Association for Computer Machinery's (ACM) special interest group on graphics known as SIGGRAPH, and, above all, the International Game Developers Association (IGDA) valuable for networking, industry information, and general support.

Tips for Entry

1. While still in college and aiming for a position in game design, you should add to your graphics and other art-related programs courses in computer programming, English composition, and basic mathematics, as you will need all these skills in game design.

2. When job searching, check game companies' Web sites for employment announcements. In addition, since many game development firms (who do contract work for larger game publishers) do not advertise, visit their Web sites, or even sites dedicated to specific game projects, to search for potential job openings.

3. Become experienced in all forms of game design (and a little game programming would help) to aid you in your technical understanding of the design process and be able to relate to, and manage, the skilled designers under your charge when you achieve the position of Lead Designer.

OTHER DESIGNER POSITIONS

CAREER PROFILE

Duties: Level Designer: build the individual levels or missions that make up the game; User Interface Designer: create the connections between the game player and the world of the game; Artificial Intelligence (AI) Designer: work with AI programmer on specifying how the characters or creatures will behave and how the game responds to the game player's actions; Assistant Designer: as the entry-level worker, learn all facets of game design by helping in specific design aspects

Alternate Title(s): Level Designer: Game World Builder, Associate Designer

Salary Range: $25,000 to $75,000 or more

Employment Prospects: Fair to Good

Advancement Prospects: Fair to Good

Prerequisites:

Education or Training—Bachelor's degree in graphic arts or technical design, with courses in computer programming required (in some cases, two-year degree with computer and art-related courses and design work experience may be acceptable); portfolio of game development work critical; for positions above the Assistant Designer, one to three years' background in game development usually required

Experience—Positions other than Assistant Designer: three to five years' previous experience in game development; hands-on familiarity with existing game engines and concepts/terminology for computer graphics; knowledge of programming scripting languages; some experience with designing and using tools for game development; Assistant Designer: some game development experience and a portfolio of design work and demos

Special Skills and Personality Traits—Ability to function within a collaborative technical design environment and to work closely with programming and artist personnel; capable of doing research, using public libraries and surfing the Web; creativity and innovative thinking; excellent interpersonal and communication skills (both verbal and writing); excitement about games and an understanding of what makes them effective; strong organizational and problem solving abilities

CAREER LADDER

```
┌─────────────────────────────────┐
│  Game Designer; Lead Designer   │
└─────────────────────────────────┘

┌─────────────────────────────────┐
│  Designer Positions (various)   │
└─────────────────────────────────┘

┌─────────────────────────────────┐
│     Apprentice Designer;        │
│     Production Assistant        │
└─────────────────────────────────┘
```

Position Description

When the design document for the planned game is done, teams of specialists work to bring its words to life. Engine programmers determine graphics pipelines and how to detect when objects in the game world might collide. Modelers build complex characters and creatures and hand them off to the animators, whose duty is to give them movement. Artificial Intelligence (AI) programmers are tasked with providing the behavior of the game's characters and creatures. Texture artists clothe the characters, create the exterior skin of creatures, and paint the world they populate. Composers dream up atmospheric music, and audio technicians twist everyday sounds to emerge from the game hardware as echoes of a wholly imagined world.

It is the Level Designers (or "LDs") who take all these pieces and stitch them together to make a game. They build the individual levels (the self-contained missions or scenarios within a game, with their own starting conditions and victory conditions) that make up the game. They are the ones who decide what the player should be trying to achieve at any given moment during the game. They set the goals for each player and choose the focus of each level, making certain there is variety from level to level (i.e., one may contain a fight, the next could involve stealth and avoiding detection, and the next might focus on sidestepping traps) in order that they work together and move the story along. They also vary the challenges from level to level to satisfy both the expert, hardcore game player and the average or novice players. Although Level Designers have the least amount of design authority over the interior mechanics of the game, they have the greatest effect on the player's actual experience of it.

Level Designers take the game elements and mechanics that the designers have created, and use a level editor, a software program designed especially for the process, to define the landscape that makes up the level and to create the challenges that players will face. In addition, Level Designers are part game tester, as, after they complete the level, they have to playtest and balance it. Level Designers report back to the game designer if there are any glitches, if certain strategies always win, or if particular units or elements of the game prove not to have any practical use. They also may be called upon to demo the product for upper management or a crowd at a trade show at various points during its development.

Like writers, most game designers tend to be generalists: they do a little of everything and seldom concentrate on one task exclusively, except for level designers. However, there are two areas that require additional knowledge: user interface design and AI design. The duties of these jobs are usually assigned to specific designers.

User Interface Designers create the conduit between the game player and the game world. They allow participants to project their own will into playing the game. To do this, User Interface Designers must establish a relationship between a set of buttons and analog controls and a fictional person, creature, vehicle, city, or whatever comprises the particular world of the particular game. This transition needs to operate smoothly and naturally, so that, after a while, game players forget they are using a machine at all, and feel truly immersed in the game world.

AI Designers basically structure artificial intelligence within the game. Designing artificial intelligence is not programming, but it comes as close to it as any area of game design ever does. AI Designers work closely with AI programmers to specify how characters or creatures will behave, and how the game as a whole will react, both strategically and tactically, to players' actions. AI Designers often write pseudo computer code for AI programmers to implement, and help to define the states of a software construct called a finite state machine. (This is a software technique used to create an artificial intelligence for autonomous or partially autonomous units, such as a soldier. The various states of a soldier might include advancing, retreating, holding ground, or dying. For each such state, a prescribed set of conditions determines under what circumstances the unit will change to a different state.)

The Assistant Designer is usually the entry point for those individuals joining the design team. They are typically assigned to specific aspects of the game, but not made responsible for the various design issues presented by working on the game in its entirety. They may also be made responsible for documenting the game's design in the game design document, which specifies all aspects of the game's design, and will be an important part of the testing process of the game. In keeping the game design document current, Assistant Designers report directly to the Lead Designer or, if there is no one in that position, the senior game designer.

Salaries

Salary ranges for Game Designers, like many other game development positions, vary greatly. Assistant Designers, an entry-level job, might make $25,000 to $35,000 annually. Level Designers may expect income in the mid-range of salaries for designers, usually from $40,000 to $70,000 or more. Specialty game designers, such as AI Designers and User Interface Designers, may expect incomes similar to those of Level Designers.

Employment Prospects

Gaining a game design job of any kind is never really easy, as the competition is always intense. On any given development team, there may be as many as 25 developers. However, most of these posts are those of programmers and artists. This means that game productions typically have many more programmers and artists working on a title than they do designers.

The job of Level Designer is seldom an entry-level position, as it is such a highly sought-after assignment, and requires much game development experience. Similarly, the positions of User Interface Designer and AI Designer require game development experience.

Applicants for openings as Assistant Designers require a strong portfolio that demonstrates their previous design work. This portfolio can take the form of completed games, design documents, design materials, and demos. Game design jobs are available, but the competition for them is heavy.

Advancement Prospects

For Assistant Designers, the first step up the career ladder in a design department is an associate designer or a Level Designer position. In turn, Level Designers look to move on to becoming game designers (and, eventually, senior game designers) or lead designers on a major game design project.

Education and Training

The basic educational requirement of most game design positions is a four-year college degree in graphics or technical design, with computer and art-related courses. Designers also need to be comfortable with mathematics. While there are relatively few educational programs that teach game design principles, trade schools and some postgraduate programs can be found that are dedicated specifically to the game and new media industries.

More importantly, actual experience in game development is a necessity. Most applicants for design positions come from other areas of game development and most likely will have to demonstrate their design abilities to obtain employment.

Experience, Skills, and Personality Traits

Level Designers should have one to two years' background in gameplay development, particularly in helping to create scenarios, scripts, and character descriptions for games. They need to know existing game engines and understand concepts and terminology for computer graphics, as well as programming/scripting languages (such as Perl or C++). In addition, they should be able to use 3-D software. Their technical awareness of computer programming need not be exhaustive, but it helps greatly to have done some programming, even if only in a scripting language.

Assistant Designers should have some experience in gameplay development and be able to maintain all project-related documents, schedules, lists, and so forth, using commercial software (such as Microsoft Office and FileMaker

Pro). They should be familiar with basic scripting programming tools and be able to implement basic components of game design as required.

Generally, game designers must be problem solvers and be highly organized. They must be able to think logically about cause and effect. They should be both creative and imaginative. They need visual and auditory imagination to invent new objects and envision how they will look and sound. They require dramatic imagination to fashion characters, plots, scenes, and relationships. Conceptual imagination enables them to visualize ideas and their interrelationships, while lateral thinking enables them to create unexpected twists on familiar formulas and material. They need excellent writing and good verbal communication talents, as design work is a highly collaborative enterprise. Above all, they must have a tremendous passion for games, and an understanding of what makes games work.

Unions and Associations

Game designers should find such associations as The American Institute of Graphic Arts (AIGA), the Association for Computer Machinery's (ACM) special interest group on graphics known as SIGGRAPH, and, above all, the International Game Developers Association (IGDA) valuable for networking, industry information, and general support.

In addition, the major annual professional conference for the game industry, the Game Developers' Conference (http://www.gdconf.com), is held every year in San Jose, California. This gathering is affiliated with the IGDA, so IGDA members get a registration discount.

Tips for Entry

1. While still in college, add classes in computer programming, English composition, and basic mathematics to your graphics and other art-related programs, as you will need these skills in game design.
2. When job searching, check game companies' Web sites for employment announcements. In addition, since many game development firms (who do contract work for larger game publishers) do not advertise, visit their Web sites, or even sites dedicated to specific game projects, to search for potential job openings.
3. One way to gain experience in level design, before you start job hunting, is to investigate games that now ship with level editors built into their programming. This way you can create your own levels to games and add what you have done to your portfolio.
4. Above all, play games endlessly to develop your understanding for what ingredients make them a hit with users.

MANAGEMENT

BUSINESS DEVELOPMENT DIRECTOR

CAREER PROFILE

Duties: Responsible for pursuing business partnership and product distribution opportunities for an electronic game developer, multimedia equipment manufacturer, or game software development company

Alternate Title(s): Business Development Manager; Development Director; Vice President of Development

Salary Range: $40,000 to $125,000 or more

Employment Prospects: Fair

Advancement Prospects: Poor to Fair

Prerequisites:

Education or Training—A bachelor's degree in business administration with some computer courses or in marketing and computer science; a Master of Business Administration (M.B.A.) frequently preferred as well

Experience—Minimum of two to four years of related online marketing (or sales) and business development expertise in launching and growing new consumer-focused technology products; experience in initiating and cultivating a wide variety of business relationships; knowledge of, or experience in, the video game industry; some project or account management experience

Special Skills and Personality Traits—Ability to work well in a team environment and manage multiple complex projects simultaneously while meeting deadlines; aggressive self-starter with good interpersonal capabilities; excellent written and verbal communication and presentation skills; highly organized with strong analytical and problem-solving strengths

CAREER LADDER

```
┌─────────────────────────────────┐
│   Vice President of Marketing    │
└─────────────────────────────────┘

┌─────────────────────────────────┐
│  Business Development Director   │
└─────────────────────────────────┘

┌─────────────────────────────────┐
│ Distribution Manager; Marketing/ │
│  Research Manager; Sales Manager │
└─────────────────────────────────┘
```

Position Description

Business Development Directors are responsible for researching, identifying, negotiating, and managing new commerce partners for their companies, as well as maintaining and developing relationships with existing associates. They act as key liaisons between upper management and the company's key business teammates. They analyze overall performance of partner deals, develop initiatives designed to expand the operation in new areas, and identify areas for future improvement.

They perform ongoing market analysis to support the company's strategic planning efforts and initiatives. They assist in the development and execution of the firm's business development strategic plan. In this process, they build market approaches to meet effectively and efficiently the goals that are set forth in that plan, and coordinate with finance and marketing teams on executing business development strategies. They operate closely with legal and financial personnel in drawing up and negotiating contracts, and are usually tasked with the documentation and contracts relating to new and existing partner relationships. They track partner contractual compliance and communicate to upper management their findings of partner performance, along with proposed courses of action to optimize partnership arrangements. In addition, they review all new development proposals, making their recommendations to senior management.

In addition, Business Development Directors work with internal department heads to ensure a total organizational understanding of partner product strategy, marketing initiatives, and other partner needs or requirements. In researching prospective business partners, they assess the competitive landscape and oversee the process of establishing these potential associations. They are the primary account management contacts for their companies. They help to integrate new partnerships throughout their organizations by communicating, managing, and coordinating with other departments within the company, including the product development, creative services, and technical sections, as well as the finance and marketing departments.

In negotiating development deals and establishing contracts, Business Development Directors have to be concerned with advances, royalties, reserves against returns, milestones (points within development marked by the completion of a certain amount of work) and deliverables, rights (to intellectual property) and proprietary technology, termination of contracts, confidentiality agreements, and ancillary revenues (for items related to the initial product). While both sides in these negotiations presume that lawyers will craft the final language of the contract, they still must agree on the various points of the deal. Such discussions and negotiations constitute a major part of the job of a Business Development Director.

Salaries

In line with their critical responsibilities in the development and management of a company, Business Development Directors are usually well paid. Yearly salaries range from a low of about $45,000 to a high of $125,000 or more. The median range for an experienced Business Development Director is approximately $75,000.

Employment Prospects

In the electronic games industry, this position is open only to candidates seasoned in marketing and sales promotion, with additional experience within the industry. It is not an entry-level position. All operations need to develop their business and development plans to guarantee financing of their projects and the successful promotion and distribution of their finished projects, so the role of Business Development Director will continue to be a necessary component of any management team.

Advancement Prospects

Due to the specific nature of the marketing and contract duties of Business Development Directors and their wide-ranging relationships with business partners and other related commerce professionals, the natural advancement step for them is to the higher management position of Vice President of Marketing. This position will place them in the upper management echelons of their firms, with added overall responsibilities and higher salaries.

Education and Training

At a minimum, an undergraduate degree—in marketing or business administration, or in computer science and marketing—is the usual requirement for this position. Many companies also prefer, or require, a master's degree in business administration.

Experience, Skills, and Personality Traits

Business Development Directors must, above all, be adept at negotiating sound commercial agreements and be experienced in negotiating complex contracts (including content licensing and distribution) in tandem with a company's legal team. They should be practiced at analyzing business opportunities and be able to make internal and external presentations of such opportunities to senior executive management. They should have at least two to four years' experience in negotiating and closing strategic partnerships, and knowledge of project account management techniques.

In addition, Business Development Directors must be able to take a business strategy and create actionable plans based upon it. They should be able to create basic financial models and be proficient in MS Office Suite, including Excel and Powerpoint. They should be aggressive and committed self-starters, with a facility of working in a competitive and fast-paced environment. They should have excellent interpersonal abilities, superior verbal and written skills, and strong problem-solving talents. They must be highly organized, able to manage multiple complex projects all at the same time, and able to meet tight deadlines.

Unions and Associations

While there are no specific unions or organizations that represent Business Development Directors, membership in such umbrella trade associations as the American Management

Association (AMA) and the American Marketing Association (AMA) may prove useful in order to share mutual concerns and to network.

Tips for Entry

1. In college, take basic computer courses along with your business and marketing courses.
2. While playing plenty of games, familiarize yourself with all aspects of the game playing community, including player preferences for genres, frequently visited sites, and all the relevant industry magazines.
3. Having some direct knowledge of game development is very useful. Learn as much as you can about the challenges faced by developers in introducing games into the marketplace.
4. Some public relations and marketing departments within game publishers have internships, which is a great gateway into a company and the industry.

CHIEF TECHNOLOGY OFFICER

CAREER PROFILE

Duties: Create and implement the overall technology strategy of a game development company or game publisher

Alternate Title(s): Chief Technical Officer; Director of Technology; Program Manager

Salary Range: $55,000 to $120,000 or more

Employment Prospects: Poor

Advancement Prospects: Poor to Fair

Prerequisites:

Education or Training—Bachelor's degree in computer science required; master's of business administration degree recommended; management training a necessity

Experience—Five to 10 years' experience in game development; significant management experience

Special Skills and Personality Traits—Ability to think laterally and spot interconnected business issues and impacts; capable of balancing business needs with game development interests; excellent verbal/written communication and presentation skills; highly organized team player with experience in collaboration with other departments; self-motivated, proactive, and a problem solver; solid business and commercial understanding

CAREER LADDER

```
┌─────────────────────────────────────┐
│  CEO of Game Development Company      │
│  or Publisher; Game Developer         │
└─────────────────────────────────────┘

┌─────────────────────────────────────┐
│      Chief Technology Officer         │
└─────────────────────────────────────┘

┌─────────────────────────────────────┐
│         Lead Programmer               │
└─────────────────────────────────────┘
```

Position Description

Chief Technology Officer (CTO) is an executive position that focuses primarily on the technical issues facing a company. Generally, the post calls for an operational executive who can make critical strategic decisions that impact the competitive position of the firm within the business sector.

For game development companies or publishers, Chief Technology Officers are responsible for creating and implementing their technological strategy. That strategy can include such decisions as whether the company should create its own proprietary game engine or license off-the-shelf components, which platforms to support technically for their games, or what technology trends in the field will impact the company in the coming year. CTOs constantly monitor new technologies as applied to the game industry and assess their potential usefulness to their firms' development processes and procedures.

As a high-ranking executive of the company, the CTO is a businessperson who measures innovation, research, and experimentation on the company's game products by the contributions they make to the operation's revenues and future competitive advantage. Thus, CTOs have to think about technology as a moneymaking asset, not as a field of exploration for its own sake. In addition, they may be required to negotiate with outside vendors and service providers to ensure that the company is receiving the resources needed for its game development but is not overpaying for these items/services. Thus, they are an integrated part of the executive staff, deeply involved in shaping and implementing overall corporate strategy, and much relied upon to assist in directing and managing the business.

As program managers, Chief Technology Officers guide each game project from its initial vision through its development, ensuring that the correct and/or breakthrough technologies are applied and that the right architecture for the product is created. They define strategy and features for all aspects of a product, from systems architecture to user experience. As such, they work with other members of the development team (programmers, artists, and sound engineers) to translate the ideas of the game into a final consumer product. (In some cases, the lead programmer reports directly to the CTO and relays decisions back to the programming personnel.) CTOs document the necessary specifications, plan schedules, and generally ensure that decisions get made in a timely fashion and that everything is being accomplished according to the project's technical plan.

A Chief Technology Officer may also act as an advocate focused on customers' experience with the company's games, as well as being consumers' contact person with the company. In this process, CTOs will work with marketing and sales personnel to translate known customer desires and requirements into product features to be added to the game design. They then create the necessary functional specifications and oversee the implementation of them, working with programming personnel and other tech support.

Media attention to the company's products plays an important role in the success of these games. Constructing the images and information released to the media and the public is primarily the responsibility of marketing and sales personnel. However, CTOs may be consulted for their technical expertise to translate accurately product details into terms that can be marketed. In addition, they may be called upon to be interviewed by the media as experts who can speak authoritatively on a subject while always representing the company's interests.

Since most CTOs possess advanced college degrees, they tend to have multiple relationships with members of academia, which can lead to fruitful partnerships and even funding for technical research for their company. As a businessperson and representative of the company, the CTO must ensure that money and time devoted to such corporate and academic partnerships has a realistic potential of contributing to the firm's competitive advantage in the marketplace. Finally, as technical representatives of their companies, Chief Technology Officers participate in professional organizations and their associated meetings.

Salaries

In a survey of game makers' salaries in 2004 done by DeVry University, it was found that technical directors (CTOs) with three years' or less experience made an average of $63,750 a year. Technical directors with three to six years' experience averaged $77,129, and technical directors with six or more years of experience averaged $115,087. The highest annual salary for a CTO was reported to be $211,500.

Employment Prospects

Employment possibilities for technical game people aspiring to become Chief Technology Officers are generally poor. Smaller game development companies most likely will not have such a position in their more modest executive hierarchy. For firms that do employ a CTO, the competition for this prestigious and much sought-after post is extremely fierce. The most logical step for a programmer to achieve this job advance is to become, first, a lead programmer. Besides actual programming, the lead programmer position also encompasses administrative and management duties, all of which are excellent training for the higher executive level of Chief Technology Officer.

Advancement Prospects

The job of Chief Technology Officer is the highest technical executive job in the development departments of a game development company or publisher. The only more senior executive position is that of chief executive officer (CEO) for the company or a game developer entrepreneur starting up his or her own company.

Education and Training

Basic educational requirements for a Chief Technology Officer are a bachelor's degree in computer science or mathematics (with an emphasis on statistics) and, usually, a Master of Business Administration degree, as well. In a few rare instances, extensive management training may be substituted for a master's degree.

Experience, Skills, and Personality Traits

A Chief Technology Officer's experience with electronic game development should extend over at least three years, and more often, the requirement is six to 10 years as a programmer and a lead programmer. Experience as an administrator and manager are crucial elements in a CTO's background.

Chief Technology Officers must have a solid business and commercial understanding of the game development industry. The must be able to identify issues, solve problems, and present ideas cogently to upper management. Their communication skills across all levels within the company and with outside professional contacts must be exemplary. They should be able to oversee several game development projects at once, be able to spot interconnected business issues with these projects, and understand their potential impact on the company's competitive position. They need to apply technical processes to solve complex issues and be able to create and manage complicated project schedules. Their focus must always be primarily on the strategic positioning of the company and, then, on perceived customer desires and requirements.

Unions and Associations

Chief Technology Officers should find it advantageous to belong to such industry umbrella organizations as the International Game Developers Association (IGDA) and the Software and Information Industry Association (SIIA). As an executive of a company, the CTO may also wish to belong to such business associations as the American Management Association (AMA).

Tips for Entry

1. During your college years working toward a bachelor's degree in computer science, be sure you take some business administration or management courses as preparation for your career move to more executive responsibilities as a lead programmer and higher.

2. Check out *Research-Technology Management*, the publication of the Industrial Research Institute (http://www.iriinc.org) which publishes regular articles from Chief Technology Officers. Another publication to examine is *InfoWorld Magazine* (http://www.infoworld.com).

3. As you move up into a management position, remember that a good manager knows when and how to delegate. One part of your duties is to hire people who can take care of the smaller details for you, leaving you free to work on the larger development management picture.

EXECUTIVE PRODUCER

Duties: Responsible for the production process of an electronic game's development

Alternate Title(s): Senior Producer

Salary Range: $50,000 to $120,000 or more

Employment Prospects: Poor to Fair

Advancement Prospects: Poor

Prerequisites:

Education or Training—Bachelor's degree in computer science, electronics, information technology, or allied field usually required; master's degree in business administration (M.B.A.) may be helpful

Experience—Five to 10 years' experience in game development processes and management; extensive background in game product development, implementation, and promotion

Special Skills and Personality Traits—Ability to sense good game products; attention to detail; excellent leadership and communication skills; knowledge of budgeting, scheduling, and project management techniques; superior negotiation and organizational capabilities; well versed in both the business and creative elements in game development

```
Vice President of Product Development
```

```
Executive Producer
```

```
Producer
```

Position Description

An Executive Producer is the lead producer in a game development company and is responsible for the efforts of other producers and their teams. In addition, Executive Producers often oversee multiple game projects and multiple teams. They handle the highest-level work relationships in production and maintain connections with marketing, public relations, sales, the legal department, and anyone else in other areas who might have any impact on the product(s) under their management control.

Executive Producers are overall project team leaders. They carry the responsibilities for the concept, design, and, usually, the development (art, audio, programming, and so on) of a game. In addition, they often are accountable for all game products in a given franchise (say, all racing games within the *Need for Speed* business franchise).

Executive Producers need to be project leaders; that is, they must have a complete understanding of the consumer audience and the creative definition of the game that is being prepared. They are often team leaders as well, which means that they maintain the focus and productivity of a large number of people on the production team. Executive Producers manage people, processes, and technology to balance the scope, resources, and time necessary to deliver the final product: hopefully, a highly rated and successful game. In any product development organization, senior executives must decide how to allocate resources across a number of potentially successful products. The Executive Producer has to present a game concept in a compelling way to upper management executives. As the approved game development progresses, Executive Producers have to report on the game's progress and present its potential sales success in an effective manner to their superiors. These presentations typically involve extensive and lengthy preparation by teams under the guidance of the Executive Producer.

As a senior development executive, the Executive Producer must be proficient in both the business and creative elements of administering an entertainment software franchise, which is what a game development company or publisher is. Executive Producers must have a complete understanding and foresight of critical business issues related to the game as a brand. (A brand is a very important part of software marketing, as it includes the distinctive name identifying the game product and the manufacturer. A game product may be a part of a brand of games produced by the company, and it must be consistent with the company's vision for the overall brand and support the main strengths of the brand and its expansion.) As a part of their responsibilities to the company, Executive Producers are tasked with managing the business profit and loss statement for the brand (and its games) and with achieving the determined fiscal corporate goals. This might mean cutting some game projects in favor of approving others. This also means that the Executive Producer always has to look at the big picture of the brand and how investing in it is going to be financially rewarding for the company. In addition, they negotiate relevant development contracts and license agreements, and they work with senior management in creating the firm's overall product plan.

Another aspect of the Executive Producer's job may be leading the global business effort and advocating the vision of the brand and its games. An Executive Producer's presentation skills (to both senior management and the media), persuasiveness, and ability to instill and inspire confidence are key abilities in these arenas. Having sufficient seasoning in the industry helps Executive Producers to distinguish between game products of high potential impact and those that will likely fail, and this experience is critical in helping them to establish their reputations and instill that confidence in their abilities for both the press and the senior management to whom they report. Complete self-assurance in determining how best to exploit the brand (and its games) on given hardware and software platforms (such as Xbox, PlayStation 2, or GameCube) to the intended game players' user base and key demographic(s) is another essential talent. This means that Executive Producers must possess a thorough understanding and vision for each game product in a brand and how it can live up to its maximum potential on each platform.

Salaries

In their survey of video game makers' 2004 earnings, DeVry University found that electronic game Executive Producers with three years' or less experience made an average of $52,533 a year. Executive Producers with three to six years of experience averaged incomes of $79,989, and those with six or more years of experience averaged $118,417 a year. The highest reported salary in this survey was $210,000.

Employment Prospects

The position of Executive Producer is not an entry-level position, and Executive Producers of other types of entertainment (or software) products (such as music, television shows, or films) are unlikely to be hired as Executive Producers in the game industry. The nature of the work is just too different. The only real way to obtain this position is by completing and shipping successful game products. Many experienced and successful game producers aspire to, and become, Executive Producers when such posts become vacant either in their own companies or by transferring to a larger game development company or game publisher.

Advancement Prospects

The position of Executive Producer is the most senior and most responsible in the production team ladder in both game development companies and game publishers. As it combines both creative and business elements, the only real advancement, open to Executive Producers is to become a vice president of product development, who generally reports directly to the company's president or CEO (chief executive officer). As this position does not become vacant often, the chances of such promotion are slim.

Education and Training

As applicants for production positions in the game industry, future Executive Producers should have a bachelor's degree in computer science, information technology, or some allied field, or even a liberal arts degree. As they advance their careers from beginning producer status to that of producer and then Executive Producer, they should take additional management courses, or even earn an M.B.A. degree, as many of their tasks as Executive Producer are administrative in nature, and they will be dealing more with business issues than with production or game development technical concerns.

In addition, Executive Producers must have a comprehensive knowledge about the game industry, its trends, patterns, and motivations. They must constantly undertake research to keep abreast of all new movements, styles, and technological changes in the industry that may affect their company's competitive edge and sales.

Experience, Skills, and Personality Traits

Executive Producers usually climb through the ranks of the production department from beginning producer to producer and then to Executive Producer, concentrating as much on the business areas as on the creative ones. Their management skills must be exemplary, as they most likely will manage the production team, and their communication skills must be excellent, as they will work closely with other sections of the development team. They need to be able to manage meetings efficiently and effectively and be able to communicate well with the public and the media.

They must have excellent leadership capabilities and exhibit integrity and the ability to inspire trust and confidence. Their techniques of project management should always include risk assessment and contingency planning. They must be able to negotiate skillfully on behalf of their companies and be highly organized in all their business activities. They should have an exceptional ability to evaluate game product, coupled with a refined intuition into what makes a game fun and what game products will do well on their targeted platforms and in their intended markets. They should also have an understanding of and facility to integrate marketing concepts with the product development's creative initiative and unite both behind the new product. Above all, their zeal for the game industry as a whole must be unqualified.

Unions and Associations

Associations useful for Executive Producers include such umbrella industry organizations as the Academy of Interac-tive Arts & Sciences (AIAS), the Association for Interac-tive Media (AIM), and, most importantly, the International Game Developers Association (IGDA).

Tips for Entry

1. As communication skills are the key to success in product management, be sure to take speech and writing courses during your college education.

2. The best way to obtain your needed game development experience is to join a game development company. In production, the job route usually starts with testers, then assistant producers, then on to higher positions. Be willing to devote the years needed to learn all the ropes, as you will call heavily on that experience when you reach the administrative positions at the top of the career ladder.

3. Keep in mind that most successful producers combine a solid understanding of game construction technology and a reasonable amount of business sense and experience.

PRODUCT DEVELOPMENT DIRECTOR

CAREER PROFILE

CAREER LADDER

Duties: Provide product analysis of new games, evaluating their potential sales; identify market needs and potentials for new product; research and represent customer/market needs and desires; on the basis of research, recommend marketing methodologies to sell new merchandise

Alternate Title(s): Director of Product Development; Product Manager; Product Planner

Salary Range: $70,000 to $140,000 or more

Employment Prospects: Fair

Advancement Prospects: Fair

Prerequisites:

Education or Training—Undergraduate degree in business, communications, or marketing; a master's degree in business administration (M.B.A.) highly desirable

Experience—Four to eight years' marketing experience or relevant technical product management experience in a software development environment

Special Skills and Personality Traits—Ability to conceptualize and think creatively; comfortable interacting with technical personnel, product and marketing groups, and senior executives; excellent written and verbal communication talents; firm analytical and quantitative capabilities; knowledge of, and experience with, a variety of game products; strong time management and organization skills including the ability to manage several projects simultaneously; team player with demonstrated history of strong leadership, initiative, and ability to meet tight deadlines

---

Vice President of Product Development

Product Development Director

Marketing Assistant; Production Assistant; Planning Assistant

Position Description

The larger game software development companies and many software publishers have on staff both marketing managers and a Product Development Director. Sometimes called product planners, Product Development Directors focus on planning and defining the future of games (or game franchises) in development. They may also plan for the array of video game console products, or even on such peripherals as controllers, remote control units, headsets, and other future items. In straddling traditional marketing and development

responsibilities, product planners bring a marketing sensibility and a research process to game development.

Product Development Directors develop analytic frameworks for analyses of game market needs. They conduct investigations and evaluations of game products and related merchandise with regard to existing and potential markets and to different ways of marketing these products and services. They research and represent game customer/marketplace needs and help to ensure identification and prioritization of appropriate design criteria, pricing strategies, costs, and manufacturing schedules throughout the game development process. They influence product strategy by defining and validating customer requirements, user needs and patterns, trends, and customer segmentation. They identify new consumer opportunities by thinking strategically and analytically about the consumer technology landscape and emergent buying trends. In effect, they are the "voice" of the game consumer within the game development process.

With their focus on the development of the game product idea, they work with the marketing, sales, and business development teams to establish the product's feasibility and shelf life. They then coordinate with the development teams to concentrate their research and market analysis on the game development process. Throughout the development stages, Product Development Directors concentrate on game features, schedules, and trade-off decisions. In conjunction with the executive producer and the production staff, they shepherd the product through each phase of development and balance the various necessary compromises by aggregating, analyzing, and communicating customer feedback and the market research to the production team. Thus, they develop a market-wide competitive understanding to aid in the implementation of the game's product development plan, which includes projected costs.

Once this development plan is completed (with schedules and budgets projected), the Product Development Director then can work with the business development director in building the business models as well as identify fresh ways to generate revenue from the projected game. In this way, the director influences change within the overall development process without actually mandating it. Teamwork is critical, and the director must have an understanding of the goals of the game development company or game publisher and what part other departments and teams play in meeting those goals. This process demands careful communication and coordination between the Product Development Director and the other groups involved with the game development process, as well as marketing, sales, and business development departments. The Product Development Director frequently work's with the business development director in defining and executing marketing partnerships, such as joint agreements with vendors and distributors.

Whether employed by a game development company or a game publisher, Product Development Directors usually report directly to senior executives.

Salaries

For their extensive and critical responsibilities, Product Development Directors are paid well. According to a 2004 job valuation report released by Salary.com, typical Product Development Directors working in the United States earn a median base annual salary of $122,022, with salaries ranging from lows of about $70,000 to highs of $140,000 or more.

Employment Prospects

There are many planning, production, or marketing assistants who would like to become Product Development Directors, so there is severe competition for this position. In addition, needed experience in research, analysis, and strategic thinking comes only with years employed in a software development environment generally, and marketing of game products specifically. Individuals interested in this position need to be methodical and thorough in gaining qualifications for this job.

Advancement Prospects

Product Development Directors/Planners can make the transition into the development company's (or the game publisher's) upper levels of management, but only after several years of success. In addition, positions within the top executive levels do not become available that frequently.

Education and Training

A four-year college degree in business, communications (with strong business emphasis), marketing, or product marketing is a basic requirement for product development work. For Product Development Directors, a Master's in Business Administration (M.B.A.) is a necessity, as well. Their educational background should include an emphasis on both the methodology of software development and management theory and practice.

Experience, Skills, and Personality Traits

Product Development Directors should have a minimum of four to six years of experience within the game industry, generally, and specifically in marketing, product planning, strategic marketing, or business development. They should be very familiar with all modes of game distribution, from online to console and vendor. They should be practiced game players and have a strong consumer focus. They need to have clear, consistent oral and written communication abilities and excellent interpersonal skills. Their analytical and quantitative abilities must be exceptionally strong, as well as their performance evaluation and interpretation abilities as applied to their game and customer research.

Product Development Directors must be self-directed, highly organized, and able to handle multiple projects simultaneously and drive them to completion effectively and on schedule. Their strong team orientation must include the ability to maintain strong working relationships and interactions with vendors, distributors, development team members, product sales and marketing teams, and senior executives. Their problem resolution and decision-making abilities must be exceptional.

Unions and Associations

Product Development Managers may find it useful to belong to such umbrella industry groups as the American Marketing Association (AMA), the Marketing Research Association (MRA), or the premier organization for the game industry, the International Game Developers Association (IGDA).

Tips for Entry

1. During college, secure a paid job, an internship, or an apprenticeship in a market research firm to gain hands-on experience in the practice, procedures, and techniques of market research.

2. College courses that are extremely useful for future product planners include mathematics, research techniques, sampling theory, statistics, and survey design.

3. As an electronic game player, consider what attracted you as a consumer to specific games and how their marketing strategy was successful in targeting you for their product. Answering this question will give you insights into consumer behavior and purchasing desires that you will need to understand in your job as a product planner.

QUALITY ASSURANCE MANAGER

CAREER PROFILE

Duties: Ensure the development of quality standards and protocols for electronic games' quality assurance verification and testing; supervise the quality assurance department

Alternate Title(s): Gameplay Testing Manager; Quality Assurance Lead

Salary Range: $35,000 to $70,000 or more

Employment Prospects: Good

Advancement Prospects: Good

Prerequisites:

Education or Training—Bachelor's degree in computer science, electronics, information technology, or allied field required; some training in game development processes suggested; in some cases, a master's degree is required as well

Experience—Minimum five years' experience (six to 10 preferred) in quality assurance and testing for software products; knowledge of test automation programs and user acceptance testing programs; some technical management experience

Special Skills and Personality Traits—Ability to communicate technical information to both technical and nontechnical personnel, orally and in writing; attention to detail and strong problem solving and analytical skills; capacity to lead and manage staff while maintaining a hands-on role in quality assurance process; good at setting priorities and able to work in a fast-paced environment; self-motivated; thorough understanding of the game development life cycle

Special Requirements—Some game developer companies or publishers may require Quality Assurance Managers, analysts, and testers to have the industry certification from the International Software Testing Qualifications Board (ISTQB)

CAREER LADDER

```
┌─────────────────────────────────┐
│   Game Designer; Lead Programmer; │
│   Product Development Director;   │
│     Producer; Game Developer      │
└─────────────────────────────────┘

┌─────────────────────────────────┐
│    Quality Assurance Manager      │
└─────────────────────────────────┘

┌─────────────────────────────────┐
│     Software Test Engineer;       │
│        Test Lead Person           │
└─────────────────────────────────┘
```

Position Description

The quality assurance (QA) department is responsible for ensuring that every electronic game is bug-free (error-free), works on every possible system, and is ready to be sent out into the world. Quality assurance and gameplay testing are two of the most important steps in bringing an electronic game to completion before its commercial release. Both these processes guarantee that the product works as designed and that it provides sufficient functionality, usability, and fun to appeal to both critics and end users.

Usually, a game goes to the quality assurance team of analysts when all the bugs have been removed through various testing procedures. Although quality assurance may sound like just a fancy name for the same kind of testing, it is, in fact, a different aspect of the process. In quality assurance, the team does not try to determine whether the game is enjoyable or well balanced. The team is concerned *only* with the question of whether it functions properly as a piece of software. If a game crashes, responds inappropriately to a command, or displays something that it is not supposed to, it fails. Thus, while testing is concerned with improving the game's playability and with finding bugs, quality assurance is more concerned with appearances and the feeling of "correctness" that the game must exude. The goal of quality assurance is to confirm that a product meets certain standards, and that it does not contain flagrant errors. (The level of acceptable errors in game products is a constant concern for quality assurance professionals.)

Quality assurance is exacting work. While no special training is required, it does demand a rigorous approach to the job. Quality assurance analysts need to be extremely detail-oriented to the point of perfection. They also have to be hard-nosed about their statements of inadequacy in a game given to them to examine. They are the last line of defense against a game going public with a mistake in it.

Before Quality Assurance Managers can guide their quality assurance and test analysts on a particular product, they need to know the full development plan for the game's design, what tools they have on hand to find the bugs, and an estimation from production as to how many bugs may still remain in the programming code of the game. The first step is to set up a bug-tracking system so that when a bug is discovered, it can be traced and tracked through the code and fixed. While there are excellent computer tools to track and fix bugs, the most effective tool is a well-trained staff.

The supervision and training of that staff is a primary task of the Quality Assurance Manager. Even more importantly, it is the manager's task to ensure the development of quality standards and protocols to be used in the quality assurance testing. These managers oversee the design and implementation of policies and procedures for that testing, as well as evaluate the precision and accuracy of the testing and of the testing software and equipment. They continuously monitor the test plans and processes and advise on how the testing system is performing. They collate and analyze performance data and chart it against defined performance parameters. In addition, they are the final arbiters of when the game should be released as "clean." They decide when testing must stop, usually when during a specific amount of time bugs of a certain priority level have not been found or by a mathematical equation that estimates the number of bugs remaining in the code as compared to a criterion of what is allowable. Throughout this process, they supervise their staff in carrying out tests and checks and work methodically to establish a defined system that their staff can apply.

Salaries

According to industry sources, Quality Assurance Managers with at least 10 years of field experience can expect annual salaries ranging from about $50,000 to $70,000 or higher. The range of salaries for starting managers (with at least five years' experience in game development and testing) can range from a low of $25,000 to a high of about $40,000. Salaries tend to vary by location, the size of the game development project (or company, or publisher), and the experience of the manager.

Employment Prospects

Employment prospects for Quality Assurance Managers are good. The quality assurance process in game development is critical. As long as new games are being made, there will be work for those involved in the testing of them. Each team of testers needs guidance, supervision, and management, so the position of Quality Assurance Manager is a guarantee. With the continuous expansion of the game development industry, the job outlook for this position remains positive.

Unlike in most other areas of game development, both full-time and part-time employment is available within most quality assurance departments. For potential game developers, this is a great way to test whether this industry is appropriate for them. Testers and analysts who are full time (with a full salary and benefits) are often the minority on the team and are the senior members. Quality assurance departments frequently rely on part-time help when the testing needs peak and then let the part-time people go after a game finishes up.

Advancement Prospects

Many game developers and game designers see the quality assurance department as a launching pad for their careers. Quality assurance allows developers and designers to observe how the game becomes truly final and how various decisions help to shape a game. Some developers become testers (and, at times, eventually managers), but really want to be artists, programmers, designers, software engineers, and so forth. This type of career move is common in the industry.

Education and Training

The basic educational requirement for Quality Assurance Managers is a bachelor's degree in computer science, electronics, information technology, or some allied field. Some game development companies may require a master's degree as well.

Special Requirements

As a tester or a quality assurance analyst, a Quality Assurance Manager may be required by some game development companies or publishers to have an industry certification. This certification is issued by the International Software Testing Qualifications Board (ISTQB) as the ISTQB Certified Tester: Foundation Level.

Experience, Skills, and Personality Traits

Quality Assurance Managers must have at least five years' (and preferably 10 years') experience in quality assurance and testing. They need to be well attuned to the entire game development process and should be familiar with the various programming tools used in this process. In addition, their own computer abilities should include basic scripting skills, such as Perl and Shell. They need to be knowledgeable about bug-tracking systems and be able to write both high level and intricate test plans.

In addition, they need to have administrative experience and to have developed the necessary management proficiency. They should possess strong project management and analytical talents, as well as excellent written and oral communication skills. As managers, their interpersonal skills must be exemplary, and they must be capable of interacting professionally with colleagues and senior management. In their work, Quality Assurance Managers also must maintain a constant awareness of the business context of the development process and budgetary control issues that may affect testing procedures and time frames.

Unions and Associations

Quality Assurance Managers do not have a union that represents them. However, there are several associations that might be useful for career development and networking, such as the American Society for Quality (ASQ), the Association for Computing Machinery (ACM), the Institute of Electrical and Electronics Engineers (IEEE), the Quality Assurance Institute (QAI), and the Society for Software Quality (SSQ).

Tips for Entry

1. Along with your other computer courses in working toward your bachelor's degree, take basic courses in programming to learn how user interfaces are designed, as they are an important part of game development. Languages like Virtual Basic are useful, as they make it easy to experiment with interface ideas.

2. While in college, seek out game development companies that need play testers. In addition, to gain practical experience, you can test "shareware" programs and correspond by e-mail with their developers, who often appreciate such feedback.

3. A course in business administration or management techniques might be of great use as background in your career move to Quality Assurance Manager, but be willing to put in three to five years as a tester or analyst to gain the necessary skills in game testing.

PRODUCTION

ASSISTANT PRODUCER

CAREER PROFILE

Duties: Provide support to the associate producer and the producer of an electronic game

Alternate Title(s): Production Assistant

Salary Range: $20,000 to $45,000 or more

Employment Prospects: Fair to Good

Advancement Prospects: Good

Prerequisites:

Education or Training—Bachelor's degree in liberal arts or computer science is suggested for all applicants for production jobs; in some cases, a high school diploma is all that is required

Experience—Computer or graphics art background; solid gameplay skills; some experience, usually two to three years, in a production environment, preferably in games development, but work in film or in advertising may also be acceptable

Special Skills and Personality Traits—Ability to fit into a dynamic, creative team environment; attention to detail; confident and motivated; excellent oral and written communication abilities; good organizational talents; comfortable with working in a deadline-prone environment and under stress

CAREER LADDER

```
┌─────────────────────────────────┐
│      Associate Producer          │
└─────────────────────────────────┘

┌─────────────────────────────────┐
│      Assistant Producer          │
└─────────────────────────────────┘

┌─────────────────────────────────┐
│  Game Tester; College Graduate   │
└─────────────────────────────────┘
```

Position Description

Assistant Producers generally are at the bottom rung of the production ladder, the first level where they begin to get involved with building games as opposed to simply testing them or aiding other more senior members of the production team. As such, Assistant Producers do a tremendous amount of tedious work, some of it creative, but much of it not. What they will find is that they soon will be waist deep in the minutiae of the development process, which, of course, is how one learns the ever-changing game business.

Assistant Producers ship and receive documents, equipment, and CDs, sending them on to development personnel. They assemble data needed by the development teams and convert them into a form usable by designers and programmers, such as athlete photographs for a new sports game.

They test the milestone deliveries (when specific parts of the game development are to be delivered, debugged, and ready to be made part of the game plan) to determine if they meet specific requirements. Assistant Producers do the actual examination of the game or the materials to ensure that all the specifications have been fulfilled and report their findings to the associate producer or the producer. They may be assigned to assist the quality assurance groups in testing a game and to maintain the bug database during testing phases as well. (The bug database is a computer record of all bugs, or problems, found by testers in the game programs, which, in turn, are turned over to programmers to fix and then to be retested for assurance.)

Assistant Producers may also be tasked with managing assets. As game projects evolve and the teams grow larger, the amount of data generated during development explodes. The typical high-end program has hundreds of thousands, or even more than a million, computer files to manage. The asset manager (in some cases, the Assistant Producer) has the seemingly impossible task of keeping track of every one of these files (assets), which ones are the latest version and where the previous versions are stored, and whether all updates have been tracked properly. Most development companies have rudimentary tools to help in asset management, but ensuring the safety and usability of data is still a time-consuming and very necessary task.

It often falls to the Assistant Producer to supervise the daily build (collection of executable data files) and maintain the backup for that work. When a game project is well under way, the Assistant Producer has to ensure that the current playable version is always on the network utilized by all development teams. In addition, Assistant Producers they are usually responsible for ensuring that a solid daily, weekly, and monthly backup plan of all material is in place and implemented. The Assistant Producer often generates most of the management paperwork associated with the game project, including submissions to console manufacturers (on whose equipment games will run) to satisfy their approvals process.

Salaries

Typical of beginning positions within the game industry, Assistant Producers usually have the lowest earnings of anyone on the production team. Their annual starting salaries may start as low as $20,000 and go only as high as $45,000. Their income depends heavily upon both their experience and the duties and responsibilities they are assigned and may vary considerably from one company to another.

Employment Prospects

Opportunities for employment as Assistant Producers are strong. It is the entry point for individuals desiring to get involved in game projects, even though they are not programmers or design artists. Many such people start out as game testers (either through an intern program or at a nominal salary), which is a good route into game design. From there they move up to the position of Assistant Producer, which will involve them even deeper in the game design and development process.

Advancement Prospects

The natural advancement step for Assistant Producers, is to become associate producers, who are the heart of the production team and the key helpers of the producer. All their skills as Assistant Producers are directly applicable to their duties as associate producers, with the added responsibilities of working with and supporting the producer.

Education and Training

A bachelor's degree in computer science, or liberal arts with computer courses, is the usual requirement for production jobs in the games industry.

Experience, Skills, and Personality Traits

Participation in some type of production environment is good seasoning for a candidate aiming for an Assistant Producer position. Some companies prefer the background to be in games development, but film or advertising at a large or multinational company may be acceptable as well. Any experience with software project development and management is a plus. Assistant Producers should be knowledgeable about computer operating systems, and have word processing, spreadsheet, and database software skills. They need to have an excellent understanding of electronic games in general, as well as the processes of developmental artwork and art production. Their game-playing experience should extend to familiarity with one or all of the HH game platforms (PSP, DS, or GBA).

Assistant Producers need to be self-confident with good motivational abilities, strong interpersonal skills, tact, and diplomacy. They must be capable of fitting smoothly into a creative team environment and be comfortable with deadlines and performing under pressure. They should be heavily detail-oriented, be well organized, and have superior written and oral communication talents.

Unions and Associations

There are several associations whose membership may be valuable for Assistant Producers, including such umbrella industry organizations as the Academy of Interactive Arts & Sciences (AIAS) and the Association for Interactive Media (AIM), and, most importantly, the International Game Developers Association (IGDA).

Tips for Entry

1. While in college, seek out intern jobs with game development companies or game publishers. Most beginning intern positions involve game testing, which is an excellent way to learn the specifics of game development, make contacts, and prepare the way for your job search for a production post.
2. As preparation for your production positions (and as an ongoing career project), learn all you can about the fast-changing game industry. When you obtain your production position, you need to quickly become well acquainted with your company and about the vision of the project on which you work. In addition, you need to keep on top of industry news, trends, and competitive game titles.
3. Never consider any task given you as Assistant Producer to be too small, as all your experience adds to your overall knowledge, and never be afraid to ask questions.

ASSOCIATE PRODUCER

CAREER PROFILE

Duties: Work in conjunction with the producer in all aspects of production of an electronic game, focusing on internal team-level communication and project-specific issues

Alternate Title(s): Assistant Producer

Salary Range: $45,000 to $85,000 or more

Employment Prospects: Good

Advancement Prospects: Good

Prerequisites:

Education or Training—Bachelor's degree in liberal arts with computer courses or in computer science with liberal arts courses is suggested for all applicants for production jobs; in some cases, a high school diploma is all that is required

Experience—Minimum of three years of production experience with one or more complete development cycles in a production role, working with software developers, artists, and designers from preproduction to shipping of final product

Special Skills and Personality Traits—Excellent people and communication abilities; exceptionally well organized with good time management skills and an aptitude for focusing on priorities, risk assessment, and problem solving; extremely detail-oriented, energetic, and good at multi-tasking; solid understanding of the entire game development process; strong technical background

CAREER LADDER

```
┌─────────────────────────────┐
│         Producer            │
└─────────────────────────────┘

┌─────────────────────────────┐
│     Associate Producer      │
└─────────────────────────────┘

┌─────────────────────────────┐
│     Assistant Producer      │
└─────────────────────────────┘
```

Position Description

Associate Producers (or APs) are at the heart of the production team, aiding the producer, overseeing all aspects of production from the start to the finish, and solving problems as they occur. They do the majority of the hands-on work, assets (data files) management, build (collection of executable data files) management, and shepherd the project through the quality assurance (QA) phase. (Most Associate Producers began working in production as testers in the quality assurance department.) Associate Producers are primarily focused on internal team-level communication and project-specific issues, freeing the producer to deal with more company-wide issues (e.g., platforms, deadlines, and financial goals).

Associate Producers assist the producer in budgeting and scheduling the game project in the preproduction phase of development. They confer with the design team about the structure of the game and the requirements as set by the developer (or the publisher). They keep continuous track of the development team's progress throughout the lifetime of the project, reporting back to the producer. They provide a comprehensive analysis of the development tasks to facilitate decisions based on accurate and measurable information about all assets utilized in the game process. They track all schedules, identifying any weaknesses, bottlenecks, or risks in the schedule and troubleshoot communication- and schedule-related problems, including the creation of contingency plans to recover from any setbacks. They monitor the day-to-day administration of the project, record and maintain project information and documentation, and report on project status to the producer on a daily basis.

Associate Producers schedule development milestones and aid the producer in overseeing internal and external expenditures. They identify all tasks' interdependencies and coordinate the effective use of staff to ensure timely and accurate flow of asset production. APs schedule regular meetings with the development team to discuss project status, resolve issues, and share information, thus facilitating team communication and ensuring the timely dissemination of information to all members. They work with the art, design, and programming department directors/managers to guarantee adequate, efficient, and effective project staffing, and help the producer to deal with any staffing conflicts. Within these consultations, APs distinguish, for team members and other departments, between high and low priority items, focusing on areas yielding the greatest return, and make sound determinations based on what requires a "sense of urgency." They participate in ongoing milestone evaluation and work with the producer in creating the production plan review and resource plan. (They may be delegated the task of facilitating this milestone review and publishing consistent documentation of the review's findings for use in future game developments.)

Associate Producers also maintain contracts with and help direct individuals or organizations outside the project in the creation of assets to be used in the project, such as independent contractors, talent, music, sound, voice, and video production. In their management of these external developers and contractors, APs ensure that the outside providers keep to their contractual requirements. In addition, APs provide support for ongoing marketing, public relations, and sales demonstrations and reviews concerning the project. This support usually includes live demonstrations of the product for retail and media purposes. They also may attend trade shows and other industry-related events, may demonstrate the product to potential buyers, and may help the marketing department in running consumer focus tests.

Salaries

Annual earnings for Associate Producers range from a low of about $45,000 to a high of $85,000 or more, according to industry sources. Salaries are inclined to vary by location, the size of the company and the project(s), and the experience of the Associate Producer.

Employment Prospects

Most assistant producers aim to become Associate Producers, a career move that is facilitated by their growing knowledge and understanding of the entire game development process. As Associate Producers, they will have to assist producers in the managing of this process, and their background usually gives them the tools with which to accomplish this task. Many game developers and/or publishers usually have more than one project in ongoing process at any one time, which guarantees the hiring of multiple Associate Producers and producers by these companies. In addition, many games are released on more than one platform (hardware on which the product is played), so that there is a need for more than one Associate Producer to take responsibility for the development for the various platforms (e.g., one handles the Xbox version, one the PS2 version). For all these reasons, employment prospects for individuals seeking the post of Associate Producer are good.

Advancement Prospects

The natural career progression for Associate Producers is to become producers. Because Associate Producers spend most of their time dealing directly with the production team and coordinating with other members of the total development group (artists, programmers, designers), they usually are in a good position to form a close bond with the team members. This bond will engender goodwill that will be advantageous for them and will follow them through the career move up the ranks. Many development companies and publishers like to "grow" their Associate Producers into producers by gradually increasing the scope of their duties. Additionally, some producers help to mentor Associate Producers by passing on their knowledge of the development process.

Education and Training

The usual educational requirement for production jobs in the game industry is a bachelor's degree in computer science with liberal arts courses or in liberal arts with computer courses. In addition, classes in business administration, project management, psychology, and human behavior may be useful to Associate Producers, as one of their primary tasks concerns human resources management and its relationship to the smooth flow of the development process.

Experience, Skills, and Personality Traits

In the vast majority of cases, Associate Producers should have a minimum of three years' experience in a production role, including the seasoning of one or more complete game development cycles. They need to demonstrate a solid understanding of the entire game development process, from preproduction planning and content creation through the budgeting and scheduling phases to the final approval stage (of testing and quality assurance) and, finally, to the marketing of the game product. In addition, they should have a working knowledge of hardware and software trends in the game industry and have a solid technical background.

(For example, they must understand game development pipelines and how various tools integrate into the game engines.) A familiarity with asset tracking software tools is an additional credit for them.

Associate Producers need to be self-directed, extremely detail-oriented, and very much problem solvers determined to contribute to the creative environment of game development. They should demonstrate exceptional organization, communication, and management skills and be able to handle multiple demands from both their superiors and their coworkers. They will need to maintain their professionalism in every adverse work condition but be flexible, receptive, and open to change.

Unions and Associations

Membership in several professional associations may be useful for Associate Producers, including such umbrella industry organizations as the Academy of Interactive Arts & Sciences (AIAS) and the Association for Interactive Media (AIM), and, most importantly, the International Game Developers Association (IGDA).

Tips for Entry

1. Consider adding business administration and human psychology courses to your college schedule of computer courses (or liberal arts classes), as these are skills that will be useful to you in handling the typical duties of an Associate Producer.

2. Learn all you can about the game industry, because, as Associate Producer, you will need to keep current on game industry news and trends, as well as competitive game titles.

3. As an Associate Producer, be both proactive (to stay on top of requests, problems, and tasks that have not yet been completed and are holding up other undertakings) and a facilitator to all members of the development teams, which will help you maintain a high morale throughout the production process.

4. Be process-oriented, as by establishing (and sticking to) processes that define how you handle your work (despite the daily disruptions that will occur) will not only translate into lessening the stress but also will make you more productive.

PRODUCER

Duties: Accountable for the entire production process of game development, and the final authority of creative decision regarding any given game

Alternate Title(s): Project Manager; Project Lead; Team Lead

Salary Range: $65,000 to $120,000 or more

Employment Prospects: Fair

Advancement Prospects: Poor

Prerequisites:

Education or Training—Bachelor's degree in liberal arts with computer courses or in computer science with liberal arts courses is the usual requirement for all production jobs; in some cases, a high school diploma is all that is required

Experience—Minimum of three to eight years of production and product management experience with five to eight game titles produced from inception to shipping

Special Skills and Personality Traits—Ability to negotiate complex agreements; excellent people and communication skills; exceptionally well-organized with good time management capabilities and an ability to manage multiple tasks as well as focus on priorities, risk assessment, and problem solving; extremely detail-oriented and energetic, with a thorough understanding of the entire game development process; strong technical background; willingness to travel when required

Special Requirements—Some employers may require a certification in project management

```
┌─────────────────────────────────────┐
│   Executive Producer; Vice President │
│       of Product Development         │
└─────────────────────────────────────┘

┌─────────────────────────────────────┐
│               Producer               │
└─────────────────────────────────────┘

┌─────────────────────────────────────┐
│ Associate Producer; Assistant Producer │
└─────────────────────────────────────┘
```

Position Description

The game development process encompasses both creative and production aspects, and these two facets are represented by game developers on the one hand and by game publishers on the other. Development companies do one thing: design and build electronic games. Most first-class games require teams of 15 to 200 people, and a development firm is a full-scale business, with design, artist, and programmer staffs, as well as administrators (but seldom any sales or marketing people, as their concentration is on development). They may have several game projects under way simultaneously, usually for one publisher with whom they have a contract to develop finished games (but sometimes with several different publishers, if the development company is sufficiently large).

A publisher is a company that funds the development of new games (by developers) and advertises them to the public. As the publisher paid for the game to be developed and placed it on the consumer market (and is responsible for its success or failure), the game is theirs. In most cases, the publisher actually owns the copyright on the source code and the artwork, making it truly their property. Publishers also usually have the final word on content. Some publishers develop and build the games themselves with their in-house staff of artists, designers, programmers, and audio engineers. Other publishers have no development staff and prefer to publish games done by development companies under contract. Many publishers work both ways concurrently, using outside developers for some projects and doing others in-house.

For the supervision of the game development process, there are two types of Producers. The first is the internal Producer who works at a development company and who is in daily contact with the development team, manages their work through the assistant producers, and, ultimately, is responsible for the team's performance. During the preproduction phase, internal Producers ensure that there is sufficient staff for the game development. They also supervise, or commission, the crucial design document for the projected game development. In addition, a project plan for the game is developed by the Producer working with the project manager. This plan defines the scope of the undertaking: how big and complicated the program will be and how much artwork, animation, and audio the game will require. Based on these conclusions, Producers will then estimate the size of staff required and how long the development should take. Throughout this process, the internal Producer manages and adjusts the schedule to stay on track. At cycle's end, the Producer works with the lead tester and lead programmer to handle the quality assurance check for bugs, and it is the Producer who decides whether the game is ready to ship. This individual represents the development team to the outside world (including the publisher's management, as well as the marketing, public relations, and sales departments). Some development companies call this Producer a project manager, product lead, or director.

The second type of producer is the one based at the publisher (the external Producer) who oversees the efforts of an external development company and manages the relationship and the development contract between the publisher and the external development team. The external Producer is responsible for getting the outside developer to deliver the game on time and within budget. While ultimately beholden to the publisher (i.e., his or her employer), the external Producer must also be seen by the developer as a valuable ally and member of the team. External Producers usually have extensive industry contacts to offer a developer in need of services, such as motion capture assets, sound design, or special programming. These contacts make the external Producer's task of seeing that the game is completed that much easier. In addition, the external Producer is the primary representative of the game project for the publisher to both the development team and to the outside world.

There are similarities in the challenges facing both internal and external Producers. They both make daily updates to the schedule and the budget. This information is generally provided by the developer, and the external Producer usually interprets it for any possible risks that must be faced to keep on schedule and within budget. They both serve as the primary contact for the development team with the publisher. They coordinate the efforts of the development team so that those efforts support the marketing initiatives of the publisher as much as possible. They manage all external contacts, such as deals with original equipment manufacturers (OEMs) and the media. (OEMs want to ensure that the projected game is compatible with their system and that their hardware includes the features that game developers need.) Keeping and managing media contacts is another demanding part of the Producer's job description. Finally, both types of Producers prepare and present progress reports and weekly updates either to the executive producer of a development company or to the executives of the publisher. This update process is critical, even during times of intense development, as it can facilitate any needed discussion of challenges to the schedule and their potential solutions.

Internal Producers define the monthly milestones with lead staffs from the development team. (Milestones are measurements of where the game project should be at certain points in time.) They maintain the team vision, resolving conflicts and maintaining harmony among all team members. Management of any outside contractors is also the Producer's duty, particularly in resolving difficulties with outside talent or vendors who deliver content or assets for the game that do not meet specifications or quality standards. In addition, they facilitate communication and decision-making at all levels with the development team and the executive management. Managing the development of new tools and procedures that enhance the development team's efficiency and ensuring that the development team is fully staffed and fully supplied with necessary equipment are also vital parts of the internal Producer's job. Producers may also work with the business development team of the developing company to evaluate new game opportunities and may also be responsible for documenting a post mortem for each project for which they are responsible to help other Producers learn from their experience.

Typically, external Producers are responsible for more than one game project at a time. They have to be sure that each of the projects is in a different stage of development to avoid conflicts on their time, as games require an enormous amount of attention on the part of the Producer. Producers' familiarity with the particulars of each game they manage has to be absolute. They need to know which features are essential to the game's success and which elements are just "nice to have." They will work with their executive management in choosing the external developer and must know all facets of each developing company's background, expertise, and capabilities. After the selection process is completed, external Producers need to get to know the development staff of the chosen company and how they work. They also need to ensure that their employer, the publisher, is responsive to the development team's needs. They must keep track of any redefinitions of what constitutes a milestone, any change in the delivery schedule, or any alteration to the payment schedule, as the contract between the publisher (their employer) and the developer may have to be amended.

Whether they are internal or external, Producers are the game's champion to the rest of the people involved in its development. They explain to members of the development team how the game fits into the publisher's plans and keep the team updated on the marketing efforts being made on behalf of the game. The Producer details the game's selling points to public relations and marketing personnel and explains to executives why a project should be kept in development even when problems arise. Producers may demonstrate the game at project review meetings and provide the product's current status.

Another crucial part of a Producer's job is risk management. Game developments never run smoothly. There are always roadblocks, and they come from both inside and outside the project. A Producer's job is to deal intelligently with the risks that threaten the game's progress and manage them to minimize any potential repercussions.

Salaries

Annual salaries for Producers, both external and internal, range from lows of about $65,000 to highs up to $120,000 or more. Incomes depend greatly upon the experience and responsibilities of the Producer.

Employment Prospects

It is unusual for an individual to enter the game business as a full-fledged Producer unless the person has already gained significant project management experience elsewhere within the software community. The most common path to becoming a Producer is to begin on the production team as a tester and learn the game business from the ground up. From testing, it is a small step to become an assistant producer and then an associate producer, who is deeply involved in the day-to-day development process and manages a significant number of individuals. The next step is to become a full-blown Producer, responsible for one or more games in development.

Advancement Prospects

The usual career advancement for a Producer is to become the lead producer in a development company: the executive producer, who has overall supervision of the entire development process. Alternatively, a Producer may advance to become vice president of product development for a publisher, with the attendant responsibilities of overseeing both the production of games and their distribution to the public.

Education and Training

Most production jobs in the games industry require the applicant to have a bachelor's degree in computer science with liberal arts courses or in liberal arts with computer courses. For aspiring Producers, courses in business administration, project management, psychology, and human behavior may prove useful with respect to the position's management duties. For most Producer posts, however, experience is more important than a specific education degree.

Special Requirements

Some employers may require their Producer to have an industry certificate in addition to formal college training. The standard certifications for project management, the Project Management Professional (PMP) certificate and the Certified Associate in Project Management (CAPM) certificate, are given by the Project Management Institute in Pennsylvania. They can be contacted by e-mail at customercare@pmi.org, or visited at their Web site, http://www.pmi.org.

Experience, Skills, and Personality Traits

Producers need to have a thorough knowledge of PC hardware, operating systems, and standard application program interfaces (APIs), which are formalized sets of software calls and routines that can be referenced by an application program to access supporting network services. They need to be familiar with PS2, Xbox, and GameCube hardware, development tools, and standard console manufacturer product submission requirements. They should have a good comprehension of all aspects of multimedia, film, the dynamic aspects of narrative, and game production—specifically graphics, design, programming, audio and video production, quality assurance procedures, and distribution (localization) processes.

When applying for a Producer job, applicants should have already completed three or more major game titles on PC or current console platforms and have a track record of on-time delivery as an assistant or associate producer. At least two to three years of experience as a project manager is usually the minimum requirement before any individual is considered for a Producer's role.

A Producer's comprehensive knowledge of game genres should guarantee the ability to spot good products and concepts prior to development. A background in competitive products, demographics, market preferences, and the biases of game players is useful in analyzing potential game projects. In addition, Producers should be familiar with standard project accounting practices, including budgets, profit and loss (P&L) statements, and *pro forma* financial analysis.

Producers should have exceptional organizational, communication, and management skills. They must be self-directed, heavily detail-oriented, and aggressive in finding fresh ways to problem solve and work through resolutions.

They need to be able to hold others accountable for their work product. They must excel as team players and strive to maximize group/department performance. Producers have to be the pillar of strength for the development team and must know the exact status of all aspects of the game project at all times. Their ability and confidence to approach the game project proactively will help them anticipate and solve problems before they detrimentally affect the project. Their enthusiasm for playing games and their keen knowledge of the software entertainment industry, game platforms, and genres will allow them to keep on top of industry trends and apply this knowledge effectively to the products developed under their management.

Unions and Associations

Membership in several professional associations may be helpful for Producers. They include such umbrella industry organizations as the Academy of Interactive Arts & Sciences (AIAS), the Association for Interactive Media (AIM), and, most importantly, the International Game Developers Association (IGDA). In addition, the Project Management Institute (PMI) offers career support, beyond their certification program, to project management professionals in all types of careers as well as useful monthly and quarterly publications.

Tips for Entry

1. During your college career, take business and psychology courses, as you will need these skills (such as dealing with persons, resolving conflicts, and managing budgets and schedules) as a Producer.
2. Keep in mind that Producers have their areas of specialty. If you are more creative (one who can lead and take a hands-on approach to designing a producible game), you are different from a Producer who goes searching for a new game title from a third-party software developer. Know your core competencies, strengths, and talents.
3. As a manager, encourage team members to tell you about problems, and, when they arise, gather all the data you can and work with the people who have the skills to come up with potential solutions.

PROJECT MANAGER

Duties: Under the supervision of the producer, keep track of all facets of a game development project and help coordinate efforts of the development team

Alternate Title(s): Production Manager, Project Coordinator, Project Planner, Schedule Coordinator, Scheduler

Salary Range: $50,000 to $105,000 or more

Employment Prospects: Fair

Advancement Prospects: Fair

Prerequisites:

Education or Training—Four-year college degree in business, communications, or computer science with a business emphasis; working knowledge of full game development process

Experience—One to two years of game production background with some responsibility on at least one completed game cycle through shipping

Special Skills and Personality Traits—Ability to work within team environment, exhibiting strong interpersonal skills with an emphasis on diplomacy; confident self-starter with motivational know-how; excellent communication and presentation talents; good understanding of game development techniques; some project coordination and scheduling seasoning; solid knowledge of electronic games in general; strong attention to detail and ease with working to meet tight deadlines

```
┌─────────────────────────────────┐
│  Producer; Executive Producer   │
└─────────────────────────────────┘

┌─────────────────────────────────┐
│        Project Manager          │
└─────────────────────────────────┘

┌─────────────────────────────────┐
│      Production Assistant       │
└─────────────────────────────────┘
```

Position Description

On most large game development projects, the producer may be too busy to keep personal track of the progress of all the development tasks. When this happens, a Project Manager is usually hired to assist. Project Managers are task and schedule checkers. It is *not* a management (or leadership) position. Rather, Project Managers' function is to manage the flow of information. They are the producer's task coordinators.

Their job is complicated due to the basic nature of game development. During game development, not just program code is being written. Still images, 3-D models and animation, music, sound effects, and user interface elements are just some of the tasks being completed concurrently with the writing of the programming code. Each of these elements requires a different procedure to bring about, and each requires different amounts of time to complete. Project management is the delicate art of balancing all these tasks, the resources (both staff and technical capabilities) with which they are accomplished, and the amount of time allotted for completion of these goals. It is the Project Manager who coordinates this according to an agreed-upon project plan.

Project planning begins during the preproduction phase of the game development process and is handled by the producer and the Project Manager. They define the scope of the project: how big and complicated the game program will be and how much artwork, animation, and audio the game will require. From these working assumptions, they estimate the size of staff required to develop the game and how long the development course will take. Thus, the project plan becomes the roadmap that describes how the game is to be built.

The plan starts with the game design document (which exhaustively details everything that will happen in the game) and establishes the interconnections between tasks, adds overhead hours, and develops a real-world schedule for accomplishing all the steps. The final project plan is usually broken down into separate components: a person power plan (usually a personnel spreadsheet), a resource plan (which calculates the project's costs), a project tracking documenting procedure (usually a software program that reveals dependencies and critical paths), a budget plan, a profit and loss (P&L) estimate (that is continuously updated), a development schedule (which is tied in with marketing and sales schedules), and a milestones definition process (in which significant points, called deliverables, in the development path are established as goals for completion time frames).

It is the ongoing task of the Project Manager to monitor the implementation of this plan throughout the development process, to keep track of any slippage in scheduling, and to report progress to the producer. This entire process is a very fluid one and that involves endless meetings to discuss issues, report on progress, and resolve problems. It is estimated that, in extreme cases, 40 percent of a programmer or artist's time and 80 percent of a manager's time is spent in meetings, making it clear that game development is an intensely collaborative activity.

Salaries

In its computer industry salary surveys, Salary.com found that annual earnings as of June 2006 for Project Managers ranged from a low of about $50,000 to a high of $105,000 or more, with a median annual salary of about $85,000, depending greatly upon the geographic location of the job and its responsibilities.

Employment Prospects

As the position of Project Manager combines production responsibilities with administrative duties (running meetings and task scheduling), the job of Project Manager is a natural career advance for production assistants. As a result, many production assistants seek to become Project Managers, so there is considerable competition for the job.

Advancement Prospects

Project Managers frequently look to become producers in their own right. Alternatively, it can be a transition move from the production development team to the higher man-

agement position of executive producer. In their scheduling and monitoring responsibilities, Project Managers are conversant with most aspects of game development, giving them the overall vision of the process needed by executive producers.

Education and Training

For Project Managers, a four-year degree in computer science or in a computer-related field with emphasis on business courses is a basic requirement. Their educational background should include a strong emphasis on both the methodology of software development and administrative management theory.

Experience, Skills, and Personality Traits

Project Managers must have an excellent understanding of the game development process and its techniques. They should have sufficient business background and computer proficiency to support their duties in scheduling and monitoring development activities. They must have strong negotiation, interpersonal, and conflict resolution skills, while exhibiting a great deal of tact. They should be accomplished communicators with excellent presentation talents. Heavily detail-oriented, they must be comfortable working within tight deadline schedules, and be able to fit into a dynamic team environment.

Unions and Associations

Project Managers may find it useful to belong to the International Game Developers Association (IGDA), the premier association of the industry. In addition, they may find membership in the Project Management Institute (PMI) useful for career support and for receiving their assorted publications.

Tips for Entry

1. College courses in business management, mathematics and statistics, along with a major in computer science, should provide a solid educational background for video games project management.
2. Exploring a wide variety of electronic games will provide the necessary broad background in gameplay and the techniques used to build today's ever more complex games.
3. As a production assistant, in order to gain experience and background, look for opportunities to assist the Project Manager of the game project in coordinating and scheduling the different aspects of the game development.

TECHNICAL DIRECTOR

CAREER PROFILE

Duties: Under the management of the producer, verify the correctness of the computer code utilized in the game development and evaluate the quality of computer programming used on the project

Alternate Title(s): Technical Advisor, Technical Producer

Salary Range: $46,000 to $110,000 or more

Employment Prospects: Fair

Advancement Prospects: Fair

Prerequisites:

Education or Training—Four-year college degree in computer science with business emphasis; graduate degree in computer programming or a computer-related field often required; working knowledge of technical aspects of game development process a necessity

Experience—One to two years of game production background with some responsibility on at least one completed game cycle through shipping

Special Skills and Personality Traits—Aptitude or working within team environment, but also operating separately as an advisor on technical issues to programming management and other executives; expert computer programming background; familiarity with game programming techniques and game hardware technology; good communication and interpersonal skills; solid knowledge of game software resources and tools

CAREER LADDER

```
┌─────────────────────────────────┐
│   Chief Technology Officer;      │
│   Director of Technology         │
└─────────────────────────────────┘

┌─────────────────────────────────┐
│      Technical Director          │
└─────────────────────────────────┘

┌─────────────────────────────────┐
│      Software Engineer           │
└─────────────────────────────────┘
```

Position Description

Producers seldom have the technical experience to judge the quality of the computer programming utilized in game development, or of the programming team as a whole. Some individual needs to check the programming code to ensure it meets software engineering standards and to advise the producer on technical issues. That person is a Technical Director, sometimes called a technical producer or a technical advisor.

Technical Directors are usually senior software engineers with a broad range of experience, which might even include management expertise. They are usually hired by a game software publisher to aid the developing company and its

producer. Technical Directors are *not* managers, but primarily advisors (though they may be given some authority by the publisher). One of their duties is to check each milestone delivery of computer code to guarantee it is as good as required. If it is not, they advise the producer not to authorize the next milestone (and its payment) until modifications are made.

In addition to examining the code and advising the producer, Technical Directors also serve as emergency resources for the game developing company. With their background, they can provide aid as needed, helping to track down particularly difficult software bugs or resolving other technical issues. They also may recommend particular technical approaches and help the program developers get the coding resources they need.

Finally, Technical Directors are used by game publishers to check out other new game development teams with whom they are considering working. Besides studying their résumés, talking with them, and examining their gear and facilities, Technical Directors often will inspect proposed technical designs of their proposed game product for its feasibility. Most Technical Directors have worked almost exclusively within the game industry, though some may have had experience programming the target hardware used in the gameplay and, thus, have experience with the industry while working primarily outside it.

Salaries

According to the U.S. Department of Labor's *Occupational Outlook Handbook,* median annual earnings of computer applications software engineers (including Technical Directors) employed by software publishers in May 2004 were about $79,930. The middle 50 percent earned between $59,130 and $92,130. The lowest 10 percent earned less than $46,520, and the highest 10 percent earned more than $113,830.

Employment Prospects

Software engineers with an enthusiasm and knowledge of electronic games in general would like to become Technical Directors for software publishers, resulting in considerable rivalry for this job. As there are a limited number of such positions available, chances of employment are only fair.

Advancement Prospects

While most Technical Directors are employed by game software publishers, some of them may advance to a higher technical management position within the development company, such as chief technology officer. Others may seek higher management positions within the publishing company.

Education and Training

For Technical Directors, a four-year degree in computer science or software engineering is essential, and a master's degree in a computer-related field is recommended. They should have a working knowledge of software applications in the game industry and a strong background in systems design.

Experience, Skills, and Personality Traits

Technical Directors must have an excellent reputation as a software engineer with superior problem-solving and analytical skills. They must be heavily detail-oriented and well organized. Their communication abilities must be strong as they will deal with both technical personnel and with management. They should have some administrative background and an extensive knowledge of available game software and related hardware.

Unions and Associations

Technical Directors should find it advantageous to belong to such industry umbrella organizations as the Association for Computing Machinery (ACM), the International Game Developers Association (IGDA), and the Software and Information Industry Association (SIIA).

Tips for Entry

1. As a software engineer, gain skills in such computer languages as C++, Java, and Visual Basic, as they are the major tools of game programming.
2. Exploring a wide variety of electronic games will provide the broad background in gameplay and the techniques used to build today's ever more complex games.
3. In your apprenticeship job, you, as a potential Technical Director, should seek to gain experience in designing programs, not just coding or testing them, so that you can be able to measure effectively the quality of the game programming you will be investigating.

PROGRAMMING

JUNIOR PROGRAMMER

CAREER PROFILE

Duties: Under supervision of a senior or lead programmer, write or revise computer programs for use in game development; test and document programs as directed

Alternate Title(s): Assistant Programmer; Entry-level Programmer

Salary Range: $45,000 to $65,000 or more

Employment Prospects: Fair to Good

Advancement Prospects: Good

Prerequisites:

Education or Training—Bachelor's degree in computer science preferred, but degree in electrical engineering, mathematics, or physics may be acceptable; in some cases, a master's degree is recommended; courses in technical writing and applications software development helpful

Experience—One to two years' experience in programming beneficial, with expertise in C programming and debugging preferred; some background in technical writing at school or elsewhere; strong knowledge of and experience with electronic games, either console-based or online

Special Skills and Personality Traits—Analytical and organizational ability; detail-oriented; good communication skills, both verbal and written; self-motivated and able to work within a team environment

CAREER LADDER

```
┌─────────────────────────────────────┐
│   Programmer (various positions)     │
└─────────────────────────────────────┘

┌─────────────────────────────────────┐
│        Junior Programmer             │
└─────────────────────────────────────┘

┌─────────────────────────────────────┐
│   Student; Amateur Programmer        │
└─────────────────────────────────────┘
```

Position Description

Computers manage much of present-day existence, from the operation of airplanes to everyday business transactions, from the automatic teller and debit card machines of banks to the diagnosis by doctors of illnesses, from the ordinary objects of life (like microwave ovens, VCRs, automobiles, and telephone answering machines) to the spectacular special effects displayed on the movie screen. Each of these devices can do little or nothing without a programmer's having first created a series of instructions (the program) to control its operation. So it is with the development and production of electronic games.

Programmers write their machine instructions in special languages, such as C++ (and other variants, all commonly used in game development programming), Java, and BASIC. The instructions specify how data will be recognized, orga-

nized, processed, and displayed. A different program, called a compiler, converts the instructions from key words and statements into low-level instructions called machine codes. These codes tell the computer processor precisely how to move each tiny piece of data and how to perform calculations. Most students taking computer courses have become familiar with the most common languages (C++ and BASIC) and have gained additional experience by writing programs for their own home computers.

As Junior Programmers for a game development company or publisher, they will work under the supervision of a senior programmer, usually the lead programmer. Some of the tasks on which they work might include writing short "utility" programs to perform simple tasks or writing a specified part of a larger program. They may be tasked to find and fix bugs in existing programs or make specified changes in an existing program (known as "program maintenance"). Most Junior Programmers will be involved in writing and/or organizing program documentation, which may consist of comments in the code itself or notes to be passed on to a technical writer. Junior Programmers usually work using detailed specifications provided by the lead programmer.

As Junior Programmers demonstrate their capabilities on the job, they may be assigned to work with more seasoned programmers on specific areas of the program development of the game. This variety of assignments provides Junior Programmers with opportunities to learn all aspects of the programming needed in game development and production. By functioning in all these areas, they may find the programming specialty that appeals most to them.

Salaries

Programming is one of the most highly paid technical professions available to recent college graduates. According to the National Association of Colleges and Employers, starting annual salary offers in 2005 for graduates with a bachelor's degree in computer science averaged about $51,000. Graduates with a bachelor's degree in computer engineering averaged $52,400 in 2005, and those with a master's degree averaged $60,300. According to Robert Half International, a firm providing specialized staffing services, starting salaries in 2005 for computer programmers ranged from $52,000 to $83,000.

Employment Prospects

Employment of programmers in general is anticipated to grow more slowly than the average for all occupations through the year 2014, according the U.S. Department of Labor, but the increasing expansion of game development and production will ensure that game development/publisher employers will continue to need programmers with strong technical skills who understand the game industry. This means that an applicant for an entry-level junior position as a programmer in game development must be skilled as a programmer and must, as a game player, be knowledgeable about various types of games. These people should enjoy working on tricky problems and love programming so much that they spend free time developing coding for their own enjoyment. One other element in their favor is that software publishers and computer systems design establishments are projected to be the fastest growing industries in the economy through the year 2014.

Advancement Prospects

As Junior Programmers become familiar with game development procedures and the game industry as a whole, they will have the chance to work with one or more of the separate modules of programming (such as AI programming, tools programming, or graphical user interface programming) and be in a better position to decide which specialty best fits

them. If they can successfully demonstrate their basic programming skills and show that they can take instruction and follow specifications exactly, their likelihood of advancing to a programmer position is greatly enhanced.

Education and Training

Besides the basic requirement of a four-year college degree in computer science or a related field, Junior Programmers should take courses in mathematics and be happy and comfortable with mathematical concepts. All electronic games are, at one level or another, mathematical models. Courses in graphic design and writing (composition) should also prove helpful in preparation for the various aspects of game software development. Junior Programmers should be knowledgeable in C++ and C computer languages, as they are *the* languages of retail game development. A familiarity with Java (which is used in Web-based games) would also be helpful.

They should have some acquaintance with the various programming tools employed in game development: a text editor designed to edit program code, a compiler (which converts program code into a high-level language like C++) and linker (which binds the different modules of a program together), and a debugger (which allows a programmer to watch the internals of a program while it is running). One way to gain this type of experience is to hire on as a game tester for the development company and then move on to an entry-level post as a programmer.

Experience, Skills, and Personality Traits

Like writing is for a writer, programming is the only way to become a programmer. Skill is developed by writing, testing, revising, and improving a variety of different kinds of programs, either in school or at home. The combination of computer science theory with practical applications builds a foundation of skills that will be necessary in seeking a programming job within the game industry, as it would be for most computer programming openings. These skills include tackling problems by breaking them into manageable parts and methodically testing program code to ensure its reliability. Other proficiencies include the know-how to transpose user specifications (such as those for game design) into appropriate objects (representations) that can be constructed into a programming language and using existing software to build into new applications.

Programmers need not only to visualize a variety of possible solutions to problems they encounter, but also to want (and look for) innovative, elegant solutions that closely fit the context of the situation. They need to communicate clearly and concisely, both verbally and in writing. In addition, they should be highly organized and self-motivated. They will need to work well with other programmers on the development team, and be able to take supervision and guidance from the lead programmer, or other manager. They must have good analytical abilities and a complete attention to detail.

Unions and Associations

Game programmers in general, and Junior Programmers in particular, should find it advantageous to belong to such industry professional organizations as the Association for Computing Machinery (ACM), the International Game Developers Association (IGDA), and the Software and Information Industry Association (SIIA).

Tips for Entry

1. Along with your technical courses in computer science, take classes in writing (composition) and/or technical writing, which can assist you both with your job appli-

cations and the documenting of program code, which will be a part of your job as a Junior Programmer.

2. Use school projects, internship programs, and any volunteer situations to gain actual programming experience that you can list on your job applications.

3. Study technical journals and publications devoted to the game industry. Use the Internet as a resource for learning programming tools and techniques, as well as finding employment possibilities. In addition, look for opportunities to be a tester for a game development company to gain experience in playing and debugging game software.

LEAD PROGRAMMER

CAREER PROFILE

Duties: Manage the programming team; be responsible for the team-based programming coding effort on all game projects; create and maintain the technical design plan

Alternate Title(s): Lead Game Programmer; Senior Programmer; Technical Lead

Salary Range: $60,000 to $100,000 or more

Employment Prospects: Good

Advancement Prospects: Fair to Good

Prerequisites:

Education or Training—Bachelor's degree in computer science or similar discipline (physics, mathematics, or electrical engineering) minimum requirement; master's degree often required, with some theoretical grounding in 2-D/3-D computer graphics

Experience—Three to five years' experience as a programmer in game development; some background in management and training of programming teams

Special Skills and Personality Traits—Ability to work with other game development personnel (artists, designers, and so forth); excellent written and verbal communication skills; experienced in programming code development, designing large scale game software, and low level engine programming; solid mathematics background (particularly linear algebra, trigonometry, and vector analysis); strong C/C++ programming skills

CAREER LADDER

```
┌─────────────────────────────────┐
│   Chief Technology Officer;      │
│   Director of Technology         │
└─────────────────────────────────┘

┌─────────────────────────────────┐
│        Lead Programmer           │
└─────────────────────────────────┘

┌─────────────────────────────────┐
│   Other Programming Positions    │
└─────────────────────────────────┘
```

Position Description

Programming is the hub around which everything revolves in game development. The software *is* the game, with the pictures and sounds its visible outward form. Because the software is the core into which all the other game assets (including animation, art, audio, text, and video) fit, programmers generally devote only about half of their work hours writing computer code. In addition to their writing, testing, and debugging software, programmers, under the leadership of the Lead Programmer, participate in meetings, design new game objects and game routines with other programmers, and smooth out details of the game development process with designers, artists, and audio team members.

Lead Programmers are usually involved with the game project from the start, along with the producer, designer, and lead artist. They indicate to this group what is technically achievable, damping down unrealistic expectations and identifying areas of innovation. They evaluate the delivery platforms planned for the game, and create an overall programming architecture that will maximize its strengths and compensate for any weaknesses. If the game is to be a multiplatform one, Lead Programmers must add special features geared to each of the different hardware platforms in order to take advantage of each system's internal structure.

During this preproduction phase, Lead Programmers create a technical plan. This is the technical design document that sets out the manner in which they plan to transform the game design from words on a page to software on a machine. The plan itemizes all the knowable tasks on the project and estimates the number of individuals needed and the time required to complete them. (From these projections it can be extrapolated what technical people are needed on the project and how long they will be involved with the project, which, in turn, directly affects the estimated budget.) These calculations must be tested continuously for their accuracy and to avoid problems that could disrupt schedules. The technical design document also describes the core tools that will be used to build the game, and it enumerates which of these are already in-house at the development company and which have to be purchased or created. These decisions about equipment and software pertain not only to the game engine but also to the collection of hardware and software tools that the programming team will use during production. In addition, the document lists any changes required to be made in the development company's infrastructure (such as storage capacity, backup capabilities, and network speed) to support the planned game development.

Preproduction is the window of time during which Lead Programmers build their programming team. They either hire them from outside the development company or select them from available programmers on staff. Assembling such a group may take some time. In addition, Lead Programmers have to ensure that the team is equipped properly and that the budget for the game project will support the best equipment and any possible needed upgrades during the project's life cycle. As managers, Lead Programmers need to provide a working area for programmers that minimizes any interruptions or distractions from their work. In addition, there has to be an infrastructure that will support the game development: a high-speed computer network for in-house use and huge amounts of data storage availability, providing the capacity of backing up everything continuously.

During production, Lead Programmers assign tasks to individual programmer and schedule their completion dates after consulting with them as to their own estimates of how long it will take to complete these chores. As the project progresses, Lead Programmers must track each programmer's estimates against actual results to load-balance the project and decide which features can be delivered on time and which ones must be deleted. During the process, Lead Programmers must become adept at explaining technical issues to management and other non-programming members of the development team so that the entire game squad can make intelligent choices together. In particular, Lead Programmers have to be practiced at explaining technical trade-offs to the producer.

As Lead Programmers have built their careers on acquiring technical proficiency and becoming excellent program coders, they may experience some frustration as they discover that the majority of their work effort is spent on administration/management issues. They must also find time to assess, mentor, and train new programmers. The larger the team, the more their work day will be devoted to administration, planning, scheduling, load balancing, reviewing code, and other management activities and the less of their time spent writing actual code for the game. However, in the end, it is their ability to estimate, schedule, inform, inspire, compromise, and lead that will determine the game's final design and what will appear on the screen for the end user: the game player.

Salaries

According to a video game salary survey conducted by DeVry University in 2005 on 2004 annual salaries, Lead Programmers with three years' or less experience made an average of $58,486 a year. Lead Programmers with three to six years of experience averaged $81,155 a year, and ones with six or more years of experience averaged $93,067 a year.

In a study made in April 2006 by *Game Developer* magazine (and available at their Web site, http://gamedeveloper.texterity.com), Lead Programmers with three years' or less experience now make an average of $76,848 a year, those with three to six years of experience now average $81,591 a year, and those with six or more years of experience now average $100,528 a year.

Employment Prospects

As every game development team needs a Lead Programmer to head up the programming group, the number of jobs available to programmers with the requisite computer background and administrative experience is dependent upon the number of games being developed both domestically and internationally. With the tremendous expansion of the game industry, vying successfully with other fields of entertainment for the attention of the public, the possibility of employment for prospective Lead Programmers is bright.

Advancement Prospects

Those Lead Programmers with six or more years' experience as team leader and a success rate of completed games may look for advancement to director of technology or chief technology officer of a game development company (or publisher). However, these posts become available only infrequently, so chances of advancement are lessened. As with other specialties, becoming an independent consultant for game developers or publishers is another possibility.

Education and Training

A bachelor's degree in computer science or a similar discipline (such as physics, mathematics, or electrical engineering) is the basic minimum requirement for this position. Many game development employers prefer their Lead Programmers to have a master's degree in computer science (or its equivalent) as well. As programmers, their math background has to be exemplary (especially in linear algebra, trigonometry, and vector analysis). A Lead Programmer's training should include solid understanding of one or more programming specialties, such as 3-D graphics and rendering, artificial intelligence (AI), networking, creature animation, audio (including real-time streaming), game logic, and game tools.

Experience, Skills, and Personality Traits

Lead Programmers need to have three to five years' experience, and preferably more, in game development and the game industry. They need to have shipped (completed the development cycle) at least one game. Their code-writing skills must be excellent. They should have some background in administrative duties and in management of different individuals all striving for a common goal. Their interpersonal skills, as well as their written and verbal communication talents must be outstanding, as they will be dealing with artists, designers, producers, and other non-programming personnel. They should be able to work with proprietary existing software technology, and build new technology when required.

As Lead Programmers are responsible for creating the user's experience on the game which they are developing, they should have some experience working on player controls for a character or game. They need an understanding of game scripting engine integration and at least a theoretical grounding in 2-D/3-D computer graphics.

Lead Programmers need to be patient and thorough and be able to envision the larger picture of the game development process from the specifics of game design and programming. Above all, their love of, and commitment to, the game design experience must be thorough.

Unions and Associations

Lead Programmers should find it advantageous to belong to such industry umbrella organizations as the Association for Computing Machinery (ACM), the International Game Developers Association (IGDA), and the Software and Information Industry Association (SIIA).

Tips for Entry

1. While working toward your Bachelor of Science or master's degree in computer science (or allied field), take courses in business administration and personnel management, as this background will greatly aid you when you apply for a position as Lead Programmer.

2. Learn as much as you can about the various types of programming necessary in game design development, as you will be leading individuals adept in these areas and must be able to communicate effectively with them.

3. Keep abreast with state of the art computer design by constant self-education. In that way, you can make the intuitive and creative decisions necessary as you lead your programming team during production.

OTHER PROGRAMMER POSITIONS

CAREER PROFILE

Duties: Artificial Intelligence (AI) Programmer: responsible for building simulated behavior patterns of characters (or creatures) in games; Audio Programmer: provide computer code to support the audio requirements of a game; Engine Programmer: in charge of building the primary technical foundation upon which a game is constructed; Gameplay Programmer: focuses on the strategy and the "feel" of the game experience; Graphics Programmer: tasked with developing and modifying 3-D graphic renderers; Input Programmer: responsible for the code specifying how input devices affect the game; Network Programmer: provides the computer code that allows game players to compete against each other connected via a local area network (LAN) or the Internet; Physics Programmer: tasked with developing the physics underlying all movements in a game; Porting Programmer: responsible for converting computer code from one operating system to work on another; Tools Programmer: accountable for building the tools that support complex game creation requirements of all kinds; User Interface (UI) Programmer: handles the building of the interface between the game player and the game

Alternate Title(s): Sound Engineer; Content Engineer; Server Programmer; 3-D Graphics Programmer; Utilities Programmer

Salary Range: $45,000 to $99,000 or more

Employment Prospects: Fair to Good

Advancement Prospects: Poor to Fair

Prerequisites:

Education or Training—Bachelor's degree in computer science, electrical engineering, mathematics, physics, or software engineering required (or equivalent work experience); in some cases, master's degree in computer science also required

Experience—At least three years, and preferably six or more years, of programming experience in game development

Special Skills and Personality Traits—Ability to work within a schedule and within a team environment; excellent written and verbal communication talents; good C/C++ programming abilities; good mathematics skills; problem-solver with a strong work ethic; self-motivated and well organized; strong background in 2-D/3-D programming techniques

Special Requirements—Licenses or certifications seldom required, but may be a helpful résumé addition and career booster

CAREER LADDER

```
Lead Programmer; Producer
```

```
Various Programming Positions
```

```
Entry-Level Programmer
```

Position Description

Programming is a creative activity, that of the computer software engineer/programmer who aims to construct something robust and useful. Programming requires a degree of what may be called *technical imagination,* that is, the ability to envision how a task can best be accomplished. Being a Programmer also requires a logical and painstaking mindset. Computers execute the instructions that a Programmer gives them, so these instructions must make sense. Programmers have to be concerned with every part of these instructions (coding) down to the minutest technical detail, as one misplaced keystroke has the potential for catastrophic consequences.

Game Programmers are the software engineers who plan and write electronic game software. They turn ideas, art, and music into a game that works. When designers describe an event that is to occur in the game, Programmers translate the idea into mathematical equations the computer understands. Game Programmers control the speed and placement of art and sound, such as how high a jeep flies over an obstacle in its path. In a low gravity environment, say on an alien world, Programmers might instruct the computer to move the car to a higher position to make the jump dramatically bouncier.

Game Programmers search for the most efficient way to write software with the fewest possible instructions and a fast processing time for those instructions. A slightly faster program could give artists hundreds of additional design polygons to use or game designers space for more features. By their very nature, online and 3-D games with their fast player response time make speed even more critical. Electronic games need to be flexible as well as fast. Good Programmers write code that can be changed without destroying the game. Some games have features allowing players to add new levels and effects. Moreover, if a program is sufficiently flexible, large portions of the software may be usable as components in other games.

There are many specialists on a programming team, each handling a different aspect of programming games. Each of these individuals works under a lead programmer, or, in some cases, a technical director.

Artificial Intelligence (AI) Programmers write programming code that will make computer-controlled characters (or creatures) perform realistically. They write the rules that will dictate how characters (and creatures) will react to the player's commands. AI Programmers develop the logic the game employs to carry out a large number of actions, such as pathfinding, strategy, and enemy tactic systems. AI programming is mostly about finding ways to allow a range of appropriate decisions in a given situation within the design and has become one of the most challenging aspects of game programming. According to *Game Developer* magazine, many contemporary games dedicate 60 percent of their programming staff to AI.

Audio (or Sound) Programmers work on programming code to support the game?s audio requirements. They may write intelligent audio spooling systems to stream music sections as background melodies for the game or develop custom-made computer code to handle specialized audio output formats. Computer audio games forego graphics altogether and use sound as their primary feedback mechanism, and many other games use advanced techniques such as 3-D positional sound. Audio Programmers dedicate most of their time to building and refining the game's sound engine, and may have a formal background in digital signal processing. In addition, scripting tools are often created and/or maintained by Audio Programmers for use by sound designers, allowing them to associate specific sounds with characters, actions, objects, and events, while also assigning music or atmospheric sounds for game environments.

Engine Programmers focus on game engine development and revision, the primary technical foundation upon which the game is built. They develop the broad architecture and the toolset for the game. They may not work on any particular game content, but rather on the software configurations that make other game content development possible. Various aspects of the game architecture may be doled out to members of the programming team. For instance, one Engine Programmer may be charged with doing all the death effects in a fighting game, and another may be responsible for implementing collision detection or integrating special effects in a fighting or sports game. Engine Programmers control how graphics are stored and reproduced by the computer. Recently, Engine Programmers have focused on making electronic games automatically reduce their level of detail when they run on a slower computer.

Though all programmers add to the content and experience that the game provides to the game player, a Gameplayer Programmer concentrates more on a game's strategy and "feel." By necessity, what this programmer does usually differs from one game to another, and they are frequently involved with the more specialized areas of development, such as sound or graphics. Gameplayer Programmers may implement strategy tables, modify input code, or adjust other facts that alter the game, but many of these duties can also be carried out by other programmers (e.g., strategy tables are often implemented by AI programmers). Large and complex games may well employ a separate Gameplayer Programmer rather than have their other programmers do these tasks.

Graphics Programmers specialize in developing and modifying the complex 3-D graphic rendering process that creates pictures from the data. Three-D rendering is a collection of software techniques that take the geometry of a three-dimensional scene made up of polygonal objects (which is the fundamental unit of graphical data which, when combined in the hundreds or thousands create a surface as seen in the picture) and display it on the screen from a particular perspective. They may also work closely with artists to preface the playback of animation designed for the game. Graphics Programmers must be well versed in advanced mathematical concepts and are highly valued members of the team. Their skills can be used for both computer games and products geared for game consoles (such as PlayStation 2).

Input programming, not necessarily a job title unto itself (or even a full-time position on any one game project), is still an important task. The Input Programmer writes the code specifying how input devices, such as a keyboard, a mouse, or a joystick, affect the game. These routines are usually developed early in the production and are modified continuously as needed. Normally, a programmer is assigned to these tasks as well as to other duties in other areas of specialty.

Network Programmers write the computer code that permits game players to compete against each other (or to play together)—connected via a local area network (LAN), the Internet, or, in rarer cases, directly connected by a modem. Network programming is one of the most challenging game programming roles, as it deals with writing computer code involving multiple game players. Network Programme have to consider network latency, packet compression, and dropped (or interrupted) connections. They must develop the networking system to be compatible with all features of the shared game framework, which may include abstracting online service user interfaces. They may help to define programming policies and guidelines to aid other programmers in creating networking-compatible software.

Physics Programmers are responsible for developing the physics behind making the movement of solid bodies in the game design look realistic. Typically, a game will only simulate a few aspects of real-world physics, those most critical to the gameplay. Since processing cycles are always at a premium, Physics Programmers usually employ shortcuts that are computationally less expensive, but look and act "good enough" for the product in development. Physics Programmers have to be entirely comfortable with both trigonometry and calculus, without which they can not understand the formulas needed for measuring distance or program even the most trivial of movements. Physics programming is used heavily in vehicle simulating games and sports games but is applicable to any game that presents solid bodies moving through it.

Porting (also called "converting") means taking a game that works on one machine and making it playable on another. Porting a game from one platform to another has always been an important activity for game developers. Porting Programmers specialize in this activity, converting computer code from one operating system to function on another or, in some instances, making the application work not for just one operating system, but a variety of devices, such as mobile phones. Often, however, the porting process can entail rewriting the entire game from scratch, as proprietary languages, tools, or hardware make converting the source code meaningless. Porting Programmers must be familiar with both the original and the target operating systems and languages (such as converting from a game origi-

nally written in C++ to Java) as well as the assets (such as artwork or sounds). Sometimes, the code has to be rewritten to scale for a wide variety of screen sizes or to implement special operator guidelines. In the process, programmers may find bugs that were never discovered in the game's original release.

Tools Programmers (sometimes called Utilities Programmers) write software for artists, designers, and audio designers to use within the development process. Some of these software tools convert art, sound, and gameplay into data that will work in the game. Other tools help developers to edit their work and see how it will look when the game is finished. Tools are used on almost every game for tasks such as scripting, importing or converting art for use in the game design, modifying behaviors of characters or objects, or building levels of the game. Some tools are proprietary to external owners (such as Photoshop and 3-D graphics modeling software), but many tools are designed specifically for a particular game and are custom-programmed by Tools Programmers. Some tools may be included with the game, but most will not. Most tools evolve with the game and can easily consume all of several Tools Programmers' time.

User interfaces in environments like the Windows or Macintosh desktop are pretty straightforward: menus and dialogue boxes, mostly supplied by operating system commands. User interfaces in electronic games, however, are far more challenging. Unlike ordinary software, games have to map a fantasy situation onto a limited input device, and they must be able to respond quickly, smoothly, accurately, and predictably at all times, regardless of the highly variable loads on the game player's CPU. User Interface (UI) Programmers specialize in this type of programming. Though some games may be designed with custom user interfaces, the User Interface Programmer is more likely to develop a library of interfaces that can be used in multiple projects. Present-day game user interfaces employ the same 3-D technology as the rest of the game, so the User Interface Programmer needs to have some knowledge of 3-D mathematics and systems.

Salaries

According to DeVry University's Video Game Makers Salary Survey, in 2005, video game programmers and engineers with three years' or less experience made an average of $54,300 a year. Game programmers and engineers with three to six years of experience averaged $68,072, and those with six or more years of experience averaged $86,243. In the April 2006 issue of *Game Developer* magazine, the magazine's fifth annual salary survey stated that programmers and engineers with three years' or less experience made an annual average of $52,989. Those with three to six years experience received an average of $73,618, and those with six or more years of experience made an average of $90,658. Some positions (such as Artificial Intelligence Programmers and Graphics Programmers) attract the highest salaries due to the expertise needed. The lowest-paid programmer is usually the Gameplay Programmer.

Employment Prospects

Employment demands for computer programmers in the game industry remain fairly strong. There is more game development in progress than ever before, which helps create that demand. However, games are getting more and more sophisticated and complex, meaning that computer programmers must have the requisite game experience (possibly as entry-level programmers or a game tester position in the quality assurance department) to even be considered. In addition, programmers need to be familiar with more than one programming specialty. It should be noted that the skills involved in game programming are very similar to those used in multimedia and Web development, so prospective programmers willing to purse all three areas have an even better chance at finding employment.

Advancement Prospects

The logical advancement for programmers in general is to expand their talents into administrative and training work, leading to a position as lead programmer. Some may decide to become producers in their own right. Low-level programmers, such as Gameplay Programmers, may advance both their careers and their salary earnings by becoming involved in one or more of other special programming jobs.

Education and Training

The basic requirement for programmers looking to work in the game industry is a bachelor's degree in computer science, software engineering, or mathematics (or getting the equivalent level of understanding on their own). Some specialties, such as engine programming, have a greater need for a superior background in mathematics, but all programmers need strong math skills, as they are translating ideas into numerical equations. As veteran game producer and designer Tom Meigs states in his book *Ultimate Game Design,* "Gathering knowledge of many games is the easy part. … The tough part seems to be gaining enough understanding of the pure foundational mathematics and physics to get the intended effect out at the other end of your code."

Many of the skills most in demand by game development companies are seldom taught in school. A student who can show exceptional skill in 3-D texture-mapped graphics may have a better chance than one who has extensive theoretical knowledge but little actual experience.

Special Requirements

While there are no certifications or licenses required in game programming, there are professional certifications available that may enhance a programmer's professional standing. The Institute of Electrical and Electronic Engineers (IEEE) offers the designation of Certified Software Development Professional (CSDP). Professional certification is also available through the Institute for the Certification of Computing Professionals (ICCP) and other professional associations devoted to computer programming.

Experience, Skills, and Personality Traits

Unlike testing and producing, which are professions that can be learned on the job while working at upward career advancement, programmers are expected to know their stuff already (which may explain the higher initial pay rate for beginning programmers). Programmers are expected to have programmed either a game or parts of one before job-hunting for a position as a programmer with a game development company. One way to gain this needed experience is to write one or more "shareware" games and make them available on the Internet. Shareware games can be downloaded and played by anyone for free (although the user is expected to pay the developer some fee upon visiting the game more than once). The objective is for the programmer to gain experience, including receiving feedback on their own programming and game design skills.

Game programmers should learn C and C++, as these are the programming languages most often used in the industry. Many jobs may also require a knowledge of assembly language. Most games, especially console games, tax the hardware to the limit, and tight, optimized computer code is required to allow the game to run at its usual target frame rate of 30 to 60 frames per second. That is why compiled rather than interpreted code is usually used. Almost all PC games also employ either the DirectX or OpenGL Application Programming Interfaces (APIs) to interface with hardware devices. In addition, most game programmers specialize on one platform (operating system) or another. For example, a programmer can concentrate on the Xbox, GameCube, or PlayStation 2. Thus, specialists in one type of game programming discipline may also specialize in development on a certain platform. Some disciplines, such as Artificial Intelligence (AI) and 3-D graphics programming are naturally transferable between platforms.

Programmers must have the ability to work within a schedule and to function comfortably within an established programming code framework. They must be self-motivated, be highly organized, have a strong work ethic, and be able to work as part of a team. Their problem-solving capabilities must be exceptional, and they should display excellent oral and written communication skills.

One nice aspect to game programming as a career is the fact that programmers can eventually gravitate in a number of directions. They can focus on areas that meet their interests: graphics or rendering, audio, tools, compression, AI development, or software development management. Another bonus to this work field is that there will always be a demand for programmers who can write *fast* code.

Unions and Associations

Many game programmers should find a professional advantage in belonging to such industry umbrella organizations as the Association for Computing Machinery (ACM), the International Game Developers Association (IGDA), and the Software and Information Industry Association (SIIA).

Tips for Entry

1. In taking your courses in computer science, look for those dealing with principles and algorithms for decision-making, data structures, and graphics. Combine them with classes in specific programming languages (especially C++ and Java, the latter in particular being popular for Internet-based games).

2. Read game magazines and search Internet newsgroups on gaming development to find development companies with entry-level programming positions. Remember to develop and constantly update your demo or portfolio of your game programming achievement, as this is absolutely critical in order to break into the industry in such a skill-based position as a programmer.

3. Create a simple game or two, then possibly work on a larger shareware game effort that will become the centerpiece of your portfolio.

4. After achieving a programming position with a game developer, become familiar with several aspects of game programming other than your own specialty so that you can expand your programming career and achieve both a higher status and a higher salary.

QUALITY ASSURANCE AND TESTING

GAME TESTER

CAREER PROFILE

Duties: Play and test games being developed to locate bugs (problems) and to identify potential changes to improve their playability; test games on various types of hardware to be sure they work on all of them

Alternate Title(s): Configuration Tester; Game Analyst; Playtester; Quality Assurance Analyst

Salary Range: $25,000 to $50,000 or more

Employment Prospects: Fair

Advancement Prospects: Fair to Good

Prerequisites:

Education or Training—While there are no formal requirements, graduation from high school is recommended, and a college education is a further enhancement

Experience—Familiarity with a wide variety of electronic games; if configuration testing, knowledge of various game platforms is recommended

Special Skills and Personality Traits—Ability to follow detailed procedures and be both thorough and systematic; good communication skills, both written and verbal; patience and persistence; some gaming ability and programming know-how

CAREER LADDER

```
┌─────────────────────────────────┐
│  Assistant Producer; Game Designer; │
│            Programmer            │
└─────────────────────────────────┘

┌─────────────────────────────────┐
│          Game Tester            │
└─────────────────────────────────┘

┌─────────────────────────────────┐
│    Student; Volunteer Tester    │
└─────────────────────────────────┘
```

Position Description

Testing is a crucial part of game development. To intrigue users, a game must allow for many possible approaches and playing styles on the part of its players (customers). Player demand and competition has led to producing games with many intricate features. The result of such complexity is that it becomes increasingly hard to make sure there are no combinations of data and player actions that will interact to cause "bugs" or errors. Problems could stem from missed pieces of key data or from testing programming routines under reasonable conditions that are insufficient benchmarks, as users are notoriously "unreasonable" in their game playing.

There are several categories of testing. Bug testing is the process of searching out possible software errors and testing the game software again after programmers claim to have fixed the existing bugs. Configuration testing is playing the game on a variety of hardware to guarantee that the game

works on all these platforms. Gameplay testing and tuning consists of trying out the game to be certain the product is both enjoyable and well balanced for users. Quality assurance testing consists of the final checks before the product is approved for shipment (and is the responsibility of the testing manager).

Testing games has its serious side. In testing, games are *not* played in order to win. There is a strict test plan (devised by the test lead and the quality assurance manager in consultation with the programming and design leads) that set forth which features are to be checked. Furthermore, gameplay testing and tuning hinges on several issues. Is the game fun and are the basic gameplay mechanisms enjoyable to use? This type of question is usually applied to the initial testing, and feedback to the designers and programmers may have impact on how the game's design is modified. Is the game easy to use, and are the controls smooth rather than awkward? As a corollary, is the game manual accurate? Then, does the game make sense, and will players have the entertainment experience the designer has in mind? In testing games after modifications have been made, the focus becomes: Is the game still fun? Is it too hard, or is it too easy? Are there points where players will be lost or will not understand what they are supposed to do next? Finally, if the tester plays through the game, doing what average users are intended to do, can they navigate successfully to the end of the game? If they do things the game player isn't expected to do, does the game work anyway? In addition, can the tester make the game crash?

As Game Testers gain experience in trying out products, they are often entrusted with the added task of testing the software for bugs and writing bug reports for the programmers. These statements detail what went wrong and supply as much information as possible about the circumstances that led up to the gameplay problem. Usually, a database for recording bugs has been set up already for the product that the Game Tester is testing. When a bug is found, the game tester creates a new entry (usually requiring only filling in a form or using a search facility on a Web site) and enters the details. In some cases, a VCR or DVD is attached to the video output of the machine on which the testing is being done so that Game Testers can record what they are doing as they go. An advantage of this system is that steps can be retraced, and the recorded documentation enables the Tester to display the particular bug to a programmer.

Testing games is fun, though. Testers get an up-close-and-personal look at the game development process because they interact with everyone involved, from audio engineers to artists, designers, and programmers. As the project proceeds, they watch a raw, unfinished piece of software turn into an actual game. It is a perfect background for individuals looking to become game designers, programmers, or involved in the production process.

Salaries

In a study made in April 2006 by *Game Developer* magazine (and available at their Web site, http://gamedeveloper.texterity.com), Game Testers with three years' or less experience made an average of $26,797 a year, while those with three to six years' experience made an average of $42,125. Those Game Testers with six or more years' experience can expect to make average annual salaries of $50,000 or more.

Employment Prospects

The attractive nature of game testing, particularly for high school or college students, means that there is considerable competition even for this entry-level, low-paying position. It helps candidates to be able to demonstrate their special experience (say, in writing game reviews) and expertise (any programming background that they may have, or customer service work that teaches patience in the workplace). As quality assurance analyst Jon Gramlich detailed, "My entry into the game business was somewhat of an accident. … I realized that he [his soon-to-be-boss] was primarily interested in my own computer experience, especially in the area of Bulletin Board Systems. He told me he was looking for someone who could set up a large BBS for technical support and other customer service inquiries. I had been running one of those from my home for years, but only added it to my résumé as an afterthought. It paid off though, since he offered me the job on the spot … and I have been in the industry ever since."

Advancement Prospects

Game testing often is what an individual does until they move into their "real" job in the industry. Many Game Testers use game testing as a stepping-stone to other game development work, such as design, programming, or production. Advancement will depend greatly upon the applicants' demonstrable skills they have gained as Testers and their good work habits.

Education and Training

While there is no formal educational experience required, a high school diploma is suggested as a minimum educational background. Many Game Testers have, in addition, associate or bachelor's degrees. Formal courses in programming may also prove useful.

Experience, Skills, and Personality Traits

Besides an abiding love of playing computer games, a Game Tester must be able to follow detailed instructions and have excellent verbal and written communication skills. To be good Testers, they need to be keen-eyed analytical observers. They must look at the whole screen to make sure everything is happening the way it is supposed to. Their close attention to detail must include knowing what exactly they were doing when things went wrong and what exactly happened on the screen when that occurred. They not only have to notice what went amiss but also be able to explain it, accurately and unambiguously, to the programmer who is tasked with fixing the bug. (A little diplomacy with prideful programmers would be a good idea as well.)

Game Testers need to be decent game players, but they should not be so good that they will not be able to tell if a game is too hard for an ordinary user. They need a lot of patience and fortitude in their work, and programming skills will help them understand the way that software works and the manners in which it can break.

Unions and Associations

Most Game Testers have never thought of joining a professional association, but they may find it advantageous to belong to the most important game development organization, the International Game Developers Association (IGDA). Other groups they might join, particularly if they are looking to make a career of game development, are the Academy of Interactive Arts and Sciences (AIAS) and the Association for Interactive Media (AIM).

Tips for Entry

1. Check Web newsgroups and other Web sites for game companies that are hiring Game Testers, and be sure you are adept at a variety of games before applying for the job.

2. Read magazines such as *Computer Gaming World* and *Game Developer* to keep abreast with trends in game design and to identify the companies that are producing the types of games you prefer to play.

3. While working as a Game Tester, ask plenty of questions and soak up as much information as you can. If you enjoy the quality assurance process, you may have found your niche in the game development industry. If you want to move into development, programming, or production, watch for opportunities and network. Remember that game developers are looking for people who genuinely enjoy building games.

SOFTWARE TEST ENGINEER

CAREER PROFILE

Duties: Test and critique game software in technical depth to assure quality and identify potential improvement opportunities; write test programs to assure quality and develop test tools to increase effectiveness of testing process

Alternate Title(s): Quality Assurance Engineer

Salary Range: $40,000 to $85,000 or more

Employment Prospects: Fair

Advancement Prospects: Poor to Fair

Prerequisites:

Education or Training—Bachelor's degree or higher in computer science, computer engineering, electrical engineering, or related subject

Experience—Two to six years' development and testing experience in electronic games industry or a commercial software equivalent; some background with imaging, animation, design, and programming procedures in game development

Special Skills and Personality Traits—Demonstrated comprehension of good software engineering and debugging practices; familiarity with performance and code optimizations techniques; knowledge of software development life cycle and the basic components of a game engine and how they work together; outstanding written and verbal communication skills; proficiency in testing client/server Windows-based applications and in the use of C, C++, and Perl software; strong interest in computer gaming

Special Requirements—Industry certification may be required

CAREER LADDER

```
┌─────────────────────────────────┐
│   Quality Assurance Manager;     │
│       Lead Programmer            │
└─────────────────────────────────┘

┌─────────────────────────────────┐
│     Software Test Engineer       │
└─────────────────────────────────┘

┌─────────────────────────────────┐
│  Applications Software Programmer; │
│  College Graduate (computer science) │
└─────────────────────────────────┘
```

Position Description

Software quality engineering is made up of two primary activities: process level quality (normally called *quality assurance*) and product-oriented quality (typically called *testing*). Process level quality (quality assurance) establishes the techniques, procedures, and tools that help promote, facilitate, and create a software development environment in which efficient, optimized, and as fault-free as possible game software code can be produced. Product level quality (testing) focuses on ensuring that the game software delivered is as error-free as possible—that it is functionally sound and meets or exceeds the actual game player's needs.

Software testing is the process used to help identify the correctness, completeness, security, and quality of developed computer software. There are many approaches to software testing, but effective testing of complex products, such as electronic games, is essentially a process of investigation, not merely a matter of creating and following rote procedures. In evaluating the game product, a software tester asks "questions" of it, and the software product "answers" with its built-in behavior in reaction to the probing of the tester. This is a dynamic analysis, as the Software Test Engineer puts the game product through its paces, attempting not to prove that the product works, but that it does *not* work properly. Testing is a negative activity conducted with the explicit purpose of creating a strong game product, and, therefore, it is focused operatively on the "weak links" within the software. In addition, there is a trend in the industry to apply testing to the earlier phases of the game software development cycle. Rather than viewing testing as something that takes place after development, adherents of this altered view focus on the testing of every component from the start, including the initial concept of operations, the specifications as laid out in the design plan, the design, the programming code as it is being written, and the test plans themselves.

Software Test Engineers help the lead test engineer to develop/maintain test plans, develop test cases (a single step in the game and its expected result), and develop/maintain internal test tools. This involves designing, documenting, writing, and executing automated and semi-automated unit tests, as well as conducting functional, compatibility, installer, performance/stress, and regression tests on the game development software. Under the guidance of the quality assurance manager, Software Test Engineers contribute to the establishment and implementation of effective practices/procedures for software testing. They may be asked to analyze design information and provide feedback during the early stages of development and to perform technical, stylistic, and grammatical reviews of user documentation aimed at the game's users.

Throughout this testing process, they provide time estimates for each task and report on project status to the quality assurance manager and project leads. They work with the development teams in providing gameplay-test feedback and documentation on software defects through the bug-tracking database made available to designers and programmers. If they work for a game publisher, they will be working with external development teams to ensure efficient and effective testing efforts.

In recent years, a new type of game has emerged that presents a unique challenge to designers, programmers, and quality assurance personnel: the massively multiplayer online game (MMOG). These are electronic games made available online that people of all ages and genders are playing. (Two very popular ones are *The Sims Online* and *Everquest.*) With the game console now an online personal computer, this type of game title provides new testing challenges full of many complex variables. Software Test Engineers are examining not only game design factors, but also hardware requirements, bandwidth issues, latency problems, error checking and error correction, server timeouts,

and dropped connections with the MMOG game player's computer downtime. The MMOG is an example of how the role of the Software Test Engineer is ever expanding and changing.

Salaries

According to the U.S. Bureau of Labor Statistics' *Occupational Outlook Handbook*, during 2004, median annual earnings of computer applications software engineers were about $74,980, with salary ranges from a low of about $46,000 to a high of $110,000 or more. For Software Test Engineers, salaries were generally lower than for software engineers (programmers) working directly in the game development process. They ranged from about $45,000 to $85,000 or higher, dependent upon their experience, the range of their responsibilities, and the number of years they have worked in this position.

Employment Prospects

According to the U.S. Bureau of Labor, employment of computer software engineers to 2014 is expected to increase much faster than the average for all occupations. Software Test Engineers are trained as computer applications software engineers, and have moved into the game industry due to their fascination and commitment to game playing and a desire to make a career in the game development field. The quality assurance team is a good place to apply their skills in applications software and gain knowledge about, and skills in, game development. Like the test lead, a Software Test Engineer position is *not* an entry-level post like that of game tester, as the programming skills needed are more advanced. Nonetheless, recent graduates with the requisite computer background and some experience in the application of testing methodologies in a computer environment may be hired to fill this position on the quality assurance team of a game developer or publisher.

Advancement Prospects

The quality assurance department is often a stepping-off job position for many different types of game personnel, from designers and artists to programmers and production management personnel. Software Test Engineers may want to make a parallel career move to the programming teams in game development. As an alternative, they may decide to take on more management responsibilities and seek a position as quality assurance manager for a game developer or publisher.

Education and Training

The minimum requirement for Software Test Engineers is a bachelor's degree in computer science, computer engineering, electrical engineering, or a related field. Some development companies may look for candidates with a higher degree in a computer-related discipline.

Special Requirements

Some game development companies or publishers may require an industry certification for software engineering testing. Certification programs include the CSQE (Certified Software Quality Engineer) program offered by the American Society for Quality (ASQ), the CSTE/CSQA (Certified Software Test Engineering/Certified Software Quality Assurance) program offered by the Quality Assurance Institute (QAI), and the ISTQB certification, offered by the International Software Testing Qualification Board.

Experience, Skills, and Personality Traits

Software Test Engineers need to have a firm understanding of the full life cycle of the software development process and software testing methodologies. Many game developers insist that they have one to three years' experience in software quality assurance. They should be proficient in such programming languages as C, C++ (Visual C++ or Visual. NET), and Perl. They should be familiar with performance and code optimization techniques, as well as understand QA metrics and benchmarking measurement techniques. They may be asked to write automation scripts and tools, so a familiarity with game engines and technologies, the SQL server, Net languages, networking, security, DirectX, and other appropriate Windows programs would be useful. In addition, any experience with imaging, animation, modeling, or rendering is a distinct advantage.

Software Test Engineers should have excellent written and verbal communication skills, as well as strong analytical and problem-solving abilities. They need to be imaginative and innovative, but also operate well as members of teams working collaboratively with, and taking direction from, others. They need to be able to take responsibility for their actions and outcomes and be able to see projects through despite obstacles and difficult circumstances. Above all, they must exhibit a strong passion and pride in their work and an overriding love of games.

Unions and Associations

There are several professional associations useful to Software Testing Engineers for career development and networking. These include the American Society for Quality (ASQ), the Association for Computing Machinery (ACM), the Institute of Electrical and Electronic Engineers (IEEE), the Quality Assurance Institute (QAI), and the Society for Software Quality (SSQ).

Tips for Entry

1. If your present company or your college uses a lot of software, they may have a testing arrangement with a software firm that releases its new and/or upgraded product to a limited audience outside its company for testing (the "beta" phase of the testing process). If so, volunteer to be a beta tester so you can practice your testing skills.
2. When playing games you may discover bugs on your own. Document them according to a standard bug report criteria (which can be found in most books on game design). Demonstrating that you can write a clean bug report might help you land a local Quality Assurance job where you can further demonstrate your software engineering know-how.
3. Remember to always update your skills, and keep current with the latest game platforms, tools, and industry trends, because all these factors will affect your "marketability," as game development is an extremely competitive industry.

TEST LEAD

CAREER PROFILE

Duties: Create a plan for electronic games quality assurance testing; build and maintain a bug database for the testing process; supervise quality assurance personnel

Alternate Title(s): Lead Quality Assurance Supervisor; Lead Test Engineer; Lead Tester; Quality Assurance Lead; Testing Manager

Salary Range: $30,000 to $65,000 or more

Employment Prospects: Fair

Advancement Prospects: Fair

Prerequisites:

Education or Training—Bachelor's degree in computer science with emphasis on quality control, quality assurance testing, and computer software and/or computer hardware

Experience—One to two years' experience as a technical lead of a team of at least five people; one to two years background as a computer programmer; some administrative background

Special Skills and Personality Traits—Ability to work effectively with diverse personalities; capacity to communicate clearly both verbally and in writing; good observational skills and close attention to detail; problem-solving abilities; self-disciplined with strong time management know-how and a proven ability to meet deadlines; systematic and thorough

Special Requirements—In some cases, an industry certification may be requested

CAREER LADDER

```
┌─────────────────────────────────────┐
│ Quality Assurance Manager; Producer  │
└─────────────────────────────────────┘

┌─────────────────────────────────────┐
│              Test Lead               │
└─────────────────────────────────────┘

┌─────────────────────────────────────┐
│ Programmer; Software Test Engineer   │
└─────────────────────────────────────┘
```

Position Description

Test Leads do some testing of game software themselves to help out during any peak period, but their primary role consists of four key duties: (1) defining the test plan for the game; (2) building and maintaining a database for documenting bugs found in the software; (3) implementing the test plan and supervising testing personnel; and (4) sustaining rapport with the game development team. These key duties constitute the Test Lead's primary responsibility of ensuring that the game works properly.

During the early stages of the game development, the testing team will be small, and will provide a continuous

(and up-to-date) feedback to the developers. On a daily basis, the programmers will implement a bit of software code, look to see whether it works, and then pass it on to the Test Lead to discover any hidden ramifications or problems within it. By providing quick feedback to the programmers, Test Leads have a real influence on the game design, as their response on these features is provided when the game software/design is still in flux.

As the game project approaches the *alpha* stage (where the game is more or less playable from start to finish), the Test Lead will bring in the rest of the test team, and at this point the Test Lead prepares the test plan.

Defining the test plan for a game is a large and extremely intricate undertaking that requires a thorough understanding of how software works and how it can be improved to operate correctly. Test Leads may consult the original design document for the game (if it is current), but a written document seldom captures all the thousands of small choices made in the course of game development. For that reason, Test Leads consult with the designers and programmers to document every function and aspect of the game that is subject to observational analysis. Then, they build a test plan for actually performing that thorough analysis.

Test Leads' second chore is to build and maintain a bug database, requiring them to have fundamental database skills and familiarity with such programs as Microsoft Access, Filemaker Pro, and Lotus Approach. This task, however, is not the same as database programming, as no software code has to be written. The bug database provides a means of uniquely recording each bug found, who found it, under what circumstances during the gameplay, and any other useful observations that may help the programmer to solve the problem posed by the bug. The database also provides a status flag on each bug described in order to indicate whether it is yet to be fixed, claimed to have been fixed, or verified that it is fixed.

In implementing this test plan, the Test Lead oversees the work of each of the testing staff and checks on their progress. When the game enters the *beta* stage of its development (when all the features are present in the software and all the assets have been created to allow the entire game to be tested), the testing team is expanded. (During this *beta* stage, selected members of the public may be allowed to help test the game.) At this point the Test Lead instructs each tester specifically what to look for that day. Sometimes, Test Leads bring fresh testers onto the project, as their new eyes may spot a different set of bugs, or they can give a new perspective on existing problems.

For every bug the testers find (at whatever stage of the development), someone on the development team (usually a programmer) has to fix it. This means that testing results are constantly flowing from quality assurance to the developers, and new, corrected, builds (program files) are constantly flowing back to the testers for verification. The Test Lead oversees this process, making certain that the testers are working on the current version. The Test Lead needs to be as diplomatic as possible in all this interaction, to avoid offending individual developers and, meanwhile, to keep their testing team focused.

At the end of the development phase, when pressure is mounting from company executives and production personnel to get the new game released, the Test Lead may well have a better idea whether the project is ready to ship than the designer, the producer, or the tech lead. At this point, Test Leads meet daily with the department heads and the producer to discuss outstanding problems and agree upon which items must still be addressed and which will be ignored. The Test Lead often has the determining say on whether the game can now be released to the public.

Salaries

According to a video game makers survey of 2004 salaries conducted by DeVry University in 2005, it was found that Test Leads (and quality assurance leads) with three years' or less experience made an average of $38,340 a year. Those with three to six years of experience averaged $43,195, and Test Leads with six or more years of experience averaged $60,929 with the highest salary reported being $225,000. In their annual salary survey, *Game Developer Magazine* found that 2005 salaries ranged from an average of $33,125 for those Test Leads with three years' or less experience, $43,125 for those with three to six years' experience, and $61,310 for those with six or more years of experience.

Employment Prospects

While there has been some decline in demand for quality assurance testing, primarily due to the use of automated test utility software suites run by low-level technicians and to the growing use of selected potential customers to do testing when at the *beta* stage in the development process, there is still a steady demand for trained, technical Test Leads with the appropriate programming and game development backgrounds. Individuals who have background managing software tests in other industries may be able to gain a position as Test Lead in the game industry.

The position of Test Lead is not one to which most testers can aspire. Most often, testers become assistant and associate producers first. Testers don't have enough administrative experience to move directly to a Test Lead post. Once they have gained some necessary management skills (while in a production position), they may be able to move laterally to become Test Leads.

Advancement Prospects

Test Leads looking to advance their careers may choose to apply to become managers of the quality assurance department, overseeing all the testing and quality assurance processes for a game development company or a publisher. Another potential professional move would be to producer, as Test Leads have the administrative, management, and technical backgrounds for such a position.

Education and Training

The usual requirement for a quality assurance department Test Lead is a bachelor's degree in computer science with an emphasis on quality control methodologies, quality assurance testing, and game computer software and hardware. Training as a computer programmer is recommended. In addition, some courses in business administration and management techniques should prove to be useful.

Special Requirements

In a few cases, an industry certification for software testing may be requested by a developer or a publisher. Certification programs include the Certified Software Quality Engineer (CSQE) program offered by the American Society for Quality (ASQ), the Certified Software Test Engineering/Certified Software Quality Assurance (CSTE/CSQA) program offered by the Quality Assurance Institute (QAI), and the ISTQB certification, offered by the International Software Testing Qualification Board.

Experience, Skills, and Personality Traits

As Test Lead is not an entry-level position, experience counts heavily. A minimum of two years' seasoning as a technical lead of a development team of at least five people is a typical requirement. Many game developers (and publishers) also insist on a minimum of two years of professional background with computer programming. Test Leads should understand the full game development cycle and have a solid understanding of the standard game operating systems and platforms. Their knowledge of accepted software and console game testing and quality assurance principles, methodologies, and best practices must be comprehensive.

Test Leads must be able to lead a team and successfully supervise different types of individuals. They must have excellent communication talents, both verbal and written. Test Leads are problem solvers who can recommend solutions and then implement the approved solutions in a resourceful manner. They should have strong time management skills with a proven track record for meeting deadlines. In addition, they need to be extremely thorough in their work and highly self-disciplined.

Unions and Associations

Like quality assurance managers, Test Leads do not have a union that represents them. However, several associations might be useful for career development and networking. These include the American Society for Quality (ASQ), the Association for Computing Machinery (ACM), the Quality Assurance Institute (QAI), and the Society for Software Quality (SSQ).

Tips for Entry

1. Seriously consider a course or two in business administration and/or management techniques to complement your computer classes, as the management skills taught will be an important part of your job as Test Lead in a quality assurance department.
2. Be willing to put in three to five years as a testing or quality control analyst to gain the necessary skills in game testing and then some additional years as a technical team leader in the game development industry.
3. Look for opportunities that allow you to interpret, analyze, and evaluate a variety of technical instructions and documents, as these skills will be instrumental in your ability to devise productive plans and instructions for the testing process.

SALES AND DISTRIBUTION

ELECTRONIC GAMES STORE CLERICAL PERSONNEL

CAREER PROFILE

Duties: Sales Clerk: sell electronic games, software, and related hardware at the retail level; Technical Salesperson: use technical skills to demonstrate special features of electronic games and related hardware in order to finalize sales at the retail level

Alternate Title(s): Clerk, Retail Salesperson; Sales Engineer

Salary Range: Sales Clerk: $17,000 to $30,000 or more; Technical Salesperson: $20,000 to $45,000 or more

Employment Prospects: Good

Advancement Prospects: Good

Prerequisites:

Education or Training—Sales Clerk: high school diploma or equivalent, training often on the job; Technical Salesperson: preferably a bachelor's degree in computer science or computer-related subject with some business emphasis or, alternatively, a degree in business with technical emphasis in a computer-related subject

Experience—Sales Clerk: some retail sales background preferable and familiarity with electronic games; Technical Salesperson: previous retail sales experience/training and technical knowledge of game development processes, techniques, software, and hardware

Special Skills and Personality Traits—Sales Clerk: attention to detail and good communication skills, basic knowledge of games and video products, initiative, dependability, and pleasing personality; Technical Salesperson: good interpersonal skills, excellent computer skills, initiative, dependability, sales aptitude, thorough technical background in electronic games techniques, processes, and related hardware products

CAREER LADDER

Assistant Manager; Store Manager; Sales Manager; Game Tester

Sales Clerk; Technical Salesperson

Graduate; Sales Trainee

Position Description

An electronic games store Sales Clerk is responsible for sales of electronic games software and related products and hardware to customers in a retail store (or in an electronics products department in a larger retail store). In operations that also specialize in video programming in addition to electronic games, the Sales Clerk is involved in the rental and/or sales of videocassettes and videodiscs as well.

Sales Clerks usually report directly to the store manager or, if in a department, to the department manager.

In large retail stores with greater staff needs, assistant managers may be assigned to supervise the Sales Clerks. In small stores (or departments), Sales Clerks are responsible for selling or renting all displayed merchandise. In larger businesses, they may be assigned to specific types of merchandise, such as electronic game software as opposed to DVDs.

It is the primary duty of Sales Clerks to service customer requests and inform the potential buyer about the merchandise offered by the store. They operate in a dynamic environment with new game software products, new related hardware merchandise, and, in some instances, new home entertainment merchandise constantly being introduced, as are new merchandising techniques, discounts, and special sales. In addition, there usually is a wide variety of customers moving through the store daily. It is the Sales Clerks' responsibility to balance all these factors and devise sales approaches that meet the needs of the customers but, above all, increase sales for the store.

Sales Clerks may also be called upon to assist in setting up in-store and window merchandising displays, help stock shelves or racks, and maintain inventory records and sales files. They may also be responsible for operating cash registers at specified times during the day, receiving cash, checks, debit, and charge payments from customers. In this process, they will bag or package the purchases and give change and receipts to customers. In some instances, they may also be responsible for handling returns and exchanges of merchandise.

In some retail stores (particularly larger chain stores) selling and/or renting electronic game software (and/or home entertainment merchandising) and hardware, there may be, in addition to the regular Sales Clerks, specialized clerks with technical backgrounds who participate in the selling process. These Technical Salespersons (sometimes called sales engineers) use their special skills to demonstrate to potential customers the use of hardware equipment and describe the features of electronic game software. They will demonstrate these products to the customers, usually by playing demos provided by game software developers or publishers. Many of their duties are similar to those of Sales Clerks, in that they must interest the customer in purchasing the game product. However, Technical Salespersons tend to employ selling techniques that are somewhat different from those used by Sales Clerks. They generally utilize a "consultative" style; that is, they focus on the customer's interests and desires, and show how the game merchandise can satisfy them.

Often, Technical Salespersons will be teamed with Sales Clerks who attend to the marketing/sales aspects, while the Technical Salespersons concentrate on demonstrating/ explaining the technical features and details to customers. Thus, by working as a sales team, each member is able to focus on his or her strengths/knowledge.

Salaries

According to the U.S. Department of Labor's Bureau of Labor Statistics, median hourly earnings of retail salespersons, including any commissions, were $8.98 in 2004. The middle 50 percent made between $7.46 and $12.22 an hour. The lowest 10 percent earned less than $6.38, and the highest 10 percent made more than $17.85 an hour. These hourly wages translate into yearly salaries ranging from $15,500 at the low end, to about $37,100 at the high end. Sales Clerks who have the responsibility of handling electronic merchandise (such as game software and hardware) should earn within the middle range of these figures. In turn, Technical Salespersons, due to their technical expertise and knowledge, will earn at the high end of these salary ranges or more.

Employment Prospects

The position of a retail Sales Clerk is an entry-level job at most retail stores. Most businesses selling electronic game software and, usually, entertainment DVD discs employ from three to eight workers in sales for various shifts and assignments. There may also be part-time employees hired during busy seasons.

According to the Bureau of Labor Statistics' *Occupational Outlook Handbook,* employment opportunities for retail salespersons remain strong because of the need to replace the large number of workers who transfer to other occupations or leave the labor force each year. In addition, firms often hire retail Sales Clerks as they seek to expand their operations and enhance their customer service. In particular, with the increase in number of electronic games being made available, the chances of sales employment in this sector are increasing. According to the Bureau, employment of retail salespersons is expected to grow about as fast as the average for all occupations through the year 2014.

Despite the growing popular support for making games available on the Internet, sales on the Internet have not decreased the need for retail salespersons. They will remain important in assuring customers that they will receive, in person, specialized service that helps to guarantee their customer satisfaction, something Internet operations cannot do easily.

Advancement Prospects

Many Sales Clerks and Technical Salespersons look to advance to positions as assistant managers and, eventually, to store managers. With a proven record of accomplishment, they may become department managers at larger chain operations; others may move into branch management for a store chain. Some aggressive Sales Clerks or Technical Salespersons may use their retail sales experience to move to more responsible positions as sales managers at stores that sell products unrelated to electronic games, DVDs, or even electronic merchandise. Some may decide to try to enter the game industry by becoming game testers within quality assurance departments of game publishers or game developers.

Education and Training

A high school diploma is usually a basic requirement of retail salespersons. For Technical Salespersons, training in computer science (either during high school or in a trade or technical college) is a prerequisite. Some of them may have a college degree in computer science or electrical engineering. It is important for both Sales Clerks and Technical Salespersons working in such a fast-changing retail environment as electronic games to continue their technical and sales education, because much of their value to their employers depends on their knowledge of the latest game technology and its products, as well as their ability to sell that technology.

Experience, Skills, and Personality Traits

Some previous experience in retail sales in any field is often required of electronic games store clerks. Background with computers, either in their personal life or during their education, is highly desirable. A basic understanding of the electronic game development process and gameplaying procedures and techniques is a necessity as well.

Because Sales Clerks and Technical Salespersons deal primarily with people, they should have outgoing personalities, have the ability to listen carefully to customers, and be able to speak clearly. A neat appearance is important. Successful individuals are friendly, very service-oriented, and, to a degree, competitive and aggressive in finalizing sales.

Unions and Associations

In larger stores or chains, retail Sales Clerks may belong to clerical or retail clerks' unions. Some retail salespersons may find it advantageous to attend periodic sales conferences and seminars held by the North American Retail Dealers Association (NARDA) or the Electronic Representatives Association (ERA) to improve their skills and share mutual concerns.

Tips for Entry

1. Look for part-time or summer jobs during high school (or college) where you can work in a store and learn how to sell merchandise and deal effectively with customers.
2. Visit video and electronic games stores to see how the merchandise is displayed. Use your gameplaying expertise to ask clerks questions to see how well organized and knowledgeable they may be (and think how you might do as well or better).
3. As a retail salesperson who wants to move forward with your career, look for community college (or technical school) programs in either computer technology (if you want to advance into technical sales support) or business and management (if you want to become a store manager).

ELECTRONIC GAMES STORE MANAGERIAL PERSONNEL

CAREER PROFILE

Duties: Merchandise Buyer: responsible for merchandise fulfillment for a retail store selling electronic games, software, and related hardware; Store Manager: manage the day-to-day operations of an individual retail store selling electronic games merchandise (or manage a department in a larger retail operation)

Alternate Title(s): Game Buyer, Merchandising Manager; Sales Worker Supervisor, Department Manager

Salary Range: Merchandise Buyer: $30,000 to $70,000 or more; Store Manager: $25,000 to $58,000 or more

Employment Prospects: Fair

Advancement Prospects: Poor to Fair

Prerequisites:

Education or Training—Merchandise Buyer: bachelor's degree with a business emphasis, some training in retailing practices; Store Manager: bachelor's degree with business emphasis, previous training in retail management principles and practices

Experience—Merchandise Buyer: two years' experience in retail sales and extensive working knowledge of electronic games industry products and related hardware products; Store Manager: minimum of two to four years' background in retail sales experience, with some supervisory experience, and familiarity with electronic games industry

Special Skills and Personality Traits—Merchandise Buyer: excellent marketing and merchandising instincts; good accounting and computer abilities; practiced game player with thorough knowledge of game industry products; Store Manager: ability to manage stock, train and supervise employees; accounting, marketing, and merchandising instincts; well organized and an energetic risk taker; thorough knowledge of game industry products

CAREER LADDER

Store Manager; Store Owner, or Higher Chain Store Management Positions

Merchandise Buyer; Store Manager

Technical Salesperson; Assistant Manager; Sales Clerk

Position Description

There are two basic retail outlet stores that sell electronic games along with other related products: the general merchandise store and specialty software stores. The general merchandise store can be either large or small (such as Wal-Mart or drugstore chains), but they seldom stockpile a large selection and seldom special order any games that are out of stock. Additionally, their sales and managerial staff usually knows little to nothing about the games, leaving customers much on their own. Another variant of this type of business is the home entertainment rental store which rents (and sells) DVDs and may carry some electronic games. Like the general merchandise store, their stock is generally confined to the latest releases and classics, and the staff is only peripherally knowledgeable about the games.

The second type of store is the specialty shop that sells only electronic games, or perhaps software in general, and offers the best service and the widest selection to the game-playing customer. The salespersons are usually specifically interested in computers, are gameplayers themselves, and are knowledgeable about which games are fun and for what age groups. Among the sales staff will be technical salespersons whose business is to be well-informed about the technical details of games and able to play available demos of games. In addition, specialty shops will have the very latest games the first day they are available, though the prices may be higher than in the large general merchandise stores.

The managerial staff in most specialty shops usually consists of one or more assistant managers and a Store Manager. In addition, there may be a Merchandise Buyer, who has the overall responsibility of product buying and inventory control that might otherwise be the sole responsibility of the Store Manager. When both jobs are filled on a store's staff, they work together in establishing merchandise levels and standards and handle the control of inventory.

Store Managers are the individuals responsible for making decisions about the store's operation and training and supervising employees. They are in charge of all income and expenses and all short- and long-range planning and responsible for the store's overall profitability level. (In some small shops, the Store Manager may also be the owner.) Store Managers schedule employees, delegate work assignments, provide regular feedback on their performance, and, frequently, are in charge of hiring and firing staff. Motivating poorly paid entry-level sales clerks is one of their more difficult tasks. In addition, they are tasked with maintaining a safe and clean environment to ensure that health and Occupational Safety Hazards Administration (OSHA) requirements are met. They analyze customer satisfaction and monitor employee contentment to identify areas needing improvement and develop processes and/or procedures to address these issues. They maintain accurate records to ensure documentation of all store activities. In addition, Store Managers need to stay informed of game industry trends, new products, and fresh techniques of advertising and merchandise display.

Store Managers in chain stores (and game department managers in larger retail merchandising stores) make fewer of these decisions, as the parent company often arranges for distribution and pricing and sets other policies. In these cases, managers concentrate on meeting sales goals.

Merchandise Buyers are responsible for developing the store's merchandising strategies for electronic game prod-

ucts that will achieve good sales levels for the store. They manage game inventories by tracking weekly sales reports and evaluating customer satisfaction reports. Their goals are to order entertainment products and supplies to meet buyers' requirements, to ensure that the most popular products are always in stock, and to maximize profits for the store. They evaluate upcoming software releases, as well as new hardware and accessory items, select the product to add to the store's existing lineup, and determine the level of inventory commitment for those items. They negotiate terms, discounts, advertising monies, returns, and markdowns with game vendors and distributors, which will aid in achieving the store's gross profit margin objectives.

They must keep aware of special promotions or other offers presented by software publishers/developers and be able to negotiate for the best wholesale price. The Merchandise Buyer works with the Store Manager to determine the appropriate retail price on game software and other related products. In addition, Merchandise Buyers devise merchandising presentation guidelines and promotional marketing strategies for games whenever such marketing strategies are left to the store by the game publisher/developer. Merchandise Buyers frequently shop in competitor stores to compare price schedules, strategies, developments, and opportunities.

Salaries

According to the U.S. Department of Labor's *Occupational Outlook Handbook,* in May 2004, the median annual earnings of salaried supervisors of retail sales workers (a category that includes Store Managers) were $32,720. The middle 50 percent had incomes between $25,120 and $43,110 a year, with the highest salaries being more than $58,400.

Earnings for Merchandise Buyers tend to be somewhat higher, due to the complexity of their financial responsibilities (the store's profits hinge upon their decisions). According to the *Occupational Outlook Handbook,* median annual earnings in May 2004 for wholesale and retail buyers were $42,230. The middle 50 percent earned between $31,550 and $57,010 and the highest 10 percent earned more than $75,340.

Employment Prospects

Chances of employment in game software specialty stores for either Store Managers or Merchandise Buyers is only fair. There are a limited number of such operations, and the competition from the large chain store companies, with their ability to buy in bulk and slash prices, significantly lessens the chances of new specialty stores being started. In addition, the sale of games over the Internet and through mail-order vendors inhibits financing of new game software specialty stores.

Employment prospects are fairly good for managers and buyers who are willing to work within a smaller department environment in a chain store, due primarily to the high turn-over rate in such operations. Better prospects for managers and buyers may be found in smaller communities or rural areas that have enough people interested in electronic games to support a small specialty store but not enough to attract a chain outlet. Such stores usually find that they have to expand their merchandise to cover other areas of computer technology or add the attraction of DVD sales and, possibly, rentals.

Advancement Prospects

Advancement prospects for Store Managers is limited, as they are already on the highest rung within the store, or, as department managers, at the top of the department. Within chain stores, advancement possibilities for those individuals who make the right contacts usually are confined to upper management positions at corporate or local headquarters.

Merchandise Buyers may advance their careers by moving to a chain store that handles a large volume of products other than electronic games and becoming merchandise managers of a bigger product base. Alternatively, they may seek to become Store Managers but must demonstrate that, beyond their expert knowledge of game industry products, they can also handle business, administrative, and supervisory responsibilities.

Education and Training

Most employers expect Store Managers and Merchandise Buyers to have a four-year college degree, preferably with a business emphasis. Individuals applying for either position should have three to five years' experience in retail sales. Store Managers need, in addition, to have been trained as supervisors and be able to demonstrate their ability to handle financial matters related to running a store. Merchandise Buyers, in turn, need to have had training on buying from vendors and distributors, usually as assistant buyers in a retail situation. They must be familiar with standard whole-saling and retailing practices.

Experience, Skills, and Personality Traits

Most Store Manager candidates will have worked for at least three years as a retail sales clerk, a support representative, or an assistant manager. General computer hardware and software skills are mandatory, and they should possess knowledge of electronic games and their industry. A Store Manager's management/supervisory experience should include budgetary control, staff recruitment and development, and working knowledge of health and safety codes within a retail or similar environment. Store Managers should be familiar with collective bargaining agreement procedures and be able to read a profit and loss statement. They need to have very strong organizational abilities and good interpersonal and communication skills (both written and verbal). Their commitment to excellent customer service must be coupled with a strong determination for success that can inspire the same in their sales team.

Merchandise Buyers should have three or more years of retail background, preferably a part of which includes buying experience in the electronic games industry. Their general computer hardware and software skills should include some know-how with spreadsheet programs. They must have strong financial analysis skills and be highly organized. They must be able to analyze technical data in game suppliers' proposals and have good communication, negotiation, and mathematical abilities. Anticipating game consumer preferences and ensuring game products are in stock when they are needed requires resourcefulness, good judgment, and self-confidence.

Unions and Associations

Many Store Managers and Merchandise Buyers in the electronic games software retail business will find it useful to belong to the Entertainment Software Association (ESA), the major trade organization representing the home DVD and game entertainment industry. They may also find it useful to belong to such retail industry organizations as the North American Retail Dealers Association (NARDA) or the Electronic Industries Alliance (EIA). The latter sponsors many forums and semiannual shows of new electronics products.

Tips for Entry

1. While in high school and/or college, gain retail experience, perhaps through a part-time job at a local chain store. While on the job, search for opportunities to help out in software buying, inventory, and customer service.
2. In high school, be sure to take business-related courses. While at your community or four-year college, consider a major in marketing or retail management.
3. Familiarize yourself with a wide variety of electronic games and be sure you have worked on your basic computer skills, even to the extent of taking courses in computer programming, software, or hardware technology.

MARKETING MANAGER AND MARKETING RESEARCH DIRECTOR

CAREER PROFILE

Duties: Marketing Manager: develop and coordinate all marketing activities for an electronic game developer or publisher; Marketing Research Director: gather and analyze information essential to marketing and advertising decisions by an electronic game developer or publisher

Alternate Title(s): Brand Manager, Marketing Director; Research Analyst, Research Specialist, Researcher/Planner

Salary Range: $35,000 to $90,000 or more

Employment Prospects: Good

Advancement Prospects: Fair

Prerequisites:

Education or Training—Undergraduate degree in advertising, communications, or marketing, and emphasis on computer-related concentration; master's in business administration (M.B.A.) degree often required

Experience—Minimum of two to four years' experience in telecommunications sales or marketing; grasp of marketing research and analysis techniques; love of the electronic game experience

Special Skills and Personality Traits—Ability to conduct market research and analysis; excellent understanding of economics, marketing principles, and the media and communications industries; good interpersonal and management skills; organizational abilities and talent for promotion

CAREER LADDER

```
┌─────────────────────────────────┐
│  Business Development Director;  │
│  Vice President of Marketing     │
└─────────────────────────────────┘

┌─────────────────────────────────┐
│  Marketing Manager; Marketing    │
│  Research Director               │
└─────────────────────────────────┘

┌─────────────────────────────────┐
│  Sales Manager; Junior Researcher │
└─────────────────────────────────┘
```

Position Description

Marketing of electronic games is *not* actually about selling the product by phone or e-mails or persuading a retailer to purchase it. Rather it is about selling the game on a large scale, advertising it, promoting it, ensuring that the public hears about it. Marketing is primarily the art of attracting attention, of making the product look beautiful and sound wonderful, of persuading consumers to buy the game.

Marketing Managers usually have a team of specialists working with them. This marketing group has two goals: to target the game for a particular market and to persuade a great many in that market to acquire the game. First, they research demographics. They advise the development team whether any features of the new game will help or hinder sales to the target audience, which of these features will affect the game's rating by reviewers, and how that ranking will affect sales. They may also advise on cultural differences that may affect how the product is received in foreign countries. Whether the game is geared to the hardcore gamer or the casual game-player will determine much of the marketing strategy. Marketing Managers suggest specific features that will give the game a broader audience and help it last longer in the marketplace.

To persuade the public to buy the game, Marketing Managers and their team create an image for the product that they promote to the target market. In creating this image, Marketing Managers are responsible for the look of the game's packaging. The marketing group usually has artists, or product designers, of its own to design the box. They also write the accompanying text, and the Marketing Manager works with the design team to decide which key features should be highlighted. They obtain screen shots and other material from the game's artists to incorporate into the marketing scheme. Marketing personnel also design and make the posters, cardboard cutouts, flyers, shelf-markers, and other items found in stores (and online) to sell the game.

If the game is based on an intellectual property, such as *Star Wars,* licensing for its use is handled by the legal staff. Once the contract has been signed, a lot of marketing coordination is required. The license-holder will have all kinds of images and other data to give to the marketing and development teams in building/selling the game. Marketing Managers often make joint marketing plans with other licensees of the same property, such as movie studios or book publishers, thus saturating the public's interest in the property to advance the sales of all participating products.

Another aspect of the Marketing Manager's job is to arrange presentation of forthcoming games at trade shows and special events. These activities demand a tremendous amount of planning and coordination by the marketing team. As in all other facets of marketing the game, Marketing Managers and their team coordinate efforts with public relations managers and with sales personnel. Typically, Marketing Managers are busy on more than one game, with some items still in (early) planning stages.

Marketing Research Directors supervise a staff concerned with the potential sales of electronic games. They gather statistical data on competitors and explore prices, sales, and methods of marketing and distribution. They analyze statistics on sales of electronic games to predict future sales. After compiling and evaluating this data, Marketing Research Directors and their staff make recommendations to the Marketing Manager and the game development team on the design, pricing, promotion, and distribution of projected games. They aid the marketing staff in developing advertising, sales plans, and product promotions for the upcoming games.

Salaries

The Bureau of Labor Statistics of the U.S. Department of Labor has found that median annual earnings in May 2004 of Marketing Managers were $87,640. Salaries can range from about $50,000 to highs of $105,000 or more, depending upon years of experience and success of past game promotional campaigns. According to a National Associa-

tion of Colleges and Employers survey, starting salaries for marketing majors graduating in 2005 averaged $33,873.

Marketing Research Directors in May 2004 were found to have median annual earnings of $56,140, with their income ranging from $30,890 to $79,990.

Employment Prospects

According to the U.S. Department of Labor's *Occupational Outlook Handbook,* employment of Marketing Managers and Marketing Research Directors, generally, is expected to increase faster than the average for all occupations through 2014. This trend is spurred by the vigorous expansion of the industry as a whole. Every game development project needs a perceptive Marketing Manager to interface with the development team. Those individuals with a love of electronic games and with the requisite education and background should have little problem in finding employment on a marketing team as a Marketing Manager or Marketing Research Director for a game developer or publisher.

Advancement Prospects

Marketing Research Directors may best advance their careers by moving to positions as Marketing Managers. Marketing Managers, in turn, may look to become vice presidents of marketing for the game publisher or the game development company or expand their management expertise into overall business development. Competition for these jobs, however, is strong, and noteworthy success in promotional campaigns is a necessary requisite for job advancement.

Education and Training

An undergraduate degree in advertising, communications, or marketing is a basic necessity for any position in a marketing team. A master's degree in Business Administration (M.B.A.) is often an additional requirement, particularly by game publishers. Courses in sales management and promotion techniques, as well as training in computer science or programming, are additional prerequisites.

Experience, Skills, and Personality Traits

A minimum of two to four years of previous experience in telecommunications sales or marketing is usually required of a Marketing Manager. This experience can frequently be gained as a sales manager or as a Market Research Director. Specific experience in sales or marketing in the game industry is a distinct advantage.

Marketing Managers need to be aggressive and capable of providing motivation and leadership to the rest of the marketing team. They need to have good organizational abilities and an outgoing and positive personality. They should have a flair for promotion and publicity and a good feel for logistics, statistics, research, and projecting industry trends. Their verbal and writing skills should be exemplary, and they need to have a working knowledge of the typical promotional aspects of the games industry.

Marketing Research Directors need to have an extensive knowledge of the game industry and be heavily detail-oriented. Computer literacy is assumed, and they should be able to write clearly and logically. Experience with marketing campaigns is essential, and analytical experience in research methodology and design is helpful.

Unions and Associations

Membership in such umbrella industry associations as the American Marketing Association (AMA) or the Computer and Electronics Marketing Association (CEMA) should prove useful for Marketing Managers. In turn, Marketing Research Directors should consider membership in the Marketing Research Association (MRA).

Tips for Entry

1. In high school and college, gain practical experience in promotional campaigns by helping to raise money for clubs or sports groups. Consider whom you are trying to reach in these campaigns and how best to appeal to them.
2. In college, as you gain your broad business background, focus also on marketing techniques as employed in the media industry. Examine case studies or simulations to gain an understanding of marketing strategies.
3. As an electronic game player, consider what attracted you to specific games and how the marketing strategy for the game was able to "target" you for its product.

PUBLIC RELATIONS MANAGER AND CUSTOMER SERVICE MANAGER

CAREER PROFILE

Duties: Public Relations Manager: direct publicity programs for an electronic game to its targeted audience, utilizing the press and other communication media; Customer Service Manager: serve as the direct point of contact between the product (the game) and its customers

Alternate Title(s): Communications Manager, Public Relations Specialist; Customer Service Representative

Salary Range: Public Relations Manager: $30,000 to $80,000; Customer Service Manager: $20,000 to $45,000

Employment Prospects: Fair

Advancement Prospects: Fair to Good

Prerequisites:

Education or Training—Undergraduate degree in advertising, communications, journalism, or public relations required; high school diploma necessary, and an undergraduate degree in communications, marketing, or public relations often essential

Experience—Working with the public and preparing materials for the media; technical expertise in, and familiarity with, game software

Special Skills and Personality Traits—Ability to communicate effectively, both verbally and in writing, essential; creativity, initiative, and good judgment; excellent decision-making, problem-solving, and research skills; self-confident with an outgoing personality; ability to interact well and patiently with customers

Special Requirements—Certifications are available but seldom required

CAREER LADDER

```
┌─────────────────────────────────────┐
│   Vice President of Marketing;       │
│ Public Relations Company Manager;    │
│           Game Tester                │
└─────────────────────────────────────┘

┌─────────────────────────────────────┐
│    Public Relations Manager;         │
│     Customer Service Manager         │
└─────────────────────────────────────┘

┌─────────────────────────────────────┐
│    Public Relations Assistant;       │
│    Customer Service Assistant        │
└─────────────────────────────────────┘
```

Position Description

Public Relations (PR) Managers and their staff deal primarily with the media in carefully orchestrated campaigns to help build public awareness of the products released by game developers and publishers. Their media targets are trade magazines, Web sites, general-interest publications, newspapers, and radio and television. Their success is measured in previews, reviews, feature coverage, and, the biggest and most influential prize of all, magazine covers.

Public Relations Managers and their staff write press releases to announce new games and events associated with them. They assemble "press kits"—documents and CDs containing demos and images—to inform journalists about the new release. They send out copies of games to magazines for review and they invite the press to attend parties and other special events to showcase the game. In addition, they use videos, concept art, interviews with members of the development team, and, above all, screenshots. The purpose of all this activity is to create "buzz"—customer interest and excitement in the months before the game product actually becomes available. The most important tools that should be made available to the PR people by the game development team are demos and screenshots.

Demos can last anywhere from just a few seconds to several hours, determined by the purpose of the demo. Audiences for such demos are primarily journalists, buyers, trade show audiences, and the public. Demos are not easy to prepare as they have a different purpose from the overall game, as well as a different rhythm, design, and execution, making them a mini-project unto themselves for the development team. Screenshots are single photo shots of scenes and locations in the game designed to exhibit the game to its maximum advantage. They have to be carefully created and controlled. Web sites are always clamoring for new and exclusive shots of upcoming games, and PR has to be careful not to overexpose the product so that consumers will *not* feel they have seen all that the game has to offer by the time of its release.

Additional tools used are interviews with members of the development team and sell sheets. The latter are usually one-page flyers that marketing and sales distribute to the retail trade with feature summaries, attractive graphics (or screenshots), and information of interest to the retail buyer.

Public Relations Managers and their staff devote much effort to cultivating relationships with media and retail people. They have the delicate task of always telling the truth about their products, even when it is embarrassing, yet doing so in a way that puts the development company and its products in the best possible light. They have to be continuously in contact with people without becoming a nuisance and must maintain a professional stance, particularly in social events. When promotional events involve both consumers and the media, PR Managers coordinate with the marketing department. Public Relations Managers and their staff must understand fully all the game products they are promoting and find exciting angles to attract media attention. They cannot merely repeat what the game developer has told them, as many of the journalists they talk with play more games than anyone else in the business.

Customer Service Managers and their staff work to support the game player base audience as a title is released and then long afterwards. They run the help phone lines or hint hotlines, Web sites, and technical support Frequently Asked Questions (FAQ) sections on Web sites. They answer questions from the game audience and assist game players with resolving installation, patching, or compatibility issues. This activity requires that they have a great familiarity with the products, considerable technical competence, and unbe-

lievable patience. It takes a fair amount of imagination and analytical skill to diagnose a software problem over the phone or through e-mails! They coordinate with the Public Relations Manager on keeping game developers informed about public sentiment and reaction to game issues and specific game particulars.

Salaries
According to the U. S. Department of Labor's Bureau of Labor Statistics, median annual incomes for salaried public relations specialists were $43,830 in May 2004. The middle 50 percent earned between $32,970 and $59,360, while the lowest 10 percent earned less than $25,750, and the top 10 percent earned more than $81,120. For customer service representatives, in this same time period, median annual earnings were $27,020. The middle 50 percent had incomes between $21,510 and $34,560. The lowest 10 percent earned less than $17,680, and the highest 10 percent received more than $44,160.

Employment Prospects
As many people are attracted to the profession of public relations because of the high profile nature of the work, keen competition continues for entry-level jobs on public relations teams. The number of qualified applicants is estimated to exceed the number of job openings. Opportunities are best for college graduates who have combined a degree in journalism, public relations, advertising, or another communications-related field with a public relations internship or other related work experience. Most Public Relations Managers must have at least five to seven years' experience working within a game public relations environment before becoming qualified for their position, and they need to demonstrate both their administrative and their managerial expertise. Nonetheless, the U.S. Department of Labor's *Occupational Outlook Handbook* expects that employment of public relations specialists will grow faster than the average for all occupations through 2014.

Likewise, the *Occupational Outlook Handbook* expects that employment of customer service representatives will increase faster than the average for all occupations through the year 2014. The increased reliance of the game development industry on these crucial individuals (who may well determine the continued success of their game products with their customer base) greatly heightens their chance of employment.

Advancement Prospects
Successful Public Relations Managers with a game development company or publisher may look for greater management and administrative responsibility by moving into a position as vice president of marketing for the entire company or publisher. Alternatively, they may decide to join a

public relations firm as its top PR specialist or management specialist or even set up their own public relations firm.

Customer Service Managers may have several different career options. They may decide to trade on their marketing and customer service experience to move forward within the marketing team to higher management positions. On the other hand, customer service is good training for a position as a production game tester, as their skills in helping customers navigate through software problems give them insight and experience in reviewing the positive and negative aspects of games. From a post as game tester, they can advance to more responsible positions within the production team.

Education and Training

The usual requirement for a public relations specialist (and a Public Relations Manager) is an undergraduate degree in advertising, communications, journalism, or public relations. Their curriculum should include courses in advertising, business administration, public affairs, public speaking, and creative and technical writing. It is also recommended that they gain some practical experience in public relations, usually through internship programs while in college.

For a customer relations representative (and a Customer Service Manager) a high school diploma is an absolute requirement, and an undergraduate degree in communications, marketing, or public relations is recommended. Courses should include business administration, computer science, English, journalism, and public relations. Training in customer relations is frequently done on the job in an entry-level position with the customer relations group or as an adjunct to the public relations team.

Special Requirements

Accredited certifications for Public Relations Managers are seldom requested or required. However, for professional satisfaction, Public Relations Managers and their specialists who are members of the Public Relations Society of America (PRSA) can participate in an examination for accreditation. The Universal Accreditation Board gives the Accredited in Public Relations (APR) designation to those who have at least five years of full-time public relations work and a bachelor's degree in a communications-related field. The International Association of Business Communicators (IABC) also has an accreditation program, resulting in the earning of the Accredited Business Communicator (ABC) designation.

Experience, Skills, and Personality Traits

Prior experience dealing with the public in some capacity or working as an assistant in a media organization is helpful for public relations specialists joining a game development company or publisher. The ability to communicate persuasively, both orally and in writing, with other members of the game development team, the public relations staff, the media, and the game public is vital. In the pursuit of their work, PR Managers need tact, good judgment, and an exceptional ability to establish and maintain effective personal relationships. They should be creative, highly motivated, resistant to stress, and be both flexible and decisive. They should be poised in their dealing with the media and the public, as well as persuasive with the technical members of the game development team in order to gain technical details to help the media better understand the game development process.

As Customer Service Managers and their staff provide the interface between the game playing customer and the game development company or publisher, they should have a friendly and professional manner. The ability to deal patiently with problems and complaints and to remain courteous when faced with difficult problems or angry customers is essential. They should have excellent vocal and written communication skills. Knowledge of one or more foreign languages is considered a plus. They must have a clear grasp of the game development process, gain a thorough knowledge of the specific games for which they will interact with the public, and exhibit an overriding love of games and game playing.

Unions and Associations

Public Relations Managers (as well as Customer Service Managers) and their staffs may find it useful to belong to the primary association of the profession, the Public Relations Society of America (PRSA). In addition, joining computer and game industry organizations and reading the trade press are other important ways to keep in touch with industry practices, technology, and trends.

Tips for Entry

1. When taking journalism classes, focus on how public relations people "manage" the media in order to plant favorable ideas about their product and key personnel and how they minimize any seemingly negative aspects of products.
2. Practice your public relations skills by volunteering to publicize school events or act as a "media contact" for a campus organization.
3. Study Internet Web sites for game companies (or other types of firms) that provide customer support for their products and observe how well thought out their postings of frequently asked questions (FAQs) are presented and how you might make such sites more customer friendly.

SALES AND DISTRIBUTION MANAGER

CAREER PROFILE

Duties: Responsible for the sales and distribution of electronic games by establishing relationships with distributors and retailers; manage sales and distribution staff of a game development company or game publisher

Alternate Title(s): Sales Director; Product Manager

Salary Range: $50,000 to $95,000 or more

Employment Prospects: Fair to Good

Advancement Prospects: Fair

Prerequisites:

Education or Training—Four-year technical degree (in engineering or a computer-related area) with business courses combined with a master's degree in business administration recommended, especially for managerial positions in game industry sales

Experience—Three to five years' experience in sales or marketing in the game industry

Special Skills and Personality Traits—Ability to glean key information from technical details; aggressiveness and perseverance; highly organized with ability to prioritize scheduling; personal drive and energy; strong interpersonal skills; supervisory, motivational, and leadership skills

CAREER LADDER

```
+---------------------------------+
|       Marketing Manager         |
+---------------------------------+

+---------------------------------+
|  Sales and Distribution Manager |
+---------------------------------+

+---------------------------------+
|       Sales Staff Person        |
+---------------------------------+
```

Position Description

The sales force of a game development company or publisher, under the direction of the Sales and Distribution Manager, maintains personal relationships with wholesalers/retailers who order the newly released games in bulk. These buyers work for chain stores, national or regional distributors, "club" stores, home entertainment rental chains, and even original equipment manufacturers (OEMs). Each of these customers requires a different sales approach, and each strategy needs different game material to support it.

Chain stores make money only if they continuously turn over their inventory. This need to move product is the driving economic force behind every retail business. While they may be eager to sell the game, what they care about more is getting enough money to pay the overhead for the space that the game is taking up. Therefore, games that do not sell quickly are sent back and replaced by ones that do. Generally, retailers do not care about a broad selection of product if most of that selection does not move. That is why there is such a push in the game industry to promote new products throughout the game development process—to build a "buzz" with customers about forthcoming titles in order to guarantee quick sales. Chain stores also require the game publisher or developer to pay for all or some of the advertising of their product in the store's ads, flyers, and newspaper circulars, as well as any special display positioning within the store. Many game development companies and publishers also send their Sales Manager and staff to annual meetings of these chain stores to put on miniature trade shows in which the sales group educates the store managers about upcoming products so that, in turn, they'll recommend them to their clerks and customers.

National or regional distributors buy games in bulk and then sell selectively to smaller stores that, then, are able to carry less inventory but still access a wide range of game products. The Sales Manager's job is to encourage the wholesaler's representatives to be aware of and promote their range of games. Game publishers frequently organize a special day at the wholesaler's place of business where their Sales Manager and staff promote the publisher's games with videos, promotional material, and other incentives so that they, in turn, will promote the game to their customers.

An OEM is a company that makes hardware, including computers, graphics or sound cards, joysticks, and mouses. These companies want to bundle the publisher's game software with their hardware to add extra value to their own products and to distinguish them from their competition. Games Sales Managers meet with OEM management to inform them about their games and to establish deals, which may require preparing special versions of the game that will work with the particular piece of hardware and show off its features. These deals may also include the hardware manufacturers' providing financial support to develop new games that will run on their hardware. Such bundling agreements are a good way for a game publisher to continue making money out of a game that is not selling well any more.

The retail and mail-order businesses (either from the publisher or from a distributor) are the traditional ways to sell game software to consumers. However, they get some serious competition from other distribution channels. Online (downloading) distribution is rapidly becoming an increasingly popular mechanism for selling less intricate games. There are still problems for the larger software game products, as most users' computer network access is too slow to download the requisite 650 megabytes of data at a time, but this situation is changing as more potential game players gain broadband access to the Internet and problems of encryption and other mechanisms are resolved. There is even a move to sell access to games over personal cell phones as the technology of that fast-expanding part of the communication industry continues to grow.

Shareware (where the game is given away free in the hope that people will like it enough to pay for it or for a more advanced version of the product) is another method used by game publishers and developers of less complex product. Some game publishers have their Sales Managers work on deals whereby their games are available as rentals in DVD stores, though, generally, this practice is discouraged by the game industry, which is more focused on the buying of games.

In all these transactions and pursuits after sales, it is Sales and Distribution Managers, in conjunction with marketing managers, who are tasked with moving the game successfully into the marketplace and attaining a favorable position for the game against its competition.

Salaries

According to the U.S. Department of Labor's Bureau of Labor Statistics, median annual earnings in May 2004 for Sales Managers, generally, were $84,220. Salaries will vary according to the level of managerial responsibility, length of service, and size of the game publisher or development company. Salaries for beginning sales staff will average about $35,000, and the income for Sales and Distribution Managers can range from $50,000 to $95,000 or more, depending upon their success rate.

Employment Prospects

Many game Sales and Distribution Managers have risen through the ranks of the sales staff after three or more years' experience in sales or marketing within the industry. However, competition for this highly sought-after position is strong. Building a strong track record in sales (together with a degree of patience) is the best path to gaining a managerial position on the sales (or marketing) team of a game publisher or developer.

Advancement Prospects

As with sales staff people, the amount of total sales is the most important factor in a Sales and Distribution Manager's career. Success at the smaller development companies can lead to a "jump" to a larger company or a publisher, with the accompanying increase in responsibility and earnings. In some situations, the Sales Manager's next career advance may be to become the marketing manager who, in this instance, has greater responsibility for the overall sales and distribution of the game product. However, once again, competition is stiff.

Education and Training

Sales and Distribution Managers generally need a four-year degree in a computer-related field (for the necessary background in understanding the technical aspects of game development) along with a strong preparation through business-related courses. Often, game employers prefer individuals applying for this position to have both a technical degree and a master's degree in business administration. Entry-level salespersons often continue their education at night or online to gain the qualifications needed for the higher post of manager.

Experience, Skills, and Personality Traits

Sales and Distribution Managers usually have several years of background in sales or marketing. They must be able to handle the administrative details of the position: managing a staff, as well as dealing with retailers, wholesalers, store personnel, and manufacturers. They need to be able to motivate, train, and lead their sales staff. They have to keep up with the many reports coming from the marketing and public relations staffs about the game products (both in production and already on the market) and be able to identify the key facts and conclusions relevant to sales projections. They need to interact professionally with retailers, wholesalers, store personnel, and manufacturers and be capable of establishing agreements with them.

Successful Sales and Distribution Managers must have outgoing personalities and a lot of drive and energy. They also have to be very well disciplined and have the ability to focus on details while keeping track of the larger picture of the sales process for their companies. They need to be aggressive supervisors who lead by example. They must be extremely persuasive, persistent, and always enthusiastic.

Unions and Associations

Sales and Distribution Managers can belong to sales and marketing organizations such as the American Marketing Association (AMA) as well as groups for the advertising and retailing industries. They may find it also useful to belong to specific trade industry associations for the game industry, such as the International Game Developers Association (IGDA).

Tips for Entry

1. In college, as you work toward your technical degree, take courses in business administration to discover if you have a vocation for selling products and managing people, both of which skills you will need to be a successful Sales Manager.

2. Get sales experience as soon as possible, whether in a store or as a sales representative or sales trainee.

3. Enhance your love of electronic game playing by playing all types of games and note how successfully (or not) they are promoted and sold to the public. Learn from the mistakes made by the unsuccessful games, and speculate how you would have handled the promotion and sales effort differently.

MULTIMEDIA AND CONSUMER ELECTRONICS: VIDEO AND DVD

DISTRIBUTION AND SALES

DISTRIBUTION MANAGER

CAREER PROFILE

Duties: Manage an office or business that distributes video and DVD software, hardware, and accessories to retail stores

Alternate Title(s): Branch Office Manager; Independent Representative

Salary Range: $49,000 to $85,000 or more

Employment Prospects: Fair

Advancement Prospects: Poor

Prerequisites:

Education or Training—High school diploma minimum requirement; undergraduate degree in advertising, business administration, or marketing preferable

Experience—Minimum of five to seven years in product or program marketing or sales

Special Skills and Personality Traits—Assertiveness and persistence; good business sense; leadership ability; organizational talent; persuasiveness

CAREER LADDER

```
┌─────────────────────────────┐
│      Marketing Manager       │
└─────────────────────────────┘

┌─────────────────────────────┐
│     Distribution Manager     │
└─────────────────────────────┘

┌─────────────────────────────┐
│  Salesperson; Store Manager  │
└─────────────────────────────┘
```

Position Description

A Distribution Manager acquires products from manufacturers or wholesalers and sells or rents them to retail stores, online outlets and e-commerce stores and is, thus, the sales executive in the middle of the chain of distribution in the consumer electronics industry. Distribution Managers are in charge of a sales organization that is the intermediary between either a national original equipment manufacturer (OEM) or a national video, DVD, or blank video tape and DVD disc wholesaler and a retail outlet. A Distribution Manager's key responsibilities are to establish and meet sales goals in the territory covered by the sales organization and to supervise the activities of salespersons within that organization.

The majority of national manufacturers and wholesalers in consumer electronics distribute their products to retail stores and online outlets in one of two ways: through company-owned district branches and/or the company's own retail Web site or through nonaffiliated, regional, independent distribution firms of various types or other e-commerce retail Web sites. These stores, in turn, then sell or rent the products to consumers.

A Distribution Manager who is employed full time by a national wholesaler or manufacturer (but is stationed away from the home office) is usually called a branch office manager. As such, this person supervises a staff that takes orders, makes sales calls, provides promotional materials, and, in some cases, even stocks the products in a retail store. Distribution Managers who are branch managers usually report to the marketing manager of the parent company. National wholesalers or manufacturers of consumer electronics video and DVD products and accessories usually employ from eight to 10 district branch office Distribution Managers. These executives supervise all the sales to the retail stores or online outlets in their specific geographic territory.

Distribution Managers employed by independent distribution companies, under contract to distribute the products or labels of one or more national wholesalers or manufacturers, are known as independent representatives (or "reps"). These independent companies usually have an exclusive distribution contract in a given territory or region. Like branch Distribution Managers, independent representatives are responsible for the sales to the retail stores and online outlets in a prescribed geographic area. Independent representatives in charge of such an independent company supervise a staff that sells and distributes to the retail store or online outlet.

In addition to their supervisory activities, Distribution Managers are responsible for providing overnight or special catalog order fulfillment to the retailers in their assigned territory and must maintain and balance the inventory of products in warehouses or distribution points for their redistribution to retail stores and online outlets. They supervise the servicing of all retail accounts and must actively seek and acquire new retail store accounts. They recommend to their retail accounts the stocking of specific accessories, equipment, and video and DVD products and suggest new products, product lines, or product improvements to manufacturers or wholesalers whose product they sell to the stores.

Salaries

The salary of a Distribution Manager who is a branch office manager will vary according to the extent of the territory, the size of the company, its employment policies, and the individual's experience. Earnings may range from $49,000 to $85,000, according to industry sources. Many branch office managers are paid a base salary and a relatively modest commission for sales made within their territories. Some managers may work according to a sales quota and receive bonuses for exceeding it, while others may work strictly on a commission basis. Fringe benefits can be relatively liberal and usually include a reasonable expense account, a company car, and the usual retirement and health benefits of the parent company.

Most independent representatives own all or a portion of their distribution company and, thus, receive all or a portion of that company's profits. They may earn considerably more than branch office managers, but their income is dependent entirely on the amount of their sales.

Employment Prospects

The job of Distribution Manager is one that individuals obtain after some sales experience and, thus, is not an entry-level position. Most job opportunities for branch office managers occur when individuals in that position move on to another industry post. While there is considerable turnover in these sales management positions, the competition for this job is intense. National wholesalers or manufacturers look primarily for bright and aggressive salespersons to fill any such openings. With the ongoing consolidation within the industry—the large-scale acquisition or elimination of smaller companies—distribution channels nationwide continue to be streamlined. The result is the removal of competition between smaller companies covering the same territory and the resultant assigning by

one national organization of a single individual to direct operations within that region.

Another change that has affected both job opportunities and traditional retail procedures is the exploding growth of Internet sales of consumer electronics directly to customers via Web sites. The full impact of these online sales on brick-and-mortar retail outlets for consumer electronic products is yet to be determined, but it has been significant and, thus, affects the job opportunities in the more traditional retail distribution industry.

Advancement Prospects

The opportunities for Distribution Managers to move upward in a career path are generally poor. Some branch managers are promoted to more responsible marketing or sales posts, such as marketing manager, in their company's home office. Other Distribution Managers may move up the career ladder by taking similar jobs at increased salaries at other industry-related firms. Some may even start their own consumer electronics operations or retail/Internet businesses.

Independent representatives usually advance their careers by expanding the territories that they cover and the product lines that they represent.

Education and Training

All national companies that employ branch office Distribution Managers require a minimum of a high school diploma. Most prefer candidates to have additional training in marketing and sales distribution or sales management. In addition, most large national employers require an undergraduate (or, in some cases, graduate) degree in advertising, business administration, or marketing. Moreover, they look for candidates that have the ability to motivate and lead a sales staff, which is just as crucial as a formal education in marketing or sales.

Experience, Skills, and Personality Traits

Employers at national companies usually require a minimum of five to seven years of sales or marketing experience when they look to promote an employee to becoming a branch office Distribution Manager. For this reason, middle management experience in sales and marketing is preferred. Most independent representatives also have had extensive sales and marketing experience before setting up (or joining others in establishing) an independent distribution operation.

Both branch office managers and independent representatives must be excellent businesspeople with solid sales and marketing backgrounds. They must be aggressive, competitive, and persistent and display good leadership qualities. They need to be persuasive and well organized, with a healthy respect for maintaining and expanding profit margins for their company.

Unions and Associations

There are no unions that serve as bargaining agents for Distribution Managers, either as independent representatives or as branch office managers. Some independent representatives may find it useful to belong to the Electronic Representatives Association (ERA) to share trade concerns and pursue career development.

Tips for Entry

1. Obtain experience in sales and marketing in a retail-oriented company.

2. Explore participation in management training programs and participation in seminars and conferences provided by professional societies related to the industry.

3. Consider opportunities for continuing education, either in-house or at local colleges and universities, in such subjects as sales management evaluation, marketing communication, or promotion to further your sales and marketing skills.

EQUIPMENT SERVICE TECHNICIAN

CAREER PROFILE

Duties: Repair and service consumer electronic equipment at a consumer electronics retail store or in the field

Alternate Title(s): Bench Technician; Electronic Home Entertainment Equipment Repairer; Field Technician; Maintenance Technician; Service Technician

Salary Range: $20,000 to $40,000 or more

Employment Prospects: Fair

Advancement Prospects: Fair to Good

Prerequisites:

Education or Training—High school diploma required; vocational or technical school training necessary

Experience—Minimum of six months to a year of electronic equipment maintenance preferable

Special Skills and Personality Traits—Electronic aptitude; good communication skills; inquisitiveness; manual dexterity; mechanical ability

Special Requirements—A certification from one of the electronics industry certification study programs usually required

CAREER LADDER

```
┌─────────────────────────────────┐
│        Maintenance Engineer;     │
│   Media Technician; Television   │
│      Engineering Technician      │
└─────────────────────────────────┘

┌─────────────────────────────────┐
│   Equipment Service Technician   │
└─────────────────────────────────┘

┌─────────────────────────────────┐
│   Vocational or Technical School │
└─────────────────────────────────┘
```

Position Description

Electronic Equipment Service Technicians are responsible for the maintenance and repair of a variety of electronic equipment, ranging from video and audio disc players to video and digital cameras, video and digital recorders, stereo system components, cell phones, mp3 players, and audiovisual equipment. Service Technicians may work in a retail electronics store or in a repair center, where they usually report to the manager of the facility. Equipped with a full array of electronic tools and parts, they repair smaller and portable equipment that is brought to the repair shops by customers for servicing. Repair technicians at such repair locations are known as bench technicians. When larger, less mobile equipment breaks down, customers may pay repairer technicians to come to their locations if the equipment does not include a service contract which covers such in-home visits. Equipment Service Technicians who travel to a customer's location with a limited set of tools and parts for such repairs are known as field technicians.

When equipment breaks down, repair service technicians check for common causes of trouble, such as dirty or defective components. Many repairs consist simply of cleaning and lubricating equipment. If routine inspections do not pinpoint the trouble, service technicians may have to refer to manufacturer schematics and specifications and must be able to interpret diagrams and charts. They also employ a variety of test equipment to diagnose and identify malfunctions. Multimeters detect short circuits, failed capacitors, and blown fuses; color-bar and dot generators provide onscreen test patterns; signal generators test signals; and oscilloscopes and digital storage scopes measure complex waveforms produced by electronic equipment. Service technicians need to be familiar with the digital electronics, microprocessors, and integrated circuitry utilized in today's highly complex electronic hardware.

At a retail store, Equipment Service Technicians usually maintain the technical equipment owned and utilized by the facility as well as handling repairs on customers' equipment.

They also are responsible for setting up and maintaining a comprehensive repair service that can be a profit center for the business. The presence of a good repair department can be instrumental in bringing back customers for new purchases and building the store's reputation.

It is usual for only one Equipment Service Technician to be employed in an average electronics retail outlet. In some instances, a group of Equipment Service Technicians will operate out of one main store and repair equipment sent to them from branch locations. From four to 10 or more service technicians may be employed at a repair center that operates as a separate (but sometimes affiliated) business, and they may provide electronic repair work for many stores, regardless of their ownership. Some of the largest organizations set up their own independent repair centers that, subsequently, deal only with their own products (or those which are contracted to be sold in their outlets).

Equipment Service Technicians work with manufacturers' field representatives or design engineers in order to isolate equipment problems. They need to attend training programs regularly to keep abreast of new equipment and maintenance/repair techniques. In addition, they are responsible for maintaining an inventory of supplies, accessories, and test gear used in their servicing of equipment.

Salaries

According to the U.S. Bureau of Labor Statistics, in 2004 the mean hourly earnings of electronic Equipment Service Technicians were $14.45, and the mean annual wage was $30,060.

Salaries often depend on the geographical location of the store or repair center and the competition from other retail outlets in the area. Usually, Equipment Service Technicians are rewarded financially upon completion of certificate training or other in-service training programs. In addition, there are usually ample opportunities for overtime work. Some of the larger retail chains who have repair facilities also offer excellent benefit programs.

Employment Prospects

The opportunities for employment are only fair. The U.S. Department of Labor's Bureau of Labor Statistics projects that employment for service technicians will grow more slowly than the average through 2012, due to a decreasing demand for repair work. As electronic equipment, particularly home entertainment hardware, becomes less expensive than in the past, the need for repairs instead of replacement of equipment becomes less viable. When malfunctions do occur in most consumer electronics equipment, it is often cheaper today for consumers to replace the equipment rather than pay for repairs (and most present-day warranty programs for such equipment are strictly limited in what repairs they cover).

Nonetheless, job openings will occur because of the need to replace technicians who have retired or who have transferred to higher paying technical jobs in other occupations. Employment opportunities will be best for applicants with hands-on experience and demonstrable knowledge of electronics.

Advancement Prospects

Many Equipment Service Technicians improve their skills and, with further training, advance their careers by moving into broadcast-related electronics as maintenance engineers or becoming technicians at television stations, networks, cable TV systems, or multichannel multipoint distribution service (MMDS) stations. A few technicians may look for advancement and security as media technicians at educational institutions or find employment at a manufacturer's facility. Some may even transition to computer and office machine repair. In all cases, competition for these higher paying positions remains stiff.

Education and Training

A high school diploma and some vocational or technical school training are the typical requirements for being hired as an Equipment Service Technician. Coursework in the basic sciences, algebra, and physics is suggested. In addition, drafting courses will help in the understanding of spatial relationships and physical characteristics of equipment. Specialized training is available at technical schools, community colleges, extension divisions of colleges and universities, and public or private vocational and technical schools. Some training may even be taken by correspondence study. In addition, some manufacturers operate their own training centers.

Special Requirements

Most Equipment Service Technicians serve an apprenticeship. After four years of work experience, an individual can qualify for a voluntary examination leading to certification as a journeyman certified electronic technician (CET) under the auspices of the International Society of Certified Electronic Technicians (ISCET). Other similar certifications are offered by such organizations as the Association of Communications Technicians (ACT), the Custom Electronic Design and Installation Association, and the Electronic Technicians Association International. Some states may require Equipment Service Technicians to pass a proficiency test.

Experience, Skills, and Personality Traits

While six months to a year in electronics or audiovisual repair work is preferred, lengthy employment experience is not generally required for entry-level positions in electronic equipment servicing. Many employers hire recent vocational or technical school graduates and train them on the job.

However, some experience in the operation of video, digital, photographic, audio, and audiovisual equipment is essential. Applicants for technician posts should have a basic knowledge of electronics. They should be familiar with schematics and have some hands-on experience repairing electronic equipment. They should have inquisitive minds and should enjoy solving technical problems. They must possess good manual dexterity and an aptitude for electronics. An ability and patience to do detailed work with a high degree of accuracy is needed, along with the ability to work independently. As field technicians work closely with customers, it is important they have good communication skills and a neat appearance. Employers also may require field technicians to have valid driver's licenses.

Unions and Associations

There are no unions that serve as bargaining agents for Equipment Service Technicians. Some may belong to the Institute of Electrical and Electronics Engineers (IEEE) or the National Electronic Service Dealers Association (NESDA). Others may also belong to ISCET or ACT to share professional concerns and networking.

Tips for Entry

1. While in high school, take courses in electronics, mechanics, physics, and math, all necessary background for a service technician.
2. While in high school look for intern programs with electronics firms to gain practical experience in the application of your studies and as a leg up on your further vocational/technical course work after high school.
3. Building electronic equipment from hobby kits is another good way of learning how to read schematics and improving dexterity with your hands.

MARKETING MANAGER

CAREER PROFILE

Duties: Supervise all national marketing and distribution for a consumer electronics product or program company

Alternate Title(s): Director of Marketing; National Sales Manager; Vice President of Marketing

Salary Range: $55,000 to $170,000 or more

Employment Prospects: Poor to Fair

Advancement Prospects: Poor

Prerequisites:

Education or Training—Undergraduate degree in advertising, communications, or marketing required; graduate degree in business administration recommended

Experience—Minimum of five years' experience in consumer electronics marketing

Special Skills and Personality Traits—Excellent business expertise; good judgment; leadership skills; organizational talents; persuasiveness; promotional abilities

CAREER LADDER

```
┌─────────────────────────────────────┐
│  President or Chief Executive Officer │
│   (Consumer Electronics Company)      │
└─────────────────────────────────────┘

┌─────────────────────────────────────┐
│         Marketing Manager             │
└─────────────────────────────────────┘

┌─────────────────────────────────────┐
│        Distribution Manager           │
└─────────────────────────────────────┘
```

Position Description

A Marketing Manager is the top sales executive in a consumer electronics firm and, as such, is in charge of all national—and, sometimes, international—marketing, sales, advertising, and promotion activities associated with the company's consumer electronics products or programs. It is the major responsibility of this individual to market aggressively and successfully the product line(s) to consumers.

There are over 500 consumer electronics companies in the United States selling videocassette and DVD equipment, audio/stereo machines, video games, traditional audiovisual equipment, blank videotapes and digital discs, and electronic accessories of all sorts. With the introduction of digital video discs (DVDs), the market demand for VHS videocassettes was seriously challenged. Additionally, with the emergence of e-commerce as a viable direct sales channel, traditional retail outlets have faced a substantial challenge, as buying electronic hardware products and software programs online has become a widespread and popular form of distribution.

The success or failure of a consumer electronics company's total sales efforts depends on the talents of the Marketing Manager in strengthening marketing strategies, improving the visibility and consumer awareness of hardware and tape/disc/video products, and maximizing the volume of sales while containing costs. The Marketing Manager must also provide marketing research to assist in product development, create the marketing strategies to introduce new merchandise and support sales, and establish company-wide policies on price, discounts, special sales, rentals, returns and exchanges, and other terms of sale.

Marketing Managers also supervise retail sales and distribution channels through company branch offices, independent firms, and authorized dealers. They oversee all print, radio-TV, and Internet advertising, promotional literature, advertising billboards, and point-of-purchase displays and other in-store merchandising. In addition, they manage all marketing and sales employees and, often, the advertising and promotion staffs.

Marketing Managers usually report directly to the company's president or chief executive officer, and they are normally located at the company's national headquarters. Marketing Managers supervise a staff that may have as few as five or more than 200 people.

Salaries

The financial remunerations for Marketing Managers are usually considerable, although they will vary according to the size of the company, its sales volume, and type of electronic hardware and/or software manufactured or distributed. The U.S. Bureau of Labor Statistics estimates that the mean annual wage of Marketing Managers, generally, during 2004 was $100,020. The lowest 10 percent of them earned $47,100 yearly, and the highest 10 percent earned $126,290 or more per year. In the electronics industry, salaries tend to be somewhat higher for this occupation, ranging from $48,000 to $150,000 or more annually, depending upon seniority and the size of the product lines.

Beyond a base salary, yearly earnings for Marketing Managers also usually include some type of bonus arrangement, a liberal expense account, stock options, profit sharing, and life insurance, health and retirement plans. Some managers also receive a small commission on overall yearly sales. Membership in social or country clubs, a company car, and other perquisites are often offered as part of a compensation package.

Employment Prospects

Opportunities for employment are only fair at best, as there are a limited number of domestic electronics products companies that employ full-time Marketing Managers. Most of these companies concentrate on the home entertainment market, but some also sell specialized software programming to the school, health, or business markets. While the electronics industry as a whole is expanding, due to the successful introduction of DVD discs and the public's enthusiastic response, competition for the coveted position of Marketing Manager remains severe. Only the most able and successful marketing professionals reach this position, and then only after a good number of years of demonstrated success. Many of them have had extensive experience as distribution managers with the company, or in a related consumer electronics firm.

Advancement Prospects

Opportunities for advancement for Marketing Managers are poor. For many of them, the attainment of this position is the peak of a successful marketing career. Some may move further upward to assume overall control of a company as its president or chief executive officer. Most such positions are still held by individuals with strong marketing backgrounds. Some Marketing Managers may advance their careers by forming their own consumer electronics firms or by joining larger companies.

Education and Training

An undergraduate degree in advertising, business administration, communications, or marketing is a basic requirement for the position of Marketing Manager. Many managers have a master's degree in business administration (MBA) as well. Courses in sales management are also highly recommended. As an additional tool, training in computer science would be helpful, as most management information systems are totally computerized. Those few managers who do not have an undergraduate degree must have considerable experience and hands-on success in marketing of electronics products.

Experience, Skills, and Personality Traits

Most Marketing Managers at major electronics products companies have obtained the post only after five to 10 years of product, program, or packaged goods marketing experience. Some smaller companies may require less experience, but an extensive background in advertising and promotion is still essential.

Marketing Managers need to be poised, confident business leaders with exceptional organizational skills. Many of them have a flair for promotion and public speaking. They are good conceptualizers and are extremely persuasive in the business environment. Successful Marketing Managers must be able to make sound business judgments and possess outstanding leadership skills.

Unions and Associations

There are no unions that represent Marketing Managers, as they are considered a part of the management team of a company. However, many firms belong to, and participate in, industry trade associations, such as the Electronic Industry Alliance (EIA), the International Communications Industries Association (ICIA), the International Recording Media Association, and the Motion Picture Association of America (MPAA). Marketing Managers often represent their companies at trade meetings of these groups. In addition, some Marketing Managers find it beneficial to belong to such umbrella organizations as the American Management Association or the American Marketing Association in order to share mutual professional concerns and discuss the developing of policies and procedures.

Tips for Entry

1. While earning your degree in advertising, communications, or marketing, be sure that you include courses in sales management as well.
2. During your undergraduate years, investigate possible internships with video/digital electronics firms to gain a hands-on familiarity with the ever-changing product line.
3. Add public speaking courses to your educational agenda, as this will be a valuable asset to your eventual career as Marketing Manager.

SALES CLERK (RETAIL)

CAREER PROFILE

Duties: Sell video and DVD products software, consumer electronic equipment, and accessories at the retail level

Alternate Title(s): None

Salary Range: $15,000 to $40,000 or more

Employment Prospects: Good to Excellent

Advancement Prospects: Good

Prerequisites:

Education or Training—High school diploma required

Experience—Some retail sales background recommended

Special Skills and Personality Traits—Dependability; good interpersonal skills; initiative and persistence; sales aptitude

Special Requirements—A certification given by the Certified Media Specialist Program of the International Communications Industries Association is available for some sales personnel in the audiovisual equipment field.

CAREER LADDER

```
┌─────────────────────────────────┐
│   Store Manager; Salesperson    │
└─────────────────────────────────┘

┌─────────────────────────────────┐
│          Sales Clerk            │
└─────────────────────────────────┘

┌─────────────────────────────────┐
│ High School/College; Retail Sales Clerk │
└─────────────────────────────────┘
```

Position Description

A Sales Clerk is responsible for selling video hardware (equipment), software (video programming), and products (videocassettes and DVD discs) to customers at a retail store. In addition, Sales Clerks also sell video and audiovisual accessories, such as connecting boxes, cables, blank videocassettes or blank DVD/CD discs, bulbs, and other such supplies. In venues that specialize in the renting of videocassettes and DVDs, the Sales Clerk is involved in that rental process with customers.

Sales Clerks usually report directly to the store manager or owner. In small stores, clerks are responsible for the selling or renting of all displayed merchandise, whereas, in larger operations, they usually specialize in either the software and products or the hardware, or in a particular line of equipment.

The major responsibility of Sales Clerks is to service customer requests and to inform customers about the merchandise offered by the store. They outline the various options available for customers, demonstrate equipment, programs, and accessories, and persuade the customer to make purchases.

Sales Clerks operate in a very dynamic environment. New products, equipment, and label lines and programs are constantly being introduced, as are new merchandising techniques, discounts, and special sales. Different customers move through the store daily, each presenting new sales challenges. A Sales Clerk must balance all these factors and devise new sales methods that meet customers' needs and maximize sales for the store.

In addition, Sales Clerks must study and understand the operation and/or user characteristics of each new product offered by the store. Often, they assist in setting up in-store and window merchandising displays. While computerized sales equipment keeps track of sales, Sales Clerks are often called upon to maintain inventory records and, in some instances, sales files.

Salaries

Compensation for Sales Clerks is relatively low. The majority of consumer electronics retailers pay either a straight salary, a salary with commission, or a salary and a bonus for good sales. Most employers start beginners with a small salary and a relatively healthy commission on each sale. As each individual progresses, the salary is raised and commissions are lowered. Some stores have incentive sales plans and rewards to motivate employees. Most Sales Clerks are paid on an hourly basis.

In 2004, the mean annual wage for retail sales clerks in electronics and appliance stores was $24,570, according to the U.S. Bureau of Labor Statistics. Beginning yearly salaries for inexperienced full-time individuals were between $14,000 and $15,000, while experienced employees with good sales track records may expect ranges from $24,000 to $40,000 or more. Benefits are usually minimal, with only the larger stores or chains sometimes offering medical and retirement plans.

Employment Prospects

Sales Clerk positions are an entry-level job at most consumer electronics venues. Most of these operations employ three to nine workers in sales for various shifts and assignments. The average store also usually employs four to eight part-time employees.

According to the U.S. Bureau of Labor Statistics, employment opportunities for retail Sales Clerks are expected to be good. There is a large turnover among consumer electronics Sales Clerks as workers transfer to other occupations, advance into higher management positions in sales or in the store, or leave the labor force altogether. In addition, there is an increasing number of openings for Sales Clerks of consumer electronics products in book, music, and drug stores, along with other mass merchandising outlets. Thus, employment opportunities are solid.

Many large stores or chains provide in-service training in sales merchandising for apprentices. Other employers seek bright, aggressive high school or college students to work part time, and, after graduation, these part-time individuals often begin working full time at the store.

Advancement Prospects

Most Sales Clerks of consumer electronics goods seek advancement in higher levels of sales or distribution management in the video/DVD, audiovisual, or other consumer electronics retail businesses. Opportunities for advancement are good. Some diligent individuals may be appointed managers of the consumer electronics department at larger chain operations, and others progress into branch management for an electronics store chain. Some aggressive Sales Clerks use their retail sales experience to move to more responsible positions as sales managers at stores that sell products other than consumer electronics. A few persistent Sales Clerks advance their careers by becoming salespersons for particular consumer electronics products or manufacturers' lines.

Education and Training

A high school diploma is the basic requirement for this position. In many cases, particularly at the larger store chains, some junior college or college course work is preferred and, occasionally, an undergraduate degree is required. Sales experience and some background or training in business computers is a further recommendation. Nonetheless, the ability to sell is more essential than a formal education or extensive training.

Special Requirements

Some Sales Clerks in the audiovisual equipment field find it beneficial to participate in the Certified Media Specialist program of the International Communications Industries Association (ICIA). Such certification is valuable in obtaining more responsible management positions within the industry.

Experience, Skills, and Personality Traits

Some previous experience in retail sales in any field is often required of applicants for this post. In addition, experience with computers is highly desirable.

Sales Clerks must have an outgoing personality, initiative, and an aptitude for selling. They should enjoy working with the public and should have the ability to deal tactfully with difficult customers. They also should be geared to handle several tasks at once, while continuing to provide friendly service. In addition, they should exhibit a neat appearance and have good oral and written communication skills. The most successful Sales Clerks are friendly, service-oriented, and, while competitive and aggressive, persuasive in manner when dealing with customers.

Unions and Associations

There are no unions that represent Sales Clerks at consumer electronics stores. Some individuals, however, may belong to the International Communications Industries Association (ICIA) to learn new sales techniques and methods and to network. ICIA also holds training seminars in sales and new products. In addition, Sales Clerks may attend periodic sales conferences and seminars held by the Electronic Representatives Association (ERA) or the North American Retail Dealers Association (NARDA) to improve their skills further.

Tips for Entry

1. While in high school or college, take courses in advertising, business management, and marketing to aid you in your future sales and marketing career.
2. Look for part-time or summer jobs in any type of store to learn how to deal with customers.
3. Visit consumer electronics stores (or departments in any of the larger department store chains) and observe how merchandising is displayed. Ask Sales Clerks questions to gain an insight into what you as a Sales Clerk will have to answer.

SALESPERSON (WHOLESALE)

CAREER PROFILE

Duties: Sell video cassettes and digital discs, consumer electronics equipment, and accessories to retail stores

Alternate Title(s): Marketing Representative; Sales Agent; Sales Representative

Salary Range: $35,000 to $60,000 or more

Employment Prospects: Good

Advancement Prospects: Fair

Prerequisites:

Education or Training—High school diploma required; some college or vocational school courses in sales or marketing recommended

Experience—Minimum of two years in consumer electronics or related sales experience

Special Skills and Personality Traits—Aggressive and persistent with initiative; extremely knowledgeable about consumer electronics products and accessories; good communication skills; persuasive and energetic

CAREER LADDER

```
┌─────────────────────────────┐
│    Distribution Manager     │
└─────────────────────────────┘

┌─────────────────────────────┐
│   Salesperson (wholesale)   │
└─────────────────────────────┘

┌─────────────────────────────┐
│  Store Manager; Sales Clerk │
└─────────────────────────────┘
```

Position Description

Salespersons (or sales representatives) are an important part of the success of manufacturers and wholesalers. Their primary duties are to interest wholesale and retail buyers and purchasing agents in their merchandise and to address any of the client's questions or concerns.

A consumer electronics Salesperson sells and services video cassettes and digital video discs (DVDs), video/DVD equipment, and consumer electronics accessories to retail outlets for resale to consumers. Most Salespersons are employed at independent video/DVD distribution companies or at branch offices of national video- and DVD-related wholesalers or manufacturers. Salespersons sell television satellite dishes, blank video tapes and DVD discs, prerecorded videocassettes and DVDs, videocassette and DVD players, video cameras, projection television units, cables, connectors, and traditional audiovisual equipment, including film cameras, projectors, and photographic supplies.

If based at a branch office, a Salesperson concentrates on selling the products of a single original equipment manufacturer (OEM) or of a video and DVD program wholesaler. A Salesperson for a hardware equipment company may handle cameras, videocassette or, increasingly, DVD hardware, and their accessories for a particular equipment company (such as Sony). A Salesperson for a video/DVD program wholesaler, on the other hand, will sell the videocassette or DVD releases of a particular label or line (such as Disney). A Salesperson working for an independent distribution company usually sells programs, videocassettes, DVD discs, or electronic equipment for a variety of national manufacturers or program wholesalers.

Salespersons usually report directly to the distribution manager (either a branch office manager or an independent representative). They are designated to work either throughout a prescribed geographic territory or with specific retail accounts. In a few cases, Salespersons report directly to the home office of the national wholesaler or manufacturer.

Their other responsibilities may include acquiring new accounts in their assigned territory, as well as delivering merchandising materials to, and collecting payment from, some stores. They distribute sales literature, point-of-purchase displays, brochures, posters, and other merchandising materials to the stores and often train the stores' retail sales clerks in the operation of new equipment and accessories.

They usually are assigned to keep track of the company's competition and their products, and are responsible for coordinating sales incentive programs, contests, and catalog (noncurrent) sales of video material. In addition, they analyze sales statistics, prepare reports, and handle administrative duties, such as filing their expense account reports, scheduling appointments, and making travel plans.

Most Salespersons travel quite a lot, visiting prospective buyers and current clients and servicing their assigned retail accounts in a given territory. Many are assigned also to phone sales duty (telemarketing) at the branch office or headquarters of the distribution manager. Salespersons usually visit or call retail stores once a week or once a month, depending upon the volume of purchases made by the store. (The marketing of products to online outlets and vendors is usually handled by an organization's e-commerce marketing and sales personnel.)

Salaries

Salespersons are paid either a straight salary, a small salary plus a commission, or a draw against commission. There is no industry-wide pattern as to which, but fewer than 20 percent of sales employees work on a straight salary basis, according to recent industry studies. Some companies offer commissions on gross sales, others on gross profits from an individual's sales, and others on a sliding scale allied with the gross profit received by the company for a particular item.

According to the U.S. Bureau of Labor Statistics, the mean annual salary in 2004 for sales representatives was $54,060, with a range from $35,100 for the lowest 10 percent to a high of $65,000 or more for the highest paid 10 percent of Salespersons. Compensation will vary according to experience and to the type of products sold by Salespersons. Since payment is usually tied to sales results in one way or another, yearly earnings are a direct result of the individual's sales success.

Most companies provide sales samples, a modest entertainment account, and phone and auto expenses for their Salespersons. Some firms provide a company car, and most of them offer hospitalization and pension plans. A few operations also offer the individual Salesperson an opportunity to participate in a company profit-sharing plan.

Employment Prospects

Many branch offices of the larger national manufacturers of electronics products for the consumer market employ seven or more Salespersons. Independent distribution companies within a specific region may have three to five Salespersons on staff, depending upon the amount of revenue generated by the company. The U.S. Bureau of Labor Statistics estimates that the employment of sales representatives, wholesale and manufacturing, is expected to grow about as fast as the average of all occupations through the year 2012. There

is considerable turnover of sales employees in consumer electronics. As a result, the job opportunities for bright, capable, sales-oriented individuals remain good.

Advancement Prospects

While the turnover rate of sales employees in the consumer electronics industry remains relatively high, the opportunities for advancement are only fair. The primary reason is that competition for more responsible sales positions is very heavy. Many Salespersons utilize their skills and sales experience in one product line or label to get a better-paying sales job at a competitive company. Some Salespersons advance within their own company, becoming distribution managers (at branch offices) or move to other middle management marketing positions at the home office. Other Salespersons, trading upon their extensive sales experience, may seek sales positions in other industries.

Education and Training

The usual educational requirement for this position is a high school education and some evidence of course work in sales or marketing at a community college or vocational school. Some employers prefer applicants to have an undergraduate degree, preferably in advertising, marketing, or sales. Some training in business management, motivation and human psychology, or sales techniques is also considered valuable. Nonetheless, the demonstrated ability to sell is more important than a specific formal college education.

Experience, Skills, and Personality Traits

Although the position of Salesperson is occasionally an entry-level one, employers tend to prefer individuals who have at least two years of direct sales experience. Some successful applicants may have gained this experience in fields other than consumer electronics, while others may have worked as store managers or sales clerks in consumer electronics stores.

Above all, Salespersons must be dependable and abundantly demonstrate their sales initiative. They must be persistent and persuasive in their sales efforts, display an outgoing, gregarious personality, and show their service orientation in their marketing efforts. A good Salesperson must have excellent verbal skills in direct contact with customers and is able to respond intuitively to the customers' cues, reactions, and product needs.

Unions and Associations

There are no unions that serve as bargaining agents for Salespersons in the consumer electronics industry. Many Salespersons attend company-sponsored sales training seminars or those that are sponsored by such industry organizations as the Consumer Electronics Group (CEG) of the Electronic

Industries Alliance (EIA) and the International Communications Industries Association (ICIA). At such meetings, Salespersons can learn new sales techniques and methods, as well as network with other sales and marketing professionals.

Tips for Entry

1. While in high school (or college) take courses in advertising, business management, market research techniques, and psychology to aid you in your future sales and marketing career.

2. Perfect your verbal and interpersonal skills by joining high school (or college) extracurricular groups in any administrative capacity where you will interact with others.

3. Work in a paid or internship capacity as a salesperson in a consumer electronics store to learn the specifics of electronics products, programs, equipment, and accessories.

4. Check trade and consumer magazines and manufacturers' Web sites to keep abreast of new product lines.

STORE MANAGER

CAREER PROFILE

Duties: Manage and operate a video/DVD or consumer electronics retail store

Alternate Title(s): Video/DVD and Electronics Retailer; Video/DVD and Electronics Dealer; Electronics Sales Worker Supervisor

Salary Range: $20,000 to $60,000 or more

Employment Prospects: Fair

Advancement Prospects: Fair

Prerequisites:

    Education or Training—High school diploma minimum requirement; business management courses required

    Experience—Minimum of two to four years' experience in retail sales

    Special Skills and Personality Traits—Business acumen; merchandising instinct; sales talent; Video/DVD and electronics consumer products knowledge

    Special Requirements—A certification from the International Communications Industries Association may be required.

CAREER LADDER

Distribution Manager; Salesperson

Store Manager

Sales Clerk

Position Description

A Store Manager is responsible for the day-to-day operation and management of a retail store that deals in consumer electronics and related accessories and supplies. A Store Manager may be the owner or part-owner of an independent store, the manager of the daily operations of a retail outlet that is part of a chain of stores, or the head of a consumer electronics department within a large department store. This individual is in charge of all income and expenses, all short- and long-range planning, the hiring, training, and supervising of employees, and the general organization, maintenance, and profitability of the store.

A Store Manager develops the store's advertising and promotional campaigns and in-store displays, establishes special sales and discount policies, and maintains inventory control of all products stocked at the store. In addition, the Store Manager, with the possible assistance of a buyer, selects what brands of equipment, software, videocassettes, DVD disks, and other related accessories and supplies to stock. This process involves dealing with vendors, distribu-

tors, and salespersons, keeping track of such things as release dates for computer games or software, and monitoring sales so that the most popular products are always in stock. The Store Manager and/or buyer must be aware of manufacturers' special promotions or offers and be able to negotiate for the best wholesale price of these products. They need to stay informed of industry trends, new products, and new rental, sales, and return policies within the industry.

Once stock is obtained, the best retail price must be determined. Prices need to be low enough to be competitive with other stores, which are always changing their own prices. Prices cannot be too low, as the store might not then be able to meet its expenses and make a profit. For independent stores, decisions must also be made about advertising—how much, what kind, and in what medium (print, broadcast, or online). Store Managers in chain stores make fewer of these decisions, as the parent company often arranges for distribution and, sometimes, pricing, as well as setting other policies (including the look and organization of the premises). A Store Manager in this case concentrates on meeting sales goals. Store Managers (or Owners) of independent stores must take full responsibility and accept the risk of business failure for the possibility of keeping more of the profits.

The Store Manager develops and supervises training and retraining programs for employees (or, if managing a chain store, oversees the correct institution of company policies regarding employees). The hiring, training, and supervision of employees are an essential part of the Store Manager's job. The attitude of sales clerks toward customers and knowledge of products sold at the store are essential to the financial well-being of the store. In addition, because sales clerks traditionally are paid low salaries (as their job is usually an entry-level position), turnover tends to be high. Motivating employees to take a genuine interest in their work can be one of the Store Manager's more difficult tasks.

Salaries

Earnings for consumer electronics Store Managers vary substantially, depending on the level of responsibility the individual has, the length of service, and the geographical location, size, and profitability of the store. According to the U.S. Bureau of Labor Statistics, in May 2004, median annual earnings of salaried managers of retail sales workers, including commissions, were $32,720. The lowest 10 percent of these managers earned less than $20,110 annually, the middle 50 percent earned between $25,120 and $43,110 a year, while the top 10 percent earned more than $58,400 per year.

The Store Manager who is also the owner (or part-owner) usually collects a weekly salary and shares in or retains any profits the store returns during the year. Such individuals may earn $65,000 or more annually, depending on the store's success. Those individuals who do not own a share of the store are usually compensated by a combination of salary and commission (a percentage of the department or store sales) or yearly bonus.

Employment Prospects

Sales of consumer electronics, games, videos, and DVDs over the Internet are increasingly placing great pressure on traditional consumer electronics stores. Together with the big retail chains (who can slash prices more easily), these trends have threatened the livelihood of many small, independently owned consumer electronics stores. Employment opportunities still exist for potential owners or co-owners of stores who have financial and sales experience in the retail trade. The best opportunities for owner-managers are outside the large urban areas in locations that still have a large enough population to support a small store, but not enough to attract a chain outlet.

Employment prospects are better with the retail chains, due to their traditional high turnover. While overall employment in the retail trade is expected to continue its steady increase through 2014, employment of managers of consumer electronics stores is expected to grow more slowly than average for all occupations through 2014, according to the U.S. Department of Labor's *Occupational Outlook Handbook.* Some job opportunities will occur in store chains when the experienced managers or supervisors move into higher levels of management, but job turnover tends to be relatively low.

Advancement Prospects

The prospects for advancement from the position of Store Manager when the store is part of a chain remain fair, due to considerable competition for higher management posts. For many Store Managers who are owners or co-owners, their position is the successful realization of their career goal of being their own boss. Many of them have moved away from the corporate world to own and operate their own venue. They may seek advancement and additional success by owning and operating more stores.

Some salaried Store Managers may use their contacts to advance their careers by becoming salespersons for particular consumer electronic products or labels. A few may become distribution managers for national wholesalers and manufacturers. For individuals who have the analogous position to that of a Store Manager of being in charge of consumer electronics departments in large department stores, they sometimes can move to more responsible middle management positions in their stores or elsewhere in the chain.

Education and Training

A high school education is a basic requirement for any type of managing position. Chains generally require Store Managers (and sometimes department managers) to have an undergraduate degree in a business-related field with courses in business management, marketing, and retailing. Independent Store Managers may go into business without any formal qualifications, but they are well advised to seek training, or hire help, if they don't have small business experience or sufficient technical knowledge of the consumer electronics products they want to sell.

Special Requirements

Some Store Managers and/or owners in the audiovisual equipment field may find it beneficial to their careers to participate in the certification program of the International Communications Industries Association (ICIA).

Experience, Skills, and Personality Traits

The consumer electronics retailing business is a unique blend of the entertainment and package goods industries. The majority of consumer electronics Store Managers have had at least two to four years of retail sales experience prior to assuming their position (or setting up their new business).

Day-to-day experience as a sales clerk is almost a requirement for this job.

Store Managers must be very well organized and display both leadership and supervisory qualities. Initiative and sound business judgment are also required. Store Managers should have a thorough understanding of the electronics products they sell, and they need to have both knowledge of and experience with business computers in order to be able to run their businesses. They need to be experts in media and video equipment and programming, understand local tastes and desires, and be good merchandisers. They must have the ability to select, train, supervise, and motivate employees, many of whom will be at entry level and have only limited skills.

Unions and Associations

There are no unions that represent consumer electronics Store Managers. Many, however, belong to such associations as ICIA, the National Association of Recording Merchandisers (NARM), or the North American Retail Dealers Association (NARDA) to keep informed about the industry and share common concerns. Many Store Managers and/or owners attend the annual trade exhibitions and seminars of the Consumer Electronics Group (CEG) of the Electronic Industries Alliance (EIA), whose semiannual show offers the largest display of new electronics products.

Some Store Managers whose stores sell both videocassettes and DVD discs may belong to the Video Software Dealers Association (VSDA). This organization for the home entertainment industry also includes the home video divisions of major and independent motion picture studios, major distributors, and many other businesses connected to the consumer video industry.

Tips for Entry

1. While in high school or college, gain retail experience, perhaps by taking a part-time job at a chain electronics store. On the job, look for opportunities to help with a variety of tasks, such as inventory or customer support.

2. In high school take business-related courses. At a community or four-year college, consider a major in marketing or retail business management.

3. If you are thinking of starting your own consumer electronics store, make sure that there are enough potential customers in the surrounding area of your planned store and not too much competition. Federal and state small business agencies can provide you with helpful information.

PRODUCTION

AUDIO ENGINEER AND VIDEO ENGINEER

<table>
<tr><td colspan="2">CAREER PROFILE</td><td colspan="2">CAREER LADDER</td></tr>
</table>

CAREER PROFILE

Duties: Responsible for all aspects of audio recording of a video production; responsible for controlling the image, color, brightness, and contrast of images recorded in a video production

Alternate Title(s): Audio Technician, Production Sound Mixer, Sound Technician; Video Technician, Color Timer

Salary Range: $20,000 to $85,000 or more

Employment Prospects: Fair to Good

Advancement Prospects: Fair to Good

Prerequisites:

Education or Training—High school diploma necessary; college degree recommended but not necessary; formal training with sound and recording equipment helpful; formal training with video equipment helpful

Experience—Work in a variety of electronics and sound areas, including mixing, recording, and editing; work with film processing laboratories or production companies

Special Skills and Personality Traits—Able to work as a team member, but also function in isolation; creativity; detail-oriented; excellent vision; good people skills; patient and precise; quick reflexes and steady hands; strong electronics background; technical ability; versatility

Special Requirements—A certification from one of the engineering industry certification study programs may be required

CAREER LADDER

Engineering Supervisor; Postproduction Supervisor; Sound Editor; Technical Director

Audio Engineer; Video Engineer

Engineering Technician; Production Assistant; Film Lab Technician; Boom Operator

Position Description

Audio Engineers and Video Engineers set up, test, and operate audio and video equipment, including microphones, sound speakers, video screens, projectors, video monitors, recording equipment, connecting wires and cables, sound and mixing boards, and related electronic equipment for video productions at studios and production companies (as well as for films, concerts, meetings and conventions, news conferences, and sports events). They also are tasked with the maintenance and repair of their respective equipment. While some cross training for both positions occurs for personnel to handle audio and video jobs, engineers typically focus on, and are more experienced in, one of these two functions.

Audio Engineers are in charge of the sound part of a production, which includes voices, music, and sound special effects. They operate audio and computer equipment to record, enhance, mix, and edit sound, either from a large audio console in the control room where they control the sound from the microphones and playback units or from the set during actual production. In either case, they select, place, and adjust microphones and instruct performers involved in the production on their proper use. On the set, Audio Engineers usually operate an audiotape recorder that runs synchronously with the cameras and attempts to record a consistent, balanced audio signal throughout all the different camera setups so a smooth, even soundtrack can be created during subsequent postproduction editing and mixing.

Audio Engineers monitor all audio signals during production to detect any quality deviations or malfunctions and operate their mixer controls to preserve correct sound levels. They prerecord all special sounds required by the script and, during production, cue in where this prerecorded material is to be utilized. Many such prerecorded sounds, such as music, applause, or other sound effects, may be added to the video production during a postproduction phase, and some portions of the material may be modified to improve the overall sound quality. In addition, Audio Engineers must log and manage all the audio production notes (to be employed in the postproduction process).

Video Engineers are in charge of the quality of the visualization of the video aspect of the production. The quality of video and film images depends on these technical specialists, who can control image, color, brightness, and contrast levels. Video Engineers are responsible for the setting up and aligning of cameras and for ensuring that all cameras are functioning properly and that multiple cameras all have comparable image qualities. Due to the sensitivity of the equipment, continuous monitoring is necessary to ensure that the best possible image is being captured. Besides cameras, Video Engineers handle video recorders, video switches, time base correctors, monitors, character generators, and other assorted video production equipment.

Video Engineers also make color corrections to individual shots during postproduction. When working at a film laboratory, the Video Engineer (frequently referred to as a "color timer") works on the finished videotaped production after it has been edited. In video postproduction, the color can be adjusted using special digital equipment. Color can also be adjusted within individual frames using computer-controlled colorizing equipment, which digitizes images and allows a colorist to control individual pixels (the smallest units, or dots, from which a picture can be built up) in the framed shot. Many digital editing software programs contain a wide range of image-control devices, permitting precise adjustments of the color, brightness, and contrast of scenes, sequences, shots, and individual frames by the Video Engineer during postproduction.

Audio and Video Engineers usually report to an engineering supervisor who makes the necessary work shift and project assignments. During rehearsals of the video production and the actual shooting of the production, Audio and Video Engineers report to the technical director, or, in some cases, the producer. This is the individual with whom they interact to achieve any special sound or visual effects required by the video production.

Salaries

According to the *Occupational Outlook Handbook* of the U.S. Department of Labor's Bureau of Labor Statistics,

median annual earnings of Video Equipment Engineers (or technicians) in May 2004 were $32,570. The middle 50 percent earned yearly between $24,180 and $44,290. The lowest 10 percent earned less than $19,110 per year, and the highest 10 percent earned more than $62,850. For Audio (or Sound) Engineers, in May 2004 their median annual earnings were $38,110. The middle 50 percent earned annually between $25,470 and $56,320. The lowest 10 percent earned less than $19,180 a year, and the highest 10 percent earned more than $80,450.

Audio and Video Engineers who belong to the International Alliance of Theatrical Stage Employees (IATSE) are covered by that union's minimum wage agreements. For audio mixers (engineers), the minimum weekly salary is set at $1,564, or a daily (eight hours) rate of $344 per day. For video controllers (engineers), the minimum weekly salary is set at $1,416, or a daily (eight hours) rate of $305 per day.

Employment Prospects

According to the U.S. Department of Labor's Bureau of Labor Statistics, employment of audio and video technicians and sound engineering technicians is expected to grow faster than the average for all other occupations through 2014. As these two jobs are essential to the production process, as well as most postproduction facilities, employment opportunities for qualified individuals are good.

Advancement Prospects

Qualified Audio and Video Engineers are in demand. Those with several years' experience, especially with digital technologies, have good opportunities to get engineering posts with greater responsibilities and higher salaries. Some may be promoted to engineering supervisor or technical director at production or postproduction companies or with television stations. In addition, chances for employment in middle management engineering jobs at production centers of corporations or educational, health, or governmental production studios are good.

Education and Training

A high school diploma and some training at a technical or vocational school is usually the bare minimum requirement to obtain a job as an engineering technician, from which the individual has the chance of being promoted to an Audio or Video Engineer position. Some video production facilities may require a bachelor's degree in electronics, or the equivalent, and two to three years of related work in electronic repair and maintenance of audio and/or video equipment.

Special Requirements

Some video production companies may insist that applicants for the positions of Audio Engineer and Video Engineer have studied and received a certificate from one of the programs offered by such industry organizations as the Institute of Electrical and Electronics Engineers (IEEE) or the Society of Broadcast Engineers (SBE).

Experience, Skills, and Personality Traits

A minimum of two to three years' experience as an engineering technician is typically required for promotion to the positions of Audio Engineer or Video Engineer. Individuals in either position must be thoroughly familiar with either audio or video equipment that is utilized in the making of a video production, and must be capable of handling routine maintenance as well as troubleshooting and correcting system problems when they occur.

Gaining experience as a boom operator (who handles and places the overhead boom microphone used to capture sound during the recording of a production) is a good way to acquire the necessary knowledge about recording equipment that an Audio Engineer must have. In addition, Audio Engineers need to have strong audio skills, a discriminating "ear" for detail in all-areas of sound, and an all-encompassing understanding of the dynamics of sound, very similar to the expertise of a musician. Video Engineers need to have an "eye" for lighting and color mix and be able to aid the effect that the director of photography was trying to achieve.

Both jobs call for quick reflexes and strong communication skills. Both have to follow the director's lead and work within and around the particular circumstances of each shot of the production. They need to be both patient and creative. Both positions involve considerable pressure, so individuals in these posts must be even-tempered and flexible in order to function smoothly in collaboration with artists and producers of each production on which they work.

Unions and Associations

Audio Engineers and Video Engineers may belong to the International Production Sound Technicians, Television Engineers, and Video Assist Technicians, Local 695, of the International Alliance of Theatrical Stage Employees (IATSE). Some may also belong to such associations as the Society of Broadcast Engineers (SBE) and the Society of Motion Picture & Television Engineers (SMPTE) or, for Audio Engineers, the Audio Engineering Society (AES).

Tips for Entry

1. During high school take courses in electronics and physics as building blocks upon which you will add your technical and vocational training.
2. As both sound and video technology are always changing, continuing education is a must.
3. A business management course somewhere in your educational background would be a plus, as you will be required to keep logs, notes, and other documentation on work accomplished on each production.
4. As a prospective Audio Engineer, consider working in a music or sound studio to acquire experience in the techniques of sound recording. As a future Video Engineer, consider working as a production assistant in the film or television industries to become familiar with video equipment and how it is utilized.

DIRECTOR

CAREER PROFILE

Duties: Integrate the creative and technical components of a video production into a completed project

Alternate Title(s): None

Salary Range: $20,000 to $120,000 or more

Employment Prospects: Fair to Good

Advancement Prospects: Good

Prerequisites:

Education or Training—Undergraduate degree in communications, radio/TV, or film production

Experience—Minimum of two years in film or television production

Special Skills and Personality Traits—Ability to collaborate; decisiveness; excellent interpersonal skills; keen judge of talent; motivational, organizational, and leadership abilities; technical knowledge of film and video production; visual creativity

CAREER LADDER

```
┌─────────────────────────────────────┐
│              Producer                │
└─────────────────────────────────────┘

┌─────────────────────────────────────┐
│              Director                │
└─────────────────────────────────────┘

┌─────────────────────────────────────┐
│  Assistant Director; Production Unit │
│   Manager; Production Assistant      │
└─────────────────────────────────────┘
```

Position Description

The function of the Director is vital in any video, film, or (live) television production. It is the Director's duty to translate creatively from an idea or the written word of a script into specific sounds and visual images. The Director establishes a point of view on the action of the video that helps to determine the selection of shots, camera placements and movements, and the staging of the action. Directors are responsible for the dramatic structure, pace, and directional flow of the sounds and visual images to maintain viewer interest throughout. Most Directors spend about half their time planning and the other half rehearsing, shooting, and/or editing. Throughout, the Director works with the performers and technical crew, staging and plotting the action, refining the script of the action in an ongoing process, supervising setups and rehearsals, and making suggestions as to the final editing of the project. It is the Director's talent, ingenuity, and vision that make for the success of a video production.

Yet, to get that success, the Director must collaborate with a large team, including the producer, scriptwriters, casting directors, performers, production designers, and directors of photography. Directors are involved in equipment and engineering decisions, as well as the design elements of the production. These encompass selection of the sets, costumes, choreography (if any), and music, as well as decisions reached about sound and lighting, and how many cameras the production requires. In interpreting the script, Directors convey their concept of the production to costume designers, production designers, makeup artists, and light and sound personnel. They audition and select the performers, review the script with them, conduct rehearsals, and direct the cast and the crew during the production. Working with floor plans, Directors plot camera shots, equipment placement, and the blocking of the performers for each scene. In short, the Director coordinates all the elements, facilities, and people during rehearsal and the actual production, whether in the studio or on location. For some of the more complex or larger video productions, an assistant or associate director may be hired to aid the Director. This individual keeps track of the time, alerts the performers and the technical crew members of upcoming events in the filming process, and sometimes relays the director's commands to the camera operators and other members of the technical crew.

Most Directors are also involved in the postproduction phase, working with the production editor and the producer in assembling and sorting the footage of the video into a cohesive sequence, ensuring both continuity of action and the maintaining of the director's vision for the production.

Directors work within a pressure-filled environment filled with crucial deadlines. They must be the unifying element during all phases of the execution of the production, and they must accomplish all this while staying within the budget set by the producer.

Salaries

According to the U.S. Bureau of Labor Statistics' *Occupational Outlook Handbook,* median annual earnings, as of May 2004, of salaried Directors throughout the performing industry were $52,840, whereas, in the motion picture and video industries, median yearly earnings in May 2004 were $75,200. The middle 50 percent of Directors in the motion picture and video industries earned between $35,550 and $87,980 per year.

Most Directors belong to the Directors Guild of America (DGA). The Guild sets minimum rates for member Directors for motion pictures, video production, and television work. Their rates are based on the budget for the production (motion pictures and video productions) or the length and type of program on which the Director is working (television). For example, for a low-budget motion picture (many video productions fall into this category) of up to $500,000, the weekly minimum compensation rate for Directors is $8,395. For medium budget motion pictures of $500,000 to $1,500,000 (and some video productions, particularly music videos, will have budgets this high), the weekly minimum salary for Directors rises to $9,541. The Guild also has guidelines for overtime, holidays, time off, and other members' benefits.

Employment Prospects

As the Director is key to every video production, employment prospects for Directors are good. However, the job requires considerable experience, and the competition for the position is always strong. Most Directors gain their career breaks after working several years as assistant directors, production assistants, or second unit directors. The increased number of independent production companies making films, television programs, and video productions provides a demand for Directors, increasing employment opportunities for individuals with the requisite experience.

Advancement Prospects

Many Directors hope to become producers themselves. Some accept more responsibility as producers/directors at independent production firms as a means to becoming a full-time producer. Such advancement is greatly dependent upon the Director's achievement with the projects he or she has headlined. A record of success as a Director helps prospects for advancement.

Education and Training

An undergraduate degree in communications or radio/TV production is the usual requirement for getting a job as a Director. Many Directors have some education in theater or film and even a degree from a film school, while others may come from the field of journalism. A broad educational background, typically in liberal arts, is extremely useful for Directors, who are usually called upon to work on a wide range of subjects, styles, and formats.

The job of Director is not an entry-level position, and very few Directors are hired as such straight out of college or film school. Training to become a Director is available from workshops and seminars that the Directors Guild of America (DGA) conducts for its members. In addition, directing commercials for independent production companies or television firms is good practice for directing video productions.

Experience, Skills, and Personality Traits

Directors have to know exactly what they are doing, which means they have to be experienced in nearly all aspects of filmmaking and production. Many Directors gain such expertise while working as production crew members, such as a camera operator, scriptwriter, unit production manager, or, eventually, assistant director. They also have to have an innate respect for the script. As veteran director Mel Damski points out, "I think the best way to become a director is through screenwriting. … Many directors come from cinematography, from acting, and from the stage. There are many different ways to approach it. The important thing is you have to understand the story. If people go into directing thinking it's all about getting sexy shots and clever angles, they are going to miss the boat."

Directors need to have a mix of creative talent, outstanding technical knowledge about film and video production, good organizational skills, and the capacity to motivate people. They have to be comfortable being in charge, because they are the guide to everything within the production. They have to be self-confident and have a clear vision of their project. They need to be able to recognize talent, whether acting, writing, or designing, because video production work is a collaborative job. In addition, Directors must have fast reflexes to give instructions to numerous individuals working in a variety of tasks under severe time constraints. Above all, Directors must always act decisively, even when under tremendous pressure, be creative and flexible, and have an excellent eye for the composition of images and sounds that will appear in the final video product.

Unions and Associations

Most Directors belong to the Directors Guild of America (DGA), and such membership is a requirement when the Director works on a studio or union film. For most video productions, this is not a requirement, but the Guild offers minimum wage guarantees to its membership, as well as support and training.

Tips for Entry

1. During your years in college and/or film school, get involved in any aspect of moviemaking available to you.
2. Consider buying or renting a digital camera and using it to direct and shoot a short video or a music video for the experience.
3. Pursue any internship or apprenticeship opportunities available to Directors, such as those given at the American Film Institute (AFI).
4. Join the Directors Guild of America, as their training programs are probably the best preparation, other than a film school education, for becoming a Director of video productions.

DIRECTOR OF PHOTOGRAPHY

Duties: Be responsible for all technical aspects of visuals involved in filming a video production

Alternate Title(s): Cinematographer; DP

Salary Range: $27,000 to $90,000 or more

Employment Prospects: Fair to Good

Advancement Prospects: Fair

Prerequisites:

Education or Training—Undergraduate degree (or advanced degree) in film or dramatic and visual arts is recommended

Experience—Minimum of one to three years of camera work and editing

Special Skills and Personality Traits—Creativity; detail oriented; excellent interpersonal skills; originality, passion, and tenacity; resourcefulness; solid photographic skills; strong visual abilities

Production Designer; Producer

Director of Photography

Camera Operator; Assistant Camera Operator; Production Assistant

Position Description

The overall control of video lighting and the creative camera work (known as cinematography) is usually given to the Director of Photography, sometimes known as the DP. This is the individual who directs the camera crew to create the moving image portion of the director's overall vision of the video. The camera crew usually consists of a senior camera operator, assistant camera operators, lighting technicians (or grips), and the electrical crew (often called gaffers) who actually control the lighting setup. The Director of Photography works closely with the director in controlling the lighting, framing, setting up, and composing of camera shots. Directors of Photography usually do not actually operate the camera, but they are the primary creative contributors to the overall look of the video production.

The Director of Photography's primary responsibility is to produce quality images and interpret exactly the needs of the director. In addition, he or she is responsible for everything involved in getting the image to be used in the production, including selecting the camera or cameras, lenses, filters, and lighting and electrical equipment. The Director of Photography is also involved in setting camera positions, framing the dramatics of each shot, and the interpretive use

of the camera in capturing each part of the video production. It is an extremely demanding and important position and one that is crucial to the overall quality of the final production.

During the preproduction phase, the Director of Photography meets with the director to discuss that individual's overall vision of the project and the specific needs of individual shots. Based upon these meetings, the Director of Photography selects the necessary cameras, lenses, equipment, and film or tape or digital resources appropriate (given the budget) and tests filming the sets, makeup, costumes, lighting, and any scenic art that will be used.

Throughout the production, Directors of Photography determine how each scene is to be lighted, what filters, lenses, film stock, or digital resources will be employed, and the position and movement of cameras for each shot. Constantly, decisions have be made, involving everything from light readings and exposures to camera angles and type of film stock, all while supervising the camera crew. Much of the DP's production time is taken blocking out each shot, figuring how to cover whatever action is to happen and what type of shot will comply with the director's wishes. The DP may or may not work from a storyboard (which has been devised in preproduction), depending upon the complexity of the shot. Throughout shooting, changes are constantly made, so the DP has to keep a continual line of communication open with the director.

In postproduction, Directors of Photography work closely with the processing laboratories to check that the footage shot is processed correctly to preserve the colors (or shades, if black and white) and moods aimed for during production.

Salaries

Salaries for Directors of Photography are relatively moderate. According to a 2006 survey, conducted by the Broadcast Employment Services, of 2005 annual earnings of Directors of Photography (which include both Cinematographers and Videographers), yearly salaries ranged from $27,000 to $140,000, with the mean yearly average salary being $58,200. Most Directors of Photography who work on video productions also do work in television and/or film.

Those Directors of Photography who do work in television and/or film are usually members of Local 600, the International Cinematographers Guild, of the International Alliance of Theatrical Stage Employees (IATSE). As such, they have minimum wages set by union contract. If hired on a daily basis, their daily rate (eight hours) is $626.56. If hired on a weekly basis (five days, 43.2 hours), their weekly rate is $3,010.55. Experienced Directors of Photography generally earn well above the minimum rates.

Employment Prospects

As the position of Director of Photography is key to any video or film production, employment opportunities are good. Both camera and assistant camera operators, or even talented and knowledgeable production assistants, can move upward to the more heavily responsible position of Director of Photography. However, as there are many aspiring cinematographers for this position, competition remains stiff.

Now that much of the video and film industry is using digital technology instead of film, it is fortunate that the techniques and skills required of Directors of Photography are easily transferable to the new methodology of using portable video and/or digital camera equipment. Lighting and the setting up of scenes for shoots remain approximately the same.

Advancement Prospects

Opportunities for Directors of Photography to advance higher in the production hierarchy are only fair. Some look to be promoted to production design positions supervising other Directors of Photography or to a position as a producer of video productions. However, prospects of advancement from DP to director are rare, as most directors need to go through the additional training that is offered by the Directors Guild of America (DGA), or they get into directing from screenwriting or producing.

Education and Training

A basic requirement for this position is an undergraduate degree in communications or film, with some additional training in video or film production. There are hundreds of college and university film programs, as well as training programs at many film and television studios. All of them are designed to help aspiring Directors of Photography learn the necessary technical skills involved in cinematography. In addition, the International Cinematographers Guild (ICG), Local 600 of the International Alliance of Theatrical Stage Employees (IATSE), has a training program that would also prove useful.

Experience, Skills, and Personality Traits

The position of Director of Photography is so critical to the success of any film, television, or video production that most employers require at least one to three years' experience in shooting and editing motion picture film and tape. Familiarity with, and an understanding of, all types of cameras and lenses is essential. A background in still camera equipment and technique, film processing, and film chemistry, in addition to film editing techniques, would also be very useful.

Directors of Photography must have a strong visual sense and visual creativity and know how to light a scene properly to achieve their vision. As veteran Cinematographer Richard Crudo points out, "Look at light in your real life, in your house, in your car, on the street at daytime and nighttime; in the bank, in the supermarket, in a restaurant—you have to look at light. You have to see how light creates feelings." In addition, Directors of Photography must be able to work with lighting, design, and color to create drama in the video.

As video production, like film production, is a highly collaborative art form, Directors of Photography have to have good interpersonal skills to assert their own creative ideas in a nonthreatening way. They need to be able to follow orders of the director but also be willing to speak up when something is not going right. They need to be original and resourceful in dealing with the variety of circumstances that occur during production and be zealous and tenacious in the pursuit of their art.

Unions and Associations

Many Directors of Photography are represented by Local 600, the International Cinematographers Guild (ICG), of the IATSE. The Guild acts as their bargaining agent. If video Directors of Photography also work in television, they may be represented by the National Association of Broadcast Employees and Technicians, AFL-CIO (NABET). Another association of value for Directors of Photography is the American Society of Cinematographers (ASC), both for networking and for sharing issues of common concern.

Tips for Entry

1. While in school, work on low-budget, independent nonunion films or student film projects to become familiar with the processes through which Directors of Photography must go.
2. Find a way to shoot as much film or video as possible to gain as much experience as you can and to learn what works and what does not.
3. Make as many personal connections as you can with Directors of Photography or camera people within the film or video industry. Since directors usually hire Directors of Photography, get to know as many directors as you can. Go to networking functions sponsored by the Directors Guild of America or other associations that attract directors to their ranks.

PRODUCER

CAREER PROFILE	CAREER LADDER

Duties: Find (or create), develop, and oversee video and media productions

Alternate Title(s): Executive Producer; Production Manager

Salary Range: $30,000 to $100,000 or more

Employment Prospects: Fair

Advancement Prospects: Fair

Prerequisites:

    Education and Training—Undergraduate degree in communications, radio/TV, or video production

    Experience—Minimum of three to five years as a director or an associate producer in film, television, or video

    Special Skills and Personality Traits—Business insight and financial expertise; creativity; detail-oriented; excellent communication, interpersonal, and leadership skills; organizational abilities; problem solving skills; thorough understanding of media production and technology

```
┌─────────────────────────────────────────┐
│  Executive Producer (Film or Television)  │
└─────────────────────────────────────────┘

┌─────────────────────────────────────────┐
│               Producer                    │
└─────────────────────────────────────────┘

┌─────────────────────────────────────────┐
│     Director; Production Assistant        │
└─────────────────────────────────────────┘
```

Position Description

Producers, generally, are tasked with turning creative ideas into practical and/or marketable video concepts. They secure financial backing for the production and manage the entire production process, including budgeting and scheduling. They oversee the scriptwriting phase and the planning of sets, lights, props, and camera work. They usually are responsible for the hiring of the director, the scriptwriter, and performers either directly or through associate producers, casting directors, or supervising producers. (The terms *television* and *video* are sometimes used interchangeably, but it is generally thought that television is a means of distributing and exhibiting video signals, usually over the air, and video is a production term. The term *video* is sometimes used to refer to the visual portion of the television signal, as opposed to the audio or sound. Video also can refer to a three- to five-minute popular song with accompanying visuals on a videotape or a CD or a videotape copy of a feature film, television broadcast, or video production made available at a video/DVD rental store or online. Nonetheless, the more general and useful definition of *video* as a production term refers to all forms of electronic production of moving images and sounds.)

Producers are risk-takers, seizing on an idea, running with it, and convincing others to participate financially and artistically in a project. They are creative administrators who serve as a link between business managers, corporate executives, distributors' financial concerns, and investors (all of whom finance video productions) and the artists who create them. They understand the diverse needs of creative people, corporate executives, investors, product buyers, and audiences. They tread a fine line between the creative talent's need for artistic expression and the necessity of providing concrete returns on production investments.

In addition to their creative supervision, Producers often handle business arrangements and contracts with performers. They expedite needed clearances and see to the acquiring of necessary technical facilities and equipment. They supervise all negotiations with talent as well as with needed production and technical people. They coordinate all production assignments and the activities of writers and technical personnel and supervise the director of the production. In short, they make many of the critical decisions about the production.

Above all, good Producers have to be effective decision-makers, as well as persuasive people-managers. If the video production runs over schedule or over budget (that is, the original time and money guidelines set for the project), it is the Producer who must step in and decide how to handle the situation. Making these judgment calls can be extremely difficult. Ultimately, the production buck stops with the Producer, who assumes full responsibility for the successful completion of the project.

Some Producers of video productions become directly involved in day-to-day production decisions, while others function as executive managers, largely delegating production duties to others while keeping general supervision over them. Regardless of the extent of their daily participation in the production, Producers have to ensure that the financial support for a production is maintained and that the project keeps within its budget. They usually represent the views of their clients, investors, or superiors, as well as those of the prospective audience, throughout the production process.

Producers often concentrate on particular types of productions. Specialists who work with television commercials, dramas, sport news, video, or interactive multimedia projects rarely work outside of their program type because success in one type of producing does not necessarily guarantee success in another. Producers are further classified by the nature and the extent of their responsibilities. Staff Producers are employed on a continuing basis by a production company or organization. Such Producers in small video or film production companies are often assigned to specific projects. Independent Producers put together and sell production ideas to production companies (and to movie studios, network and cable television executives, and electronic publishers). They put together marketable story, staff, and talent as a package and work on a freelance basis. Executive Producers usually are less involved in day-to-day production decisions and, instead, focus on project development and evaluation. Finally, Producer "hyphenates" combine the role of Producer with those of writer and/or director. A writer-producer-director immerses him- or herself in the preplanning and the day-to-day production process in order to control the quality of the final product and preserve the integrity of the original idea.

Salaries
According to the U.S. Bureau of Labor's *Occupational Outlook Handbook,* median annual earnings of salaried producers throughout the performing industry were $52,840 as of May 2004, whereas in the motion picture and video industries, median yearly earnings in May 2004 were $75,200. The middle 50 percent of producers in the motion picture and video industries had annual incomes of between $35,550 and $87,980.

Employment Prospects
The position of Producer is a highly coveted one, and the competition in the video industry is intense. While nearly

anyone can become a Producer, it does not mean that it is easy to be employed or become successful. In fact, a Producer's job may be one of the hardest jobs around, since so much is involved in just getting a video production up and running. Nonetheless, the continued growth and development of media and multimedia outlets for video productions, such as the Web, help guarantee the need for successful Producers.

Advancement Prospects
Many Producers consider their jobs as the ultimate step in their careers, particularly as competition for higher positions of executive producer or production manager in motion picture organizations or at major market television stations/networks is extremely tough. Some Producers may seek administrative or production posts at independent production companies or at private education, health, or governmental media organizations.

Education and Training
A college degree in communications, radio/TV, or video technology is a usual requirement for a Producer in the video production field. A broad liberal arts background and/or a business degree may also be extremely helpful. A Producer should be knowledgeable about all aspects of filmmaking and video production, from screenwriting to directing and action, as well as about the more technical elements of photographic work, camera operations, sound design, and digital editing.

Experience, Skills, and Personality Traits
To be prepared to take on the responsibilities of a full-fledged Producer, an aspirant to this position should have a minimum of three to five years' experience as an associate producer or a director, having already gained production experience and knowledge as a production assistant. Producers need to be extremely familiar with budget estimation methodologies and should have background in all phases of video production, from the original conception of an idea for a video to the final editing processes.

Producers require excellent leadership qualities to head the team of production collaborators (writers, directors, production designers, lighting and sound personnel, and other technical personnel) through the often-laborious production process. Creativity is important, and Producers need to be fast problem solvers. They have to be well organized, highly detail-oriented, and financially astute. Above all, they must be decisive at all times and posses solid business and industry judgment.

Unions and Associations
Although a few Producers (who are also directors) may belong to the Directors Guild of America (DGA), there are no unions representing Producers. Membership in the Pro-

ducers Guild of America may be useful for networking and enhancing of skills through educational seminars. The guild attempts to provide a forum for its members, whether they work in films, television, video, or multimedia.

Tips for Entry

1. Gain a solid liberal arts education along with your concentration on communications, radio/TV, or video production to give you a better scope of the industry as a whole.

2. Take additional business and financial courses, as knowledge of business affairs and finances is extremely important in a Producer's job.

3. Be willing to start out as a production assistant, secretary, or assistant to a producer to learn the business and make industry contacts.

PRODUCTION DESIGNER

CAREER PROFILE

Duties: Envisage and create the style for a video production, establishing and planning the visual design

Alternate Title(s): Scenic Designer

Salary Range: $22,000 to $95,000 or more

Employment Prospects: Fair

Advancement Prospects: Poor

Prerequisites:

Education and Training—Minimum of an undergraduate degree in commercial arts, fine arts, or design

Experience—Minimum of three to five years working in as many design positions on a production as possible, such as graphic artist or set designer and/or two to three years as art director

Special Skills and Personality Traits—Artistic and highly creative; excellent basic design abilities; good communication skills; supervisory and administrative abilities; visually acute

CAREER LADDER

```
┌─────────────────────────────┐
│    Production Manager        │
└─────────────────────────────┘

┌─────────────────────────────┐
│    Production Designer       │
└─────────────────────────────┘

┌─────────────────────────────┐
│ Art Director; Production Assistant │
└─────────────────────────────┘
```

Position Description

The position of Production Designer in the video production industry is quite similar to that found in both the film and television industries. A Production Designer has the overall responsibility for creating the style of a video production and establishing and planning the visual design of the project. In conjunction with the director and/or producer, the Production Designer chooses the colors, textures, and tone of the production and then supervises the drawing of blueprints, the construction and dressing of any sets needed, and the coordination of all personnel involved in the artistic design, which includes set design, construction, and decoration, as well as costume design, hair and makeup, props, and special effects. It is a highly creative and conceptual role and a key position in the production team. Production Designers provide an integrated whole, an environment in which the on-camera action will occur. In addition, they typically decide which scenes of the video production will be shot at existing locations and which can be shot on a soundstage.

In preproduction, Production Designers meet with the producer and the director to determine the goals of the project and discuss their expectations for the production. Next, the Production Designer devises an appropriate visual concept within agreed-upon budgetary parameters and presents them to the producer and the director. Once these are approved, the designer will work with (and frequently hire) an art director (if such a position is required) and the craftspeople (which include the set designer, the costume designer, and the property master) to construct sets, purchase or rent needed furniture and props, and, generally, oversee the realization of the design.

While most of Production Designers' work is accomplished during the preproduction phase of the video production, their involvement may extend into the actual production stage as well. If so, during this part of the making of the production, the Production Designer will work closely with the director, the producer (or production manager), and the director of photography to establish the final "look" of the video production.

Salaries

While salaries may vary from one video production to another, based on the complexity of the project as well as the individual Production Designer's reputation, compensation of designers tends to be higher than that of art directors but less than most producers. According to Broadcast Employment Services, annual salaries in 2005 for Production Designers in general ranged from a low of $22,000 to a high of $125,000, and the median yearly salary is $41,000. (For video production designers, the high end of this salary range was closer to $100,000 per year.) Beginner designers may earn little or nothing but the experience of the work and the establishment of a credit to aid in their advance to higher-paid positions on later productions.

Employment Prospects

The chance of employment as a Production Designer is fair for those individuals who have had design experience, as an art director or a graphic designer, in the film or television industries. Trainee graphic artists often move on to become assistant art directors and then art directors as the next step toward becoming Production Designers.

Advancement Prospects

Chances for advancement for Production Designers are only fair. The next logical step for them is to become producers or, trading on their knowledge of production and their management experience, to look for a position as a production manager for a television station. These positions, however, are highly desirable and hard to come by. Production Designers in the video field may add to their experience by expanding their work into either film or television work.

Education and Training

An undergraduate degree in commercial art, fine arts, or design is the usual background for an individual looking for a position as a Production Designer. Some liberal arts background in literature, history, and theater is also recommended, as are courses in drafting and graphic design. Many Production Designers have studied architecture and environmental design as well. Most Production Designers start in graphic design positions within the art department of a television station to gain experience and production training before moving into similar positions in the video production industry.

Experience, Skills, and Personality Traits

Production Designers have to be highly creative and possess basic design skills, as well as be good communicators of their ideas, able to explain what they visualize and how it is to be accomplished. They must be skilled environmental designers, have a thorough knowledge of video production, and be able to supervise the multiple components and people of the artistic part of such a production. They need to have the ability to draw plans and sketch the design of the production from words and notes provided by either the director or producer, providing the script for the production with their own strong visual creative sense. Their design will affect the way the audience of the video will view it, just by the color and texture that the designer has chosen and the way objects and actions are arranged.

As a Production Designer is also a supervisor of the various art and design positions in the preproduction phase of a video production, some management experience is required. This experience is exactly what can be gained as an art director or an assistant art director.

Unions and Associations

While membership in the International Alliance of Theatrical Stage Employees (IATSE) is seldom required of Production Designers of video productions, such membership is beneficial for industry networking. Many Production Designers, however, may not be represented by a union. Some Production Designers who also work in commercial television may be members of the Broadcast Designers Association International (BDA International) in order to share mutual professional concerns and to network.

Tips for Entry

1. While a broad educational background is very helpful, you need to have an inherent artistic sense and enhance it by training in the aesthetic use of color, shapes, and light.
2. While in college, volunteer to work on student films or low-budget movies being shot in your area to gain practical experience, build your résumé, and make contacts for your future work as a designer.
3. Consider enrolling in a film or television school to add to your educational background. The production techniques you will learn there are applicable to video production as well.

PRODUCTION EDITOR

CAREER PROFILE

Duties: Choose the best shots and takes of a video production and assemble them in the most effective manner to reflect the director's vision of the project

Alternate Title(s): Video Editor; Film Editor

Salary Range: $21,000 to $110,000 or more

Employment Prospects: Fair to Good

Advancement Prospects: Fair

Prerequisites:

Education or Training—Undergraduate degree required; advanced degree recommended, with courses in video production and all phases of filmmaking

Experience—Editing experience with student films recommended; successful completion of Editors Guild training program

Special Skills and Personality Traits—Creativity; effective communication skills; good vision; sense of pacing; strong judgment and decision-making abilities

CAREER LADDER

```
┌─────────────────────────────────────┐
│   Director; Director of Photography; │
│            Producer                  │
└─────────────────────────────────────┘

┌─────────────────────────────────────┐
│         Production Editor            │
└─────────────────────────────────────┘

┌─────────────────────────────────────┐
│ Assistant Editor; Production Assistant│
└─────────────────────────────────────┘
```

Position Description

The craft of editing consists of selecting, combining, and trimming sounds and visual images after they have been recorded. In consultation with the director, Production Editors are responsible for the complex process of assembling and sorting the film, video, or digital footage of a video production into a cohesive sequence to ensure continuity and to execute the director's vision.

Today, film is seldom used as a medium within the video industry (but still used to a degree in motion pictures). Videotape quickly became the preferred medium. Up until the 1980s, the only process of editing videotape was linear (or online) editing. In this process, the videotaped footage is mounted onto the source (video) deck. Then a second, blank tape is mounted on the master deck. They both then are plugged into an editing controller, a device which tells the deck what to do. The Production Editor chooses and tags the beginning and end of each shot in both decks, and the controller then transfers the picture and sound from the source to the master. Each shot had to be handled separately and in sequence, which made transposing scenes difficult. Transi-

tions, or fades, from one shot to the next were not possible, unless a separate process, called offline editing, was set up. The offline editor put together the edit of the video without any fancy transitions, and the online editor, using the Edit Decision List (EDL)—a computer-generated list of which shots would be used in what order—would program multiple-source decks to recreate the whole program with all the required transitions. In either case, linear editing systems require a Production Editor to add visual images and sounds in consecutive order from the beginning to the end of a piece. The entire process remained unwieldy and time-consuming.

In the early 1980s, nonlinear editing was introduced along with the development of a new format called a "music video." This exciting and creative medium utilized an extremely fast method of editing. At the same time, a new machine, the Avid editing system, was introduced. It digitized the videotape footage, loading it into a computer. Because digitizing video (or film) requires tremendous storage capacity, only those shots and takes of the production that are very likely to be used during editing are digitized, using a computer board or card. A digitizing or capture card or board consists of hardware that rapidly samples electrical signals during videotape playback. These signals carry analog video and audio information, and the capture board converts them to digital information. Capturing video and audio signals requires fairly sophisticated hardware and considerable storage capacity, especially when high-quality images and sounds must be digitized. In nonlinear or "off-line" editing, the overall duration of a video production can be lengthened or shortened at any time, and images and sounds do not have to be edited in consecutive order from beginning to end.

The Production Editor, sitting at a computer terminal, now can arrange the shots on a time line, accurately trim frames, do quick searches for scenes, shifting them around at will, and rapidly create new sequences. The Avid editing system has allowed Production Editors (and directors) unlimited ability to change, manipulate, and make their final product more intricate. Under the new procedure, the editor can add new shots, moving all other shots aside to make room, or let the new shot wipe out part of an older one. The editor can add effects, split screens, graphics, and color effects, as well as all kind of slick transitions from one shot to another. One of the great advantages of the off-line system is that the editor, at any point, can see how the project is coming together, complete with at least rudimentary dissolves, fades, titles, color correction, and other effects. However, the effects created in this off-line system can be used only as a gauge, as the end product will be only as good as the information going into the system. Without accurate footage counts to give to the processing lab, these effects will become useless until they fit into the negative properly. The Production Editor must work closely with lab technicians to ensure the effects are translated properly.

The concept of on- and off-line editing still exists in nonlinear editing. Once the EDL is complete on the nonlinear computer, it is sent to an online editor who does a high-quality edit using the original video footage at its full resolution, attaching the final sound track at the same time.

Another method is sometimes used by low-budget filmmakers and video production directors, borrowing from the news media, by working with digital video (DV) cameras. These DV cameras can be plugged into a desktop or laptop computer and the images downloaded. Then, editing can be accomplished right on the desktop or laptop computer.

Thus, today's sophisticated editing hardware, software, and networking capabilities allow for segments of tape to be digitized, cut, pasted, and manipulated by Production Editors to create a seamless and imaginative content flow. This editing can occur during production itself, or in the postproduction phase.

Salaries

Wages for Production Editors are moderate to good. According to the U.S. Department of Labor's *Occupational Outlook Handbook,* median annual earnings for film and video Production Editors in May 2004 were $43,590. The middle 50 percent earned between $29,310 and $63,890 yearly. The lowest 10 percent earned less than $21,710 per year, and the highest 10 percent earned more than $93,950. Median annual earnings were $44,710 in the motion picture and video industries, which employed the largest number of film and video Production Editors.

For those Production Editors who belong to Local 700 of the International Alliance of Theatrical Stage Employees (IATSE), their hourly minimum wage, as set by union contract, is $42.20. If they are hired on a weekly basis (total of 48.6 hours), their minimum hourly wage is $38.92 or $1,891.33 per week. If they are put on an "on call" basis, their five-day minimum rate is $2,387.23.

Employment Prospects

As the video production industry is a growth industry, and since the Production Editor is a central position within the production process, employment prospects for Production Editors are relatively fair to good. Editors who have the needed skills to work with all the new digitizing processes have the best chance for continued employment. For many Production Editors, membership in the Editors Guild of IATSE can bolster and broaden their employment prospects, as they can shift their work between video productions and film and television work. Job security is further enhanced by how well Production Editors work with directors and/or producers.

Advancement Prospects

Many Production Editors remain in their position as the job itself is so demanding as well as rewarding. A few editors open their own editing firms. Others may want to become directors of photography, producers, or directors. Their post as Production Editor is one of the best ways to learn about directing (particularly as they work so closely with directors) and the entire production process. Generally, the skills and aesthetics learned as a Production Editor are applicable to many other higher-level production jobs in video production or film and television work. While opportunities for those with skill, dedication, and ambition are good, the competition is always stiff. It should also be noted that a good director has to be a good editor, but a good editor is not necessarily a good director.

Education and Training

A high school diploma is a basic requirement. In addition, prospective Production Editors should have some college training in film and video production and editing, as well as an undergraduate degree. The Motion Picture and Video Tape Editors Guild has training programs designed to help the aspiring Production Editor. These programs train members in the latest editing equipment and software programs. The American Cinema Editors society offers an internship program to college graduates who have majored in film, providing excellent background for Production Editors who want to work on video productions as well.

Experience, Skills, and Personality Traits

The process of editing is both an art and a craft. Production Editors need to be visual storytellers and must be able to reorganize visual shots to tell the same or different stories in different ways. They need to be both highly organized and logical in their thinking. They must have strong creative and artistic abilities (both visual and auditory), be able to communicate well, and have excellent manual dexterity.

Production Editors have to work well with strong ego-centered individuals, such as directors and producers, who may be counting upon them to fix a shot and improve on the video production as recorded. Production Editors need to be good listeners and collaborators and still have the ability to work long hours on a complex task alone. As veteran television editor M. Edward Salier observes, "You can't allow your own ego to get in the way … it's not what I want to see, it's what the director wants to see. I really have to be able to sit and listen to him, get a sense of what he wants to accomplish, and deliver that as quickly and efficiently as possible. … It's an intense job. It's a long workday. You have to be able to work on your own."

Unions and Associations

Many Production Editors belong to the International Alliance of Theatrical Stage Employees (IATSE). If Production Editors want to work on a studio or union motion picture as well as their video production work, they must be members of IATSE. Some Production Editors may find it beneficial to belong to the Association of Independent Video and Film-makers (AIVF) for networking purposes.

Tips for Entry

1. During your educational years, become involved in any aspect of filmmaking available to you, such as creating student films with a video or digital camera, and then edit the footage.
2. Consider starting out in an internship, where you can learn the basic editing skills, meet people, and build relationships that will be critical to advancing your career. Look for these internships at commercial production houses or postproduction facilities.
3. Attend film/video festivals to meet directors, as they usually are the ones who hire Production Editors. At such functions, network with Production Editors who may be seeking assistants.

MULTIMEDIA AND EDUCATION

DIRECTOR OF MEDIA SERVICES

CAREER PROFILE

Duties: Supervise media services, including television, video, DVD, and multimedia/Internet support, in a school district, college, or university

Alternate Title(s): Director of Educational Media; Director of Instructional Technology; Director of Library Media Services; Director of Media and Technology; Media Director/Supervisor; Media Instructional Coordinator

Salary Range: $35,000 to $75,000 or more

Employment Prospects: Fair to Good

Advancement Prospects: Poor

Prerequisites:

Education or Training—Master's or doctorate degree in education or media library services; special courses in Internet and media technology

Experience—Minimum of three to five years of educational media experience; two to three years of classroom teaching

Special Skills and Personality Traits—Excellent verbal, written, and interpersonal communication skills; inquisitiveness; leadership qualities; persuasiveness; supervisory ability

Special Requirements—Teaching license usually required; an education administrator license may also be required

CAREER LADDER

```
┌─────────────────────────────────────┐
│      Director of Media Services      │
│  (Larger Institution); Dean; Assistant │
│    Superintendent (School System)    │
└─────────────────────────────────────┘

┌─────────────────────────────────────┐
│      Director of Media Services      │
└─────────────────────────────────────┘

┌─────────────────────────────────────┐
│     Media Specialist Librarian;      │
│ Instructional Designer; Director of ITV │
│     (Instructional Television)       │
└─────────────────────────────────────┘
```

Position Description

A Director of Media Services is the senior administrative individual in charge of providing instructional support materials to schools, colleges, and universities that utilize multimedia services as part of their curricula and training. The person holding this post must ensure that well-selected multimedia materials and equipment are easily accessible to teachers and students for classroom use. Directors of Media Services often also manage a multimedia center within the educational setting. They work in elementary and secondary schools, community and four-year colleges, and universities.

In addition to the traditional audiovisual equipment and material used in the classroom, such as films, videocassettes, slides, charts, filmstrips, overhead transparencies, audio tape cassettes, and CDs, there is a large array of relatively new technological devices that can be used. These new media include computers and DVD equipment and programs, as well as the Internet and World Wide Web. It is the responsibility of the Director of Media Services to coordinate the use of this new technology within the instructional process and supervise all appropriate media staff. This individual must be an educational and technological generalist who views all these devices as components of a multimedia service and provides leadership for all facets of the media program of the school district, college, or university.

As a part of the overall responsibility of the job, the Director of Media Services must evaluate and purchase (or recommend) media equipment and programs to supplement and enhance classroom instruction and often supervises the operation of the equipment and programs in the classroom. In addition, the director supervises the maintenance of media equipment and provides technical assistance in troubleshooting any hardware, software, closed-circuit systems, telecommunications, or online service problems.

Directors of Media Services are also responsible for preparing budgets, coordinating with other departments or agencies to assure maximum use of media services and resources, and maintaining records, reports, and inventories in accordance with the school's policies and local, state, and federal guidelines. They may research, initiate, and encourage the obtaining of a wide range of grants and external funding for the support and enhancement of the media center. They also serve as liaisons between the school and both the public and other agencies, acting as advocates for the institution's media programs within the school system, the college (or university) environment, and the community.

Directors of Media Services operate in a variety of administrative ways. In some instances, they have overall responsibility for instructional television (ITV) operations, including the production of programs that are shown through a school-owned closed-circuit TV system. Sometimes, the director oversees all print (library) and non-print (media center) services for a school or college and is in charge of the day-to-day distribution of multimedia programs and equipment and other instructional programs. Directors often assist school principals or college personnel directors in the recruitment and hiring of qualified media specialists, as well as supervise staff development and training for media specialists and clerks.

In both higher education and some larger school districts, media services departments (or centers) are complex organizations and often employ more than 30 individuals who handle a variety of tasks, all under the supervision of the Director of Media Services. In smaller school systems, these functions may be carried out by as few as five people. In a school system, the Director of Media Services typically reports to an assistant superintendent. At a college or university, the director usually reports to a vice president of academic affairs or an equivalent administrative position.

Salaries

According to the U.S. Bureau of Labor Statistics, median annual earnings of instructional coordinators (which includes directors of media educational centers) in May 2004 were $48,790. The middle 50 percent earned between $35,940 and $65,040 yearly. The lowest 10 percent earned less than $27,300 annually, and the highest 10 percent earned more than $81,210 per year. The average salary for most Directors of Media Services for schools and school districts will depend to a degree upon the extent of their duties, and will range between $40,000 and $65,000 yearly. Similar positions at the college or university level have sal-

ary ranges slightly lower, again dependent upon the extent of their responsibilities.

Employment Prospects

According to the U.S. Bureau of Labor Statistics' 2004–05 *Occupational Outlook Handbook,* employment of instructional coordinators is expected to grow much faster than the average for all occupations through the year 2014. Although budget restraints may limit employment growth to some extent, the continuing emphasis on developing new curricula to meet the demands of a changing society and in training the teacher workforce, as well as providing instruction on the use of technology in the classroom, will all contribute to fair to good employment opportunities for administrators of media services in schools and colleges.

Although some small school systems may employ as Directors of Media Services individuals who have just received their college degrees, most systems look for more experienced people. In some organizations, the media specialist librarian or an instructional designer is promoted to the post of Director of Media Services.

Most states have a unit or department concerned with statewide media coordination and services, and many of these units circulate classroom and in-service media materials to schools. In addition, most school districts, community and four-year colleges, and universities have media centers. However, there is relatively little turnover in the position of director of these centers, and openings are often filled from within the unit or department.

Advancement Prospects

Opportunities for advancement are somewhat poor compared to most other video and electronic media communications areas. For many senior-level Directors of Media Services at large school systems or at higher education institutions, the position is the pinnacle of a successful career in educational communications and media. A few Directors of Media Services may be able to take administrative posts at larger colleges or universities as deans of instructional resources or at larger school systems as assistant superintendents.

Most directors move their careers forward by transferring to larger school systems, colleges, or universities that offer higher salaries and more prestige. Some directors obtain higher-paying positions in business, government, or health media centers. However, such a move usually requires a willingness to specialize in a particular field of interest.

Education and Training

A bachelor's degree in education is the bare minimum requirement for this position, and all but the very smallest school systems require a master's degree (in education or library services media). For colleges and universities, a master's degree is the minimum requirement, but most higher education institutions prefer a doctorate degree.

A candidate for the position of Director of Media Services should have earned a degree in education with the major field of study in educational media, instructional technology, or library media services. In addition, courses in computer technology and operations, curriculum design, educational administration and fiscal management, educational psychology, and information management are essential.

Special Requirements

Director/supervisor (at the master's degree level) certification is required for employment as Director of Media Services in most school systems. Certification is based on eligibility to hold the media coordinator (076) certificate plus 12 graduate semester hours of credit in administration, curriculum development, and supervision, as well as three years of acceptable experience as a media coordinator.

Most states require teacher certifications for the position of Director of Media Services in school systems or in higher educational institutions.

Experience, Skills, and Personality Traits

While some small schools or colleges may employ recent graduates as media directors, the majority require three to five years educational media experience, and, in some cases, two to three years of actual classroom teaching. This classroom experience provides insight into the day-to-day instructional process and environment. In addition, the candidate must have a broad knowledge of electronic media technology, including both traditional audiovisual equipment and more advanced uses of digital technology as applied to the learning process.

Most good Directors of Media Services are expert in various teaching and learning techniques and are well motivated to discover new methods that work. To this end, most directors participate in both media and educational profes-sional organizations. Directors must possess strong verbal and writing abilities, must be extremely articulate and persuasive, and have excellent interpersonal skills, as they need to coordinate well with other departments within their educational environment. They should be extremely well organized, have good leadership qualities, and be able to supervise a variety of individuals in various tasks.

Unions and Associations

There are no unions that specifically represent Directors of Media Services. Some directors may belong to the National Education Association (NEA) or the American Association of University Professors (AAUP), which may represent them as faculty members.

Most Directors of Media Services belong to the American Association of School Administrators, the Association for Educational Communications and Technology (AECT), the International Society for Technology in Education (ISTE), or the American Library Association (ALA) in order to share mutual concerns and network.

Tips for Entry

1. Consider getting your master's degree in education and a doctorate degree in library media as the best educational background for a position of Director of Media Services.

2. It is advisable to learn all you can about media technology, including basic computer programming, Internet search techniques, educational software, electrical wiring, and basic electrical repairs, as all these skills will be important to your career in media services.

3. While completing your education, join professional organizations that support the electronic media industry and network with technology directors and other professionals to gain insights into the latest technological choices that educational institutions need to consider.

INSTRUCTIONAL DESIGNER

CAREER PROFILE

Duties: Assist teachers in the design of new technology-based instructional materials and techniques using video, media technologies, and computers

Alternate Title(s): Curriculum Specialist; Curriculum Writer

Salary Range: $27,000 to $65,000 or more

Employment Prospects: Good

Advancement Prospects: Good

Prerequisites:

Education or Training—Undergraduate degree in education required; master's degree in education preferable, with courses in multimedia technology and equipment

Experience—Minimum of two to three years in media, training, and instruction; teaching experience recommended

Special Skills and Personality Traits—Analytical, writing, organizational, and project management abilities; interpersonal and teamwork skills; knowledge of media equipment and materials; patient, tolerant, tactful, and flexible; self-motivated; statistical aptitude

CAREER LADDER

```
┌─────────────────────────────────┐
│     Director of Media Services    │
└─────────────────────────────────┘

┌─────────────────────────────────┐
│       Instructional Designer      │
└─────────────────────────────────┘

┌─────────────────────────────────┐
│   Graduate Assistant; Teacher;    │
│          Media Intern             │
└─────────────────────────────────┘
```

Position Description

Instructional Designers are learning facilitators who help faculty members (in colleges and universities), teachers (in schools), and trainers (in business, health, and government) to create effective means of instruction and teaching by the use of media techniques and materials. They provide the basic framework for the development and design of non-broadcast training videotapes, satellite television courses, online courses, telecommunications systems in education, and other instructional materials.

The position of Instructional Designer includes the traditional functions of an educational curriculum specialist and curriculum writer. They are employed by schools and school systems, colleges and universities, as well as by private industry, health, and, occasionally, government training projects and programs. Some Instructional Designers are employed in educational publishing companies and software companies, providing instructional expertise for

the development of educational software and course work projects.

In higher educational institutions, they support the faculty in developing technology resources (such as Webpages on the Internet) for their courses and assist faculty in the design and development of online courses. They are tasked with assisting experts (in particular subjects) to design—or redesign—entire courses of study, specific lessons, individual lectures, or professional training sessions. They help to develop the content and to design the most effective methods of teaching it, making use of media technology. Instructional Designers develop units, modules, and courses of instruction. They recommend and update instructional materials, such as video or digital programs. When appropriate, they may organize and plan new media fare, and they often write, edit, and rewrite scripts for instructional video use. In this process, they consult with faculty and supervisors about instructional needs and designs, develop cost-benefit and accountability studies for the utilization of media, and evaluate the effectiveness of new instructional techniques, equipment, and programs.

Instructional Designers may work independently, but, more often, they work as part of a team of experts, each responsible for different aspects of the project. Other likely team members would include a content or subject specialist (usually a faculty member in a specific discipline), a multimedia editorial person (writer), a media technician, a media specialist librarian, a graphic design artist, a software engineer or programmer, and, often, a producer or director.

When developing multimedia materials, Instructional Designers examine the process of instructing from the perspective of the students (or learners) in order to best meet their specific needs. They must take into account the target audience for this learning process, the educational goals and objectives of the program, the settings in which the proposed material would be utilized, the appropriate instructional strategies to employ, and the most effective media and/or formats to present the instruction. In the creation of instructional projects, designers might write or edit text, develop layouts, make videotapes or digital disks, or, even, write programming codes. Instructional Designers often have the responsibility of managing a program through completion, tracking the project's progress, and testing a sampling of the participants to evaluate whether the program has met the learning objectives.

The position of Instructional Designer is not, generally, a supervisory position, and the individual usually reports to a director of media services or a director of instructional television.

Salaries

Wage earnings vary and depend on factors such as the education or experience of the individual and the budget of the educational institution. According to the U.S. Bureau of Labor Statistics, in May 2004, the median annual earnings of instructional coordinators (which include Instructional Designers) were $48,790. The middle 50 percent earned between $35,940 and $65,040 yearly. The lowest 10 percent earned less than $27,300 annually, and the highest 10 percent earned more than $81,210 per year.

In addition to a salary, most Instructional Designers receive fringe benefits, such as vacation leave, medical insurance, and retirement benefits.

Employment Prospects

Instructional Designers work for schools, colleges, and universities, as well as educational publishers, businesses, corporations, government agencies/departments, the U.S. military, nonprofit groups, and various other types of organizations and associations. They and their expertise are in demand, and employment prospects for this type of work are good. Increasing costs have prompted administrators in education and business to examine all possible ways to improve teaching and training and to manage the process more effectively. The effective application of new technology by Instructional Designers is one of the more viable approaches.

Job openings in education are available at the larger school districts, colleges, and universities, which are involved with extensive media programs, as well as video and telecommunications usage in the classroom. Some elementary and secondary school teachers who have worked in curriculum development undertake further training in the use of the latest electronic media equipment and materials and find jobs in their schools or school districts as Instructional Designers.

In addition to the opportunities in education, there are an increasing number of positions available in private business, industries (such as the health sector), and government. This field is expected to continue growing due to the explosion of public interest in online distance education programs available on the Internet and the resultant need for the creation of new online courses as well as the redesign of existing online courses.

Advancement Prospects

Some Instructional Designers serve in joint academic appointments and teach instructional development, educational psychology, or other allied courses in schools, colleges, or universities. As teachers, their career advancement is often tied to their academic achievements (papers, research, teaching competence, and so forth) as well as their abilities as designers or program developers.

Some Instructional Designers advance their careers by moving to more responsible positions as lead project managers or directors of media services at smaller colleges or school systems. Still others join private industry for better-paid positions, become self-employed, or start their own media development companies. Thus, the opportunities for advancement are good.

Education and Training

In general, the minimum requirement for Instructional Designers is a bachelor's degree in education, instructional design, or instructional technology. In many cases, a master's degree is also required. Individuals who are looking for employment at a major college or university may have to have a doctorate as well.

Course work in computer design and technology, curriculum development and design, educational psychology, and sociology are highly recommended. In addition, courses in educational media, including television, video and digital technologies, cable, and other nonbroadcast technology are mandatory.

Experience, Skills, and Personality Traits

Requirements vary among the different types of employers of Instructional Designers. Educational institutions usually require two to three years' experience, either as a graduate assistant or as an elementary school, secondary school or college teacher.

Knowledge of, and experience with, educational multimedia design principles and the use of a wide range of media resources and technology is essential. Skill in the operation and use of video and digital equipment and in writing and editing video and television instructional programs is another requirement. Candidates should have a working knowledge of such appropriate technology as HTML programming, educational software, and Web-based instructional systems.

Instructional Designers need superior analytical, writing, organizational, and program management skills. They must possess good communication, interpersonal, and teamwork skills, as they are in daily contact with, and must work well with, faculty and staff members of an organization. The Instructional Designers should have an inquisitive mind, a penchant for creative and logical thought, and an aptitude for statistical analysis. Successful Instructional Designers have had some teaching experience and are excellent motivators and cooperative leaders.

Unions and Associations

There are no unions that serve as bargaining agents for Instructional Designers. Those individuals who also serve as faculty members at schools, colleges, and universities may belong to the American Association of University Professors (AAUP) or the National Education Association (NEA).

Many Instructional Designers join local, state, and national professional associations to take advantage of professional resources, continuing education programs, networking opportunities, and other professional services. Such organizations may include the American Society for Training and Development (ASTD) and its Media Design and Production Division, the Association for Educational Communication and Technology (AECT) and its Division of Instructional Development, the Association for the Advancement of Computing in Education (AACE), the Association of Internet Professionals, or the International Society for Performance Improvement.

Tips for Entry

1. During your high school years, gain teaching experience by working (part time or as a volunteer) as a tutor, teacher's aide, summer camp counselor, or Sunday school teacher.
2. To acquire know-how in instructional design work, look for intern positions while finishing your college education.
3. Keep knowledgeable about the many advances in multimedia technology and materials by reading literature about technology, participating in training workshops and continuing education courses, attending professional conferences to network with colleagues, and keeping abreast of pertinent news/user groups (and Web sites) on the Internet.

MEDIA INSTRUCTOR

CAREER PROFILE

Duties: Teach college-level classes in educational multimedia technology and techniques; provide training and support in integrating media technology into curriculum and instruction

Alternate Title(s): Assistant Professor; Associate Professor; Instructional Technology Specialist; Professor

Salary Range: $30,000 to $65,000 or more

Employment Prospects: Good

Advancement Prospects: Fair

Prerequisites:

Education or Training—Minimum of a master's degree in education; doctorate degree preferable

Experience—Minimum of two to three years in teaching and media laboratory supervision

Special Skills and Personality Traits—Ability to motivate others; excellent verbal and writing skills; knowledge of educational media technology, techniques, and materials; leadership qualities

CAREER LADDER

```
┌─────────────────────────────────────┐
│   Department Chairperson; Dean       │
└─────────────────────────────────────┘

┌─────────────────────────────────────┐
│         Media Instructor             │
└─────────────────────────────────────┘

┌─────────────────────────────────────┐
│ Graduate Assistant; Graduate School  │
└─────────────────────────────────────┘
```

Position Description

Media Instructor is a general title for an individual who teaches college courses on the educational uses of a wide range of electronic media, including television, video, computers and the Internet, and other multimedia materials. The courses are offered for undergraduate, graduate, or in-service teacher education credit at a community college, four-year college, or university. A Media Instructor instructs teachers and teachers-in-training as to when, how, and why to utilize media technology, techniques, and materials as a facet of the classroom instructional procedure.

Theoretical courses taught by Media Instructors investigate how media technology and materials operate in the learning process to spark interest, complement classroom training, and supplement printed materials. Practical courses and laboratories focus on specific types of media technology (such as computers, closed-circuit television, videotapes, and DVD discs) and their advantages, availabilities, limitations, and costs. Media Instructors make clear what kinds of media technology are appropriate for assorted learning situations,

how to work electronic equipment, what software is best, and how to devise media projects as inexpensively as possible.

While traditional supplementary classroom materials such as filmstrips, slides, overhead projection equipment, and 16 mm films are still used in some situations, most Media Instructors today emphasize newer multimedia resources including computer-assisted instruction by using the Internet, digital CD-Rom disks, television, and video. It is the Media Instructor's primary duty to educate and train students (and, in some cases, educators) in the theory, utilization, and techniques of all such teaching aids.

A Media Instructor not only teaches classes but also may be involved in the educational institution's media center, which is where multimedia materials are produced and equipment obtained for the use of other faculty members teaching any subject. Instructors also conduct laboratory sessions detailing how to operate specific multimedia equipment, hold seminars on new media techniques, and present lectures in other education classes to highlight the use of state-of-the-art multimedia equipment and materials. They evaluate and select instructional media material and equipment for classroom use and lab training and supervise student workers at the educational institution's media instructional or learning resource center. They may be tasked to maintain equipment at their center and even prepare grant proposals for additional media financial support for their institution.

In addition, Media Instructors advise other faculty members about multimedia applications in the teaching of their subject areas and guide them on appropriate hardware, software, and peripherals (such as scanners and digital cameras) that can be used in completing teacher projects. They also help faculty develop and design computer-assisted instruction and presentations, which may include interactive Web-based applications. As a result, a Media Instructor is typically both a member of the faculty and an administrative and support employee of the educational institution. In some cases, they may not actually teach any classes but, instead, act as consultants in their assistance to faculty members and the administration. When Media Instructors are members of the faculty of a school or a department of education, they may hold any rank, from that of lecturer to full professor.

Media Instructors also work in secondary and elementary schools and school districts, usually as consultants in instructional technology. They are generally based in computer laboratories, sometimes as managers of the lab, and are in charge of coordinating technology training in their schools.

Salaries

Earnings for college faculty vary according to rank and type of institution, geographic area, and field. According to a 2004–05 survey by the American Association of University Professors, salaries for full-time faculty averaged $68,505 annually. By rank, the yearly average was $91,548 for professors, $65,113 for associate professors, $54,571 for assistant professors, $38,899 for instructors, and $45,647 for lecturers. According to the U.S. Bureau of Labor Statistics, median annual earnings of all postsecondary (college-level) teachers in May 2004 were $51,800, with the salaries ranging from the lowest of $25,460 to the highest of $99,980 per year.

Salaries for Media Instructors will also vary according to their education, experience, and the institution's budget. They can earn from $30,000 to $65,000 per year according to industry sources. In addition to a salary, they receive fringe benefits such as sick pay, medical insurance, and retirement benefits.

Employment Prospects

Media Instructors generally are in demand, as educational institutions are in need of qualified individuals who can counsel and teach the new techniques of instruction that multimedia technology offers. With the advent of the Internet and the almost universal use of the World Wide Web, the need for qualified Media Instructors in academic settings is high throughout the United States. In fact, some educational institutions find themselves in competition with business and industry (where the salary rates are usually higher) in recruiting and retaining media experts.

Candidates for this position are usually screened by a search committee. Selection is made based on the candidate's academic credentials, references, professional writing, research reputation, knowledge of media technology, and whether the particular academic strengths of the candidate match the instructional need at the institution. There are always a considerable number of adjunct or part-time teaching positions available at both four-year and community colleges. Many Media Instructors are chosen from the ranks of graduate school students or graduate teaching assistants.

Advancement Prospects

Opportunities for advancement are fair. Teachers usually progress from assistant professor to associate professor and, finally, to full professor. Promotion is highly competitive and is based largely on an individual's research, publication of papers, and teaching abilities. A Media Instructor may become chairperson of the media or education department or, in some cases, become dean. Some leave the educational profession for higher-paying jobs in private industry. Others use their multimedia, video, computer, and training skills to obtain more financially rewarding jobs in business or health media operations or become freelance owners of their own consulting firms.

Education and Training

A Media Instructor must have at least a master's degree in education, and a doctorate is generally preferred. Courses in communications, curriculum design, educational psychology, instructional technology, and learning theory are required subjects.

Experience, Skills, and Personality Traits

Media Instructors must have experience operating all kinds of multimedia equipment, such as audio gear, television cameras, and videotape and digital disc players and accessories. A thorough familiarity with computer-assisted instruction and interactive Web-based techniques is also required. At least two to three years' experience in teaching and media laboratory supervision is another requirement. Many Media Instructors are excellent teachers with a thorough knowledge of both the more traditional instructional support equipment and that of the new multimedia technology, as well as their operation and use in education.

Unions and Associations

There are no unions that serve as bargaining agents for Media Instructors. Those who have teaching positions may belong to the American Association of University Professors (AAUP), the American Federation of Teachers (AFT), or the National Education Association (NEA), which act as bargaining agents for salary increases and benefits. In addition, most Media Instructors are active in the Association for Educational Communications Technology (AECT) to share mutual concerns and network, while some may also belong to the University Film and Video Association (UFVA).

Tips for Entry

1. As a college student, obtain part-time work with media centers or with media technology production companies to become familiar with the technology, its hardware and software.

2. Gain as much teaching experience as you can so you have an understanding of what teachers want to accomplish with their instruction and where these needs may be met by multimedia techniques and materials.

3. To learn about job listings, contact professional organizations that support Media Instructors. Many of them have job hotlines as well as job banks on their Web sites. Another source for job listings can be found in the *Chronicle of Higher Education,* a professional journal, and on its Web site, http://chronicle.com/jobs.

MEDIA SPECIALIST LIBRARIAN

CAREER PROFILE

Duties: Manage the school (or college) library media center, instructing students, teachers, and others on how to access and use library media resources; develop and maintain collections of print and non-print materials (including online access to databases).

Alternate Title(s): Learning Information Specialist; Learning Resource Specialist; Media Specialist; Audiovisual Librarian

Salary Range: $29,000 to $70,000 or more

Employment Prospects: Fair to Good

Advancement Prospects: Poor to Fair

Prerequisites:

Education or Training—Undergraduate degree in communications or English; master's degree in library science usually required

Experience—Minimum of one to two years of library cataloging, classifying, and circulating media materials

Special Skills and Personality Traits—Communication and interpersonal skills; computer and online searching aptitude; detail orientation; organizational and problem solving talents; patient, caring, creative, curious, enthusiastic, flexible, and resourceful

Special Requirements—A library media specialist credential may be required; a teaching certificate may be required

CAREER LADDER

```
┌─────────────────────────────────────────┐
│   Media or Library Administrator;         │
│   Library Supervisor or Coordinator       │
│   (school district or central office level)│
└─────────────────────────────────────────┘

┌─────────────────────────────────────────┐
│        Media Specialist Librarian         │
└─────────────────────────────────────────┘

┌─────────────────────────────────────────┐
│          Librarian; Teacher               │
└─────────────────────────────────────────┘
```

Position Description

The traditional concept of a library is changing from a place to access paper records, recordings, books, or microfilm/microfiche to one that also houses the most advanced multimedia equipment and materials, including CD-ROM, the Internet, virtual libraries, and remote access to a wide range of multimedia resources. In public and private educational facilities, the school library is often known as the library media center. The library media center personifies the change in the concept of a library, in that along with book collections and other print collections (such as photo or microfilm/microfiche), it also holds in its collection video, DVD, software, CD-ROM, and other nonprint material for students (and teachers) to use. Most library media centers also have multimedia workstations available so that students and other users can take advantage of electronic resources like the Internet. Media Specialist Librarians, who are professional librarians, manage these centers.

Media Specialist Librarians are responsible for acquiring, previewing, categorizing, cataloging, scheduling, and circulating films, videocassettes, DVDs, and other nonprint materials, as well as maintaining records detailing the location and disposition of all such material. They select media materials from a variety of sources, including reviews in professional literature, producer or distributor sales or promotional literature, and exhibits.

Another of their responsibilities is to provide reference services to students and help them locate appropriate resources for their research projects. They also teach students essential library skills, such as searching for information in print and technology resources and evaluating the information they find. In addition, Media Specialist Librarians instruct students on how properly to use and care for computers, printers, copiers, and other media equipment in the library media center. They provide consulting services to teachers on the utilization of the various print and electronic media resources at the library media center. Frequently, they collaborate with teachers on using these materials to enhance instructors' class lessons. They may also provide in-service training to teachers, administrators, and other school staff.

An additional part of their job is to make sure the center policies on hours of operation, library rules, circulation procedures, and rules for Internet access are in place and are followed by students, teachers, and other users. They may perform many administrative duties, such as evaluating their center's goals and performance; overseeing budgets; writing reports and completing required paperwork; supervising the preparation and publication of the media center's film, video, and DVD rental/sale catalogs; keeping an inventory of hardware and other multimedia equipment and materials; and maintaining accurate records on circulation and general use of the media center.

Media Specialist Librarians are employed by schools and colleges, private industry, and government and health media centers and, increasingly, are important staff members at most major public libraries. Many media librarians at small schools are in charge of print, photo, and multimedia collections. In some large media centers that have extensive collections of multimedia materials or in public libraries, Media Specialist Librarians are also responsible for off-campus or public circulation.

Media Specialist Librarians frequently supervise many part-time student workers and, in large media centers, are often responsible for the management of one to three full-time employees. In some schools, colleges, or universities, media librarians may participate in faculty meetings and serve on academic committees. Media Specialist Librarians employed by schools or colleges usually report to a Director of Media Services, whereas a media librarian working at a public library typically reports to the head librarian.

Salaries

Salaries of librarians generally vary according to the individual's qualifications and duties, and the type, size, and location of the library. The salaries of Media Specialist Librarians similarly reflect the type and size of the media center and the extent of duties that the librarian must perform.

According to the U.S. Bureau of Labor Statistics, median annual earnings of librarians in May 2004 were $45,900. The middle 50 percent earned between $36,980 and $56,960 per year. The lowest 10 percent earned less than $29,930 yearly, and the highest 10 percent earned more than $70,200 annually. The study further noted that librarians with primarily administrative duties often had the higher salaries. In colleges, universities, and professional schools, median annual earnings in May 2004 for librarians were $47,830, in comparison to those employed by elementary and secondary schools, whose earnings were $47,580 per year. However, in public library settings, the median annual earnings were $40,000.

Employment Prospects

Media Specialist Librarians are employed by both public and private schools. Most job opportunities occur when Media Specialist Librarians retire, resign, or transfer to other positions. The creation of such a position at small to medium schools is usually dependent upon the availability of school funds. Nonetheless, most school and college administrators find it preferable to hire professional librarians with a master's in library science to run their media centers. Positions as Media Specialist Librarians in private industry and at health media centers are increasingly available.

Advancement Prospects

Many Media Specialist Librarians obtain advancement through increases in pay. In library media centers with more than one staff member, Media Specialist Librarians can move on to supervisory and managerial positions. By obtaining further licensing, media librarians can advance to positions as library supervisors or coordinators at the district (or central office) level or at larger media centers. Those with higher administrative ambitions can look for positions as principals (of schools), program directors, assistant superintendents, and school superintendents.

Another avenue of advancement for Media Specialist Librarians can be the pursuit of other librarian careers in academic libraries, public libraries, research libraries, or business media centers. They can pursue related careers, such as systems analysts, webmasters, information scientists, or information brokers.

Education and Training

Media Specialist Librarians must have a bachelor's degree and, in most instances, a master's degree in library science (M.L.S.). Most employers insist that the master's degree comes from a school accredited by the American Library Association (ALA).

In smaller media operations where the position has less responsibility for the selection and acquisition of media equipment and materials, a bachelor's degree may be all that is necessary. Nonetheless, courses in media, cataloging, and classification of materials are required, and a broad liberal arts background is encouraged.

Special Requirements

In public schools, Media Specialist Librarians must hold a valid Library Media Specialist credential. They may also be required to have a teaching credential in some states. In addition, licensed Media Specialist Librarians must have completed an approved school library media program that leads to licensure in the state in which they practice. The program usually includes a supervised field practicum (a course devoted to practical experience in the field).

Many private schools require state licensure as well as a librarian credential, or professional certification from school accreditation organizations.

Experience, Skills, and Personality Traits

Most public schools require that Medial Specialist Librarians have some previous classroom teaching experience. In addition, a minimum of one to two years of cataloging and classifying media equipment and materials, as well as handling circulation procedures related to the distribution of nonprint materials, is usually required. Since most media centers use computers in their circulation operations, familiarity with appropriate computer hardware/software is essential. However, both public and private schools look for candidates who have traditional library skills as well as knowledge about the latest media technology.

Media Specialist Librarians need to have excellent teaching, communication, interpersonal, management, organizational, and problem-solving skills. They must be detail-oriented, responsible, and inquisitive. They need superior computer skills and effective online skills for searching CD-ROM and Internet databases. They should be caring, curious, enthusiastic, flexible, creative, and resourceful. They must be committed to helping students to find the enjoyment of reading and researching, as well as assisting them to become successful independent information seekers.

Unions and Associations

While there are no national unions that represent and bargain for Media Specialist Librarians, most of them belong to the American Library Association and one or more of its divisions, such as the American Association of School Librarians (AASL) or the Library and Information Technology Association (LITA). Others hold membership in the Special Libraries Association (SLA). Additional organizations that Media Specialist Librarians may wish to join are the Association for Educational Communications and Technology (AECT), the Association of Visual Communicators (AVC), and the American Film and Video Association (AFVA), where they can share common concerns and network.

Media Specialist Librarians in public schools may be eligible to join teacher unions, such as the American Federation of Teachers (AFT) or the National Education Association (NEA).

Tips for Entry

1. While earning your bachelor's degree or your master's degree in library science, visit a school library media center and talk with librarians about their job. In addition, volunteer or intern at a school library media center during your undergraduate or graduate years to learn firsthand about what such a center and its librarians do.

2. Contact public and/or private schools where you might want to work, and be ready to complete job applications with all your information (résumé, education, work history, and references).

3. Upon being hired as a Media Specialist Librarian, be sure to continue your professional development through self-study, networking with colleagues, attending professional conferences, and enrolling in continuing education courses and keep current on copyright regulations and any licensing agreements attached to your media equipment and materials.

MEDIA TECHNICIAN

CAREER PROFILE

CAREER LADDER

Duties: Repair and maintain multimedia equipment in a library media center at a school, college, or university

Alternate Title(s): Audiovisual Technician; Library Technical Assistant; Maintenance Technician; Media Aide

Salary Range: $15,000 to $40,000 or more

Employment Prospects: Excellent

Advancement Prospects: Good

Prerequisites:

   Education or Training—High school diploma required; some vocational or technical school training recommended

   Experience—Minimum of six months to a year of multimedia equipment repair preferable

   Special Skills and Personality Traits—Accuracy; electronics skills; inquiring mind; mechanical aptitude; problem-solving capacity

   Special Requirements—A certification as an electronics technician may be required

Director of Media Services; Television Technician; Video Service Technician

Media Technician

Video Equipment Repairperson; Technical School

Position Description

Media Technicians maintain, repair, and service the multimedia equipment at a school or college media facility. They repair traditional audiovisual equipment, including 16 mm projectors and cameras, slide and film-strip machines, Microfiche readers, opaque and overhead projectors, and television sets (used for closed-circuit television programming), as well as videocassette, audio cassette, and DVD players. In media centers that utilize television studio equipment, the technician's duties reside in repairing cameras, switchers, and associated appliances. While many difficulties that arise are mechanical in nature, others may require the technician to have knowledge about digital electronics, integrated circuit boards, and computer equipment and to be able to interpret schematic charts and diagrams detailing television, video, DVD, and other media electronic components and systems.

   One of the most important of the Media Technician's responsibilities is to develop and maintain a methodical and consistent system of preventive maintenance to guarantee

that all media equipment is operating well at all times. In addition, technicians have to keep an inventory of all parts, accessories, and supplies. They interact with manufacturers' field service representatives and attend periodic seminars and training sessions to keep current about new equipment and techniques. From this ongoing knowledge, they are able to recommend the replacement of outdated equipment or machinery that should be discarded rather than fixed.

   Media Technicians usually operate out of a single maintenance equipment room at the media center. In some large media operations with more than one site, Media Technicians may be assigned to a specific branch or office. Occasionally, they may be sent on location to handle repair work in classrooms or other buildings where equipment is located.

   Increasingly, Media Technicians are assuming greater responsibilities, in some cases taking on tasks previously performed by librarians. With the widespread use of computerized information storage and retrieval systems, Media Technicians may handle technical services, such as entering into the library's computer cataloging and coding of library and media materials, retrieving information from computer databases and storing it in the library's computer system, and even supervising media support staff. Media Technicians may assist with customizing library databases and, in some instances, instruct patrons on how to utilize the library's media computer systems to access data.

Small media centers at schools usually employ only one full-time Media Technician, while at larger centers (at colleges or universities), two or three technicians are required full time to keep the equipment in good working order and carry out other duties assigned to them. In some instances, high school or college students are hired on a part-time basis to supplement the services of the Media Technician, who then supervises and trains them. In turn, Media Technicians usually report directly to a director of media services in small to medium-sized media operations and to that person's assistant (if there is one) at large media centers.

Salaries

According to the U.S. Bureau of Labor Statistics in its *Occupational Outlook Handbook,* median annual earnings of library technicians (which include Media Technicians) in May 2004 were $24,940. The middle 50 percent earned yearly between $18,640 and $32,600. The lowest 10 percent earned less than $14,760 per year, and the highest 10 percent earned more than $40,730 annually.

While such salaries are generally lower than those of similar equipment maintenance posts in multichannel multipoint distribution (MMDS) companies or in the home video/DVD field, the fringe benefits and security offered are often distinctly better. All school, college, and university media centers offer good employee health, life, insurance, and pension plans. An employee credit union is frequently available as well, and reasonable vacation schedules are the norm.

Employment Prospects

Opportunities for employment are excellent. To a degree, there is a lack of sufficient qualified technical people in established media centers, and the position does not usually require as much electronics knowledge and training as comparable positions of video/DVD service technicians (in home video/DVD) or cable TV technicians, although the basic skills are similar. The increasing use of library automation and the expansion of library service to include media equipment and materials for students and the public will continue to spur job growth among Media Technicians working within the library field. In addition to jobs opening up through employment growth, some jobs will result from the need to replace Media Technicians who leave for better-paid jobs in the private sector, or leave the (particular) job market altogether. According to the U.S. Bureau of Labor

Statistics, employment of library technicians is expected to grow about as fast as the average for all occupations through 2014.

While the continuing efforts of educational institutions to contain costs could dampen employment growth of Media Technicians in school, public, college, and university libraries, cost containment efforts can just as easily result in hiring more technicians than librarians, due to the increased use of the library's multimedia equipment and materials. In addition, the growth in the number of professionals and other workers who use special libraries should result in good job opportunities for Media Technicians in those settings.

Advancement Prospects

Opportunities for advancement are good. Library technicians (including Media Technicians) often advance by assuming added responsibilities within the library. They often start at the circulation desk, checking books and other materials in and out, then move on to become responsible for storing and verifying information. They may also become involved in budget and personnel matters at the media center. Some Media Technicians advance to supervisory positions, such as director of media services.

As in most technical positions in electronics, there is some turnover in the field. Individual Media Technicians who combine their mechanical and electronic experience with further study may move on to better paid positions as technicians in MMDS or cable TV operations. Some may get jobs in the consumer electronics field as video/DVD service technicians with higher pay but, usually, with fewer benefits.

Education and Training

While training requirements for Media Technicians in libraries may vary widely, the usual requirement is that of a high school diploma and some evidence of postsecondary training in a trade, technical, or vocational school. Classes in the basic sciences, math, and algebra are considered vital, and courses in drafting (to be able to read technical specification charts), basic electronics, and electrical engineering are considered helpful. Most employers prefer to hire technicians who have an associate degree or some other postsecondary training. Given the rapid spread of automation in libraries, computer skills are required. In addition, knowledge of databases, library automation systems, online library systems, online public access systems, and circulation systems may be particularly valuable.

Specialized training is available at technical institutes, community colleges, extension divisions of colleges and universities, and public or private vocational/technical schools. Some training may be taken by correspondence study. In addition, a number of community colleges offer an associate degree or certificate programs designed for library Media Technicians, in which students learn about library and media organization and operation, as well as how to order, process, catalog, locate, and circulate library materials and work with library automation.

Special Requirements

While a Federal Communications Commission (FCC) license is not required of Media Technicians, many of them study for exams and become certified by the Association of Communications Technicians (ACT) or the International Society of Certified Electronics Technicians (ISCET).

Experience, Skills, and Personality Traits

Most employers prefer to hire those with some experience, usually a minimum of six months to a year, in the repair of audiovisual and other media equipment. Others may prefer to employ individuals with technical school training but little experience and then train these technicians on the job.

An understanding of the operation of various types of media equipment, from traditional audiovisual machines to television sets to newer technologies, such as CD-ROM machines and computers, is required. Also important is the ability to diagnose mechanical and electronic problems. Media Technicians need to have inquisitive minds, have mechanical dexterity, and exhibit an intuitive feel for problem solving. An ability to do detailed work with a high degree of accuracy is a basic requirement, and Media Technicians must be able to work independently.

Unions and Associations

There are no national unions that represent or serve as bargaining agents for Media Technicians. Technicians working in government and in some health areas are in local or federal civil service positions and may be represented by appropriate governmental unions.

Some Media Technicians belong to the Association of Communications Technicians (ACT), the International Society of Certified Electronics Technicians (ISCET), the International Television Association (ITVA), or the National Electronic Service Dealers Association (NESDA) to share mutual concerns with colleagues and to network.

Tips for Entry

1. While finishing your high school and/or vocational training education, check at local electronics stores for part-time jobs that can give you more experience in the technology of media electronics.
2. In addition, look for technical internships or work-study jobs in electronics (these are sometimes available at local, state, or federal government agencies).
3. While working as a Media Technician, attend periodic seminars and training sessions to keep informed about new equipment and techniques that you can suggest for your media center.

APPENDIXES

APPENDIX I
EDUCATIONAL INSTITUTIONS

For those candidates entering the Internet, video game, and multimedia industries (especially in senior level and/or highly technical posts), a college degree (whether from a two- or four-year program) is generally preferred and, often, a requirement. Many institutions offer degrees in such relevant majors as applied mathematics, communication technology, computer engineering, computer graphics, design/visual communications, drafting and design technology, electrical and communications engineering, electrical engineering technology, information technology, LAN/WAN management, mathematics/computer science multimedia, sales/distribution, software engineering, and web/multimedia management. Some institutions are now offering a degree in video game design. A good place to search for such burgeoning programs is online at http://www.technical-schools. us/videogamedesign.htm. In addition, a growing number of schools offer other degrees appropriate to multimedia, the Internet, and video game design, online as well as at their physical locations. A useful starting point to locate such institutions is online at http://www.onlinedegreedirect.com.

The following is a selected list of many of the U.S. colleges and universities that offer bachelor's degrees in various areas of the multimedia and Internet industries. (We have *not* included computer science, marketing, or other such overlapping general majors, which most colleges and universities offer, or such tangential specialties as creative writing, fine/studio arts, physics, or speech and communication.) Many of these establishments also offer master's and other higher degrees which are *not* detailed herein.

For the undergraduate schools included in this appendix, the listings below provide addresses, telephone numbers, fax numbers, e-mail addresses, and Web sites. Also provided (in alphabetical order) are each school's majors and specialties allied to the multimedia and Internet industries. For further information about courses offered and admission requirements as well as such topics as scholarships, campus housing, and academic calendar, contact the institution(s) of choice. Since the e-mail addresses of college admissions offices frequently change, it is advised to check the institution's Web site. (Increasingly, colleges now provide a link/form on their Web site for directly contacting school departments.)

For a listing of those institutions offering two-year programs dealing with majors appropriate to the multimedia, video game, and Internet industries, please check such directories as *Peterson's Two-Year Colleges,* published annually by Thomson Peterson.

ALABAMA

Alabama A&M University
P.O. Box 908
Normal, AL 35762
Phone: (256) 851-5245
Fax: (256) 851-5249
E-mail: aboyle@asnaam.aamu.edu
http://www.aamu.edu
Communications technology.

Auburn University—Auburn
202 Mary Martin Hall
Auburn, AL 36849
Phone: (334) 844-4080
Fax: (334) 844-6179
E-mail: admissions@auburn.edu
http://www.auburn.edu
Applied mathematics, computer
    engineering, design/visual
    communications, electrical and
    communications engineering, software
    engineering.

Auburn University—Montgomery
P.O. Box 244023
Montgomery, AL 36124
Phone: (334) 244-3611
Fax: (334) 244-3795
E-mail: mmoore@mail.aum.edu
http://www.aum.edu
Design/visual communications, electrical
    and communications engineering,
    software engineering.

Birmingham-Southern College
900 Arkadelphia Road
Birmingham, AL 35254
Phone: (205) 226-4696
Fax: (205) 226-3074
E-mail: admission@bsc.edu
http://www.bsc.edu
Mathematics/computer science.

Faulkner University
5345 Atlanta Highway
Montgomery, AL 36109
Phone: (334) 386-7200
Fax: (334) 386-7137
E-mail: admissions@faulkner.edu
http://www.faulkner.edu
Drafting and design technology.

Huntingdon College
1500 East Fairview Avenue
Montgomery, AL 36106
Phone: (334) 833-4497
Fax: (334) 833-4347
E-mail: admiss@huntingdon.edu
http://www.huntingdon.edu
Computer graphics.

Jacksonville State University
700 Pelham Road North
Jacksonville, Al 36265
Phone: (256) 782-5268
Fax: (256) 782-5953
E-mail: info@jsucc.jsu.edu
http://www.jsu.edu
Electrical engineering technology.

Oakwood College
7000 Adventist Boulevard
Huntsville, AL 35896
Phone: (800) 824-5312
Fax: (256) 726-7154
E-mail: admission@oakwood.edu
http://www.oakwood.edu
Applied mathematics, multimedia.

South University
South University
709 Mall Boulevard
Savannah, GA 31406-4805
Phone: (888) 444-3404
Fax: NA
E-mail: syaghoubi@southuniversity.edu
http://www.online.southuniversity.edu
Information technology.

Spring Hill College
4000 Dauphin Street
Mobile, AL 36608
Phone: (251) 380-3030
Fax: (251) 460-2186
E-mail: admit@shc.edu
http://www.shc.edu
Graphic design.

Tuskegee University
Old Administration Building, Suite 101
Tuskegee, AL 36086
Phone: (334) 727-8500
Fax: (334) 727-5750
E-mail: adm@tuskegee.edu
http://www.tuskegee.edu
Electrical and communications
    engineering.

University of Alabama—Birmingham
HUC 260
1530 3rd Avenue South
Birmingham, AL 35294
Phone: (205) 934-8221
Fax: (205) 975-7114
E-mail: undergradadmit@uab.edu
http://www.uab.edu
Electrical and communications
    engineering.

University of Alabama—Huntsville
301 Sparkman Drive
Huntsville, AL 35899
Phone: (256) 824-6070
Fax: (256) 824-6073
E-mail: admitme@email.uah.edu
http://www.uah.edu
Computer engineering, electrical and
    communications engineering, software
    engineering.

University of South Alabama
182 Administration Building
Mobile, AL 36688
Phone: (334) 460-6141
Fax: (334) 460-7023
E-mail: admiss@jaguari.usouthal.edu
http://www.usouthal.edu
Computer engineering, e-commerce,
    electrical and communications
    engineering.

ALASKA

University of Alaska—Anchorage
3211 Providence Drive
Anchorage, AK 99508
Phone: (907) 786-1480
Fax: (907) 786-4888
E-mail: At Web site
http://www.uaa.alaska.edu
Computer programming—specific
    applications, drafting and design
    technology, electrical and
    communications engineering,
    electrical engineering technology.

University of Alaska—Fairbanks
P.O. Box 757480
Fairbanks, AK 99775
Phone: (907) 474-7500
Fax: (907) 474-5379
E-mail: fyapply@uaf.edu
http://www.uaf.edu
Applied mathematics, computer
    engineering, electrical and
    communications engineering.

ARIZONA

Arizona State University East
P.O. Box 870112
Tempe, AZ 85387
Phone: (480) 965-7788
Fax: (480) 727-1008
E-mail: Stacie.dana@asu.edu.
http://www.east.asu.edu
Applied mathematics, computer
    engineering, electrical and
    communications engineering,
    multimedia.

Arizona State University West
4701 West Thunderbird Road
Phoenix, AZ 85306-4908
Phone: (602) 543-9378
Fax: (602) 543-8312
E-mail: west-admissions@asu.edu
http://www.west.asu.edu
Applied mathematics, computer
    engineering, electrical and

communications engineering,
    multimedia.

Arizona Western College
2020 South Avenue 8 East
P.O. Box 929 Yuma, AZ 85366
Phone: (888) 293-0392
Fax: (928) 344-7543
E-mail: At Web site
http://www.azwestern.edu
Computer graphics, drafting and design
    technology, LAN/WAN management.

**Embry-Riddle Aeronautical
    University—Prescott Campus**
3700 Willow Creek Road
Prescott, AZ 86301
Phone: (928) 777-6600
Fax: (928) 777-6605
E-mail: pradmit@erau.edu
http://www.embryriddle.edu
Computer engineering, electrical and
    communications engineering.

Northern Arizona University
P.O. Box 4080
Flagstaff, AZ 86011
Phone: (926) 523-5511
Fax: (928) 523-0226
E-mail: undergraduate.admissions@nau.
    edu
http://www.nau.edu
Computer engineering, digital media,
    electrical and communications
    engineering.

University of Advancing Technology
2625 West Baseline Road
Tempe, AZ 85283
Phone: (602) 383-8228
Fax: (602) 383-8222
E-mail:admissions@uat.edu
http://www.uat.edu
Computer graphics, design/visual
    communications, multimedia,
    software engineering.

ARKANSAS

Arkansas State University
P.O. Box 1630
State University, AR 72467
Phone: (870) 972-3024
Fax: (870) 910-8094
E-mail: admissions@astate.edu
http://www.astate.edu
Communications technology, data
    processing technology, digital
    media, electrical engineering
    technology.

Arkansas Tech University
Doc Bryan #141
Russellville, AR 72801
Phone: (479) 968-0343
Fax: (479) 964-0522
E-mail: tech.enroll@mai.atu.edu
http://www.atu.edu
Electrical and communications
   engineering, electrical engineering
   technology.

Central Baptist College
1501 College Avenue
Conway, AR 72034
Phone: (501) 329-6872
Fax: (501) 329-2941
E-mail: ccalhoun@cbc.edu
http://www.cbc.edu
Data processing technology.

Harding University
P.O. Box 12255
Searcy, AR 72149
Phone: (501) 279-4407
Fax: (501) 279-4865
E-mail: admissions@harding.edu
http://www.harding.edu
Computer engineering, digital media,
   graphic design, information
   technology, sales/distribution.

Henderson State University
1100 Henderson Street
HSU P.O. Box 7560
Arkadelphia, AR 71999
Phone: (870) 230-5028
Fax: (870) 230-5066
E-mail: hardwrv@hsus.edu
http://www.hsu.edu
Computer programming—specific
   applications.

John Brown University
2000 West University Street
Siloam Springs, AR 72761
Phone: (800) 634-6969
Fax: (479) 524-4196
E-mail: jbuinfo@jbu.edu
http://www.jub.edu
Design/visual communications, electrical
   and communications engineering,
   graphic design, illustration.

Ouachita Baptist University
410 Ouachita Street
Arkadelphia, AR 71998
Phone: (870) 245-5110
Fax: (870) 245-5500
E-mail: admissions@alpha.obu.edu
http://www.obu.edu
Graphic design.

Philander Smith College
812 West 13th Street
Little Rock, AR 72202
Phone: (501) 370-5221
Fax: (501) 370-5225
E-mail: admission@philander.edu
http://www.philander.edu
Mathematics/computer science.

University of Arkansas—Fayetteville
232 Silas Hunt Hall
Fayetteville, AR 72701
Phone: (479) 575-5346
Fax: (479) 575-7515
E-mail: uofa@uark.edu
http://www.uark.edu
Communications computer engineering,
   data processing technology, electrical
   and communications engineering.

University of Arkansas—Fort Smith
5210 Grand Avenue
P.O. Box 3649
Fort Smith, AR 72913
Phone: (888) 512-LION
Fax: NA
E-mail: information@uafortsmith.edu
http://www.uafortsmith.edu
Drafting and design technology, electrical
   and communications engineering.

University of Arkansas—Little Rock
2801 South University Avenue
Little Rock, AR 72204
Phone: (501) 569-3127
Fax: (501) 569-8915
E-mail: admissions@ualr.edu
http://www.ualr.edu
Applied mathematics, communications
   technology, computer engineering,
   data processing technology,
   electrical and communications
   engineering, electrical engineering
   technology, technical and business
   writing.

University of Arkansas—Pine Bluff
1200 North University Drive, Mail Slot
   4981
Pine Bluff AR 71601
Phone: (870) 575-8000
Fax: (870) 543-8014
E-mail: fulton_E@uapb.edu
http://www.uapb.edu
Applied mathematics, computer
   engineering, data processing

technology, electrical and
   communications engineering.

University of Central Arkansas
201 Donaghey Avenue
Conway, AR 72035
Phone: (501) 450-3128
Fax: (501) 450-5228
E-mail: admissions@mail.uca.edu
http://www.uca.edu
Data processing technology.

University of Phoenix
Mail Stop 10-0030
4615 East Elwood Street
Phoenix, AZ 85040
Phone: (480) 317-6000
Fax: (480) 594-1758
E-mail: At Web site
http://www.uofphx.info
Web/multimedia management.

CALIFORNIA

Academy of Art University
79 New Montgomery Street
San Francisco, CA 94105
Phone: (415) 274-2222
Fax: (415) 263-4130
E-mail: info@academyart.edu
http://www.academyart.edu
Cinematography and film/video
   production, design/visual
   communications, graphic design,
   illustration, multimedia, photographic/
   film/video technology.

Allan Hancock College
800 South College Drive
Santa Maria, CA 93454
Phone: (805) 922-6966, ext. 3272
Fax: (805) 922-3477
E-mail: At Web site
http://www.hancock.cc.ca.us
Design/visual communications.

Art Center College of Design
1700 Lida Street
Pasadena, CA 91103
Phone: (626) 396-2373
Fax: (626) 795-0578
E-mail: admissions@artcenter.edu
http://www.artcenter.edu
Animation, cinematography and film/
   video production, graphic design,
   illustration.

Azusa Pacific University
901 East Alosta Avenue
Azusa, CA 91702

Phone: (626) 812-3016
Fax: (626) 812-3096
E-mail: admissions@apu.edu
http://www.apu.edu
Computer programming—specific applications, webpage/multimedia design.

Bakersfield College
1801 Panorama Drive
Bakersfield, CA 93305
Phone: (661) 395-4011
Fax: (661) 395-4500
E-mail: bcadmission@bc.cc.ca.us
http://www.http://bc.cc.ca.us
Data processing technology.

Bethesda Christian University
730 North Euclid Street
Anaheim, CA 92801
Phone: (714) 517-1945
Fax: NA
E-mail: NA
http://www.bcu.edu
Design/visual communications, information technology.

Brooks Institute of Photography
801 Alston Road
Santa Barbara, CA 93108
Phone: (805) 966-3888
Fax: (805) 564-1475
E-mail: admissions@brooks.edu
http://www.brooks.edu
Cinematography and film/video production.

Butte College
3536 Butte Campus Drive
Oroville, CA 95965
Phone: (530) 895-2511
Fax: NA
E-mail: At Web site
http://www.butte.edu
Cinematography and film/video production, communications technology, computer programming—specific applications.

California College of the Arts
1111 Eighth Street
San Francisco, CA 94107
Phone: (415) 703-9523
Fax: (415) 703-9539
E-mail: enroll@cca.edu
http://www.cca.edu
Cinematography and film/video production, graphic design, illustration.

California Institute of Technology
Caltech Office of Undergraduate Admissions
Mail Code 1-94
Pasadena, CA 91125
Phone: (626) 395-6341
Fax: (626) 683-3026
E-mail: ugadmissions@caltech.edu.
http://www.caltech.edu
Applied mathematics, computer engineering, electrical and communications engineering.

California Institute of the Arts
24700 McBean Parkway
Valencia, CA 91355
Phone: (661) 255-1050
Fax: (661) 255-7710
E-mail: admiss@calarts.edu
http://www.calarts.edu
Animation, cinematography and film/video production, computer graphics, graphic design.

California Lutheran University
60 West Olsen Road, 1350
Thousand Oaks, CA 91300
Phone: (805) 493-3135
Fax: (805) 493-3114
E-mail: cluadm@clunet.edu
http://www.clunet.edu
Computer graphics, mathematics/computer science.

California Polytechnic State University—San Luis Obispo
Admissions Office
Cal Poly
San Luis Obispo, CA 93407
Phone: (805) 756-2311
Fax: (805) 756-5400
E-mail: admissions@calpoly.edu
http://www.calpoly.edu
Computer engineering, computer graphics, electrical and communications engineering.

California State Polytechnic University—Pomona
3801 West Temple Avenue
Pomona, CA 91768
Phone: (909) 468-5020
Fax: (909) 869-5020
E-mail: cppadmit@csupomona.edu
http://www.csu.pomona.edu
Computer engineering, graphic design, information technology.

California State University—Chico
400 West First Street
Chico, CA 95929

Phone: (530) 898-4428
Fax: (530) 898-6456
E-mail: info@csuchico.edu
http://www.csuchico.edu
Accounting/computer science, applied mathematics, computer engineering, computer graphics, design/visual communications, electrical and communications engineering, graphic design, information technology, organizational communication.

California State University—Fresno
5150 North Maple Avenue M/S JA 57
Fresno, CA 93740
Phone: (559) 278-2261
Fax: (559) 278-4812
E-mail: vivian_franco@csufresno.edu
http://www.csufresno.edu
Applied mathematics, communication, computer engineering, electrical and communications engineering, electrical engineering technology.

California State University—Fullerton
800 North State College Boulevard
Fullerton, CA 92834
Phone: (714) 773-2370
Fax: (714) 278-2356
E-mail: admissions@fullerton.edu
http://www.fullerton.edu
Electrical and communications engineering.

California State University—Hayward
25800 Carlos Bee Boulevard
Hayward, CA 94542
Phone: (510) 885-2624
Fax: (510) 885-4059
E-mail: adminfo@csuhayward.edu
http://www.csuhayward.edu
Applied mathematics, software engineering.

California State University—Long Beach
1250 Bellflower Boulevard
Long Beach, CA 90840
Phone: (562) 985-5471
Fax: (562) 985-4973
E-mail: eslb@csulb.edu
http://www.csulb.edu
Applied mathematics, cinematography and film/video production, computer engineering, design/visual communications, electrical and communications engineering, electrical engineering technology.

**California State University—
Los Angeles**
5151 State University Drive
Los Angeles, CA 90032
Phone: (323) 343-3901
Fax: (323) 343-6306
E-mail: admission@calstatela.edu
http://www.calstatela.edu
Communications technology, electrical
and communications engineering.

**California State University—
Monterey Bay**
100 Campus Center
Seaside, CA 93955
Phone: (831) 582-3000
Fax: NA
E-mail: onestop@csumb.edu
http://www.csumb.edu
Computer graphics.

**California State University—
Northridge**
P.O. Box 1286
Northridge, CA 91328
Phone: (818) 677-3773
Fax: (818) 677-4665
E-mail: lorraine.newlon@csun.edu
http://www.csun.edu
Applied mathematics, communications
technology, computer engineering,
electrical and communications
engineering.

**California State University—
Sacramento**
6000 J Street
Lassen Hall
Sacramento, CA 95819
Phone: (916) 278-3901
Fax: (916) 279-5603
E-mail: admissions@csus.edu
http://www.admissions@csus.edu
Computer engineering, design/visual
communications, electrical and
communications engineering, graphic
design.

Chapman University
One University Drive
Orange, CA 92866
Phone: (714) 997-6711
Fax: (714) 997-6713
E-mail: admit@chapman.edu
http://www.chapman.edu
Cinematography and film/video
production, graphic design,
playwriting/screenwriting.

Claremont McKenna College
890 Columbia Avenue
Claremont, CA 91711
Phone: (909) 621-8088
Fax: (909) 621-8516
E-mail: admissions@claremontmckenna.
edu
http://www.claremontmckenna.edu
Mathematics/computer science.

Columbia College—Hollywood
18618 Oxnard Street
Tarzana, CA 91356
Phone: (818) 345-8414
Fax: (818) 345-9053
E-mail: cchadfin@columbiacollege.edu
http://www.columbiacollege.edu
Cinematography and film/video production,
communications technology.

DeVry University—Long Beach
3880 Kilroy Airport Way
Long Beach, CA 90806
Phone: (562) 427-4162
Fax: (562) 997-5371
E-mail: cblas@socal.devry.edu
http://www.devry.edu
Information technology.

Dominican University of California
Office of Admissions
50 Acacia Avenue
San Rafael, CA 94901
Phone/Fax: (415) 485-3214
E-mail: enroll@dominican.edu
http://www.dominican.edu
Computer graphics, drafting and design
technology.

Fresno Pacific University
1717 South Chestnut Avenue
Fresno, CA 93702
Phone: (559) 453-2039
Fax: (559) 453-2007
E-mail: ugadmis@fresno.edu
http://www.fresno.edu
Applied mathematics.

Harvey Mudd College
301 East Twelfth Street
Claremont, CA 91711
Phone: (909) 621-8011
Fax: (909) 621-8360
E-mail: admission@hmc.edu
http://www.hmc.edu
Applied mathematics.

La Sierra University
4700 Pierce Street
Riverside, CA 92515
Phone: (909) 785-2176
Fax: (909) 785-2447
E-mail: ivy@lasierra.edu
http://www.lasierra.edu
Animation, communications technology,
computer programming—specific
applications, data processing
technology, design/visual
communications, digital media.

Loyola Marymount University
One LMU Drive, Suite 100
Los Angeles, CA 90045
Phone: (310) 338-2750
Fax: (310) 338-2797
E-mail: admissions@lmu.edu
http://www.lmu.edu
Cinematography and film/video
production, communications
technology, electrical and
communications engineering.

Mills College
5000 MacArthur Boulevard
Oakland, CA 94613
Phone: (510) 430-2135
Fax: (510) 430-3314
E-mail: admission@mills.edu
http://www.mills.edu
Mathematics/computer science.

Mount St. Mary's College
12001 Chalon Road
Los Angeles, CA 90049
Phone: (845) 569-3248
Fax: (845) 562-6762
E-mail: mtstmary@msmc.edu
http://www.msmc.edu
Applied mathematics.

National University
11255 North Torrey Pinos Road
La Jolla, CA 92037
Phone: (858) 642-8180
Fax: (858) 642-8710
E-mail: advisor@nu.edu
http://www.nu.edu
Digital media, drafting and design
technology.

Northwestern Polytechnic University
47671 Westinghouse Drive
Fremont, CA 94539
Phone: (510) 657-5913
Fax: (510) 657-8975
E-mail: admission@npu.edu
http://www.npu.edu
Electrical and communications
engineering, software engineering.

Occidental College
Office of Admission
1600 Campus Road
Los Angeles, CA 90041
Phone: (323) 259-2700
Fax: (323) 341-4875
E-mail: admission@oxy.edu
http://www.oxy.edu
Cognitive science.

Otis College of Art & Design
9045 Lincoln Boulevard
Los Angeles, CA 90045
Phone: (310) 665-6820
Fax: (310) 665-6821
E-mail: admissions@otis.edu
http://www.otis.edu
Animation, computer graphics, design/
    visual communications, digital media,
    graphic design, illustration, webpage/
    multimedia design.

Pacific Union College
Enrollment Services
One Angwin Avenue
Angwin, CA 94508
Phone: (800) 862-7080
Fax: (707) 965-6432
E-mail: enroll@puc.edu
http://www.puc.edu
Cinematography and film/video
    production, computer graphics, data
    processing technology.

Pepperdine University
24255 Pacific Coast Highway
Malibu, CA 90263
Phone: (310) 456-4861
Fax: (310) 506-4861
E-mail: admission-seaver@pepperdine.
    edu
http://www.pepperdine.edu
Mathematics/computer science.

Pitzer College
1050 North Mills Avenue
Claremont, CA 91711
Phone: (909) 621-8129
Fax: (909) 621-8770
E-mail: admissions@pitzer.edu
http://www.pitzer.edu
Cinematography and film/video
    production.

Pomona College
333 North College Way
Claremont, CA 91711
Phone: (909) 621-8134
Fax: (909) 621-8952

E-mail: admissions@pomona.edu
http://www.pomona.edu
Cognitive science, mathematics/computer
    science.

Saint Mary's College of California
P.O. Box 4800
Moraga, CA 94575-4800
Phone: (925) 631-4224
Fax: (925) 376-7193
E-mail: smcadmit@stmarys-ca.edu
http://www.stmarys-ca.edu
Computer graphics, mathematics/
    computer science.

San Diego State University
5500 Campanile Drive
San Diego, CA 92182
Phone: (619) 594-7800
Fax: (619) 594-1250
E-mail: At Web site
http://www.sdu.edu
Applied mathematics, computer
    engineering, design/visual
    communications, electrical and
    communications engineering.

San Francisco Art Institute
800 Chestnut Street
San Francisco, CA 94133
Phone: (415) 749-4500
Fax: (415) 749-4592
E-mail: admissions@sfai.edu
http://www.sfai.edu
Multimedia.

San Francisco State University
1600 Holloway Avenue
San Francisco, CA 94132
Phone: (415) 338-6486
Fax: (415) 338-7196
E-mail: ugadmit@sfsu.edu
http://www.sfsu.edu
Applied mathematics, electrical and
    communications engineering,
    technical and business writing.

San Jose State University
1 Washington Square
San Jose, CA 95112
Phone: (408) 283-7500
Fax: (408) 924-2050
E-mail: contact@sjsu.edu
http://www.sjsu.edu
Accounting/computer science,
    computer engineering, electrical and
    communications engineering, graphic
    design, information technology,
    quality control technology.

Santa Clara University
500 El Camino Real
Santa Clara, CA 95053
Phone: (408) 554-4700
Fax: (408) 554-5255
E-mail: none@scu.edu
http://www.scu.edu
Applied mathematics, computer
    engineering, electrical and
    communications engineering,
    electrical engineering technology,
    mathematics/computer science.

Sonoma State University
1801 East Cotati Avenue
Rohnert Park, CA 94928
Phone: (707) 664-2778
Fax: (707) 664-2060
E-mail: admitme@sonoma.edu
http://www.sonoma.edu
Computer engineering.

Stanford University
Undergraduate Admission
Old Union 232
Stanford, CA 94305
Phone: (650) 723-2091
Fax: (650) 723-6050
E-mail: admissions@stanford.edu
http://www.stanford.edu
Electrical and communications
    engineering.

University of California—Berkeley
110 Sproul Hall
Berkeley, CA 94720
Phone: (510) 642-3175
Fax: (510) 642-7333
E-mail: ouars@uclink.berkeley.edu
http://www.berkeley.edu
Applied mathematics, electrical and
    communications engineering.

University of California—Davis
178 Mrak Hall
Shields Avenue
Davis, CA 95616
Phone: (530) 752-2971
Fax: (530) 752-1280
E-mail: freshmanadmissiosn@ucdavis.
    edu
http://www.ucdavis.edu
Computer engineering, design/visual
    communications, electrical and
    communications engineering.

University of California—Irvine
204 Administration Building
Irvine, CA 92697

Phone: (949) 824-6703
Fax: (949) 824-2711
E-mail: admissions@uci.edu
http://www.uci.edu
Computer engineering, electrical and
    communications engineering.

University of California—Los Angeles
405 Hilgard Avenue
P.O. Box 951436
Los Angeles, CA 90095
Phone: (310) 825-3101
Fax: (310) 206-1206
E-mail: ugadm@saonet.ucla.edu
http://www.ucla.edu
Applied mathematics, computer
    engineering, design/visual
    communications, electrical and
    communications engineering.

University of California—Riverside
1138 Hinderaker Hall
Riverside, CA 92521
Phone: (909) 787-3411
Fax: (909) 787-6344
E-mail: ugadmiss@pop.ucr.edu
http://www.ucr.edu
Applied mathematics, computer
    engineering, electrical and
    communications engineering.

University of California—San Diego
9500 Gilman Drive, 0021
La Jolla, CA 92093
Phone: (858) 534-4831
Fax: (858) 534-5723
E-mail: admissionsinfo.ucsd.edu
http://www.ucsd.edu
Applied mathematics, cognitive science,
    computer engineering, digital media,
    electrical and communications
    engineering.

**University of California—Santa
    Barbara**
Office of Admissions
1210 Cheadle Hall
Santa Barbara, CA 93106
Phone: (805) 893-2881
Fax: (805) 893-2676
E-mail: appinfo@sa.ucsb.edu
http://www.ucsb.edu
Applied mathematics, cinematography
    and film/video production,
    computer engineering, electrical and
    communications engineering.

University of California—Santa Cruz
Office of Admissions, Cook House

1156 High Street
Santa Cruz, CA 95064
Phone: (831) 459-4008
Fax: (831) 459-4452
E-mail: admissions@ucsc.edu
http://www.admissions.ucsc.edu
Applied mathematics, computer
    engineering, design/visual
    communications, electrical and
    communications engineering.

University of San Diego
5998 Alcala Park
San Diego, CA 92110
Phone: (619) 260-4506
Fax: (619) 260-6836
E-mail: admissions@sandiego.edu
http://www.sandiego.edu
Electrical and communications
    engineering,

University of San Francisco
2130 Fulton Street
San Francisco, CA 94117
Phone: (415) 422-6563
Fax: (415) 422-2217
E-mail: admission@usfca.edu
http://www.usfca.edu
Drafting and design technology, graphic
    design, illustration.

University of Southern California
700 Childs Way
Los Angeles, CA 90089
Phone: (213) 740-1111
Fax: (213) 740-6364
E-mail: admitusc@usc.edu
http://www.usc.edu
Computer engineering, electrical and
    communications engineering,
    playwriting/screenwriting.

University of the Pacific
3601 Pacific Avenue
Stockton, CA 95211
Phone: (209) 946-2211
Fax: (209) 946-2413
E-mail: admissions@pacific.edu
http://www.pacific.edu
Applied mathematics, computer
    engineering, electrical and
    communications engineering.

**Vanguard University of Southern
    California**
55 Fair Drive
Costa Mesa, CA 92626
Phone: (714) 556-3601
Fax: (714) 966-5471

E-mail: admissions@vanguard.edu
http://www.vanguard.edu
Digital media.

Woodbury University
7500 Glenoaks Boulevard
Burbank, CA 91510
Phone: (818) 767-0888
Fax: (818) 767-7520
E-mail: info@woodbury.edu
http://www.woodbury.edu
Technical and business writing.

COLORADO

Art Institute of Colorado
1200 Lincoln Street
Denver, CO 80203
Phone: (800) 275-2420
Fax: NA
E-mail: aicadm@aii.edu
http://www.aic.artinstitutes.edu
Cinematography and film/video
    production, communications
    technology, computer graphics,
    multimedia.

**Colorado Mountain College—
    Timberline Campus**
Admissions Office
901 South Highway 24
Leadville, CO 80461
Phone: (800) 621-8559
Fax: (719) 947-8324
E-mail: joinus@coloradomtn.edu
http://www.coloradomtn.edu
Data processing technology,
    photographic/film/video technology.

Colorado School of Mines
Weaver Towers, 1811 Elm Street
Golden, CO 80401
Phone: (303) 273-3220
Fax: (303) 273-3509
E-mail: admit@mines.edu
http://www.mines.edu
Applied mathematics.

Colorado State University—Pueblo
Office of Admissions and Records
2200 Bonforte Boulevard
Pueblo, CO 81001
Phone: (719) 549-2461
Fax: (719) 549-2419
E-mail: info@colostate-pueblo.edu
http://www.colostate-pueblo.edu
Electrical and communications
    engineering, electrical engineering
    technology, graphic design.

Colorado Technical University
4435 North Chestnut Street
Colorado Springs, CO 80907
Phone: (719) 598-0200
Fax: (7190) 598-3740
E-mail: cosadmissions@coloradotech.
edu
http://www.coloradotech.edu
Computer engineering, computer
graphics, digital media, e-commerce,
electrical and communications
engineering, information technology.

DeVry University—Colorado Springs
225 South Union Boulevard
Colorado Springs, CO 80910
Phone: (719) 632-3000
Fax: (719) 632-1909
E-mail: admitcs@cs.devry.edu
http://www.devry.edu
Electrical engineering technology.

DeVry University—Denver
1870 West 122nd Avenue
Westminster, CO 90234
Phone: (303) 280-7600
Fax: (3030) 280-7606
E-mail: info@devry.edu
http://www.devry.edu
Computer engineering, electrical
engineering technology.
Fort Lewis College
1000 Rim Drive
Durango, CO 91301
Phone: (970) 247-7184
Fax: (970) 247-7179
E-mail: admission@fortlewis.edu
http://www.fortlewis.edu
Applied mathematics, mathematics/
computer science.

Jones International University
9697 East Mineral Avenue
Englewood, CO 80112
Phone: (800) 811-5663
Fax: (303) 799-0966
E-mail: admissions@international.edu
http://www.jonesinternational.edu
Communications technology, computer
engineering, digital media, e-
commerce, information technology.

National American University—Denver
1325 South Colorado Boulevard
Denver, CO 80222
Phone: (303) 876-7100
Fax: (303) 876-7105
E-mail: At Web site
http://www.national.edu/DenverCampus

Computer programming—specific
applications, data processing
technology.

University of Colorado—Boulder
Campus Box 30
Boulder, Co 90309
Phone: (303) 492-6301
Fax: (303) 492-7115
E-mail: apply@colorado.edu
http://www.colorado.edu
Applied mathematics,
telecommunications technology,
computer engineering, electrical and
communications engineering.

**University of Colorado—Colorado
Springs**
Admissions Office
P.O. Box 7150
Colorado Springs, CO 80933
Phone: (719) 262-3383
Fax: (719) 262-3116
E-mail: admrec@mail.uccs.edu
http://www.uccs.edu
Applied mathematics, computer
engineering, electrical and
communications engineering.

University of Colorado—Denver
P.O. Box 173304
Campus Box 167
Denver, CO 80217
Phone: (303) 556-3287
Fax: (303) 556-4838
E-mail: admissions@carbon.cudenver.
edu
http://www.cudenver.edu
Applied mathematics, electrical and
communications engineering.

University of Denver
University Hall, Room 110
2197 South University Boulevard
Denver, CO 80208
Phone: (303) 871-2036
Fax: (303) 871-3301
E-mail: admission@du.edu
http://www.du.edu
Computer engineering, electrical and
communications engineering.

Westwood College of Technology
7350 North Broadway
Denver, CO 80221
Phone: (303) 426-7000
Fax: (303) 426-1832
E-mail: bsimms@westwood.edu
http://www.westwood.edu

Computer engineering, computer
graphics, computer programming
(specific applications), electrical
engineering technology, web/
multimedia management, webpage/
multimedia design.

CONNECTICUT

Central Connecticut State College
1615 Stanley Street
New Britain, CT 06050
Phone: (860) 832-2278
Fax: (860) 832-2295
E-mail: admissions@ccsu.edu
http://www.ccsu.edu
Design/visual communications, sales/
distribution.

Fairfield University
1073 North Benson Road
Fairfield, CT 06824
Phone: (203) 254-4100
Fax: (203) 254-4199
E-mail: admis@mail.fairfield.edu
http://www.fairfield.edu
Computer engineering, electrical and
communications engineering.

Paier College of Art
20 Gorham Avenue
Hamden, CT 06514
Phone: (203) 287-3031
Fax: NA
E-mail: At Web site
http://www.paiercollegeofart.edu
Design/visual communications, illustration.

Quinnipiac University
275 Mount Carmel Avenue
Hamden, CT 06518
Phone: (203) 582-8600
Fax: (203) 582-8906
E-mail: admissions@quinnipiac.edu
http://www.quinnipiac.edu
Computer graphics, digital media,
mathematics/computer science.

Sacred Heart University
5151 Park Avenue
Fairfield, CT 06432
Phone: (203) 371-7880
Fax: (203) 365-7607
E-mail: enroll@sacredheart.edu
http://www.sacredheart.edu
Design/visual communications.

Trinity College
300 Summit Street
Hartford, CT 06016

Phone: (860) 297-2180
Fax: (860) 297-2287
E-mail: admissions.office@trincoll.edu
http://www.trincoll.edu
Electrical and communications
    engineering.

University of Bridgeport
380 University Avenue
Bridgeport, CT 06601
Phone: (203) 576-4552
Fax: (203) 576-4941
E-mail: admit@bridgeport.edu
http://www.bridgeport.edu
Computer engineering, graphic design,
    illustration.

University of Connecticut
2131 Hillside Road, Unit 3088
Storrs, CT 06286
Phone: (860) 486-3137
Fax: (860) 486-1476
E-mail: beahusky@uconn.edu
http://www.uconn.edu
Applied mathematics, cinematography
    and film/video production,
    computer engineering, electrical and
    communications engineering.

University of Hartford
200 Bloomfield Avenue
West Hartford, CT 06117
Phone: (860) 768-4296
Fax: (860) 768-4961
E-mail: admissions@mail.hartford.edu
http://www.hartford.edu
Computer engineering, design/visual
    communications, electrical and
    communications engineering,
    electrical engineering technology,
    technical and business writing.

University of New Haven
300 Orange Avenue
West Haven, CT 06516
Phone: (203) 932-7319
Fax: (203) 931-6093
E-mail: adminfo@newhaven.edu
http://www.newhaven.edu
Data processing technology, electrical
    and communications engineering,
    sales/distribution.

Western Connecticut State University
Undergraduate Admissions Office
181 White Street
Danbury, CT 06810
Phone: (203) 837-9000
Fax: NA

E-mail: At Web site
http://www.wcsu.edu
Mathematics/computer science.

Yale University
P.O. Box 208234
New Haven, CT 06520
Phone: (203) 432-9316
Fax: (203) 432-9392
E-mail: undergraduate_admissions@
    yale.edu
http://www.yale.edu
Applied mathematics, electrical and
    communications engineering,
    mathematics/computer science.

DELAWARE

Delaware State University
1200 North DuPont Highway
Dover, DE 19901
Phone: (302) 857-6361
Fax: (302) 857-6362
E-mail: admissions@dsu.edu
http://www.dsu/edu
Electrical engineering technology.

University of Delaware
Admissions Office
116 Hullihen Hall
Newark, DE 19716
Phone: (302) 831-8123
Fax: (302) 931-6095
E-mail: admissions@udel.edu
http://www.udel.edu
Computer engineering, electrical and
    communications engineering.

Wilmington College
320 Dupont Highway
New Castle, DE 18720
Phone: (302) 328-9401
Fax: (302) 328-5902
E-mail: mlee@wilmcoll.edu
http://www.wilmcoll.edu
Communications technology.

DISTRICT OF COLUMBIA

American University
4400 Massachusetts Avenue NW
Washington, DC 20016
Phone: (202) 885-6000
Fax: (202) 885-1025
E-mail: afa@american.edu
http://www.american.edu
Animation, applied mathematics,
    cinematography and film/video
    production, computer graphics, data

processing technology, design/visual
    communications, graphic design,
    multimedia, recording arts, web/
    multimedia management.

Catholic University of America
Office Enrollment Services
Washington, DC 20064
Phone: (202) 319-6305
Fax: (202) 319-6533
E-mail: cua-admissions@cua.edu
http://www.cua.edu
Computer engineering, electrical and
    communications engineering.

George Washington University
2121 I Street NW, Suite 201
Washington, DC 20052
Phone: (202) 994-6040
Fax: (202) 994-0325
E-mail: gwadm@gwu.edu
http://www.gwu.edu
Applied mathematics, computer
    engineering, electrical and
    communications engineering.

Howard University
2400 Sixth Street NW
Washington, DC 20059
Phone: (202) 806-2700
Fax: (202) 806-4462
E-mail: admission@howard.edu
Computer engineering, design/visual
    communications, electrical and
    communications engineering.

University of the District of Columbia
4200 Connecticut Avenue NW
Washington, DC 20008
Phone: (202) 274-6110
Fax: (202) 274-5552
E-mail: lflannagna@udc.edu
http://www.udc.edu
Electrical and communications
    engineering, electrical engineering
    technology.

FLORIDA

Bethune-Cookman College
640 Dr. Mary McLeod Bethune
    Boulevard
Daytona Beach, FL 32114
Phone: (386) 481-2600
Fax: (386) 481-2601
E-mail: admissions@cookman.edu
http://www.bethune.cookman.edu
Computer engineering.

DeVry University—Miramar
2300 SW 145th Avenue
Miramar, FL 33027
Phone: (954) 499-9700
Fax: (954) 499-9723
E-mail: openhouse@mir.devry.edu
http://www.devry.edu
Electrical engineering technology.

DeVry University—Orlando
4000 Millenia Boulevard
Orlando, FL 32839
Phone: (407) 370-3131
Fax: (407) 370-3198
E-mail: krochford@orl.devry.edu
http://www.devry.edu
Electrical engineering technology.

Embry Riddle Aeronautical University
600 South Clyde Morris Boulevard
Daytona Beach, FL 32114
Phone: (386) 226-6100
Fax: (386) 226-7070
E-mail: dbadmit@erau.edu
http://www.embryriddle.edu
Computer engineering, software
    engineering.

Everglades University
5002 T-REX Avenue, #100
Boca Raton, FL 33431
Phone: (888) 772-6077
Fax: (561) 912-1191
E-mail: admissions-boca@
    evergladesuniversity.edu
http://www.evergladesuniversity.edu
Information technology.

Florida A&M University
Suite G-9, Foote-Hilyer Administration
    Center
Tallahassee, FL 32307
Phone: (850) 599-3796
Fax: (950) 599-3069
E-mail: adm@famu.edu
http://www.famu.edu
Electrical engineering technology.

Florida Atlantic University
777 Glades Road
P.O. Box 3091
Boca Raton, FL 33431
Phone: (561) 297-3040
Fax: (561) 297-3758
E-mail: admisweb@fau.edu
http://www.fau.edu
Computer engineering, digital media,
    electrical and communications
    engineering.

Florida Institute of Technology
150 West University Boulevard
Melbourne, FL 32901-6975
Phone: (321) 674-8030
Fax: (321) 723-9468
E-mail: admissions@fit.edu
http://www.fit.edu
Applied mathematics, computer
    engineering, electrical and
    communications engineering,
    software engineering.

Florida International University
University Park, PC 140
Miami, FL 33119
Phone: (305) 348-2363
Fax: (305) 348-3648
E-mail: admiss@flu.edu
http://www.flu.edu
Applied mathematics, electrical and
    communications engineering,
    information technology.

Florida State University
2500 University Center
Tallahassee, FL 32306
Phone: (850) 644-6200
Fax: (850) 644-0197
E-mail: admissions@admin.fsu.edu
http://www.fsu.edu
Cinematography and film/video
    production, computer engineering,
    electrical and communications
    engineering, information technology,
    software engineering.

Jacksonville University
700 Pelham Road North
Jacksonville, AL 36252
Phone: (904) 256-7000
Fax: (904) 256-7012
E-mail: admissions@ju.edu
http://www.jacksonville.edu
Design/visual communications, electrical
    and communications engineering.

Jones College
11430 North Kendall Drive
Suite 200, Kendall Summit
Miami, FL 33176
Phone: (904) 743-1122
Fax: NA
E-mail: admissions@jones.edu
http://adm.jones.edu
Accounting/computer science.

Palm Beach Atlantic University
P.O. Box 24708
901 South Flagler Drive

West Palm Beach, FL 33416
Phone: (561) 803-2100
Fax: (561) 803-2115
E-mail: admit@pba.edu
http://www.pba.edu
Graphic design, organizational
    communication, playwriting/
    screenwriting.

Stetson University
421 North Woodland Boulevard, Unit
    8378
DeLand, FL 32723
Phone: (386) 822-7100
Fax: (386) 822-7112
E-mail: admissions@stetson.edu
http://www.stetson.edu
E-commerce, webpage/multimedia design.

University of Central Florida
P.O. Box 160111
Orlando, FL 32816
Phone: (407) 823-3000
Fax: (407) 823-5625
E-mail: admission@mail.ucf.edu
http://www.ucf.edu
Cinematography and film/video
    production, computer engineering,
    electrical and communications
    engineering, electrical engineering
    technology, information technology,
    multimedia.

University of Florida
201 Criser Hall, P.O. Box 11400
Gainesville, FL 32611-4000
Phone: (352) 392-1365
Fax: (352) 392-3987
E-mail: At Web site
http://www.ufl.edu
Computer engineering, electrical and
    communications engineering.

University of Miami
P.O. Box 248025
Coral Gables, FL 33124
Phone: (305) 284-4323
Fax: (305) 284-2507
E-mail: admission@miami.edu
http://www.miami.edu/admissions
Cinematography and film/video
    production, computer engineering,
    electrical and communications
    engineering, organizational
    communication.

University of North Florida
4567 St. Johns Bluff Road, South
Jacksonville, FL 32224

Phone: (904) 620-2624
Fax: (904) 620-2414
E-mail: osprey@unf.edu
http://www.unf.edu
Electrical and communications
    engineering.

**University of South Florida—
    St. Petersburg**
140 Seventh Avenue South
St. Petersburg, FL 33701
Phone: (813) 974-3352
Fax: (813) 974-9689
E-mail: admissions@stpt.usf.edu
http://www.usf.edu
Computer engineering, information
    technology.

University of South Florida—Tampa
4202 East Fowler Avenue SVC-1036
Tampa, FL 33620-9951
Phone: (813) 874-3350
Fax: (813) 974-9689
E-mail: jglassma@admin.usf.edu
http://www.usf.edu
Computer engineering, electrical and
    communications engineering,
    information technology.

University of Tampa
401 West Kennedy Boulevard
Tampa, FL 33606
Phone: (813) 253-6211
Fax: (813) 258-7398
E-mail: admissions@ut.edu
http://www.ut.edu
Computer graphics, graphic design,,
    mathematics/computer science.

University of West Florida
11000 University Parkway
Pensacola, FL 32514
Phone: (850) 474-2230
Fax: (850) 474-3360
E-mail: admissions@uwf.edu
http://uwf.edu
Applied mathematics, computer
    engineering, electrical and
    communications engineering,
    electrical engineering technology,
    organizational communication,
    technical and business writing.

GEORGIA

Armstrong Atlantic State University
11935 Abercorn Street
Savannah, GA 31419
Phone: (912) 927-5277

Fax: (912) 927-5462
E-mail: adm-info@mail.armstrong.edu
http://www.armstrong.edu
Applied mathematics, information
    technology.

Atlanta College of Art
1280 Peachtree Street Northeast
Atlanta, GA 30309
Phone: (404) 733-5100
Fax: (404) 733-5107
E-mail: acinfo@woodruffcenter.org
http://www.aca.edu
Cinematography and film/video
    production, computer graphics, design/
    visual communications, multimedia,
    webpage/multimedia design.

Augusta State University
2500 Walton Way
Augusta, GA 30904?
Phone: (706) 737-1632
Fax: (706) 667-4355
E-mail: admission@aug.edu
http://www.aug.edu
Multimedia.

Brenau University Women's College
1 Centennial Circle
Gainesville, GA 30501
Phone: (770) 534-6100
Fax: (770) 538-4306
E-mail: wcadmissions@lib.brenau.edu
http://www.brenau.edu
Applied mathematics, e-commerce,
    graphic design.

Clark Atlanta University
223 James P. Brawley Drive
Atlanta, GA 30314
Phone: (404) 880-8000
Fax: (404) 880-6174
E-mail: admissions@panthernet.cau.edu
http://www.cau.edu
Communications technology,
    mathematics/computer science.

Clayton College and State University
5900 North Lee Street
Morrow, GA 30206
Phone: (770) 961-3500
Fax: (770) 961-3752
E-mail: ccsu-info@mail.clayton.edu
http://www.clayton.edu
Data processing technology.

Columbia State University
4225 University Avenue
Columbus, GA 31907

Phone: (866) 264-2035
Fax: NA
E-mail: At Web site
http://www. colstate.edu
Applied mathematics, technical and
    business writing.

DeVry University—Alpharetta
2555 Northwinds Parkway
Alpharetta, GA 30005
Phone: (770) 664-9520
Fax: (770) 664-8824
E-mail: info@devry.edu
http://www.devry.edu
Electrical engineering technology.

DeVry University—Atlanta
3575 Piedmont Road NE, # P100
Atlanta, GA 30305
Phone: (770) 671-1744
Fax: NA
E-mail: admissions@devry.com
http://www.devry.edu
Electrical engineering technology.

Emory University
Boisfeuillet Jones Center
201 Dowman Drive NE
Atlanta, GA 30322
Phone: (404) 727-6036
Fax: (404) 727-4303
E-mail: admiss@emory.edu
http://www.emory.edu
Mathematics/computer science.

Fort Valley State University
1005 State University Drive
Fort Valley, GA 31030
Phone: (912) 825-6307
Fax: (912) 875-6394
E-mail: fordd@fvsu.edu
http://www. fvsu.edu
Electrical engineering technology.

Georgia Institute of Technology
219 Uncle Heine Way
Atlanta, GA 30332
Phone: (404) 894-4154
Fax: (404) 894-9511
E-mail: admissions@gatech.edu
http://www.gatech.edu
Computer engineering, electrical and
    communications engineering.

Georgia Southern University
P.O. Box 8024
Statesboro, GA 30460
Phone: (912) 681-5391
Fax: (912) 486-7240

E-mail: admissions@georgiasouthern.edu
http://www.georgiasouthern.edu
Electrical and communications
    engineering.

Georgia Southwestern State University
800 Wheatley Street
Americus, GA 31709
Phone: (912) 928-1273
Fax: (912) 931-2983
E-mail: gswapps@canes.gsw.edu
http://www.gsw.edu
Computer programming—specific
    applications.

Georgia State University
P.O. Box 4009
Atlanta, GA 30302
Phone: (404) 651-2365
Fax: (404) 651-4811
E-mail: admissions@gsu.edu
http://www.gsu.edu
Applied mathematics.

Macon State College
100 College Station Drive
Macon, GA 31206
Phone: (800) 272-7619
Fax: NA
E-mail: mscinfo@mail.maconstate.edu
http://www.maconstate.edu
Computer programming—specific
    applications.

Mercer University—Macon
Admissions Office
1400 Coleman Avenue
Macon, GA 31207
Phone: (478) 301-2650
Fax: (478) 301-2828
E-mail: admissions@mercer.edu
http://www.mercer.edu
Computer engineering, electrical and
    communications engineering.

Piedmont College
P.O. Box 10
Demorest, GA 30535
Phone: (706) 776-0103
Fax: (706) 776-6635
E-mail: ugrad@piedmont.edu
http://www.piedmont.edu
Mathematics/computer science.

Savannah College of Art and Design
P.O. Box 3146
Savannah, GA 31402
Phone: (912) 525-5100
Fax: (912) 525-5986

E-mail: admission@scad.edu
http://www.scad.edu
Animation, cinematography and film/
    video production, computer graphics.

Savannah State University
College Station, P.O. Box 20209
Savannah, GA 31404
Phone: (912) 356-2181
Fax: (912) 356-2256
E-mail: SSUAdmission@savstate.edu
http://www.savstate.edu
Electrical engineering technology.

Southern Polytechnic State University
1100 South Marietta Parkway
Marietta, GA 30060
Phone: (678) 915-4188
Fax: (678) 915-7292
E-mail: admissions@spsu.edu
http://www.spsu.edu
Electrical engineering technology,
    quality control technology, software
    engineering, technical and business
    writing, telecommunications
    technology.

South University
709 Mall Boulevard
Savannah, GA 31406
Phone: (888) 444-3404
Fax: NA
E-mail: At Web site
http://online.southuniversity.edu.
Information technology.

University of Georgia
Terrell Hall
Athens, GA 30602
Phone: (706) 542-8776
Fax: (706) 542-1466
E-mail: undergrad@admissions.uga.edu
http://www.uga.edu
Communications technology, multimedia.

Valdosta State University
1500 North Patterson Street
Valdosta, GA 31698
Phone: (229) 333-5791
Fax: (229) 333-5482
E-mail: admissions@valdosta.edu
http://www.valdosta.edu
Applied mathematics.

HAWAII

Hawaii Pacific University
1164 Bishop Street
Honolulu, HI 96813

Phone: (808) 544-0238
Fax: (808) 544-1136
E-mail:admissions@hpu.edu
http://www.hpu.edu
Applied mathematics, data processing
    technology.

University of Hawaii—Manoa
2600 Campus Road, QLCSS Room 001
Honolulu, HI 96822
Phone: (808) 956-8975
Fax: (808) 956-4148
E-mail: ar-info@hawaii.edu
http://www.uhm.hawaii.edu
Electrical and communications engineering.

IDAHO

Boise State University
1910 University Drive
Boise, ID 83725
Phone: (208) 426-1156
Fax: (208) 426-3765
E-mail: bsuinfo@boisestate.edu
http://www.boisestate.edu
Electrical and communications
    engineering.

Brigham Young University
Admissions Office
KIM 120
Rexburg, ID 83460
Phone: (208) 496-1020
Fax: (208) 496-1220
E-mail: admissions@byui.edu
http://www.byui.edu
Computer engineering, electrical and
    communications engineering,
    electrical engineering technology.

Idaho State University
Admissions Office
Campus P.O. Box 8270
Pocatello, ID 93208
Phone: (208) 282-2475
Fax: (208) 282-4231
E-mail: info@isu.edu
http://www.isu.edu
Computer programming—specific
    applications, drafting and design
    technology, electrical and
    communications engineering,
    electrical engineering technology.

Lewis-Clark State College
500 Eighth Avenue
Lewiston, ID 83501
Phone: (208) 792-2210
Fax: (208) 792-2876

E-mail: admissions@lcsc.edu
http://www.lcsc.edu
Drafting and design technology, web/
multimedia management.

North Idaho College
1000 West Garden Avenue
Coeur d'Alene, ID 83814
Phone: (877) 404-4536
Fax: NA
E-mail: At Web site
http://www.nidc.edu
Computer programming—specific
applications, electrical and
communications engineering.

University of Idaho
UI Admissions Office
P.O. Box 44264
Moscow, ID 83844
Phone: (308) 885-6326
Fax: (308) 885-9119
E-mail: admappl@uidaho.edu
http://www.uidaho.edu
Applied mathematics, design/visual
communications, electrical and
communications engineering.

ILLINOIS

Augustana College
639 38th Street
Rock Island, IL 61201
Phone: (309) 794-7341
Fax: (309) 794-7422
E-mail: admissions@augustina.edu
http://www.augustina.edu
Mathematics/computer science.

Bradley University
1501 West Bradley Avenue
Peoria, IL 61625
Phone: (309) 677-1000
Fax: (309) 677-2797
E-mail: admissions@bradley.edu
http://www.bradley.edu
Computer engineering, digital media,
electrical and communications
engineering.

Chicago State University
9501 South Street King Drive, ADM-200
Chicago, IL 60628
Phone: (773) 995-2513
Fax: (773) 995-3820
E-mail: ug-Admissions@csu.edu
http://www.csu.edu
Data processing technology, technical and
business writing.

Columbia College—Chicago
600 South Michigan Avenue
Chicago, Il 60605
Phone: (312) 344-7130
Fax: (312) 344-8024
E-mail: admissions@colum.edu
http://www.colum.edu
Cinematography and film/video
production, communications
technology, design/visual
communications, multimedia,
playwriting/screenwriting, recording
arts, webpage/multimedia design.

DePaul University
1 East Jackson Boulevard
Chicago, IL 60604
Phone: (312) 362-8300
Fax: (312) 362-5749
E-mail: admitdpu@depaul.edu
http://www.depaul.edu
Computer graphics, playwriting/
screenwriting.

DeVry University—Addison
1221 North Swift Road
Addison, IL 60101
Phone: (630) 953-2000
Fax: (630) 953-1236
E-mail: info@devry.edu
http://www.devry.edu
Electrical engineering technology,
information technology,

DeVry University—Chicago
3300 North Campbell Avenue
Chicago, IL 60618
Phone: (773) 697-2155
Fax: (773) 697-2710
E-mail: keaster@chi.devry.edu
http://www.devry.edu
Electrical engineering technology,
information technology.

DeVry University—Tinley Park
18624 West Creek Drive
Tinley Park, IL 60477
Phone: (708) 342-3100
Fax: (708) 342-3505
E-mail: imccauley@tp.devry.edu
http://www.tp.devry.edu
Electrical engineering technology.

Dominican University
7900 West Division
River Forest, IL 60305
Phone: (708) 524-6800
Fax: (708) 524-5990
E-mail: domadmis@dom.edu

http://www.dom.edu
Computer engineering, computer
graphics, electrical and
communications engineering,
mathematics/computer science,
technical and business writing.

Eastern Illinois University
600 Lincoln Avenue
Charleston, IL 61920
Phone: (217) 581-2223
Fax: (217) 581-7060
E-mail: cdadmit@www.eiu.edu
http://www.eiu.edu
Mathematics/computer science.

East-West University
816 South Michigan Avenue
Chicago, IL 60605
Phone: (312) 939-0111
Fax: (312) 939-0083
E-mail: admissions@eastwest.edu
http://www.eastwest.edu
Electrical engineering technology.

Greenville College
315 East College Avenue
Greenville, IL 62246
Phone: (618) 664-7100
Fax: (618) 664-9841
E-mail: admissions@greenville.edu
http://www.greenville.edu
Web/multimedia management.

Illinois Institute of Technology
10 West Thirty-third Street
Chicago, IL 60616
Phone: (312) 567-3025
Fax: (312) 567-6939
E-mail: admission@iit.edu
http://www.iit.edu
Information technology.

Illinois State University
Admissions Office
Campus P.O. Box 2200
Normal, IL 61790
Phone: (309) 438-2181
Fax: (309) 438-3932
E-mail: ugradadm@ilstu.edu
http://www.ilstu.edu
Electrical and communications
engineering, information technology.

Lewis University
One University Parkway
P.O. Box 297
Romeoville, IL 60446
Phone: (815) 836-5250

Fax: (815) 836-5002
E-mail: admissions@lewisu.edu
http://www.lewisu.edu
Communications technology, computer
graphics, e-commerce.

Loyola University of Chicago
Admissions Office
820 North Michigan Avenue
Chicago, IL 60611
Phone: (312) 915-6500
Fax: (312) 915-7216
E-mail: admission@luc.edu
http://www.luc.edu
E-commerce, mathematics/computer
science.

Millikin University
1184 West Main Street
Decatur, IL 62522
Phone: (217) 424-6210
Fax: (217) 425-4669
E-mail: admis@mail.millikin.edu
http://www.millikin.edu
Applied mathematics.

National-Louis University
2840 Sheridan Road
Evanston, IL 60201
Phone: (847) 465-0575
Fax: NA
E-mail: ninuinfo@wheeling1.nl.edu
http://www.nl.edu
Applied mathematics, computer
programming—specific applications.

North Central College
30 North Brainard Street
P.O. Box 3063
Naperville, IL 60506
Phone: (630) 637-5800
Fax: (630) 637-5819
E-mail: ncadm@noctrl.edu
http://www.northcentralcollege.edu
Applied mathematics.

Northern Illinois University
Office of Admissions
Williston Hall 101, NIU
DeKalb, IL 60115
Phone: (815) 753-0446
Fax: (815) 753-1783
E-mail: admissions-info@niu.edu
http://www.reg.niu.edu
Applied mathematics, electrical and
communications engineering.

North Park University
3225 West Foster Avenue
Chicago, IL 60625

Phone: (773) 244-5500
Fax: (773) 244-4953
E-mail: admission@northpark.edu
http://www.northpark.edu
Applied mathematics.

Northwestern University
P.O. Box 3060
1801 Hinman Avenue
Evanston, IL 60208
Phone: (847) 491-7271
Fax: (847) 491-5565
E-mail: ug-admission@northwestern.edu
http://www.nrthwestern.edu
Applied mathematics, communications
technology, computer engineering,
e-commerce, electrical and
communications engineering.

Quincy University
1800 College Avenue
Quincy, IL 62301
Phone: (217) 228-5215
Fax: (217) 228-5479
E-mail: admissions@quincy.edu
http://www.quincy.edu
Graphic design.

Rockford College
Office of Undergraduate Admission
5050 East State Street
Rockford, IL 61108
Phone: (815) 226-4050
Fax: (815) 226-2822
E-mail: admission@rockford.edu
http://www.rockford.edu
Mathematics/computer science.

Roosevelt University
430 South Michigan Avenue
Chicago, IL 60605
Phone: (312) 341-3515
Fax: (312) 341-3523
E-mail: applyRU@roosevelt.edu
http://www.roosevelt.edu
Electrical engineering technology.

School of the Art Institute of Chicago
37 South Wabash Avenue
Chicago, IL 60603
Phone: (312) 899-5219
Fax: (312) 899-1840
E-mail: admiss@artic.edu
http://www.artic.edu
Cinematography and film/video
production, design/visual
communications, digital media,
graphic design, recording arts.

**Southern Illinois University—
Carbondale**
Admissions & Records, MC 4710
Carbondale, IL 62901
Phone: (618) 453-4405
Fax: (618) 453-3250
E-mail: joinsiuc@siuc.edu
http://www.siuc.edu
Cinematography and film/video production,
computer engineering, design/visual
communications, electrical and
communications engineering.

**Southern Illinois University—
Edwardsville**
P.O. Box 1600
Edwardsville, IL 62026
Phone: (618) 650-3705
Fax: (618) 650-5013
E-mail: admis@siue.edu
http://www.siue.edu
Computer engineering, electrical and
communications engineering.

University of Chicago
1116 East 59th Street
Chicago, IL 60637
Phone: (773) 702-8650
Fax: (773) 702-4199
E-mail: toneill@uchicago.edu
http://www.uchicago.edu
Applied mathematics.

University of Illinois—Chicago
P.O. Box 5220
Chicago, IL 60680
Phone: (312) 996-4350
Fax: (312) 413-7628
E-mail: uicadmit@uic.edu
http://www.uic.edu
Computer engineering, electrical and
communications engineering,
mathematics/computer science.

**University of Illinois—
Urbana-Champaign**
901 West Illinois Street
Urbana, IL 61801
Phone: (217) 333-0302
Fax: (217) 333-9758
E-mail: admissions@oar.uiuc.edu
http://www.uiuc.edu
Computer engineering, electrical and
communications engineering, graphic
design, mathematics/computer
science, sales/distribution.

University of Saint Francis
500 Wilcox Street
Joliet, IL 60435

Phone: (815) 740-5037
Fax: (815) 740-5032
E-mail: admissions@stfrancis.edu
http://www.stfrancis.edu
Information technology, web/multimedia
management.

Wheaton College
501 College Avenue
Wheaton, IL 60187
Phone: (630) 752-5005
Fax: (630) 752-5285
E-mail: admissions@wheaton.edu
http://www.wheaton.edu
Mathematics/computer science.

INDIANA

Anderson University
1100 East Fifth Street
Anderson, IN 46012
Phone: (765) 641-4080
Fax: (765) 641-4091
E-mail: info@anderson.edu
http://www.anderson.edu
Mathematics/computer science.

Ball State University
Office of Admissions
2000 West University Avenue
Muncie, IN 47306
Phone: (765) 285-8300
Fax: (765) 285-1632
E-mail: askus@bsu.edu
http://www.bsu.edu
Communications technology, design/
visual communications.

Bethel College
1001 West McKinley Avenue
Mishawaka, IN 46545
Phone: (574) 257-3339
Fax: (574) 257-3335
E-mail: admissions@bethelcollege.edu
http://www.bethel.college.edu
Design/visual communications.

Goshen College
1700 South Main Street
Goshen, IN 46526
Phone: (574) 535-7535
Fax: (574) 535-7609
E-mail: admissions@goshen.edu
http://www.goshen.edu
Applied mathematics.

Huntington College
2303 College Avenue
Huntington, IN 46750

Phone: (260) 359-4000
Fax: (260) 358-3699
E-mail: admissions@huntington.edu
http://www.huntington.edu
Digital media, e-commerce.

Indiana Institute of Technology
1600 East Washington Boulevard
Fort Wayne, IN 46803
Phone: (260) 422-5561
Fax: (260) 422-7696
E-mail: admissions@indtech.edu
http://www.indtech.edu
Computer engineering, electrical and
communications engineering.

Indiana State University
Office of Admissions
Trey Hall 134
Terra Haute, IN 47809
Phone: (812) 237-2121
Fax: (812) 237-8023
E-mail: admissions@indstate.edu
http://www.indstate.edu
Electrical engineering technology.

Indiana University—Bloomington
300 North Jordan Avenue
Bloomington, IN 47405
Phone: (812) 855-0661
Fax: (812) 855-5102
E-mail: iuadmit@indiana.edu
http://www.indiana.edu
Digital media.

Indiana University—Kokomo
Office of Admissions
P.O. Box 9003, KC 230A
Kokomo, IN 46904
Phone: (765) 455-9217
Fax: (765) 455-9537
E-mail: iuadmis@iuk.edu
http://www.iuk.edu
Data processing technology.

Indiana University—Northwest
3400 Broadway
Hawthorn 100
Gary, IN 46408
Phone: (219) 980-6991
Fax: (219) 981-4219
E-mail: admit@iun-edu
http://www.iu.edu
Data processing technology.

**Indiana University—Purdue University
Fort Wayne**
2101 East Coliseum Boulevard
Fort Wayne, IN 46805

Phone: (260) 481-6812
Fax: (260) 481-6880
E-mail: ipfwadms@ipfw.edu
http://www.ipfw.edu
Computer engineering, computer
graphics, electrical and
communications engineering,
electrical engineering technology,
graphic design, LAN/WAN
management, mathematics/
computer science, organizational
communication, quality control
technology, technical and business
writing, webpage/multimedia design.

**Indiana University—Purdue University
Indianapolis**
425 North University Boulevard
Cavanaugh Hall, Room 129
Indianapolis, IN 46202
Phone: (317) 274-4591
Fax: (317) 278-1862
E-mail: apply@iupui.edu
http://www.iu.edu
Communications technology,
computer engineering, computer
software technology, drafting and
design technology, electrical and
communications engineering,
electrical engineering technology.

Indiana University South Bend
1700 Mishawaka Avenue
P.O. Box 7111, A169
South Bend, IN 46634
Phone: (574) 237-4840
Fax: (219) 237-4834
E-mail: admission@iusb.edu
http://www.iusb.edu
Applied mathematics.

Indiana Wesleyan University
4201 South Washington Street
Marion, IN 46953
Phone: (800) 332-6901
Fax: (317) 677-2333
E-mail: admissions@indwes.edu
http://www.indwest.edu
Computer programming—specific
applications.

Manchester College
604 College Avenue, North
Manchester, IN 46962
Phone: (260) 982-5055
Fax: (260) 982-5239
E-mail: admitinfo@manchester.edu
http://www.manchester.edu
Mathematics/computer science.

Marian College
3200 Cold Spring Road
Indianapolis, IN 46222
Phone: (317) 955-6300
Fax: (317) 955-6401
E-mail: admit@marian.edu
http://www.marian.edu
Mathematics/computer science.

Oakland City University
143 North Lucretia Street
Oakland City, IN 47660
Phone: (812) 749-4781
Fax: (812) 749-1233
E-mail: ocuadmit@oak.edu
http://www.oak.edu
Applied mathematics, drafting and design
technology.

Purdue University—Calumet
Office of Admissions
2200 169th Street
Hammond, IN 46323
Phone: (219) 989-2213
Fax: (219) 989-2775
E-mail: adms@calumet.purdue.edu
http://www.calumet.purdue.edu
Applied mathematics, computer
engineering, computer graphics,
design/visual communications,
drafting and design technology,
electrical and communications
engineering, electrical engineering
technology.

**Purdue University—North Central
Campus**
1401 South U.S. Highway 421
Westville, IN 46391
Phone: (219) 785-5458
Fax: (219) 785-5538
E-mail: admissions@purduenc.edu
http://www.pnc.edu
Computer graphics, computer
programming—specific applications,
data processing technology, design/
visual communications, drafting
and design technology, electrical
and communications engineering,
electrical engineering technology,
mathematics/computer science.

Purdue University—West Lafayette
1080 Schleman Hall
West Lafayette, IN 47907
Phone: (765) 494-1776
Fax: (765) 494-0544
E-mail: admissions@purdue.edu
http://www.purdue.edu

Computer graphics, design/visual
communications, drafting and
design technology, electrical and
communications engineering,
electrical engineering technology.

Saint Joseph's College
P.O. Box 890
Rensselaer, IN 47978
Phone: (219) 866-6170
Fax: (219) 866-6122
E-mail: admissions@saintjoe.edu
http://www.saintjoe.edu
Mathematics/computer science.

Saint Mary-of-the-Woods College
Office of Admissions
Guerin Hall
Saint Mary-of-the-Woods, IN 47876
Phone: (812) 535-5106
Fax: (812) 535-4900
E-mail: smwcadms@smwc.edu
http://www.smwc.edu
Communications technology, design/
visual communications, graphic
design, information technology.

Saint Mary's College
Admission Office
Notre Dame, IN 46556
Phone: (219) 284-4587
Fax: (219) 284-4841
E-mail: admission@saintmarys.edu
http://www.saintmarys.edu
Applied mathematics, mathematics/
computer science.

Taylor University—Fort Wayne Campus
1025 West Rudisill Boulevard
Fort Wayne, IN 46807
Phone: (800) 233-3922
Fax: (260) 744-8660
E-mail: admissions_f@tayloru.edu
http://www.tayloru.edu/fw
Computer engineering, mathematics/
computer science.

Taylor University—Upland
236 West Reade Avenue
Upland, IN 46989
Phone: (765) 998-5134
Fax: (765) 998-4925
E-mail: admissions_U@tayloru.edu
http://www.tayloru.edu
Computer engineering, mathematics/
computer science.

Tri-State University
1 University Avenue
Angola, IN 46703

Phone: (260) 665-4132
Fax: (260) 665-4578
E-mail: admit@tristate.edu
http://www.tristate.edu
Data processing technology, drafting
and design technology, electrical and
communications engineering.

University of Evansville
1800 Lincoln Avenue
Evansville, IN 47722
Phone: (812) 479-2468
Fax: (812) 474-4076
E-mail: admission@evansville.edu
http://www.evansville.edu
Applied mathematics, computer
engineering, design/visual
communications, electrical and
communications engineering.

University of Indianapolis
1400 East Hanna Avenue
Indianapolis, IN 46227
Phone: (317) 788-3216
Fax: (317) 788-3300
E-mail: admissions@uindy.edu
http://www.indy.edu
Design/visual communications.

University of Notre Dame
230 Main Building
Notre Dame, IN 46556
Phone: (574) 631-7505
Fax: (574) 631-8865
E-mail: admissio.1@nd.edu
http://www.nd.edu
Design/visual communications, electrical
and communications engineering.

University of Saint Francis
2701 Spring Street
Fort Wayne, IN 46808
Phone: (260) 434-3279
Fax: (260) 434-7590
E-mail: admis@sf.edu
http://www.sf.edu
Animation, graphic design.

University of Southern Indiana
8600 University Boulevard
Evansville, IN 47712
Phone: (812) 464-1765
Fax: (812) 465-7154
E-mail: enroll@usi.edu
http://www.usi.edu
Communications technology.

Valparaiso University
Office of Admissions, Kretzman Hall

1700 Chapel Drive
Valparaiso, IN 46383-4520
Phone: (219) 464-5011
Fax: (219) 464-6898
E-mail: undergrad.admissions@valpo.edu
http://www.valpo.edu
Computer engineering, digital media, electrical and communications engineering, organizational communication.

IOWA

Briar Cliff University
Admissions Office
P.O. Box 100
Sioux City, IA 51104
Phone: (712) 279-5200
Fax: (712) 279-1632
E-mail: admissions@briarcliff.edu
http://www.briarcliff.edu
Graphic design.

Buena Vista University
610 West Fourth Street
Storm Lake, IA 50588
Phone: (712) 749-2235
Fax: (712) 749-1459
E-mail: admissions@bvu.edu
http://www.buv.edu
Organizational communication.

Central College
812 University Street
Pella, IA 50219
Phone: (877) 462-3687
Fax: (641) 628-5316
E-mail: admission@central.edu
http://www.central.edu
Mathematics/computer science.

Coe College
1220 First Avenue NE
Cedar Rapids, IA 52402
Phone: (319) 399-8500
Fax: (319) 399-8816
E-mail: admissioin@coe.edu
http://coe.edu
Mathematics/computer science.

Dordt College
498 Fourth Avenue Northeast
Sioux Center, IA 51250
Phone: (712) 722-6080
Fax: (712) 722-1987
E-mail: admissions@dordt.edu
http://www.dordt.edu
Computer engineering, data processing technology, design/visual

communications, electrical and communications engineering, LAN/WAN management.

Drake University
2507 University Avenue
Des Moines, IA 50311
Phone: (515) 271-3181
Fax: (515) 271-2831
E-mail: admission@drake.edu
http://www.choose.drake.edu
Information technology.

The Franciscan University
400 North Bluff Boulevard
P.O. Box 2967
Clinton, IA 52793
Phone: (563) 242-4153
Fax: (563) 243-6102
E-mail: admissns@tfu.edu
http://www.ffu.edu
Mathematics/computer science.

Graceland University
1 University Place
Lamoni, IA 50140
Phone: (641) 784-5196
Fax: (641) 784-5480
E-mail: admissions@graceland.edu
http://www.graceland.edu
Computer engineering.

Grand View College
1200 Grandview Avenue
Des Moines, IA 50316
Phone: (515) 263-2810
Fax: (515) 263-2974
E-mail: admiss@gvc.edu
http://www.gvc.edu
Applied mathematics.

Iowa State University
100 Alumni Hall
Ames, IA 50011
Phone: (515) 294-5836
Fax: (515) 294-2592
E-mail: admissions@iastate.edu
http://www.iastate.edu
Computer engineering, design/visual communications, electrical and communications engineering, graphic design, technical and business writing.

Maharishi University of Management
1000 North Fourth Street
Fairfield, IA 52557
Phone: (641) 472-7000

Fax: (641) 472-1179
E-mail: admissions@mum.edu
http://www.mum.edu
Electrical and communications engineering, webpage/multimedia design.

Saint Ambrose University
518 West Locust Street
Davenport, IA 52803
Phone: (563) 444-6300
Fax: (563) 333-6297
E-mail: admit@sau.edu
http://www.sau.edu
Graphic design, LAN/WAN management, multimedia.

University of Dubuque
2000 University Avenue
Dubuque, IA 52001
Phone: (319) 589-3200
Fax: (319) 589-3690
E-mail: admssns@dbq.edu
http://www.dbq.edu
Computer graphics.

University of Iowa
107 Calvin Hall
Iowa City, IA 52242
Phone: (319) 335-3847
Fax: (319) 335-1535
E-mail: admissions@uiowa.edu
http://www.uiowa.edu
Applied mathematics, cinematography and film/video production, electrical and communications engineering, graphic design, LAN/WAN management, multimedia, organizational communication.

University of Northern Iowa
1227 West 27th Street
Cedar Falls, IA 50614
Phone: (319) 273-2281
Fax: (319) 273-2885
E-mail: admissions@uni.edu
http://www.uni.edu
Digital media, organizational communication.

Waldorf College
106 South Sixth Street
Forest City, IA 50436
Phone: (641) 585-8112
Fax: (641) 585-8125
E-mail: admissions@waldorf.edu
http://www.waldorf.edu
Communications technology.

KANSAS

Central Christian College of Kansas
1200 South Main Street
McPherson, KS 67460
Phone: (800) 835-0078
Fax: (620) 241-6032
E-mail: admissions@centralchristian.edu
http://www.centralcollege.edu
Communications technology, computer
    programming—specific applications,
    mathematics/computer science,
    photographic/film/video technology,
    playwriting/screenwriting, recording
    arts.

Haskell Indian Nations University
155 Indian Avenue
Lawrence, KS 66046
Phone: (785) 749-8404
Fax: NA
E-mail: admissions@haskell.edu
http://www.haskell.edu
Data processing technology.

Kansas State University
119 Anderson Hall
Manhattan, KS 66506
Phone: (785) 532-6250
Fax: (785) 532-6393
E-mail: kstate@ksu.edu
http://www.consider.k-state.edu
Computer engineering, electrical and
    communications engineering.

Ottawa University
1001 South Cedar Street
Ottawa, KS 66067
Phone: (785) 242-5200
Fax: (785) 229-1008
E-mail: admiss@ottawa.edu
http://www.ottawa.edu
Information technology.

Pittsburg State University
1701 South Broadway
Pittsburg, KS 66762
Phone: (620) 235-4251
Fax: (620) 235-6003
E-mail: psuadmit@pittstate.edu
http://www.pittstate.edu
Computer graphics, electrical engineering
    technology, graphic design,
    information technology, technical and
    business writing.

Southwestern College
100 College Street
Winfield, KS 67156

Phone: (620) 229-6236
Fax: (620) 229-6344
E-mail: scadmit@sckans.edu
http://www.sckans.edu
Digital media, LAN/WAN management,
    radio/television broadcasting,
    recording arts, software engineering.

Tabor College
400 South Jefferson Street
Hillsboro, KS 67063
Phone: (620) 947-3121
Fax: (620) 947-6276
E-mail: admissions@tabor.edu
http://www.tabor.edu
Mathematics/computer science,
    organizational communication.

University of Kansas
Office of Admissions and Scholarships
1502 Iowa Street
Lawrence, KS 66045-7575
Phone: (785) 864-3911
Fax: (785) 864-5017
E-mail: adm@ku.edu
http://www.ku.edu
Computer engineering, design/visual
    communications, electrical and
    communications engineering, graphic
    design, illustration, organizational
    communication.

Washburn University
1700 SW College Avenue
Topeka, KS 66621
Phone: (785) 231-1030
Fax: (785) 296-7933
E-mail: zzdpadm@washburn.edu
http://www.washburn.edu
Electrical engineering technology.

Wichita State University
1845 Fairmount Street
Wichita, KS 67260
Phone: (316) 978-3085
Fax: (316) 978-3174
E-mail: admissions@wichita.edu
http://www.wichita.edu
Computer engineering, electrical and
    communications engineering,
    electrical engineering technology.

KENTUCKY

Asbury College
1 Macklem Drive
Wilmore, KY 403390
Phone: (859) 858-3511
Fax: (859) 858-3921

E-mail: admissions@asbury.edu
http://www.asbury.edu
Communications technology.

Bellarmine University
2001 Newburg Road
Louisville, KY 4025
Phone: (502) 452-8131
Fax: (502) 452-8002
E-mail: admissions@bellarmine.edu
http://www.bellarmine.edu
Computer engineering.

Berea College
CPO 2220
Berea, KY 40404
Phone: (859) 985-3500
Fax: (859) 985-3512
E-mail: admissions@berea.edu
http://www.berea.edu
Mathematics/computer science.

Eastern Kentucky University
Coates, P.O. Box 2A
Richmond, KY 40475
Phone: (859) 622-2106
Fax: (606) 622-8024
E-mail: stephen.byn@eku.edu
http://www.eku.edu
Data processing technology, drafting and
    design technology.

Kentucky State University
400 East Main Street, Third Floor
Frankfort, KY 40601
Phone: (502) 597-6813
Fax: (502) 597-5814
E-mail: jburrell@gwmail.kysu.edu
http://www.kysu.edu
Data processing technology, drafting
    and design technology, electrical
    engineering technology.

Kentucky Wesleyan College
3000 Frederica Street
P.O. Box 1039
Owensboro, KY 42302
Phone: (270) 852-3120
Fax: (270) 852-3133
E-mail: admitme@kwc.edu
http://www.kwc.edu
Computer engineering.

Murray State University
P.O. Box 9
Murray, KY 42071
Phone: (270) 762-3741
Fax: (270) 762-3780

E-mail: admissions@murraystate.edu
http://www.murraystate.edu
Drafting and design technology, electric
  engineering technology, organizational
  communication.

Northern Kentucky University
Administrative Center 400
Nunn Drive
Highland Heights, KY 41099
Phone: (859) 572-5220
Fax: (859) 572-6665
E-mail: admitnku@nku.edu
http://www.nku.edu
Communications technology, electrical
  and communications engineering,
  electrical engineering technology.

Sullivan University—Louisville
3101 Bardstown Road
Louisville, KY 40205
Phone: (502) 456-6504
Fax: NA
E-mail: At Web site
http://www.sullivan.edu
Computer programming—specific
  applications.

Thomas More College
333 Thomas More Parkway
Crestview Hill, KY 40107
Phone: (859) 344-3332
Fax: (859) 344-3444
E-mail: admissions@thomasmore.edu
http://www.thomasmore.edu
Data processing technology.

University of Kentucky
100 Funkhouser Building
Lexington, KY 40506
Phone: (859) 257-2000
Fax: (859) 257-3823
E-mail: admission@uky.edu
http://www.uky.edu
Electrical and communications
  engineering.

University of Louisville
Admissions Office
Louisville, KY 40292
Phone: (502) 852-6531
Fax: (502) 852-4776
E-mail: admitme@louisville.edu
http://www.louisville.edu
Applied mathematics, computer
  engineering, electrical and
  communications engineering.

Western Kentucky University
Potter Hall 117

1 Big Red Way
Bowling Green, KY 42101
Phone: (270) 745-2551
Fax: (270) 745-6133
E-mail: admission@wku.edu
http://www.wku.edu
Data processing technology, electrical
  and communications engineering,
  electrical engineering technology.

LOUISIANA

Centenary College of Louisiana
P.O. Box 41188
Shreveport, LA 71134
Phone: (318) 869-5131
Fax: (318) 869-5005
E-mail: admissions@centenary.edu
http://www.centenary.edu
Cinematography and film/video
  production, digital media.

Grambling State University
P.O. Box 864
Grambling, LA 71245
Phone: (318) 274-6423
Fax: (318) 274-3292
E-mail: taylorn@gram.edu
http://www.gram.edu
Drafting and design technology, electrical
  engineering technology.

Grantham University
34641 Grantham College Road
Slidell, LA 70460
Phone: (985) 649-4191
Fax: (985) 649-4183
E-mail: admissions@grantham.edu
http://www.grantham.edu
Computer engineering, computer
  programming (specific applications),
  computer software technology, data
  processing technology, drafting
  and design technology, electrical
  and communications engineering,
  electrical engineering technology,
  information technology, LAN/WAN
  management, software engineering,
  web/multimedia management,
  webpage/multimedia design.

Louisiana College
1140 College Drive
P.O. Box 560
Pineville, LA 71359
Phone: (318) 487-7259
Fax: (318) 487-7550
E-mail: admissions@lacollege.edu
http://www.lacollege.edu
Web/multimedia management.

**Louisiana State University—
  Baton Rouge**
110 Thomas Boyd Hall
Baton Rouge, LA 70803
Phone: (225) 578-1175
Fax: (225) 578-4433
E-mail: admissions@lsu.edu
http://www.lsu.edu
Computer engineering, electrical and
  communications engineering.

Louisiana Tech University
P.O. Box 3178
Ruston, LA 71272
Phone: (318) 257-3036
Fax: (318) 257-2499
E-mail: bulldog@latech.edu
http://www.latech.edu
Electrical and communications engineering,
  electrical engineering technology.

Loyola University—New Orleans
6363 St. Charles Avenue, P.O. Box 18
New Orleans, LA 70811
Phone: (504) 865-3240
Fax: (504) 865-3383
E-mail: admit@loyno.edu
http://www.loyno.edu
Communications technology.

McNeese State University
P.O. Box 92495
Lake Charles, LA 90609
Phone: (318) 475-5146
Fax: (318) 475-5189
E-mail: info@mail.mcneese.edu
http://www.mcneese.edu
Data processing technology.

Nicholls State University
P.O. Box 2004
Thibodaux, LA 70310
Phone: (985) 448-4507
Fax: (985) 448-4929
E-mail: nicholls@nicholls.edu
http://www.nicholls.edu
Technical and business writing.

Northwestern State University
209 Roy Hall
Natchitoches, LA 71497
Phone: (318) 357-4078
Fax: (318) 357-4660
E-mail: admissions@nsula.edu
http://www.nsula.edu
Electrical engineering technology.

Southern University—New Orleans
6801 Press Drive
New Orleans, LA 70126

Phone: (504) 286-5314
Fax: NA
E-mail: At Web site
http://www.suno.edu
Computer programming (specific
    applications).

Southern University—Shreveport
3050 Martin Luther King Jr. Drive
Shreveport, LA 71107
Phone: (318) 674-3342
Fax: (318) 674-3338
E-mail: admissions@susla.edu
http://www.susla.edu
Computer programming—specific
    applications, drafting and design
    technology, electrical engineering
    technology.

Tulane University
6823 St. Charles Avenue
New Orleans, LA 70118
Phone: (504) 865-5731
Fax: (504) 862-8715
E-mail: undergrad.admission@tulane.edu
http://www.tulane.edu
Computer engineering, electrical and
    communications engineering,
    multimedia.

University of Louisiana—Lafayette
P.O. Drawer 41210
Lafayette, LA 70504
Phone: (337) 482-6457
Fax: (337) 482-6195
E-mail: admissions@louisiana.edu
http://www.louisiana.edu
Computer engineering, electrical and
    communications engineering,
    telecommunications technology.

University of Louisiana—Monroe
700 University Avenue
Monroe, LA 71209
Phone: (318) 342-5252
Fax: (318) 342-5274
E-mail: rehood@ulm.edu
http://www.ulm.edu
Communications technology.

University of New Orleans
Admissions Office
Lakefront, New Orleans, LA 70148
Phone: (504) 280-6595
Fax: (504) 280-5522
E-mail: admissions@uno.edu
http://www.uno.edu
Electrical and communications
    engineering.

Xavier University of Louisiana
One Drexel Drive
Attn: Admissions Office
New Orleans, LA 70125
Phone: (504) 483-7388
Fax: (504) 485-7941
E-mail: apply@xula.edu
http://www.xula.edu
Computer engineering.

MAINE

Bowdoin College
5000 College Station, Bowdoin College
Brunswick, ME 04011
Phone: (207) 725-3100
Fax: (207) 725-3101
E-mail: admissions@bowdoin.edu
http://www.bowdoin.edu
Mathematics/computer science.

Colby College
4000 Mayflower Hill
Waterville, ME 04091
Phone: (207) 872-3168
Fax: (207) 872-3474
E-mail: admissions@colby.edu
http://www.colby.edu
Mathematics/computer science.

Husson College
One College Circle
Bangor, ME 04401
Phone: (207) 941-7100
Fax: (207) 941-7935
E-mail: admit@husson.edu
http://www.husson.edu
Computer programming—specific
    applications, data processing
    technology, sales/distribution.

**New England School of
    Communications**
1 College Circle
Bangor, ME 04401
Phone: (888) 877-1876
Fax: NA
E-mail: GrantL@nescom.edu
http://www.nescom.edu
Cinematography and film/video
    production, communications
    technology, digital media,
    photographic/film/video technology,
    recording arts, webpage/multimedia
    design.

St. Joseph's College
278 Whites Bridge Road
Standish, ME 04084

Phone: (207) 893-7746
Fax: (207) 893-7862
E-mail: admission@sjcme.edu
http://www.sjcme.edu
Digital media.

Thomas College
180 West River Road
Waterville, ME 04901
Phone: (207) 859-1101
Fax: (207) 859-1114
E-mail: admiss@thomas.edu
http://www.thomas.edu
Software engineering.

University of Maine—Augusta
46 University Drive
Augusta, ME 04330
Phone: (207) 621-3185
Fax: (207) 621-3116
E-mail: umaar@maine.edu
http://www.uma.maine.edu
Computer engineering, electrical and
    communications engineering,
    electrical engineering technology.

University of Maine—Farmington
246 Main Street
Farmington, ME 04938
Phone: (207) 778-7050
Fax: (207) 778-8182
E-mail: umfadmit@maine.edu
http://www.umf.maine.edu
Mathematics/computer science.

University of Maine—Fort Kent
23 University Drive
Fort Kent, ME 04743
Phone: (207) 834-7500
Fax: (207) 834-7609
E-mail: umfkadm@maine.edu
http://www.umfk.maine.edu
E-commerce, electrical and
    communications engineering,
    electrical engineering technology,
    information technology, mathematics/
    computer science.

University of Maine—Orono
5713 Chadbourne Hall
Orono, ME 04469
Phone: (207) 581-1561
Fax: (207) 581-1213
E-mail: um-admit@maine.edu
http://www.maine.edu
Computer engineering, electrical and
    communications engineering,
    electrical engineering technology.

University of Southern Maine
37 College Avenue
Gorham, ME 04038
Phone: (207) 780-5670
Fax: (207) 780-5640
E-mail: usmadm@usm.maine.edu
http://usm.maine.edu
Cinematography and film/video
production, computer programming—
specific applications, electrical
and communications engineering,
electrical engineering technology,
mathematics/computer science.

MARYLAND

Bowie State University
14000 Jericho Park Road
Henry Administration Building
Bowie, MD 20715
Phone: (301) 860-3415
Fax: (301) 860-3438
E-mail: schanaiwa@bowiestate.edu
http://www.bowiestate.edu
Communications technology,
organizational communication.

Capitol College
11301 Springfield Road
Laurel, MD 20708
Phone: (800) 950-1992
Fax: (301) 953-1442
E-mail: admissions@capitol-college.edu
http://www.capitol-college.edu
Computer engineering, software
engineering.

Johns Hopkins University
3400 North Charles Street
140 Garland Hall
Baltimore, MD 21218
Phone: (410) 516-8171
Fax: (410) 516-6025
E-mail: gotojhu@jhu.edu
http://www.jhu.edu
Applied mathematics, computer
engineering, electrical and
communications engineering.

Loyola College in Maryland
4501 North Charles Street
Baltimore, MD 21210
Phone: (800) 221-9107
Fax: (410) 617-2176
E-mail: admissions@loyola.edu
http://www.loyola.edu
Applied mathematics.

Maryland Institute College of Art
1300 Mount Royal Avenue
Baltimore, MD 21217
Phone: (410) 225-2222
Fax: (410) 225-2337
E-mail: admissions@mica.edu
http://www.mica.edu
Graphic design, illustration, multimedia.

Morgan State University
1700 East Cold Spring Lane
Baltimore, MD 21251
Phone: (800) 332-6674
Fax: (410) 319-3684
E-mail: tjenness@moac.morgan.edu
http://www.morgan.edu
Electrical and communications
engineering.

**University of Maryland—Baltimore
County**
1000 Hilltop Circle
Baltimore, MD 21250
Phone: (410) 455-2291
Fax: (410) 455-1094
E-mail: admissions@umbc.edu
http://www.umbc.edu
Cinematography and film/video
production, computer engineering,
e-commerce, electrical and
communications engineering.

University of Maryland—College Park
Mitchell Building
College Park, MD 20742
Phone: (301) 314-8385
Fax: (301) 314-9693
E-mail: um-admit@uga.umd.edu
http://www.maryland.edu
Computer engineering, electrical and
communications engineering.

**University of Maryland—
Eastern Shore**
Office of Admissions
Backbone Road
Princess Anne, MD 21853
Phone: (410) 651-6410
Fax: (410) 651-7922
E-mail: ccmills@mail.umes.edu
http://www.umes.edu
Electrical engineering technology.

Villa Julia College
1525 Greenspring Valley Road
Stevenson, MD 21153
Phone: (410) 486-7001
Fax: (410) 602-6600

E-mail: admissions@vjc.edu
http://www.vjc.edu
Cinematography and film/video production,
communications technology, design/
visual communications.

MASSACHUSETTS

**Ai: The New England Institute of Art
and Design**
10 Brookline Place West
Brookline, MA 02445
Phone: (617) 739-1700
Fax: NA
E-mail: At Web site
http://www.education.org/artinstitutes/
boston.php
Graphic design, illustration.

Amherst College
Campus Box 2231, P.O. Box 5000
Amherst, MA 01002
Phone: (413) 542-2328
Fax: (413) 542-2040
E-mail: admission@amherst.edu
http://www.amherst.edu
Mathematics/computer science,
multimedia, recording arts.

Anna Maria College
50 Sunset Lane, Box O
Paxton, MA 01612
Phone: (508) 849-3260
Fax: (508) 849-3362
E-mail: admission@annamaria.edu
http://www.annamaria.edu
Graphic design.

**Art Institute of Boston at
Lesley University**
700 Beacon Street
Boston, MA 02215
Phone: (617) 585-6700
Fax: (617) 437-1226
E-mail: admission@aiboston.edu
http://www.aiboston.edu
Graphic design, illustration.

Assumption College
500 Salisbury Street
Worcester, MA 01609
Phone: (508) 767-7285
Fax: (508) 799-4412
E-mail: admiss@assumption.edu
http://www.assumption.edu
Organizational communication.

Babson College
Lunder Hall
Babson Park, MA 02457

Phone: (781) 239-5522
Fax: (781) 239-4136
E-mail: ugradadmission@babson.edu
http://www.babson.edu
Sales/distribution.

Boston University
121 Bay State Road
Boston, MA 02215
Phone: (617) 353-2300
Fax: (617) 353-9695
E-mail: admissions@bu.edu
http://www.bu.edu
Cinematography and film/video
    production, computer engineering,
    electrical and communications
    engineering, mathematics/computer
    science.

Clark University
950 Main Street
Worcester, MA 01610
Phone: (508) 793-7431
Fax: (508) 793-8821
E-mail: admissions@clarku.edu
http://www.clarku.edu
Mathematics/computer science.

College of the Holy Cross
Admissions Office
1 College Street
Worcester, MA 01610
Phone: (313) 664-7425
Fax: (313) 872-2739
E-mail: admissions@ccscad.edu
http://www.ccscad.edu
Cinematography and film/video
    production.

Eastern Nazarene College
23 East Elm Avenue
Quincy, MA 02170
Phone: (617) 745-3000
Fax: (617) 745-3490
E-mail: admissions@enc.edu
http://www.enc.edu
Computer engineering.

Emerson College
120 Boylston Street
Boston, MA 02116
Phone: (617) 824-8600
Fax: (617) 824-8609
E-mail: admission@emerson.edu
http://www.emerson.edu
Cinematography and film/video
    production, communications
    technology, playwriting/
    screenwriting.

Emmanuel College
400 The Fenway
Boston, MA 02115
Phone: (617) 735-9715
Fax: (617) 735-9801
E-mail: enroll@emmanuel.edu
http://www.emmanuel.edu
Design/visual communications,
    organizational communication.

Endicott College
376 Hale Street
Beverly, MA 01915
Phone: (978) 921-1000
Fax: (978) 232-2520
E-mail: admissio@endicott.edu
http://www.endicott.edu
Design/visual communications.

Fitchburg State College
160 Pearl Street
Fitchburg, MA 01420
Phone: (978) 665-3144
Fax: (978) 665-4540
E-mail: admissions@fsc.edu
http://www.fsc.edu
Cinematography and film/video
    production, technical and business
    writing.

**Franklin W. Olin College of
    Engineering**
Olin Way
Needham, MA 02492
Phone: (781) 292-2222
Fax: (781) 292-2210
E-mail: info@olin.edu
http://www.olin.edu
Computer engineering.

Hampshire College
Admissions Office
893 West Street
Amherst, MA 01002
Phone: (413) 559-5471
Fax: (413) 559-5631
E-mail: admissions@hampshire.edu
http://www.hampshire.edu
Applied mathematics, cinematography
    and film/video production,
    computer graphics, design/visual
    communications, communications,
    mathematics/computer science,
    multimedia playwriting/screenwriting.

Harvard College
Byerly Hall
8 Garden Street
Cambridge, MA 02138
Phone: (617) 495-1551

Fax: (617) 495-8821
E-mail: college@fas.harvard.edu
http://www.fas.harvard.edu
Applied mathematics, cinematography
    and film/video production, computer
    engineering, computer graphics,
    design/visual communications,
    mathematics/computer science.

Lasell College
Office of Admissions
1844 Commonwealth Avenue
Newton, MA 02406
Phone: (617) 243-2225
Fax: (617) 243-2380
E-mail: info@lasell.edu
http://www.lasell.edu
Graphic design.

Massachusetts College of Art
621 Huntington Avenue
Boston, MA 02115
Phone: (617) 879-7222
Fax: (617) 879-7250
E-mail: admissions@massart.edu
http://www.massart.edu
Cinematography and film/video
    production, design/visual
    communications.

Massachusetts Institute of Technology
MIT Admissions Office Room 3108
77 Massachusetts Avenue
Cambridge, MA 02139
Phone: (617) 253-4791
Fax: (617) 258-8304
E-mail: admissions@mit.edu
http://www.mit.edu
Mathematics/computer science.

Merrimack College
Office of Admission
Austin Hall
North Andover, MA 01845
Phone: (978) 837-5100
Fax: (978) 837-5133
E-mail: admission@merrimack.edu
http://www.merrimack.edu
Computer engineering, electrical and
    communications engineering.

Mount Ida College
777 Dedham Street
Newton, MA 02459
Phone: (617) 928-4500
Fax: NA
E-mail: admissions@mountida.edu
http://www.mountida.edu
Sales/distribution.

Northeastern University
260 Huntington Avenue, 150 Richards
    Hall
Boston, MA 02115
Phone: (617) 373-2200
Fax: (617) 373-8780
E-mail: admissions@neu.edu
http://www.neu.edu
Computer engineering, design/visual
    communications, electrical and
    communications engineering,
    electrical engineering technology.

Salem State College
352 Lafayette Street
Salem, MA 01970
Phone: (978) 542-6200
Fax: (978) 542-6893
E-mail: admissions@salemstate.edu
http://www.salemstate.edu
Mathematics/computer science.

School of the Museum of Fine Arts
230 The Fenway
Boston, MA 02115
Phone: (617) 369-3626
Fax: (617) 369-4264
E-mail: admissions@smfa.edu
http://www.smfa.edu
Cinematography and film/video
    production, graphic design,
    illustration, multimedia.

Simmons College
300 The Fenway
Boston, MA 02115
Phone: (617) 521-2051
Fax: (617) 521-3190
E-mail: ugadm@simmons.edu
http://www.simmons.edu
Sales/distribution.

Simon's Rock College of Bard
84 Alford Road
Great Barrington, MA 01230
Phone: (413) 528-7312
Fax: (413) 528-7334
E-mail: admit@simons-rock.edu
http://www.simons-rock.edu
Cinematography and film/video
    production, cognitive science,
    mathematics/computer science,
    photographic/film/video technology,
    playwriting/screenwriting.

Smith College
17 College Lane
Northampton, MA 01063
Phone: (413) 585-2500

Fax: (413) 585-2527
E-mail: admission@smith.edu
http://www.smith.edu
Computer engineering, electrical and
    communications engineering.

Stonehill College
320 Washington Street
Easton, MA 02357
Phone: (508) 565-1373
Fax: (508) 565-1545
E-mail: admissions@stonehill.edu
http://www.stonehill.edu
Computer engineering.

Suffolk University
8 Ashburton Place
Boston, MA 02108
Phone: (617) 573-8460
Fax: (617) 742-4291
E-mail: admission@suffolk.edu
http://www.suffolk.edu
Communications technology,
    computer engineering, electrical
    and communications engineering,
    organizational communication.

Tufts University
Bendetson Hall
Medford, MA 02156
Phone: (617) 627-3170
Fax: (617) 627-3860
E-mail: inquiry@ase.tufts.edu
http://www.tufts.edu
Applied mathematics, computer
    engineering, electrical and
    communications engineering,
    mathematics/computer science.

**University of Massachusetts—
    Amherst**
University Admissions Center
Amherst, MA 01003
Phone: (413) 545-0222
Fax: (413) 545-4312
E-mail: mail@admissions.umass.edu
http://www.umass.edu
Computer engineering, electrical and
    communications engineering.

University of Massachusetts—Boston
100 Morrissey Boulevard
Boston, MA 02125
Phone: (617) 287-6000
Fax: (617) 287-5999
E-mail: undergrad@umb.edu
http://www.umb.edu
Applied mathematics.

**University of Massachusetts—
    Dartmouth**
285 Old Westport Road
North Dartmouth, MA 02747
Phone: (508) 999-9605
Fax: (508) 999-8755
E-mail: admissions@umassd.edu
http://www.umassd.edu
Computer engineering, design/visual
    communications, electrical and
    communications engineering,
    electrical engineering technology,
    multimedia.

University of Massachusetts—Lowell
Office of Undergraduate Admissions
883 Broadway Street Room 110
Lowell, MA 01854
Phone: (978) 934-3931
Fax: (978) 934-3086
E-mail: admissions@uml.edu
http://www.uml.edu
Applied mathematics, computer
    engineering, electrical and
    communications engineering,
    electrical engineering technology.

Wentworth Institute of Technology
555 Huntington Avenue
Boston, MA 02115
Phone: (800) 556-0610
Fax: (6117) 989-4591
E-mail: admissions@wit.edu
http://www.wit.edu
Electrical engineering technology,
    telecommunications technology.

Worcester Polytechnic Institute
100 Institute Road
Worcester, MA 01609
Phone: (508) 831-5286
Fax: (508) 831-5875
E-mail: admissions@wpi.edu
http://www.wpi.edu
Applied mathematics, electrical and
    communications engineering,
    technical and business writing.

MICHIGAN

Albion College
611 East Porter Street
Albion, MI 49224
Phone: (517) 629-0321
Fax: (517) 629-0569
E-mail: admissions@albion.edu
http://www.albion.edu
Mathematics/computer science.

Alma College
614 West Superior Street
Alma, MI 48801
Phone: (989) 463-7139
Fax: (989) 463-7057
E-mail: admissions@alma.edu
http://www.alma.edu
Design/visual communications, graphic
design.

Andrews University
Office of Admissions
Berien Springs, MI 49104
Phone: (800) 253-2874
Fax: (616) 471-3228
E-mail: enroll@andrews.edu
http://www.andrews.edu
Communications technology, design/
visual communications, electrical
and communications engineering,
electrical engineering technology,
multimedia.

Baker College of Auburn Hills
1500 University Drive
Auburn Hills, MI 48326
Fax:
Phone: (248) 340-0600
E-mail: Bohleh_j@auburnhills.baker.edu
http://www.baker.edu
Computer graphics, data processing
technology.

Baker College of Cadillac
9600 East 13th Street
Cadillac, MI 49601-9169
Phone: (888) 313-3463
Fax: (231) 775-8505
E-mail: adm-ca@baker.edu
http://www.baker.edu
Computer programming—specific
applications.

Baker College of Clinton Township
34950 Little Mack Avenue
Clinton Township, MI 48035
Phone: (888) 272-2842
Fax: (586) 790-9580
E-mail: adm-ct@baker.edu
http://www.baker.edu
Data processing technology.

Baker College of Flint
1050 West Bristol Road
Flint, MI 48507-5508
Phone: (800) 964-4299
Fax: (810) 766-4293
E-mail: adm-fl@baker.edu
http://www.baker.edu

Data processing technology, electrical
engineering technology.

Baker College of Jackson
2800 Springport Road
Jackson, MI 49202
Phone: (517) 788-7800
Fax: (517) 789-7331
E-mail: kelli.stepka@baker.edu
http://www.baker.edu
Data processing technology, webpage/
multimedia design.

Baker College of Muskegon
1903 Marquette Avenue
Muskegon, MI 49442
Phone: (231) 777-5200
Fax: (231) 777-5201
E-mail: Kathy.jacobson@baker.edu
http://www.baker.edu
Computer graphics, computer
programming—specific applications,
electrical engineering technology,
quality control technology, webpage/
multimedia design.

Baker College of Owosso
1020 South Washington Street
Owosso, MI 48867
Phone: (989) 729-3350
Fax: (989) 723-3355
E-mail: mike.konopacke@baker.edu
http://www.baker.edu
Computer graphics, data processing
technology, electrical engineering
technology.

Baker College of Port Huron
3403 Lapeer Road
Port Huron, MI 48060
Phone: (810) 985-7000
Fax: (810) 985-7066
E-mail: Kenny_d@porthuron.baker.edu
http://www.baker.edu
Computer graphics, computer
programming—specific applications,
data processing technology, electrical
engineering technology, webpage/
multimedia design.

Calvin College
3201 Burton Street Southeast
Grand Rapids, MI 49546
Phone: (616) 526-6106
Fax: (616) 526-6777
E-mail: admissions@calvin.edu
http://www.calvin.edu
Digital media.

Central Michigan University
205 Warriner Hall
Mount Pleasant, MI 48859
Phone: (989) 774-3076
Fax: (989) 774-7267
E-mail: cmuadmit@cmich.edu
http://www.cmich.edu
Design/visual communications, electrical
engineering technology, sales/
distribution, technical and business
writing.

Cleary University
3750 Cleary Drive
Howell, MI 48843
Phone: (517) 548-3670
Fax: (517) 548-7805
E-mail: admissions@cleary.edu
http://www.cleary.edu
E-commerce.

College for Creative Studies
201 East Kirby
Detroit, MI 48202
Phone: (313) 664-7425
Fax: (313) 872-2739
E-mail: admissions@ccscad.edu
http://www.ccscad.edu
Animation, cinematography and film/
video production, computer graphics,
design/visual communications, digital
media, graphic design, illustration,
multimedia.

Eastern Michigan University
400 Pierce Hall
Ypsilanti, MI 48197
Phone: (734) 487-3060
Fax: (734) 487-1484
E-mail: admissions@emich.edu
http://www.emich.edu
Communications technology, computer
engineering, electrical engineering
technology.

Ferris State University
1201 South State Street
Center for Student Services
Big Rapids, MI 49307
Phone: (231) 591-2100
Fax: (231) 591-3944
E-mail: admissions@ferris.edu
http://www.ferris.edu
Applied mathematics, communications
technology, design/visual
communications, electrical
engineering technology, sales/
distribution.

Finlandia University
601 Quincy Street
Hancock, MI 49930
Phone: (877) 202-5491
Fax: (906) 487-7383
E-mail: At Web site
http://www.finlandia.edu
Design/visual communications, graphic
    design, illustration.

Grace Bible College
P.O. Box 910
1011 Aldon Street SW
Grand Rapids, MI 49509
Phone: (800) 968-1887
Fax: (616) 538-0599
E-mail: At Web site
http://www.gbcol.edu
Digital media, information technology,
    recording arts.

Grand Valley State University
1 Campus Drive
Allendale, MI 49401
Phone: (616) 331-5000
Fax: (616) 331-2000
E-mail: go@gvsu@gvsu.edu
http://www.gvsu.edu
Electrical and communications
    engineering, technical and business
    writing.
Hillsdale College
35 East College Street
Hillsdale, MI 49242
Phone: (517) 607-2377
Fax: (517) 607-2223
E-mail: admissions@hillsdale.edu
http://www.hillsdale.edu
Mathematics/computer science.

Kendall College of Art and Design of
    Ferris State University
17 Fountain Street Northwest
Grand Rapids, MI 49503
Phone: (616) 451-2787
Fax: (616) 831-9689
E-mail: brittons@ferris.edu
http://www.kcad.edu
Design/visual communications.

Kettering University
1700 West Third Avenue
Flint, MI 48504
Phone: (810) 762-7865
Fax: (810) 762-9837
E-mail: admissions@kettering.edu
http://www.kettering.edu
Applied mathematics, computer
    engineering, electrical and

communications engineering, LAN/
WAN management.

Lawrence Technological University
21000 West Ten Mile Road
Southfield, MI 48075
Phone: (248) 204-3160
Fax: (248) 204-3188
E-mail: admissions@ltu.edu
http://www.ltu.edu
Computer engineering, electrical and
    communications engineering,
    illustration, information technology,
    mathematics/computer science.

Madonna University
36600 Schoolcraft Road
Livonia, MI 48150
Phone: (734) 432-5339
Fax: (734) 432-5393
E-mail: muinfo@smtp.munet.edu
http://www.munet.edu
E-commerce, technical and business
    writing.

Michigan State University
250 Administration Building
East Lansing, MI 48824-1046
Phone: (517) 355-8332
Fax: (517) 353-1647
E-mail: adis@msu.edu
http://www.msu.edu
Applied mathematics, computer
    engineering, electrical and
    communications engineering,
    technical and business writing.

Michigan Technological University
1400 Townsend Drive
Houghton, MI 49931
Phone: (906) 487-2335
Fax: (906) 487-2125
E-mail: mtu4u@mtu.edu
http://www.mtu.edu
Computer engineering, drafting and
    design technology, electrical and
    communications engineering,
    electrical engineering technology,
    organizational communication,
    software engineering.

Northern Michigan University
1401 Presque Isle Avenue
304 Cohodas
Marquette, MI 49855
Phone: (906) 227-2650
Fax: (906) 227-1747
E-mail: admiss@nmu.edu
http://www.nmu.edu

Applied mathematics, cinematography
    and film/video production,
    computer graphics, design/visual
    communications, drafting and design
    technology, electrical engineering
    technology, technical and business
    writing.

Oakland University
Office of Admissions
101 North Foundation Hall
Rochester, MI 48309
Phone: (248) 370-3360
Fax: (248) 370-4462
E-mail: ouinfo@oakland.edu
http://www.oakland.edu
Computer engineering, electrical and
    communications engineering.

Saginaw Valley State University
7400 Bay Road
University Center, MI 48710
Phone: (989) 964-4200
Fax: (989) 790-0180
E-mail: admissions@svsu.edu
http://www.svsu.edu
Communications technology, design/
    visual communications, electrical
    and communications engineering,
    mathematics/computer science.

University of Detroit—Mercy
P.O. Box 19900
Detroit, MI 48219
Phone: (313) 993-1245
Fax: (313) 993-3326
E-mail: admissions@udmercy.edu
http://www.udmercy.edu
Applied mathematics, computer
    engineering, electrical and
    communications engineering,
    technical and business writing.

University of Michigan—Ann Arbor
1220 Student Activities Building
Ann Arbor, MI 48109
Phone: (734) 764-7433
Fax: (734) 936-0740
E-mail: ugadmiss@umich.edu
http://www.umich.edu
Applied mathematics, electrical and
    communications engineering,
    multimedia, playwriting/
    screenwriting.

University of Michigan—Dearborn
4901 Evergreen Road
Dearborn, MI 48128
Phone: (313) 593-5100

Fax: (313) 436-9167
E-mail: admissions@umd.umich.edu
http://www.umd.umich.edu
Computer engineering, design/visual
    communications, electrical and
    communications engineering,
    multimedia.

University of Michigan—Flint
University Pavilion, Suite 245
Flint, MI 48502
Phone: (810) 762-3300
Fax: (810) 762-3272
E-mail: admissions@umflint.edu
http://www.flint.umich.edu
Design/visual communications,
    electrical and communications
    engineering, information technology,
    multimedia.

Wayne State University
656 West Kirby Street
Detroit, MI 48202
Phone: (313) 577-3577
Fax: (313) 577-7536
E-mail: admissions@wayne.edu
http://www.wayne.edu
Computer engineering, electrical and
    communications engineering,
    electrical engineering technology.

Western Michigan University
1903 West Michigan Avenue
Kalamazoo, MI 49008
Phone: (269) 387-2000
Fax: (269) 387-2096
E-mail: ask-wmu@umich.edu
http://www.wmich.edu
Applied mathematics, computer
    engineering, electrical and
    communications engineering.

MINNESOTA

Art Institute International—Minnesota
15 South Ninth Street
Minneapolis, MN 55402
Phone: (612) 332-3361
Fax: (612) 332-3934
E-mail: kozela@aii.edu
http://www.aii.edu
Animation, computer graphics, digital
    media, graphic design, multimedia,
    web/multimedia management.

Capella University
222 South Ninth Street, 20th Floor
Minneapolis, MN 55402
Phone: (888) 227-3552

Fax: (612) 339-8022
E-mail: info@capella.edu
http://www.capellauniversity.edu
Computer graphics, e-commerce,
    information technology, LAN/
    WAN management, quality control
    technology.

Carleton College
100 South College Street
Northfield, MN 55057
Phone: (507) 646-4190
Fax: (507) 646-4526
E-mail: admission@acs.carleton.edu
http://www.carleton.edu
Mathematics/computer science.

College of St. Benedict
P.O. Box 7155
Collegeville, MN 56321
Phone: (320) 363-2196
Fax: (320) 363-2750
E-mail: admission@csbsju.edu
http://www.csbsju.edu
Mathematics/computer science.

College of St. Scholastica
1200 Kenwood Avenue
Duluth, MN 55811
Phone: (218) 723-6000
Fax: (218) 723-5991
E-mail: admissions@css.edu
http://www.css.edu
Organizational communication.

College of Visual Arts
344 Summit Avenue
St. Paul, MN 55102
Phone: (800) 224-1536
Fax: (651) 224-8854
E-mail: info@cva.edu
http://www cva.edu
Design/visual communications,
    illustration.

Concordia College—oorhead
901 Eighth Street South
Moorhead, MN 56562
Phone: (218) 299-3004
Fax: (218) 299-4720
E-mail: admissions@cord.edu
http://www.goconcordia.com
Applied mathematics, mathematics/
    computer science.

Metropolitan State University
1501 Hennepin Avenue
Minneapolis, MN 55403
Phone: (612) 659-6000

Fax: NA
E-mail: At Web site
http://www.metrostate.edu
Applied mathematics, sales/distribution,
    technical and business writing.

Minneapolis College of Art and Design
2501 Stevens Avenue
Minneapolis, MN 55404
Phone: (612) 874-3760
Fax: (612) 874-3701
E-mail: admissions@mcad.edu
http://www.mcad.edu
Design/visual communications.

Minnesota College of Art and Design
2501 Stevens Avenue
Minneapolis, MN 55404
Phone: (612) 874-3760
Fax: (612) 874-3701
E-mail: admissions@mcad.edu
http://www.mcad.edu
Cinematography and film/video
    production.

Minnesota State University—Mankato
Mankato, TC 122
Mankato, MN 56001
Phone: (507) 389-1822
Fax: (507) 389-1511
E-mail: admissions@mnsu.edu
http://www.mnsu.edu
Computer engineering, electrical
    engineering technology.

Northwestern College
3003 Snelling Avenue North
Saint Paul, MN 55113
Phone: (651) 631-5111
Fax: (651) 631-5680
E-mail: admissions@nwc.edu
http://www.nwc.edu
Graphic design.

Saint Cloud State University
720 South Fourth Avenue
Saint Cloud, MN 56301
Phone: (320) 308-2244
Fax: (320) 308-2243
E-mail: scsu4u@stcloudstate.edu
http://www.stcoudstate.edu
Computer engineering, data
    processing technology, electrical
    and communications engineering,
    electrical engineering technology.

St. John's University
P.O. Box 7155
Collegeville, MN 56321

Phone: (320) 363-2196
Fax: (320) 363-2750
E-mail: admission@csbsju.edu
http://www.csbsju.edu
Mathematics/computer science.

Saint Mary's University of Minnesota
700 Terrace Heights #2
Winona, MN 55987
Phone: (507) 457-1600
Fax: (507) 457-1722
E-mail: admissions@smumn.edu
http://www.smumn.edu
Communications technology, information
    technology, mathematics/computer
    science.

University of Minnesota—Crookston
170 Owen Hall
2900 University Avenue
Crookston, MN 56716
Phone: (218) 281-8569
Fax: (218) 281-8575
E-mail: info@umcrookston.edu
http://www.umcrookston.edu
LAN/WAN management, technical and
    business writing, webpage/multimedia
    design.

University of Minnesota—Duluth
23 Solon Campus Center
1117 University Drive
Duluth, MN 55812
Phone: (218) 726-7171
Fax: (218) 726-7040
E-mail: undadmis@d.umn.edu
http://www.d.umn.edu
Computer engineering, electrical and
    communications engineering,
    mathematics/computer science.

University of Minnesota—Twin Cities
240 Williamson Hall
231 Pillsbury Drive SE
Minneapolis, MN 55455
Phone: (612) 625-2008
Fax: (612) 626-1693
E-mail: admissions@tc.umn.edu
http://www1.umn.edu/twincities
Computer engineering, design/visual
    communications, electrical and
    communications engineering. sales/
    distribution.

University of Saint Thomas
2115 Summit Avenue, Mail #32-F1
St. Paul, MN 55105
Phone: (651) 962-6150
Fax: (651) 962-6160

E-mail: admissions@stthomas.edu
http://www.stthomas.edu
Electrical and communications
    engineering.

Winona State University
Office of Admissions
P.O. Box 5838
Winona, MN 55987
Phone: (507) 457-5100
Fax: (507) 457-5620
E-mail: admissions@winona.edu
http://www.winona.edu
Applied mathematics, communications
    technology, computer programming—
    specific applications, data
    processing technology, design/visual
    communications, mathematics/
    computer science.

MISSISSIPPI

Belhaven College
1500 Peachtree Street
Jackson, MS 39202
Phone: (601) 968-59040
Fax: (601) 968-8946
E-mail: admissions@belhaven.edu
http://www.belhaven.edu
Mathematics/computer science.

Jackson State University
1400 Lynch Street
P.O. Box 17330
Jackson, MS 39217
Phone: (601) 979-2100
Fax: (601) 979-3445
E-mail: schatman@ccaix,jsums.edu
http://www.jsums.edu
Communications technology, computer
    engineering, data processing
    technology, electrical and
    communications engineering.

Mississippi College
P.O. Box 4026
Clinton, MS 39058
Phone: (601) 925-3800
Fax: (601) 925-3950
E-mail: enrollment-services@mc.edu
http://www.mc.edu
Mathematics/computer science.

Mississippi State University
P.O. Box 6305
Mississippi State, MS 39762
Phone: (662) 325-2224
Fax: (662) 325-7360
E-mail: admit@admissions.msstate.edu

http://www.msstate.edu
Computer engineering, electrical and
    communications engineering, software
    engineering.

Tougaloo College
500 West Country Line Road
Tougaloo, MS 39174
Phone: (888) 424-2566
Fax: (601) 977-6185
E-mail: slaterJa@mail.tougaloo.edu
http://www.tougaloo.edu
Mathematics/computer science.

University of Mississippi
145 Martindale
University, MS 38677
Phone: (662) 915-7226
Fax: (662) 915-5869
E-mail: admissions@olemiss.edu
http://www.olemiss.edu
Communications technology, electrical
    and communications engineering.

University of Southern Mississippi
P.O. Box 5166
Southern Station
Hattiesburg, MS 38406
Phone: (601) 266-5000
Fax: (601) 266-5148
E-mail: admissions@usm.edu
http://www.usm.edu
Data processing technology, electrical
    engineering technology.

MISSOURI

Central Methodist College
411 CMC Square
Fayette, MO 65248
Phone: (660) 248-6251
Fax: (660) 248-1872
E-mail: admissions@cmc.edu
http://www.cmc.edu
Applied mathematics.

Central Missouri State University
Office of Admissions
WDE 1401
Warrensburg, MO 64093
Phone: (660) 543-4290
Fax: (660) 543-8517
E-mail: admit@cmsuvmb.cmsu.edu
http://www.cmsu.edu
Data processing technology, electrical
    engineering technology.

DeVry University—Kansas City
11224 Homes Street

Kansas City, MO 64131
Phone: (816) 941-2810
Fax: (816) 941-0896
E-mail: ssmeed@kc.devry.edu
http://www.devry.edu
Electrical engineering technology.

Drury University
900 North Benton Avenue
Springfield, MO 65802
Phone: (417) 873-7205
Fax: (417) 866-3873
E-mail: druryad@drury.edu
http://www.drury.edu
Design/visual communications.

Evangel University
1111 North Glenstone Avenue
Springfield, MO 65802
Phone: (417) 865-2811
Fax: (417) 520-0545
E-mail: admissions@evangel.edu
http://www.evangel.edu
Communications technology.

Kansas City Art Institute
44415 Warwick Boulevard
Kansas City, MO 64111
Phone: (816) 474-5225
Fax: (816) 802-3309
E-mail: admiss@kcai.edu
http://www.kcai.edu
Cinematography and film/video
    production, graphic design, illustration.

Lincoln University
Admissions Office, P.O. Box 29
Jefferson City, MO 65102
Phone: (573) 681-5599
Fax: (573) 681-5889
E-mail: enroll@lincolnu.edu
http://www.lincolnu.edu
Drafting and design technology.

Lindenwood University
309 South Kingshighway Street
St. Charles, MO 63301
Phone: (314) 949-4949
Fax: (314) 949-4989
E-mail: admissions@lindenwood.edu
http://www.lindenwood.edu
Computer graphics, graphic design,
    information technology, mathematics/
    computer science, organizational
    communication.

Maryville University of Saint Louis
13550 Conway Road
Saint Louis, MO 63141

Phone: (314) 529-9350
Fax: (314) 529-9927
E-mail: admissions@maryville.edu
http://www.maryville.edu
Applied mathematics, e-commerce,
    graphic design.

Missouri Southern State University
3950 East Newman Road
Joplin, MO 64801
Phone: (417) 625-9378
Fax: (417) 659-4429
E-mail: admissions@mssu.edu
http://www.mssu.edu
Drafting and design technology, graphic
    design, quality control technology.

Park University
8700 River Park Drive, Campus Box 1
Parkville, MO 64152
Phone: (816) 741-2000
Fax: (816) 741-4462
E-mail: admissions@mail.park.edu
http://www.park.edu
Graphic design.

Saint Louis University
221 North Grand Boulevard
Saint Louis, MO 63103
Phone: (314) 977-2500
Fax: (314) 977-7136
E-mail: admitme@slu.edu
http://www.slu.edu
Applied mathematics, electrical and
    communications engineering,
    organizational communication.

Southeast Missouri State University
One University Plaza
Mail Stop 3550
Cape Girardeau, MO 63701
Phone: (573) 651-2590
Fax: (573) 651-5936
E-mail: admissions@semo.edu
http://www.semo.edu
Communications technology, electrical
    engineering technology.

Southwest Missouri State University
901 South National Avenue
Springfield, MO 65804
Phone: (417) 836-5517
Fax: (417) 836-6334
E-mail: smsuinfo@smsu.edu
http://www.smsu.edu
Design/visual communications, drafting
    and design technology, electrical
    engineering technology, technical and
    business writing.

Stephens College
1200 East Broadway
P.O. Box 2121
Columbia, MO 65215
Phone: (573) 876-7207
Fax: (573) 876-7237
E-mail: apply@wc.stephens.edu
http://www.stephens.edu
Mathematics/computer science.

Truman State University
McClain Hall 205
100 East Normal Street
Kirksville, MO 63501
Phone: (660) 785-4114
Fax: (660) 785-7456
E-mail: admissions@truman.edu
http://www.admissions.truman.edu
Applied mathematics.

University of Missouri—Columbia
230 Jesse Hall
Columbia, MO 65211
Phone: (573) 882-7786
Fax: (573) 882-7887
E-mail: admissions@missouri.edu
http://www.missouri.edu
Computer engineering, electrical and
    communications engineering.

University of Missouri—Kansas City
5100 Rockhill Road, 101 AC
Kansas City, MO 64114
Phone: (816) 235-1111
Fax: (816) 235-5544
E-mail: admit@umkc.edu
http://www.umkc.edu
Electrical and communications
    engineering.

University of Missouri—Rolla
106 Parker Hall
Rolla, MO 65409
Phone: (573) 341-4165
Fax: (573) 341-4082
E-mail: admissions@umr.edu
http://www.umr.edu
Applied mathematics, computer
    engineering, electrical and
    communications engineering,
    information technology, technical and
    business writing.

University of Missouri—Saint Louis
351 Millennium Student Center
9001 Natural Bridge Road
Saint Louis, MO 63121
Phone: (314) 516-8675
Fax: (314) 516-5310

E-mail: admissions@umsl.edu
http://www.umsl.edu
Applied mathematics, electrical and
   communications engineering.

Washington University in Saint Louis
Campus Box 1089
One Brookings Drive
Saint Louis, MO 63130
Phone: (314) 935-6000
Fax: (314) 935-4290
E-mail: admissions@wustl.edu
http://www.wustl.edu
Applied mathematics, computer
   engineering, data processing
   technology, design/visual
   communications, electrical and
   communications engineering, graphic
   design, illustration, mathematics/
   computer science.

Webster University
470 East Lockwood Avenue
Saint Louis, MO 63119
Phone: (314) 968-6991
Fax: (314) 968-7115
E-mail: admit@webster.edu
http://www.webster.edu
Cinematography and film/video
   production.

William Jewell College
500 College Hill
Liberty, MO 64068
Phone: (816) 781-7700
Fax: (816) 415-5040
E-mail: admission@william.jewell.edu
http://www.jewell.edu
Mathematics/computer science,
   organizational communication.

William Woods University
Office of Enrollment Services
One University Avenue
Fulton, MO 65251
Phone: (573) 592-4221
Fax: (573) 592-1146
E-mail: admissions@williamwoods.edu
http://www.williamwoods.edu
Design/visual communications, graphic
   design.

MONTANA

Montana State University—Billings
1500 University Drive
Billings, MT 59101
Phone: (406) 657-2158
Fax: (406) 657-2051

E-mail: keverett@msubillings.edu
http://www.msubillings.edu
Computer programming—specific
   applications, data processing
   technology, drafting and design
   technology.

Montana State University—Bozeman
New Student Services
P.O. Box 172190
Bozeman, MT 59717
Phone: (406) 994-2452
Fax: (406) 994-1923
E-mail: admissions@montana.edu
http://www.montana.edu
Cinematography and film/video
   production, computer engineering,
   electrical and communications
   engineering.

Montana State University—Northern
P.O. Box 7751
Havre, MT 59501
Phone: (406) 265-3704
Fax: (406) 265-3777
E-mail: msuadmit@msun.edu
http://www.msun.edu
Drafting and design technology, electrical
   engineering technology.

**Montana Tech of the University of
   Montana**
1300 West Park Street
Butte, MT 59701
Phone: (406) 496-4178
Fax: (406) 496-4710
E-mail: admissions@mtech.edu
http://www.mtech.edu
Applied mathematics, communications
   technology, computer engineering,
   computer programming—specific
   applications, computer software
   technology, data processing
   technology, electrical and
   communications engineering,
   information technology, LAN/WAN
   management, technical and business
   writing.

University of Great Falls
1301 20th Street South
Great Falls, MT 59405
Phone: (406) 791-5200
Fax: (406) 791-5209
E-mail: enroll@ugf.edu
http://www.ugf.edu
Computer graphics, computer
   programming—specific applications,

data processing technology, LAN/
   WAN management.

University of Montana—Missoula
103 Lodge Building
Missoula, MT 59812
Phone: (406) 243-6266
Fax: (406) 243-5711
E-mail: admiss@selway.umt.edu
http://www.umt.edu
Data processing technology, electrical
   engineering technology, mathematics/
   computer science.

University of Montana—Western
710 South Atlantic
Dillon, MT 59725
Phone: (406) 683-7331
Fax: (406) 683-7493
E-mail: admissions@umwestern.edu
http://www.umwestern.edu
Applied mathematics, information
   technology.

NEBRASKA

Bellevue University
1000 Galvin Road South
Bellevue, NE 68005
Phone: (402) 293-2000
Fax: (402) 293-3730
E-mail: info@bellevue.edu
http://www.bellevue.edu
E-commerce, information technology,
   webpage/multimedia design.

Creighton University
2500 California Plaza
Omaha, NE 68178
Phone: (402) 280-2703
Fax: (402) 280-2685
E-mail: admissions@creighton.edu
http://www.creighton.edu
Applied mathematics, organizational
   communication.

Dana College
2848 College Drive
Blair, NE 68008
Phone: (402) 426-7222
Fax: (402) 426-7386
E-mail: admission@dana.edu
http://www.dana.edu
Animation, webpage/multimedia design,
   organizational communication.

Doane College
1014 Boswell Avenue
Crete, NE 68333

Phone: (402) 826-8222
Fax: (402) 826-8600
E-mail: admissions@doane.edu
http://www.doane.edu
Organizational communication.

Hastings College
800 Turner Avenue
Hastings, NE 68901
Phone: (402) 461-7403
Fax: (402) 461-7490
E-mail: mmollicon@hastings.edu
http://www.hastings.edu
Communications technology.

Nebraska Wesleyan University
Admissions Office
5000 Saint Paul Avenue
Lincoln, NE 68504
Phone: (402) 465-2218
Fax: (402) 465-2177
E-mail: admissions@nebrwesleyan.edu
http://www.nebrwesleyan.edu
Webpage/multimedia design.

University of Nebraska—Lincoln
313 North 13th Street
Van Brunt Visitors Center
Lincoln, NE 68588
Phone: (402) 472-2023
Fax: (402) 472-0670
E-mail: nuhusker@unl.edu
http://www.unl.edu
Computer engineering, electrical and
communications engineering,
electrical engineering technology,
information technology,
telecommunications technology.

University of Nebraska—Omaha
Office of Admissions
6001 Dodge Street, EAB Room 103
Omaha, NE 68182
Phone: (402) 554-2393
Fax: (402) 554-3472
E-mail: unoadm@unomaha.edu
http://www.unomaha.edu
Computer engineering, electrical and
communications engineering,
information technology.

Wayne State College
1111 Main Street
Wayne, NE 68787
Phone: (402) 375-7234
Fax: (402) 375-7204
E-mail: admit1@wsc.edu
http://www.wsc.edu
Graphic design.

NEVADA

Sierra Nevada College
999 Tahoe Boulevard
Incline Village, NV 89451
Phone: (775) 831-1314
Fax: (702) 831-1347
E-mail: admissions@sierranevada.edu
http://www.sierranevada.edu
Computer graphics.

University of Nevada—Las Vegas
4505 Maryland Parkway
P.O. Box 451021
Las Vegas, NV 89154
Phone: (702) 774-8658
Fax: (702) 774-8008
E-mail: undergraduate.recruitment@
ccmail.nevada.edu
http://www.unlv.edu
Applied mathematics, computer
engineering, electrical and
communications engineering, software
engineering.

University of Nevada—Reno
1664 North Virginia Street
Reno, NV 89557
Phone: (775) 784-4700
Fax: (775) 784-4283
E-mail: asknevada@unr.edu
http://www.unr.edu
Electrical and communications
engineering, software engineering.

NEW HAMPSHIRE

Chester College of New England
40 Chester Street
Chester, NH 03036
Phone: (800) 974-6372
Fax: (603) 887-1777
E-mail: At Web site
http://www.chestercollege.edu
Graphic design, webpage/multimedia
design.

Colby-Sawyer College
541 Main Street
New London, NH 03257
Phone: (603) 526-3700
Fax: (603) 526-3452
E-mail: csadmiss@colbysawyer.edu
http://www.colby-sawyer.edu
Graphic design.

Franklin Pierce College
Admissions Office
P.O. Box 60
20 College Road
Rindge, NH 03461

Phone: (603) 899-4050
Fax: (603) 889-4394
E-mail: admissions@fpc.edu
http://www.fpc.edu
Computer graphics, design/visual
communications, information
technology.

Keene State College
229 Main Street
Keene, NH 03435
Phone: (603) 358-2276
Fax: (603) 358-2767
E-mail: admissions@keene.edu
http://www.keene.edu
Applied mathematics, graphic design,
mathematics/computer science.

Plymouth State University
17 High Street, MSC 52
Plymouth, NH 03264
Phone: (603) 535-2237
Fax: (603) 535-2714
E-mail: plymouthadmit@plymouth.edu
http://www.plymouth.edu
Information technology.

Rivier College
420 Main Street
Nashua, NH 03060
Phone: (603) 897-8507
Fax: (603) 891-1799
E-mail: rivadmit@rivier.edu
http://www.rivier.edu
Design/visual communications,
mathematics/computer science.

Southern New Hampshire University
2500 North River Road
Manchester, NH 03108
Phone: (603) 645-9611
Fax: (603) 645-9693
E-mail: admission@snhu.edu
http://www.snhu.edu
Sales/distribution.

University of New Hampshire—Durham
4 Garrison Avenue
Durham, NH 03024
Phone: (603) 862-1360
Fax: (603) 862-0077
E-mail: admissions@unh.edu
http://www.unh.edu
Computer engineering, drafting and
design technology, electrical and
communications engineering,

**University of New Hampshire—
Manchester**
400 Commercial Street
Manchester, NH 03101

Phone: (603) 629-4150
Fax: (603) 629-2745
E-mail: unhm-admissions@unh.edu
http://www.unh.edu/unhm
Computer engineering, drafting and design technology, electrical and communications engineering, electrical engineering technology.

NEW JERSEY

The College of New Jersey
P.O. Box 7718
Ewing, NJ 08628
Phone: (609) 771-2131
Fax: (609) 637-5174
E-mail: admiss@vm.tcj.edu
http://www.tcnj.edu
Computer engineering.

Farleigh Dickinson University—College at Florham
285 Madison Avenue
Madison, NJ 07940
Phone: (800) 338-8803
Fax: (973) 443-8088
E-mail: globaleducation@fdu.edu
http://www.fdu.edu
Cinematography and film/video production, computer engineering, sales/distribution.

Farleigh Dickinson University—Metropolitan Campus
1000 River Road
Teaneck, NJ 07666
Phone: (201) 692-2553
Fax: (201) 692-7319
E-mail: globaleducation@fdu.edu
http://www.fdu.edu
Electrical and communications engineering, electrical engineering technology, sales/distribution.

Kean University
P.O. Box 411
Union, NJ 07083
Phone: (908) 737-7100
Fax: (908) 737-7105
E-mail: admitme@kean.edu
http://www.kena.edu
Design/visual communications.

New Jersey Institute of Technology
University Heights
Newark, NJ 07102
Phone: (973) 596-3300
Fax: (973) 596-3461
E-mail: admissions@njit.edu
http://www.njit.edu
Applied mathematics, computer engineering, electrical and communications engineering, technical and business writing.

Princeton University
P.O. Box 430, Admission Office
Princeton, NJ 08544
Phone: (609) 258-3060
Fax: (609) 258-6743
E-mail: uaoffice@princeton.edu
http://www.princeton.edu
Computer engineering, electrical and communications engineering.

Ramapo College of New Jersey
505 Ramapo Valley Road
Mahwah, NJ 07430
Phone: (201) 684-7300
Fax: (201) 684-7964
E-mail: admissions@ramapo.edu
http://www.ramapo.edu
Multimedia.

Rowan University
201 Mullica Hill Road
Glassboro, NJ 08028
Phone: (856) 256-4200
Fax: (856) 256-4430
E-mail: admissions@rowan.edu
http://www.rowan.edu
Communications technology, data processing technology, electrical and communications engineering.

Rutgers, The State University of New Jersey—Newark
249 University Avenue
Newark, NJ 07102
Phone: (973) 353-5205
Fax: (973) 353-1440
E-mail: newarkadmission@ugadm.rutgers.edu
http://www.rutgers.edu
Applied mathematics, electrical and communications engineering.

Rutgers, The State University of New Jersey—University College at New Brunswick
65 Davidson Road
Piscataway, NJ 08854
Phone: (732) 932-4636
Fax: (732) 445-0237
E-mail: admissions@ugadm.rutgers.edu
http://www.rutgers.edu
Electrical and communications engineering.

Stevens Institute of Technology
Castle Point on Hudson
Hoboken, NJ 07030
Phone: (201) 216-5194
Fax: (201) 216-8348
E-mail: admissions@stevens.edu
http://www.stevens.edu
Applied mathematics, computer engineering, computer graphics, design/visual communications, electrical and communications engineering, mathematics/computer science, software engineering, webpage/multimedia design.

Thomas Edison State College
101 West State Street
Trenton, NJ 08608
Phone: (609) 984-1150
Fax: (609) 984-8447
E-mail: info@tesc.edu
http://www.tesc.edu
E-commerce.

NEW MEXICO

College of Santa Fe
1600 St. Michaels Drive
Santa Fe, NM 87505
Phone: (505) 473-6133
Fax: (505) 473-6129
E-mail: admissions@csf.edu
http://www.csf.edu
Multimedia, technical and business writing.

New Mexico Highlands University
NMHU Office of Student Recruitment
P.O. Box 900
Las Vegas, NM 87701
Phone: (505) 454-3593
Fax: (505) 454-3511
E-mail: recruitment@nmhu.edu
http://www.nmhu.edu
Design/visual communications.

New Mexico Institute of Mining and Technology
Campus Station
801 Leroy Place
Socorro, NM 87801
Phone: (505) 835-5424
Fax: (505) 835-5989
E-mail: admission@admin.nmt.edu
http://www.nmt.edu
Applied mathematics, information technology, technical and business writing.

New Mexico State University
P.O. Box 30001, MSC 3A
Las Cruces, NM 88003
Phone: (505) 646-3121
Fax: (505) 646-6330
E-mail: admissions@nmsu.edu
http://www.nmsu.edu
Computer engineering, electrical and
   communications engineering,
   electrical engineering technology,
   photographic/film/video technology.

San Juan College
4601 College Boulevard
Farmington, NM 87402
Phone: (505) 566-3318
Fax: (505) 566-3500
E-mail: At Web site
http://www.sjc.cc.nm.us
Communications technology, computer
   graphics, data processing technology.

University of New Mexico
Office of Admissions
Student Services Center 150
Albuquerque, NM 87131
Phone: (505) 277-2446
Fax: (505) 277-6686
E-mail: apply@unm.edu
http://www.unm.edu
Computer engineering, electrical and
   communications engineering.

Western New Mexico University
P.O. Box 680
Silver City, NM 88062
Phone: (800) 872-9668
Fax: (505) 538-6127
E-mail: At Web site
http://www.wnmu.edu
Drafting and design technology.

NEW YORK

Alfred University
Alumni Hall
1 Saxon Drive
Alfred, NY 14802
Phone: (607) 871-2115
Fax: (607) 871-2198
E-mail: admwww@alfred.edu
http://www.alfred.edu
Electrical and communications
   engineering, mathematics/computer
   science.

Bard College
Office of Admissions
Annandale-on-Hudson, NY 12504

Phone: (845) 758-7472
Fax: (845) 758-5208
E-mail: admissions@bard.edu
http://www.bard.edu
Cinematography and film/video
   production, multimedia, playwriting/
   screenwriting.

Barnard College
3090 Broadway
New York, NY 10027
Phone: (212) 854-2014
Fax: (212) 854-6220
E-mail: admissions@barnard.edu
http://www.barnard.edu
Applied mathematics.

Canisius College
2001 Main Street
Buffalo, NY 14208
Phone: (716) 888-2200
Fax: (716) 888-3230
E-mail: inquiry@canisius.edu
http://www.canisius.edu
Digital media, information technology.

Cazenovia College
13 Nickerson Street
Cazenovia, NY 13035
Phone: (315) 655-7208
Fax: (315) 655-4860
E-mail: admissions@cazenovia.edu
http://www.cazenovia.edu
Design/visual communications.

**City University of New York—
   Baruch College**
Undergraduate Admissions
1 Bernard Baruch Way
P.O. Box H-0720
New York, NY 10010
Phone: (646) 312-1400
Fax: (646) 312-1361
E-mail: admissions@baruch.cuny.edu
http://www.baruch.cuny.edu
Design/visual communications, sales/
   distribution.

**City University of New York—
   Brooklyn College**
3000 Bedford Avenue
Brooklyn, NY 11210
Phone: (718) 951-5001
Fax: (718) 951-4506
E-mail: adminqry@brooklyn.cuny.edu
http://www.brooklyn.cuny.edu
Cinematography and film/video
   production, computer graphics,
   mathematics/computer science,

multimedia, playwriting/
   screenwriting.

**City University of New York—
   City College**
Convent Avenue at 138th Street
New York, NY 10031
Phone: (212) 650-6977
Fax: (212) 650-6417
E-mail: admissions@ccny.cuny.edu
http://www.ccny.cuny.edu
Cinematography and film/video
   production, computer engineering,
   electrical and communications
   engineering, graphic design.

**City University of New York—College
   of Staten Island**
2800 Victory Boulevard, Building 2A,
   Room 104
Staten Island, NY 10314
Phone: (718) 982-2010
Fax: (718) 982-2500
E-mail: recruitment@postbox.csi.cuny.edu
http://www.csi.cuny.edu
Cinematography and film/video
   production.

**City University of New York—
   Hunter College**
695 Park Avenue
New York, NY 10021
Phone: (212) 772-4490
Fax: (212) 650-3336
E-mail: admissions@hunter.cuny.edu
http://www.hunter.cuny.edu
Cinematography and film/video
   production.

**City University of New York—
   Lehman College**
350 Bedford Park Boulevard West
Bronx, NY 10468
Phone: (718) 960-8000
Fax: (718) 960-8712
E-mail: wilkes@alpha.lehman.cuny.edu
http://www.lehman.cuny.edu
Computer graphics.

**City University of New York—
   New York City College of Technology**
300 Jay Street, NG17
Brooklyn, NY 11201
Phone: (718) 260-5500
Fax: (718) 260-5504
E-mail: admissions@citytech.cuny.edu
http://www.citytech.cuny.edu
Data processing technology, drafting and
   design technology.

Clarkson University
P.O. Box 5605
Potsdam, NY 13699
Phone: (315) 268-6479
Fax: (315) 268-7647
E-mail: admission@clarkson.edu
http://www.clarkson.edu
Applied mathematics, computer
   engineering, digital media,
   e-commerce, electrical and
   communications engineering, software
   engineering.

Colgate University
13 Oak Drive
Hamilton, NY 13346
Phone: (315) 228-7401
Fax: (315) 228-7544
E-mail: admission@mail.colgate.edu
http://www.colgate.edu
Mathematics/computer science.

Columbia University—
   Columbia College
212 Hamilton Hall MC 2807
1130 Amsterdam Avenue
New York, NY 10027
Phone: (212) 854-2521
Fax: (212) 894-1209
E-mail: At Web site
http://www.college.columbia.edu
Applied mathematics.

Columbia University—Fu Foundation
   School of Engineering and Applied
   Science
212 Hamilton Hall, MC 2807
1130 Amsterdam Avenue
New York, NY 10027
Phone: (212) 854-2521
Fax: (212) 894-1209
E-mail: ugrad-ask@columbia.edu
http://www.engineering.columbia.edu
Applied mathematics, computer
   engineering, electrical and
   communications engineering.

Cornell University
Undergraduate Admissions
410 Thurston Avenue
Ithaca, NY 14850
Phone: (607) 255-5241
Fax: (607) 255-0659
E-mail: admissions@cornell.edu
http://www.cornell.edu
Applied mathematics, cognitive science,
   electrical and communications
   engineering, organizational
   communication.

Daemen College
4380 Main Street
Amherst, NY 14226
Phone: (716) 839-8225
Fax: (716) 839-8229
E-mail: admissions@daemen.edu
http://www.daemen.edu
Graphic design.

DeVry Institute of Technology
3020 Thomson Avenue
Long Island City, NY 11101
Phone: (718) 472-2728
Fax: (718) 361-0004
E-mail: leads@ny.devry.edu
http://www.devry.edu
Electrical engineering technology,
   information technology.

Eugene Lang College/New School
   University
Office of Admission
65 West Eleventh Street
New York, NY 10011
Phone: (212) 229-5665
Fax: (212) 229-5166
E-mail: lang@newschool.edu
http://www.lang.edu
Design/visual communications.

Five Towns College
305 North Service Road
Dix Hills, NY 11746
Phone: (631) 424-7000
Fax: (631) 424-7008
E-mail: admissions@ftc.edu
http://www.fivetowns.edu
Cinematography and film/video
   production, communications
   technology, recording arts.

Hobart and William Smith College
629 South Main Street
Geneva, NY 14456
Phone: (315) 781-3472
Fax: (315) 781-3471
E-mail: admissions@hws.edu
http://www.hws.edu
Mathematics/computer science.

Hofstra University
Admission Center
Bernon Hall
1000 Fulton Avenue
Hempstead, NY 11549
Phone: (516) 463-6700
Fax: (516) 463-5100
E-mail: admitme@hofstra.edu
http://www.hofstra.edu

Applied mathematics, cinematography
   and film/video production,
   computer engineering, electrical
   and communications engineering,
   mathematics/computer science.

Iona College
715 North Avenue
New Rochelle, NY 10801
Phone: (914) 633-2502
Fax: (914) 633-2642
E-mail: icad@iona.edu
http://www.iona.edu
Applied mathematics.

Ithaca College
100 Job Hall
Ithaca, NY 14850
Phone: (607) 274-3124
Fax: (607) 274-1900
E-mail: admission@ithaca.edu
http://www.ithaca.edu
Cinematography and film/video
   production, information technology,
   recording arts.

Long Island University—C. W. Post
   Campus
720 Northern Boulevard
Brookville, NY 11548
Phone: (516) 299-2900
Fax: (519) 299-2137
E-mail: enroll@cwpost.liu.edu
http://www.liu.edu
Applied mathematics, cinematography
   and film/video production,
   multimedia.

Manhattan College
Manhattan College Parkway
Riverdale, NY 10471
Phone: (718) 862-7200
Fax: (718) 862-8019
E-mail: admit@manhattan.edu
http://www.manhattan.edu
Electrical and communications
   engineering.

Marist College
3399 North Road
Poughkeepsie, NY 12601
Phone: (845) 575-3226
Fax: (845) 575-3215
E-mail: admissions@marist.edu
http://www.marist.edu
Animation, computer engineering,
   computer graphics, computer
   programming—specific applications,
   digital media, graphic design,

information technology, mathematics/ computer science, organizational communication, web/multimedia management, webpage/multimedia design.

Medaille College
18 Agassiz Circle
Buffalo, NY 14214
Phone: (716) 884-3281
Fax: (716) 884-0291
E-mail: jmatheny@medaille.edu
http://www.medaille.edu
Technical and business writing, webpage/ multimedia design.

Mount Saint Mary College
330 Powell Avenue
Newburgh, NY 12550
Phone: (845) 569-3248
Fax: (845) 562-6762
E-mail: mtstmary@msmc.edu
http://www.msmc.edu
Information technology.

New York Institute of Technology
P.O. Box 8000
Northern Boulevard
Old Westbury, NY 11568
Phone: (516) 686-7520
Fax: (516) 686-7613
E-mail: admissions@nyit.edu
http://www.nyit.edu
Communications technology, computer engineering, computer graphics, data processing technology, electrical and communications engineering, technical and business writing.

New York University
22 Washington Square North
New York, NY 10011
Phone: (212) 998-4500
Fax: (212) 995-4902
E-mail: admissions@nyu.edu
http://www.nyu.edu
Cinematography and film/video production, communications technology, digital media, playwriting/ screenwriting.

Pace University
1 Pace Plaza
New York, NY 10038
Phone: (212) 346-1323
Fax: (212) 346-1040
E-mail: infoctr@pace.edu
http://www.pace.edu
Data processing technology.

Pace University—Pleasantville/ Briarcliff
861 Bedford Road
Pleasantville, NY 10570
Phone: (914) 773-3746
Fax: (914) 773-3851
E-mail: infotr@pace.edu
http://www.pace.edu
Data processing technology, mathematics/ computer science.

Parsons School of Design/New School University
66 Fifth Avenue
New York, NY 10011
Phone: (877) 528-3321
Fax: (212) 229-5166
E-mail: inquiry@newschool.edu
http://www.parsons.edu
Design/visual communications.

Polytechnic University
6 Metrotech Center
Brooklyn, NY 11201
Phone: (718) 260-3100
Fax: (718) 260-3446
E-mail: admitme@poly.edu
http://www.poly.edu
Computer engineering, electrical and communications engineering.

Pratt Institute
200 Willoughby Avenue
Brooklyn, NY 11205
Phone: (718) 636-3660
Fax: (718) 636-3670
E-mail: admissions@pratt.edu
http://www.pratt.edu
Cinematography and film/video production, computer graphics, graphic design, illustration.

Rensselaer Polytechnic Institute
110 Eighth Street
Troy, NY 12180
Phone: (518) 276-6216
Fax: (518) 276-4072
E-mail: arpi.edu
http://www.rpi.edu
Computer engineering, digital media, electrical and communications engineering, information technology.

Rochester Institute of Technology
60 Lomb Memorial Drive
Rochester, NY 14623
Phone: (585) 475-6631
Fax: (585) 475-7424
E-mail: admissions@rit.edu

http://www.rit.edu
Animation, applied mathematics, cinematography and film/video production, computer engineering, computer graphics, computer programming—specific applications, design/visual communications, digital media, electrical and communications engineering, electrical engineering technology, graphic design, illustration, information technology, LAN/WAN management, mathematics/computer science, software engineering, telecommunications technology, web/ multimedia management, webpage/ multimedia design.

Saint Francis College
180 Remsen Street
Brooklyn Heights, NY 11201
Phone: (718) 489-5200
Fax: (718) 802-0453
E-mail: admissions@stfranciscollege.edu
http://www.stfranciscollege.edu
Data processing technology, information technology.

St. John's University
8000 Utopia Parkway
Jamaica, NY 11439
Phone: (718) 990-2000
Fax: (718) 990-5728
E-mail: admissions@stjohns.edu
http://www.stjohns.edu
Accounting/computer science, cinematography and film/video production, communications technology, data processing technology.

St. Lawrence University
23 Romoda Drive
Canton, NY 13617
Phone: (800) 285-1856
Fax: NA
E-mail: admissions@stlawu.edu
http://www.stlawu.edu
Mathematics/computer science.

Saint Thomas Aquinas College
125 Route 340
Sparkill, NY 10976
Phone: (845) 398-4100
Fax: (845) 398-4224
E-mail: admissions@stac.edu
http://www.stac.edu
Applied mathematics, graphic design, mathematics/computer science.

Sarah Lawrence College
One Mead Way
Bronxville, NY 10708
Phone: (914) 395-2510
Fax: (914) 395-2676
E-mail: slcadmit@slc.edu
http://www.slc.edu
Cinematography and film/video
    production, playwriting/screenwriting.

School of Visual Arts
209 East 23rd Street
New York, NY 10010
Phone: (212) 592-2100
Fax: (212) 592-2116
E-mail: admissions@sva.edu
http://www.sva.edu
Cinematography and film/video
    production, design/visual
    communications.

Siena College
515 Loudon Road
Loudonville, NY 12211
Phone: (518) 783-2423
Fax: (518) 783-2436
E-mail: admit@siena.edu
http://www.siena.edu
Applied mathematics, data processing
    technology.

State University of New York at Albany
Office of Undergraduate Admissions
1400 Washington Avenue
Albany, NY 12222
Phone: (518) 442-5435
Fax: (518) 442-5383
E-mail: ugadmissions@albany.edu
http://www.albany.edu
Applied mathematics.

**State University of New York at
    Binghamton**
P.O. Box 6001
Binghamton, NY 13902
Phone: (607) 777-2171
Fax: (607) 777-4445
E-mail: admit@binghamton.edu
http://www.binghamton.edu
Computer engineering, electrical and
    communications engineering.

**State University of New York at
    Stony Brook**
Office of Admissions
Stony Brook, NY 11794
Phone: (631) 632-6868
Fax: (631) 632-9898
E-mail: enroll@stonybrook.edu

http://www.stonybrook.edu
Applied mathematics, electrical and
    communications engineering.

**State University of New York College
    at Buffalo**
1300 Elmwood Avenue
Buffalo, NY 14222
Phone: (716) 878-4017
Fax: (716) 878-6100
E-mail: admissions@buffalostate.edu
http://www.buffalostate.edu
Computer engineering, electrical and
    communications engineering,
    electrical engineering technology.

**State University of New York College at
    Cortland**
P.O. Box 2000
Cortland, NY 13045
Phone: (607) 753-4712
Fax: (607) 753-5998
E-mail: admissions@cortland.edu
http://www.cortland.edu
Organizational communication.

**State University of New York College at
    New Paltz**
75 South Manheim Boulevard, Suite 1
New Paltz, NY 12561
Phone: (845) 257-3200
Fax: (914) 257-3209
E-mail: admissions@newpaltz.edu
http://www.newpaltz.edu
Computer engineering, electrical and
    communications engineering.

**State University of New York College at
    Oneonta**
Alumni Hall 116
State University College
Oneonta, NY 13820
Phone: (607) 436-2524
Fax: (607) 436-3074
E-mail: admissions@oneonta.edu
http://www.oneonta.edu
Animation, computer graphics,
    multimedia.

**State University of New York College
    at Oswego**
211 Culkin Hall
Oswego, NY 13126
Phone: (315) 312-2250
Fax: (315) 312-3260
E-mail: admiss@oswego.edu
http://www.oswego.edu
Applied mathematics.

**State University of New York College at
    Plattsburgh**
1001 Kehoe Building
Plattsburgh, NY 12091
Phone: (518) 564-2040
Fax: (518) 564-2045
E-mail: admissions@plattsburgh.edu
http://www.plattsburgh.edu
Communications technology.

**State University of New York College at
    Purchase**
Admissions Office
735 Anderson Hill Road
Purchase, NY 10577
Phone: (914) 251-6300
Fax: (914) 251-6314
E-mail: admissn@purchase.edu
http://www.purchase.edu
Cinematography and film/video
    production, mathematics/computer
    science, playwriting/screenwriting.

**State University of New York College
    of Agriculture and Technology at
    Cobleskill**
Office of Admissions
Cobleskill, NY 12043
Phone: (518) 255-5525
Fax: (518) 255-6769
E-mail: admissions@cobleskill.edu
http://www.cobleskill.edu
Computer engineering, computer
    programming—specific applications,
    data processing technology, electrical
    engineering technology.

**State University of New York College of
    Technology at Alfred**
Huntington Administration Building
Alfred, NY 14802
Phone: (800) 425-3733
Fax: (607) 587-4299
E-mail: admissions@alfredstate.edu
http://www.alfredstate.edu
Electrical and communications
    engineering.

Syracuse University
201 Tolley
Administration Building
Syracuse, NY 13244
Phone: (315) 443-3611
Fax: (315) 443-4226
E-mail: orange@syr.edu
http://www.syracuse.edu
Cinematography and film/video
    production, computer engineering,
    computer graphics, electrical and

communications engineering, graphic design, illustration, information technology.

Union College
Grant Hall, Union College
Schenectady, NY 12308
Phone: (518) 388-6112
Fax: (518) 388-6986
E-mail: admissions@union.edu
http://www.union.edu
Electrical and communications engineering.

University of Rochester
300 Wilson Boulevard
P.O. Box 270251
Rochester, NY 14627
Phone: (585) 275-3221
Fax: (585) 461-4595
E-mail: admit@admissions.rochester.edu
http://www.rochester.edu
Applied mathematics, electrical and communications engineering.

Utica College of Syracuse University
1600 Burnstone Road
Utica, NY 13502
Phone: (315) 792-3006
Fax: (315) 792-3003
E-mail: admiss@utica.ucsu.edu
http://www.utica.edu
Electrical and communications engineering.

Vassar College
124 Raymond Avenue
Poughkeepsie, NY 12604
Phone: (845) 437-7300
Fax: (845) 437-7063
E-mail: admissions@vassar.edu
http://www.vassar.edu
Cognitive science.

NORTH CAROLINA

Appalachian State University
Office of Admissions
P.O. Box 32004
Boone, NC 28608
Phone: (828) 262-2120
Fax: (828) 262-3296
E-mail: admissions@appstate.edu
http://www.appstate.edu
Electrical and communications engineering.

Campbell University
P.O. Box 546
Buies Creek, NC 27506

Phone: (910) 893-1320
Fax: (910) 893-1288
E-mail: adm@mailcenter.campbell.edu
http://www.campbell.edu
Computer graphics, computer programming—specific applications.

Chowan College
200 Jones Drive
Murfreesboro, NC 27855
Phone: (252) 398-1236
Fax: (252) 398-1190
E-mail: admissions@chowan.edu
http://www.chowan.edu
Graphic design.

Duke University
2138 Campus Drive
Durham, NC 27708
Phone: (919) 684-3214
Fax: (919) 681-8941
E-mail: undergrad.admissions@duke.edu
http://www.duke.edu
Design/visual communications, electrical and communications engineering.

Elon University
2700 Campus Box
Elon, NC 27244
Phone: (336) 278-3566
Fax: (336) 278-7699
E-mail: admissions@elon.edu
http://www.elon.edu
Computer engineering.

Johnson C. Smith University
100 Beatties Ford Road
Charlotte, NC 28216
Phone: (704) 378-1011
Fax: (704) 378-01242
E-mail: admissions@jcsu.edu
http://www.jcsu.edu
Applied mathematics, computer engineering.

Mount Olive College
634 Henderson Street
Mount Olive, NC 29365
Phone: (919) 658-7164
Fax: (919) 658-7180
E-mail: admissions@moc.edu
http://www.moc.edu
Design/visual communications.

North Carolina A&T University
1601 East Market Street
Greensboro, NC 27411
Phone: (336) 334-7946
Fax: (336) 334-7478

E-mail: uadmit@ncat.edu
http://www.ncat.edu
Electrical and communications engineering.

North Carolina Central University
1891 Fayetteville Street
Durham, NC 27707
Phone: (919) 560-6298
Fax: (919) 530-7625
E-mail: ebridges@wpo.nccu.edu
http://www.nccu.edu
Design/visual communications.

North Carolina School of the Arts
1433 South Main Street
P.O. Box 12189
Winston-Salem, NC 27127
Phone: (336) 770-3290
Fax: (336) 770-3370
E-mail: admissions@ncarts.edu
http://wwwncarts.edu
Cinematography and film/video production.

North Carolina State University
P.O. Box 7103
Raleigh, NC 27695
Phone: (919) 515-2434
Fax: (919) 515-5039
E-mail: undergrad_admissions@ncsu.edu
http://www.ncsu.edu
Applied mathematics, computer engineering.

Peace College
15 East Peace Street
Raleigh, NC 27604
Phone: (800) 732-2306
Fax: (919) 508-2306
E-mail: mmcleery@peace.edu
http://www.peace.edu
Design/visual communications.

Saint Augustine's College
1315 Oakwood Avenue
Raleigh, NC 27610
Phone: (919) 516-4016
Fax: (919) 516-5805
E-mail: admissions@st-aug.edu
http://www.st-aug.edu
Applied mathematics, cinematography and film/video production.

Queen's University of Charlotte
1900 Selwyn Avenue
Charlotte, NC 28274
Phone: (704) 337-2212
Fax: (704) 337-2403

E-mail: admissions@queens.edu
http://www.queens.edu
Organizational communication.

**University of North Carolina—
    Chapel Hill**
Office of Undergraduate Admissions
Jackson Hall 153A
Campus P.O. Box 2220
Chapel Hill, NC 27599
Phone: (919) 966-3621
Fax: (919) 962-3045
E-mail: uadm@email.unc.edu
http://www.unc.edu
Applied mathematics.

**University of North Carolina—
    Charlotte**
9201 University City Boulevard
Charlotte, NC 28223
Phone: (704) 687-2213
Fax: (704) 687-6483
E-mail: uncadm@email.uncc.edu
http://www.uncc.edu
Computer engineering, electrical and
    communications engineering,
    electrical engineering technology.

**University of North Carolina—
    Greensboro**
123 Mossman Building
Greensboro, NC 27402
Phone: (336) 334-5243
Fax: (336) 334-4180
E-mail: undergrad_admissions@uncg.
    edu
http://www.uncg.edu
Cinematography and film/video
    production.

**University of North Carolina—
    Pembroke**
One University Drive
P.O. Box 1510
Pembroke, NC 28372
Phone: (910) 521-6262
Fax: (910) 521-6407
E-mail: admissions@papa.uncp.edu
http://www.uncp.edu
Mathematics/computer science.

Western Carolina University
232 HFR Administration
Cullowhee, NC 28723
Phone: (828) 227-7317
Fax: (828) 227-7319
E-mail: cauley@emai.wcu.edu
http://www.wcu.edu
Electrical engineering technology.

Wingate University
Campus Box 3059
Wingate, NC 28174
Phone: (704) 223-8200
Fax: (704) 233-8130
E-mail: admit@wingate.edu
http://www.wingate.edu
Mathematics/computer science.

NORTH DAKOTA

Jamestown College
6081 College Lane
Jamestown, ND 58405
Phone: (701) 252-3467
Fax: (701) 253-4318
E-mail: admissions@jc.edu
http://www.jc.edu
Applied mathematics.

Minot State University—Minot
500 University Avenue
West Minot, ND 58707
Phone: (701) 858-3350
Fax: (701) 858-3386
E-mail: msu@minotstateu.edu
http://www.minotstateu.edu
Communications technology.

North Dakota State University
P.O. Box 5454
Fargo, ND 58105
Phone: (701) 231-8643
Fax: (701) 231-8802
E-mail: ndsu.admission@ndsu.nodak.edu
http://www.ndsu.edu
Computer engineering, electrical and
    communications engineering.

University of North Dakota
Enrollment Services
Twamley Hall Room 312
P.O. Box 8135
Grand Forks, ND 58202
Phone: (701) 777-4463
Fax: (701) 777-2696
E-mail: enrolser@sase.und.nodak.edu
http://www.und.edu
Electrical and communications
    engineering.

OHIO

Antioch College
795 Livermore Street
Yellow Springs, OH 45387
Phone: (937) 769-1100
Fax: (937) 769-1111
E-mail: admissions@antioch-college.edu

http://www.antioch-college.edu
Cinematography and film/video
    production, mathematics/computer
    science.

Bowling Green State University
110 McFall Center
Bowling Green, OH 43403
Phone: (419) 372-2478
Fax: (419) 372-6955
E-mail: admissions@bgnet.bgsu.edu
http://www.bgsu.edu
Design/visual communications, digital
    media, electrical engineering
    technology, quality control technology,
    technical and business writing.

Brescia University
717 Frederica Street
Owensboro, KY 42301
Phone: (270) 686-4241
Fax: (270) 686-4314
E-mail: admissions@brescia.edu
http://www.brescia.edu
Mathematics/computer science.

Capital University
Admission Office, Yochum Hall
1 College and Main
Columbus, OH 43209
Phone: (614) 236-6101
Fax: (614) 236-6926
E-mail: admissions@capital.edu
http://www.capital.edu
Technical and business writing.

Case Western Reserve University
103 Tomlinson Hall
10900 Euclid Avenue
Cleveland, OH 44106
Phone: (216) 368-4450
Fax: (216) 368-5111
E-mail: admission@case.edu
http://www.case.edu
Applied mathematics, computer
    engineering, electrical and
    communications engineering.

Cedarville University
251 North Main Street
Cedarville, OH 45314
Phone: (937) 766-7700
Fax: (937) 766-7575
E-mail: admissions@cedarville.edu
http://www.cedarville.edu
Communications technology, computer
    engineering, electrical and
    communications engineering, graphic
    design, technical and business writing.

Cleveland State University
East 24th and Euclid Avenue
Cleveland, OH 44114
Phone: (216) 687-2100
Fax: (216) 687-9210
E-mail: admissions@csuohio.edu
http://www.csuohio.edu
Electrical and communications
    engineering, electrical engineering
    technology.

College of Mount Saint Joseph
5701 Delhi Road
Cincinnati, OH 45233
Phone: (513) 244-4531
Fax: (513) 244-4629
E-mail: peggy_minnich@mail.msj.edu
http://www.msj.edu
Mathematics/computer science.

Denison University
P.O. Box H
Granville, OH 43023
Phone: (740) 587-6276
Fax: (740) 587-6306
E-mail: admissions@denison.edu
http://www.denison.edu
Digital media.

DeVry University—Columbus
1350 Alum Creek Drive
Columbus, OH 43209
Phone: (614) 253-1525
Fax: (614) 253-0843
E-mail: admissions@devry.edu
http://www.devry.edu
Electrical engineering technology,
    information technology.

Franklin University
201 South Grant Avenue
Columbus, OH 43215
Phone: (614) 797-4700
Fax: (614) 224-8027
E-mail: info@franklin.edu
http://www.franklin.edu
Digital media.

Hiram College
P.O. Box 96
Hiram, OH 44234
Phone: (330) 569-5169
Fax: (330) 569-5944
E-mail: admission@hiram.edu
http://www.hiram.edu
Mathematics/computer science.

Kent State University
161 Michael Schwartz
Kent, OH 44242

Phone: (330) 672-2444
Fax: (330) 672-2499
E-mail: kentadm@admissions.kent.edu
http://www.knet.edu
Animation, applied mathematics,
    computer graphics, computer
    programming—specific applications,
    design/visual communications, digital
    media, electrical and communications
    engineering, electrical engineering
    technology, illustration, information
    technology, quality control
    technology.

Malone College
515 25th Street NW
Canton, OH 44709
Phone: (330) 471-8145
Fax: (330) 471-8149
E-mail: admissions@malone.edu
http://www.malone.edu
Recording arts.

Marietta College
215 Fifth Street
Marietta, OH 45750
Phone: (740) 376-4600
Fax: (740) 376-8888
E-mail: admit@marietta.edu
http://www.marietta.edu
Organizational communication.

**Miami University—Middletown
    Campus**
4200 East University Boulevard
Middletown, OH 45042
Phone: (513) 727-3200
Fax: NA
E-mail: mumadmission@muohio.edu
http://www.mid.muohio.edu
Computer programming—specific
    applications, electrical engineering
    technology.

Miami University—Oxford Campus
301 South Campus Avenue
Oxford, OH 45056
Phone: (513) 529-2531
Fax: (513) 529-1550
E-mail: admissions@muohio.edu
http://www.muohio.edu
Sales/distribution.

Mount Union College
1972 Clark Avenue
Alliance, OH 44601
Phone: (800) 334-6682
Fax: (330) 823-3457
E-mail: admissn@muc.edu

http://www.muc.ed
Design/visual communications, digital
    media, technical and business writing.

Mount Vernon Nazarene University
800 Martinsburg Road
Mount Vernon, OH 43050
Phone: (740) 392-6868
Fax: (740) 393-0511
E-mail: admissions@mvnu.edu
http://www.mvnu.edu
Data processing technology, design/visual
    communications.

Ohio Dominican University
1216 Sunbury Road
Columbus, OH 42319
Phone: (614) 251-4500
Fax: (614) 251-0156
E-mail: admissions@ohiodominican.
    edu
http://www.ohiodominican.edu
Graphic design.

Ohio Northern University
525 South Main Street
Ada, OH 45810
Phone: (419) 772-2260
Fax: (419) 772-2313
E-mail: admissions-ug@onu.edu
http://www.onu.edu
Computer engineering, computer
    graphics, electrical and
    communications engineering,
    organizational communication,
    technical and business writing.

Ohio State University—Columbus
Third Floor Lincoln Tower
1800 Cannon Drive
Columbus, OH 43210
Phone: (614) 292-3980
Fax: (614) 292-4818
E-mail: askabuckeye@osu.edu
http://www.osu.edu
Computer engineering, design/visual
    communications, electrical and
    communications engineering.
Ohio University—Athens
120 Chubb Hall
Athens, OH 45701
Phone: (740) 593-4100
Fax: (740) 593-0560
E-mail: admissions.freshmen@ohiou.edu
http://www.ohiou.edu
Applied mathematics, cinematography
    and film/video production,
    computer engineering, design/visual
    communications, illustration.

Ohio University—Southern
Office of Enrollment Services
1804 Liberty Avenue
Ironton, OH 45638
Phone: (740) 533-4600
Fax: (740) 533-4632
E-mail: askousc@mail_southern.ohiou.
edu
http://www.southern.ohiou.edu
Applied mathematics, computer
engineering, design/visual
communications, illustration.

Ohio University—Zanesville
Office of Admissions
1425 Newark Road
Zanesville, OH 43701
Phone: (740) 588-1439
Fax: (740) 588-1444
E-mail: tumbling@ohiou.edu
http://www.zanesville.ohiou.edu
Digital media, illustration, organizational
communication.

Shawnee State University
940 Second Street
Portsmouth, OH 45662
Phone: (740) 351-4SSU
Fax: (740) 351-3111
E-mail: to_ssu@shawnee.edu
http://www.shawnee.edu
Data processing technology.

University of Akron
381 Buchtel Common
Akron, OH 44325
Phone: (330) 972-7100
Fax: (330) 972-7022
E-mail: admissions@uakron.edu
http://www.uakron.edu
Applied mathematics, computer
engineering, data processing
technology, drafting and design
technology, electrical and
communications engineering,
electrical engineering technology,
graphic design, mathematics/computer
science.

University of Cincinnati
P.O. Box 210091
Cincinnati, OH 45221
Phone: (513) 556-1100
Fax: (513) 556-1105
E-mail: admissions@uc.edu
http://www.uc.edu
Computer engineering, design/visual
communications, information
technology.

University of Dayton
300 College Park
Dayton, OH 45469
Phone: (937) 229-4411
Fax: (937) 229-4729
E-mail: admission@udayton.edu
http://www.udayton.edu
Computer engineering, digital media,
electrical engineering technology.

University of Findlay
1000 North Main Street
Findlay, OH 45840
Phone: (419) 424-4732
Fax: (419) 434-4898
E-mail: admissions@findlay.edu
http://www.findlay.edu
Cinematography and film/video
production, communications
technology, LAN/WAN management,
multimedia.

University of Northwestern Ohio
1441 North Cable Road
Lima, OH 45805
Phone: (419) 998-3120
Fax: (419) 229-6926
E-mail: info@unoh.edu
http://www.unoh.edu
Computer programming—specific
applications.

University of Rio Grande
218 North College Avenue, Admissions
Rio Grande, OH 45774
Phone: (740) 245-7206
Fax: (740) 245-7260
E-mail: mabell@urgrgcc.edu
http://www.rio.edu
Drafting and design technology.

University of Toledo
2801 West Bancroft Street
Toledo, OH 43606
Phone: (419) 530-8700
Fax: (419) 530-5713
E-mail: enroll@utnet.utoledo.edu
http://www.utoledo.edu
Computer engineering, data processing
technology, drafting and design
technology, electrical engineering
technology.

Ursuline College
2550 Lander Road
Pepper Pike, OH 44124
Phone: (440) 449-4203
Fax: (440) 684-6138
E-mail: admission@ursuline.edu

http://www.ursuline.edu
Graphic design.

Wilberforce University
1055 North Bickett Road
P.O. Box 1001
Wilberforce, OH 45384
Phone: (800) 367-8568
Fax: (937) 376-4751
E-mail: kchristm@shorter.wilberforce.edu
http://www.wilberforce.edu
Electrical and communications engineering.

Wilmington College
Pyle Center, Box 1325
251 Ludovic Street
Wilmington, OH 45117
Phone: (937) 382-6661
Fax: (937) 382-7077
E-mail: admission@wilmington.edu
http://www.wilmington.edu
Sales/distribution.

Wittenberg University
P.O. Box 720
Springfield, OH 45501
Phone: (800) 677-7558
Fax: (937) 327-6379
E-mail: admission@wittenberg.edu
http://www.wittenberg.edu
Mathematics/computer science.

Wright State University
3640 Colonel Glenn Highway
Dayton, OH 54435
Phone: (937) 775-5700
Fax: (937) 775-5795
E-mail: admissions@wright.edu
http://www.wright.edu
Applied mathematics, computer
engineering, drafting and design
technology, electrical and
communications engineering,
electrical engineering technology,
organizational communication.

Youngstown State University
One University Plaza
Youngstown, OH 44555
Phone: (330) 941-2000
Fax: (330) 941-3674
E-mail: enroll@ysu.edu
http://www.ysu.edu
Computer engineering, data processing
technology, Electrical and
communications engineering,
electrical engineering technology,
information technology, mathematics/
computer science, sales/distribution

selling/sales operations, technical and business writing.

Xavier University
3800 Victory Parkway
Cincinnati, OH 45207
Phone: (513) 745-3301
Fax: (513) 745-4319
E-mail: xuadmit@xavier.edu
http://www.xavier.edu
Organizational communication.

OKLAHOMA

Cameron University
2800 West Gore Boulevard
Lawton, OK 73505
Phone: (580) 581-2230
Fax: (580) 581-5514
E-mail: admiss@cua.cameron.edu
http://www.cameron.edu
Data processing technology, drafting and design technology.

East Central University
Office of Admissions & Records
1100 E 14 PMB J8
Ada, OK 74820
Phone: (580) 332-8000
Fax: (580) 436-5495
E-mail: pdenny@mailclerk.ecok.edu
http://www.ecok.edu
Applied mathematics, sales/distribution, technical and business writing.

Langston University
P.O. Box 728
Langston, OK 73050
Phone: (405) 466-2231
Fax: (405) 466-3381
E-mail: admissions@lunet.edu
http://www.lunet.edu
Communications technology, drafting and design technology.

Northeastern State University
Office of Admissions and Records
600 North Grand Avenue
Tahlequah, OK 74464
Phone: (918) 456-5511
Fax: (918) 458-2342
E-mail: nsinfo@nsuok.edu?
http://www.nsuok.edu
Communications.

Northwestern Oklahoma State University
709 Oklahoma Boulevard
Alva, OK 73717

Phone: (580) 327-8545
Fax: (580) 327-1881
E-mail: krschroc@ranger1.nwalva.edu
http://www.nwalva.edu
E-commerce.

Oklahoma Baptist University
2501 North Blackwelder Avenue
Oklahoma City, OK 73106
Phone: (405) 521-5050
Fax: (405) 521-5264
E-mail: uadmission@okcu.edu
http://www.okcu.edu
Computer programming—specific applications, mathematics/computer science, software engineering.

Oklahoma Christian University
P.O. Box 11000
Oklahoma City, OK 73136
Phone: (405) 425-5050
Fax: (405) 425-5269
E-mail: info@oc.edu
http://www.oc.edu
Computer engineering, electrical and communications engineering, mathematics/computer science.

Oklahoma City University
2501 North Blackwelder Avenue
Oklahoma City, OK 73106
Phone: (405) 521-5050
Fax: (405) 521-5264
E-mail: uadmission@okcu.edu
http://www.okcu.edu
Cinematography and film/video production.

Oklahoma State University
323 Student Union
Stillwater, OK 74078
Phone: (405) 744-6858
Fax: (405) 744-5285
E-mail: admit@okstate.edu
http://www.okstate.edu
Computer engineering, drafting and design technology, electrical and communications engineering, electrical engineering technology, LAN/WAN management, technical and business writing.

Oral Roberts University
7777 South Lewis Avenue
Tulsa, OK 74171
Phone: (918) 495-0518
Fax: (918) 495-6222
E-mail: admissions@oru.edu
http://www.oru.edu

Computer engineering, design/visual communications, electrical and communications engineering.

Rogers State University
1701 West Will Rogers Boulevard
Claremore, OK 74017
Phone: (800) 256-7511
Fax: (918) 343-7550
E-mail: At Web site
http://www.rsuonline.edu
Communications technology, electrical and communications engineering, information technology.

St. Gregory's University
1900 West MacArthur
Shawnee, OK 74804
Phone: (405) 878-5100
Fax: (405) 878-5198
E-mail: info@stgregorys.edu
http://www.stgregorys.edu
Computer programming—specific applications.

Southeastern Oklahoma State University
1405 North Fourth Avenue, PMB 4225
Durant, OK 74701
Phone: (580) 745-2060
Fax: (580) 745-7502
E-mail: admissions@sosu.edu
http://www.sosu.edu
Electrical engineering technology.

University of Central Oklahoma
100 North University Drive
Edmond, OK 73034
Phone: (405) 974-2338
Fax: (405) 341-4964
E-mail: admituco@ucok.edu
http://www.ucok.edu
Applied mathematics.

University of Oklahoma
1000 Asp Avenue
Norman, OK 73019
Phone: (405) 325-2252
Fax: (405) 325-7124
E-mail: admrec@ou.edu
http://www.ou.edu
Cinematography and film/video production, computer engineering, electrical and communications engineering.

University of Tulsa
500 South College Avenue
Tulsa, OK 74104

Phone: (918) 631-2307
Fax: (918) 631-5003
E-mail: admission@utulsa.edu
http://www.utulsa.edu
Applied mathematics, electrical and
    communications engineering,
    information technology.

OREGON

The Art Institute of Portland
1122 NW Davis Street
Portland, OR 97209
Phone: (888) 228-6528
Fax: (503) 227-1945
E-mail: aipdadm@aii.edu
http://www.artinstitutes.edu/portland
Animation, graphic design, multimedia,
    webpage/multimedia design.

George Fox University
414 North Meridian Street
Newberg, OR 97132
Phone: (503) 554-2240
Fax: (503) 554-3110
E-mail: admissions@georgefox.edu
http://www.georgefox.edu
Computer programming—specific
    applications, electrical and
    communications engineering.

Lewis & Clark College
0615 SW Palatine Hill Road
Portland, OR 97219
Phone: (503) 768-7040
Fax: (503) 768-7055
E-mail: admissions@lclark.edu
http://www.lclark.edu
Mathematics/computer science.

Oregon Institute of Technology
3201 Campus Drive
Klamath Falls, OR 97601
Phone: (541) 885-1150
Fax: (541) 885-1115
E-mail: oit@oit.edu
http://www.oit.edu
Computer software technology, electrical
    engineering technology.

Oregon State University
104 Kerr Administration Building
Corvallis, OR 97331
Phone: (541) 737-4411
Fax: (541) 737-2482
E-mail: osuadit@orst.edu
http://www.oregonstate.edu
Computer engineering, electrical and
    communications engineering.

Pacific Northwest College of Art
1241 North West Johnson Street
Portland, OR 97209
Phone: (503) 821-8972
Fax: (503) 821-8978
E-mail: admissions@pnca.edu
http://www.pnca.edu
Graphic design, illustration, multimedia.

Pacific University
2043 College Way
Forest Grove, OR 97116
Phone: (503) 352-2218
Fax: (503) 352-2975
E-mail: admissions@pacificu.edu
http://www.pacificu.edu
Multimedia.

Portland State University
P.O. Box 751
Portland, OR 97207
Phone: (503) 725-3511
Fax: (503) 725-5525
E-mail: admissions@pdx.edu
http://www.pdx.edu
Computer engineering, design/visual
    communications, electrical and
    communications engineering.

Southern Oregon University
Office of Admissions
1250 Siskiyou Boulevard
Ashland, OR 97520
Phone: (541) 552-6411
Fax: (541) 552-6614
E-mail: admissions@sou.edu
http://www.sou.edu
Mathematics/computer science.

University of Oregon
1217 University of Oregon
Eugene, OR 97403
Phone: (541) 346-3201
Fax: (541) 346-5815
E-mail: uoadmit@oregon.uoregon.edu
http://www.uoregon.edu
Mathematics/computer science,
    multimedia, software engineering.

University of Portland
5000 North Willamette Boulevard
Portland, OR 97203
Phone: (503) 943-7147
Fax: (503) 283-7315
E-mail: admission@up.edu
http://www.up.edu
Computer engineering, electrical and
    communications engineering.

Western Oregon University
345 North Monmouth Avenue
Monmouth, OR 97361
Phone: (503) 838-8211
Fax: (503) 838-8067
E-mail: wolfgram@wou.edu
http://www.wou.edu
Mathematics/computer science.

PENNSYLVANIA

Albright College
P.O. Box 15234
13th and Bern Streets
Reading, PA 19612
Phone: (610) 921-7512
Fax: (610) 921-7294
E-mail: admissions@albright.edu
http://www.albright.edu
Webpage/multimedia design.

Allegheny College
Office of Admissions
Meadville, PA 16335
Phone: (814) 332-4351
Fax: (814) 337-0431
E-mail: admissions@allegheny.edu
http://www.allegheny.edu
Software engineering, technical and
    business writing.

Arcadia University
450 South Easton Road
Glenside, PA 19038
Phone: (215) 572-2910
Fax: (215) 572-4049
E-mail: admiss@arcadia.edu
http://www.arcadia.edu
Computer graphics, graphic design.

**Bloomsburg University of
    Pennsylvania**
104 Student Services Center
400 East Second Street
Bloomsburg, PA 17815
Phone: (570) 389-4316
Fax: (570) 389-4741
E-mail: buadmiss@bloomu.edu
http://www.bloomu.edu
Electrical and communications
    engineering.

Bucknell University
Freas Hall
Bucknell University
Lewisburg, PA 17837
Phone: (570) 577-1101
Fax: (570) 577-3538

E-mail: admissions@bucknell.edu
http://www.bucknell.edu
Computer engineering, electrical and
    communications engineering.

California University of Pennsylvania
250 University Avenue
California, PA 15419
Phone: (724) 938-4404
Fax: (724) 938-4564
E-mail: inquiry@cup.edu
http://www.cup.edu
Applied mathematics, communications
    technology, design/visual
    communications, drafting and design
    technology, electrical engineering
    technology, technical and business
    writing.

Carlow College
3333 Fifth Avenue
Pittsburgh, PA 15213
Phone: (412) 578-6059
Fax: (412) 578-6668
E-mail: admissions@carlow.edu
http://www.carlow.edu
Technical and business writing.

Carnegie Mellon University
5000 Forbes Avenue
Pittsburgh, PA 15213
Phone: (412) 268-2082
Fax: (412) 268-7838
E-mail: undergraduateadmissions@
    andrew.cmu.edu
http://www.cmu.edu
Design/visual communications, electrical
    and communications engineering,
    information technology, mathematics/
    computer science, technical and
    business writing.

Chatham College
Woodland Road
Pittsburgh, PA 15232
Phone: (412) 365-1290
Fax: (412) 365-1609
E-mail: admissions@chatham.edu
http://www.chatham.edu
Animation, design/visual
    communications, technical and
    business writing.

Chestnut Hill College
9601 Germantown Avenue
Philadelphia, PA 19118
Phone: (215) 248-7001
Fax: (215) 248-7082
E-mail: chcapply@chc.edu

http://www.chc.edu
Mathematics/computer science.

Cheyney University of Pennsylvania
Cheyney and Creek Roads
Cheyney, PA 19319
Phone: (610) 399-2275
Fax: (610) 399-2099
E-mail: jbrowne@cheyney.edu
http://www.cheyney.edu
Communications technology.

DeSales University
2755 Station Avenue
Center Valley, PA 18034
Phone: (610) 282-4443
Fax: (610) 282-0131
E-mail: admiss@desales.edu
http://www.desales.edu
E-commerce.

DeVry University—Ft. Washington
1140 Virginia Drive
Ft. Washington, PA 19034
Phone: (866) 338-7934
Fax: NA
E-mail: info.devry.edu
http://www.devry.edu
Electrical engineering technology,
    information technology.

Drexel University
3141 Chestnut Street
Philadelphia, PA 19104
Phone: (215) 895-2400
Fax: (215) 895-5939
E-mail: enroll@drexel.edu
http://www.drexel.edu
Cinematography and film/video
    production, computer engineering,
    design/visual communications,
    electrical and communications
    engineering, playwriting/screenwriting,
    technical and business writing.

Duquesne University
600 Forbes Avenue
Pittsburgh, PA 15282
Phone: (412) 396-5000
Fax: (412) 396-5644
E-mail: admissions@duq.edu
http://www.duq.edu
Mathematics/computer science.

Eastern University
1300 Eagle Road
St. Davids, PA 19087
Phone: (610) 341-5967
Fax: (610) 341-1723

E-mail: ugadm@eastern.edu
http://www.eastern.edu
Multimedia.

**East Stroudsburg University of
    Pennsylvania**
200 Prospect Street
East Stroudsburg, PA 18301
Phone: (570) 422-3542
Fax: (570) 422-3933
E-mail: undergrads@po-box.esu.edu
http://www.esu.edu
Communications technology, graphic
    design.

Edinboro University of Pennsylvania
Biggers House
Edinboro, PA 16444
Phone: (814) 732-2761
Fax: (814) 732-2420
E-mail: eup_admissions@edinboro.edu
http://www.edinboro.edu
Information technology.

Elizabethtown College
Leffler House
One Alpha Drive
Elizabethtown, PA 17022
Phone: (717) 361-1400
Fax: (717) 361-1365
E-mail: admissions@etown.edu
http://www.etown.edu
Computer engineering, technical and
    business writing.

Gannon University
University Square
Erie, PA 16541
Phone: (814) 871-7240
Fax: (814) 871-5803
E-mail: admissions@gannon.edu
http://www.gannon.edu
Communications technology, computer
    engineering, data processing
    technology, electrical and
    communications engineering, software
    engineering.

Geneva College
3200 College Avenue
Beaver Falls, PA 15010
Phone: (724) 847-6500
Fax: (724) 847-6776
E-mail: admissions@geneva.edu
http://www.geneva.edu
Applied mathematics.

Gettysburg College
300 North Washington Street
Gettysburg, PA 17325

Phone: (717) 337-6100
Fax: (717) 337-6145
E-mail: admiss@gettysburg.edu
http://www.gettysburg.edu
Computer engineering, electrical and
communications engineering,
mathematics/computer science.

Grove City College
100 Campus Drive
Grove City, PA 16127
Phone: (724) 458-2100
Fax: (724) 458-3395
E-mail: admissions@gcc.edu
http://www.gcc.edu
Computer programming—specific
applications, electrical and
communications engineering,
mathematics/computer science.

Holy Family University
Grant and Frankford Avenue
Philadelphia, PA 19114
Phone: (215) 637-3050
Fax: (215) 281-1022
E-mail: undergrad@hfu.edu
http://www.holyfamily.edu
E-commerce.

Immaculata University
1145 King Road
P.O. Box 642
Immaculata, PA 19345
Phone: (610) 647-4400
Fax: (610) 647-0836
E-mail: admiss@immaculata.edu
http://www.immaculata.edu
Communications technology.

Indiana University of Pennsylvania
216 Pratt Hall
Indiana, PA 15075
Phone: (724) 357-2230
Fax: (724) 357-6281
E-mail: admissions-inquiry@iup.edu
http://www.iup.edu
Applied mathematics, multimedia.

Kutztown University of Pennsylvania
Admission Office
P.O. Box 730
Kutztown, PA 19530
Phone: (610) 683-4060
Fax: (610) 683-1375
E-mail: admission@kutztown.edu
http://www.kutztown.edu
Digital media, information technology,
technical and business writing.

Lafayette College
118 Markle Hall
Easton, PA 18042
Phone: (610) 330-5100
Fax: (610) 330-5355
E-mail: admissions@lafayette.edu
http://www.lafayette.edu
Electrical and communications
engineering.

La Roche College
9000 Babcock Boulevard
Pittsburgh, PA 15237
Phone: (412) 536-1271
Fax: (412) 536-1048
E-mail: admissions@laroche.edu
http://www.laroche.edu
Applied mathematics, graphic design.

La Salle University
1900 West Olney Avenue
Philadelphia, PA 19141
Phone: (215) 951-1500
Fax: (215) 951-1656
E-mail: admiss@lasalle.edu
http://www.lasalle.edu
Cinematography and film/video
production, computer graphics,
computer programming—specific
applications, digital media, information
technology, mathematics/computer
science, technical and business writing,
webpage/multimedia design.

Lebanon Valley College
101 North College Avenue
Annville, PA 17003
Phone: (717) 867-6181
Fax: (717) 867-6026
E-mail: admission@lvc.edu
http://www.lvc.edu
Communications technology, digital
media, recording arts.

Lehigh University
27 Memorial Drive West
Bethlehem, PA 18015
Phone: (610) 758-3000
Fax: (610) 758-4361
E-mail: admissions@lehigh.edu
http://www.lehigh.edu
Computer engineering, digital media,
electrical and communications
engineering.

Lock Haven University of Pennsylvania
Lock Haven University
Office of Admissions, Akeley Hall
Lock Haven, PA 17745

Phone: (570) 893-2027
Fax: (570) 893-2201
E-mail: admissions@lhup.edu
http://www.lhup.edu
Computer engineering, electrical and
communications engineering,
electrical engineering technology.

Marywood University
2300 Adams Avenue
Scranton, PA 18509
Phone: (570) 348-6234
Fax: (570) 961-4763
E-mail: ugadm@ac.marywood.edu
http://www.marywood.edu
Design/visual communications, digital
media, electrical and communications
engineering, graphic design,
organizational communication.

Mercyhurst College
Admissions
501 East 38th Street
Erie, PA 16546
Phone: (800) 825-1926
Fax: (814) 824-2071
E-mail: admug@mercyhurst.edu
http://www.mercyhurst.edu
Data processing technology.

Mount Aloysius College
7373 Admiral Peary Highway
Cresson, PA 16630
Phone: (814) 886-6383
Fax: (814) 886-6441
E-mail: admissions@mtaloy.edu
http://www.mtaloy.edu
Computer programming—specific
applications, information technology,
mathematics/computer science.

Peirce College
420 Pine Street
Philadelphia, PA 19102
Phone: (888) 467-3472
Fax: (215) 545-6400
E-mail: info@peirce.edu
http://www.peirce.edu
Computer programming—specific
applications, LAN/WAN management.

**Pennsylvania State University—
Abington**
106 Sutherland
Abington, PA 19001
Phone: (215) 881-7600
Fax: (215) 881-7317
E-mail: abingtonadmissions@psu.edu
http://www.abington.psu.edu

Cinematography and film/video production, computer engineering, electrical and communications engineering, technical and business writing, telecommunications technology.

Pennsylvania State University— Altoona
East 108 Raymond Smith Building
Altoona, PA 16601
Phone: (814) 949-5466
Fax: (814) 949-5564
E-mail: aaadmit@psu.edu
http://www.aa.psu.edu
Cinematography and film/video production, computer engineering, electrical and communications engineering, electrical engineering technology, telecommunications technology.

Pennsylvania State University— Beaver
100 University Drive
Monaca, PA 15061
Phone: (724) 773-3800
Fax: (724) 773-3658
E-mail: br-admissions@psu.edu
http://www.br.psu.edu
Cinematography and film/video production, computer engineering, electrical and communications engineering, electrical engineering technology, telecommunications technology.

Pennsylvania State University—Berks
14 Perkins Student Center
Reading, PA 19610
Phone: (610) 396-6060
Fax: (610) 396-6077
E-mail: admissions@psu.edu
http://www.bk.psu.edu
Cinematography and film/video production, computer engineering, electrical and communications engineering, electrical engineering technology, telecommunications technology.

Pennsylvania State University— Delaware County
25 Yearsley Mill Road
Media, PA 19083
Phone: (610) 892-1200
Fax: (610) 892-1357
E-mail: admissions-delco@psu.edu
http://www.de.psu.edu

Computer engineering, electrical and communications engineering, information technology, telecommunications technology.

Pennsylvania State University—Dubois
College Place
Dubois, PA 15801
Phone: (866) 374-3378
Fax: (814) 375-4784
E-mail: ds-Admissions@psu.edu
http://www.ds.psu.edu
Cinematography and film/video production, computer engineering, electrical and communications engineering, electrical engineering technology, telecommunications technology.

Pennsylvania State University—Erie, The Behrend College
5091 Station Road
Erie, PA 16563
Phone: (814) 898-6100
Fax: (814) 898-6044
E-mail: behrend.admissions@psu.edu
http://www.pserie.psu.edu
Computer engineering, electrical and communications engineering, electrical engineering technology, telecommunications technology.

Pennsylvania State University—Fayette
P.O. Box 519
Route 119 North
108 Williams Building
Uniontown, PA 15041
Phone: (724) 430-4130
Fax: (724) 430-4175
E-mail: feadm@psu.edu
http://www.fe.psu.edu
Cinematography and film/video production, electrical engineering technology, telecommunications technology.

Pennsylvania State University— Harrisburg
Swatara Building
777 West Harrisburg Pike
Middletown, PA 17057
Phone: (717) 948-6250
Fax: (717) 948-6325
E-mail: hbgadmit@psu.edu
http://www.hhb.psu.edu
Applied mathematics, electrical and communications engineering, electrical engineering technology, telecommunications technology.

Pennsylvania State University— Hazelton
110 Administrative Building
76 University Drive
Hazelton, PA 18202
Phone: (570) 450-3142
Fax: (570) 450-3182
E-mail: admissions-hn@psu.edu
http://www.hn.psu.edu
Cinematography and film/video production, computer engineering, electrical engineering technology, telecommunications technology.

Pennsylvania State University— Lehigh Valley
8380 Mohr Lane
Academic Building
Fogelsville, PA 19051
Phone: (610) 285-5035
Fax: (610) 285-5220
E-mail: admission-lv@psu.edu
http://www.an.psu.edu
Cinematography and film/video production, computer engineering, telecommunications technology.

Pennsylvania State University— McKeesport
100 Frable Building
4000 University Drive
McKeesport, PA 15132
Phone: (412) 675-9010
Fax: (412) 675-9056
E-mail: psumk@psu.edu
http://www.mk.psu.edu
Cinematography and film/video production, computer engineering, electrical and communications engineering, telecommunications technology.

Pennsylvania State University— Mont Alto
1 Campus Drive
Mont Alto, Pennsylvania 17237
Phone: (717) 749-6130
Fax: (717) 749-6132
E-mail: psuma@psu.edu
http://www.ma.psu.edu
Cinematography and film/video production, computer engineering, electrical and communications engineering, telecommunications technology.

Pennsylvania State University— New Kensington
3550 Seventh Street Road, Route 780
Upper Barrell, PA 15068

Phone: (724) 334-5466
Fax: (724) 334-6111
E-mail: nkadmissions@psu.edu
http://www.nk.psu.edu
Cinematography and film/video
    production, computer engineering,
    electrical and communications
    engineering, electrical engineering
    technology, telecommunications
    technology.

**Pennsylvania State University—
    Schuylkill**
200 University Drive
A102 Administrative Building
Schuylkill Haven, PA 17072
Phone: (570) 385-6252
Fax: (570) 385-6272
E-mail: sl-admissions@psu.edu
http://www.sl.psu.edu
Cinematography and film/video
    production, computer engineering,
    electrical and communications
    engineering, electrical engineering
    technology, telecommunications
    technology.

**Pennsylvania State University—
    Shenango**
147 Shenango Avenue
Sharon, PA 16146
Phone: (724) 983-2803
Fax: (724) 983-2820
E-mail: psushenango.psu.edu
http://www.shenango.psu.edu
Electrical and communications
    engineering.

**Pennsylvania State University—
    University Park**
201 Shields Building
P.O. Box 3000
University Park, PA 16802
Phone: (814) 865-5471
Fax: (814) 863-7590
E-mail: admissions@psu.edu
http://www.psu.edu
Computer engineering, drafting and
    design technology, electrical and
    communications engineering, electrical
    engineering technology, information
    technology, quality control technology,
    technical and business writing,
    telecommunications technology.

**Pennsylvania State University—
    Wilkes-Barre**
P.O. Box PSU
Lehman, PA 18627

Phone: (570) 675-9238
Fax: (570) 675-9113
E-mail: wbadmissions@psu.edu
http://www.psu.edu
Cinematography and film/video
    production, computer engineering,
    electrical and communications
    engineering, information technology,
    telecommunications technology.

**Pennsylvania State University—
    Worthington Scranton**
120 Ridge View Drive
Dunmore, PA 18512
Phone: (570) 963-2500
Fax: (570) 963-2524
E-mail: wsadmissions@psu.edu
http://www.sn.psu.edu
Cinematography and film/video
    production, computer engineering,
    electrical and communications
    engineering, telecommunications
    technology.

Pennsylvania State University—York
1031 Edgecomb Avenue
York, PA 17403
Phone: (717) 771-4040
Fax: (717) 771-4005
E-mail: ykadmisson@psu.edu
http://www.yk.psu.edu
Cinematography and film/video
    production, computer engineering,
    electrical and communications
    engineering, telecommunications
    technology.

Philadelphia University
School House Lane & Henry Avenue
Philadelphia, PA 19144
Phone: (215) 951-2800
Fax: (215) 951-2907
E-mail: admissions@PhilaU.edu
http://www.PhilaU.edu
Animation, data processing technology,
    e-commerce, graphic design, sales/
    distribution.

Point Park College
201 Wood Street
Pittsburgh, PA 15222
Phone: (412) 392-3430
Fax: (412) 391-1980
E-mail: enroll@ppc.edu
http://www.ppc.edu
Cinematography and film/video
    production, design/visual
    communications, information

technology, webpage/multimedia
    design.

Robert Morris University
6001 University Boulevard
Moon Township, PA 15108
Phone: (412) 262-8206
Fax: (412) 299-2425
E-mail: enrollmentoffice@rmu.edu
http://www.rmu.edu
Applied mathematics, design/visual
    communications, multimedia,
    software engineering.

Saint Francis University
P.O. Box 600
Loretto, PA 15940
Phone: (814) 472-3000
Fax: (814) 472-3335
E-mail: admissions@francis.edu
http://www.francis.edu
Mathematics/computer science.

Saint Joseph's University
5600 City Avenue
Philadelphia, PA 19131
Phone: (610) 660-1300
Fax: (610) 660-1314
E-mail: admit@sju.edu
http://www.sju.edu
Communications, sales/distribution.

Saint Vincent College
3000 Fraser Purchase Road
Latrobe, PA 10650
Phone: (724) 537-4540
Fax: (724) 532-5069
E-mail: admission@stvincent.edu
http://www.stvincent.edu
Communications technology.

**Slippery Rock University of
    Pennsylvania**
Office of Admissions
146 North Hall Welcome Center
Slippery Rock, PA 16057
Phone: (724) 738-2015
Fax: (724) 738-2913
E-mail: apply@sru.edu
http://www.sru.edu
Information technology.

Susquehanna University
514 University Avenue
Susquehanna, PA 17870
Phone: (570) 372-4260
Fax: (570) 372-2722
E-mail: suadmiss@susque.edu
http://www.susque.edu
Graphic design.

Temple University
1801 North Broad Street
Philadelphia, PA 19122
Phone: (215) 204-7200
Fax: (215) 204-5694
E-mail: tuadm@mail.temple.edu
http://www.temple.edu
Electrical and communications
    engineering, graphic design,
    information technology.

University of Pennsylvania
1 College Hall
Philadelphia, PA 19104
Phone: (215) 898-7507
Fax: (215) 898-9670
E-mail: info@admissions.ugao.upenn.edu
http://www.upenn.edu
Cognitive science, computer engineering,
    computer graphics, e-commerce,
    electrical and communications
    engineering, sales/distribution.

University of Pittsburgh—Bradford
Office of Admissions—Hanley Library
300 Campus Drive
Bradford, PA 16701
Phone: (814) 362-7555
Fax: (814) 362-7578
E-mail: admissions@www.upb.pitt.edu
http://www.upb.pitt.edu
Applied mathematics, computer
    engineering, electrical and
    communications engineering.

University of Pittsburgh—Greensburg
150 Finoli Drive
Greensburg, PA 15601
Phone: (724) 836-9880
Fax: (724) 836-7160
E-mail: upgadmit@pitt.edu
http://www.upg.pitt.edu
Applied mathematics, computer
    engineering, electrical and
    communications engineering.

University of Pittsburgh—Johnstown
157 Blackington Hall
450 Schoolhouse Road
Johnstown, PA 15904
Phone: (814) 269-7050
Fax: (814) 269-7044
E-mail: upjadmit@pitt.edu
http://www.upj.pitt.edu
Computer engineering, electrical and
    communications engineering.

University of Pittsburgh—Pittsburgh
4227 Fifth Avenue

First Floor Alumni Hall
Pittsburgh, PA 15260
Phone: (412) 624-7488
Fax: (412) 648-8815
E-mail: oafa@pitt.edu
http://www.pitt.edu
Computer engineering, electrical and
    communications engineering.

The University of Scranton
800 Linden Street
Scranton, PA 18501
Phone: (570) 941-7540
Fax: (570) 941-5928
E-mail: admissions@scranton.edu
http://www.scranton.edu
Electrical and communications
    engineering.

Villanova University
800 Lancaster Avenue
Villanova, PA 19085
Phone: (610) 519-4000
Fax: (610) 519-6450
E-mail: gotovu@villanova.edu
http://www.villanova.edu
Computer engineering, electrical and
    communications engineering.

Waynesburg College
51 West College Street
Waynesburg, PA 15370
Phone: (724) 852-3248
Fax: (724) 627-8124
E-mail: admissions@waynesburg.edu
http://www.waynesburg.edu
Digital media, information technology.

Westminster College
319 South Market Street
New Wilmington, PA 16172
Phone: (724) 946-7100
Fax: (724) 946-7171
E-mail: admis@westminster.edu
http://www.westminster.edu
Mathematics/computer science.

Widener University
One University Place
Chester, PA 19013
Phone: (610) 499-4126
Fax: (610) 499-4676
E-mail: admissions.office@widener.edu
http://www.widener.edu
Electrical and communications
    engineering.

Wilkes University
84 West South Street

Wilkes-Barre, PA 18766
Phone: (570) 408-4400
Fax: (570) 408-4904
E-mail: admissions@wilkes.edu
http://www.wilkes.edu
E-commerce, electrical and
    communications engineering.

RHODE ISLAND

Brown University
P.O. Box 1876
45 Prospect Street
Providence, RI 02912
Phone: (401) 863-2378
Fax: (401) 863-9300
E-mail: admission_undergraduate@
    brown.edu
http://www.brown.edu
Applied mathematics, cognitive science,
    computer engineering, electrical
    and communications engineering,
    mathematics/computer science.

Bryant College
50 Douglas Pike
Smithfield, RI 02917
Phone: (401) 232-6100
Fax: (401) 232-6741
E-mail: admission@bryant.edu
http://www.bryant.edu
Information technology.

**Johnson & Wales University—
    Providence**
8 Abbott Park Place
Providence, RI 02903
Phone: (401) 598-2310
Fax: (401) 598-2948
E-mail: admissions@jwu.edu
http://www.jwu.edu
Drafting and design technology, electrical
    engineering technology, sales/
    distribution.

Providence College
549 River Avenue and Eaton Street
Providence, RI 02918
Phone: (401) 865-2535
Fax: (401) 865-2826
E-mail: pcadmiss@providence.edu
http://www.providence.edu
Organizational communication.

Rhode Island School of Design
2 College Street
Providence, RI 02903
Phone: (401) 454-6300
Fax: (401) 454-6309

E-mail: admissions@risd.edu
http://www.risd.edu
Cinematography and film/video
    production, graphic design,
    illustration, multimedia.

Roger Williams University
One Old Ferry Road
Bristol, RI 02809
Phone: (401) 254-3500
Fax: (401) 254-3557
E-mail: admit@rwu.edu
http://www.rwu.edu
Computer engineering.

Salve Regina University
100 Ochre Point Avenue
Newport, RI 02840
Phone: (401) 341-2908
Fax: (401) 848-2823
E-mail: sruadmis@salve.edu
http://www.salve.edu
Communications technology.

University of Rhode Island
Undergraduate Admissions Office
14 Upper College Road
Kingston, RI 02881
Phone: (401) 874-7100
Fax: (401) 874-5523
E-mail: uriadmit@etal.uri.edu
http://www.uri.edu
Computer engineering, electrical and
    communications engineering.

SOUTH CAROLINA

Benedict College
Harden and Blanding Streets
Columbia, SC 29204
Phone: (803) 253-5143
Fax: (803) 253-5167
E-mail: admission@benedict.edu
http://www.benedict.edu
Multimedia.

Charleston Southern University
Enrollment Services
P.O. Box 118087
Charleston, SC 29433
Phone: (843) 863-7050
Fax: (843) 863-7070
E-mail: enropll@csuniv.edu
http://www.charlestonsouthern.edu
Applied mathematics, mathematics/
    computer science.

Claflin University
400 Magnolia Street
Orangeburg, SC 29115

Phone: (803) 535-5339
Fax: (803) 535-5387
E-mail: kboyd@clafl.claflin.edu
http://www.claflin.edu
Applied mathematics, mathematics/
    computer science.

Clemson University
106 Sikes Hall, Box 345124
Clemson, SC 29634
Phone: (864) 656-2987
Fax: (864) 656-2464
E-mail: cuadmissions@clemson.edu
http://www.clemson.edu
Computer engineering, design/visual
    communications, electrical and
    communications engineering.

Coastal Carolina University
P.O. Box 261954
Conway, SC 29528
Phone: (843) 349-2026
Fax: (843) 349-2127
E-mail: admissions@coastal.edu
http://www.coastal.edu
Applied mathematics.

Coker College
300 East College Avenue
Hartsville, SC 29550
Phone: (843) 383-8050
Fax: (843) 383-8056
E-mail: admissions@coker.edu
http://www.coker.edu
Technical and business writing.

Francis Marion University
Office of Admissions
P.O. Box 100547
Florence, SC 29501
Phone: (843) 661-1231
Fax: (843) 661-4635
E-mail: admissions@marion.edu
http://www.marion.edu
Electrical engineering technology.

Furman University
3300 Poinsett Highway
Greenville, SC 29613
Phone: (864) 294-2034
Fax: (864) 294-3127
E-mail: admissions@furman.edu
http://www.furman.edu
Mathematics/computer science.

Limestone College
1115 College Drive
Gaffey, SC 29340
Phone: (864) 488-4549

Fax: (864) 487-8706
E-mail: admiss@limestone.edu
http://www.limestone.edu
Applied mathematics, graphic design,
    web/multimedia management.

Newberry College
2100 College Street
Newberry, SC 29108
Phone: (803) 321-5127
Fax: (803) 321-5138
E-mail: admissions@newberry.edu
http://www.newberry.edu
Mathematics/computer science.

North Greenville College
P.O. Box 1892
Tigerville, SC 29688
Phone: (864) 977-7001
Fax: (864) 977-7177
E-mail: admissions@ngc.edu
http://www.ngc.edu
Accounting/computer science.

South Carolina State University
300 College Street Northeast
Orangeburg, SC 29117
Phone: (800) 260-5956
Fax: (803) 536-8990
E-mail: admissions@scsu.edu
http://www.scsu.edu
Electrical engineering technology.

Southern Wesleyan University
1907 Wesleyan Drive
P.O. Box 1020
Central, SC 29630
Phone: (864) 644-5550
Fax: (864) 644-5972
E-mail: admissions@swu.edu
http://www.swu.edu
E-commerce, web/multimedia
    management.

University of South Carolina—Aiken
471 University Parkway
Aiken, SC 29801
Phone: (803) 641-3366
Fax: (803) 641-3727
E-mail: admit@sc.edu
http://www.usca.edu
Applied mathematics, computer
    engineering, electrical and
    communications engineering,
    mathematics/computer science.

**University of South Carolina—
    Columbia**
Office of Undergraduate Admissions

902 Sumter Street Access
Columbia, SC 29208
Phone: (803) 777-7000
Fax: (803) 777-0101
E-mail: admissions-ugrad@sc.edu
http://www.sc.edu
Computer engineering.

**University of South Carolina—
    Spartanburg**
800 University Way
Spartanburg, SC 29303
Phone: (864) 503-5246
Fax: (864) 503-5727
E-mail: dstewart@uscs.edu
http://www.uscs.edu
Accounting/computer science, applied
    mathematics, computer engineering,
    design/visual communications.

SOUTH DAKOTA

Black Hills State University
1200 University Avenue, USB 9502
Spearfish, SD 57799
Phone: (605) 642-6343
Fax: (605) 642-6022
E-mail: admissions@bhsu.edu
http://www.bhsu.edu
Drafting and design technology.

Dakota State University
820 North Washington Avenue
Madison, SD 57042
Phone: (605) 256-5139
Fax: (605) 256-5020
E-mail: yourfuture@dsu.edu
http://www.dsu.edu
Computer graphics, e-commerce,
    webpage/multimedia design.

Dakota Wesleyan University
1200 West University Avenue
Mitchell, SD 57301
Phone: (605) 995-2650
Fax: (605) 995-2699
E-mail: admissions@dwu.edu
http://www.dwu.edu
Webpage/multimedia design.

Northern State University
1200 South Jay Street
Aberdeen, SD 57401
Phone: (605) 626-2544
Fax: (605) 626-2431
E-mail: admissions@northern.edu
http://www.northern.edu
Information technology.

Sinte Gleska University
101 Antelope Lake Circle
P.O. Box 105
Mission, SD 57555
Phone: (605) 856-8100
Fax: NA
E-mail: At Web site
http://www.sinte.edu
Data processing technology.

**South Dakota School of Mines and
    Technology**
501 East Saint Joseph Street
Rapid City, SD 57701
Phone: (605) 394-2414
Fax: (605) 394-6131
E-mail: admissions@sdsmt.edu
http://www.sdsmt.edu
Computer engineering, electrical and
    communications engineering.

South Dakota State University
P.O. Box 2201
Brookings, SD 57007
Phone: (605) 688-4121
Fax: (605) 688-6891
E-mail: admissions@sdstate.edu
http://www.sdstate.edu
Electrical and communications
    engineering, electrical engineering
    technology, software engineering.

University of Sioux Falls
1101 West 22nd Street
Sioux Falls, SD 57105
Phone: (605) 331-6600
Fax: (605) 331-6615
E-mail: admissions@usiouxfalls.edu
http://www.usiouxfalls.edu
Applied mathematics.

TENNESSEE

Bethel College
325 Cherry Avenue
McKenzie, TN 38201
Phone: (731) 352-4030
Fax: (731) 352-4069
E-mail: admissons@bethel-college.edu
http://www.bethel-college.edu
Applied mathematics.

Bryan College
P.O. Box 7000
Dayton, TN 37321
Phone: (423) 775-204
Fax: NA
E-mail: info@bryan.edu
http://www.bryan.edu
Mathematics/computer science.

Christian Brothers University
Admissions
P.O. Box T-6
650 East Parkway South
Memphis, TN 38104
Phone: (901) 321-3205
Fax: (901) 321-3202
E-mail: admissions@chu.edu
http://www.chu.rfu
Computer engineering, electrical and
    communications engineering,
    mathematics/computer science.

King College
1350 King College Road
Bristol, TN 37620
Phone: (423) 652-4861
Fax: (423) 652-4727
E-mail: admissions@king.edu
http://www.king.edu
Digital media.

Lambuth University
705 Lambuth Boulevard
Jackson, TN 38301
Phone: (731) 425-3223
Fax: (731) 425-3496
E-mail: admit@lambuth.edu
http://www.lambuth.edu
Design/visual communications.

Maryville College
502 East Lamar Alexander Parkway
Maryville, TN 37804
Phone: (865) 981-8092
Fax: (865) 981-8005
E-mail: admissions@maryvillecollege.
    edu
http://www.maryvillecollege.edu
Mathematics/computer science, technical
    and business writing.

Memphis College of Art
Overton Park
1930 Poplar Avenue
Memphis, TN 38104
Phone: (800) 727-1088
Fax: (901) 726-9371
E-mail: info@mca.edu
http://www.mca.edu
Computer graphics, design/visual
    communications, graphic design,
    illustration, multimedia.

Middle Tennessee State University
Office of Admissions
1301 East Main Street
Murfreesboro, TN 37132
Phone: (800) 433-6878

Fax: (615) 898-5478
E-mail: admissions@mtsu.edu
http://www.mtsu.edu
Sales/distribution.

Sewanee—University of the South
735 University Avenue
Sewanee, TN 37383
Phone: (931) 598-1238
Fax: (931) 538-3248
E-mail: collegeadmission@sewanee.edu
http://www.sewanee.edu
Mathematics/computer science.

Southern Adventist University
P.O. Box 370
Collegedale, TN 37315
Phone: (423) 238-2844
Fax: (423) 238-3005
E-mail: admissions@southern.edu
http://www.southern.edu
Cinematography and film/video production,
    communications technology.

Tennessee State University
3500 John A. Merritt Boulevard
Nashville, TN 37209
Phone: (615) 963-3101
Fax: (615) 963-5108
E-mail:jcade@tnstate.edu
http://www.tnstate.edu
Electrical and communications
    engineering.

Tennessee Technological University
P.O. Box 5006
Cookeville, TN 38505
Phone: (931) 372-3888
Fax: (931) 372-6250
E-mail: admissions@tntech.edu
http://www.tntech.edu
Communications technology,
    computer engineering, electrical
    and communications engineering,
    technical and business writing,
    webpage/multimedia design.

Trevecca Nazarene University
333 Murfreesboro Road
Nashville, TN 37210
Phone: (888) 210-4868
Fax: NA
E-mail: At Web site
http://www.trevecca.edu
Communications technology.

Union University
1050 Union University Drive
Jackson, TN 38305

Phone: (731) 661-5000
Fax: (731) 661-5017
E-mail: cgriffin@uu.edu
http://www.uu.edu
Digital media, electrical and
    communications engineering.

University of Memphis
Office of Admissions
101 Wilder Tower
Memphis, TN 38152
Phone: (901) 678-2111
Fax: (901) 678-3053
E-mail: recruitment@memphis.edu
http://www.memphis.edu
Computer engineering, electrical and
    communications engineering,
    electrical engineering technology,
    sales/distribution.

University of Tennessee—Chattanooga
615 McCallie Avenue
131 Hooper Hall
Chattanooga, TN 37403
Phone: (423) 425-4662
Fax: (423) 425-4157
E-mail: yancy-freeman@utc.edu
http://www.utc.edu
Applied mathematics.

University of Tennessee—Knoxville
320 Science Building
Circle Park Drive
Knoxville, TN 37996
Phone: (865) 974-2184
Fax: (865) 974-6341
E-mail: admissions@tennessee.edu
http://www.utk.edu
Electrical and communications
    engineering.

Vanderbilt University
2305 West End Avenue
Nashville, TN 37203
Phone: (615) 322-2561
Fax: (615) 343-7765
E-mail: admissions@vanderbilt.edu
http://www.vanderbilt.edu
Computer engineering, electrical and
    communications engineering.

TEXAS

Abilene Christian University
ACU P.O. Box 29000
Abilene, TX 79699
Phone: (325) 674-2650
Fax: (325) 674-2130
E-mail: info@admissions.acu.edu

http://www.acu.edu
Digital media.

Austin College
90 North Grand Avenue, Suite 6N
Sherman, TX 75090
Phone: (903) 813-3000
Fax: (903) 813-3198
E-mail: admissions@austincollege.edu
http://www.austincollege.edu
Data processing technology.

Baylor University
P.O. Box 97056
Waco, TX 76798
Phone: (254) 710-3435
Fax: (254) 710-3436
E-mail: admissions_serv_office@baylor.
    edu
http://www.baylor.edu
Applied mathematics, electrical and
    communications engineering, sales/
    distribution.

DeVry University—Irving
4800 Regent Boulevard
Irving, TX 75063
Phone: (972) 929-5777
Fax: (972) 929-2860
E-mail: cwilliams@mail.dal.devry.edu
http://www.devry.edu
Electrical engineering technology,
    information technology.

Houston Baptist University
7502 Fondren Road
Houston, TX 77074
Phone: (281) 649-3211
Fax: (281) 649-3217
E-mail: unadm@hbu.edu
http://www.hbu.edu
Accounting/computer science, electrical
    and communications engineering.

Lamar University
P.O. Box 10009
Beaumont, TX 77710
Phone: (409) 880-8888
Fax: (409) 880-8463
E-mail: admissions@hal.lamar.edu
http://www.lamar.edu
Applied mathematics, electrical and
    communications engineering, sales/
    distribution.

LeTourneau University
P.O. Box 7001
Longview, TX 75607
Phone: (903) 233-3400

Fax: (903) 233-3411
E-mail: admissions@letu.edu
http://www.letu.edu
Computer engineering, drafting and
    design technology, electrical
    engineering technology, mathematics/
    computer science.

Lubbock Christian University
5601 19th Street
Lubbock, TX 79407
Phone: (800) 720-7151
Fax: (806) 720-7162
E-mail: admissions@lcu.edu
http://www.lcu.edu
Computer graphics, design/visual
    communications, electrical and
    communications engineering,
    organizational communication.

McMurray University
South 14th and Sayles Boulevard
Abilene, TX 79697
Phone: (915) 793-4700
Fax: (915) 793-4718
E-mail: admissions@mcm.edu
http://www.mcm.edu
Data processing technology, graphic
    design, mathematics/computer
    science.

Prairie View A&M University
P.O. Box 3089
University Drive
Prairie View, TX 77446
Phone: (936) 857-2626
Fax: (936) 857-2699
E-mail: admissions@pvamu.edu
http://www.pvamu.edu
Computer engineering, drafting and
    design technology, electrical and
    communications engineering,
    electrical engineering technology.

Rice University
P.O. Box 1892
Houston TX 77251
Phone: (713) 348-7423
Fax: (713) 348-5952
E-mail: admission@rice.edu
http://www.rice.edu
Applied mathematics, cognitive science,
    computer engineering, electrical and
    communications engineering.

St. Edward's University
3001 South Congress Avenue
Austin, TX 78704
Phone: (512) 448-8400

Fax: NA
E-mail: infostedwards.edu
http://www.stedwards.edu
Graphic design.

St. Mary's University
One Camino Santa Maria
San Antonio, TX 78228
Phone: (210) 436-3126
Fax: (210) 431-6742
E-mail: uadm@stmarytx.edu
http://www.stmarytx.edu
Computer engineering, electrical and
    communications engineering.

Sam Houston State University
P.O. Box 2418, SHSU
Huntsville, TX 77341
Phone: (936) 294-1828
Fax: (936) 294-3758
E-mail: admissions@shsu.edu
http://www.shsu.edu
Drafting and design technology, electrical
    engineering technology.

Southern Methodist University
P.O. Box 750296
Dallas, TX 75275
Phone: (214) 768-2058
Fax: (214) 768-2507
E-mail: enroll_serv@mail.smu.edu
http://www.smu.edu
Computer engineering, electrical and
    communications engineering.

Southwestern Adventist University
P.O. Box 567
Keene, TX 76059
Phone: (800) 433-2240
Fax: (817) 645-3921
E-mail: illingworth@swac.edu
http://www.swac.edu
Applied mathematics.

Stephen F. Austin State University
P.O. Box 13051, SFA Station
Nacogdoches, TX 75962
Phone: (936) 468-2504
Fax: (936) 468-3849
E-mail: admissions@sfasu.edu
http://www.sfasu.edu
Data processing technology.

Tarleton State University
P.O. Box T-0030
Tarleton Station
Stephenville, TX 76402
Phone: (254) 968-9125
Fax: (254) 968-9951

E-mail: uadm@tarleton.edu
http://www.tarleton.edu
Sales/distribution.

Texas A&M University—Commerce
P.O. Box 3011
Commerce, TX 75429
Phone: (903) 886-5106
Fax: (903) 886-5888
E-mail: admissions@tamu-commerce.edu
http://www.tamu-commerce.edu
Applied mathematics, design/visual
    communications, digital media,
    electrical engineering technology.

**Texas A&M University—Corpus
    Christi**
6300 Ocean Drive
Corpus Christi, TX 78412
Phone: (361) 825-2624
Fax: (361) 825-5887
E-mail: judith.perales@mail.tamucc.edu
http://www.tamucc.edu
Applied mathematics, computer
    engineering, electrical engineering
    technology.

Texas A&M University—Kingsville
700 University Boulevard, MSC 128
Kingsville, TX 78363
Phone: (361) 593-2315
Fax: (361) 593-2195
E-mail: ksossrx@tamuk.edu
http://www.tamuk.edu
Applied mathematics, computer
    engineering, electrical and
    communications engineering,
    electrical engineering technology.

Texas Christian University
Office of Admissions
TCU, P.O. Box 297013
Fort Worth, TX 76129
Phone: (817) 257-7490
Fax: (817) 257-7268
E-mail: frogmail@tcu.edu
http://www.tcu.edu
Graphic design, telecommunications
    technology.

Texas Southern University
3100 Cleburne Street
Houston, TX 77004
Phone: (713) 313-7420
Fax: (713) 313-4317
E-mail: admissions@tsu.edu
http://www.tsu.edu
Drafting and design technology, electrical
    engineering technology.

Texas State University—San Marcos
429 North Guadalupe Street
San Marcos, TX 78666
Phone: (512) 245-2364
Fax: (512) 245-9020
E-mail: admissions@txstate.edu
http://www.txstate.edu
Data processing technology, recording arts.

Texas Tech University
P.O. Box 45005
Lubbock, TX 79409
Phone: (806) 742-1480
Fax: (806) 742-0062
E-mail: admissions@ttu.edu
http://www.ttu.edu
Computer engineering, electrical and
    communications engineering,
    electrical engineering technology,
    telecommunications technology.

University of Houston—Clear Lake
2700 Bay Area Boulevard
Houston, TX 77058
Phone: (281) 283-7600
Fax: (281) 283-2530
E-mail: admissions@cl.uh.edu
http://www.uhcl.edu
Computer engineering, electrical
    engineering technology, mathematics/
    computer science, sales/distribution.

University of Houston—Downtown
Admissions Office
One Main Street
Houston, TX 77002
Phone: (713) 221-8522
Fax: (713) 221-8157
E-mail: uhdadmit@dt.uh.edu
http://www.uhd.edu
Applied mathematics, computer
    engineering, electrical engineering
    technology, sales/distribution,
    technical and business writing.

University of Houston—Houston
Office of Admissions
122 East Cullen Building
Houston, TX 77204
Phone: (713) 743-1010
Fax: (713) 743-9633
E-mail: admissions@uh.edu
http://www.uh.edu
Applied mathematics, communications
    technology, computer engineering,
    sales/distribution.

University of Houston—Victoria Campus
Enrollment Management Office, UHV
Victoria, TX 77901

Phone: (361) 788-6222
Fax: (361) 572-9377
E-mail: urbanom@jade.vic.uh.edu
http://www.vic.uh.edu
Computer engineering, electrical
    engineering technology, sales/
    distribution.

University of North Texas
P.O. Box 311277
Denton, TX 76203
Phone: (940) 565-2681
Fax: (940) 565-2408
E-mail: undergrad@unt.edu
http://www.unt.edu
Communications technology, electrical
    engineering technology.

University of Texas—Arlington
Office of Admissions
P.O. Box 19111
Arlington, TX 76019
Phone: (817) 272-6287
Fax: (817) 272-3435
E-mail: admissions@uta.edu
http://www.uta.edu
Computer engineering, electrical and
    communications engineering.

University of Texas—Austin
P.O. Box 8058
Austin, TX 78713
Phone: (512) 475-7440
Fax: (512) 475-7475
E-mail: frmn@uts.cc.utexas.edu
http://www.utexas.edu
Design/visual communications,
    electrical and communications
    engineering.

University of Texas—Dallas
P.O. Box 830688, MC 11
Richardson, TX 75083
Phone: (972) 883-2342
Fax: (972) 883-6803
E-mail: admissions-status@utdallas.
    edu
http://www.utdallas.edu
Applied mathematics, computer
    engineering, electrical and
    communications engineering, software
    engineering.

University of Texas—El Paso
500 West University Avenue
El Paso, TX 79968
Phone: (915) 747-5576
Fax: (915) 747-8893

E-mail: admission@utep.edu
http://www.utep.edu
Applied mathematics, computer
    engineering, electrical and
    communications engineering, graphic
    design, technical and business
    writing.

University of Texas—Pan American
Office of Admissions and Records
1201 West University Drive
Edinburgh. TX 78541
Phone: (956) 381-2201
Fax: (956) 381-2212
E-mail: admissions@panam.edu
http://www.panam.edu
Electrical and communications
    engineering, illustration.

University of Texas—San Antonio
6900 North Loop 1604 West
San Antonio, TX 78249
Phone: (210) 458-4530
Fax: (210) 458-7716
E-mail: prospects@utsa.edu
http://www.utsa.edu
Computer engineering, electrical and
    communications engineering, sales/
    distribution, technical and business
    writing.

University of Texas—Tyler
3900 University Boulevard
Tyler, TX 75799
Phone: (903) 566-7202
Fax: (903) 566-7068
E-mail: admissions@mail.uttyl.edu
http://www.uttyler.edu
Sales/distribution.

University of the Incarnate Word
4301 Broadway, Box 285
San Antonio, TX 78209
Phone: (210) 829-6005
Fax: (210) 829-3921
E-mail: admis@universe.uiwtx.edu
http://www.uiw.edu
Computer graphics, information
    technology.

West Texas A&M University
P.O. Box 60907
Canyon, TX 79016
Phone: (806) 651-2020
Fax: (806) 651-5268
E-mail: admissions@mail.wtamu.edu
http://www.wtamu.edu
Graphic design.

UTAH

Brigham Young University
A-153 ASB
Provo, UT 84602
Phone: (801) 422-2507
Fax: (801) 422-0005
E-mail: admissions@byu.edu
http://www.byu.edu
Animation, cinematography and film/video production, computer engineering, design/visual communications, electrical and communications engineering, graphic design, illustration, information technology, organizational communication, playwriting/screenwriting.

Southern Utah University
Admissions Office
351 West Center Street
Cedar City, UT 84720
Phone: (435) 586-7740
Fax: (435) 865-8223
E-mail: Adminfo@suu.edu
http://www.suu.edu
Computer programming—specific applications, data processing technology, drafting and design technology.

University of Utah
210 South 1460 East, Room 250 South
Salt Lake City, UT 84112
Phone: (801) 581-7281
Fax: (801) 585-7864
E-mail: admiss@sa.utah.edu
http://www.utah.edu
Computer engineering, electrical and communications engineering, mathematics/computer science.

Utah State University
0160 Old Main Hill
Logan, UT 84322
Phone: (435) 797-1079
Fax: (435) 797-3708
E-mail: admit@cc.usu.edu
http://www.usu.edu
Computer engineering, drafting and design technology, electrical and communications engineering, electrical engineering technology.

Weber State University
1137 University Circle
Ogden, UT 84408
Phone: (801) 626-6744
Fax: (801) 626-6747
E-mail: admissions@weber.edu
http://www.weber.edu
Applied mathematics, computer programming—specific applications, design/visual communications, drafting and design technology, electrical engineering technology, technical and business writing.

VERMONT

Bennington College
Office of Admissions and Financial Aid
Bennington, VT 05201
Phone: (802) 440-4312
Fax: (802) 440-4320
E-mail: admissions@bennington.edu
http://www.bennington.edu
Applied mathematics, cinematography and film/video production, computer graphics, design/visual communications, mathematics/computer science, multimedia, playwriting/screenwriting.

Burlington College
95 North Avenue
Burlington, VT 05401
Phone: (802) 862-9616
Fax: (802) 660-4331
E-mail: admissions@burcol.edu
http://www.burlingtoncollege.edu
Animation, cinematography and film/video production, photographic/film/video technology.

Castleton State College
Office of Admissions
Castleton, VT 05735
Phone: (802) 468-1213
Fax: (802) 468-1476
E-mail: info@castleton.edu
http://www.castleton.edu
Digital media, e-commerce, mathematics/computer science, web/multimedia management.

Champlain College
163 South Willard Street
P.O. Box 670
Burlington, VT 05402
Phone: (802) 860-2727
Fax: (802) 860-2767
E-mail: admission@champlain.edu
http://www.champlain.edu
Animation, cinematography and film/video production, computer graphics, design/visual communications, digital media, e-commerce, graphic design, information technology, LAN/WAN management, multimedia, organizational communication, software engineering, webpage/multimedia design.

Lyndon State College
1001 College Road
Lyndonville, VT 05851
Phone: (802) 626-6200
Fax: (802) 626-6335
E-mail: admissions@lyndonstate.edu
http://www.lsc.vsc.edu
Graphic design.

Marlboro College
P.O. Box A, South Road
Marlboro, VT 05344
Phone: (802) 258-9236
Fax: (802) 451-7555
E-mail: admissions@marlboro.edu
http://www.marlboro.edu
Cinematography and film/video production, mathematics/computer science, playwriting/screenwriting.

Middlebury College
Emma Willard House
Middlebury, VT 05763
Phone: (802) 443-3000
Fax: (802) 443-2056
E-mail: admissions@middlebury.edu
http://www.middlebury.edu
Cinematography and film/video production.

Norwich University
Admissions Office
158 Harmon Drive
Northfield, VT 05663
Phone: (802) 485-2001
Fax: (802) 485-2032
E-mail: nuadm@norwich.edu
http://www.norwich.edu
Electrical and communications engineering.

University of Vermont
Admissions Office
194 South Prospect Street
Burlington, VT 05401
Phone: (802) 656-3370
Fax: (802) 656-8611
E-mail: admissions@uvm.edu
http://www.uvm.edu
Electrical and communications engineering.

VIRGINIA

Art Institute of Washington
1820 North Fort Myer Drive
Arlington, VA 22209
Phone: (703) 358-9550
Fax: (703) 358-9759
E-mail: aiwadm@aii.edu
http://www.aii.edu
Animation, graphic design, webpage/
   multimedia design.

Averett University
420 West Main Street
Danville, VA 24541
Phone: (434) 791-4996
Fax: (434) 797-2784
E-mail: admit@averett.edu
http://www.averett.edu
Applied mathematics, e-commerce,
   mathematics/computer science.

Christopher Newport University
1 University Place
Newport News, VA 23608
Phone: (757) 594-7015
Fax: (757) 594-7333
E-mail: admit@cnu.edu
http://www.cnu.edu
Computer engineering.

DeVry University—Crystal City
2341 Jefferson Davis Highway
Arlington, VA 22202
Phone: (703) 414-4100
Fax: (703) 414-4040
E-mail: admissions@devry.edu
http://www.devry.edu
Electrical engineering technology.

George Mason University
Undergraduate Admissions Office
400 University Drive, MSN 3A4
Fairfax, VA 22030
Phone: (703) 993-2400
Fax: (703) 993-2392
E-mail: admissions@gmu.edu
http://www.gmu.edu
Electrical and communications
   engineering, mathematics/computer
   science.

Hampden-Sydney College
P.O. Box 667
Hampden-Sydney, VA 23943
Phone: (434) 223-6120
Fax: (434) 223-6346
E-mail: hsapp@hsc.edu
http://www.hsc.edu

Applied mathematics, mathematics/
   computer science.

Hampton University
Office of Admissions
Hampton, VA 23668
Phone: (757) 727-5328
Fax: (757) 727-5095
E-mail: admissions@hamptonu.edu
http://www.hamptonu.edu
Computer engineering, electrical and
   communications engineering.

James Madison University
Sonner Hall, MSC 0101
Harrisonburg, VA 22807
Phone: (540) 568-5681
Fax: (540) 568-3332
E-mail: gotojmu@jmu.edu
http://www.jmu.edu
Technical and business writing.

Liberty University
1971 University Boulevard
Lynchburg, VA 24502
Phone: (434) 582-5985
Fax: (800) 542-2311
E-mail: admissions@liberty.edu
http://www.liberty.edu
Graphic design.

Mary Baldwin College
P.O. Box 1500
Staunton, VA 24402
Phone: (540) 887-7019
Fax: (540) 887-7279
E-mail: admit@mbc.edu
http://www.mbc.edu
Applied mathematics.

Marymount University
2807 North Glebe Road
Arlington, VA 22207
Phone: (703) 284-1500
Fax: (703) 522-0349
E-mail: admissions@marymount.edu
http://www.marymount.edu
Graphic design.

Norfolk State University
700 Park Avenue
Norfolk, VA 23504
Phone: (757) 823-8396
Fax: (757) 823-2078
E-mail: admissions@nsu.edu
http://www.nsu.edu
Electrical engineering technology, electrical
   and communications engineering,
   electrical engineering technology.

Old Dominion University
108 Rollins Hall
5215 Hampton Boulevard
Norfolk, VA 23529
Phone: (757) 683-3685
Fax: (757) 683-3255
E-mail: admit@odu.edu
http://www.odu.edu
Computer engineering, electrical and
   communications engineering,
   electrical engineering technology,
   graphic design.

Radford University
P.O. Box 6903
RU Station
Radford, VA 24142
Phone: (540) 831-5371
Fax: (540) 831-5038
E-mail: ruadmiss@radford.edu
http://www.radford.edu
Design/visual communications.

University of Virginia
Office of Admission
P.O. Box 400160
Charlottesville, VA 22906
Phone: (434) 982-3200
Fax: (434) 924-3587
E-mail: undergradadmission@virginia.
   edu
http://www.virginia.edu
Applied mathematics, computer
   engineering, electrical and
   communications engineering,
   mathematics/computer science.

Virginia Commonwealth University
821 West Franklin Street
P.O. Box 842526
Richmond, VA 23284
Phone: (804) 828-1222
Fax: (804) 828-1899
E-mail: vcuinfo@vcu.edu
http://www.vcu.edu
Computer engineering, design/visual
   communications, electrical and
   communications engineering.

**Virginia Polytechnic Institute and State
   University**
7054 Haycock Road
Blacksburg, VA 24061
Phone: (540) 231-6267
Fax: (540) 231-3242
E-mail: admissions@vt.edu
http://www.vt.edu
Computer engineering, electrical and
   communications engineering.

Virginia State University
One Hayden Street
P.O. Box 9018
Petersburg, VA 23806
Phone: (804) 524-5902
Fax: (804) 524-5056
E-mail: admiss@vsu.edu
http://www.vsu.edu
Computer engineering.

Virginia Union University
1500 North Lombardy Street
Richmond, VA 23220
Phone: (804) 342-3570
Fax: NA
E-mail: admissions@vuu.edu
http://www.vuu.edu
Sales/distribution.

Virginia Wesleyan College
1584 Wesleyan Drive
Norfolk/Virginia Beach, VA 23052
Phone: (757) 455-3208
Fax: (757) 461-5238
E-mail: admissions@vwc.edu
http://www.vwc.edu
Mathematics/computer science.

WASHINGTON

Art Institute of Seattle
2323 Elliott Avenue
Seattle, WA 98121
Phone: (800) 275-2471
Fax: (206) 269-0275
E-mail: aisadm@ais.edu
http://www.ais.edu
Cinematography and film/video
    production, graphic design, multimedia.

Central Washington University
Admissions Office
400 East Eighth Avenue
Ellensburg, WA 98926
Phone: (509) 963-1211
Fax: (509) 963-3022
E-mail: cwuadmis@cwu.edu
http://www.cwu.edu
Electrical engineering technology.

Cornish College of the Arts
710 East Roy Street
Seattle, WA 98102
Phone: (800) 726-5016
Fax: (206) 720-1011
E-mail: admissions@cornish.edu
http://www.cornish.edu
Cinematography and film/video
    production, design/visual

communications, illustration,
    playwriting/screenwriting.

DeVry University—Seattle
3600 South 344th Way
Federal Way, WA 98001
Phone: (253) 943-2800
Fax: (253) 943-3291
E-mail: admissions@sea.devry.edu
http://www.devry.edu
Electrical engineering technology,
    information technology.

Eastern Washington University
526 Fifth Street
Cheney, WA 99004
Phone: (509) 359-2397
Fax: (509) 359-6692
E-mail: admissions@mail.ewu.edu
http://www.ewu.edu
Communications technology, computer
    engineering, electrical engineering
    technology, technical and business
    writing.

The Evergreen State College
2700 Evergreen Parkway NW
Office of Admissions
Olympia, WA 98505
Phone: (360) 867-6170
Fax: (360) 867-6576
E-mail: admissions@evergreen.edu
http://www.evergreen.edu
Cinematography and film/video
    production, multimedia.

Gonzaga University
502 East Boone Avenue
Spokane, WA 99258
Phone: (509) 323-6572
Fax: (509) 324-5780
E-mail: admissions@gonzaga.edu
http://www.gonzaga.edu
Computer engineering, electrical and
    communications engineering,
    mathematics/computer science.

Henry Cogswell College
3002 Colby Avenue
Everett, WA 98021
Phone: (425) 258-3351
Fax: (425) 257-0405
E-mail: admissions@henrycogswell.edu
http://www.henrycogswell.edu
Electrical and communications
    engineering.

Northwest College
P.O. Box 579
Kirkland, WA 98083

Phone: (425) 889-5231
Fax: (425) 889-5224
E-mail: admissions@ncag.edu
http://www.nwcollege.edu
Organizational communication.

Pacific Lutheran University
Office of Admissions
12180 Park Street South
Tacoma, WA 98447
Phone: (253) 535-7151
Fax: (253) 536-5136
E-mail: admissions@plu.edu
http://www.plu.edu
Computer engineering.

Seattle Pacific University
3307 3rd Avenue West
Seattle, WA 98119
Phone: (206) 281-2021
Fax: (206) 281-2669
E-mail: admissions@spu.edu
http://www.spu.edu
Computer engineering, electrical and
    communications engineering.

Seattle University
Admissions Office
900 Broadway
Seattle, WA 98122
Phone: (206) 296-2000
Fax: (206) 296-5656
E-mail: admissions@seattleu.edu
http://www.seattleu.edu
Applied mathematics, electrical and
    communications engineering.

University of Washington
1410 NE Campus Parkway
320 Schmitz, P.O. Box 355840
Seattle, WA 98195
Phone: (206) 543-9686
Fax: (206) 685-3655
E-mail: askuwadm@u.washington.edu
http://www.washington.edu
Applied mathematics, computer
    engineering, electrical and
    communications engineering,
    information technology, technical and
    business writing.

Walla Walla College
Office of Admissions
204 South College Avenue
College Place, WA 99324
Phone: (509) 527-2327
Fax: (509) 527-2397
E-mail: info@wwc.edu
http://www.wwc.edu

Computer engineering, computer graphics, data processing technology, electrical and communications engineering.

Washington State University
370 Lighty Student Services
Pullman, WA 99164
Phone: (509) 335-5586
Fax: (509) 335-4902
E-mail: admiss2@wsu.edu
http://www.wsu.edu
Applied mathematics, computer engineering, electrical and communications engineering, mathematics/computer science.

Western Washington University
Mail Stop 9009
Bellingham, WA 98225
Phone: (360) 650-3440
Fax: (360) 650-7369
E-mail: admit@cc.wwu.edu
http://www.www.edu
Accounting/computer science, design/visual communications, electrical engineering technology, graphic design, multimedia, technical and business writing.

Whitworth College
300 West Hawthorne Road
Spokane, WA 99251
Phone: (509) 777-4786
Fax: (509) 777-3758
E-mail: admission@whitworth.edu
http://www.whitworth.edu
Applied mathematics.

WEST VIRGINIA

Alderson-Broddus College
P.O. Box 2003
Philippi, WV 26416
Phone: (800) 263-1549
Fax: (304) 457-6239
E-mail: admissions@ab.edu
http://www.ab.edu
Applied mathematics, technical and business writing.

Bethany College
Office of Admissions
Bethany, WV 26032
Phone: (304) 829-7611
Fax: (304) 829-7142
E-mail: admission@bethanywv.edu
http://www.bethanywv.edu
Design/visual communications, mathematics/computer science.

Concord College—Athens
1000 Vermillion Street
P.O. Box 1000
Athens, WV 24712
Phone: (304) 384-5248
Fax: (304) 384-9044
E-mail: admissions@concord.edu
http://www.concord.edu
Graphic design.

Davis & Elkins College
100 Campus Drive
Elkins, WV 26241
Phone: (304) 637-1230
Fax: (304) 637-1800
E-mail: admiss@davisandelkins.edu
http://www.davisandelkins.edu
Computer programming—specific applications.

Fairmount State University
1201 Locust Avenue
Fairmont, WV 26554
Phone: (800) 641-5678
Fax: NA
E-mail: At Web site
http://www.fairmontstate.edu
Drafting and design technology, electrical engineering technology.

Mountain State University
609 South Kanawha Street
Beckley, WV 25801
Phone: (304) 929-1433
Fax: (304) 253-3463
E-mail: gomsu@mountainstate.edu
http://www.mountainstate.edu
Electrical and communications engineering, electrical engineering technology.

Ohio Valley College
1 Campus View Drive
Vienna, WV 26105
Phone: (304) 865-6200
Fax: (304) 865-6001
E-mail: admissions@ovc.edu
http://www.ovc.edu
Information technology.

Salem International University
223 West Main Street
Salem, WV 26426
Phone: (304) 782-5336
Fax: (304) 782-5592
E-mail: admissions@salemiu.edu
http://www.salemiu.edu
Mathematics/computer science.

Shepherd College
Office of Admissions
P.O. Box 3210
Shepherdstown, WV 25443
Phone: (304) 876-5212
Fax: (304) 876-5165
E-mail: admoff@shepherd.edu
http://www.shepherd.edu
Communications technology, computer programming—specific applications. design/visual communications, electrical engineering technology.

University of Charleston
2300 MacCorkle Avenue Southeast
Charleston, WV 25304
Phone: (304) 357-4750
Fax: (304) 357-4781
E-mail: admissions@uchaswv.edu
http://www.uchaswv.edu
Information technology.

West Virginia State University
P.O. Box 1000
Institute, WV 25112
Phone: (800) 987-2112
Fax: NA
E-mail: At Web site
http://www.wvstateu.edu
Applied mathematics, drafting and design technology, electrical and communications engineering, electrical engineering technology, technical and business writing.

West Virginia University
Admissions Office
P.O. Box 6009
Morgantown, WV 26506
Phone: (304) 293-2121
Fax: (304) 293-3080
E-mail: wvuadmissions@arc.wvu.edu
http://www.wvu.edu
Computer engineering, drafting and design technology, electrical and communications engineering.

West Virginia University Institute of Technology
Box 10, Old Main
Montgomery, WV 25136
Phone: (304) 442-3167
Fax: (304) 442-3097
E-mail: admissions@wvutech.edu
http://www.wvutech.edu
Electrical and communications engineering, electrical engineering technology.

Wheeling Jesuit University
316 Washington Avenue
Wheeling, WV 26003
Phone: (304) 243-2359
Fax: (304) 243-2397
E-mail: admiss@wju.edu
http://www.wju.edu
Sales/distribution.

WISCONSIN

Cardinal Stritch University
6801 North Yates Road, Box 237
Milwaukee, WI 53217
Phone: (414) 410-4040
Fax: (414) 410-4058
E-mail: admityou@stritch.edu
http://www.stritch.edu
Mathematics/computer science.

Carroll College
100 North East Avenue
Waukesha, WI 53186
Phone: (262) 524-7220
Fax: (262) 951-3037
E-mail: ccinfo@ccadmin.cc.edu
http://www.cc.edu
Applied mathematics, organizational
    communication, software
    engineering.

Concordia University—Wisconsin
12800 North Lakeshore Drive
Cequon, WI 53097
Phone: (262) 243-5700
Fax: (262) 243-4545
E-mail: admission@cuw.edu
http://www.cuw.edu
Graphic design.

Lawrence University
P.O. Box 599
Appleton, WI 54912
Phone: (920) 832-6500
Fax: (920) 832-6782
E-mail: excel@lawrence.edu
http://www.lawrence.edu
Cognitive science, mathematics/computer
    science.

Marian College of Fond du Lac
45 South National Avenue
Fond du Lac, WI 54935
Phone: (920) 923-7650
Fax: (920) 923-8755
E-mail: admissions@mariancollege.edu
http://www.mariancollege.edu
Organizational communication.

Marquette University
P.O. Box 1881
Milwaukee, WI 53201
Phone: (414) 288-7302
Fax: (414) 288-3764
E-mail: admissions@marquette.edu
http://www.marquette.edu
Computer engineering, e-commerce,
    electrical and communications
    engineering, mathematics/computer
    science.

Milwaukee School of Engineering
1025 North Broadway
Milwaukee, WI 53202
Phone: (414) 277-6763
Fax: (414) 277-7475
E-mail: explore@msoe.edu
http://www.msoe.edu
Computer engineering, electrical and
    communications engineering, software
    engineering, technical and business
    writing.

Mount Mary College
2900 North Menomonee River Parkway
Milwaukee, WI 53222
Phone: (414) 256-1219
Fax: (414) 256-0180
E-mail: admiss@mtmary.edu
http://www.mtmary.edu
Computer graphics, design/visual
    communications, technical and
    business writing.

St. Norbert College
100 Grant Street
De Pere, WI 54115
Phone: (920) 403-3005
Fax: (920) 403-4072
E-mail: admit@snc.edu
http://www.snc.edu
Computer programming—specific
    applications, mathematics/computer
    science.

University of Wisconsin—Madison
Red Gym and Armory
716 Langdon Street
Madison, WI 53706
Phone: (608) 262-3961
Fax: (608) 262-7706
E-mail: onwisconsin@admissions.wisc.edu
http://www.wisc.edu
Cinematography and film/video
    production, computer engineering,
    design/visual communications,
    electrical and communications
    engineering.

University of Wisconsin—Milwaukee
P.O. Box 749
Milwaukee, WI 53201
Phone: (414) 229-3800
Fax: (414) 229-6940
E-mail: uwmlook@uwm.edu
http://www.uwm.edu
Applied mathematics, electrical and
    communications engineering,
    multimedia.

University of Wisconsin—Oshkosh
Dempsey Hall 135
800 Algoma Boulevard
Oshkosh, WI 54901
Phone: (920) 424-0202
Fax: (920) 424-1098
E-mail: oshadmuw@uwosh.edu
http://www.uwosh.edu
Cinematography and film/video
    production.

University of Wisconsin—Parkside
P.O. Box 2000
Kenosha, WI 53141
Phone: (262) 595-2355
Fax: (262) 595-2008
E-mail: matthew.jensen@uwp.edu
http://www.uwp.edu
Mathematics/computer science.

University of Wisconsin—Platteville
1 University Plaza
Platteville, WI 53818
Phone: (608) 342-1125
Fax: (608) 342-1122
E-mail: schumacr@uwplatt.edu
http://www.uwplatt.edu
Electrical and communications
    engineering.

University of Wisconsin—Stevens Point
Student Services Center
Stevens Point, WI 54481
Phone: (715) 346-2441
Fax: (715) 346-3957
E-mail: admiss@uwsp.edu
http://www.uwsp.edu
Webpage/multimedia design.

University of Wisconsin—Stout
Admissions, UW—Stout
Menomonie, WI 54751
Phone: (715) 232-1411
Fax: (715) 232-1667
E-mail: admissions@uwstout.edu
http://www.uwstout.edu
Applied mathematics, sales/distribution,
    technical and business writing.

University of Wisconsin—Superior
Belknap and Catlin
P.O. Box 2000
Superior, WI 54880
Phone: (715) 394-8230
Fax: (715) 394-8107
E-mail: admissions@uwsuper.edu
http://www.uwsuper.edu
Communications technology,
    mathematics/computer science.

**University of Wisconsin—
    Whitewater**
800 West Main Street
Baker Hall
Whitewater, WI 53190
Phone: (414) 472-1234
Fax: (414) 472-1515

E-mail: uwwadmit@uww.edu
http://www.uww.edu
Information technology.

Viterbo University
900 Viterbo Drive
La Crosse, WI 54601
Phone: (608) 796-3010
Fax: (608) 796-3020
E-mail: admission@viterbo.edu
http://www.viterbo.edu
Design/visual communications, graphic
    design.

WYOMING

University of Wyoming
Admissions Office

P.O. Box 3435
Laramie, WY 82071
Phone: (307) 766-5160
Fax: (307) 766-4042
E-mail: why-wyo@uwyo.edu
http://www.uwyo.edu
Computer engineering, e-commerce,
    electrical and communications
    engineering.

APPENDIX II
PERIODICALS, NEWSLETTERS,
AND DIRECTORIES

A. PERIODICALS AND NEWSLETTERS

The following is a selected list of periodicals and newsletters devoted to electronic games, the Internet, and multimedia. In addition, a large number of Internet Web sites and blogs are dedicated to providing information and news about electronic games, as well as about issues relating to multimedia and to the Internet. A search on any major Internet search engine, such as Google, will provide access to this multiplicity of material. In addition, many magazines (both in print and online) from Canada and the United Kingdom are devoted exclusively to information about electronic games. A visit to local newsstands/bookstores that carry imported periodicals should provide an abundance of titles for the interested gamer.

Available in print only *
Available in print and online **
Available online only ***

Abyss Magazine *
Ragnarok Enterprises
P.O. Box 14033
Austin, TX 78714
Phone: (512) 472-6535
Fax: (512) 472-6220
E-mail: NA
Web site: NA

Beckett Massive Online Gamer *
P.O. Box 350
Big Sandy, TX 75755
Phone: (800) 840-3137
Fax: NA
E-mail: At Web site
http://www.beckett.com/beckettMOG/
    default.

**Brandweek Video Gaming Directory—
    2006 Edition (PDF File only) ****
VNU Business Media
770 Broadway
New York, NY 10003
Phone: (646) 654-4500
Fax: NA
E-mail: bmcomm@vnuinc.com
http://store.vnuemedia.com

The Broadband Report **
CMP Media, LLC
600 Community Drive
Manhasset, NY 11030
Phone: (516) 562-5000
Fax: (516) 562-7123
E-mail: cmp@cmp.com
http://www.cmp.com

**Cheats: 12,000 Killer Tips, Tricks,
    Codes and Secrets ****
Future Network USA
150 North Hill Drive
Brisbane, CA 94005
Phone: (415) 468-4684
Fax: (415) 656-2483
E-mail: info@futurenetworkUSA.com
http://www.futurenetworkUSA.com

Code Vault Powered by Brady Games **
IDG Entertainment
555 Twelfth Street, Suite 1100
Oakland, CA 94607
Phone: (510) 768-2700
Fax: (510) 768-2703
E-mail: At Web site
http://www.gamerhelp.com

Communications Daily *
Warren Communications News
2115 Ward Court, NW
Washington, DC 20037
Phone: (202) 872-9200
Fax: (202) 293-3435
E-mail: sales@warren-news.com
http://www.warren-news.com

Computer Game Magazine **
65 Millet Street, Suite 203
Richmond, VT 05477
Phone: (802) 434-6493
Fax: (802) 434-6493
E-mail: editor@cgonline.com
http://www.cgonline.com

Computer Games Magazine **
Strategy Plus, Inc.
63 Millet Street, Suite 203
Richmond, VT 05477
Phone: (802) 434-3060
Fax: (802) 434-6493
E-mail: editor@cgonline.com
http://www.cgonline.com

Computer Games Online Newsletter **
Strategy Plus, Inc.
63 Millet Street
Richmond, VT 05477
Phone: (815) 739-5861
Fax: (802) 434-6493
E-mail: editor@cgonline.com
http://www.cgonline.com

Computer Gaming World **
Ziff-Davis Video Game Group
Ziff-Davis Media, Inc.
101 Second Street, Eighth Floor
San Francisco, CA 94105
Phone: (415) 547-8000
Fax: (415) 547-8777
E-mail: info@ziffdavis.com
http://www.ziffdavis.com

Computer Graphics World **
PennWell Corporation
1421 South Sheridan Road
Tulsa, OK 74112
Phone: (847) 246-1971
Fax: (847) 291-4816
E-mail: cgw@omeda.com
http://www.omeda.com

The Cursor: Game Developer Life *
7001 Winedale Drive, Suite A-100
Austin, TX 78759
Phone: (512) 249-8543
Fax: (512) 249-8592
E-mail: NA
http://www.cursor.com

Digital Media Wire ***
Digital Media Wire, Inc.
1737 Whitley Avenue, Suite 500
Los Angeles, CA 90128
Phone: (323) 464-0793
Fax: (323) 372-3849
E-mail: editorial@digitalmediawire.com
http://www.digitalmediawire.com

Dungeon *
Paizo Publishing, LLC
2700 Richards Road, Suite 201
Bellevue, WA 98005
Phone: (425) 289-0060
Fax: (425) 289-0075
E-mail: advertising@paizo.com
http://www.paizo.com

802.11 Planet ***
Jupiter Media
23 Old Kings Highway South
Darien, CT 06820
Phone: (203) 662-2800
Fax: (203) 655-4686
E-mail: news@jupitermedia.com
http://www.e-newsletters.internet.com

Electronic Gaming Monthly **
Ziff-Davis Media Game Group
Ziff-Davis Media, Inc.
101 Second Street, Eighth Floor
San Francisco, CA 94105
Phone: (415) 547-8000
Fax: (415) 547-8777
E-mail: info@ziffdavis.com
http://www.egmmag.com

Electronic Information Report (IDP Report) *
Simba Information
60 Long Ridge Road, Suite 300
Stamford, CT 06902
Phone: (203) 325-8193
Fax: (203) 325-8915
E-mail: info@simbanet.com
http://www.simbanet.com

eWeek: The Computer Newsweekly **
Ziff-Davis Media Enterprise Group
Ziff-Davis Media, Inc.
28 East 28th Street, 11th Floor
New York, NY 10016

Phone: (212) 503-3500
Fax: (212) 503-5680
E-mail: info@ziffdavis.com
http://www.eweek.com

Game Developer *
CMP Media, LLC
600 Harrison Street
San Francisco, CA 94107
Phone: (415) 947-6000
Fax: (415) 947-6027
E-mail: pmcglinchey@cmp.com
http://www.cmp.com

Game Market Watch ***
Jupiter Media
23 Old Kings Highway, South
Darien, CT 06870
Phone: (203) 662-2800
Fax: (203) 655-4686
E-mail: news@jupitermedia.com
http://www.e-newsletters.internet.com

GameNow **
Ziff-Davis Video Game Group
Ziff-Davis Media, Inc.
101 Second Street, Eighth Floor
San Francisco, CA 94105
Phone: (415) 547-8000
Fax: (415) 547-8777
E-mail: info@ziffdavis.com
http://www.ziffdavis.com

Game Pro Magazine **
IDG Entertainment
555 Twelfth Street, Suite 1100
Oakland, CA 94607
Phone: (510) 768-2700
Fax: (510) 768-2703
E-mail: letters@gamepro.com
http://www.idg.com

Gamer Informer **
Sunrise Publications
724 North First Street, Fourth Floor
Minneapolis, MN 55401
Phone: (612) 486-6155
Fax: (612) 486-6101
E-mail: customerservice@gameinformer.
    com
http://www.gameinformer.com

GameSpot.com ***
CNET Networks, Inc.
235 Second Street
San Francisco, CA 94105
Phone: (415) 344-2000
Fax: NA
E-mail: info@gamespot.com
http://www.gamespot.com

Global Media and Communication *
Sage Publications, Inc.
2455 Teller Road
Thousand Oaks, CA 91320
Phone: (805) 499-0721
Fax: (805) 499-8096
E-mail: At Web site
http://www.sagepub.com

Global Media News *
Center for Global Media Studies
3107 East 62nd Street
Spokane, WA 99223
Phone: (509) 443-2057
Fax: (509) 448-2191
E-mail: gmn@cgms.org
http://www.cgms.org

GMR **
Ziff-Davis Video Game Group
Ziff-Davis Media, Inc.
101 Second Street, Eighth Floor
San Francisco, CA 94105
Phone: (415) 547-8000
Fax: (415) 547-8777
E-mail: info@ziffdavis.com
http://www.ziffdavis.com

Hardcore Games Magazine *
DoubleJump Publishing Inc.
21407 NE Union Hill Road
Redmond, WA 98053
Phone: (706) 369-3743
Fax: NA
E-mail: customerservice@
    hardcoregamermag.com
http://www.hardcoregamermag.com

HDRI 3D Magazine *
DMG Publishing
2756 North Green Valley Parkway,
    Suite 261
Henderson, NV 89014
Phone: (702) 900-8656
Fax: (702) 992-0471
E-mail: At Web site
http://www.hdri3d.com

ieMagazine *
Cyberactive Media Group, Inc.
64 Danbury Road, Suite 500
Wilton, CT 06897
Phone: (203) 761-6150
Fax: (203) 761-6184
E-mail: NA
http://www.iemag.com

IGN Entertainment Game Magazines
DirectaDrive ***

File Planet ***
Gamer Metrics ***
GameSpy ***
GameStats.com ***
IGN.com ***
TeamXbox ***
3D Gamers ***
Vault Network ***
Unit of Fox Interactive Media, Inc.
8000 Marina Boulevard, Fourth Floor
Brisbane, CA 94005
Phone: (413) 508-2000
Fax: (413) 508-2001
E-mail: At Web site
http://www.ign.com

InQuest Gamer *
Gareh Shamus Enterprises, Inc.
Wizard Entertainment Group
151 Wells Avenue
Congers, NY 10920
Phone: (845) 268-2000
Fax: (845) 268-0053
E-mail: NA
http://www.wizarduniverse.com

Inside Report on New Media *
Conference Communications
1320 18th Street
San Francisco, CA 94107
Phone: (415) 776-8667
Fax: (603) 963-5957
E-mail: customerservice@
    wizarduniverse.com
http://www.insiderep.com

**International Journal of
    Communication Systems** *
John Wiley & Sons, Inc.
111 River Street
Hoboken, NJ 07030
Phone: (201) 748-6645
Fax: (201) 748-6021
E-mail: subinfo@wiley.com
http://www.wiley.com

**International Journal on Media
    Management** *
(Official journal of the Institute for Media
    & Communication Management)
Lawrence Erlbaum Associates, Inc.
10 Industrial Avenue
Mahwah, NJ 07430
Phone: (201) 258-2200
Fax: (201) 236-0072
E-mail: journals@erlbaum.com
http://www.erlbaum.com

Internet Business Information ***
Gatekeepers, Inc.

320 Washington Street, Suite 302
Boston, MA 02135
Phone: (617) 782-5033
Fax: (617) 782-5735
E-mail: info@igigroup.com
http://www.igigroup.com

Internet Media Review *
Digital Media Advisors, LLC
121 Boston Post Road
Sudbury, MA 01776
Phone: (508) 881-6442
Fax: (508) 881-5604
E-mail: don@dmapeople.com
http://www.digitalmediaadvisors.com

Multimedia Services *
Elsevier—Academic Press
6277 Sea Harbor Drive
Orlando Beach, FL 32887
Phone: (407) 345-4100
Fax: (407) 363-1354
E-mail: usjes@elsevier.com
http://www.harcourt-international.com

New Media and Society *
Sage Publications, Inc.
2455 Teller Road
Thousand Oaks, CA 91320
Phone: (805) 499-0721
Fax: (805) 499-8096
E-mail: At Web site
http://www.sagepub.com

New Media Magazine
ClickZ
Incisive Media Plc.
270 Lafayette Street, Suite 700
New York, NY 10012
Phone: (212) 925-6990
Fax: (212) 925-7505
E-mail: NA
http://www.newmedia.com

The New Media Report *
New Media Report
12500 Fair Lakes Circle, Suite 155
Fairfax, VA 22033
Phone: (800) 631-8883
Fax: (703) 802-2163
E-mail: NA
http://www.newmediareport.com

Nintendo Power *
Nintendo of America, Inc.
4870 150th Avenue, NE
Redmond, WA 98032
Phone: (425) 861-2876
Fax: (425) 882-3583

E-mail: info@nintendopower.com
http://www.nintendopower.com

Official U.S. Play Station Magazine **
Ziff-Davis Video Game Group
101 Second Street, 8th Floor
San Francisco, CA 94105
Phone: (415) 547-8000
Fax: (415) 547-8777
E-mail: info@ziffdavis.com
http://www.ziffdavis.com

Official Xbox Magazine *
Future US, Inc.
4000 Shoreline Court, Suite 400
South San Francisco, CA 94080
Phone: (650) 872-1642
Fax: NA
E-mail: letters@officialboxmagazine.
    com
http://www.futurenetworkusa.com

Online Media Daily ***
Media Post Communications
16 West 19th Street, Ninth Floor
New York, NY 10011
Phone: (212) 204-2000
Fax: (212) 204-2038
E-mail: feedback@mediapost.com
http://www.mediapost.com

Online Publishing Update Newspaper ***
Association of America
1921 Gallows Road, Suite 600
Vienna, VA 22182
Phone: (703) 902-1600
Fax: (703) 902-1616
E-mail: fedletters@naa.org
http://www.naa.org

PC Game Buyer—s Guide *
Sendai Publishing Group, Inc.
1920 Highland Avenue, Suite 222
Lombard, IL 60148
Phone: (818) 712-9400
Fax: NA
E-mail: NA
Web site: NA

PC Gamer **
Future Network USA
150 North Hill Drive, Suite 40
Brisbane, CA 94005
Phone: (415) 468-4684
Fax: (415) 468-4686
E-mail: letters@pcgamer.com
http://www.pcgamer.com

PC Magazine **
Ziff-Davis Computer Tech Group

Ziff-Davis Media, Inc.
28 East 28th Street, 11th Floor
New York, NY 10016
Phone: (212) 503-3500
Fax: (212) 503-5680
E-mail: info@ziffdavis.com
http://www.pcmag.com

Phaze *
Amalgam Media, Inc.
1388 Haight Street, Suite 105
San Francisco, CA 94117
Phone: (415) 861-7583
Fax: (415) 861-7584
E-mail: NA
Web site: NA

Play Magazine *
Fusion Publishing, Inc.
29229 Canwood Street, Suite 200
Agoura Hills, CA 91301
Phone: (818) 707-7786
Fax: (818) 707-7212
E-mail: play@espcomp.com
http://www.playmagazine.com

PSM: Independent Playstation
Magazine **
Future US, Inc.
4000 Shoreline Court, Suite 400
South San Francisco, CA 94080
Phone: (646) 723-5410
Fax: NA
E-mail: NA
http://www.futureus-inc.com

PSM: Playstation 2 Code Book **
Future Network USA
150 North Hill Drive, Suite 40
Brisbane, CA 94005
Phone: (415) 468-4684
Fax: (415) 468-4686
E-mail: NA
http://www.pcgamer.com

Publish E-Newsletter ***
Publish Media, LLC
462 Boston Street
Topsfield, MA 01983
Phone: (978) 887-7900
Fax: (978) 887-6117
E-mail: NA
http://www.publish.com

Pulse Online ***
Telecommunications Industry Association
2500 Wilson Boulevard, Suite 300
Arlington, VA 22201
Phone: (703) 907-7700

Fax: (703) 907-7727
E-mail: At Web site
http://www.tiaonline.org

Signal Processing: Image
Communication *
Elsevier Publishing
360 Park Avenue South
New York, NY 10010
Phone: (212) 989-5800
Fax: (212) 633-3990
E-mail: At Web site
http://www.elsevier.com

Surge—The Pulse of Gaming **
Bedford Communications
1410 Broadway, 21st Floor
New York, NY 10018
Phone: (212) 807-8220
Fax: (212) 807-1098
E-mail: NA
http://www.surgemag.com

Tips & Tricks *
L.F.P., Inc.
8484 Wilshire Boulevard, Suite 800
Beverly Hills, CA 90211
Phone: (323) 951-5400
Fax: (323) 651-0651
E-mail: amaine@lfp.com
http://www.lfp.com

VB (Video Business) **
Reed Business Information
5700 Wilshire Boulevard, Suite 120
Los Angeles, CA 90036
Phone: (323) 965-2402
Fax: (323) 965-2423
E-mail: At Web site
http://www.videobusiness.com

Video Game Buyers Guide *
Ziff-Davis Video Game Group
Ziff-Davis Media, Inc.
101 Second Street, Eighth Floor
San Francisco, CA 94105
Phone: (415) 547-8000
Fax: (415) 547-8777
E-mail: info@ziffdavis.com
http://www.ziffdavis.com

Video Games Underground *
London Publishing Company
1002 West Butler Pike
Ambler, PA 19002
Phone: (215) 643-6385
Fax: (215) 540-0146
E-mail: londonpub@aol.com
Web site: NA

Video Games Underground Digest *
London Publishing Company
1002 West Butler Pike
Ambler, PA 19002
Phone: (215) 643-6385
Fax: (215) 540-0146
E-mail: londonpub@aol.com
Web site: NA

Videography **
CMP Information, Inc.
460 Park Avenue South, Ninth Floor
New York, NY 10016
Phone: (212) 378-0400
Fax: (212) 378-2160
E-mail: cmp@cmp.com
http://www.cmpmedia.com

Videomaker *
York Publishing
1350 East Ninth Street
Chico, CA 95938
Phone: (530) 891-8410
Fax: (530) 891-8443
E-mail: sales@videomaker.com
http://www.videomaker.com

Video Systems Newsmagazine **
Primedia Business Corporate
9800 Metcalf Avenue
Overland Park, KS 66212
Phone: (913) 341-1300
Fax: (913) 967-1898
E-mail: custserv@primediabusiness.com
http://www.primediabusiness.com

Web Content Report *
Lawrence Ragan Communications, Inc.
316 North Michigan Avenue, Suite 400
Chicago, IL 60601
Phone: (312) 960-4100
Fax: (312) 960-4105
E-mail: cservice@ragan.com
http://www.ragan.com

Worldwide Videotex Update **
Worldwide Videotex Company
P.O. Box 3273
Boynton Beach, FL 33429
Phone: (501) 736-2276
Fax: NA
E-mail: markedit@juno.com
http://www.wrpubs.com

Xbox Nation **
Ziff-Davis Video Game Group
Ziff-Davis Media, Inc.
101 Second Street, Eighth Floor
San Francisco, CA 94105

Phone: (415) 547-8000
Fax: (415) 547-8777
E-mail: info@ziffdavis.com
http://www.ziffdavis.com

DIRECTORIES

Brandweek Video Gaming Directory, 2006 Edition *
Vnu Business Media, Inc.
770 Broadway
New York, NY 10003
Phone: (888) 900-3782
E-mail: infomarketplace@vnuemedia.com
http://store.vnuemedia.com

Internet Media Directory *
Bacon's Information, Inc.
332 South Michigan Avenue, Suite 900
Chicago, IL 60604
Phone: (312) 922-2400
Fax: (312) 922-3126
E-mail: info@bacons.com
http://www.bacons.com

Internet Tollfree National Directory *
(also available on CD-Rom)
Volt Information Sciences, Inc.

One Sentry Parkway, Suite 1000
Blue Bell, PA 19422
Phone: (610) 825-7720
Fax: NA
E-mail: At Web site
http://www.internettollfree.com

**Plunkett's Entertainment and Media Industry Almanac ** (also available on CD-Rom)
Plunkett Research, Ltd.
P.O. Drawer 541737
Houston, TX 77254
Phone: (713) 932-0000
Fax: (713) 932-7080
E-mail: customersupport@plunkettresearch.com
http://www.plunkettresearch.com

**Plunkett's Telecommunications Industry Almanac ** (also available on CD-Rom)
Plunkett Research, Ltd.
P.O. Drawer 541737
Houston, TX 77254
Phone: (713) 932-0000
Fax: (713) 932-7080
E-mail: customersupport@plunkettresearch.com
http://www.plunkettresearch.com

Scala—Multimedia Directory *
Address: NA
Phone: NA
Fax: NA
E-mail: At Web site
http://www.scala.com/multimedia

Telecommunications Directory *
Thomson Gale Group—HQ
27500 Drake Road
Farmington Hills, MI 48331
Phone: (248) 699-4253
Fax: (800) 414-5043
E-mail: galeord@gale.com
http://www.gale.com

**Video & Television Blue Book ** (also available on CD-Rom)
Orion Research Corporation
14555 North Scottsdale Road, Suite 330
Scottsdale, AZ 85254
Phone: (480) 951-1114
Fax: (480) 951-1117
E-mail: orion@orionbluebook.com
http://www.orionbluebook.com

APPENDIX III
PROFESSIONAL, INDUSTRY, AND
TRADE ASSOCIATIONS

Since many of these organizations operate on limited budgets, be sure to enclose a self-addressed, stamped envelope when querying any of them for data not available online. Not all of these groups maintain full-time offices, so some cannot be reached via phone, fax, or e-mail. In addition, contact information for some of these organizations may change when a new president or director is selected.

When an organization has several branch offices listed but only a general e-mail and/or Web site, this latter data is placed flush left *after* the various branch listings.

**Academy of Interactive Arts &
    Sciences (AIAS)**
23622 Calabasas Road, Suite 220
Calabasas, CA 91302
Phone: (818) 876-0826
Fax: (818) 876-0850
E-mail: nicole@interactive.org
http://www.interactive.org

**American Association for Artificial
    Intelligence (AAAI)**
445 Burgess Drive
Menlo Park, CA 94025
Phone: (650) 328-3123
Fax: (650) 321-4457
E-mail: info@aaai.org
http://www.aaai.org

American Business Association (ABA)
Hillsboro Executive Center North
350 Fairway Drive, Suite 200
Deerfield Beach, FL 33441
Phone: (954) 571-1877
Fax: (954) 571-8582
E-mail: membership@assnservices.com
http://www.aba-assn.com

**American Federation of Musicians
    (AFM)**

New York Office:
1501 Broadway, Suite 600
New York, NY 10036
Phone: (212) 869-1330
Fax: (212) 764-6134

Legislative Office:
910 17th Street NW, Suite 1070
Washington, DC 20006
Phone: (202) 463-0772
Fax: (202) 463-7441

West Coast Office:
3550 Wilshire Boulevard, Suite 1900
Los Angeles, CA 90010
Phone: (213) 251-4510
Fax: (213) 251-4520
E-mail: At Web Site
http://www.afm.org

**American Institute of Graphic Arts
    (AIGA)**
154 Fifth Avenue
New York, NY 10010
Phone: (212) 807-1990
Fax: (212) 807-1799
E-mail: comments@aiga.org
http://www.aiga.org

**American Management Association
    (AMA)**
1601 Broadway
New York, NY 10019
Phone: (212) 586-8100
Fax: (212) 903-8168
E-mail: customerservice@amanet.org
http://www.amanet.org

**American Marketing Association
    (AMA)**
250 South Wacker Drive, Suite 200
Chicago, IL 60606
Phone: (312) 542-9000
Fax: (312) 542-9001
E-mail: info@ama.org
http://www.marketingpower.com

**American Society for Information
    Science and Technology (ASIST)**
1320 Fenwick Lane, Number 510
Silver Spring, MD 20910
Phone: (301) 495-0900
Fax: (301) 495-6810

E-mail: asis@asis.org
http://www.asis.org

American Society for Quality (ASQ)
600 North Plankinton Avenue
Milwaukee, WI 53203
Phone: (800) 248-1946
Fax: (414) 272-1734
E-mail: help@asq.org
http://www.asq.org

**American Society of Composers,
    Authors, and Publishers (ASCAP)**
1 Lincoln Plaza
New York, NY 10023
Phone: (212) 621-6000
Fax: (212) 724-9064
E-mail: info@ascap.com
http://www.ascap.com

**American Society of Journalists and
    Authors (ASJA)**
1501 Broadway, Suite 302
New York, NY 10036
Phone: (212) 997-0947
Fax: (212) 768-7414
E-mail: staff@asja.org
http://www.asja.org

**American Software Testing
    Qualifications Board (ASTQB),
    North American Affiliate of the
    International Software Testing
    Qualifications Board (ISTQB)**
13153 North Dale Mabry Highway,
    Suite 105
Tampa, FL 33618
Phone: (813) 319-0890
Fax: (813) 968-3597
E-mail: info@astqb.org
http://www.astqb.org

**Association for Applied Interactive
    Multimedia (AAIM)**
P.O. Box 182
Charleston, SC 29402
Phone: (843) 953-1428
Fax: NA
E-mail: seayj@cofc.edu
http://www.aaim.org

**Association for Computing Machinery
    (ACM)**
2 Penn Plaza, Suite 701
New York, NY 10121
Phone: (800) 342-6626
Fax: (212) 302-5826
Phone: (212) 669-7440
Fax: (212) 944-1318
E-mail: acmhelp@acm.org
http://www.acm.org

**Association for Computing Machinery:
    Special Interest Group on Artificial
    Intelligence (SIGART)**
2 Penn Plaza, Suite 701
New York, NY 10121
Phone: (800) 342-6626
Fax: (212) 302-5826
E-mail: acmhelp.org
http://www.acm.org/sigart

**Association for Computing Machinery:
    Special Interest Group on Graphics
    and Interactive Technology
    (SIGGRAPH)**
c/o Alyn Rockwood, VP
1837 Highland Estates Drive
Colorado Springs, CO 80908
Phone: (719) 495-7073
Fax: NA
E-mail: acmhelp@acm.org
http://www.siggraph.org

**Association for Computing Machinery:
    Special Interest Group on
    Multimedia (SIGMM)**
2 Penn Plaza, Suite 701
New York, NY 10121
Phone: (800) 342-6626
Fax: (212) 302-5826
E-mail: acmhelp@acm.org
http://www.sigmm.org

**Association for Computing
    Machinery: Special Interest Group
    on Programming Languages
    (SIGPLAN)**
c/o Jack W. Davidson
Department of Computer Science
151 Engineer's Way

Charlottesville, VA 22904
Phone: (434) 982-2209
Fax: (434) 982-2214
E-mail: chair_sigplan@acm.org
http://www.acm.org/sigs/sigplan

**Association for Computing Machinery:
    Special Interest Group on Security,
    Audit and Control (SIGSAC)**
2 Penn Plaza, Suite 701
New York, NY 10121
Phone: (800) 342-6626
Fax: (212) 302-5826
E-mail: sigs@acm.com
http://www.acm.org/sigs/sigsac

**Association for Computing Machinery:
    Special Interest Group on Software
    Engineering (SIGSOFT)**
2 Penn Plaza, Suite 701
New York, NY 10121
Phone: (800) 342-6626
Fax: (212) 302-5826
E-mail: ignatoff@acm.org
http://www.acm.org/sigs/sigsoft

**Association for Interactive Media
    (AIM)**
1430 Broadway, Eighth Floor
New York, NY 10018
Phone: (886) 337-0008
Fax: (212) 391-9233
E-mail: At Web site
http://www.InteractiveMarketing.org

**Association for Multimedia
    Communications**
P.O. Box 10645
Chicago, IL 60610
Phone: (773) 276-9320
Fax: NA
E-mail: At Web site
http://www.amcomm.org

**Association for Women in
    Communications (AWC)**
780 Ritchia Highway, Suite 28-S
Severna Park, MD 21146
Phone: (410) 544-7442
Fax: (410) 544-4640
E-mail: pat@womcom.org
http://www.womcom.org

**Association of Cinema and Video
    Laboratories (ASVL)**
c/o Beverly Weed, President
1377 Serrano Avenue
Hollywood, CA 90027
Phone: (323) 462-6171

Fax: (323) 401-0601
E-mail: Beverly_weed@rank.com
http://www.acvl.org

**Association of Graphic
    Communications (AGC)**
330 Seventh Avenue, Ninth Floor
New York, NY 10001
Phone: (212) 279-2100
Fax: (212) 279-5381
E-mail: info@agcomm.org
http://www.agcomm.org

**Association of Information Technology
    Professionals (AITP)**
P.O. Box 809189
Chicago, IL 60611
Phone: (312) 245-1070
Fax: (312) 527-6636
E-mail: aitp_hq@aitp.org
http://www.aitp.org

Audio Engineering Society (AES)
60 East 42nd Street, Room 2520
New York, NY 10165
Phone: (212) 661-8528
Fax: (212) 602-0477
E-mail: hq@aes.org
http://www.aes.org

Authors Guild
31 East 28th Street
New York, NY 10016
Phone: (212) 563-5904
Fax: (212) 564-5363
E-mail: staff@authorsguild.com
http://www.authorsguild.org

Automated Imaging Association (AIA)
P.O. Box 3724
Ann Arbor, MI 48106
Phone: (734) 994-6088
Fax: (734) 994-3330
E-mail: aia@automated-imagig.org
http://www.machinevisiononline.org

Broadcast Music, Inc. (BMI)
320 West 57th Street
New York, NY 10019
Phone: (212) 586-2000
Fax: (212) 245-8986
E-mail: info@bmi.com
http://www.bmi.com

**Computer and Communications
    Industry Association (CCIA)**
666 Eleventh Street, NW
Washington, DC 20001
Phone: (202) 783-0070

Fax: (202) 783-0534
E-mail: ccia@ccianet.org
http://www.ccianet.org

**Computer Event Marketing
    Association (CEMA)**
1512 Weiskopf Loop
Round Rock, TX 78664
Phone: (512) 310-8330
Fax: (512) 682-0555
E-mail: info@cemaonline.com
http://www.cemaonline.com

**Computing Technology Industry
    Association (CompTIA)**
1815 South Meyers Road, Suite 300
Oak Brook Terrace, IL 60181
Phone: (630) 678-8300
Fax: (630) 268-1384
E-mail: info@comptia.org
http://www.comptia.org

**Copywriter's Council of America
    (CCA)**
CCA Building
7 Patter Lane
P.O. Box 102
Middle Island, NY 11953
Phone: (631) 929-8555
Fax: (631) 929-3890
E-mail: cca4dmcopy@att.net
http://adr.com/freelance.htm

Cyber Angels
P.O. Box 3171
Allentown, PA 18106
Phone: (610) 377-2966
Fax: (610) 377-3381
E-mail: katya@cyberangels.org
http://www.cyberangels.org

**Digital Printing and Imaging
    Association (DPI)**
c/o Specialty Graphic Imaging
    Association
10015 Main Street
Fairfax, VA 22034
Phone: (703) 385-1339
Fax: (703) 273-0450
E-mail: assist@sgia.org
http://www.sgia.org

DVD Association (DVDA)
1130 Kingston Pike, Suite I-347
Knoxville, TN 37922
Phone: NA
Fax: (865) 675-5231
E-mail: president@dvda.org
http://www.dvda.org

Electronic Retailing Association (ERA)
2000 North 14th Street, Suite 300
Arlington, VA 22201
Phone: (703) 841-1751
Fax: (703) 841-1860
E-mail: contact@retailing.org
http://www.retailing.org

eMarketing Association
105 Franklin Street, Suite 16-129
Westerly, RI 02891
Phone: (401) 315-2194
Fax: (408) 884-2461
E-mail: admin@emarketingassociation.
    com
http://www.emarketingassociation.com

**Enterprise Communications
    Association (ECA)**
1901 Pennsylvania Avenue, NW, Fifth
    Floor
Washington, DC 20006
Phone: (202) 467-4868
Fax: (202) 872-1331
E-mail: sally.stanton@ingrammicro.com
http://www.encomm.org

**Entertainment Software Association
    (ESA) [Formerly Interactive
    Digital Software Association
    (IDSA)]**
1211 Connecticut Avenue, NW,
    Suite 800
Washington, DC 20030
Phone: (202) 223-2400
Fax: NA
E-mail: esa@theesa.com
http://www.theesa.com

**Federal Communications Commission
    (FCC)**
445 12th Street SW
Washington, DC 20554
Phone: (888) 225-5322
Fax: (202) 418-0232
E-mail: fccinfo@fcc.gov
http://www.fcc.gov

**Graphic Arts Technical Foundation
    (GATF)**
200 Deer Run Road
Sewickley, PA 15143
Phone: (412) 741-6860
Fax: (412) 741-2311
E-mail: info@piagatf.org
http://www.gain.net

**Graphic Communications Association
    (GCA)**
100 Dangerfield Road
Alexandria, VA 22314

Phone: (703) 519-8160
Fax: (703) 548-2867
E-mail: info@gca.org
http://www.gca.org

HTML Writers Guild (HWG)
119 East Union Street
Pasadena, CA 91103
Phone: NA
Fax: NA
E-mail: kef@hwg.org
http://www.hwg.org

**Information Resources Management
    Association (IRMA)**
701 East Chocolate Avenue, Suite 200
Hershey, PA 17033
Phone: (717) 533-8879
Fax: (717) 533-8661
E-mail: member@irma-international.org
http://www.irma-international.org

**Information Technology Association of
    America (ITAA)**
1401 Wilson Boulevard, Suite 1100
Arlington, VA 22209
Phone: (703) 522-5055
Fax: (703) 525-2279
E-mail: hmiller@itaa.org
http://www.itaa.org

**Institute for Certification of
    Computing Professionals (ICCP)**
2350 East Devon Avenue, Suite 115
Des Plaines, IL 60018
Phone: (847) 299-4227
Fax: (847) 299-4280
E-mail: office@iccp.org
http://www.iccp.org

**Institute of Electrical and Electronics
    Engineers (IEEE)**
445 Hoes Lane
Piscataway, NJ 08854
Phone: (732) 981-0060
Fax: (732) 981-1721
E-mail: corporate-communications@
    ieee.org
http://www.ieee.org

**Institute of Electrical and Electronics
    Engineers Communications Society
    (COMSOC)**
3 Park Avenue, 17th Floor
New York, NY 10016
Phone: (212) 705-8900
Fax: (212) 705-8999
E-mail: society@comsoc.org
http://www.comsoc.org

**Institute of Electrical and Electronics
    Engineers Computer Society (CS)**
1730 Massachusetts Avenue, NW
Washington, DC 20036
Phone: (202) 371-0101
Fax: (202) 728-9614
E-mail: csinfo@computer.org
http://www.computer.org

Interactive Advertising Bureau (IAB)
116 East 27th Street, Seventh Floor
New York, New York 10016
Phone: (212) 380-4700
Fax: (212) 202-4780
E-mail: At Web site
http://www.iab.net

Interactive Media Alliance (IMA)
GCATT Building
250 14th Street, NW, Fourth Floor
Atlanta, GA 30318
Phone: NA
Fax: NA
E-mail: brian@tima.org
http://www.tima.org

**International Alliance of Theatrical
    Stage Employees, Moving Picture
    Machine Operators of the United
    States and Canada (IATSE):
    Production Sound Technicians,
    Local 695**

General Office:
1430 Broadway, 20th floor
New York, NY 10018
Phone: (212) 730-1770
Fax: (212) 921-7699

West Coast Office:
10045 Riverside Drive
Toluca Lake, CA 91602
Phone: (818) 980-3499
Fax: (818) 980-3496
http://www.iatse-intl.org

**International Association for
    Computer Systems Security
    (IACSS)**
8 Swarthmore Lane
Dix Hills, NY 11746
Phone: (631) 499-1616
Fax: (631) 462-9178
E-mail: iacssjulex@aol.com
http://www.iacss.com

**International Association of Business
    Communicators (IABC)**
1 Hallidie Plaza, Suite 600
San Francisco, CA 94102

Phone: (415) 544-4700
Fax: (415) 544-4747
E-mail: service_centre@iabc.com
http://www.iabc.com

**International Association of
    Webmasters and Designers (IAWD)**
13833-E4 Wellington Trace,
    PMB Suite 214
Wellington, FL 33414
Phone: (561) 533-9001
Fax: (561) 828-0495
E-mail: At Web site
http://www.iawd.com

**International Communication
    Association (ICA)**
1730 Rhode Island Avenue, NW, Suite 300
Washington, DC 20036
Phone: (202) 530-9855
Fax: (202) 530-9851
E-mail: icahdq@icahdq.org
http://www.icahdq.org

**International Game Developers
    Association (IGDA)**
870 Market Street, Suite 1181
San Francisco, CA 94102
Phone: (415) 738-2104
Fax: (415) 738-2178
E-mail: info@igda.org
http://www.igda.org

**International Information Systems
    Security Certification Consortium
    (ISC2)**
2494 Bayshore Boulevard, Suite 201
Dunedin, FL 34698
Phone: (888) 333-4458
Fax: (727) 738-8522
E-mail: infoisc2@isc2.org
http://www.isc2.org/cgi-bin/index.cgi

**International Recording Media
    Association (IRMA)**
182 Nassau Street, Suite 204
Princeton, NJ 08542
Phone: (609) 279-1700
Fax: (609) 229-1999
E-mail: info@recordingmedia.org
http://www.recordingmedia.com

**International Simulation and Gaming
    Association (ISAGA)**
c/o John F. Lobatts
George Washington University
School of Business and Public
    Management
Monroe Hall
Washington, DC 20052

Phone: (202) 994-6918
Fax: (202) 994-4930
E-mail: lobats@gwu.edu
http://www.isaga.info

**International Society of Applied
    Intelligence (ISAI)**
Texas State University, San Marcos
Department of Computer Science
6 University Drive
San Marcos, TX 78606
Phone: (512) 295-3409
Fax: (512) 245-8750
E-mail: cs@txstate.edu
http://www.isai.cs.txstate.edu

**International Society of Certified
    Electronics Technicians (ISCET)**
3008 Pershing Avenue
Fort Worth, TX 76107
Phone: (817) 921-9101
Fax: (817) 921-3741
E-mail: info@iscet.org
http://www.iscet.org

**International Webmasters Association
    (IWA)**
119 East Union Street, Suite F
Pasadena, CA 91103
Phone: (626) 449-3709
Fax: (212) 944-1318
E-mail: acmhelp@acm.org
http://www.acm.org

**Internet Corporation for Assigned
    Names and Numbers (ICANN)**
4676 Admiralty Way, Suite 330
Marina del Rey, CA 90292
Phone: (310) 023-9358
Fax: (310) 823-8649
E-mail: icann@icann.org
http://www.icann.org

**Internet Professional Publishers
    Association (IPPA)**
c/o Digital Minute
P.O. Box 670446
Coral Springs, FL 33067
Phone: (954) 426-3507
Fax: NA
E-mail: info@ippa.org
http://www.ippa.org

Internet Society (IS)
1775 Wiehle Avenue, Suite 102
Reston, VA 20190
Phone: (703) 326-9880
Fax: (703) 326-9881
E-mail: isoc@isoc.org
http://www.isoc.org

Marketing Research Association (MRA)
1344 Silas Deane Highway, Suite 306
P.O. Box 230
Rocky Hill, CT 06067
Phone: (860) 257-4008
Fax: (860) 257-3990
E-mail: email@mra-net.org
http://www.mra-net.org

Media Alliance (MA)
1904 Franklin Street, Suite 500
Oakland, CA 94612
Phone: (510) 832-9000
Fax: (510) 236-8557
E-mail: information@media-alliance.org
http://www.media-alliance.org

Media Resource Service (MRS)
3106 East NC Highway 54
P.O. Box 13975
Research Triangle Park, NC 27709
Phone: (919) 547-5259
Fax: (919) 549-0090
E-mail: mediaresource@sigmaxi.org
http://www.mediaresource.org

MIDI (Musical Instrument Digital Interface) Manufacturers Association (MMA): Interactive Audio Special Interest Group (IASIG)
P.O. Box 3173
La Habra, CA 90632
Phone: (714) 736-9774
Fax: (714) 736-9775
E-mail: info@iasig.org
http://www.iasig.org

National Academy of Recording Arts and Sciences (NARAS)
3402 Pico Boulevard
Santa Monica, CA 90405
Phone: (310) 392-3777
Fax: (310) 392-9262
E-mail: losangeles@grammy.com
http://www.grammy.com

National Association of Communication Systems Engineers (NASCE)
5445 DTC Parkway, Penthouse 4
Greenwood Village, CO 80111
Phone: (303) 488-3450
Fax: (720) 269-4756
E-mail: at Web site
http://www.nasce.com

National Association of Photoshop Professionals (NAPP)
c/o Jeff Kelby, Director

333 Douglas Road East
Oldsmar, FL 34677
Phone: (813) 433-5006
Fax: (813) 433-5015
E-mail: info@photoshopuser.com
http://www.photoshopuser.com

National Association of Video Distributors (NAVD)
1092 North Forest Oak
Henderson, KY 42420
Phone: (270) 826-9423
Fax: (270) 826-9424
E-mail: info@navd.com
http://www.navd.com

National Business Association (NBA)
5151 Beltline Road, Suite 1150
Dallas, TX 75254
Phone: (972) 458-0900
Fax: (972) 960-9149
E-mail: info@nationalbusiness.org
http://www.nationalbusiness.org

National Writers Association (NWA)
3140 South Peoria Street, Suite 295
Aurora, CO 80014
Phone: (303) 841-0246
Fax: (303) 841-2607
E-mail: ExecDirSandyWhelchel@nationalwriters.com
http://www.nationalwriters.com

North American Retail Dealers Association (NARDA)
4700 West Lake Avenue
Glenview, IL 60020
Phone: (800) 621-0298
Fax: (866) 879-7505
E-mail: nardasvc@narda.com
http://www.narda.com

North American Simulation and Gaming Association (NASAGA)
P.O. Box 78636
Indianapolis, IN 46278
Phone: (317) 387-1424
Fax: (317) 387-1921
E-mail: info@nasaga.org
http://www.nasaga.org

NPES—The Association for Suppliers of Printing, Publishing, and Converting Technologies (NPES)
1899 Preston White Drive
Reston, VA 20191
Phone: (703) 264-7200
Fax: (703) 620-0994
E-mail: npes@npes.org
http://www.npes.org

Open Applications Group
P.O. Box 4897
Marietta, GA 30061
Phone: (770) 943-8364
Fax: (770) 234-6036
E-mail: info@openapplications.org
http://www.openapplications.org

Open DeviceNet Association (ODVA)
c/o Technology and Training Center
1099 Highland Drive, Suite A
Ann Arbor, MI 48108
Phone: (734) 975-8890
Fax: (734) 922-0027
E-mail: odva@odva.org
http://www.odva.org

The Open Group
44 Montgomery Street, Suite 960
San Francisco, CA 94104
Phone: (415) 374-8280
Fax: (415) 374-8293
E-mail: memnews-feedback@opengroup.com
http://www.opengroup.com

Producer's Guild of America (PGA)
8530 Wilshire Boulevard, Suite 450
Beverly Hills, CA 90211
Phone: (310) 358-9020
Fax: (310) 358-9520
E-mail: info@producersguild.org
http://www.producersguild.org/index2.shtml

Programmers Guild (PG)
P.O. Box 1250
Summit, NJ 07902
Phone: NA
Fax: NA
E-mail: info@programmersguild.org
http://www.programmersguild.org

Project Management Institute (PMI)
Four Campus Boulevard
Newton Square, PA 19073
Phone: (610) 356-4600
Fax: (610) 356-4647
E-mail: customercare@pmi.org
http://www.pmi.org

Public Relations Society of America (PRSA)
33 Maiden Lane, 11th Floor
New York, NY 10038
Phone: (212) 460-1400
Fax: (212) 995-0757
E-mail: exec@prsa.org
http://www.prsa.org

Quality Assurance Institute (QAI)
7575 Dr. Phillips Boulevard, Suite 350
Orlando, FL 32819
Phone: (407) 363-1111
Fax: NA
E-mail: At Web site
http://www.qaiusa.com

SESAC, INC.

Headquarters Office:
55 Music Square East
Nashville, TN 37203
Phone: (615) 320-0055
Fax: (615) 329-9627
E-mail: info@sesac.com
http://www.sesac.com

New York Office:
152 West 57th Street
New York, NY 10019
Phone: (212) 586-3450
Fax: (212) 489-5699

Los Angeles Office:
501 Santa Monica Boulevard, Suite 450
Santa Monica, CA 90401
Phone: (310) 393-9671
Fax: (310) 393-6497

Society for Quality Assurance (SQA)
2365 Hunters Way
Charlottesville, VA 22904
Phone: (434) 297-4772
Fax: (434) 999-8899
E-mail: sqa@sqa.com
http://www.sqa.com

Society for Technical Communication (STC)
901 North Stuart Street, Suite 904
Arlington, VA 22203
Phone: (703) 522-4114
Fax: (703) 522-2075
E-mail: stc@stc.org
http://www.stc.org

Society of Illustrators
128 East 63rd Street
New York, NY 10021
Phone: (212) 939-2560
Fax: (212) 838-2561
E-mail: info@societyillustrators.org
http://www. societyillustrators.org

Software & Information Industry Association (SIIA)
1090 Vermont Avenue, NW, Sixth Floor
Washington, DC 20005

Phone: (202) 209-7442
Fax: (202) 289-7097
E-mail: At Web site
http://www.siia.net

Software Publishers Association (SPA)
1730 M Street, NW, Suite 700
Washington, DC 20036
Phone: (202) 452-1600
Fax: (202) 289-7097
E-mail: info@spa.org
http://www.spa.org

Telecommunications Industry Association (TIA)
2500 Wilson Boulevard, Suite 300
Arlington, VA 22201
Phone: (703) 907-7700
Fax: (703) 907-7727
E-mail: tia@tiaonline.org
http://www.tiaonline.org

United States Internet Service Provider Association (USISPA)
c/o Kate Dean
1330 Connecticut Avenue, NW
Washington, DC 20036
Phone: (202) 862-3816
Fax: (202) 261-0604
E-mail: kdean@steptoe.com
http://www.usispa.org

University Film and Video Associates (UFVA)
c/o Cheryl Jestis
University Film/Video Arts
462 Broadway, Suite 570
New York, NY 10013
Phone: (212) 941-8787
Fax: NA
E-mail: info@ufva.org
http://www.ufva.org

Usenix: The Advanced Computing Systems Association
2560 Ninth Street, Suite 215
Berkeley, CA 94710
Phone: (510) 528-8649
Fax: (510) 598-5738
E-mail: office@usenix.org
http://www.usenix.org

U.S. Internet Industry Association (USIIA)
PMP 212
5810 Kingstowne Center Drive, Suite 120
Alexandria, VA 22315
Phone: (703) 924-0006
Fax: (703) 924-4203

E-mail: info@usiia.org
http://www.usiia.org

Video Software Dealers Association (VSDA)
16530 Ventura Boulevard, Suite 400
Encino, CA 91436
Phone: (818) 385-1500
Fax: (818) 385-0587
E-mail: vsdaoffice@vsda.org
http://www.vsda.org

Virtual Private Network Consortium (VPNC)
127 Segré Place
Santa Cruz, CA 95060
Phone: (831) 426-9827
Fax: NA
E-mail: paul.hoffman@vpnc.org
http://www.vpnc.org

Web Developers Association of America (WDAA)
221 Liberty Street
New York, NY 10201
Phone: NA
Fax: NA
E-mail: At Web site
http://www.wdaa.org

Web Producers Organization (WPO)
E-mail: info@webproducers.org
http://www.webproducers.org

Web 3D Consortium
225 Bush Street, 16th Floor
PMB # 8900
San Francisco, CA 94104
Phone: (650) 722-0659
Fax: (415) 439-8304
E-mail: At Web site
http://www.web3d.org

Women in Animation
P.O. Box 17706
Encino, CA 91416
Phone: (818) 759-9596
Fax: NA
E-mail: info@womeninanimation.org
http://www.womeninanimation.org

Women in Film and Video (WIFV)
1233 20th Street, NW, Suite 401
Washington, DC 20036
Phone: (202) 429-9438
Fax: (202) 429-9440
E-mail: membership@wifv.org
http://www.wifv.org

**World Organization of Webmasters
(WOW)**
9580 Oak Avenue Parkway, Suite 7-177
Folsom, CA 95630
Phone: (916) 989-2933
Fax: (916) 987-3022
E-mail: info@joinwow.org
http://www.joinwow.org

**World Wide Web Chamber of
Commerce**
17232 Pickwick Drive
Purcellville, VA 20132

Phone: NA
Fax: (703) 763-0511
E-mail: President@WebChamber.com
http://www.webchamber.com

World Wide Web Consortium (W3C)
c/o Susan Westhaver
Massachusetts Institute of Technology
Laboratory for Computer Science and
   Artificial Intelligence
32 Vassar Street, Room 32-G515
Cambridge, MA 02139
Phone: (617) 253-2613

Fax: (617) 258-5999
E-mail: susan@w3.org
http://www.w3.org

APPENDIX IV
USEFUL WEB SITES FOR
MULTIMEDIA, THE INTERNET, AND
VIDEO GAMES INDUSTRIES

The Internet has become an increasingly valuable resource in today's high-tech electronic age. The following are a selection of useful Web sites to help in your industry research, such as job searching, trade news gathering, and networking. (Web sites which do *not* have self-explanatory names are annotated with a brief explanation situated between the site name and its URL.)

You may wish to bookmark and/or list the following URLs in your Favorites folder. In addition, by utilizing one or more of the search engines listed below, you can easily research any organization, individual, or topic.

As has always been true, the Internet is in a constant state of flux. As such even well-established Web sites often change their Web address. If a link is not working, use a search engine to search for the Web site in question. Most times this step will lead you to the new home page of the desired site. (As always, when using a search engine, if your query is more than one word place the name/term in quotes to narrow and target the search.)

While the Internet and e-mail are great tools to employ in starting/furthering your career in the Multimedia, the Internet, and the Video Games industries, do not ignore traditional person-to-person contact with colleagues, mentors, family, friends, and others within your support network. They are equally vital in keeping you on track in your work and life.

A. SEARCH ENGINES

How to Use Search Engines

Bare Bones 101
http://www.sc.edu/beaufort/library/pages/
  bones/bones.shtml

Organic SEO Wiki
http://www.organicseo.org

Search.com
http://www.search.com

SearchEngineWatch
http://searchenginewatch.com

Spider's Apprentice
http://www.monash.com/spidap4.html

WebRef
http://webreference.com/content/search

Search Engines (By Country)
http://www.philb.com/countryse.htm

Search Engines (General)

Alltheweb
http://alltheweb.com

Alta Vista
http://www.altavista.com

A9
http://a9.com

Answers.com
http://www.answers.com

AOL
http://www.aol.com

Ask.com
http://www.ask.com

AT1
http://www.at1.com

Blogs
An increasingly important venue for
  industry news and trends; note that
  many general search engines now
  provide a subcategory targeted for
  locating blogs by subject matter

Blogflux
http://dir.blogflux.com

Bloggernity
http://www.bloggernity.com

BlogSearchEngine
http://www.blogsearchengine.com

Bloogz: World Wide Blog
http://www.bloogz.com

Feedster
http://www.feedster.com

Game/Life
http://blog.wired.com/games

Google Blog Search
http://blogsearch.google.com

IceRocket.com
http://blogs.icerocket.com

LS Blog
http://www.lsblogs.com

QuackTrack
http://quacktrack.com

Technorati
http://www.technorati.com

Web Images
http://blog.searchenginewatch.com/
blog/060103-180848

Wired Magazine Blogs
http://blog.wired.com

Yahoo Blog Search
http://ysearchblog.com

Clusty
http://clusty.com
Copernic
Free and paid versions of special
    download software available at
    site; generally does not work with
    Macintosh system
http:copernic.com

Ditto
http://www.ditto.com

Dogpile
http://www.dogpile.com

Excite
http://www.excite.com

Findspot
http://www.findspot.com

Galaxy
http://www.galaxy.com

Gigablast
http://www.gigablast.com

Gimpsy
http://www.gimpsy.com

GoFish
http://www.gofish.com

Google
http://www.google.com

Google Scholar
http://scholar.google.com

HotBot
http://www.hotbot.com

HotSheet
http://www.hotsheet.com

Itool
http://www.itools.com

KartOO
http://www.kartoo.com

LookSmart
http://search.looksmart.com

Lycos
http://www.lycos.com

Metacrawler
http://metacrawler.com

Mr. Sapo
http://mrsapo.com

MSN
http://www.msn.com

Nokodo
http://www.nokodo.com

Omgili Beta 2
Search engine for discussion forums
http://omgili.com

Singingfish
http://www.singingfish.com

Soople
http://www.soople.com

Starting Page
http://www.startingpage.com

Starting Point
http://www.stpt.com

Teoma
http://www.directhit.com

WebCrawler
http://webcrawler.com

Wikipedia
http://en.wikipedia.org

WiseNut
http://www.wisenut.com

Yahoo
http://www.yahoo.com

B. EDUCATION WEB SITES

Curriculum framework
A curriculum framework as a conceptual
    guide for game-related educational
    programs presented by the IGDA
    (International Game Developers
    Association) Education Committee
http://www.igda.org/academia/
    curriculum_framework.php

David Perry
A veteran of the video game business
    lists educational institutions

offering courses in game design and
    development
http://www.dperry.com

Technical Schools
Guide to Web development training
    schools
http://www.technical-schools.us/
    videogamedesign.htm

Videogametimes
Guide to electronic game schools
http://www.videogametimes.com

Yahoo! Education
Guide to courses and degrees in
    Engineering and Technology,
    Networking, and Security
http://degrees.education.yahoo.com/sub2-
    engineering_and_technology

C. JOB SEARCH/SALARY SURVEY/CAREER INFORMATION WEB SITES
Some of these Web sites require a
subscription fee for their use.

BreakingIn
Preparing for a career in game
    development
http://www.igda.org/breakingin/home.htm

CareerPage
http://www.careerpage.org

Careers: Wall Street Journal
http://www.careers.wsj.com

Center for Mobility Resources
http://www.homefair.com/homefair/cmr/
    salcalc.html

Creative Hot List
http://www.creativehotlist.com

David Perry
A contact directory to computer game
    developers, written and researched by
    Simon Dew
http://www.dperry.com/jobs/directory.
    htm

Electronics Art Jobs
http://jobs.ea.com

Employnow
http://www.employnow.com

Entertainmentcareers.net
http://www.entertainmentcareers.net

Entertainment Jobs Now.com
http://www.entertainmentcareers.net

Gamasutra
http://www.gamasutra.com

GameDaily
http://biz.gamedaily.com/classifieds/
?id=1481

Hot Jobs
http://www.hotjobs.com

InternetIndustryJobs
http://www.internetindustryjobs.com

Job Hunt
http://www.job-hunt.org

Job Profiles
http://www.jobprofiles.org

Jobs.aol.com
http://jobs.aol.com/sem=1&ncid=AOLC
AR00170000000004

Job Search
http://jobsearch.monster.com

Jobsearchtech.about
http://jobsearchtech.about.com/od/
salary6/index.htm

JobSmart Salary Info
http://jobsmart.org/tools/salary/sal-prof.
htm

Jobs Search
http://jobs.ea.com

JobStar Central
http://www.jobstar.org/tools/salary/sal-
prof.cfm#PR

Magin & Associates—Career FAQ
Electronic game industry career guidance
and information
http://www.edmagnin.com/careers.html

Media Internship Book
http://www.internships-usa.com

Media Recruiter
http://www.mediarecruiter.com

MediaStar
http://www.medialandjobs.com

Monster
http://www.monster.com

MSN Careerbuilder
http://jobs.msn.careerbuilder.com/
Custom/MSN/FindJobs.aspx

The Real Rate Survey
http://www.realrates.com/survey.htm

Salary.com
http://www.salary.com

Salary Wizard
http://swz-hoovers.salary.com

TheLadders
Job site for $100K+ job listings
http://www.TheLadder.com

TopUSAjobs.com
http://topusajobs.com

True Careers
General career information
http://www.truecareers.com/jobseeker/
careerresources/default.shtml

Wageweb Salary Survey Data Online
http://www.wageweb.com/index.htlm

Wetfeet
http://www.wetfeet.com

Yahoo
http://careers.yahoo.com/employment/
carrer_resources/salaries_and_benefits

D. MULTIMEDIA/INTERNET/ VIDEO GAME RESOURCES

Adrenaline Vault
This site, featuring The Developer's
Corner, is dedicated to, and written by,
people in the gaming industry.
http://www.avault.com/developer

Answers.com
http://www.answers.com

Arcade Flyers
Video game brochures
http://www.arcadeflyers.net

BabelFish
Language translator for users of the Internet
http://world.altavista.com/tr

ClickZ Internet Marketing
Resource for online marketing topics
http://www.clickz.com

Computeruser
A high tech computer terminology
dictionary
http://www.computeruser.com/resources/
dictionary/index.html

David Perry
A veteran of the video game business
gives advice and information to help
future game developers
http://www.dperry.com

Dictionary.com
Free online English dictionary, thesaurus
and reference guide, and online
translator
http://www.dictionary.com

DVD FAQ (and Answers)
Extensive information about DVDs and
DVD technology
http://dvddemystified.com/dvdfaq.html

E-mail newsletters
Some are free, others are subscription-based.
Sign-up is at the publication's Web site.

(Daily) Variety
http://www.variety.com

Electronic Arts
http://www.ea.com

Gamasutra
http://www.gamasutra.com

GameCareerGuide.com
http://info.gamanetwork.com

GameDailyBIZ
http://biz.gamedaily.com

Gamesindustry.biz
http://www.gamesindustry.biz

GameSlice
Reporting on events within the game
industry, with feature stories, including
interviews
http://www.gameslice.com

Google Zeitgeist
User search behavior and search
patterns, trends, and surprises
according to Google
http://www.google.com/press/zeitgeist.
html

Hollywood Reporter
http://www.hollywoodreporter.com

Jupitermedia Newsletters
Portal to e-mail newsletters on
assorted topics
http://e-newsletters.internet.com

Mediabistro
http://www.mediabistro.com

Mediaweek
Contains a listing to check off to
receive a video game newsletter
http://www.mediaweek.com/mw/
newsletters/email.jsp

NetFuture
Concerned with technology and
human responsibility on the Internet
http://www.netfuture.org

Tomalak's Realm
Covers the Web daily with selected
links to stories about e-commerce,
usability, journalism, tools, design,
and other selected topics
http://www.tomalak.org/
todayslinks/2001/02/22.html

Windows IT Pro
Targeted to the Internet technology
(IT) community
http://www.windowsitpro.com/email

EMedia
News and feature articles on the digital
video equipment industry
http://www.emedialive.com

Everything2.com
http://www.everything2.com/index.
pl?node_id=598967

Flip Code
Articles, coding techniques, news,
and interviews relating to game
programming
http://flipcode.com

Foldoc
http://foldoc.org

Gamasutra
A major resource for the electronic game
industry
http://www.gamasutra.com

Game Developer
Game development information for
video game development news,
game development tutorials, game
development tool reviews, and game
developer editorials
http://www.digitalgamedeveloper.com

GamePlayer
http://www.gamesinvestor.com/Glossary/
glossary.html

GamePro
Gaming news, reviews, the latest cheats,
codes, strategies, pro tips, and previews
http://www.gamepro.com

GameProgrammer
http://www.gameprogrammer.com/
glossary.html

Gamespot
History of electronic games
http://www.gamespot.com

Geekcomix
History of electronic games
http://www.geekcomix.com/vgh/main.shtml

Google News Site
Google news site with group links to
other Web sites
http://deja.com/news

Inside Video Games
Video game industry articles
http://www.insidevideogames.com/vgp/
news/index.jso

I Want Media
Media news and resources
http://www.iwantmedia.com/news/index.
html

Jakob Nielsen's site
Column on Web usability, usability
engineering, and Web quality
http://useit.com
The Java Tutorial
Example-based guide to the Java
programming language
http://java.sun.com/docs/books/tutorial

MakeGames
Game developer information
http://www.makegames.com

MSN Tech & Gadgets
Covers the spectrum of the video game
industry
http://tech.msn.com/games

Multimedia Web Ring
http://www.members.tripod.com/2lotto_
number/multimedia.htm

Nielsen Media Research
http://www.nielsenmedia.com

**NIST (National Institute of Standards
and Technology) Reference Site**
Reference tool on physical constants and
units
http://www.physics.nist.gov/cuu

Noslang
Internet slang translator
http://www.noslang.com

ProductionHub.com
This leading online resource and
industry directory for film,
television, video and digital media
production was developed as a tool
for people to locate production
products, services and professionals
http://www.productionhub.com

Rentrak
Information on game ratings, rentals, and
sales
http://www.rentrak.com/es_homevideo.pby

Sloperama.com
http://www.sloperama.com/advice/
lesson28.html

Usable Web
Collection of links and accompanying
information about HCI (human
computer interaction) centered on the
Web
http://www.usableweb.com

Webopedia.com
http://www.webopedia.com

Web Price Index
Standard guide to how much marketers
can expect to pay for Web services
http://www.netb2b.com/webPriceIndex/
index.html

Webring
Contains a list of game programming
webrings, each of which concentrates
on a particular area of game
development
http://www.webring.com

WebWord
Usability and human factors for the
Internet
http://www.webword.com

WhatIs
Definitions and explanations for
thousands of the most current
information technology-related words
http://www.whatis.com

GLOSSARY

Terms that appear in a definition that also are defined separately will appear as capital letters in that definition.

Above-the-Line Costs Production costs relating to producer, director, writers, and talent.

A/D Analog-to-digital conversion. Also called digitization.

ADR (Automatic Dialogue Replacement) A process of re-recording dialogue by performers in a sound studio during POST-PRODUCTION, typically performed against a playback of the edited production to match lip movements on screen. ADR is frequently used to replace production sound track of poor quality or to insert fresh lines of dialogue. Also known as looping.

ADSL (Asymmetrical Digital Subscriber Loop) A digital transmission technology that allows local telephone companies to deliver video services to homes and businesses over copper wires.

AI See ARTIFICIAL INTELLIGENCE (AI).

Alpha Testing In electronic game development, an early stage of product development. Alpha testing is usually geared toward resolving gameplay issues.

Ambient The prevailing location environment; in audio, the background noise present at a location.

Animation A process of creating the illusion that inanimate objects are moving.

Animation stand The mounting for the animation camera, lights, and table for shooting animation cells. Sometimes called a rostrum.

API (Application Programming Interface) A pre-written software package of routines that a programmer can build into his program for an electronic game to accomplish certain tasks. An API is usually designed to provide an interface between the game (application program) and input or output device.

Application A computer program designed to permit particular types of work to be accomplished.

Application Programming Interface See API (APPLICATION PROGRAMMING INTERFACE).

Armature A collection of data that defines the skeletal structure of a 3-D model in an electronic game that is intended to be animated. The armature indicates to the software how the joints move and how they are related to one another.

Artificial Intelligence (AI) (1) A computer program that mimics the human mind. (2) In electronic games, a method of inserting text-based dialogue.

Assembler A programming tool that converts a file of ASSEMBLY LANGUAGE machine instructions into an OBJECT FILE.

Assembly language A human-readable form of a computer's internal machine language.

Assets A collective term for the audio, video, animation, and other data files required by an electronic game. Also known as the content of a game.

Asymmetrical Digital Subscriber Loop See ADSL (ASYMMETRICAL DIGITAL SUBSCRIBER LOOP).

Asynchronous (1) A sound that does not match its actual or presumed on-screen source. (2) In computers, signals operating at different speeds.

Audio console An audio board through which sounds are channeled, amplified, and mixed during production or post-production. Also known as a mixer.

Automatic Dialogue Replacement See ADR (AUTOMATIC DIALOGUE REPLACEMENT).

Bandwidth Volume of information that can be transmitted through a communications link—measured in bits, or binary digits, per second (bps).

Banner Ad The most visible of all WORLD WIDE WEB advertisements in the style of a long skinny ad running along the top of a Web site page.

Baud Number of symbols per second. A measure of data-transmission speed.

Below-the-line costs Those production costs associated with a cast and crew and their work, with the exception of the producers, directors, writers, and performers.

Beta testing In electronic game development, a late stage of product development, when the game is nearly complete. Beta testing generally focuses on finding/fixing bugs (errors).

Binary A number in base 2; an either/or comparison. Computer systems are binary systems.

Biotechnology See ERGONOMICS.

Bit A binary digit, the smallest piece of information usable by a computer, either on or off.

Bits Per Second (BPS) The measurement of the speed of data transfer in a communications system.

Branching In multimedia, various paths that a viewer may take by following links on a Web page.

Broadband carrier A high-capacity transmission system used to carry large blocks of data on one cable or carrier (coaxial cable, microwave, or optical fiber).

Browser A computer program that is used to look at various kinds of information on the WORLD WIDE WEB and navigate the sites.

Bug database A database of bugs (errors) found during electronic game development, maintained by the testing manager. All bugs found by testers are logged in the bug database, telling the programmers what they still need to fix.

346 CAREER OPPORTUNITIES IN THE INTERNET, VIDEO GAMES, AND MULTIMEDIA

Build A collection of the files needed to play an electronic game, for example, the EXECUTABLE program plus all the data files that it reads. In a build, the files required as of the current time are assembled in one place, guaranteeing that the program will not crash because data is missing. When a build is assembled, the features that have been implemented so far can be tested.

Byte Made up of eight BITS, this is the standard amount of data used to define a single character in a computer.

CD A (digital) compact disc, originally for music; also used for computer data, in which case it is called a CD-ROM, for "read-only memory."

Cel Short for celluloid. The base material used to draw individual animation frames. Each cel is a drawing on a clear acetate sheet.

Cel animation The process of drawing and shooting as many as 24 cels per second. Cels showing foreground, mid-ground, and background may be layered to give the impression of three dimensions.

Central Processing Unit (CPU) The main circuits that process digital information in a computer.

CGI See COMPUTER-GENERATED IMAGERY (CGI).

Character generator A computerized device that electronically creates titles or any other numeric or alphanumeric graphics which can be combined with a video signal. The text is created with a keyboard and a program that has a selection of fonts and backgrounds.

Codec A library of software routines that a program can call upon to compress or decompress data (usually audio and video data) for playback to a video frame, or to speakers and a screen. Also a device (such as sound cards or video cards) that converts analog signals to digital to be read by a computer or transmitted over a network and converts the digital signals back to analog.

Compiler A programming tool which takes as input a file of program code (a source file) written in a high-level language, processes it, and produces as output a file of machine code for a particular machine (an OBJECT FILE).

Computer-generated imagery (CGI) Images created totally within a computer system.

Computer graphics Pictorial images and illustrations created on a computer to be used in video and/or film productions.

Cost Per Click See CPC (COST PER CLICK).

CPC (Cost Per Click) The cost an advertiser pays a host Web site for one click, or hit, on the advertiser's online advertisement.

C++ An OBJECT-ORIENTED PROGRAMMING LANGUAGE commonly used in many present-day computer programming operations, including electronic game development and Web site development.

CPU See CENTRAL PROCESSING UNIT (CPU).

Cross-fade A transition in which one sound source fades out at the same rate another is phased in.

Cutscene An animated or live action sequence in an electronic game over which the game player has no control. Cutscenes are employed to advance the plot, present character development, and provide background information, atmosphere, dialogue, and clues.

Data Compression Any of a wide variety of algorithms for an encoding process that reduces the amount of space that data require in a given storage medium, such as a video frame. This is accomplished by throwing away information the eye cannot see and/or redundant information in areas of the video frame that do not change.

Decompression The decoding of a compressed video data stream to allow playback.

Demo (1) A freely distributed demonstration or preview of an upcoming or recently released computer or electronic game. Demos are typically released by the game's publisher to help consumers get the feel of the product before deciding whether to buy the full version. (2) A collection of a job-seeker's previous work, used to demonstrate the applicant's skills and experience to potential employers. It can be a portfolio of drawings, a computer program, a CD or tape of music or other types of audio, a videotape or DVD of animations or other video data, or a Web site.

Digital Subscriber Line See DSL (DIGITAL SUBSCRIBER LINE).

Digitization The process of converting a continuous analog video or audio signal to digital data for computer storage and manipulation.

Download The process of transferring electronic information from one source, circuit, or storage medium to another.

Download and play A way of viewing Web video that requires a user to DOWNLOAD a video before playing it. Download and play files are usually higher quality than streamed video.

DSL (Digital Subscriber Line) A system designed to allow a standard telephone line to carry digital information at a rate much faster than using a standard digital modem.

E-commerce Commerce (buying and selling) that is transacted electronically, as over the INTERNET.

E-mail Text messages created and viewed on PCs and other hardware transmitted electronically, usually over an office network or over the INTERNET.

Engine A subset of a computer program that performs a particular task, usually on an ongoing basis. In electronic game development, engines are designed in such a way that they can be employed in several different games, saving the cost of redeveloping that part of the code for each new product. The most common types of game engines are graphics engines (which display 3-D spaces on the screen) and physics engines (which compute the behavior, including collisions) of moving objects in a 3-D space.

Equalization The process of emphasizing specific audio or video frequencies and eliminating others as signal control measure, usually to produce particular sonic qualities, by using an equalizer.

Ergonomics The applied science of equipment design as for the workplace, intended to maximize productivity by reducing operator fatigue and discomfort. Also called biotechnology, human engineering, and human factors engineering.

Executable A file of machine code that is ready to be run by a computer. This is the end product of the programming process.

FCC See FEDERAL COMMUNICATIONS COMMISSION (FCC).

Federal Communications Commission (FCC) The U.S. federal government agency charged with the supervision and regulation of all electronic communication media in this country.

Fiber optics Glass strands designed to carry (high-speed) communication signals modulated on pulses of light waves rather than radio waves.

File Transfer Protocol See FTP (FILE TRANSFER PROTOCOL).

Finite state machine In electronic game development, a software technique that can be used to create the artificial intelligence for autonomous, or partially autonomous, units. At any given time, each unit is in exactly one of a number of states defined by the finite state machine. For example, a soldier could be in one of the states of advancing, retreating, holding ground, or dead. The state will determine what behavior the soldier exhibits within the game.

Firewall Any of a number of security schemes that prevent unauthorized users from gaining access to a computer network or that scrutinize transfers of information to and from the network.

FTP (File Transfer Protocol) A procedure for transmitting files of computer data over the INTERNET.

F/X Special effects. Visual tricks and illusions—electronic or on camera—employed in film and video to define, distort, or defy reality.

Game Development Company A firm that designs and builds electronic games, but seldom advertises, sells, or distributes them to the public.

Game Publisher A firm that funds the development and building of new electronic games (by game developers) and advertises and sells them to the public. Some publishers may also develop and build the games themselves.

Genre A group of electronic games possessing similar gameplay, though not necessarily similar settings. Games are categorized into genres by how the player plays the game, regardless of the setting.

Geometry Collectively, all the POLYGONS that make up a 3-D scene or model in an electronic game.

Graphics generator A digital unit designed to create and combine pictures with type. Sometimes called a paint box.

Hardware Mechanical, electronic, or magnetic equipment rather than SOFTWARE, the material recorded or computer programs.

HTML (Hypertext Markup Language) A computer language used for formatting documents to be transferred through the WORLD WIDE WEB.

Hyperlink The computer action whereby a user can jump (by pressing a key or keys on a keyboard or by pressing a button on a remote control) from one area on a Web site to another area.

Hypertext Markup Language See HTML (HYPERTEXT MARKUP LANGUAGE).

Icon A graphic symbol.

IDE (Integrated Development Environment) In electronic games, a suite of programming tools that work together to help a software engineer write, compile, and debug program code.

Integrated Development Environment See IDE (INTEGRATED DEVELOPMENT ENVIRONMENT).

Interactive media Communication systems that permit two-way interaction between electronic stations (video monitors, computers). May depend on stored programs, such as electronic games or Web shopping networks.

Internet A public computer network, comprising thousands of smaller networks, linking home, education, science, and business computers. Communication is possible because of voluntary agreements to use certain common communication techniques.

Intranet Interconnected information processing networks confined within an organization, enterprise, or membership group. Intranets may also be connected to the INTERNET.

Java An OBJECT-ORIENTED PROGRAMMING LANGUAGE commonly used in many present-day computer programming operations, including electronic game development and Web site development.

Joint Photographic Experts Group See JPEG (JOINT PHOTOGRAPHIC EXPERTS GROUP).

Joystick A manual control or cursor device attached to a computer or an electronic game.

JPEG (Joint Photographic Experts Group) An industry standards organization set up by the ISO/CCITT (the International Organization for Standardization and the Comté Consultatit International Téléphonique et Télégraphique, the latter now known as ITU, or the International Telecommunications Union). The group is charged with setting the standard for the definition of data storage of, and methods of compression for, photographic and still image data. Its Web site is: http://www.jpeg.org.

Kinematics The branch of mechanics that studies the motion of a body or a system of bodies without concern given to its mass or the forces acting upon it.

LAN   See LOCAL AREA NETWORK (LAN).

Level   (1) In electronic games, a self-contained mission or scenario with its own starting conditions and victory condition. The term comes from arcade gaming, in which the game usually proceeds in a series of stages at increasing levels of difficulty. (2) The volume at which a sound is recorded (audio level). When mixing sounds that were recorded separately, audio engineers must adjust their levels to make aesthetic sense (a dropped pencil should not be louder than a train wreck).

Linear editing   Tape-based VCR-to-VCR editing. Called linear because scenes are recorded in chronological order on the tape. This is in contrast to NONLINEAR EDITING.

Linker   A programming tool that takes as input multiple OBJECT FILES and links them all together to form a working EXECUTABLE.

Local Area Network (LAN)   A network that connects (linked by cable) computers that are in proximity to one another, typically in the same building.

Localization   In electronic game development, the process of modifying a game for sale in a different country with a different language and potentially different cultural norms.

MIDI (Musical Instrument Digital Interface)   A data format for recording the notes played by a musical instrument and storing this information in a program file. A SYNTHESIZER uses the information about which key was struck to play back a pre-recorded sample of a musical instrument, creating synthetic music. With the advent of efficient music compression via MP3 files, most electronic games do not ship with MIDI files, but composers use MIDI files to record and edit their compositions. MIDI files are edited with a piece of software called a sequencer.

Milestone   A date upon which an electronic game development team is supposed to deliver a BUILD to the game publisher, usually containing certain features established in the development contract.

MMDS (Multichannel Multipoint Distribution System)   A local wireless terrestrial video broadcast technology that relies on line-of-sight transmission (instead of non-terrestrial satellites).

MoCap   See MOTION CAPTURE (MOCAP).

Motion capture (MoCap)   An animation technique used to duplicate movement by fastening electronic or magnetic sensors on the body of a performer, allowing a computer to record and manipulate the motions.

Motion Picture Experts Group   See MPEG (MOTION PICTURE EXPERTS GROUP).

MPEG (Motion Picture Experts Group)   An industry standards organization, set up by the ISO/IEC (the International Organization for Standardization and the International Electrotechnical Commission), which is charged with the development of video and audio encoding standards and the definition of data storage formats for video data (which also includes embedded audio data). Its Web site is: http://www.chiariglione.org/mpeg.

MP3   A highly compressed audio file format system defined by the MPEG organization. It enables the audio to be compressed to different levels and is also used to download music from the WORLD WIDE WEB.

Multichannel Multipoint Distribution System   See MMDS (MULTICHANNEL MULTIPOINT DISTRIBUTION SYSTEM).

Multimedia   A program combining text, graphics, sound, animation, video, or a combination of any of them.

Musical Instrument Digital Interface   See MIDI (MUSICAL INSTRUMENT DIGITAL INTERFACE).

Network   The collection of links that connects end users (of computers) with one another and with devices such as servers, switches, and routers.

Nonlinear editing   Digital random access editing that uses a hard drive instead of tape to store video. Random access allows easy arrangement of scenes in any order. This is in contrast to LINEAR EDITING.

Nonsynchronous sound   Audio without precisely matching visuals. Usually recorded separately, it may include wild sound, sound effects, or music incorporated in POST-PRODUCTION.

Object file   The output of a COMPILER or ASSEMBLER, an object file contains machine code, but not in a form that can be run by the computer. The object files must be linked together first into an EXECUTABLE by the LINKER.

Object-oriented programming languages   A newer generation of programming languages and techniques in which programmers are encouraged to think about a program in terms of data structures (called objects) and various manipulations that can be done to them (called "methods") rather than as one giant mechanism for accomplishing a variety of tasks (as in older programming languages such as FORTRAN or C). This approach is thought to make the program code more understandable and reusable and less prone to bugs. C++ and Java are both object-oriented programming languages.

Operating system   SOFTWARE responsible for controlling the HARDWARE in use.

Pay Per Click   See PPC (PAY PER CLICK).

PC   Personal computer.

PERT (Program Evaluation and Review Technique) chart   In electronic game development, a project management tool that shows tasks and the dependencies between them.

Pixel   A single element of a computer or television picture. Picture resolution may be measured by the number of pixels in a set space.

Polygon   In an electronic game, the fundamental unit of graphic data displayed by a 3-D graphics ENGINE. A polygon is a region in 3-D space described by three or four points called VERTICES. These points make up a triangle or a quadrilateral, each called a polygon. Three-dimensional models in the game are built up out of hundreds or thousands of polygons to create a surface as seen in the game.

Porting   Taking a computer program that works on one kind of computer or operating system and making it work on a different kind of computer or operating system. Also called conversion.

Post-production   The final stage of the production process, during which recorded images and sounds are edited, background music, VOICEOVER, sound effects, titles, and/or various electronic visual effects are added, and the production is completed for distribution.

PPC (Pay Per Click)   The cost to advertisers for the number of clicks or hits received on their ads on the WORLD WIDE WEB.

Preproduction   The preparatory stage of production planning prior to actually recording sounds and visual images.

Production   The stage of the process during which production materials and equipment are set up and sounds and images are actually recorded.

Program Evaluation and Review Technique Chart   See PERT (PROGRAM EVALUATION AND REVIEW TECHNIQUE) CHART.

RAM (Random access memory)   The short-term memory of a computer, which temporarily holds information while the computer is on. Distinct from storage, which is more permanent and is held on hard disks or some other media.

Random access memory   See RAM (RANDOM ACCESS MEMORY).

Rendering   A computerized process in electronic game development of converting the GEOMETRY that represents a scene or spatial location into a visible image of the scene. Rendering creates the picture from the data.

Search engine   Software that facilitates the discovery of relevant information in distant databases or Websites.

Search Engine Marketing   See SEM (SEARCH ENGINE MARKETING).

Search Engine Optimization   See SEO (SEARCH ENGINE OPTIMIZATION).

SEM (Search Engine Marketing)   The process of researching, submitting, and positioning a Web site within search engines to achieve maximum exposure.

SEO (Search Engine Optimization)   The process of designing a Web site so that search engines easily find the pages and index them. This is accomplished by targeting keywords so that the pages rank higher in search engine protocols, with the ultimate goal of generating more revenue from the Web site.

Software   Material recorded on audio, video, and/or computer media. Also refers to computer programs, as opposed to computer HARDWARE.

Sprite   In electronic game development, a small 2-D image of an object or character that can be drawn on the screen at different locations over time to give the impression of movement.

Storyboard   A series of drawings or cartoon-like sketches illustrating key visual stages (shots, scenes) of planned production accompanied by corresponding audio information.

Streaming   A collection of data (sound or video in real time) sent in a sequential fashion through the system used to send audio, video, and other digital signals through the Internet as opposed to storing it in a local file first.

SWOT analyses   Studies that look at the Strengths and Weaknesses of the organization, as well as Opportunities and Threats that are external to the organization that are either helpful or harmful to the group's achievement of its objectives.

Synthesizer   An electronic device capable of reproducing the sound of one or more musical instruments. Modern synthesizers contain a digital recording of the sound that a real instrument makes, and they manipulate the sample mathematically to change its pitch and duration for each note to be played.

Texture   In computer graphics, a 2-D image that is mapped onto the surface of a POLYGON in a 3-D environment in order to create the appearance of its surface.

3-D graphics   Refers to graphical data in an electronic game presented by means of 3-D RENDERING. Three-D graphics includes GEOMETRY, TEXTURES, and other data. These graphics are designed so that they can be displayed from any perspective, as if the game player were actually inside the scene. See also 2-D GRAPHICS.

3-D rendering   A collection of software techniques in electronic game development for taking the GEOMETRY of a three-dimensional scene made up of POLYGONS and displaying it on the screen from a particular perspective.

Turnkey system   Any computer system that is considered ready-to-use right out of the box, needing only trivial changes to its configuration.

2-D Graphics   Refers to graphical data in an electronic game presented without a 3-D display ENGINE, including backgrounds, user interface elements, and SPRITES. See also 3-D GRAPHICS.

Uniform Resource Locator   See URL (UNIFORM RESOURCE LOCATOR).

URL (Uniform Resource Locator)   The address system used to access sites on the WORLD WIDE WEB.

Vertex (plural Vertices)   A point in three-dimensional space in an electronic game that defines part of the surface of a 3-D model.

Vertex Coloring   The assignment of colors to the VERTICES of each POLYGON that makes up the pictorialization of objects in electronic games.

Vertex Lighting   The blending of uneven light cast on a POLYGON. Each POLYGON has a minimum of three VERTICES. If light is cast toward the POLYGON, each VERTEX will usually receive a different light level and intensity. The blending of the light level on the surface of the POLYGON is based on the program setting of the vertex light levels.

Virtual reality (VR)   Video and audio sensory computer-controlled effects, designed to create an artificial environment and/or movement.

Vlog   A BLOG containing video images.

VO   See VOICEOVER (VO).

Voiceover (VO)   Audio from an unseen narrator accompanying video, heard above background.

VR   See VIRTUAL REALITY (VR).

WAN (Wide Area Network)   A communications network that employs such devices as telephone lines, radio waves, or satellite dishes to span a greater geographic area than can be covered by a LAN.

Webpage   A webpage is typically a file written in HYPERTEXT MARKUP LANGUAGE (HTML), stored on a server for use on the INTERNET. A webpage generally has links to other web pages. Each web page has its own address called a URL (UNIFORM RESOURCE LOCATOR) and is referenced in the form http://www.sample-forbook.com.

Wide Area Network   See WAN (WIDE AREA NETWORK).

World Wide Web (WWW)   A distribution information network consisting of Web sites accessed through individual URL addresses offering text, graphics, and sound.

WWW   See WORLD WIDE WEB (WWW).

BIBLIOGRAPHY

Adams, Ernest. *Break Into the Game Industry: How to Get a Job Making Video Games.* New York: McGraw-Hill/Osborne, 2003.

Ahearn, Luke. *3D Game Textures: Create Professional Game Art Using Photoshop.* Burlington, Mass.: Focal Press/Elsevier, 2006.

Arntson, Amy E. *Graphic Design Basics.* 5th ed. Belmont, Calif.: Wadsworth Publishing, 2006.

Bartle, Richard. *Designing Virtual Worlds.* Berkeley, Calif.: New Riders Games/Peachpit Press, 2003.

Bates, Bob. *Game Design.* 2nd ed. Boston, Mass.: Premier Press/Thomson Course Technology, 2004.

Bergeron, Bryan. *Developing Serious Games.* Hingham, Mass.: Charles River Media, Inc., 2006.

Bethke, Erik. *Game Development and Production.* Plano, Tex.: Wordware Publishing, Inc., 2003.

Bourg, David. *Physics for Game Developers.* Cambridge, Mass.: O'Reilly & Associates, Inc., 2001.

Brinck, Tom, Darren Gergle, and Scott D. Wood. *Usability for the Web: Designing Web Sites That Work.* San Francisco, Calif.: Morgan Kaufmann, 2001.

Bureau of Labor Statistics, U.S. Department of Labor. *November 2004 National Industry-Specific Occupational Employment and Wage Estimates.* Available online at http://stats.bls.gov/oes/current/naics3_443000.htm.

Bureau of Labor Statistics, U.S. Department of Labor. *Occupational Employment and Wages, November 2004.* Available online at http://www.bls.gov/oes/current/oes112021.htm.

Bureau of Labor Statistics, U.S. Department of Labor. *Occupational Outlook Handbook, 2006–07 Edition.* Available online at http://www.bls.gov/oco/.

Busby, Jason, Zak Parrish, and Joel Van Eenwyk. *Mastering Unreal Technology: The Art of Level Design.* Indianapolis, Ind.: Sams Publishing, 2004.

Byrne, Ed. *Game Level Design.* Hingham, Mass.: Charles River Media, Inc., 2004.

Carter, Ben. *The Game Asset Pipeline.* Hingham, Mass.: Charles River Media, Inc., 2004.

Chandler, Heather M. *Game Production Handbook.* Hingham, Mass.: Charles River Media, Inc., 2006.

Clark, Mike, Mark Waterhouse, and Peter Fletcher, eds. *Web Service Business Strategies and Architectures.* Berkeley, Calif.: APress, Inc., 2003.

Co, Phil. *Level Design for Games : Creating Compelling Game Experiences.* Berkeley, Calif.: New Riders Publishing, 2006.

Computer Videomaker Magazine Editors. *The Videomaker Guide to Digital Video and DVD Production.* 3rd ed. Burlington, Mass.: Focal Press/Elsevier, 2004.

Crawford, Chris. *Chris Crawford on Game Design.* Berkeley, Calif.: New Riders Publishing, 2003.

Crowder, David A., and Andrew Bailey. *Creating Web Sites Bible.* 2nd ed. New York: John Wiley and Sons, 2004.

Eccher, Clint, Eric Hunley, and Erik Simmons. *Professional Web Design: Techniques and Templates.* 2nd ed. Hingham, Mass.: Charles River Media, Inc., 2004.

Erl, Thomas. *Service-Oriented Architecture: A Field Guide to Integrating XML and Web Services.* Upper Saddle River, N.J.: Prentice-Hall, 2004.

———. *Service-Oriented Architecture (SOA): Concepts, Technology, and Design.* Upper Saddle River, N.J.: Prentice-Hall, 2005.

Everett, Anna, and John Caldwell, eds. *New Media: Theories and Practices of Digitextuality.* New York: Routledge, 2003.

Finney, Kenneth C. *3D Game Programming All in One.* Boston.: Premier Press/Thomson Course Technology, 2004.

Fox, Brent. *Game Interface Design.* Boston: Premier Press/Thomson Course Technology, 2004.

Fullerton, Tracy, Christopher Swain, and Steven Hoffman. *Game Design Workshop: Designing, Prototyping, and Playtesting Games.* San Francisco, Calif.: CMP Books, 2004.

Garrand, Timothy. *Writing for Multimedia and the Web: A Practical Guide to Content Development for Interactive Media.* 3rd ed. Burlington, Mass.: Focal Press/Elsevier, 2006.

Gee, James Paul. *What Video Games Have to Teach Us About Learning and Literacy.* New York: Palgrave/Macmillan, 2004.

Gershenfeld, Alan, Mark Loparco, and Cecilia Barajan. *Game Plan: The Insider's Guide to Breaking in and Succeeding in the Computer and Video Game Business.* New York: St. Martin's Griffin, 2003.

Gordon, Bob, and Maggie Gordon, eds. *The Complete Guide to Digital Graphic Design.* New York: Watson-Guptill, 2002.

Griffin, Hedley. *The Animator's Guide to 2-D Animation.* Burlington, Mass.: Focal Press/Elsevier, 2001.

Irish, Dan. *The Game Producer's Handbook.* Boston, Mass.: Premier Press/Thomson Course Technology, 2005.

Iuppa, Nicholas. *Interactive Design for New Media and the Web.* 2nd ed. Burlington, Mass.: Focal Press/Elsevier, 2001.

Jones, David. *Web Site Design & Architecture: From Concept to Delivery to Redesign.* 2nd ed. Arvada, Colo.: WestNet Learning, 2002.

Jorgensen, David. *Developing .Net Web Services with XML.* Rockland, Mass.: Syngrest Publishing, 2002.

Kent, Steven L. *The Ultimate History of Video Games: From Pong to Pokemon—The Story Behind the Craze That Touched Our Lives and Changed the World.* New York: Three Rivers Press, 2001.

Kerlow, Isaac V. *The Art of 3-D Computer Animation and Effects.* Hoboken, N.J.: John Wiley and Sons, 2004.

Kim, Amy Jo. *Community Building on the Web : Secret Strategies for Successful Online Communities.* Berkeley, Calif.: Peachpit Press, 2000.

Kindem, Gorham, and Robert B. Musburger. *Introduction to Media Production: The Path to Digital Media Production.* 3rd ed. Burlington, Mass.: Focal Press/Elsevier, 2005.

King, Brad, and John Borland. *Dungeons and Dreamers: The Rise of Computer Game Culture from Geek to Chic.* New York: McGraw-Hill/Osborne, 2003.

Koster, Ralph. *A Theory of Fun for Game Design.* Scottsdale, Ariz.: Paraglyph Press, 2004.

Krug, Steve. *Don't Make Me Think: A Common Sense Approach to Web Usability.* 2nd ed. Berkeley, Calif.: New Riders Publishing, 2005.

Kuperberg, Marcia. *A Guide to Computer Animation for TV, Games, Multimedia, and the Web.* Burlington, Mass.: Focal Press/Elsevier, 2002.

Landa, Robin. *Graphic Design Solution.* 3rd ed. Albany, N.Y.: Thomson Delmar Learning, 2005.

Laramée, François Dominic, ed. *Secrets of the Game Business.* 2nd ed. Hingham, Mass.: Charles River Media, Inc., 2005.

Lengyel, Eric. *Mathematics for 3D Game Programming and Computer Graphics.* Hingham, Mass.: Charles River Media, Inc., 2002.

Maciuba-Koppel, Darlene. *The Web Writer's Guide.* Burlington, Mass.: Focal Press/Elsevier, 2002.

McAlpine, Rachel. *Web Word Wizardry: A Net-Savvy Writing Guide.* Berkeley, Calif.: Ten Speed Press, 2001.

McGovern, Gerry, Rob Norton, and Catherine O'Dowd. *The Web Content Style Guide: An Essential Reference for Online Writers, Editors and Managers.* Indianapolis, Ind.: Financial Times Prentice Hall, 2001.

Meigs, Tom. *Ultimate Game Design: Building Game Worlds.* New York: McGraw-Hill/Osborne, 2003.

Mencher, Marc. *Get in the Game! Careers in the Game Industry.* Berkeley, Calif.: New Riders Publishing, 2002.

Miller, Philip. *Media Law for Producers.* 4th ed. Burlington, Mass.: Focal Press/Elsevier, 2002.

Morville, John, and Louis Rosenfeld. *Information Architecture for the World Wide Web.* 2nd ed. Cambridge, Mass.: O?Reilly & Associates, Inc., 2002.

Mulligan, Jessica, and Bridgette Patrovsky. *Developing Online Games: An Insider's Guide.* Berkeley, Calif.: New Riders Publishing, 2003.

Nichols, David, Tom Fairand, Rom Rowley, and Matt Avery. *Brands and Gaming: The Computer Gaming Phenomenon and the Impact of Brands on Gaming.* New York: Palgrave/Macmillan, 2006.

Novak, Jeannie. *Game Development Essentials: An Introduction.* Clifton Park, N.Y.: Thomson Delmar Learning, 2004.

Omernick, Matthew. *Creating the Art of the Game.* Berkeley, Calif.: New Riders Publishing, 2004.

Owen, B. M. *The Internet Challenge to Television.* Cambridge, Mass.: Harvard University Press, 1999.

Pagani, Margherita. *Multimedia and Interactive Digital TV: Managing the Opportunities Created by Digital Convergence.* Hershey, Penn.: IRM Press, 2003.

Platten, John Z. *Ultimate Guide to Video Game Writing & Design.* Hollywood, Calif.: Lone Eagle Publishing, 2006.

Price, Jonathan, and Lisa Price. *Hot Text: Web Writing that Works.* Berkeley, Calif.: New Riders Publishing, 2002.

Rollings, Andrew, and Dave Morris. *Game Architecture and Design: A New Edition.* Rev. ed. Berkeley, Calif.: New Riders Publishing, 2002.

Rose, Jay. *Audio Postproduction for Digital Video.* San Francisco, Calif.: CMP Books, 2002.

Rosenfeld, Louis, and Peter Morville. *Information Architecture for the World Wide Web: Designing Large-Scale Web Sites.* Cambridge, Mass.: O'Reilly & Associates, Inc., 2002.

Rouse, Richard, III. *Game Design: Theory and Practice.* 2nd ed. Plano, Tex.: Wordware Publishing, 2001.

Rumsey, Francis, and Tim McCormick. *Sound and Recording: An Introduction.* 5th ed. Burlington, Mass.: Focal Press/Elsevier, 2005.

Ryan, Marie-Laure. *Narrative as Virtual Reality: Immersion and Interactivity in Literature and Electronic Media.* Baltimore, Md.: The Johns Hopkins University Press, 2003.

Salen, Katie, and Eric Zimmerman. *Rules of Play: Game Design Fundamentals.* Cambridge, Mass.: MIT Press, 2003.

Saltzman, Marc. *Game Creation and Careers: Insider Secrets from Industry Experts.* Berkeley, Calif.: New Riders Publishing, 2003.

Sheldon, Lee. *Character Development and Storytelling for Games.* Boston: Premier Press/Thomson Course Technology, 2004.

Shelford, Thomas J., and Gregory A. Remillard. *Real Web Project Management: Case Studies and Best Practices from the Trenches.* Boston: Addison-Wesley, 2002.

Szuprowicz, B. *Multimedia Networking.* New York: McGraw-Hill, 1995.

Taylor, T. L. *Play Between Worlds: Exploring Online Game Culture.* Cambridge, Mass.: MIT Press, 2006.

Tull, Chris. *Web Designer's Guide to Adobe Photoshop.* Plano, Tex.: Wordware Publishing, 2006.

Wardrip-Fruin, Noah, and Pat Harrigan, eds. *First Person: New Media as Story, Performance, and Game.* Boston, Mass.: The MIT Press, 2004.

Waters, John. *The Real Business of Web Design.* New York: Allworth Press, 2004.

Watkinson, John. *The Art of Digital Video.* Woburn, Mass.: Focal Press, 2000.

Whitaker, Jerry. *Master Handbook of Video Production.* New York: McGraw-Hill Professional, 2002.

White, Tony. *Animation from Pencils to Pixels: Classical Techniques for the Digital Animator.* Burlington, Mass.: Focal Press/Elsevier, 2006.

Wolf, Mark J. P., and Bernard Perron, eds. *The Video Game Theory Reader.* New York: Routledge, 2003.

Yanker, John. *Beyond Borders: Web Globalization Strategies.* Berkeley, Calif.: New Riders Publishing, 2002.

INDEX

ABOUT THE AUTHORS

ALLAN TAYLOR, a freelance editor, indexer, and researcher, comes from a family long involved in the publishing and newspaper industries, and, as a production manager, has participated in the computerization of bibliographic databases. He is the coauthor of *Career Opportunities in Writing, Career Opportunities in Television and Cable,* and *The Encyclopedia of Ethnic Groups in Hollywood* (all Facts on File), and he has created special bibliographic indexes for such volumes as *The Great Spy Pictures, Hollywood Songsters, 101 Things I Don't Know About Art, Questions and Answers About Community Associations,* and *Women Doctors Guide to Health and Healing.*

Mr. Taylor's publishing industry posts include tenures at the R. R. Bowker Company (Bibliographic Services), Engineering Information, Inc. (Production Manager), and Graphic Typesetting Services (Proofreading/Technical Specifications Department Manager). He resides in Los Angeles, California. His Web site is at http://www.tataylor.net.

JAMES ROBERT PARISH, a former entertainment reporter, publicist, and book series editor, is the author of many published biographies and reference books about the entertainment industry including *It's Good to Be the King: The Seriously Funny Life of Mel Brooks, The Hollywood Book of Breakups, Fiasco: Hollywood's Iconic Flops, The Hollywood Songsters, The Hollywood Book of Scandals, The Hollywood Book of Death, Prison Pictures From Hollywood, The RKO Gals, Katharine Hepburn, Whitney Houston, Gus Van Sant,* and *Whoopi Goldberg.* With Allan Taylor he coauthored *Career Opportunities in Writing, Career Opportunities in Television and Cable,* and *The Encyclopedia of Ethnic Groups in Hollywood* (all Facts on File) and has written several entries in the Ferguson Young Adult biography series (including Gloria Estefan, Jim Henson, Twyla Tharp, Denzel Washington, Katie Couric, Stan Lee, Halle Berry, Steven Spielberg, Tom Hanks, and Stephen King).

Mr. Parish is a frequent on-camera interviewee on cable and network TV for documentaries on the performing arts both in the United States and in the United Kingdom. He resides in Studio City, California. His Web site is at http://www.jamesrobertparish.com.